Casi Nada
A Study of Agrarian Reform
in the Homeland of Cardenismo

Studies on Culture and Society

CASI NADA
A STUDY OF AGRARIAN REFORM
IN THE HOMELAND OF CARDENISMO

John Gledhill
Department of Anthropology
University College London

Studies on Culture and Society
Volume 4

Institute for Mesoamerican Studies
The University at Albany
State University of New York

Distributed by
University of Texas Press

For submission of manuscripts address the publisher:
Institute for Mesoamerican Studies
The University at Albany
State University of New York
Albany, New York 12222

For copies address the distributor:
University of Texas Press
Post Office Box 7819
Austin, Texas 78713-7819

Cover: Photograph of the interior of the old sugar mill and remains of the feeding troughs from the ill-fated cattle cooperative of Guaracha.

Library of Congress Catalog Card Number: 91-07176C
ISBN: 0-942041-13-5
Printed in the United States of America

A Spanish version of this book,
*Casi Nada: La Reforma Agraria en
la Tierra Natal del Cardenismo* is published by:

El Colegio de Michoacán
Martinez de Navarrete #505
Esq. Avenida del Arbol
59690, Zamora, Michoacán
México

ISBN: 968-7230-68-1

To the campesinos of the Bolsa de Guaracha

How much utilidad did you get sowing with
the hacienda as a mediero?

Hardly anything—a few hanegas.

And when you sowed with Don Gabriel?

The same. In fact I almost always ended up in debt.

But it's better today, isn't it?

*Well, you see, we were ignorant then, we hadn't been to school.
Now we're educated, but it's the same thing, only a little worse.*

TABLE OF CONTENTS

LIST OF TABLES

LIST OF FIGURES

PREFACE

This book has been written over a period of seven years, in what have been very brief periods of respite from many other commitments. Though it would certainly have been nice to have had more time free for my own research throughout this period, the extended writing process has at least brought the compensation of extending the period of time covered by the study. I first visited Michoacán in 1979, with some financial help from my department at University College London, then headed by Andrew Strathern. The main fieldwork was conducted between March 1982 and April 1983, with the aid of a project grant received from the Social Science Research Council (subsequently renamed the Economic and Social Research Council) of the United Kingdom. I returned briefly in December 1986 and in August 1988 at my own expense, although the 1986 visit was made possible by the fact that the British Academy gave me a grant to present a paper at the American Anthropological Association meeting in Philadelphia, cutting out the cost of the transatlantic leg of the journey. My most recent visit, from September to December 1989, gave me the opportunity to revise the manuscript and to bring the conclusion up-to-date through a direct study of the processes surrounding the municipal election process. This was made possible by invitations to teach from the Centro de Estudios Antropológicos of the Colegio de Michoacán and the Centro de Investigaciones de Movimientos Sociales of the University of Guadalajara, supplemented by sabbatical leave from UCL. I also wish to acknowledge the accumulated debt both I and my students owe to these two Mexican university institutions, which have offered us their support in innumerable ways over the years.

In the periods in which I was in England, I was able to keep in touch with events in the study region through correspondence with friends in the village of Guaracha. I owe a special debt of gratitude to two of the ejidatarios, Jesús Prado Inocencio and Roberto Avalos Soria, who compiled data on cultivation in the ejido on my behalf, extending the data base of this aspect of the study to 1986. Jesús also supplied me with updated information on many other matters covered in the study through his letters, and my original fieldwork was made very much easier by his willingness to let me share his wide circle of *amistades* in the community.

My account of the period prior to land reform owes much to the work of the historian Heriberto Moreno García, of the Colegio de Michoacán, himself a native of Guaracha. Heriberto introduced me to the village, found me housing, and showed me innumerable other personal kindnesses, in addition to giving freely of his incomparable knowledge of the region's history. Jesús Pérez Sandoval not only refused to accept an economic rent for the rooms he let to me and frequently entertained me in his own house, but also helped me greatly with information during my research. Juan Figueroa, one of the original ejidatarios, spent days walking over the ejido with me, and played a key role in giving me a preliminary understanding of the history and organization of the agrarian community. So many other Guaracheños, ejidatarios and non-ejidatarios, have become friends over the years that it would be dangerous to attempt to make a more complete list, for fear of inadvertently excluding someone. The list would need to be extended to include people who provided me with lengthy interviews and an equal measure of hospitality in Totolán, San Antonio Guaracha and Villamar. Although it is little to offer in return for such warmth and friendship, I dedicate this book to all those whose history it tells, in the hope that they will at least judge it an honest attempt to convey to the outsider what I was able to understand of them and their world thanks to the *confianza* they granted me, even if they do not agree with all my judgment. When I am in the Ciénega I truly feel that I am home.

I would also like to take this opportunity to thank my many academic friends in Mexico for their intellectual inspiration and unending hospitality over the years. Guillermo de la Peña and Pastora Rodríguez, Juan Manuel Durán and Esmeralda Matute, Brigitte Boehm and José Lameiras have all played a major role in making this book possible over the past seven years and have influenced my thinking on almost everything. I have also benefited from the friendship and intellectual stimulus of Patricia Arias, Margarita Calleja, Jorge Durand, Humberto González, Cristina Padilla, Luis Ramírez, Fernando Salmerón and Jaime Tamayo. Paul Kersey and Salud Maldonado have been an unfailing source of kindnesses during my stays in Zamora and have helped me to understand something of the Meseta Tarasca. Lucia García worked with me for a month early in my fieldwork, conducting a series of interviews with women in the community. The census data were collected with the help of the staff of the Guaracha primary school. Many present and former colleagues at University College and other schools of London University have influenced my thinking over the years, but I hope no offense will be given if I make special mention of Barbara Bender, Joel Kahn, Bruce Kapferer, Steven Nugent, Michael and Nanneke Redclift, Paul Richards, Michael Rowlands, Maila Stivens and June Wyer. From the beginning of my career, the work of Eric Wolf has represented my paradigm for what anthropology should be about, and I hope that he will not find this assertion an embarrassment in the context of the present volume. Tom Patterson, of Temple University, has also encouraged me to persevere with my endeavors over the past few years, and continues to shame me into action by his own vastly greater productivity in publication. Kathy Powell played a central role in the final revisions of the manuscript, saving me many embarrassments, linguistic and ideological, and forcing me to transform gibberish into an argument on all too many occasions. To Caroline and James I owe apologies for the time I was preoccupied with writing and thanks for their support and understanding.

Lastly, I must express my gratitude to the Institute for Mesoamerican Studies and above all to James Wessman, who voluntarily took on the arduous task of doing a final editing job on my manuscript. An author who has a friend for an editor is fortunate, but even more so when the editor is fellow anthropologist so knowledgeable about the Mexican *Occidente* and so sympathetic to the work's objectives and theoretical orientations.

John Gledhill
Department of Anthropology
University College London

CHAPTER 1

INTRODUCTION:
AGRARIAN CYCLES, SOCIAL
TRANSFORMATION

On the 29th October 1935, Lázaro Cárdenas, President of the Mexican Republic, signed a Presidential Resolution granting an ejido to 316 beneficiaries to be drawn from the *peones acasillados* of the Great Hacienda of Guaracha in the Ciénega de Chapala. Though the President was to sign many more such resolutions in the coming months, and the redistribution of land to contracted wage-laborers represented an important new phase in agrarian policy nationally, this one had a very personal significance for him. The boundaries of the 35,000 hectare Guaracha estate had run up to the outskirts of Jiquilpan, the small provincial administrative town where Don Lázaro had grown up.

This book examines the history and contemporary results of land reform in the backyard of Mexico's greatest reforming President as seen through the eyes of the peasantry who are its supposed beneficiaries. My empirical objectives therefore appear straightforward enough, though the facts of the case turn out to be less so. But there are now innumerable studies of Mexico's ejidos, a vast theoretical literature on the "Agrarian Question" as it pertains to the Mexican case, and an equally extensive corpus of writings on the relationship between Mexican peasants and the Mexican state. Before I make any specific claims for this particular work by sketching out the arguments and lines of analysis it presents, I should begin by addressing the question of why it is worth adding another book, especially one based on the apparently narrow horizons of an anthropological field study.

THE LIMITS AND POSSIBILITIES OF
ETHNOGRAPHIC KNOWLEDGE

This book is an ethnography. Its historical analysis is based mainly on the oral testimony of local people, and its basic data were collected through structured interviews, supplemented by questionnaires, casual spontaneous conversation and the direct observation of formal and informal occasions of social interaction during fieldwork. It is also an ethnography which focuses primarily on a single community. Yet I am going to use the material I have collected to address and try to advance general arguments, some of which are intended to be relevant not only to other regions of Latin America, but to other parts of the world. The reader is quite entitled to feel that these claims seem contradictory and implausible, for, in a sense, they are.

I do not claim that Guaracha represents rural Mexico in microcosm. Nor do I claim it portrays a "typical" peasant community within its own microregion. It was because this community and its region had certain specific historical and contemporary characteristics that I chose to undertake my research here. All too often, theorizing about the peasantry and its place in developing capitalist societies abstracts from the diversity of regional agrarian structures, a diversity which is particularly marked in the Mexican case, and has been a persistent factor in the social landscape since the dawn of the colonial era. It is equally common for empirical studies of particular regions at particular moments of time to become transformed into ahistorical position markers in polemical debates. This is certainly the fate which has tended to befall Chayanov, and to an even greater extent those Mexican Chayanovians who can less easily be accused of sharing their mentor's essentialism: it is the reward, but also the curse, of original and profound insights into historically bounded reality. Studies conducted in particular places twenty years ago or more can certainly still convey insights of contemporary relevance, but it is necessary to recognize that the world moves on, perhaps at an accelerating rate.

Anthropologists are particularly beset by the problem of the historicity of their endeavors. Fieldwork takes a long time. Analyzing field data takes even longer. And at the end of the day, the individual anthropological researcher can accomplish so little, if he or she persists with the intensive, microscopic examination of human reality characteristic of the so-called method of "participant observation." Anthropologists can, and have, adopted larger frames of reference, and the particular virtues of anthropological research at the regional level as an antidote to the excesses of the "micro" and "macro" poles of analysis have been abundantly demonstrated in terms of practical results as well as justified methodologically at a more abstract level (Wolf 1955, De la Peña 1981, Long and Roberts 1984). I have no quarrel with these arguments. In fact I insist that anthropologists must be prepared to work with national, international and, as this study seeks to demonstrate, transnational, units of analysis. Nor am I at all enthusiastic for the argument that anthropological perspectives can or should be autonomous with respect to work in other disciplines. Little of what any of us has to say has (thankfully) yet become so esoteric as to be unintelligible to scholars in other fields (and *vice versa*), nor are our professionally inculcated methodologies so arcane as to be beyond at least reasonably effective replication by scholars trained in other fields when analytical need arises. But more importantly, the human problems with which we are all grappling in our several ways are far too serious to be reduced to the objects of professionalization and the commoditization of knowledge, even if such a reduction is to some extent inevitable given the world we live in. Yet we may perhaps make a more modest and legitimate claim for the more detailed kind of knowledge produced by anthropological fieldwork of a traditional kind.

There are genuine virtues in the close analysis of human sociocultural realities through micro-level field studies, and there are ways of looking analytically at those realities which are the collective legacy of the discipline's exploration of the cross-cultural variety of human experience. We can

embody those virtues and strengths in our work without self-delusion by systematically addressing the limitations of the different types of knowledge
produced by different types of empirical enquiry and levels of analysis. This
is what this book sets out to do. Analysis of the specific data on Guaracha
will frequently lead me to pose questions which cannot possibly be answered
empirically on the basis of the data acquired by this, or any other, case study.
My response to this dilemma is to indicate the extent to which collectively
accumulated knowledge leads us towards a particular answer at this moment
of time, and what further investigation would be desirable in order to pursue
the issue. Much of the argument of the book is critical of established ways of
looking at "the problem of the peasantry," and I use my particular data to
demonstrate the usefulness of other conceptualizations in this specific case.
In looking beyond the immediate empirical and historical horizons of my
field study, I offer what are simply pointers as to how to proceed with larger
arguments which must, of necessity, be conducted on a different basis and at
a different level of abstraction. There is a justification for moving towards
these issues from an anthropological field study: the local is inevitably con-
ceptualized from the standpoint of prior conceptions of the global, and any
limitations in existing higher level abstractions revealed through grappling
with the concrete should therefore merit attention.

We can, however, make one final and straightforward claim for anthropological research at the micro-level. Though anthropologists have made all
manner of dubious epistemological claims for the profundity of the knowledge of "other cultures" produced by fieldwork, we might do better to tell our
paymasters about the more mundane advantages of living in a place and gaining the confidence of those we study. The data on such matters as ejidal land
tenure or international migration provided in this book could not have been
obtained in any other way. Though there are more "exotic" kinds of data in
the book of which the same would be equally true, and much of the data
obtained requires a degree of filtering in presentation on my part for ethical
reasons, if one wishes to provide an accurate picture of the mundane realities
of the social reproduction of a *campesino* community it is hard to see how
such a picture could be obtained without doing anthropological fieldwork.
Readers can judge this particular claim for themselves, but there is one type
of reader whose judgment is, for me, particularly important. Many
campesinos in Guaracha themselves read books (or have them read to them).
They gave me information on the understanding that I would try to transmit
the reality of their historical experience to the outside world in as accurate a
way as I could. Neither they, nor I, are so naive as to imagine that there is a
"truth" here which stands above particular points of view and interests,
including my own. Since the *campesinos* are not socially homogeneous, the
truth of their history is a contested domain of facts and meanings. But I have
tried to write the book in a way which provides a vehicle for these various
truths to find expression, without trying to pretend such expression is

unmediated by making use of the literary and rhetorical devices which are currently so much in vogue in Anglo-Saxon anthropology or abandoning the objectifying thrust I would maintain is the only honest response on the part of the outside observer of other social realities.

I hope that this volume will convey something of the human experience underlying its more abstract analytical concerns, an experience which is worth documenting in its own right, as a testament to the remarkable nature of "ordinary people." What is at issue here, I hope, is more than a populist enthusiasm for being on the side of the oppressed, or guilty conscience on the part of the privileged bourgeois whose career is advanced by prying into other people's misfortunes. People and their social worlds are multidimensional. Yet much of our academic literature reduces the peasant to one dimension—the occupant of an economic, social or political niche in a larger social world where he (or she, but usually he!) is interesting only as a victim of history and the various structures of domination which define his or her place in the larger totality. It is not that these perspectives are incorrect, since adopting them does raise significant issues. But they are certainly incomplete, and predispose us to lose sight of much that is essential to understanding both the objective and subjective reproduction of the peasantry as a social category.

This, then, is a study which unashamedly embraces the particular facts of a historical social situation, and uses those facts to address generalizations about contemporary agrarian realities in Mexico and their wider determinants and significance. My approach will generally be one of chiselling away at the apparently idiosyncratic and contingent aspects of social existence to identify the social facts which constitute them and the determinants and effects of those social facts in terms of the larger movement of Mexican society since the Revolution. I believe this approach has its virtues. But some might still argue that the entire object of study here is an illusion. What is the place of peasant studies, and especially anthropological peasant studies, in the world of the 1990s? It is well worth posing this question, especially in the Mexican case, since the answer is not at all self-evident, and critics of anthropologists' work in this field muster serious arguments which demand a response.

THE PEASANTRY—A PROBLEM FOR HISTORIANS?

At the end of a short paper discussing the impact of the urbanization of agricultural land in the state of Morelos, Michael Redclift despairingly remarks:

> In the case of Morelos, part of the reason for the demise of "peasant" movements and the restructuring of the peasantry lies in the urbanization of agricultural land, a process which has been ignored by all but a handful of social scientists...while hundreds of Mexican and foreign scholars still descend on ejidos or communities to record their history and internal dynamics, it is left to

a few journalists and students from the Universidad Autónoma
Metropolitana Ixtapalapa to study *fraccionamiento* development.
(Redclift 1986:100)

This particular facet of changing "rural" reality is scarcely central to the
Ciénega de Chapala at the present time, though much of the capital generated
in the agrarian economy does end up being sunk into urban real estate, often
in Zamora, Morelia, Guadalajara or Mexico City. But there are a number of
other respects in which the entrenched rural-urban divides of so much of the
traditional literature are as unsatisfactory even in what is supposedly still a
predominantly rural state as they evidently are in contemporary Morelos.
Moreover, the short answer to the puzzle posed by Redclift—to what do we
owe our ignorance, despite all these armies of rural researchers?—is quite
simple. Rural research and peasant studies are an academic specialization.

There is, however, a much longer, more complex, and possibly more
meaningful answer. There are intensely practical, political determinants of
the various types of literature which have appeared over the decades on the
Mexican peasantry, brilliantly surveyed for an English-speaking audience by
Cynthia Hewitt (1984). While some, mainly foreign, anthropologists may
have dedicated themselves to the study of the peasantry in search of an object
of analysis sharing some of the characteristics of the "primitive" small-scale
society, or even out of pure romanticism, Mexico's variant on the long-standing debate on "The Agrarian Question" has a genuinely substantial content.
The link between agrarian policy and the political strategy of the post-revolutionary elite before Cárdenas becomes somewhat more intelligible if one
credits its authors with the conviction that the peasantry was doomed to
extinction through the operation of inexorable economic forces. The Mexican
state's contribution to the conservation of the peasantry through land reform
posed questions which leftward-leaning analysts could hardly have ignored,
even in abstraction from the general awakening of interest in the problem of
the peasantry's survival throughout the capitalist world during the 1960s.
What was the ultimate position of this reconstituted peasantry with respect to
the prospects for socialist advance through class-based mass politics? Perhaps
land reform is ultimately a conservative force, even if, as in the Mexican
case, it originates in a context of genuine popular struggle rather than as a
purely manipulative intervention from above.

Mexican neo-populist arguments which denied an ultimate coincidence of
interest between "rural" *campesinos* and "urban" workers at least grappled
with some of the evident contradictions between classical Marxist theory and
reality on two fronts: the explanation of actual mass politics, and the more
normative but politically crucial issue of what constituted an acceptable form
of "development" from the point of view of rural people. Though the
Marxist-structuralist literature of the late 1960s and 1970s often tended
towards economism and frequently degenerated into formalism, the debates

on "modes" versus "forms" of production, characterization of peasants as "disguised proletarians," "peasantization" and "depeasantization" and so forth, represented genuine, and in comparison with the absurdities of modernization theories, extremely fruitful advances, advances which to some extent recognized the changing nature of rural reality. Most of these writers also addressed the implications of their attempt at "objective" analysis of class structures for political behavior and the development of mass-based social movements.

It would be an error to dismiss these traditions of politically committed and scholarly work as transcended by the relentless march of a process of social transformation on which they were silent because this would be patently untrue. If, for example, the Morelos studied by Arturo Warman and his associates in the 1960s was a different Morelos from that of the 1980s, Warman's contribution to the Chayanovian tradition was precisely to demonstrate that the logic of peasant economy was to be found in its capacity to adapt and innovate in response to changing circumstances which were changes in urban-rural and peasant-state relationships (Alonso *et al.* 1974, Warman 1976). It might, of course, seem that one of the fundamental problems with the whole field of peasant studies is that defining peasants as "farmers" (especially "family farmers") is less and less meaningful as more and more of the peasant household reproduction process becomes tied to other activities—including new forms of urban-derived non-agricultural production in rural locations as well as various forms of rural-urban migration—and the residual "peasant" labor process becomes increasingly subsumed by the agro-industrial complex of modern transnational capitalism. But as Shanin points out, the argument may cut both ways:

> Peasants still form a major part of mankind, but their numbers are stationary while their share in the population of the "developing societies" is rapidly in decline. They are also being "incorporated" while the livelihoods of those who survive as rural smallholders increasingly include what has been considered as "nonpeasant" characteristics. A decline in the significance and particularity of peasantries leading to a parallel depeasantation [*sic*] of the social sciences can be predicted, with Chayanov assigned eventually to the archives. Or can it? ...A central element of contemporary global society is the failure of the capitalist economies as well as of state economies to advance unlimitedly and to secure general welfare in ways expected by the nineteenth century theories of progress, liberal and socialist alike...While in the "developing societies" islands of precapitalism disappear, what comes instead is mostly not the industrial proletariat of Europe's nineteenth century but strata of plebeian survivors ... another extracapitalist pattern of social and economic existence

under capitalism and/or third-worldish types of state
economy...Theoretically the analysis of modes of incorporation
by a dominant political economy is in increasing need of being
supplemented by the parallel study of modes of nonincorporation
operating in the worlds we live in. [Shanin 1986: 22-23]

One might quarrel with some of the phrasing and conceptualization of
Shanin's argument in these passages, but it is harder to reject the essential
logic of what he is arguing. The demise of the "farmer-peasant" is not necessarily equivalent to the demise of the problems posed by this "awkward
class." If anything, they have now become the problems posed by the once
unproblematic "working classes." It may be helpful to add a quantitative
dimension to the picture as it stands for Mexico at this juncture. We should
bear in mind here that Mexico is one of the most industrialized countries in
the contemporary Third World, and that its modern industrialization process
had its beginnings, albeit limited ones, in the Porfirian era, though we should
also remember that only a quarter of the Mexican working population is classified as being in industrial employment of any kind in official statistics, and
that the real structures of industrial production in all its forms—including
unregulated workshops, domestic outwork and so on—are often associated
with patterns of household labor mobility from factory work to other forms of
activity which make the association of "sectors" with discrete social classes
highly problematic (Connolly 1985). Table 1 provides a superficial picture
based on aggregate data.

Though the Mexican state's definition of rural population is hardly ideal
from the point of view of grasping socio-economic realities, the gross figures
have certain advantages over more specific kinds of measures. They underscore the fact that, however they actually earn a living, a very large absolute
number of modern Mexicans may still think of themselves as *campesinos*.
From the political point of view, this may be significant, even though only a
tiny minority of *campesinos* is incorporated into the framework of agrarian
reform or engaged in family farming outside the land reform sector. It is now
a commonplace to observe that there are more Mexicans theoretically entitled
to benefit under the agrarian reform legislation alive today than there were at
the time of the Mexican revolution, while both land concentration and rural
family income distributive inequality measures have actually risen since 1940
(Tirado de Ruíz 1971, Ginneken 1980). How relevant these facts might be
politically is something which I will attempt to assess in the conclusions of
this book, but it is important to keep absolute numbers of people in mind
rather than proportions and percentages when considering "the problem of
the countryside."

Again, however, the argument cuts both ways. According to the Fifth
Agricultural Census of 1970, more than two million Mexicans held rights to
land as ejidatarios under the Land Reform program. Though in theory

Table 1

URBANIZATION AND POPULATION GROWTH
IN MEXICO, 1900-1977

Year	Population (thousands)		As percentage of Total Population		Rate of Growth
	Urban	Rural	Urban	Rural	(%)
1900	1,657	11,950	12.18	87.82	1.3
1910	2,034	13,126	13.42	86.58	1.3
1925	—	—	—	—	6.6
1930	3,272	13,281	19.77	80.23	—
1935	—	—	—	—	19.7
1940	4,298	13,356	21.87	78.13	—
1945	—	—	—	—	25.4
1950	7,453	18,338	29.90	71.10	—
1955	—	—	—	—	31.8
1960	13,751	21,239	39.30	60.70	—
1965	—	—	—	—	34.7
1970	23,811	25,182	48.60	51.40	—
1975	—	—	—	—	32.5
1977	34,524	27,648	55.53	44.47	—

Source: Dirección General de Estadística, Secretaría de Programación y Presupuesto

ejidatarios outnumber "small private farmers with less than 5 hectare" by more than three to one, the 1970 population census only records around 800,000 of the former as "working their own plot of land during most of the year" (Ginneken 1980:63). Even these figures should be taken with a pinch of salt, since the official census can take little effective cognizance of the rental of ejidal land to private entrepreneurs. In a real sense "the problem of the countryside" is not the problem of the ejidatarios, who constitute a relatively privileged minority, but the problems of the landless who remain in the countryside, or move between countryside, city and the United States. These include, of course, a high proportion of the ejidatarios' own children.

THE NATURE OF THE PROBLEM
POSED BY THE EJIDOS

This study does address itself to the "problem of the countryside" in the larger sense. Nevertheless, the ejidatarios remain a not insignificant problem in their own right. Politically, the land reform peasantry has been a major prop to the regime of the PRI in times past, and while they are becoming an increasingly small percentage of the State's mass clientele in terms of occupational and sectoral divisions, it would perhaps be simplistic to assume that their condition is no longer of any moment. Many of the people who belong to the other, numerically preponderant, "mass" sectors which the PRI seeks to mobilize are, of course, the close kin of ejidatarios and retain regular contact with their rural communities of origin even if they were born in the cities. But more significantly, perhaps, land reform is of enormous ideological significance to the regime. Despite repeated attempts to declare land redistribution a process which has reached its practical historical limits, the Mexican state has been forced to acknowledge its continuing responsibility for generating employment and "development" for the populations of rural areas. When all is said and done, despite all the changes, the ejido, that "peculiarly Mexican institution," with its archaic colonial name, remains at the heart of the state's claims to legitimacy.

Furthermore, the issue of land redistribution cannot be disposed of too readily. Not only are the gross violations of Mexico's agrarian legislation a feature of the rural social landscape and a symbol of the injustice and duplicity of the country's political class, but the increasing emphasis on land reform elsewhere in the Americas helps to perpetuate the principle of struggle for the land as it is diffused through the mass media. As Martínez-Alier (1977) has suggested, it would be wrong to think of the demand for land as a "primordial" peasant demand which requires no explanation since it is universal and natural: land may not necessarily be preferred to employment and a salary, and, as we will see, the major goal of many Guaracheño ejidatarios has been to emancipate their children from the peasant life. On the other hand, the picture from Latin America suggests that some of the most vigorous struggles for the land today are pursued by those who have seen the urban future and have found it wanting. Given the alternatives presented by modern Third World socio-economic systems, it seems unlikely indeed that land reform will cease to be one of the major directions of popular struggle for the foreseeable future. In the time it takes to read this introduction, someone, somewhere will probably have died for the land.

This is not a book about "development policy." There are, of course, powerful arguments concerning the advantages of land reform as a means of securing a form of "development" which achieves progress towards establishing the mimimum levels of general social welfare that were so patently not achieved in the early epoch of post-war economic growth (Griffin 1974). In reviewing the Mexican experience, it is hard not to dwell on its negative aspects. One of my reasons for deciding to work in a region like the Ciénega was to take what would appear to provide a favorable context for ejidal farming. Although not all the ejidatarios in Guaracha and neighboring communities have access to prime agricultural land, a majority does possess rights to land which is fertile and irrigated. The entire terrain of the ex-hacienda on the plain was distributed among ejidos. Though the region was relatively neglected in terms of infrastructural investments by the central government until the 1960s, in more recent years substantial investments have been made to improve on what was already a comparatively good base. Yet until the 1970s, the region was scarcely a success story for the ejidal system. Vast numbers of peasant plots were rented long-term to a capitalist neolatifundist whom the ejidatarios referred to as their new *patrón*. If the epoch of *neolatifundismo* of this kind ended with the introduction of the new state policies to "refunctionalize" the ejidos, and a large proportion of ejidatarios returned to sowing their land in the 1970s, they did so under conditions which set strict limits on the income which could be derived from peasant farming by those dependent on the official credit system, promoted new forms of subsumption of the peasant process by capital, fostered capital accumulation in other sectors, and left the peasants, as most of them see it, where they have always been, "at the bottom of Mexican society."

During my fieldwork, I was able to observe what were probably the last moments of this phase of the region's agrarian history, since the deepening crisis into which the country was sliding was already producing signs of change: on my subsequent visits in 1986 and 1988, rental of ejidal land (and international migration) had shown a further increase. But rental of ejidal land today is a somewhat different phenomenon from that of the earlier period of *neolatifundismo*. Today's farmers include numerous members of the state's own agrarian bureaucracy or investors from outside the agrarian sector, like restaurant owners from the regional towns, as well as longer established elements of the regional agrarian bourgeoisie. In the 1960s, large-scale capitalist tomato growers entered the region from the Bajío, primarily with a view to expanding production for the growing Guadalajara metropolitan market. Today vegetable production on a large scale is increasingly orientated to export. The "modernization" and internationalization of local production systems hands local economic power to truckers and owners of machines, though such people are, in reality, only the immediate local manifestations of much larger and infinitely more powerful forces. As another facet of these larger processes, *emigrados* with steady jobs in the U.S. acquire titles to ejidal land. The 1980s therefore have brought a multitude of "new men" into the contest to capture control of the patrimony of peasant communities.

These brief observations give an indication of the framework which underpins the analysis of this book: the notion that the post-revolutionary agrarian history of the Ciénega corresponds to a sequence of agrarian cycles characterized by the ebb and flow of peasant commitment to farming the land, and the expansion and contraction of various forms of capitalism and state intervention. The nature of the cycles is more complex than these brief and superficial statements can indicate, but it is important to emphasize from the outset that there are irreversible secular processes of change at work beneath these apparently cyclical phenomena.

From the point of view of the reproduction of the ejidal system, one such secular trend is the rising value of the land. In theory, ejidatarios receive only (inalienable) rights to use the land, which can only be transferred in perpetuity through direct inheritance or the nomination of an eligible successor approved by the agrarian community in the event of no heir being available. In practice, land rights are commoditized.[1] Competition between capitalist renters, and the prospect of securing good returns to investment in production available to those who have the capital, has driven up the going rate for definitive sale of ejidal rights, and acquiring such rights has progressively become beyond the means of the children of peasant families. In past decades, "new ejidatarios" were able to acquire land through savings from seasonal migration to the United States or other forms of work outside the community. Today's "new ejidatarios" are often people earning professional salaries and state employees. If yesterday's purchasers of ejidal titles included such evidently ineligible figures as the ex-neolatifundist, a resident of another community, what is striking about the situation today is that the same entrepreneur has been able to add to his holdings in Guaracha and, worse, has been joined by members of the agrarian bureaucracy. Though the changing land tenure situation is far from being the only secular tendency at work, and is one which could theoretically be reversed at a stroke simply by an agrarian census and purging of the ejidal rolls in conformity with the agrarian laws, the point is, of course, that nothing has ever been done in this region in this sphere. At the present rate, half the ejidatarios may be holders of university degrees by the end of the century.

In the light of what I have already said about the role of "the problem of the countryside" and the place of the ejidal system in Mexico's system of political control, it becomes apparent that we are not simply looking at land reform's "failures" from the point of view of the criteria defined by development policy. We are looking at the wholesale perversion of theory by practice and the incipient total disintegration of the framework of land reform agriculture in a productive and fertile region of the country. In the past, the peasants were exploited by merchant capital while they tried to farm their land, and ceased to be "real ejidatarios" when they rented their land for long periods. But the situation was reversible to a degree: the reexpansion of the state made the ejidatarios "work for capitalism" in new ways, but they were, to an extent, reconstituted as a rural underclass of a specific type, enjoying clear advantages over the landless day-laborers as *dueños* of their land. It is the possibility of this recurring in the future which is now increasingly in question. The more the ranks of the peasant ejidatarios are eroded, the more dangerous the situation may become politically in the long-term in the absence of an alternative and comprehensive solution to the country's mounting social problems.

In writing about the negative side of Mexico's land reform program, my objective is not really to provoke feelings of righteous indignation but to direct analysis towards a realistic and concrete view of the realities of peasant life. It is pointless to discuss these matters as if they were pathologies with respect to the normal functioning of the system, as many analyses seem to do. If one wants to ask what determined the income from farming of a significant number of ejidatarios in Guaracha in certain years, it would be meaningless to do the calculation in terms of harvest volume multiplied by price minus costs: what in fact determined it was that the inspectors of BANRURAL, the official credit bank, and the ANAGSA, the state agricultural insurance agency, volunteered to record harvests as a total loss, allowing the ejidatarios to sell their crops at the free market price without repaying their debts to the state.

The question immediately at issue here is how much the peasants are willing to pay the inspectors for this service, and how much public money can be wasted or stolen by the bureaucracy without exciting action from a higher level. These questions in turn invite us to explain the social and political conditions which promote such behavior on the part of the servants of the state, on the one hand, and a lack of effective collective resistance on the part of the ejidatarios when it is they who are the chief victims of such abuses—as they often are—on the other. In posing these questions, one begins to see that there is more to these phenomena than a term like "corruption" would imply, and that the nature of bureaucracy in Mexico may be one of several effects of the structures of social power determining the basis and limits of state power in the country. Similarly, the vicissitudes of agrarian policy, with their spectacular effects on agrarian structures, demand an explanation in terms of the complex shifts in national and international social forces which underlie them.

A concern with the scandalous becomes an analytical necessity if one wishes to explain the realities of Mexican social and political life and, by extension, that of many other parts of the world. Nevertheless, it must be conceded that many Mexicans are understandably irritated when foreigners come to their country to do studies which belittle their achievements and dwell only on the negative. Though I could offer an additional defense of such a focus by observing that a majority of the peasantry express themselves dissatisfied with their treatment, I would prefer to emphasize a different point. If one compares the situation I describe for the early 1980s with earlier epochs, especially that of the hacienda, or with the situation obtaining to the south in Central America, then the positive achievements of Mexico's land reform program are apparent enough. Land reform has not solved the problems of rural poverty. It only assists a minority of rural people, and peasants who hold irrigated land in the Ciénega de Chapala are clearly better placed than the many who hold resources of inferior quality. What emerges from this often dismal history is that land reform is capable of improving the lot of rural people. It is the very failures of Mexico's land reform program which underscore what might have been achieved, and what might yet be achieved.

My purpose is not to suggest what would be desirable in the abstract: it is to describe what has been and is and address the problem of causes. The future will be, and must be, determined by what Mexicans choose to do about their situation, though the simplistic voluntarism of the use of the word "choice" here abstracts utterly from the powerful historical forces which are likely to foreclose on many developmental possibilities being realized. Nevertheless, if voluntarism, to some extent a hallmark of western Marxism in the post-war period (Skocpol 1979), is indefensible, so is the idea that history is determined by blind, mechanistic historical forces immune to the impact of human struggles to transform reality. The ideas and data presented by this and other studies may or may not play a minor role in the evolving stream of social and political action which will determine Mexico's future. But what is certain is that such action will shape the future as much as it has shaped the past. Furthermore, as this book will seek to demonstrate, social struggles in which peasants engage cannot be defined in terms of self-conscious collective political action alone, the visible struggles accompanied by slogans and banners. Had the Mexican peasantry's survival been determined solely by its participation in social movements of an overtly "politicized" kind, movements which history demonstrates are so susceptible to the processes of cooptation and incorporation by other strata, today's reality might be very different from what it is. There are other ways in which peasants have contested the forces of capitalist expansion and political domination which can only be discerned in the less visible history of the practice of daily life. They are unromantic forms of social action, and quite ineffective by conventional definitions of what class struggles are supposed to achieve: their effects are neither "conservative" in the strict sense, since survival has been accompanied by transformation, nor are they "revolutionary", either in effect or intent. But they are, I will argue, significant determinants of historical reality.

AGRICULTURAL CHANGE AND RURAL TRANSFORMATIONS

The larger problem of which the ejidos constitute a facet, that of Mexican agriculture as a whole, certainly remains of undiminished significance. Though the contribution of agro-pastoral activities to Mexico's GDP fell from 20.6% to 8.4% in the years between 1939 and 1980, while that of manufacturing industry rose from 14.7% to 23.1% over the same period, the agricultural sector made a prominent contribution to the process of industrialization, and the impact of the burdens placed upon the peasant sector in pursuit of industrialization eventuated in a crisis of basic foodstuffs production which, together with mounting rural unrest, forced significant responses from the Mexican state in the late 1960s and 1970s. Today, in another epoch of crisis, the problems of sustaining agricultural productivity and balancing earnings derived from exports of meat, fruit and vegetables against the import and wider social costs entailed in the transfer of resources from basic grains production have scarcely diminished in significance. Now, however, we are in an era where industrialization has transformed agriculture itself.

For the majority of the population of the "developed" world, agriculture has become a profoundly mysterious phenomenon, about which people know little and care less, except in so far as they feel compassion for those they see starving or resentment when politicians draw their attention to the extent to which their taxes are being used to subsidize farmers. Agriculture is also rather boring and "natural." Unfortunately, modern agriculture is a highly unnatural activity, and the functioning of agricultural systems is much more dependent on political economies than the vagaries of the climate, while the man-made ecosystems which such political economies create generate their own share of unnatural disasters. It is vitally important to understand that the political economy which shapes Mexican agriculture is not entirely located within the country's national boundaries, and that Mexican *campesinos* gain a livelihood from a larger agrarian political economy whose center lies in the United States, whether or not the production of the raw crop is carried out there or to the south.

The impact on agriculture of the internationalization of capital has been subject to some penetrating analyses in the Mexican case (Barkin and Suárez 1985, Sanderson 1986, Durán 1988). This is perhaps to be expected given that while a large part of what has happened in Mexico has also happened in other regions as a consequence of the developmental dynamics of the capitalist world economy, Mexico enjoys the unique privilege of a land frontier with the heartland of northern economic power, whose own "core" is now located to the west, articulated to the new web of relationships which have shifted the center of gravity of the world economy from the Atlantic to the Pacific Rim. Questions pertaining to the internationalization of Mexican agriculture can scarcely be avoided in a study of Michoacán, since the regions of Zamora and Apatzingán have been the sites of particularly significant North American agribusiness developments (Feder 1978). The Zamora strawberry agro-industry's direct influence spread as far west as the Ciénega, from which it has recruited large numbers of young girls and more mature women workers, though on a declining scale in recent years. But the entire productive structure of Mexican agriculture has been changed through more indirect processes of "internationalization". Direct investment in production, contract farming systems and processing facilities by North American capitalism may wax and then wane, as it has done in Zamora, where the *congeladoras* have now been sold off to local entrepreneurs. But there are more subtle relations of transformation and domination at work in the evolution of the modern agro-industrial complex, and the nature of the Mexican state's "refunctionalization" of the ejidal system has played an important role in ensuring that these tendencies have impacted with maximum vigor. The initial phases of the decline in the marketed surplus of basic foodstuffs offered by the peasant producer appeared to be the result simply of the domestic policy of squeezing the peasantry to accelerate the pace of industrialization, and therefore correctable by a change of policy. But it is no longer clear whether the improvements the implementation of changes brought about can stem the impact of these deeper forces in the long term. As Barkin and Suárez have argued, the "end of food self-sufficiency" seems to be a general trend throughout the Third World, and a normal consequence of capitalist expansion and the integration of peasants into the world market (1985:240-242). That the situation in Mexico is not worse than it is may owe more to the forms of economic rationality pursued by peasant households under adverse conditions than to official policy. But the real issue is how far the objective social conditions for such behavior are being progressively eroded.

The Ciénega provides a useful test case for pursuing these questions in a number of respects. As I have already noted, ejidal land includes fertile irrigated terrain, capable of producing large commercial surpluses and susceptible to the unfettered pursuit of the processes of agricultural "modernization." The ejidal farmers who possess such lands have theoretically been the prime beneficiaries of state policies aimed at refunctionalizing the ejidal system. The Guaracha case does not permit an analysis of the alternative policy of ejidal collectivization in its modern forms, since it remains an ejido based on individual tenure and cultivation. It is, however, important to stress that the ejido did begin as a collective enterprise producing sugar. Furthermore, it was a particularly important case of early ejidal collectivization under Cárdenas, because the newly emancipated peasants received the ex-hacienda's mill, to be run as a cooperative venture, as well as the land. Since the early and spectacular failure of this experiment, all further attempts to promote cooperative projects have failed in an equally radical fashion in this community. Though this is in itself of more than passing interest, it does foreclose on certain avenues of discussion. What the case does offer is the possibility of a fairly full reflection on the situation with respect to individualized forms of cultivation, since some ejidatarios in Guaracha must dry-farm *parcelas* located on the stoney lower slopes of the hills surrounding the plain, and cannot in practice opt for the mechanized styles of cultivation which have become dominant on the plain itself. Furthermore, both ejidatarios and non-ejidatarios have access to rain-fed plots higher up in the hills, which were assigned to the hacienda peons as subsistence plots to supplement their cash wages and maize rations. These plots, still known by their Purhépecha name as *ecuaros*, have in some cases been made suitable for plow cultivation by animals through clearance of larger stones and terracing, a transformation which represents a considerable investment of labor. From the techno-ecological point of view, therefore, Guaracha and its neighboring communities provide a cross-section of the different conditions of agricultural production faced by Mexico's peasant farmers today.

Non-ecological conditions of production, in particular access to credit, also vary for this aggregate of farmers in a way which reflects the general shifts in financial aid offered to the peasantry at national level under changing state policy orientations and national economic conditions. Where the marginal farming enterprise is located at a particular moment of time is, however, influenced by the conjunction of local conditions: besides the impact of regional price structures, official credit levels have been set in accordance with average regional costs of production, penalizing those farmers with inferior resource endowments given the official bank's assumptions about appropriate technical inputs, degree of mechanization, etc. Furthermore, official policy also influences the location of peasant agriculture as a whole in relation to the margins which can be identified for the agricultural production system as a totality: the real cost of credit determines which, if any, peasant producers are capable of sharing in the appropriation of differential rents and whether they can recover the value of unpaid labor-time which has been embodied in output whose market price is related to average enterprise productivity in a given crop sector—which may be international—and the relative market share of enterprises with different cost structures (Margulis 1979, Gledhill 1981).

Although these matters are usually discussed in terms of a gross division between "capitalist" and "peasant" enterprises, on the assumption that these forms of production are distinguished by their total and secondary dependence on wage labor respectively, peasants in the Ciénega, and by implication elsewhere, are really far too heterogeneous a category for this style of analysis to be totally satisfactory. This point of view will be reinforced when we consider the actual use of wage-labor by peasant farmers in the Ciénega and the extent to which peasant reproduction is commoditized under contemporary conditions. Furthermore, household reproduction is based on the combination of a variety of different income sources, arising from the different contributions of individual family members. Internal household distributive relations, and the constitution of the effective income-sharing consumption unit, vary, as does the combination of activities which together provide overall disposable income. All this leads to varying possibilities for substituting family for paid labor and reducing cash expenditures by household production and pooling arrangements. Thus, beyond the basic differences in possible family economic strategies determined by the unequal distribution of farming resources of varying quality, and the differing possibilities for access to credit determined by these agricultural resource endowments, part of the variability in the overall economic strategies of households is determined by their non-agricultural activities.

To make matters more complex still, additional agro-pastoral activities such as goat-herding may be combined with farming, and are occasionally pursued in preference to it. Though one might expect a considerable variety in the economic strategies of the poorer non-ejidatarios, there is, in fact, a very substantial variation among the ejidatarios themselves. Nevertheless, one can still identify a particularly significant margin in the case of the ejidal producers whose land is of sufficient quality to secure a rental income, that at which the ejidatario decides to withdraw from direct involvement in production. Ejidatarios are often unable to secure a family livelihood from the *parcela* and are constantly faced with choices about how to allocate their labor time between different activities and employment possibilities which have long since become integral to what is generally a semi-proletarian form of peasant existence. One of the most striking features of the current situation in the Ciénega, from the point of view of those peasants whose position was significantly improved under the new state agrarian regime of the 1970s, is the rapid and accelerating increase in the costs of irrigation water and non-labor inputs: though they may never have been able to secure a family livelihood from their farming, the huge sums to be repaid at the present time have produced a wave of defaults and voluntary withdrawals from the official system, and frequently the total abandonment of farming the *parcela*. Though short-term expectations shift in accordance with general economic uncertainty, consumer price inflation, and problems with the state guaranteed farm price system, there seems to be little doubt that the margin relevant to levels of peasant participation in production has been shifted in structural terms.

The implications from the point of view of Mexico's agricultural problems are clear: peasant farming of high quality land tends to give way to disguised capitalist farming unless the state intervenes to make it worthwhile for such farmers to farm. The variations in resource endowments, which apparently make the ejidatarios with irrigated land less marginal farmers than those sweating with their horse-drawn plows on unirrigated rocky terrain, do not, in fact, provide a reliable guide to the political economy of peasant agriculture under modern conditions. Of course it might be argued, cynically, that it does not really matter whether a crop is grown by an poor ejidatario, a restaurant-owner from the town of Sahuayo, an Inspector from BANRURAL in Jiquilpan, or the village primary school headmaster. Indeed, since the ejidatario is probably in a better position to borrow money to take a trip to California, and may not need to do so if he uses the money from renting his land, the situation could prove quite satisfactory from the national point of view. The displaced ejidatario exports his unemployment, while the possessor of capital who takes over his agricultural role may have the financial wherewithal to produce a splendid harvest at no risk or cost to the harrassed federal treasury.[2]

The problem is that, aside from any considerations relating to the supposed social policy objectives of agrarian policy, restauranteurs are more likely to be interested in sowing high-value vegetables than basic grains, and there is always the danger that speculative capital entering the ejidos may not husband its ecological resources as it should, as Díaz-Polanco and Montandon (1978) demonstrated for the case of neolatifundist production of sorghum in the Bajío. In practice, this latter problem has not been too serious in the Ciénega. Capitalist entrepreneurs have tended to pursue cultivation practices which would be deemed superior by the standards of modernizers, partly because they have frequently rented long-term, even if their heavy use of chemical fertilizers and pesticides might be subject to a broader kind of environmentalist critique. Renters from the ranks of the agrarian bureaucracy sometimes make improvements to the land (often, of course, without cost to themselves through "creative accounting" with the use of public resources). This was a carrot which was frequently offered to peasants to encourage them to rent in days when land was in shorter supply. From the ecosystemic point of view, the sorghum monocropping regime which a majority of ejidatario farmers chose to pursue in years gone by, in consequence of their undercapitalization, shortage of disposable family labor and the official credit system, has been far more damaging. But suppose we discount the ecological aspect and ignore the possible social and political implications of a renewed disintegration of the ejidal system, given the expectations aroused by the improved situation of the previous decade. It is still hard to conduct an agricultural policy on this *laissez-faire* basis. Market forces, national and international, will continue to transform the structure of Mexican agricultural production in a way which the state cannot control.

In the longer term, the cost may be high. It would certainly be high if technologically modernized peasant producers can indeed provide supplies of basic grains to the domestic market at lower cost than the alternatives of fully-fledged capitalist production or importation. And if the cost of persuading capitalists to reenter the sector of basic grains production most abandoned a decade ago (Appendini and Salles 1979) were deemed prohibitive, the balance of export earnings over import costs after further reallocation of resources to high value crops for urban and export production would have to become more favorable than it is at present. Furthermore, the agribusiness agro-pastoral sector itself would be affected by the end of peasant production of sorghum for balanced feedstuffs: whether this sector should be promoted at all may be open to doubt, but the impact of a decline of peasant production of raw materials for the agro-industrial system would be unlikely to lead to a retrenchment of that system rather than adjustments to prices and an increase in its already high social cost. The implication of present trends is that any sort of coherent agricultural policy is becoming increasingly problematic. I will seek to demonstrate that official policy has to a degree been premised on a series of misconceptions about the nature of the modern peasantry, partly as a result of the phantasmagorical representations of "the peasant" which have become embedded in the rhetoric of the post-revolutionary regime. But one might still argue that having the possibility of implementing even an imperfect policy is preferable to lacking any possibility of implementing one and letting matters take an uncertain and perilous course by refusing to acknowledge that anything is happening.

But it is already apparent that the analysis of the situation of today's *campesinos* cannot be identified solely with the analysis of peasant farming. The working ejidatarios' households are seldom sustained exclusively by agro-pastoral production activities. Income remissions from migrant children are frequently crucial to the quality of life enjoyed by mature peasant households and may, indeed, play a key role in financing the farm. In the earlier stages of family development, most ejidatarios must supplement agro-pastoral production with wage-labor for others. The types of wage-labor undertaken by ejidatarios are typically but not exclusively agricultural and the "others" for whom they labor are varied. They may work for other peasants of similar socio-economic status, for capitalist farmers and machine owners who have emerged from the ranks of the ejidatarios, or for rural entrepreneurs of various kinds from outside the ejidos. Some obtain work locally in the public sector, while others seek work in some more distant location—including that offered by the rural and urban *patrones* north of the border in the United States.

PEASANTS AS PROLETARIANS

Michoacán has been one of the major sources of international migrant labor to the United States in general, and to California in particular. This relationship figures repeatedly in the analysis which follows. A few of the better-off ejidatarios of today are *emigrados* who invest their earnings from the U.S. in rental of land, purchase of machinery, and family education. From one case, this apparent "success story" should be qualified by the information that the person concerned now faces a premature death as the result of twenty years of inhaling the pesticides used by his unionized, multinational employer in Arizona. Nor should we imagine that all *emigrados* have prospered to any great extent: those who have worked as casual laborers in agriculture may be little better off than those who have gone illegally, and the journey *"al Norte"* has not been, as we will see, a generally enriching experience for the majority. We will also see, however, that the flow of labor has not been solely (or in some periods even predominantly) directed towards agriculture, and from the agricultural perspective, it is important to see that there has been an emergent tendency for what is essentially the agricultural production of the United States to be relocated south of the border.

Where this study differs from most accounts of this larger relationship between national entities is in taking seriously the idea that we are dealing with a single social formation. It is not simply economic interdependence across national boundaries which needs to be taken into account, but the cumulative development of a population of Mexican origin in the United States and a persistent structure of social interaction linking families north and south of the border. This transnational community remains such because its articulation to the dominant society militates against the abandonment of its cultural capital and identity, though not without inducing severe contradictions, particularly for young people who are forced to return to Mexico after growing up in the North.

As well as going *"al Norte,"* quite a number of ejidatarios and their children have undertaken seasonal migration to other parts of Mexico, cutting sugar cane in Costa Rica, Sinaloa, for example. This type of migratory movement is also a socially structured one: personal contacts are established with the employer, leading to systematic recruitment of workers from this particular, if distant, locale. Such processes are the essence of the Mexican labor market, which seldom functions on the basis of random, impersonal contact between the buyers and sellers of labor power. But a "semi-proletarian" strategy within the agricultural sector, whether or not it involves internal or international migration, is not the only one to be found in communities like Guaracha. Many of the ejidatarios have, at some time during their lives, experienced work in the cities, either as workers or, in a few cases, as self-employed people. One of the original ejidatarios has spent his entire life working in factories, returning to his land only as a pensioner. Some of the more active farmers in the history of the ejido turned out to have experimented with wage-labor before returning to the land. Although there are non-ejidatarios who have spent their entire lives sowing an *ecuaro* and working as *jornaleros* in the region, perhaps occasionally making a foray to cut cane in the Tierra Caliente, the life histories of many landless people in Guaracha also show a marked pattern of past mobility, though there are differences between the migration patterns characteristic of members of ejidatario and non-ejidatario households. But a full understanding of the process of social transformation experienced by the *campesinos* of Guaracha cannot be obtained simply by taking a snapshot of the community of residence at the time of fieldwork and the working careers of male household heads. We need a larger historical perspective.

The first point to be emphasized is that the Guaracheños did not begin the twentieth century as "peasants" in the conventional sense. Although the hacienda's agrarian regime allowed the limited reconstitution of the peasant form of production within it after achieving an effective monopoly of land based on the complete expropriation of the peasant communities it encapsulated, the *peones acasillados* were essentially proletarianized, albeit in a somewhat contradictory way. Land reform did not, at the outset, reconstitute them as peasants, since the state capitalist organization of the collective ejido did not fundamentally transform the hacienda regime, it eliminated some of its barbarities and exacerbated existing forms of spontaneous resistance to the direct subsumption of their labor power on the part of the ex-*peones*. Nevertheless, while one of the problems with the Collective was that Don Lázaro had originally promised the *peones* individual land rights and the life of a peasant farmer, many had difficulties in making the practical adjustment to the new regime when it was finally introduced in 1940. Though the ex-peons had been imperfect proletarians, many became imperfect peasants, since they had become habituated to certain conditions of proletarian existence of which they were suddenly, and unexpectedly, deprived at the end of the Cárdenas era. More significantly, in the immediate term, the creation of an individual ejido and the progressive collapse of the sugar industry in Guaracha created an employment crisis for the majority who did not obtain land. The closure of the mill was accompanied by substantial rural-urban migration.

But it was not simply those who did not receive land who left for the cities. So did a significant proportion of those who became ejidatarios. The post-war period was one of substantial industrial growth and growing demand for labor, but the emigration was not simply a spontaneous response to the effects of a state policy which increasingly favored the urban over the peasant sector. To an extent, Cárdenas himself promoted it, by arranging for the creation of various employment-generating schemes oriented towards satisfying those who had not benefited from land reform. Political patronage relationships also led to people finding work in the public sector. Later on, such patronage created further opportunities indirectly: Cárdenas personally assisted in the education of some of the children of his former peasant allies and clients, but he also offered opportunities to the community at large through the establishment of an *Escuela Práctica de Agricultura* in the *casco* of the former hacienda. It produced more urban professionals than farmers, and they found their less fortunate *paisanos* manual jobs in both the public and private sectors in the cities. The family of the ex-*hacendado* also offered Guaracheños positions in its houses in Mexico. Given that even relatively menial occupations were often "opportunities," relative to what the countryside offered the majority in this period, and that many of them were allocated by particularistic social networks in which ejidatarios were firmly inserted, it is not surprising that they were taken up by families who had land as well as those who lacked it.

From the outset, then, land reform in Guaracha did not only constitute a process of "repeasantization". A form of agrarian capitalism characterized by a high demand for labor was replaced by a peasant agricultural regime which absorbed much less of the disposable labor-power of the community, promoting rural-urban migration of relative surplus population. This was then reinforced by the abandonment of land by a number of ejidatarios who opted for the urban alternatives, generally another form of proletarianization. But the relative surplus population continued to grow as a result of "natural increase" (despite the fact that the intensified production of the *neolatifundio* increased local demand for labor, at least in its early stages). Although mechanization was very limited until the late 1950s and early 1960s, and the *bracero* program encouraged people to attempt the combination of seasonal international migration and continued residence in the village, the rural-urban drift accelerated as ejidatarios' children grew up in a climate unfavorable to farming prosperity and holders of land titles continued to rent their land. The landless had poorer prospects of going "al Norte" than landholders, who found it much easier to raise the loans necessary to pay the bribes needed to receive a place on the official lists. This factor favored their transition to the cities, but the movement was not restricted to the landless, and cannot be explained simply in terms of "unemployment" initially, though it is certainly related to the hardships of rural life in this period and lack of expectations of improvement.

Over the last two decades relative surplus population has been increased by technical transformation: mechanization, the increasing use of labor saving chemical inputs such as herbicides, and the increasing substitution of the industrialized crops like sorghum and safflower for the more labor intensive wheat, maize and beans. The trend was countered to only a marginal extent by government programs to promote cultivation of basic foodstuffs. Declining local demand for labor has been offset somewhat more by the penetration of labor intensive capitalist vegetable production into the ejidal system of the Ciénega. But the trend in adult male employment remains a downward one. In contrast to earlier decades, the increasing relative surplus population can no longer be absorbed by expanding domestic urban demand for labor.

Though the roots of this problem are structural, and scarcely confined to Mexico, the end of the *bracero* program in 1964 marked the beginning of a new epoch, as millions of mestizo rural Mexicans flooded back into the domestic labor market, and the crisis of the 1980s has created pressures of a new order of magnitude as existing jobs have disappeared throughout the economy. Since during the 1970s the ejidatarios themselves reduced their absorption of labor, most now see the solution to their dilemma as a need to create "rural industries": some even focus their attention on the idea of returning to a regime of sugar cultivation and processing, an ironic demand in historical terms. International migration has continued to offer the region a vent for its surplus population, despite the increasing problems inherent in "crossing the line," technological change in North American agriculture, and the increasing number of people competing for jobs.[3] Although agricultural demand for labor in the North is falling, making life hard for older people, younger men and women have found new niches in the American labor market, in restaurants, catering, supermarket checkouts and the expanding service sectors of this ever more affluent, and ever more unequal, society. Factory or workshop jobs in manufacturing are also to be obtained: in one case, a Guaracheño ejidatario in his sixties was found work by his sons in a factory making furniture in Bernais. But even if it is simply a fantasy to imagine that there is a "solution" to the problem of "undocumented" migration in the sense that effective action could be taken from the American side to stop it, there are increasingly disturbing signs that the U.S. economy is now finally reaching a point of saturation in its demand for what monthly becomes an increasing number of Mexican migrants.

It is important to see what these various different routes out of peasant society amount to as a macro-social process. *Campesino* communities like Guaracha are precisely the kind of communities which historically produced the modern Mexican urban working class. While it is true that the bulk of urban population growth since the 1960s has come from natural increase among urban resident families rather than from rural-urban migration, there is scarcely a household in Guaracha which does not have children working in the cities, and most of the older people have siblings or other close relatives who are deeply entrenched in the urban milieu. Many of the ejidatarios who gave up their land definitively did so because relatives or children offered them a niche in the urban economy. One of the implications of this simple fact about most mestizo rural communities is that urban crisis and rural crisis may not be as discrete as those who argue that the peasants will remain contented while they have beans and tortillas imagine (leaving aside the fact that many rural people today, even the farmers, *buy* their beans and tortillas). Rural households feel the impact of declining urban living standards when supplementary income derived from urban resident members of the family declines. Similarly, these same communities are locked into economic networks which involve relatives working in non-agricultural activities north of the border. What is different about the modern rural exodus from that of years past, to return to Shanin's point, is that it is increasingly a matter of the expansion of membership of social underclasses whose incorporation into classical forms of capitalist wage-labor relationships is at most transitory.

Studies of the contemporary working class of core countries have demonstrated an increasing polarization between households which are stably incorporated into the ranks of salaried labor, generally with multiple wage-earners of both sexes, and those which are not (Pahl 1984). Though such studies suggest that classical models of the proletariat may be becoming increasingly irrelevant, their inadequacy for countries like Mexico may not stem from any convergence between the different patterns of capitalist development. A number of recent studies suggest that the typical urban working class household moves over its development cycle from a greater to a lesser involvement in wage-labor (Connolly 1985, González de la Rocha 1986). What are generally low absolute levels of remuneration for all forms of labor power generate a working class which is relatively homogeneous in living standards in comparison with the situation envisaged by advocates of the "labor aristocracy" versus "marginalized mass/informal sector" distinction, though it is fragmented in terms of the relations of production and inter- and intra-household relations which organize its social existence.

I contend that the reproduction of the peasantry is an aspect of a much larger process of class formation, which is, in this particular case, not even restricted to a single national territorial space. The dominant tendency is rural-urban outmigration: most of the Ciénega peasantry of 1940 ultimately left for the cities. Period. But they were, of course, demographically replaced. In terms of the processes which occur within the rural milieu itself, there is an apparent cycle of recomposition and decomposition at work, but underneath this cycle is a secular process in which the nature of peasant life changes profoundly. It is not simply that an original population is redistributed, as its numbers grow, into a series of differentiated socio-economic niches corresponding to transformations in the larger economic system. Not only individual households, but single human individuals, move between niches and create a process in which they are linked together, not only as material modes of reproduction of labor power, but as alternative conditions of social existence which impact on the consciousness of the human actors.

Thus, on the one hand, we can study the "reproduction of the peasantry" as an objectified process which is a condition for various types of capitalist and state capitalist accumulation: peasant households are reproduced over time through combinations of urban and rural wage labor and production and in their turn supply products and labor power to various branches of capitalist enterprise. The complex combination of rural and urban activity sustains a laboring population exploited in a number of different ways at different times and in different places, and is not the unique responsibility of any particular faction or sector of the international capitalism which draws upon its labors. Traditional concepts, in particular the notion of a "reserve army of labor," do not fully capture the complexity of the processes involved. A son's wage-labor in a factory in Los Angeles may be a condition for a father's production of sorghum for processing by a balanced-feedstuffs plant in Jalisco controlled by a multinational company. The cultivation of sorghum in the Ciénega provides possibilities for capital accumulation by local machine-owners, who buy machines whose components are fabricated in Mexico City and Seattle. And so on. There is no "grand design" here on the part of the capitalist system, but a complex series of adaptations to evolving circumstances on the part of different sectors or fractions of a heterogeneous and to some extent conflictive capitalism, national state apparatuses and the rural underclasses themselves.

In consequence of these adaptations, which shift over time, capitalism and a peasantry reproduce themselves through a process of transformation. The peasants reproduce themselves through an existence which is generally semi-proletarian, and capitalism extracts surplus-value from them in any way it can get it, but with an increasing emphasis on means which are characteristic of the agro-industrial era rather than merchant capitalist subsumption of a more autonomous peasant production process. In the last analysis the peasantry of the Ciénega de Chapala has been reproduced through the allocation of its labor power to activities outside the farm. In some cases, these activities have involved social mobility for household members, giving those who remain access to capital otherwise unobtainable. In other cases, peasant households have transformed themselves totally by wholesale migration. There have, however, been some moves in the opposite direction, and more significantly, polarization of life chances in the countryside today may be increasing as the lowest strata of the rural underclasses find themselves facing increasingly restricted migratory opportunities both domestically and internationally.[4] But beyond the effects of peasants' own economic strategies, significant though they are, in the long term the intervention of the state has clearly played a central role in the process of peasant "conservation" in the Ciénega. This intervention has been a response both to economic pressures caused by the withdrawal of capitalist production from certain key sectors and to the political pressures created by peasant unrest outside the region.

This last observation brings us on to the second dimension of "peasant reproduction," that which involves peasant action which places demands on "the system": the conscious striving after the goal of survival as "peasants" rather than as people. There is a social category *"campesinos"* which exists, not only in the minds of academics and politicians, but in the minds of real people who use it to define their social identity. These people are not socially homogeneous: some of them could, in a meaningful way, be described as "rural capitalists" and in some contexts some of these people define themselves as having other, alternative, identities. They paint the word *agricultor* on the side of their pickups, and feel different from the *campesinos* who are not, as they are, "businessmen." Yet there are other contexts in which these same people also see themselves as part of a *campesino* community. What is interesting to investigate is why, despite the profound social cleavages and antagonisms in communities like Guaracha, the *campesino* identity retains its force. There is, of course, no guarantee that to be a *campesino* today means the same thing to the people who see themselves as having such an identity as it meant twenty or forty years ago, or even that people who occupy different places in the local system understand being a *campesino* in the same way even if they acknowledge each other's claims to the status. The socio-economic conditions of peasant reproduction have clearly had a substantial impact on the consciousness of the less well-off peasants, landed and landless.

In a region like the Ciénega we must consider processes of relatively long duration. Besides the experience of what might well be accurately defined by Wallerstein's phrase "coerced cash-crop labor" during the epoch of the hacienda, a significant number of local people in the Ciénega experienced industrial wage-labor of the classical kind in the foundries of Chicago and other American cities during the first great wave of emigration terminated by the mass deportations of 1929. The conditions of *bracero* labor were more cognate with peonage, though they generally permitted far higher standards of male personal consumption and a very different quality of life in the dance halls, bars and whorehouses. For many, the experience, relatively speaking, was liberating. But this was only one facet of a wider experience which also involved very substantial movement between countryside and city within Mexico. As the years have gone by, and participation in non-agricultural urban activities has increased, ample scope for conscious reflection on the basis of experience has been created. Today, people spontaneously discuss the pros and cons of the different conditions of laboring existence notionally available to them. No ejidatario thinks it odd to be asked whether they would rather have the land or work as they did in the U.S.: opinions differ, but the most frequent response is to give a precise definition of the sort of stable wage labor which would be more satisfactory than sowing with BAN-RURAL. Casual speculations on the nature of Castro's socialism over a beer are not uncommon.

Ultimately, of course, behavior is determined by what people see as the realistic possibilities before them, and it is in this context that we should understand their desire to remain *campesinos,* given that they cannot become doctors, teachers or lawyers. Being a *campesino* may mean going *al alambre* to the North, or it may mean being relatively poor but not having to do much work by tending the *parcela,* but either of these things may be preferable to being another member of the urban underclasses.

I have argued elsewhere that the generic term *campesino* cannot be reduced to a simple socio-economic category (Gledhill 1985). To be a *campesino* is to be politically dominated. In an important sense, it is this which unites rich and poor peasants: both are subordinated within larger structures of social power and see themselves as subordinated in that way. So the argument I have just advanced about the impact of occupational experience on forms of consciousness cannot be complete. I have not outlined the broader web of significations attached to the different modes of the peasant-worker's experience. The U.S. is not simply a place where one has to work hard but gets better wages. It is a place which peasants see as having a different system of law and government, again with its pros and cons. *Campesino* consciousness is a product of the synthesis of different experiences, in which the contradictions of one social situation are weighed against the contradictions of another. The result is that the different constructions of reality form in opposition to each other, in their mutual contrasts.

Since the experiences of different generations are not identical, it is difficult to believe that forms of consciousness can remain stable. Equally obviously, the political socialization of the younger generation in an epoch of extended schooling and mass media has clearly been very different from that of the older generation. In the end, therefore, the oscillatory and cyclical dimensions of peasant reproduction as part-farmer, part-proletarians, may be overridden by the effects of cumulative social transformation, as new forms of consciousness develop. Simply for pragmatic reasons, anything this book has to say about attitudes is focussed on older men: those born in the hacienda era and their mature children. It is possible to describe the objective and subjective effects of structures of political control. We can produce explanations which account for the views people express directly and for the kinds of actions and responses they are observed to display when confronted with particular kinds of situation, which are often discrepant with what they say they think, of course. This sort of analysis provides a "theory" of peasant identity, and of peasant action and its limitations in the present. What it cannot do is predict how the next generation will react to the circumstances they find themselves in, since this would have to rely totally on their expressed attitudes and aspirations. Mature people do tend to see the world in a different way. To this extent, even the contemporary analysis of this book is, in a sense, historical, and its discussion of the determinants of social and political action will be inevitably more effective when we deal with the past.

By emphasizing the extent to which cyclical processes have also been ones of secular transformation, we can perhaps get a clearer idea of the possible future shape of peasant communities in Mexico. Unless the future is mechanistically predestined by the past, there must remain a vast number of uncertainties, the greatest of which is how the young people of today will react to the future which larger social forces seem to be creating for them. History does not really repeat itself, even as farce.

THE MEXICAN PEASANTRY AND THE POWER STRUCTURE

It must be conceded that the picture of peasant reproduction sketched in the previous section, corresponds to a process of social disintegration. As a result of regional developments and the extension of international migration, mechanisms of reciprocal aid between households and non-commodity allocation of resources progressively broke down in Guaracha from the 1950s onwards. Though there are still some individuals who practice these forms of economic behavior, they have become a minority in a community in which commodity relations dominate all social intercourse.

Many have, of course, viewed such practices as central to the resilience of the peasant community, and the means by which reproduction of the *campesino* population at large is secured despite unequal distribution of land and substantial wealth differentiation (Scott 1976, Warman 1976). In the case of Guaracha, commodity relations have penetrated deep into the heart of the domestic unit itself, causing an increasing atomization of units of consumption. There is sometimes severe inter-generational conflict over the right of the parental generation to share in the income acquired by their unmarried children or to have access to their labor power directly. As Arizpe (1985) has observed, though primarily with reference to small-holding agriculture in rain-fed areas, transformation of the social structures of rural communities has reached a stage where simply pumping funds into rural areas cannot be sufficient to revive the social structural conditions of viable small family farming. She suggests "giving back the social and political intiative to the communities" so that they can "rebuild their social networks" and "regain their bargaining power" in the political sphere (1985:219). Although I have every sympathy with the sentiments expressed here, they remain strikingly voluntaristic and idealistic from the standpoint of the historical experience discussed in this book. The lesson of the Guaracha case is that the essence of the post-revolutionary experience is the removal of initiative and bargaining power from the base: even developments in state policy towards the ejidos which might be considered "improvements" in a narrowly material sense are increasingly negative from this point of view.

The singular interest of the Guaracha case lies in its association with the phenomenon of *Cardenismo*. The literature on the Cárdenas era as it is conventionally understood in Mexican historiography has now become so voluminous that it virtually defies summary. I have argued elsewhere that the Mexican revolution must be seen as a process of long duration, its roots deep in the nineteenth century (Gledhill 1987). It was not the Obregón years, nor the epoch of Calles, which saw the crystallization of the post-revolutionary state, but the Cárdenas presidency. This is not to say that *Cardenismo* established a fixed structural pattern for Mexico's future: it is simply to agree with Theda Skocpol's contention that social revolutions of the Mexican type are consummated with the establishment of an effective mass-incorporating state. By describing the Cardenista achievement in these terms, I in no way imply that "mass incorporation" rests on the system's achieving high levels of legitimacy. Indeed, I shall argue that the regime now possesses very little legitimacy in the conventional sense of the term. Nor will I ignore the arguments which have been advanced against seeing the Cardenista state as a "relatively autonomous" moment in the history of national state formation in Mexico: this case will in large measure reinforce the general arguments of Nora Hamilton (1982) on the extent to which the social power of an existing economic oligarchy was conserved through this epoch of apparent radicalism. Throughout my discussion, the emphasis will be on the ultimate weakness and compromised nature of Mexico's national state structure. It is, in retrospect, rather ironic that the region where Cárdenas himself grew up has proved particularly recalcitrant to the processes of incorporation into the national state, and provides an exemplary demonstration of the way the social projects of the Cardenista state could be thwarted by both old and new regional bourgeoisies, which the center could only subsume through accommodation.

As we will see, the reality of *Cardenismo* viewed from this particular regional context, is a morass of contradictions. *Cardenismo* promised the peasants liberation but it brought new forms of arbitrary power and *caciquismo* to the communities it emancipated. It would be tempting to say that the experience of Guaracha reflected special features of the case. One might be the role of Don Lázaro's brothers, who acted as the region's political bosses during and after his presidency. Then there is the crucial fact that there was no large-scale spontaneous rural mass-movement here: the *peones* of Guaracha, along with a majority of their neighbors, rejected the Cardenista program. There was substantial support for the Cristero cause in the Ciénega, and opposition to the Cardenista program was aggravated by the excesses of some of Cárdenas's followers in pursuit of the anti-clerical cause. But I will argue that these "special" factors are not really special at all, but merely symptoms of the underlying limitations of *Cardenismo* as a revolutionary movement.

This is, in my view, not a matter of its ideological orientation in the programmatic sense—the fact that it was not a socialist movement. Some of the limitations of *Cardenismo* were also limitations of the so-called "proletarian revolutionary" movements. It is clear that neither the Cardenistas nor the

Bolsheviks were from the social underclasses they claimed to represent, and that neither the Mexican nor the Russian revolutions produced outcomes which accorded with the objectives and world-views which can be imputed to the spontaneous agrarian movements which underpinned the radical turn taken by what began as political revolutions and ended as social revolutions from above. I take no real issue here with conventional Marxist accounts of the historical limitations of agrarian movements, but I take strong issue with the naivety of traditional Marxist perceptions of the nature of proletarian revolutions and the largely negative view of the objectives pursued by agrarian social movements which are entailed in the fantastic vision of the "world-historical" roles of social classes this delusion promotes. The *Zapatistas* may have "failed" because they were not state builders, but they could not have been state builders without failing to be a popular agrarian movement. In the case of the Ciénega, we need to do some yet more radical thinking about the nature of class struggle and popular reactions to the experiences of oppression and dispossession if we are to produce a positive account of the behavior of the rural underclasses rather than simply another negative appraisal of the reasons for the absence of large-scale popular social movement dedicated to agrarian issues. But I will argue that it is necessary to make such an attempt, for two reasons.

Firstly, it is simply not the case that even the *peones* of Guaracha were "apathetic," "passive" or "fatalistic" in the face of exploitation and oppression: though the majority were against land reform, they were *for* religion in a way which cannot be explained simply in terms of the ideological hegemony of the clergy and "false consciousness." Secondly, it is vital to see that both the *Cardenismo* of Don Lázaro and the *Cardenismo* of his egregiously corrupt brothers alike was ultimately, and from the beginning, antagonistic to genuine self-organization on the part of its peasant clients. What popular leadership and genuinely popular mobilization did emerge from among unrevolutionary peasants of the Ciénega was suppressed, and at times quite ruthlessly suppressed. This is not, I contend, a matter of bad faith, duplicity, or the perversion of principle by the exigencies of practice, though Cárdenas was certainly a consummate political realist. And my intention is certainly not to slight the personal reputation of Lázaro Cárdenas: no one who interviews peasants who knew the man personally could fail to appreciate his quite remarkable personal qualities, which amounted to much more than mere personal charisma. What is at issue here is the nature of the revolutionary process, and the vision of social transformation which dominated it. Cárdenas was ultimately just as much of a modernizer as Calles had been, and *Cardenismo* represented simply another (though perhaps more attractive) variant of the repeated revolts of the provincial urban periphery against the monopolistic structures of economic, social and political power which had characterized Mexico from the colonial epoch to the Porfirian era. Although the resurgence of such movements in the Mexican revolution was, in a sense, a rerun of earlier conflicts of the nineteenth century, what differentiated the developments of the twentieth century from their predecessors was precisely the fact that the building of a viable national state was increasingly seen as dependent on the incorporation of the masses into the process. *Cardenismo*'s peculiarity was its vision of the possibility of a novel and humane solution to the Agrarian Question. But this elevated objective did not eliminate its authoritarian outlook on the way the peasantry should be trained to fulfill their new historical destiny, or entail any fundamental disagreement with other viewpoints on the relationship between "modernization," technical rationality, and urban-industrial development. In fact, despite the peculiarly Mexican facet of Cárdenas's agrarian policy, it had much more in common with the Soviet perspective on modernization than most analysts seem willing to acknowledge.

At another level of abstraction, it becomes clear that *Cardenismo* was characterized by a complex of contradictions which reflected the way in which modernizing, state-building revolutionary elites have to grope their way through short-term crises and unexpected difficulties as best they can, whatever paradigmatic precepts guide their actions. *Cardenismo* was never equipped with a hugely coherent ideological program in the first place, and had to deal with entrenched power structures which the revolutionary process had only disrupted in a limited way. In the end, in the face of renewed international and internal pressures, muddling through was not sufficient to consolidate the main Cardenista social project in the countryside. The Ciénega was allowed to go its own way at a relatively early stage, and more or less ignored by the center for the next twenty-five years. Nevertheless, we will find Lázaro Cárdenas reentering our local history in person in the final years of his life, and once again striving to reshape the agrarian order. Ironically, Cárdenas's prestige in peasant circles is higher today than it was at the time of land reform, and even in 1940. The significance of *Cardenismo* gradually changed after Don Lázaro left office and began to dedicate himself to new projects in the Tierra Caliente. It has endured in Michoacán, undergoing further transformations, after the General's death, and taken new directions under the leadership of his son Cuauhtémoc, who was state governor from 1980 to 1986, prior to his break with the PRI and ascent to national leadership of the left-leaning opposition.

It is not the purpose of this book to provide the more specific, complex and multi-faceted history of *Cardenismo* in Michoacán which would be required if we were to analyze the way myth, representation and practice enter into a dialectic which has reconstituted the significance of *Cardenismo* for later generations and given it a renewed vigor as the source of legitimacy and inspiration for genuinely oppositional practices with spontaneous popular roots. Nor do I dispose of more than fragments of the data required to undertake such a study. But it is important to recognize that the myth *has* been reconstituted in the years since 1940, simply because it does provide the basis for a continuing reflection of the gulf between what is and what ought to be in the minds of those involved with the agrarian sector, an effect which becomes all the more powerful the more detached it becomes from the reality of the Cárdenas years. I pronounce no final judgment at this stage on whether the possession of this peculiar political culture may provide a vehicle for challenging the *status quo* or ultimately serves to defuse such challenges. The latter day interventions of *Cardenismo* in the life of the region remain as pregnant with ambiguities as the earlier ones, but the belated transformation of the ex-peons of Guaracha into *Cardenistas* can scarcely be dismissed as insignificant in the light of their past history and present place in Mexico's agrarian structure. I think that this local history, for all its specificities and idiosyncracies, does reveal something of the mechanics of the power structures which have enabled the Mexican "system" to stagger successfully through crisis after crisis since the 1940s—and it may also provide some insights into the ultimate limits of adaptation of that system.

This final issue returns us from the terrain of the cyclical to that of the long-term, secular tendency. If the Mexican social system has changed as radically over time as this book argues that it has, to what extent can the political system, originally adapted to a very different social world, endure without itself undergoing more radical structural change than it has thus far experienced? It would be naive to imagine that we are talking here of the possibility of a "classical" type of social revolution. But it may well be that we lack imagination when it comes to the kind of scenarios which will ultimately prove relevant to the Mexican case: there appear to be no real historical analogies available for the type of social formation which confronts us today. That, in the last analysis, is why it is worth preoccupying ourselves with the details of concrete histories and concrete social situations. Though they can never supply complete answers to the "big" issues, they can at least help us to avoid the grosser errors of conceptualization which emerge from a lack of detailed knowledge of the nature of contemporary social reality.

Although the community of Guaracha is now named "Emiliano Zapata," I have generally used the archaic name in the text. It is impossible to disguise the community's identity effectively. "Emiliano Zapatas" are legion in Mexico, and the name would have afforded a convenient enough disguise. But many local people still prefer the old name, and no harm can be done by leaving the village as a whole with its specific historical identity. The names of individuals, living and dead, have, however, often been changed in order to preserve their anonymity.

CHAPTER 2

CARDENISMO AND THE END OF AGRARIAN REVOLUTION

Cárdenas's granting of an ejido to the *peones acasillados* of the *latifundio* which dominated his natal region had a political as well as personal significance: the brother-in-law of Guaracha's owner, Don Manuel Moreno Corcuera, was son-in-law to none other than Plutarco Elías Calles. No doubt Guaracha's value as a symbol increased Cárdenas's determination to assign its expropriation a high priority in the implementation of the shift in agrarian policy initiated by the Agrarian Code of 1934. The new legislation extended the right to receive land grants to the permanent workers of haciendas, a policy which had been at the heart of the Cardenista brand of agrarianism in Michoacán.

Up to this moment, Manuel Moreno had repeatedly protested that the solicitants of land in Guaracha were ineligible to receive an ejido because they were contracted *peones*. Such objections were no longer legally valid *tout court*. But the 1934 legislation, product of the PNR convention at Querétaro the previous year, fell short of a definitive abolition of the private capitalist agro-industrial enterprise. Land sown in sugar and various industrial crops remained subject to significant exempting clauses. The extension of land grants to the peons seemed to spell the end of the systems of "tied" labor exploitation associated with the traditional hacienda. Some feared it might threaten the procurement of adequate labor supplies by free market mechanisms. But it did not, in itself, constitute a definitive new strategy of agricultural development since it was still possible to conceive of the new policy being restricted in application.

The developments which followed execution of the Presidential Decree on Guaracha—which began in March 1936— however, were to prove indicative of the more radical substance of *Cardenismo* in the field of agrarian policy, for which the change represented by the new Agrarian Code was simply a necessary first step. What was created in Guaracha was not simply a collective ejido which took over the cultivation side of a "modernized" agro-industrial enterprise. Within months of the expropriation of the land, the peasants were told that the had agreed to sell his sugar mill to the newly created Banco Nacional de Crédito Ejidal. It would be run henceforth as an Ejidal Industrial Cooperative, jointly controlled by the ejidatarios of Emiliano Zapata and their neighbors in the ejido of Totolán, on whose terrains the hacienda had also planted cane. Enterprise profits would enable the cooperative to buy the mill outright from the bank in four annual installments of a little over 100,000 pesos (Banco Nacional de Crédito Ejidal 1937: 10). The cooperative was named after the late Rafael Picazo, local promoter of agrarian reform and beloved compañero of Don Lázaro, cruelly assassinated in 1931 on the orders of the Cuesta Gallardo brothers, one of whom was married to a sister of Manuel Moreno. Don Rafael had incurred the enmity of the

Cuesta Gallardos by attempting, as federal deputy, to strip them of the land reclamation concession in the Chapala zone granted to them by Porfirio Díaz in 1905 (Ochoa n.d.:5).

Rafael Picazo was neither the first, nor the last, of Don Lázaro's lieutenants to be marked for death by the local Porfirian elite. In 1936, the Porfirian era seemed to be drawing to a belated close in the Ciénega de Chapala. Together with his mill, Don Manuel divested himself of the remaining 300 hectare of irrigated land to which he had been entitled as owner of a rural industry. In Guaracha, Cárdenas seemed to have advanced along what appeared to be truly a radically new road in agrarian policy and the social transformation of the countryside: the ejido would become a permanent institution, not a transitory stage along a path which would end in the universality of private property relations. It would constitute a higher form of socialized production than the large-scale capitalist enterprise, without imposing, Cárdenas continued to insist, the culturally alien principle of state communism on the Mexican rural masses. As some of the older ejidatarios of today wistfully remark, Guaracha has as much claim to have been in the vanguard of this new national project as the larger-scale, and more enduring, reform of the cotton agro-industry of La Laguna. The Guaracha project actually preceded Cárdenas's attempt to implement similar programs in the sugar sector in Morelos, though here there was admittedly more work of reconstruction to be done in the aftermath of more than two decades of *Zapatismo*.

THE PROBLEM POSED BY GUARACHA

The Cardenista triumph in Guaracha was consummated in inauspicious circumstances. To the last, the majority of the 563 *peones acasillados* and 176 other permanent employees of the *casco* community had been not simply apathetic, but actively hostile to land reform. Cárdenas had visited them in person as state governor five years earlier. He patiently explained that if they failed to petition for the land, their birth-right would pass into the hands of people from other communities. He was rebuffed, but with a counter-demand: "No queremos tierra, queremos culto."

The immediate context of the peons' demand was that anti-clerical measures had again been enacted by the Cardenistas in Michoacán: the churches were closed. But the peon's response to Cárdenas's social program had somewhat menacing implications in a state which had produced 12,000 armed *Cristeros* (Meyer 1976:85), and in a region whose upland *ranchitos*, along with the commercial center of Sahuayo, had proved fertile soil for the rebellion. Even the armed struggle was to revive here after 1929, in the early years of Cárdenas's presidency. Those who renewed it might be former *agraristas*, like the movement's leader, Ramón Aguilar, once a collaborator of the famous Tarascan leader Primo Tapia, though the relationship between the two men had already soured in the course of the factional struggles within the agrarian reform movement which preceded Tapia's assassination in 1926

(Friedrich 1977, Hernández 1982:21). This "second" Cristiada seemed to raise earlier conflicts amongst *agraristas*, and between *agraristas* and *Cristeros*, to a new level: it presented itself as an overt reaction against *agrarismo*, or at least as a critique of the substance of what *Cardenismo* had wrought (Meyer 1981:254-269). The rapid suppression of *La Segunda* might suggest that either the extension of land reform, or the consolidation of political control, had resolved the problem. Yet the comprehensiveness of the solution is brought into question by the influence of Acción Católica, *sinarquismo*, the PAN (Partido de Acción Nacional) and the PDM (Partido Demócrata Mexicano) in the homeland of *Cardenismo*.

Equally inauspicious was the apparently unbroken economic and political strength of the hacienda adversary in Guaracha. The first decade of revolution inflicted little direct economic damage, though the mill was temporarily under repair following an incident in 1917, to which I will return in the next chapter. The *latifundio*'s historian, Heriberto Moreno, describes the 1920s as passing "en trabajo y paz" (Moreno 1980:122). In the epoch of Porfirio Díaz, the owner of the hacienda had proposed the names of those the governor appointed *jefes políticos* of Jiquilpan, political center of the district, and Guarachita, head-town of the *municipio* in which Guaracha itself was situated. Don Manuel Moreno's influence was still being felt in the appointment of municipal presidents and deputies in the 1920s (Benítez 1977:11).

Admittedly, the closing months of 1919 did see the first blow against a situation which had apparently changed very little since the formal end of the Porfiriato. At last came the belated implementation of a 1917 decree of Carranza for the restitution of 1,397 hectare to the "indigenous pueblo" and *cabecera municipal* of Guarachita, whose very name, changed from San Miguel Guaracha in the 17th century, reflected the humiliation which it had suffered, and continued to suffer, at the hands of the *hacendados*: by the end of the nineteenth century, Guarachita had been reduced to a tiny island of habitations, totally dispossessed of its land by the engulfing sea of Guaracha. In 1918, the *hacendado*, accompanied by a judge from Jiquilpan, a lawyer, engineer and small army, had been able to declare the federal order "null and void." The final success of 1919 was largely due to the efforts of Francisco Múgica, friend and patron of the Guarachita agrarian leader, Filiberto Ruíz. Múgica was then languishing in the Department of General Provisions, to which an alarmed Carranza consigned him following his challenge to the liberal Ortiz Rubio in the Michoacán gubernatorial elections of November 1917 (Fowler Salamini 1980:174). But when Múgica did finally appropriate the governorship, no further advance was secured against Guaracha in the fourteen months of office he enjoyed before Obregón removed him in 1922.

The assault on the core of Guaracha only began in earnest after Cárdenas became governor in September 1928. Four months after entering office, he presided at the founding of the Confederación Revolucionaria Michoacana del Trabajo, which brought together radical intellectuals, the peasantry and such few urban workers as Michoacán possessed. The agrarian platform of the CRMDT was most decisively land redistribution to hacienda peons rather than simply land restitution to communities with prior title to it. Now an *agrarista* group was finally established under the shadow of the Great House in Guaracha itself, largely through Cárdenas's personal efforts. Even the governor knew that he lacked guarantees within the portals of the hacienda, and prudently brought his *pistoleros* with him on his visit to address the *peones*, thereby escaping the assassination which he correctly surmised awaited him. The leader of the tiny band of Guaracha *agraristas*, Pablo Canela, was not so lucky. He perished at the hands of an assassin hired from the ranks of the peons, early in 1934.

The partisans of *Cardenismo* might argue that it took a visionary leadership, pursuing an innovative, and perhaps more "modern," strategy for mobilizing the popular classes, to change the balance of forces in this region sufficiently to break down the remaining defenses of what had, in national terms, already become an anachronism—a *hacendado* class with pretensions to political dominance and seemingly defiant of all reform. The more jaundiced might agree that the situation in western Michoacán—though hardly unique—*was* anachronistic in terms of the overall movement of the structures of national society, but draw what may seem to be the easier, and more obvious, conclusion: that the demise of the Porfirian hacienda in the Ciénega was the consequence not of local agrarian mobilization but of Cárdenas's capture of the national state machinery, albeit with the support of the more "revolutionary" popular forces of other regions and social sectors. Either view would be consistent with the perspective that *Cardenismo* represented an advance or development within an unfolding, cumulative revolutionary process. *Cardenismo* might also, in displaying a radicalism which showed "tendencies to go beyond bourgeois limits," represent the closure of a long historical cycle: the final passage from an era of peasant and bourgeois revolutions to a new epoch, beginning in the 1940s, in which the proletariat alone could constitute a revolutionary force in Mexican society (Semo 1978:303-304).

The problem with looking at *Cardenismo* as the realization of a stage in a general historical movement of society is that we lose interest in its specific nature and pragmatic practices and are, perhaps, in danger of making analytically dangerous assumptions, assumptions about the degree of "fit" between revolutionary ideology and praxis, and between such ideologies and "popular" aspirations and forms of consciousness. In doing so, we may misconstrue the historical mechanisms which produced the national political triumph of *Cardenismo* and determined the scope and results of its intervention in the development of Mexican society.

For some, the Guaracheños themselves may be relatively uninteresting because they were not "revolutionary." The non-rebellious nature of *peones acasillados* is a familiar theme throughout the literature on peasant movements in Latin America, and most authorities opt for the generalization that agrarian revolt was spearheaded by the "free" village community subject to the pressures of landlord expansion (Miller 1985:82-83). But as Alan Knight observes, in fact "peon docility ... was not immutable or absolute" (Knight 1986a:86-87). One might have expected peons to be less docile in the late Twenties than in earlier periods, given the shocks which landlordism had sustained nationally from rebellion on the part of the underclasses, other things being equal. Perhaps the Guaracheños were simply too ignorant to comprehend the inevitable march of world-historical time, locked within the total social institution of the hacienda and mystified by the ideological domination of the clergy. Or perhaps the problem lies more in our tendency to *judge* the actions of particular segments of the social underclasses in terms of a hypothetical "universal" class consciousness and the teleology of the necessary movement of history (Kahn 1985, Laclau 1985).

The answer given in the next chapter to the question of why the majority of the Guaracha peons rejected the Cardenista social program is somewhat more elaborate, and rather less economistic, than conventional accounts of peon non-rebelliousness. It is important to preface such a discussion with some observations on the limitations of the question. To express the problem posed by the Guaracheños' rejection of Cárdenas simply in negative terms—the explanation of their failure to embrace land reform—is, in my view, to commit two potential errors. Firstly, in defining the peons as "non-revolutionary" and highlighting the clash between hacienda and village community, we assume too much about the nature and orientations of those elements of rural society which were supposedly "objectively revolutionary" in their demands. Secondly, in focussing only on the peons' rejection of Cardenista land reform, we close our eyes to other respects in which their behavior may have been active and oppositional, rather than simply passive, subservient to authority and "docile."

Closer examination of the behavior of the Guaracha *peones* does suggest that some of them, in their own way, participated in the "class struggle" taking place in the countryside of Michoacán. Popular struggles were of a heterogeneous nature, imperfectly captured by dichotomies between "backward-looking" versus "forward-looking" and "economistic" versus "revolutionary" orientations.

The great irony of *Cardenismo* in Michoacán is that its local rural support came from a very different type of peasantry than that placed at the forefront of the new agrarian system Cárdenas sought to create. In reality *Cardenismo* in Michoacán did not arise organically from local rural society and popular organizations, though it did receive reinforcement through one significant regional social process: emigration to the U.S. Returned migrants were prominent in the ranks of the *agraristas* and were clearly more sympathetic to this kind of program. *Cardenismo* was built on the existence of genuinely popular grievances and aspirations: but its success rested on the political facilities it offered to peasant leaders for the pursuit of their objectives through alliance with outside social forces. And "success" was not unqualified. Not only did Cárdenas's achievements in Michoacán suffer significant reverses after he left the governorship, but a degree of resistance persisted even after his national triumph.

In order to comprehend the situation in Guaracha on the eve of land reform, it is necessary to place it in the context of the larger history of agrarian revolution in Michoacán, not least because the *peones acasillados* themselves did not live in a closed social world. New families periodically entered the village from both urban and rural locations in the surrounding region. Guaracheños could interact with a variety of people from other parts of Michoacán and Jalisco when they visited Guarachita to take advantage of its petty commerce and modest diversions. The international migrants were sufficiently numerous to have been a major source of information about the larger world in the latter half of the 1920s. The knowledge obtained from these various sources was filtered and interpreted in imagination, through the spontaneous preconceptions of ordinary folk in the hacienda community and through motivated clerical commentaries. But it may have played a very significant role in shaping the attitudes of the peons to the unfolding patterns of social and political change.

A CENTURY OF CLASS STRUGGLES

Periodization of the Mexican revolution depends on identification of discontinuities in processes of long duration which transcend the revolutionary period itself. In western Michoacán, the logic of the events which I have outlined thus far leads one to see the Cárdenas years as a culminating point. But there are, of course, alternative logics which emerge from consideration of other events and processes. In the view of Enrique Semo, what *Cardenismo* represents nationally is the closure of a cycle of "bourgeois" revolutions which began with the Insurgency of Hidalgo and Morelos, and continued with the Wars of the Reform (1854–67) and the popular mobilizations of 1910–17 and 1935–39 (Semo 1978).

Although the Insurgency began as a movement launched against Spanish imperial rule by lower-ranking members of the Creole elite who had suffered as a result of the metropolis's imposition of a forced loan on its colonies in order to finance international war, Hidalgo's invocation of the power of popular forces immediately transformed its character. It became a popular rebellion marked by violent assaults on landed property and mercantile exploitation, showing scant respect for its leadership's initial distinction between Spaniards and "Americans." The characterization of the long-cycle of rebellions initiated by the Insurgency as one of "bourgeois" revolution can be challenged on two fronts. It is inadequate as a characterization in its original European context, even with respect to the paradigmatic case of France (Skocpol 1979), though the French Revolution certainly does offer a number of interesting parallels with events in nineteenth century Mexico. And the conventional model of "bourgeois" revolution suffers from additional problems of Eurocentricity when it is extended to deal with the social forces entangled in the revolutionary process in Latin America. But Semo's emphasis on the role of low-level "class struggle" as a determinant both of the course of Mexico's nineteenth century history as a whole and of the *distinctiveness* of that history in comparison with other parts of Latin America has much to recommend it. It provides an essential complement to Knight's more historically restricted defense of the agrarian dimension of the revolution of 1910–20 against "revisionist" interpretations which over-react against the mythologizing associated with the official revolutionary tradition (Knight 1986a,b); providing, that is, we recognize that "class struggle" in its conventional sense cannot provide an adequate characterization of all the insurrectionary social movements which emerged in any of these periods, and requires rather careful substantive definition even where it is more directly applicable.

The Insurgency, Reform, Revolution and *Cardenismo* all reflect an enduring opposition between political center and political periphery. Their leaderships are provincial, and "bourgeois" or "petty bourgeois," in the loose sense. Within the "estamental" structure of colonial society (Pearse 1975), social and political position was not defined simply in terms of wealth and ownership of property, although the position of the colonial upper class rested on the mutually reinforcing combination of proprietary wealth and venal wealth extracted from office-holding (Gledhill 1988a). The inadequacy of definitions of the interests represented by revolutionary leaderships in terms of position with respect to property, the market or means of production is immediately apparent in the case of the Insurgency. The upsurge of popular violence against property and commerce reunified Creoles and Peninsulars with a class interest to defend. It created a political divide between what Hamnett has termed an "entrepreneurial bourgeoisie" or a "Mexican or resident elite of merchant-investors, mine-operators, municipal councilors and landowners", on the one hand, and a provincial "professional bourgeoisie" of lawyers, clerics, intellectuals, writers and doctors, on the other (Hamnett 1986:24, 44-45).

Precisely the same kinds of opposition between metropolitan center and provinces emerge in the period of the *Reforma*, where once again the Liberal leadership is recruited from the professions, reinforced by intermediate rural strata such as the *rancheros* of the Bajío and Western Mexico. The position of the latter is more readily defined in economic terms, though one must continue to recognize the overdetermining role of status assignments in defining social position in the broader sense (Sinkin 1979). The conflicts between Liberals and Conservatives were again marked by moments when class anxieties over the unleashing of popular forces transcended political conflict, especially when the specter of "caste war" was evoked in elite mentalities by uprisings centered on Indian communities (Bazant 1977:58-60). Even if the appellation "bourgeois" is not a very precise or useful conceptual term, the notion of a cumulative cycle of revolution does gain a certain plausibility, at

Nor can we describe the mine workers as a proletariat. They considered themselves to be, in effect, participants in the ownership of the mines they operated, and regarded the share-out (*partido*) of ore among them as evidence of this special status. Efforts to reduce or abolish this privilege as in 1766, the 1790s, 1800s or, later, in 1827 produced conflict in the mining zone. (Hamnett 1986:25)

At the level of the leaderships themselves, each revolutionary generation contains a mix of (relatively and contextually) more or less "radical" and more or less wealthy leaders. In the case of the Liberals, the division was recognized at the time in the distinction between the "puros" and the "moderados." Semo characteristically associates this division with the representation of differing class interests:

The first [The *puros*, whom Semo also describes as "the Left"] received their support, above all, from the *rancheros* and the urban petty bourgeoisie; the second [the *moderados*] is identified more with sectors of the commercial bourgeoisie, liberal officialdom and above all, a certain portion of *hacendados*. (Semo 1978:311)

Though the *moderados*—along with the Conservatives—destroyed themselves politically by aligning with Maximilian, the "Left," as Semo sees it, collapsed on their achievement of state power, failing to honor the promises which had given the movement a mass base, and thereby allowed the pendulum of history to swing back to the "Right" (Semo 1978:313). For Semo, it is the "revolutionary action of the masses" which creates the "plebeian-revolutionary" current in the Independence movement and the radical wing of Liberalism. It is certainly valid to argue that the social programs articulated by the radical leaderships of the Insurgency and the Reform were a response to the way these political revolutionaries were forced to base their struggle for power on the insurrectionary struggles of the underclasses. It is much less acceptable to assume that the leaderships or their programs represented the social movements underlying them in the sense that they expressed the objectives and aspirations of the heterogeneous social forces which fought under their banners.

Perceived political crisis at the center, which included that associated with military defeats at the hands of the United States, provided the context in which the popular social conflicts which marked the nineteenth century were likely to flare up into open rebellion and ramify throughout different regions. Local social movements would attach themselves to the banners of political rebels for their own particular reasons, which might not be directly linked to the latters' ideological positions: in the case of Indian communities, this might be indeed, as the whites and mestizos feared, very much a calculated, if ultimately millenarian, attempt to wrest some advantage from factional conflict within the dominant society with the longer term aim of ridding themselves of white (class) domination. Liberalism's brand of radicalism was scarcely attractive to the majority within Indian communities, faced with the threat posed by the Reform's drive to abolish corporate land tenure in favor of the universalization of private property relations. In reality, many of the urban Liberal Left knew little about the heart of the Mexican countryside, particularly the Indian countryside and its problems. What knowledge they possessed was evaluated through the optic of a "modernizing" ideology borrowed from a North American world where private property relations and possessive individualism were deemed synonymous with progress. They loathed the colonial principles of status hierarchization and the Church as structural barriers to their own ascent: but they still knew the difference between *gente decente* and those who would only be truly worthy of citizenship once they had been subjected to the forces of modernization and civilization.

Bazant has summed up the practical effect of Liberal orientations in stark terms: Liberalism had an "antirural bias" in that it was uninterested in "protecting Indians from *hacendados*" (Bazant 1977:75).

The social conflicts of the Independence period had their roots in the colonial order but, as in 1910, it was the dislocation of the central apparatus of state power which enabled what were, in reality, a heterogeneous set of localized conflicts to coalesce into the Insurgency, turning it into a broad social revolutionary movement (Hamnett 1986:202). The problems of the Bajío miners, tenant farmers and artisans (Brading 1978) were not, however, the same materially or cognitively as the problems of Indian communities pleading to receive exemption from tribute payments, like the villagers of Tancícuaro in Michoacán after the drought of 1809. Neither were identical to those of communities struggling to defend their lands, water resources or customary rights from encroaching haciendas—the problem in the Bolsa de Guaracha. For some, the grievance was material, a declining standard of living, for some it was material, social and cultural. For many Indians, the threat was to the survival of a community as an autonomous entity, whose place in the cosmic scheme had been guaranteed by traditions predating the Hispanic conquest, validated by the King of Spain himself in earlier centuries (Gledhill 1988a). Others faced the threat of being thrust beyond the margin in terms of white or mestizo values—loss of the small-holding or rented land, and possible descent into the rootless world of the unemployed, vagrant or criminal. Among non-Indian peasants too, resistance to proletarianization could be premised on notions of social identity and self-realization: where the practice of autonomous or quasi-autonomous peasant labor was the necessary mark of a man of honor, while wage labor for a *patrón* represented a form of servility, humiliation and emasculation, even relatively good wages and working conditions could not compensate for the loss of social value entailed by self-alienation (Alonso 1988). But there were other roots of insurgency in 1810 beyond these conflicts rooted in class structure, just as there were a century later. Part of the insurgent phenomenon corresponded to that class of rural social movements Knight has defined as *serrano* movements—localized rebellions of entire communities under the leadership of their *caciques*. Knight's concept of a *serrano* movement builds on Eric Wolf's notion of a "tactically mobile" peasantry "located in a peripheral area outside the domains of landlord control" (Wolf 1969: 269). Although some revolts on the part of "people of the hills" at the time of the 1910 revolution were related to the ever-ramifying expansion of commodity relations and agrarian grievances, particularly those resulting from the disentailment of community land, Knight emphasizes the way *serrano* movements tended to cross-cut divisions based on internal stratification and represented a revolt of the periphery against incursions of the power of central government (Knight 1980: 27; 1986a). It is often difficult to make a sharp separation between the impact of macro-economic changes and other dimensions of the integration of local communities into the wider socio-political system, but the general historical importance of this type of *serrano* reaction cannot be underestimated.

Though there were large areas where royal writ scarcely ran in late colonial Mexico, the Bourbon regime had been displaying significant centralizing pretensions in comparison with its Habsburg predecessor, at least by the standards of an imperial state (Gledhill 1987). Such pretensions were exhibited in the spheres of administration, taxation and the imposition of mercantilist policy, in relations with the Church (Meyer 1976), and in the form of a limited interference in agrarian property relations, which mainly took the form of redistributing land between the village communities in order to maintain their tributary viability. Such policies generated many different kinds of contradictions. Whether the power of the local military *caciques* was based on interclass conflict or represented a *serrano* revolt against the center, the dependence of the movement as a whole on this network, fraught as it was by local rivalries, was in turn a source of major internal contradictions for the Insurgent cause: these escalated with the death of Morelos, who had acted as a *caudillo* unifying the military wing of the movement in his zone of operations by virtue of his control over the localized network of chieftains (Hamnett 1986:209).

The Insurgency was an important moment in the agrarian history of Michoacán in general and in the local history of the Ciénega de Chapala and the hacienda of Guaracha in particular. A brief outline of the development of the hacienda up to the time of the Insurgency will supply the background to these dramatic events. Guaracha emerged from the division of a larger, but scarcely exploited, domain in the seventeenth century, when the Zamoran Salceda family acquired three properties stretching from La Palma, to the northwest on the Lake, to Santiago Tangamandapio, 16 kilometers from Zamora. In the eighteenth century, ownership passed to a Mexico City grandee, who possessed estates in several regions, all run by administrators and heavily mortgaged. Most cultivation was performed by tenants, although Guaracha had a primitive *trapiche* served by a small cane plantation worked by 233 mulattos—whose genetic heritage is still evident in the population of Guaracha today—aided by tenant seasonal labor. In addition to cultivating cereals and sugar, the hacienda herded 9,000 head of cattle (Moreno 1980:72-91). The basic principle of this form of latifundism was the acquisition of rental income to support a social position by means of extensive landholding.

The hacienda engrossed the land of indigenous communities continually as it expanded to encompass 96,000 hectare by the late eighteenth century. The Bourbon authorities encouraged Guarachita, in which thirteen Spanish families now resided alongside sixty-one Indian tributaries, to seek to recover its patrimony in the courts (Moreno 1980:84-88). The case illustrates the centralizing element in the political economy of the Bourbon imperial state noted above: intervention of this kind was motivated by a concern to maintain the viability of the state's tributary system in a world in which the expansion of the landed estate threatened to erode it. But it also demonstrates the limited capacity of that state to move against the decentralized social power of the landlord class in practice. This situation ensured that Bourbon "agrarian reform" would consist mainly in redistributing resources between different tributary communities, a sharing out of poverty which might bring more prosperous Indian communities into conflict with the colonial regime, though it more usually exacerbated inter-communal, horizontal conflicts and local *caciquismo*. Decentralized social power certainly triumphed in the case of Guarachita versus Guaracha. The court proceedings came to nothing. In 1790 the estate was bought by Don Victorino Jaso, a powerful merchant from Tangancícuaro, whose influence over the local judiciary proved decisive.

Don Victorino reorganized the estate's production to serve his interregional commerce. Though tenants (*arrendatarios*) continued to perform most of the cultivation, old modes of accumulation were now supplemented by mercantile profits, and the expansionary thrust of the *latifundio* against the encapsulated indigenous communities continued. There were also other elements within the regional society who might hope to benefit from the destruction of the merchant-investor stratum represented by Don Victorino. One of the local leaders of the Insurgency was a Cotija muleteer:[1] muleteers were persons of variable economic position, but they were notable activists in the Insurgency in Mexico, just as they figured as the leaders of rebellions in other parts of Latin America, including some of the most celebrated Indian uprisings. Located socially in a liminal position, crossing the boundaries between local community and the larger society in a role which highlighted the possibilities and limitations of the existing structure of social relationships, the *arriero* played a role in insurrection which was unlikely to have corresponded to a defensive reaction. It is interesting to note that *arrieros* also tended to support twentieth century *agrarismo* in the Ciénega, though by this stage their livelihood was under direct threat from the revolution in transport systems and the hacienda's eagerness to monopolize the new opportunities that revolution provided.

The price of demographic growth accompanied by hacienda expansion and the increasing commercialization of the regional economy was that social banditry escalated in the region of Jiquilpan in the late Bourbon period. It is perhaps significant that local legend has painted one of the most famous bandit groups of the period as a precursor of the struggle against Spanish exploitation (Moreno 1980:95, Hamnett 1986:61). When that struggle began in earnest, the of Guaracha was singled out as the prime target for the fulfillment of the initial Insurgent program—"¡*a matar gachupines!*" The forces which attacked the hacienda—after burning Don Victorino's properties at Tangancícuaro—were commanded by Luis Macías and Marcos Castellanos, *cura* of Ocotlán, across the Jalisco border, but a native of Sahuayo (Moreno 1980:96). Subsequently, Castellanos established a base on the island of Mezcala in Chapala, which was defended with vigor from December 1812 to November 1816. In this context, Indian communities around the Lake continued to supply the rebels despite measures of repression and pre-emptive seizures of Indian property (which had almost certainly been counterproductive). It seems clear that agrarian issues played an important role in generating support for the Insurgent cause here: village lands had been captured by Guadalajara-resident merchants (identified as *gachupines*) and by neighboring communities, while there was also an internal process of land concentration within the communities (Hamnett 1986:190). In the lake communities, the issue was not one of conflict between hacienda and village, but one of the destruction of the community through transformation of its land base into smaller scale private property. The same type of phenomenon provided the basis for twentieth century agrarian movements in parts of the upland Meseta Tarasca of Michoacán, which had never experienced the expansion of *latifundios*, nor suffered commercial penetration from urban centers at the same early stage as the indigenous villages of the lake.

The difficulties which Royalist forces experienced in subduing Mezcala ensured that the region in which Guaracha was located would remain unpacified until 1817, during which time the hacienda, its mill destroyed and despoiled of most of its livestock and draft animals, was left to its tenants. In the circumstances, it is not surprising that they failed to pay their rents, but as Hamnett notes, elsewhere during the Insurgency hacienda owners were able to form self-defense forces among their *peones acasillados*, suggesting that it was generally possible to count on the loyalty of at least this part of the workforce:

> ...the *peones acasillados* were a relatively privileged group, with their secure labor, their wage and maize ration, their housing and integration into the structure of hacienda patronage. They would have much to lose if they joined itinerant rebel bands. Perhaps it

would take only exceptional circumstances, such as the break-down of food supply, to throw into jeopardy the security they had gained. Even then, there was no guarantee that life outside the hacienda would be any better than life within. Furthermore, a subsistence crisis, no matter how momentarily severe, did not alter the long term trends that weakened the rural workers' position: population growth, rising prices, competition for land. Only when the resident work force was confronted with the realities of insurgent incursions and the flight of the owners to the cities would the issue of changed allegiances become uppermost. Such arguments suggest that the problem for the hacienda was not as a rule the dissidence of the internal labor force. Most probably, the prime source of insurgent support in areas in which haciendas and *pueblos* existed side by side, derived from aggrieved and hard pressed village communities, particularly where peasants were short of subsistence lands or deprived of their traditional pasture, cultivation or water rights. Village resentment at private proprietors' pressure on the labor force added further fuel to the fire. The threat presented by the hacienda may well have been the decisive factor in revolutionizing the peasant. Within the hacienda, it is probable that the patriarchal bonds remained intact. There would, of course, be many exceptions. Once insurgency had died down, these bonds would, however, last another century. (Hamnett 1986:72-73)

In the period 1812–17, Guaracha fits some of Hamnett's exceptional circumstances. The owner's son-in-law, who formally took charge of the hacienda on the owner's death, did indeed abandon the region for Mexico City and only returned to working the hacienda when a royalist garrison was installed on his property after the fall of Mezcala. Guaracha had already been involved in a conflict for restitution of land with the indigenous community of Guarachita. Clearly the assault on Guaracha came in the first instance from the periphery of the hacienda—in particular from Sahuayo and its environs—while the military struggle which devastated the estate's capital stock was fueled by the dissident indigenous communities of the lakeside, whose grievance was distinct from that of the indigenous communities of the Bolsa de Guaracha. The mulatto peons of Guaracha could not readily merge with the local population. One of the original local insurgent leaders named by Moreno was a hacienda tenant from the hills on its western side (Moreno 1980:96). The position of hacienda tenants by the end of the Bourbon period was certainly less attractive than that of *peones acasillados*: rents increased, security of tenure diminished, and contracts were tightened to reduce customary access to estate resources without charge (Hamnett 1986:7-8, Brading 1978:197-200).

CARDENISMO AND THE END OF AGRARIAN REVOLUTION

Parts of Mexico were already experiencing the kind of changes in rural social relationships associated with colonial transformation of traditional agrarian systems in Asia in a much later period (Scott 1976). The complexity of the Insurgent phenomenon reflects the heterogeneity of Mexico's regional agrarian structures and the role of ethnostratification within the Hispanic imperial state colonial formation (Gledhill 1987, 1988a), but it was surely no accident that the cradle of the Insurgency was the highly commercialized Bajío. After order was finally restored in Guaracha, agricultural production recovered rapidly in the period between 1818 and 1820 (Moreno 1980: 98-99), though how far the speed and scale of the recovery reflected the effects of pacification and reconstruction (such as the replacement of draft animals) rather than the restoration of landlords' surplus extractive capacity remains an open question. As the Insurgency had demonstrated, Don Victorino's wealth depended not simply on the rational management of his enterprise, but on the coercive power afforded to his class by the state. And his heirs were not to continue in the business-like manner of their forebear.

In 1830, the property passed to Don Victorino's grandson, Diego Moreno Jaso, son of the *Administrador de Rentas* in La Barca, Jalisco. Don Diego resorted to mortgages in order to finance a political career which led him to the governorship, but his financial difficulties deepened, and he was forced to rent the secondary hacienda of Cojumatlán, to the northwest of Guaracha, behind Sahuayo (Moreno 1980:109). After Don Diego's death, the estate passed to his widow, and then to his eldest daughter, who added a passion for cards to the problems created by tenant rent defaults during the Wars of the Reform. The estate was now in crisis and the ultimate source of the malaise was not so much Doña Antonia's gambling, nor even the unsettled times, but the utter maladministration of what had now become a largely unproductive and parasitic rentier enterprise. In 1862, she sold off the 50,000 hectare of the Cojumatlán hacienda in parcels. This did nothing to relieve land hunger in the region: most of the new ranches went to *ricos* from Jiquilpan, Sahuayo and Cotija, rather than to humble tenants (Moreno 1980:111), and the main hacienda continued its encroachment on the land of the indigenous pueblos. But it did save the estate from total disintegration until its revival as a productive enterprise during the Porfiriato.

The period of armed conflict surrounding the Wars of the Reform and French Intervention was, admittedly, an unpropitious one for landlord enterprise, though landed property sustained the decentralized clientalistic power of the *caudillos* throughout the era from Independence to the Porfiriato, and, whatever the fate of individual *hacendados*, the landlord class emerged from the epoch of Reform not only freed of the burden of Church mortgages, but in possession of a greater proportion of the nation's agricultural and pastoral resources. Most of this expansion was at the expense of the peasant community rather than the Church (Sinkin 1979). Liberalism created not the rural middle class beloved of its ideologists but a speculative boom in real estate which absorbed capital which might otherwise have been invested productively. The political climate remained unconducive to landlord direct investment in production, capital stock and infrastructure. But the situation still favored the capture of land—as an income-yielding asset and an investment in its own right. Since the other side of land monopolization was proletarianization, this process also laid the basis for a revival of landlord agriculture under the more favorable climate created by Porfirian political stabilization. In launching their attack on communal village landholding and criminalizing poverty through vagrancy laws, the Liberal administrations acted as the midwives of a new era (Semo 1978:77).

The promulgation of the *Ley Lerdo* provoked immediate violent resistance from Indian communities. The governor of Michoacán petitioned Mexico City for the exemption of the indigenous communities of his state from the application of the Law (García Mora 1981:50). This particular petition was rejected, but Bazant has suggested that the violence of the Indian reaction did bring a temporary halt to disentailment of communal land in the country as a whole shortly afterwards (Bazant 1977:75). It seems more likely that the slowing of the pace of the Reform in the countryside was a temporary expedient during the epochs of civil war. Once the failure of the French Intervention had shifted the balance decisively, implementation of this facet of the Reform was resumed with vigor. Its consequences went beyond a further escalation of banditry in regions of hacienda dominance such as Chalco, where a major peasant uprising in 1869 developed into armed conflict extending over state boundaries into Puebla and Morelos (Sánchez 1981:33).

Hard on the heels of these risings in Central Mexico, the populations of Tarejero and Zipiajo, villages located in the same part of Michoacán as Primo Tapia's Naranja, launched an attack on Zacapu, capturing and disarming some of its *acordada*. During the 1870s, peasant risings occurred in such widely separated regions of the state as Pátzcuaro, in the lake region to the southeast of Zacapu and southwest of Morelia, and Tancítaro and Taretan, to the west and southeast of Uruapan respectively, in the zone of transition between the Meseta Tarasca and the Tierra Caliente (Sánchez 1981). In the case of the Valley of Taretan, the communities formed themselves into a *Gran Comunidad Agrícola*, took back their lost land and forcibly defended their rights of possession. But *comuneros* armed with machetes and pitchforks could not defy the Federal Army, which sent a large detachment to evict them and restored the land to the landlords in January of 1879 (Sánchez 1981:34). As the data on Guaracha and the Chapala zone have indicated, agrarian conflict involving the mobilization of indigenous communities was nothing new in Michoacán. Already, by the end of the eighteenth century, one-fifth of Michoacán's villages had lost even the legal minimum of 101 hectare of *fundo legal* prescribed under colonial legislation. But all of them were located in a triangle between Pátzcuaro, Zacapu and Cocupao, the zone where fertile soil, water supplies and proximity to the main urban markets had favored cereal production by haciendas (Hamnett 1986:6). The Tarascan sierra, in contrast, was unattractive to Spanish commercial enterprise, and retained its communal landholdings into the late nineteenth century (García Mora 1981:48).[2]

By the 1870s, agrarian problems were more widespread than they had ever been before. Though hacienda expansion and land monopolization could have a purely *rentier* dynamic, the mounting problems of the village community also reflected the extension of processes of commercialization into zones which had previously been unaffected. If extensive agrarian revolt is made up, in reality, of a number of localized struggles, then it follows that the sum constituted by the parts will be affected by the uneven development of agrarian change. Communities at the forefront of earlier struggles may be definitively vanquished, even destroyed. As the cases of the Ciénega and Zacapu indicate, this is far from invariably the case: some communities survived to experience still more severe despoliation, communities which had fared better in earlier epochs found themselves repeating the earlier experience of some of their neighbors, and entirely new areas were subjected to the pressures of agricultural commercialization. The large commercial estate was not the only beneficiary of those developments, nor at the root of all agrarian unrest. The Porfirian pattern of commercialization linked to the development of a national market as well as the export economy spelled ruin for some— local craft producers displaced by foreign imports or industrial products from Mexico City, for example (De la Peña 1978). But it also offered opportunities to a range of other agents, prosperous *rancheros*, merchants who controlled village lands, and some of the well-to-do village peasants (*acomodados*). Changes in transport arteries and market structures could produce expansion or revival in community economies as well as marginalization and recession (Knight 1986a:81).

Taretan's development in the period of Independence was dominated by the expansion of sugar haciendas, but this development was also accompanied by the emergence of a small agrarian bourgeoisie (Salmerón 1984:64-65). The agrarian content of the peasant mobilizations in this zone during the 1870s is primarily one of *comuneros* facing dispossession and proletarianization. But the existence of multiple contradictions even in those contexts where hacienda expansion was an important element in the situation is evidenced by the fact that the rebellious communities displayed divisions. Sánchez notes that:

> Not all members of the communities participated in the struggle in defense of communal property, since some of them belonged to the ranks of the usurpers or were their accomplices. When it was a question of dividing up the land on an individual basis, some opposed this roundly, seeing that private, individual, property would only lead them to ruin, while others accepted it with

enthusiasm, arguing that communal organization was a "backward and uneconomic" form. It is clear, then, that these differences revealed the internal social contradictions of the communities, which were in no way homogeneous. (Sánchez 1981:34)

In the late colonial period, communal tenure of arable land in the Tarascan
community was characterized by the possession of hereditary rights of
usufruct by individual families. Woods and pasture lands remained communal in the stricter sense. Prohibitions on voluntary alienation of rights to outsiders remained effective: despoliation by outside forces aside, the agrarian
community reproduced itself over the generations. Nevertheless, internal
inequalities developed in terms of quantities of land held in traditional fashion by different households (García Mora 1981:48-49). Chayanovian "demographic differentiation" does not seem a plausible explanation of this pattern,
since there is no evidence of the periodic redistribution of land by the community, but internal mechanisms for temporary redistribution of use rights
might still have played an important role in equilibrating access to resources
and family subsistence needs. Nor was land necessarily at the root of all
forms of rural inequality: community office-holding was intimately linked to
the accumulation of wealth and economic resources. Political *caciquismo*
might counteract tendencies to "multi-directional mobility" embedded in
demographic fluctuations, the vagaries of fortune in a fragile village economy, and the periodic intrusions of the violence of wider social conflicts into
communal life.

In the last analysis, the fact that the community divided, violently, in the
epoch of disentailment suggests that the transformation between the two
agrarian systems was perceived as marking a new phase—the end of a "moral
economy" perhaps—which drew on forces of disintegration which were
already latent in the traditional system. Though some communities joined
together to pursue a common struggle, the Reform also produced an escalation of long-standing inter-communal land disputes, many of which had their
origins in Bourbon interference with communal land tenure. The effect of the
Reform legislation was radical, since the retention or acquisition of definitive
rights of ownership now became a matter of a commodity transaction, and
constraints on the alienation of former community land could only be a matter of the informal practices of the community's members as a collectivity of
individuals. Generally such practices were not implemented; it was in any
case difficult to make them effective since outsiders found it relatively easy
to obtain legal sanction for their ownership of land from the courts. Internal
differentiation within the communities clearly aided implementation of the
transition to the new proprietary regime: internally stratified communities
were likely to display full corporate solidarity only when confronted with a
common external enemy.

Those who could not buy the land assigned to them under the division of the former community's holdings lost possession of it, although various systems of sharecropping and rental provided access to land for a portion of the disadvantaged, not on very attractive terms. Under the new regime of private property relations, better-off members of the communities could accumulate land holdings in a more definitive manner than under the old system of hereditary possession, but land could also be more readily acquired by outsiders, either at the time of disentailment itself, or in the course of time. In the Cañada de los Once Pueblos, located between Zacapu and Zamora and a hotbed of *agrarismo* in the Twenties, and in the Meseta Tarasca, there were no neighboring large estates to appropriate the communities' lands. Disentailment produced a fragmentation of their holdings into small parcels: here it was the use of debt by mestizo merchants and usurers to appropriate the land of small peasants which lay at the heart of the agrarian problem of the Cárdenas epoch. (García Mora 1981:67-70). By the end of the Porfiriato, the best irrigated lands of the indigenous communities of the Cañada were concentrated in the hands of a few mestizo families from Chilchota, who also controlled the mills that ground the peasants' wheat and maize, might have additional land in Tangancícuaro, and had their main houses there or in Zamora (Ramírez 1986b:126-127). If the absolute extensions of land involved were relatively small by the standards of the commercial estates of the neighboring Valley of Zamora, they constituted more than half of the total cultivated area of the zone. In addition to the arable land, the previously communal pastures and woods of the Sierra now became the objects of private exploitation and exclusionary proprietary relations. By the end of the nineteenth century, community representatives were petitioning the state governor for exemption from cadastral contributions, since:

> The community no longer exists, and the majority of the Indians sold the fractions [of land] assigned to them under the *reparto* to private individuals and did not present themselves as before to meet their share of the payment of each quarter's contributions. (García Mora 1981:55)

The process of dividing up the lands of those villages which still retained significant corporate landholdings in the later nineteenth century therefore benefited a number of different strata of the agrarian bourgeoisie, established and emergent. Alongside the Great Estates, *rancheros*, merchants, shopkeepers and village *caciques* were able to usurp control of portions of community land. Some of those against whom the *comuneros* struggled were outsiders from other social strata, others people from neighboring communities. Some of them sprang from within the community itself.

It is worth reflecting on the experience of the *repartos* which took place under the Liberal Reform, since at least some of the communities concerned may have looked on official "revolutionary" land reform as a case of history repeating itself. Not only were the bureaucratic mechanics of the process rather similar, but we should bear in mind that land reform did not restore the old communal landholding system to the communities. Theoretically, of course, there was one enormous difference between the nineteenth and twentieth century *repartos*: land distributed under the revolutionary reform was given in perpetual usufruct to its beneficiaries, in a manner that might, in principle, have recalled the precedent of the extinct village community. But it was the state, not the community itself, which claimed *dominium eminens* over the land, and the *practice* of land reform in the modern era may have seemed closer to the logic of inequality embedded in the *repartos* based on commodity transactions than its juridical form might suggest. Revolutionary land distributions in Michoacán often patently violated the principle of just and equal redistribution of land, and it was a case of simply replacing one set of *caciques* with another. But even where it was not imposed through the violent and arbitrary land-grabbing of *caciques* and their clients, official reform again represented the intervention of an alien state apparatus in the life of communities whose historical experiences had produced a substantial measure of *desconfianza* with regard to such interventions.

The liberal *repartos* began with a survey to delineate the former communal lands of the villages. The authorities then determined individual households' entitlement to receive a plot in private tenure: single men and widowers might readily be disenfranchised (Sánchez 1981: 35). The kinds of complaints which *comuneros* voiced in the wake of the *repartos* were that there were "irregularities" in the determination of the relevant boundaries of the village's holdings; that the best land had been sold to *hacendados,* ranchers and other outsiders, or to better-off members of the community before the conclusion of the *reparto*; that land entitlements had been assigned unequally without regard to variations in family size, and that some families had ended up with the right to acquire land which was agriculturally worthless. The disposal of land to pastoralists could, in itself, wreak havoc with the peasant economy of the village, as the animals of non-members of the community invaded cultivated plots (Sánchez 1981:36). As Knight has observed, the legal process of disentailment was the foundation of many local *cacique* careers:

> ...in many cases, the inhabitants sought to comply with the law, while safeguarding the community's lands, by vesting the titles in the name of trustworthy *vecinos*, who proved they could not be trusted. Many of Guerrero's "village elite" made their fortunes in this way. Clemente Unzueta of Tlaxmalac exploited his position as representative of the community to acquire the best lands, augmented them by shrewd combination of purchase, marriage and *baldio* denunciations, and thus established himself as the cacique "in whose hand power was always held, directly or indirectly."

> Of sixteen similar representatives chosen by the communities of
> Chaucingo and Quetzalapa, only one proved trustworthy, while
> the others used their position to confine the rest of the inhabitants
> to inferior land. (Knight 1986a:113)

Thus, the process of land division itself could constitute a process of dispossession, before any tendencies towards further impoverishment, differentiation and land engrossment got under way. Under the firmer rule of the
Porfiriato, the *comuneros* had every incentive to attempt to gain redress
through legal channels. Pleas for new distributions of land were generally
rejected on the grounds that the Indians were now "equal before the Law",
and could not expect to receive special treatment if they were too thriftless to
retain control of their land. It was difficult to press *collective* denunciations of
land usurpation within a legal system that recognized only *individual* claims
on property. The failure of efforts to obtain legal redress led to further land
invasions, repression and assassinations in the last decade of the century,
which were accompanied by renewed and, to the authorities, alarming, signs
of collaboration between communities in mounting resistance (Sánchez
1981:44-45). The Michoacán of the Indian village community was therefore a
turbulent one in the pre-revolutionary period. But not all the turbulence was
to prove symptomatic of the struggle between classes in the revolutionary
sense: *agrarismo* was, in the new climate created by the revolution, to prove
as efficacious a vehicle for self-serving *caciquismo* as the disentailment process had been, and the agrarian struggle was marked by considerable intra-
communal violence as well as violence directed against *agraristas* by the
ricos they attacked. In both contexts, the outcome was built into the rules of
the game, which I will now turn to explore.

AGRARISTAS, CAUDILLOS AND *CACIQUES*

The best-known case of agrarian revolt in Michoacán is that of Naranja, in
the Ciénega de Zacapu, immortalized for an anthropological readership by
the classic monograph of Paul Friedrich. Naranja had retained its village
lands and access to the resources of the neighboring lake and marshes up to
the 1880s. In 1883 the Spanish Noriega brothers succeeded in usurping the
village's title to the marsh land, which had hitherto provided the community
with a good income from weaving mats and baskets. They did so with the
assistance of two mestizo families resident in the community: the head of one
of them held the office of mayor at the time, and the two lines of mestizo
cacique were henceforth to alternate control of the local militia (Friedrich
1977:43, 48). Invoking the *baldio* laws, the Noriegas drained the marsh and
appropriated or alienated the rich arable land this operation produced. Loss of
subsistence resources was not compensated by employment of the villagers
as peons or sharecroppers on the Noriega estate: the *hacendados* soon began

to replace Tarascan hired labor with that of more loyal mestizo *acasillados* (Friedrich 1977:44). Dispossession did not invariably lead to incorporation into the wage-labor force in this epoch, any more than it does today. But poverty was not shared equally among the Naranjeños: some Indian *acomodados* owning plows and oxen were allowed access to Noriega land as sharecroppers, while seven wealthy families used the lever of debt to engross most of the land still held by their poorer neighbors (Friedrich 1977:45).

Participation in agrarian revolt did not, however, correlate directly with this pattern of intra-village economic stratification, even though the latter was a source of violent antagonisms within the community. Friedrich discovered that "many impoverished but fanatically Catholic Indians supported the ruling class," while the agrarian movement was launched by Joaquín de la Cruz, the university-educated son of a wealthy community *cacique* of the previous century (Friedrich 1977:48). Joaquín had studied Law "in order to help his [widowed] mother, who had her enemies, as everyone does, and was losing land and cattle" (Friedrich 1977:52-53). Joaquín was particularly well-educated, the beneficiary of Díaz's policy of awarding scholarships to a few children of "superior" Indian families: he became a student radical and rewarded the regime which patronized him by participating in the oppositional Liberal Clubs (Friedrich 1977: 64). The community agrarian leaders of this period— including those of Guarachita—generally belonged to the literate and educated village economic elite. Friedrich succumbs to a characteristic dash of "deviant personality" explanation in accounting for Don Joaquín's motivations. But the final limb of his analysis of the roots of this individual's agrarianism might pass muster as a generalization about the role of many other community leaders:

> Implicitly, his was a conservative reaction against economic and social changes that were proving detrimental to indigenous culture and *to the dominant place of his own family in Naranja political life*. (Friedrich 1977:53, my emphasis)

It cannot, however, be said that all agrarian leaders in village communities were of this type: in some cases, like Guarachita, mestizos joined the struggle against the hacienda, not in order to reclaim power they had lost, but to create new possibilities for the future. Guarachita was much more acculturated and mestizoized than a community like Naranja, the product of its longer experience of encapsulation by the Great Estate. Since Naranja's few mestizos had been the instrument of the community's despoliation, they could hardly become *agraristas*, although they did, of course, have their indigenous collaborators, whose own eyes had been on the future, not the past. How far the highly educated and politically sophisticated Don Joaquín was simply pursuing the chimera of a return to "tradition" is perhaps open to question. It may, however, be reasonable to describe his resistance as a "conservative reaction." In the next generation of leadership in Naranja, there is no doubt that we are dealing with a leadership which sought to recover what it had lost in a *new* world created by social revolution. Such visions might not, ultimately, be too concerned with the practice of social justice and economic equality: they were compatible with the ruthless pursuit of particularistic local vendettas. But they did embody some definitive cultural breaks with the past. Whether those who followed shared the whole of the vision is another matter.

As an example of agrarian revolt, the case of Naranja was neither isolated nor unusual. Its special significance resides in the larger regional role of Don Joaquín's nephew, Primo Tapia, who took over the leadership two years after his uncle had been assassinated in Colima by his own military escort, suborned by local sugar planters colluding with the Noriegas (Friedrich 1977:56). In December 1922 Tapia became the Secretary General of the state-wide *Liga de Comunidades y Sindicatos Agraristas de Michoacán*.

Primo Tapia, like the majority of the *agraristas* in Guaracha, was a migrant, a Norteño. The Tarascan communities were in the historical vanguard of the emigrant movement from Michoacán (and the migrant flow was to increase as a result of violence by revolutionary armies, the *hacendados*, *Cristeros* and *agraristas*). Tapia's absence from Naranja lasted, with only a few brief interludes, from 1907 to 1921. In the North, Tapia made contact with the Flores Magón brothers, the leadership-in-exile of the now anarcho-syndicalist PLM, married a "huera" from Sonora, and became an activist in the IWW (Friedrich 1977:64-70). From the outset, the revolutionary leadership in Naranja had enjoyed wider social and political connections, but these extended as the struggle developed. Friedrich again lapses into psychologism in seeking to explain Tapia's politics, but his juvenile restlessness, insistent flouting of sexual conventions, and subsequent ideological orientations were perhaps not so unusual for men with his social background, which placed them in the liminal zone of "Indian" society.

The politics certainly represented a trend. Not long after he assumed the leadership in Naranja, Tapia was forced to take refuge in Morelia in the face of the threat to his life posed by the "White Guards" of the local haciendas. The *Liga de Comunidades* was been founded on the initiative of the *Federación de Sindicatos de Obreros y Campesinos*. This had been one of the founding organizations of the CROM, and had acted as its daughter organization in Michoacán since 1918, enjoying close ties with the *Partido Socialista Michoacano*, the urban political sponsors of Francisco Múgica (Hernández 1982:14). The platform of the *Liga de Comunidades*, which was established in the wake of the fall of the reforming Múgica administration, embraced the creation of collective ejidos, financed by the state, the extension of rights to land grants to *peones acasillados*, and, symptomatically, the technical modernization of agriculture and the establishment of rationalist, as opposed to clerical, education in Michoacán. Tapia also dedicated himself to promotion of women's organizations, albeit from the somewhat patriarchal standpoint that the hegemony of the clergy over the female mind posed an ever-present threat to the security of the movement (Hernández 1982:15). The gulf between what was now being offered to "los compañeros indios" and the aspirations and worldview of the risings of the *comuneros* in the late nineteenth century is readily apparent.

While the *Liga de Comunidades* was the first attempt to organize the agrarian movement at the grass roots on a state-wide basis to have any real impact, there had been one precursor organization of a rather different kind. After the fall of Huerta, the constitutionalist general in command of Michoacán, Gertrudis Sánchez, expropriated some haciendas owned by *Huertistas*, in the manner of Villa's expropriations in the North. Sánchez then embarked upon a program of restitution of resources to indigenous communities, appointing Trinidad Regalado, a former companion in arms and native of the village of Atacheo, near Zamora, to head the Investigative Commission which would adjudicate on claims. Regalado had represented his village in its pre-revolutionary struggle against the hacienda of Santiaguillo. Like the village elite which initially led the struggle in Guarachita, he had attempted to prosecute the campaign through legal channels, leaving for Mexico City in 1906. Towards the end of the Madero administration, Regalado had presided over the foundation, in the capital, of the *Sociedad Unificadora de los Pueblos de la Raza Indígena de los Estados de la República* (Hernández 1982:12). The founding meeting of the organization was attended by non-Michoacano representatives—one each from the states of Veracruz, Puebla, and Guerrero, and nine from communities in the state of Mexico—but the majority were from Michoacán, including representatives from Naranja and Ciénega communities ranged against Guaracha: Guarachita, San Pedro Caro and Pajacuarán.

As its name implies, this earlier umbrella organization had a much more limited program than the *Liga de Comunidades* of 1922. It had initially embarked upon a futile campaign of legalistic petitioning through what were still essentially Porfirian municipal authorities, terminated by Huerta's *coup d'état*. Although Gertrudis Sánchez did not retain control of the state for many months, and the properties which he expropriated from the *Huertistas* were returned to their owners, the Carrancista administration which succeeded a short-lived *Villista* regime did establish a Local Agrarian Commission and a Michoacán branch of the *Casa del Obrero Mundial*. Working within the new official framework, Regalado continued his activity, achieving some modest restitutions of land, until December 1917, when he was assassinated by landlord *pistoleros*, early in the administration of Ortíz Rubio, whose agrarian perspective was very much cast within the classical Liberal paradigm of promoting the expansion of a rural middle class (Hernández 1982:13).

Although a few communities, including Guarachita, did receive land via official channels of restitution during the Ortíz Rubio administration, the total figures did not exceed 12,000 hectare (Moreno 1980:58-59). Furthermore, Ortíz Rubio was to continue to be a thorn in the side of the agrarian movement during the governorship of his successor Múgica, directing the anti-*Mugiquista* activities of his allies in Michoacán from his new post as Secretary of Communications and Transport in the Provisional Government of Adolfo de la Huerta (Hernández 1980:15-16). Múgica might well have been denied his triumph at the outset had it not been for the support of Lázaro Cárdenas, whom De la Huerta appointed Chief of Military Operations in the state. And Cárdenas's replacement—Obregón's man—proved actively hostile to the agrarian cause, simultaneously disarming *agraristas* and failing to disarm the *Defensas Civiles* which Ortiz Rubio had established in some of the state's larger haciendas (Hernández 1980:16). Múgica was powerless to prevent the armed instruments of *hacendado* power carrying out acts of murder and intimidation against the cadres of the Liga de Comunidades, and had equal difficulties securing funds for his programs from the Federal Treasury. Even in the early 1920s, the power of the center, effected through its military appointments, was not negligible. After Múgica's fall, the power of the Military Chiefs was to prevail over that of the Governor in Michoacán until the entry of Cárdenas into the governor's chair in 1928: Cárdenas himself had the inestimable advantage of being able to combine both offices, using the pretext of the "emergency" created by the recrudescence of the Cristiada to take provisional leave of absence from the governorship to assume the post of *Jefe Militar* in 1929 (Zepeda 1986:235).

Múgica did succeed, despite these obstacles, in creating a significant number of new ejidos: some 23,000 hectares were distributed during his brief period of office, though this remained below the national average for the period (Fowler Salamini 1980:192). Múgica also pressed forward with his educational program, devoting half the state budget to it, and introduced a *Ley de Trabajo* applicable to both urban and rural workers. At the time, Michoacán's urban working class was scarcely the epitome of the modern proletariat: even in 1932, the largest industrial enterprise in Morelia employed only thirty-five persons, and the proletariat of the state was to be found not in urban centers but in mining and agriculture (Hernández 1982: 35, Zepeda 1985:240). The agrarian dimension of the new legislation was considerably less radical in content than the program of the future Liga de Comunidades. It was a modest, reformist, regulation of the relationships between hacienda workers, sharecroppers and tenants and the propertied class which posed no threat whatsoever to their proprietary rights: indeed, the law was drafted in a way which recognized the corresponding rights of employers (Hernández 1982:17-20). That it provoked such ferocious resistance on the part of the *hacendados* and their administrators is, perhaps, an indication of the nature of the latifundist phenomenon in the region, a line of argument which I will pursue in the next chapter. Nor did Múgica's removal terminate the development of the agrarian movement in the state. It seems likely that the *Liga de Comunidades* was a response to the deterioration of the situation produced by the installation of hostile political authorities.

In March of 1923, a year in which the *Liga* mustered a demonstration of 8,000 persons from its hundred affiliated organizations to greet Obregón on a journey through Pátzcuaro, pleading for the restoration of Múgica, Primo Tapia led the Michoacán delegation to the first meeting of the *Confederación Nacional Agraria* in Mexico City (García Mora 1981:66, Hernández 1982:20–1). The new organization brought together *agraristas* of several different hues and orientations. It included ideologists like Andrés Molina Enríquez and Gildardo Magaña. Also a Michoacano by birth, and the governor chosen by Cárdenas to end the autonomous local power of the CRMDT in Michoacán in 1936 (Zepeda 1986:252-253), Magaña is better-known to history as the would-be "modernizer" of *Zapatismo*. Alongside them sat the "old style" *ranchero* caudillo from San Luis Potosí, Saturnino Cedillo, who was ultimately to perish in rebellion against the government of Lázaro Cárdenas in 1939 (Ankerson 1980). Knight has summarized the significance of the development represented by leaders such as Magaña, and by extension, the creation of national agrarian organizations, as follows:

> Peasant revolt, under ... traditional leadership ... was parochial, lacking a national vision, and it was here that the "outside agitators," so keenly seized on by contemporary landlords as well as by latter-day sociologists, could play a valuable role, as Magaña did for Zapatismo—not in generating political awareness, which already existed, but rather in "provid[ing] the power, assistance and supralocal organization which helps peasants *act*." (Knight 1986a:161)

The problem was, however, that the leaders who assembled in Mexico City in 1923 did not share a common agrarian perspective, nor an identical commitment to a "national" perspective. Still less were such perspectives necessarily shared by those they claimed to represent. Furthermore, identification with a national perspective and recourse to help from other quarters brought problems as well as advantages in its wake.

In April 1926, Primo Tapia joined the long list of agrarian leaders to be assassinated by the local forces of reaction. But in this case the orders came from the center, direct from Plutarco Elías Calles (García Mora 1981:67, Hernández 1982:21). This was, perhaps, the price of Primo Tapia's optimistic boast, in a letter written the previous year, that:

> I have some influence with the local government, I can get something from it for my friends ... my followers [*cuates*] haven't lost faith in me, we're close to controlling all Michoacán. (Hernández 1982:21)

The quotation suggests that Calles's decision to eliminate Tapia might have been motivated not so much by anxiety about his radicalism, but by a concern that he was succeeding in creating a regional movement answerable only to himself, outside the political control of the center. But it also hints at some of the additional circumstances surrounding his demise. By 1926, the *Liga de Comunidades* was riven by emergent divisions and factionalism.

In 1924, during the rebellion of De la Huerta, Tapia had given his support to its local leaders, Enrique Estrada, the general who had orchestrated the deposition of Múgica, and Alfredo García. Tapia's motives were certainly cynical, but various different levels of cynicism are evident: Naranja received additional land (García Mora 1981:66), while the rebellion also offered Tapia a pretext to "eliminate his enemies from the pueblo of Tiríndaro" (Hernández 1982:21). The indigenous leader of Tarejero, Juan de la Cruz, and the future *Cristero*, Ramón Aguilar of Zacapu, had both supported the government, and now became openly critical of Tapia. The *Casa del Obrero Mundial* in Morelia also challenged Tapia's leadership. This background explains why the *Liga de Comunidades* under Tapia aligned itself, just before his death, with the new *Liga Nacional Campesina*. Despite its title, this organization was led and dominated by the radical *agraristas* of Veracruz under Ursulo Galván, at that time under communist influence, although Galván's Veracruz League was also patronized by Governor Adalberto Tejeda. Tejeda was very much in Múgica's mold politically, and his socialism was very unmarxist, though what it offered went far beyond what the central government offered at the time (Fowler Salamini 1980: 191, Falcón 1977:32-41). Múgica and Tejeda represented a type of revolutionary *caudillaje* which anticipated the ultimate direction of "official" political control, despite their oppositional status in the 1920s. So Tapia aligned himself with the future, albeit in an ironic sense. But by opposing himself and the Michoacán League to the contemporary central regime, he created divisions within his own local movement which damaged his attempt to preserve a radical, autonomous regional movement.

The disintegration of the *Liga de Comunidades* was marked by escalating violence between *agraristas* as well as the violent settling of scores between village "agrarians" and their family enemies. It is evident that ruling class violence impelled *agraristas* along the same path. One should perhaps not restrict the definition of "ruling class violence" to acts of murder alone: the entire agrarian system represented a form of violence against the underclasses. But its structural effects permeated insidiously through all social relationships. As the Liga collapsed, the perpetual counter-violence of the *s* was complemented by a new factor, the *Cristero* rebellion, which brought the toll of death and destruction to unprecedented levels even by the standards of the time. Almost half the population of the Ciénega de Zacapu resolved their difficulties by emigration (García Mora 1981:67). It was in this apparently unpropitious climate that Cárdenas assumed the governorship.

In contrast to Múgica, Cárdenas began his governorship with the inestimable advantage of enjoying the support of the center in the person of
Calles, as well as local political support (Zepeda 1985:234-235). But the significance of the CRMDT was that it represented a successful attempt by
Cárdenas to create an autonomous regional power base for himself, which in
turn made a significant contribution to the enhancement of his personal position within the national revolutionary elite: now a state governor with a
proven capacity to mobilize popular forces, he had moved from the second
rank of revolutionary military caudillos to President of the PNR two years
after his appointment. A year later he was Secretary of Defense (Zepeda
1985:242). What distinguished Cárdenas from other caudillos who built up
regional power bases only to finish their careers in a losing confrontation
with central power was that he knew when it was time to sacrifice old allies
to the logic of the national revolution.

Cárdenas's personal biography is of some relevance to understanding the
genesis of *Cardenismo*, although it would be perverse not to recognize the
way that *Cardenismo* developed out of the logic of the social revolutionary
process, already apparent enough in the sequence of developments in
Michoacán. Cárdenas's grandfather, Francisco, born in Jalisco, had been a
Juarista. He ended his military career against the French as a propertyless
itinerant salesman, marrying into an equally unaffluent Jiquilpan family.
Francisco dedicated himself to Jiquilpan's principal artisan craft, shawl making, renting two hectare of land. His son Dámaso, who died in 1910, had married an orphaned Guarachiteña, who inherited a house from her godmother.
In it Dámaso established a shop and billiard table, having begun his working
life running a rented grocery shop (Benítez 1977:11-12). Jiquilpan's claims to
being "urban" resided less in its economic base than in its politico-administrative function and the cultural characteristics of its population. The young
Lázaro Cárdenas had combined personal experience of agricultural labor with
a primary education which reinforced his patriline's *Juarista* sympathies
against his mother's religiosity. Distinguished mainly by the excellence of his
handwriting, after a period of work in the local bureaucracy, he formed a
cooperative which took over the local printshop "La Económica," an occupation which provided the immediate circumstances which impelled him into
the Revolution. In May 1913, the Carrancista forces of José Rentería took
temporary control of the Guaracha hacienda and asked "La Ecónomica" to
print a manifesto, only to be annihilated almost immediately by the forces of
Huerta (Benítez 1977: 28-30).

Don Lázaro's maternal uncle was a hacienda administrator in the Tierra
Caliente, whither his nephew went in the first stage of the military peregrinations which marked the first stage of his revolutionary career. Socially,
Cárdenas was scarcely a "plebeian": his background was that of the provincial, urbanized, "professional" and small-scale commercial class, whose kin
and affinal networks would embrace persons of differing levels of affluence.

But it was his revolutionary military career and the patronage relationships established through it—with Calles in particular—which laid the basis for his career as a caudillo, to a much greater extent than someone like Múgica, who made a poor soldier and remained an essentially civilian "político." It was, however, clearly the influence of friends like Múgica, originally a journalist, and his involvement in the developing movement towards mass politics in Michoacán and elsewhere which constituted the political formation of this individual brought up in the tradition of popular *Juarismo*. His political perspective, even on Liberalism, would always have been a more Jacobin one than that of the even more popular, but yet more mythological, *Juarismo* reflected in the phrasing of Zapata's Plan de Ayala (Knight 1986a:309). As Cárdenas's governorship of Michoacán was to demonstrate, he was also a master of the art of the politically possible and of the politically necessary.

The CRMDT was initially supported by the Communists, as well as by the rump of the *Mugiquistas* and the *Liga de Comunidades*. But the Communists became disaffected with what appeared to be the line of class conciliation adopted by Cárdenas, suspecting that the CRMDT was simply to prove another organ of "official" reformism (Zepeda 1985:236). A number of commentators have emphasized the "moderation" of Cárdenas's own position in this period, relative to that of more radical elements associated with his administration and the CRMDT itself (see, for example, González 1979). The program of the first assembly of the CRMDT did include a *recommendation* that land redistributed should be worked collectively, albeit "respecting the decision of each community on the matter," which suggests that hostility towards the idea of collective ejidos on the part of the Michoacán peasantry was already apparent at this early stage. It also insisted that arming the *campesinos* was essential. But beyond additional rhetorical flourishes drawn from the discourse of the international labor movement, no great advance appeared to be offered relative to earlier agrarian programs. The CRMDT continued the emphasis on education and the organization of women which had been integral to Tapia's program: teachers played a crucial role within the new organization, in a sense providing the urban wing which could not be supplied by organized labor in the Michoacán context (Zepeda 1985:240-241). The *agraristas* still supplied the mass base of the organization—whose membership had reached 100,000 by 1932—but their representation in leadership positions was not proportional to their numerical strength among the rank-and-file (Hernández 1982:36).

The impact of the CRMDT was almost inconsequential in comparison with the scope of reform during Cárdenas's tenure of the presidency. But it did represent a very significant advance on the gains of previous movements within Michoacán, and extended its influence into neighboring regions where *agrarista* organization was weak, such as Los Altos de Jalisco (Craig 1983:82-83). Almost 16,000 Michoacano beneficiaries, in 181 communities, received 141,663 hectares in four years, during much of which time Cárdenas himself was otherwise engaged and left the state government to others, notably his brother Dámaso (Zepeda 1985:242-243). Almost the whole of this advance was secured within the legal framework of "official" agrarian reform, pushed to its limits with such measures as the 1930 *Ley de Tierras Ociosas*, a 1931 decree nullifying the contracts between the communities of the Meseta Tarasca and foreign timber companies, and a 1932 decree invoking earlier state legislation which established conditions under which *latifundios* might be divided (Hernández 1982:42). But all this highly "constitutional" reform was made possible by the fact that the Cardenistas were determined to wrest control of the local administrative apparatus from the landlord interest by whatever means were necessary: this often meant violence or electoral fraud. Some of the resistance came from established *caciques*, but the *peones acasillados* of Guaracha were not the only community, nor the only type of community, to refuse to receive land at the hands of Cárdenas in this period, and not all communities wished to vote for the candidates of Cárdenas and the CRMDT (Zepeda 1985:244).

There was a substantial quotient of landlord and clerical manipulation, not to say intimidation, physical and spiritual, in this process of resistance. But the Cardenistas did provoke quite genuine kinds of popular resistance. Cardenista anti-clericalism sometimes took shockingly sacrilegious and murderous forms: the *Cristero* problem notwithstanding, this was largely counter-productive in terms of liberating the masses from the supposed ideological hegemony of the clergy. The resolution by undemocratic means of conflicts between Cardenistas and the other "progressive" forces with which they competed may also have caused a certain disenchantment. Above all, the reliance of the new movement on *caciques* with personal ties to the governor created obvious contradictions. What could anyone make of the continued ascent of a figure like Ernesto Prado, the murderous *agrarista* boss of the Cañada who was to become "federal deputy by the will of Don Lázaro" (García Mora 1981:69)? Prado had occupied a position of authority since 1919, by virtue of "his indiscriminate violence and formal devotion to the state government in turn" (Ramírez 1986:129). As for the agrarian problem in the Cañada in the 1920s and 1930s:

> ...the conflict was not just between Indians and old proprietors. Within each of the communities there formed bands of "agraristas" and "traditionalists," unleashing a factional struggle in all the villages of the Cañada, which only began to dampen down in the middle of the Forties. The causes of this struggle had agrarian origins. The redistributed lands were not only those of "landlords" or proprietors, much communal land was distributed and the indigenous minifundists were expropriated. The distribution of the land was not exactly equitable. Those who participated most in the armed movement, received most, generating disaffec-

tion and hatred among those who received little or nothing. But after some years, it became clear that the agrarian argument was nothing more than a pretext for maintaining political control and access to institutional positions, like the municipal presidency and the *representación de bienes comunales*, since that allowed the Pradista group to create a clientele of loyal followers among the various villages of the Cañada and make themselves into brokers and protectors in relation to the political groups in Morelia, thus establishing a clear *cacicazgo*. (Ramírez 1986:128-129)

The CRMDT was ultimately a machine for monopolizing political control, and where it found that such control was already in the hands of men who would suit its purposes, particularly in places which were not, in terms of their social characteristics, at the cutting edge of its predilect social program, the destruction of the Great Estate, it left them in place or promoted them. It is not surprising that the slogan of the disenchanted Ramón Aguilar, *agrarista* turned *Cristero*, became: "¡Viva el agrarismo! ¡Mueran el agrarismo y el pillaje!" (González 1984:146). But, as the previous experience of attempts at "legal" reform demonstrated, control of the political and bureaucratic machine was a *sine qua non* for progress, it was not a sufficient condition for success. In the face of the Cardenista assault, and now deprived of the countervailing protection of a sympathetic Chief of Military Operations, the landlords might concede the political victory, at least for the moment, to *Cardenismo*. After all, retreat from the political stage was already the norm for the *hacendado* class in many other areas. But they conserved their economic power in Michoacán for the time being (Zepeda 1985:244), and with only minimal and sporadic concessions to the kind of "modernization" which was already apparent in some other areas—unilateral land reform, change to capital intensive techniques, acceptance of unqualified "free" wage labor and reformist labor laws (Knight 1986b:515). Those who had expected more radical things of Cárdenas were, for the moment, to be disappointed.

Cárdenas might offer the peons the land of Guaracha, but it is interesting to reflect on what he would, or could, have done had they greeted the offer with greater enthusiasm: such a response would certainly have pushed the agrarian movement in Michoacán into a quite different kind of confrontation with the center. His subsequent behavior suggests that he was only prepared to face the challenge of emancipating the peon once the apparatus of central power itself was in his grasp. There is also, as we will see, the problem of Cárdenas's implicit conception of the capabilities of the agrarian masses, his commitment to modernizing national ideologies, and the natural tendency of revolutionary leaderships of this type to see "progress" as synonymous with their own political dominance over an orderly process of change. All this may, however, simply demonstrate that Lázaro Cárdenas was realistic, and that a statist solution was the only historically viable one. The fate of

Zapatismo had, after all, already demonstrated the limitations of even the most intense, authentic, autonomous and, above all, uncompromising, of regional popular mobilizations, and therewith the limits of the agrarian revolutions of this epoch.

Cárdenas's legalism did, however, bring him other benefits besides that of keeping his mobilization of popular forces within the "rules of the game" as it stood during the Calles era. Together with the drive towards monopolization of access to political posts, it reestablished a state-wide, centralized chain of clientelist relations linking popular organizations to Morelia and the person of the governor. Cárdenas was now a caudillo commanding a regional power base, albeit one which included petty *cacicazgos* like the domain of the Prados, whose accommodation with the "política de masas" was opportunistic and self-serving.

Cárdenas was succeeded in office by General Benigno Serrato, who had been *Jefe de Operaciones Militares* in the state since August 1930 (Hernández 1982:48). The assumption that Serrato's appointment was the work of Calles would be plausible if one assumed that Calles wished to undermine Cárdenas's regional political base because he saw him as a political or social menace. The problem with this type of argument is that it is made with the benefit of hindsight. There is some evidence to support the alternative hypothesis, that Cárdenas himself arranged for Serrato to succeed him, in order to block the rise of the CRMDT leader Soto Reyes, who would have become a rival for control of Cárdenas's regional power base (Zepeda 1985:246). If so, then Cárdenas seriously misjudged the extent to which Serrato would attempt to dismantle what he had created. Since Serrato was already in Michoacán, it seems likely that, in his role as a potential countervailing power to the governor, he would already have been sounded out on his attitudes to the Cardenista reforms by members of the local elite and clergy. Once in office, he received direct orders from the then President, Abelardo Rodríguez, to deal with those who had been disturbing public order in the region and disarm the agrarian *Defensas Sociales* (Zepeda 1985:247-248). An attack on the Cardenista leadership of the CRMDT was launched at the very beginning of Serrato's governorship, pursued through a campaign of assassinations of agrarian leaders. Serrato himself asked Calles to ensure that Cárdenas was moved out of the state (Zepeda 1985:248). Cárdenas subsequently had little scope to defend his *cuates* in Michoacán against the thrust of Serrato's policies since, as Secretary of Defense, he was charged with a national policy of disarming *agraristas*, and there was little practical support he could offer against the Serratistas' installation of their own men into leadership positions in the CRMDT. This and other maneuvers did not so much create an alternative organization as disorganize that which existed and create confusion.

More significant than the question of Cárdenas's personal role in these events is what they demonstrate about the nature of the movement represented by the CRMDT: stripped of the support of a hegemonic *caudillo* in the governor's chair, to counterbalance the power of the landlord and clerical interests, the Cardenista leadership could not even mobilize its popular base to defend the integrity of its own organization. The entire popular movement was critically compromised by pursuing its objectives through the channels of the official system. But the Cardenista CRMDT did not disintegrate totally; once Cárdenas was the presidential candidate, it regained much of the ground it had lost politically and in the popular organizations. The *Serratistas* retained control of the local PNR, and Cárdenas avoided open conflict by agreeing to a share-out of federal and local parliamentary representatives, conceding a local majority to the opposition in exchange for federal supremacy (Zepeda 1985:250-251). Two days after Cárdenas's assumption of presidential power, Serrato was to perish in a timely aircrash.

This event, one of a number of happy chances that marked the Cárdenas era, saved the president the labor of embarking on the more drawn-out process of centralizing control by installing a client as Military Chief in order to counterbalance gubernatorial power—a key tactic in other regions at the start of Cárdenas's conquest of real control over the state apparatus of which he became titular head (Hernández Chávez 1979:74). With Serrato gone, the CRMDT completed its return to power, capturing control of the PNR and achieving—for the moment—a monopoly of representation of popular demands to the authorities (Zepeda 1985:252). But the triumph was short-lived. Cárdenas chose Gildardo Magaña as the next governor in lieu of the candidate of the CRMDT, despite the protests of the latter. Magaña had his own reasons for wanting to promote factionalism within the organization, whose relationship with *Cardenismo* left this distinguished revolutionary *caudillo* with no autonomous political base of his own in his natal state. But what finally killed the CRMDT was the fact that *Cardenismo* had shifted from the periphery to the center, from building the base for the triumph of a caudillo to building a state apparatus which would finish with *caudillaje*, and agrarian revolution, definitively.

In January 1937, the workers of Michoacán were affiliated to the CTM and the peasants to the CNC (Zepeda 1985:253). The final moment of incorporation of the regional agrarian movement into the cooptative apparatus of the state had arrived. But it was the culmination, not the beginning, of a trend. Entangled as it was in the logic of revolutionary politics and the processes of state-building, the CRMDT itself had embodied a contradiction. It encapsulated genuinely popular struggles and aspirations with deep historical roots. At the same time it sought to achieve its goals through the type of clientage relationships which were ultimately, when implemented on a national scale, to bring relative stability to the order of post-revolutionary society. Given the practical difficulties of attempting to pursue "uncompromised" popular struggle in this historical context there was, perhaps, little alternative but to go down this road. There was opposition to the centralization of the peasant movement from the more ideologically motivated local agrarian leaders, men like the remarkable José Romero, master carpenter turned labor and agrarian leader, "the eternal rebel" whose career is charted in Ann Craig's study of Lagos de Moreno, Jalisco (Craig 1983:162-163). José seems to have resigned himself to the futility of seeking further radical gains through the system before the end of the Cárdenas presidency. But as Craig shows, the foot soldiers of the agrarian movement in Los Altos never shared the same kind of political visions as their principal leader, and have proved strong "system loyalists" in a pragmatic sense (Craig 1983:222-224). The same is true of the surviving Cardenista foot soldiers I met in the Ciénega. But no Ciénega equivalent of José Romero has lived to enjoy an embittered retirement in Mexico City. The leading urban Cardenista activists of this region proved to be men of a different stamp.

SOCIAL REVOLUTION AND GUARACHA

In reflecting on the substance of their emancipation, many Guaracheño peasants may have had their doubts about whether the Porfiriato had terminated even in 1940. There was a considerable gap between the rhetoric accompanying the foundation of the Collective Ejido and the reality of its administration. Furthermore, as *Jefe de Tenencia* in the newly emancipated village, Cárdenas installed an *amigo conocido* from Tarecuato, complete with *pistoleros* and accompanied by a detachment of federal troops, given to drunkenness and abuse of the *gente humilde* and community leaders alike. If *Cardenismo* finally brought about something resembling a social revolution from above throughout Michoacán, it was in large measure experienced by those below as arbitrariness, corruption and *caciquismo*. One might understand an obsessive concern with the "pacification" of the unrevolutionary peons of Guaracha, but the experience was quite general throughout the state, and beyond. Nor, as we have seen, was this side of *Cardenismo* exactly new. But even if the pistol remained a potent political argument, by the end of the Cárdenas presidency a new institutional order of political control had replaced the order and dynamic of *caudillaje*, ensuring a definitive end to the orgiastic macro-social violence of the armed phase of the Revolution and the Cristiada. Although agrarian discontent has never been totally eliminated, the capacity of that order to endure despite its manifest injustices testifies to the scope of the transformation which *Cardenismo* wrought at the national level.

One might argue that the post-revolutionary trajectory of the Ciénega, dominated as it was by *neolatifundismo* in the three decades following the collapse of the Collective Ejido, raises the question of whether any sort of *social* revolution was really consummated, rather than simply a restructuring of capital, brought about by a bureaucratic state whose consolidation was the natural end of the socio-economic and political crisis which disrupted the Porfirian trajectory of modernization. *Cardenismo*'s provincial social base certainly looks like a repetition of a long-run cyclical pattern. The upper echelons of the leadership of the agrarian movement in the Ciénega were urban, and comprised minor functionaries, journalists and professionals (including the hacienda doctors), with a sprinkling of petty bourgeois tradesmen, artisans and some small landowners: in other words, social elements at the forefront of every phase of political agitation since Independence. Naturally, they had their personal economic rewards, including private ranches on land in Jiquilpan which had been assigned to ejidatarios by presidential decree, and a share in the irrigation waters of Guaracha after the collapse of the ejidal sugar industry. Such "abuses" might be seen as a reflection of the continuing relative weakness of the central state, and to an extent such a judgment would be valid. But it should be tempered by recognition of the increased level of effective intervention in social relations achieved by the Cardenista form of post-revolutionary state. Informal mechanisms of resource redistribution to new strata and accommodations with dominant class power played a key role in cementing a stable, if still segmented, "national" society together, and informal patronage networks and structures of intermediation remain essential conditions for the maintenance of central state power today (De la Peña 1986). By making the state the effective focal point of class struggles, *Cardenismo* secured significant changes in the *structures* of social power, albeit by checking the expression of genuinely popular power. The expansion of the economic role of the state, together with the ever-ramifying structures of intermediation between state and masses, offered new opportunities for social mobility to sectors which had previously remained unsatisfied. The Cárdenas reorganization also permitted the state as mediator to undertake reformist economic adjustments so often impossible for private capital, especially landlords. Finally, the extension of land reform made possible a more definitive incorporation of the organs of popular struggle into the new political structure. The social content of *Cardenismo* is crucial, not because it resolved the problems of the rural poor, but because it was politically effective. The creation of the PNR by Calles may have been an important step towards the triumph of institutions over *caudillaje*. Some, like Adolfo Gilly, would see Obregón as the author of a new political basis for bourgeois social power, "the model to which all subsequent Mexican governments have clung" (Gilly 1983:323). A trend clearly exists. Yet there seems to be a great deal of unfinished long-term business in 1920, or even in 1934: with the *hacendados*, the rural masses in their various guises, with the urban and especially provincial petty bourgeoisie, with the Church, with the military, and as a result of all this, with the process of building a national state which was relatively effective, at least from the standpoint of internal control (Hernández Chávez 1979).

It is difficult to argue that the agrarian regime which emerged in the longer term in post-revolutionary Mexico was not different from its predecessor from the standpoint of political economy and qualitative human social experience alike. It is scarcely germane to judgment on the objectivity of change that the new structures which emerged failed to accord with either the dreams of the rural masses and or, for that matter, the plans and expectations of the various revolutionary leaderships. If there was a high degree of continuity with respect to the projects of post-revolutionary state-builders and the social (as distinct from political) power of the pre-revolutionary elite, there was also a sea change with respect to the incorporation of "the masses" into national life, that is to say a change in the relationship between state and society premised on the "massification" of politics and the penetration of central state power into the daily lives of ordinary people throughout the national territory. Cárdenas's personal political style reflected his dedication to this transformation: his 16,000 mile presidential campaign was the first to reach into the heart of rural Mexico, and he continued to tour the country extensively after assuming the presidency. The style remained clientalistic, and some recall that a man with a satchel full of *billetes* was an integral part of the Cardenista campaign apparatus. But Cárdenas transmitted the impression that he genuinely *cared* about the fate of ordinary people, and thereby made a significant personal contribution to awakening the idea that the function of government was to provide services to the whole of society.

Some doubted whether this new style of government would outlast the Cárdenas sexennial, and many remained resolutely hostile to the General's platform. But more significantly, the approachability of Cárdenas the man was, of course, no true reflection of the real mechanics of the state's conquest of the masses. "Incorporation" entails little in terms of democratic participation or social equity. Personalistic forms of clientalism may continue to play an important role within the structures of domination. Informal social networks which provide the basis for the continuing coherence of old social elites, and mediate emergent informal alliances with new political power-holders, may play an important part in the distribution of social power, as the survival of the great Porfirian families in Mexico, and the eventual reentry of some of these elements into national politics, indicates (Hamilton 1982). Nor is "mass incorporation" incompatible with relatively high levels of mass dissatisfaction with the regime. What makes it the crucial moment of the social revolutionary process is that—for the time being, at least—it ends an era in which the *generality* of social movements are implicitly or explicitly antagonistic towards the claims of the central state and national integrity. The incorporated address their complaints to the center. They seek redress through changes in policy or government. Viewed through this optic, the Cárdenas era completes a process which had been incipient through the Twenties, carrying the state's conquest of control over civil society to completion. This achievement depended on the implementation of a more radical agrarian policy, because that alone could extend the clientelistic dependence of the countryside on the state to a level which would ensure that any continuing tensions would ultimately be resolved within and through "the system."

In the end, the triumph was sufficient, but it was by no means complete or uncontested. Resistance to the new dispensation continued partly because land reform failed in practice to provide a comprehensive solution to the problems of the countryside. Of particular significance was the support amassed by the *sinarquista* movement in the rural communities of the Center-North. Formally founded in León, Guanajuato, in 1937, the Unión Nacional Sinarquista reached the apogee of its power in the period 1940–1941: thereafter its coherence was reduced by conflict between its public political leadership and the secret organization known as *La Base*, the latter being the means by which the Church intervened in the direction of the movement (Aguilar *et al.* 1981:163-166). Pressured into a more overt anti-government stance by its internal problems, the UNS provoked direct official repression in 1944 and subsequently fragmented, losing half its members by the end of the decade, a period which saw a marked improvement in Church-State relations. It has also been argued that the key factor in sinarquism's decline was the state's ability to ameliorate the pressures created by the shortcomings of the agrarian reform through the *Bracero* program (Cross and Sandos 1981:41–42). But episodes of intra-communal violence recounted to me in the course of fieldwork suggest that the specter represented by sinarquism was not vanquished entirely even during the years of its relative decline. Today it is the UNS's modern successor, the PDM, which represents the quintessentially "*campesino*" face of the Right in Michoacán, one of its areas of greatest strength nationally (Nava 1987:35).

A recalcitrant region such as western Michoacán perhaps gives some useful indications of the conditions which permitted the emergence of a more effective centralized state, and at the same time set limits on its effectiveness. If we ask how *Cardenismo* finally triumphed in the apparently adverse circumstances of its birthplace in the Ciénega, "by achieving state power" would seem the shortest possible answer. But both Cárdenas's becoming the candidate of the PNR, and his ability to break Calles and push through his program, reflect the tensions of "unfinished business" at national level, and the continuing contribution to the course of the revolution of pressure from below, if not purely pressure from "the masses." Pressures were not entirely absent in Serrato's Michoacán, even in the unrevolutionary Ciénega de Chapala.

CHAPTER 3

THE DEMISE OF A PORFIRIAN HACIENDA

The final expropriation of the Guaracha hacienda seems, on closer inspection, to have been somewhat less than a revolutionary act, despite the armed seizure of a tract of hacienda land by a group of thirty or so Guaracha *agraristas* in August 1933, a triumph which was almost immediately negated by a suspicious breach of the Chapala flood defenses and consequent inundation of the land (Moreno, 1980:179-180). With Cárdenas installed in the Presidency, negotiations took place behind the scenes. Don Manuel Moreno received a refinery concession in Uruapan in compensation for his sugar mill. When this new enterprise went badly, Don Lázaro helped him out by arranging a contract to supply his resin to the Soviet Union (Brigitte Boehm, personal communication) Don Manuel, scion of a Guadalajaran banking family, may also have already begun to acquire the new industrial assets in Mexico City in which much of the family's capital was subsequently invested. Not only the owner who had an economic stake in Guaracha: his administrators, all local men, also had something to lose. The penultimate administrator, Eudoro Méndez, was a leading light of the Jiquilpan political faction dubbed "La Seda" (those dressed in silk), which the town's landowners formed to combat the menace posed by Cárdenas"s own party, known as "La Hilacha" (the party of the ragged).

What had appeared so menacing about the Hilachento program was its promise of land to the *peón* as well as, if not actually in preference to, the dispossessed indigenous community (Ochoa n.d.:9). Along with the likes of Don Eudoro, Jiquilpan's leading families, the Quiroz and Villaseñor, shared in their infinitely more modest way in the same system of agrarian exploitation as the Morenos (Benítez 1977:8). Politics has always been pursued with true passion in Jiquilpan. But in 1926, Cárdenas was photographed at a fiesta in Guaracha, dancing most contentedly with Don Eudoro's daughter.

By this stage in his career, of course, Don Lázaro had been Jefe de Operaciones Militares and provisional governor. Yet perhaps the social links and common aspirations had always been there in these provincial towns whose urban status was so tied to their cultural, rather than economic, opposition to the rural hinterland. A glance at the names which have figured in Jiquilpan's political life over the years would be sufficient to demonstrate that in the longer term an accommodation was not difficult to achieve.

The events, however, may be obscuring significant underlying contradictions. For the rural population of Michoacán, this was, as we have seen, a period of profound social crisis. There was substantial mass mobilization, even if it took a variety of apparently contradictory forms, in particular that of *Cristero* versus *agrarista*. Nationally, agrarian class conflict continued to add up in a cumulative process accompanied by new stirrings from organized labor and the perpetual restlessness of the provincial professionals. And the long term viability of those latifundist enterprises like Guaracha which thus far appeared to have remained immune from the reformist tendencies of the post-revolutionary period may not have been as beyond question as appearances and their eventual political suppression from above might suggest.

THE POLITICAL ECONOMY OF *LATIFUNDISMO* AND CLASS STRUGGLE

At the outbreak of revolution, Guaracha and its three annexes, San Antonio Guaracha, El Platanal and Cerrito Pelon, controlled a total land area approaching 35,000 hectare. Two thousand forty hectare were permanently irrigated, but a greater area could receive water when the dams achieved their total capacity, and the humid subsoil permitted permanent cultivation of almost a third of the *latifundio's* terrain (Moreno 1980:117, 125-126). Guaracha compared in size and organization with the famous agro-industrial enterprises of the Tierra Caliente to the south: Los Bancos, Lombardia and Nueva Italia. As well as cane, it planted wheat, maize, chickpea, barley, sweet potatoes, and cotton. The estate had 20,000 head of cattle: alfalfa supplemented hill pasture for its fine dairy herd, improved by American bloodstock. All production was commercial. The ex-*peones* recall having to make their tortillas with chickpea when maize rations were withdrawn to meet market demand.

Guaracha in 1910 was very much a product of the Porfiriato. The mill, with its imported steam-driven machinery, was built in the 1890s, following the acquisition of the estate by Don Manuel's father, Diego Moreno Leñero. New varieties of cane and Cuban technicians were brought in. By 1896, Guaracha accounted for 10% of the sugar production of Michoacán (Moreno 1980:119). Don Diego also made substantial investments in irrigation, and while cultivation remained largely unmechanized, Guaracha did possess most of the district's modern plows and mechanical implements draw by oxen: some still survive on the ejido today, as rusting relics which people seem loath to disturb.

Private investments, which often included funds from other sources, especially the Church, were supplemented by public ones. In 1905, the Cuesta Gallardo brothers were authorized to reclaim 500 square km. from Lake Chapala. Don Diego married off a daughter to one of the Cuesta Gallardos, and thereby secured himself spectacular gains from the project in the form of extra land, in addition to much needed improvements in defenses against flooding, which had hitherto reduced the economic value of large parts of his terrain. The railway reached the eastern boundary of Guaracha in 1900. At this point, the authorities agreed to abandon their original plan to extend the line across the hacienda to Jiquilpan and Sahuayo, routing it instead to Los Reyes, via a second hacienda station in San Antonio. Guaracha acquired a bulk transport system on which to base expansion of its own agro-pastoral business; its environs were relatively marginalized, although Sahuayo, whose more prosperous elements had already benefited from the disposal of the

Cojumatlán hacienda, did at least continue to enjoy direct access to the steamer service permitting bulk transport north across the lake.

It is tempting to describe the evolution of Guaracha during the Porfiriato as a transition towards agrarian capitalism. It represented at least a step along Lenin''s "Junker Road" in the sense that what remained of an "internal peasantry" enjoyed no security of access to estate resources. Though individual peasant families might be expelled, there was no mass expulsion of the internal peasantry. A form of sharecropping was the dominant mode of working the hacienda's terrains and the seasonal labor reserve was mostly contained within the boundaries of the estate. One might describe sharecropping in Porfirian Guaracha as a capitalist form of exploitation, albeit one which pursued capitalist accumulation by maximizing absolute rather than relative surplus value. Lenin himself would have been the first to acknowledge the inadequacy of ideal type formulations. He continually emphasized the way "archaic and backward" forms of exploitation could be conserved in a slow and incomplete transition to "pure" capitalist relations in peripheral regions of the modern world. It may be preferable to approach the analysis of the internal organization of agrarian estates and their transformation over time in terms of concrete economic conditions and class relations, without making any prior assumptions about the progressive realization of "transitions."

Taking a long term perspective, there was certainly a significant shift in both the internal political economy of the *latifundio* and its relationship with its region during the late nineteenth century. By 1910, the hacienda's control of the land within its extensive boundaries had become total: it controlled the hills bordering the plain as well as the plain itself. The people of the indigenous village communities of the Bolsa de Guaracha today recount the archetypical story of the feast at which they drunkenly surrendered their birthright for a dance with the Spaniard's daughter—only *hacendados* consummate the sexual relations which are the central metaphors of agrarian class relations.[1] In reality, they did not give up their rights without a struggle. Monopoly of land now ensured a "tied" labor force reduced to a proletarian class position in a regime of absolute private property. The villagers of Totolán, for example, were permitted access to their former community land in the hills only on condition of working for the hacienda for three days a week: if they declined this contract, they had to seek employment elsewhere. Though a few found work as sharecroppers in Jiquilpan, such opportunities were limited, and the children of better-off peasants were foremost in the surge of international migration after 1918. Inhabitants of the independent communities were harassed by the hacienda guard, the *acordada*, if they set foot on its terrain without business there.

Within Guaracha itself, the employment of the *peones acasillados* was regulated by a contract which provided them with a specified wage and a house in return for, in effect, such work as the administration would determine. Clause 2a stipulated that: "The worker is obliged to render his services as *jor-*

nalero or *peón* whenever he is required." (Moreno 1980:142-145). The contract distinguished work paid by the hour, at 12.5 centavos, and by the tarea, paid "in accordance with the tariffs customary in the region" (1980:142-5). In practice the hourly rate was a dead letter, though the much lower daily wage rate did vary in accordance with age and marital status. Almost everyone I met who had worked on the hacienda, *acomodados* as well as *agraristas,* related what was often a catalogue of personal stories of what they considered arbitrariness or injustice in work assignment or payment at the hands of the administration. One, son of the foreman in charge of the oxen, did take his case to the *patrón* himself on one of his rare visits to the estate and obtained limited redress, but the majority made no such effort: "En aquel tiempo, no podía uno reclamar nada."

Along with such delicts as rustling cattle, violent altercations with authority were deemed serious and menacing offenses against landlord power, to be treated through the public display of the offender's punishment. This sometimes took the form of execution, though my evidence for this relates to the years of intensifying *agrarismo,* when the administration also turned to more covert practices of murder and assassination—the visit in the night, the assault in the darkness of the street. More routinely, delinquents were filed in procession through the surrounding communities in the chain-gang. But the actual work process itself was surrounded by its own litany of "disciplinary exercises" in Foucault's sense of the term (Foucault 1979). Woe betide those who failed to respond to the *mayordomo's* "¡Ave Maria!" as they set to their labors or those who literally "stepped out of line" as their bodies were formed into parts of a living machine. Supervision was ubiquitous on the hacienda as a whole, but particularly in Guaracha itself: it seems that a child could not pass through one of the gates without being interrogated as to his or her purpose. And yet sometimes, despite everything, the living machine was unwilling to function. Additional brute coercion was necessary to enforce clause 2a of the contract: at moments of crisis, such as a breach in the flood defenses, exhausted men would try, albeit in vain, to escape an *acordada* determined to drive them from their homes again at the dead of night. But in an environment of extensive proletarianization, exemplary punishments were needed only to demonstrate the absolute nature of hacienda authority and control of resources. The general sanction against workers who simply failed to display the docility and discipline in the labor process demanded by their employer was to expel them from the estate. The hacienda constructed the houses of its permanent workforce from reeds and poles, so that the Guard could demolish them simply by running their rifle butts along the frontage.

The dispossession of the local peasantry was also accompanied by increased direct landlord control over the productive process, use of wage labor and capital investment. The mill was particularly significant. Investment in a processing facility for a commercial crop susceptible to significant bulk reduction implies an increase in the proportion of revenue generated by industrial capitalist mechanisms of accumulation, as distinct from land monopoly and pre-capitalist forms of rent (Paige 1975:14-16). Such developments reflected more than local social change. The Porfiriato offered the *hacendado* class new opportunities, but it also increased the selective pressure of market forces upon the processes of landlord wealth accumulation, particularly in sectors where foreign investment presented a direct threat to those who failed to modernize through lack of commercial judgment or, more commonly, undercapitalization (Gledhill 1985). It is clearly unwise to attempt to generalize about "the Porfirian hacienda" as an economic type in abstraction from the scale of the enterprise: Guaracha's owners possessed access to considerable financial capital and a diversified portfolio of investments. Their class position was scarcely comparable with that of a landlord whose only asset was a single maize hacienda serving a local market. It is therefore even more significant that closer examination of the internal organization of the Guaracha enterprise suggests that monopoly of land, possession of physical coercive power and the absence of "free" commodity markets for productive inputs, may all have remained crucial to its profitability, despite its high level of technical rationality.

Direct exploitation of wage-labor was supplemented by the exploitation of sharecroppers sowing temporal crops, through mechanisms more typically associated with agrarian capital as a commercial intermediary financing "independent" peasant production. Adult men in village communities beyond the hacienda core such as Las Zarquillas, just north of Estación Moreno, were assigned land to sow as sharecroppers, though the younger generation was employed as peons, and each community had a resident *mayordomo* who exercised an absolute control over the disposition of their labor resources. Moreno's apparent acceptance of an informant's contention that "there were few sharecroppers on the plain" (Moreno 1980:142) is the opposite of the generalization made by Benítez on the basis of his own conversation with another former *peón acasillado* (Benítez 1977: 10). But the discrepancy arises in the context of the interpretation which the people themselves put on the system of *mediería* as it existed in Guaracha.

On the main hacienda, the majority of the *medieros* were recruited from the ranks of the field-workers, on annual contracts which were not necessarily renewed. There was a more privileged group which always sharecropped hacienda land and generally achieved good returns. These were people who enjoyed relationships of personal patronage with the hierarchy and performed supervisory functions, like that of *caporal* of the oxen. Informants belonging to this group freely acknowledged that their situation was atypical. Ordinary *medieros* seldom achieved more than the equivalent of a subsistence wage. The last administrator of the San Antonio annex of Guaracha remarked that the Twenties were years when the climate had given particularly bountiful harvests—and that almost all his *medieros* had been perpetually in debt.[2] Such an outcome was a consequence of the "rules of the game" as it was played, increasingly in defiance of reformist legislation, not only in the domain of the Morenos, but, it seems, elsewhere in the larger region, as I discovered when interviewing some ejidatarios who had worked on a much smaller maize-producing hacienda across the state border near La Barca, Jalisco.

The Guaracha hacienda advanced land, seed and a plow team of oxen, means of production over which its monopoly was complete, since it forced its employees to surrender any male calves born to their animals. It also advanced money and items of consumption from the *tienda de raya,* thereby treating the *mediero* as an ordinary worker, with the difference that he could theoretically look forward to his extra *"utilidad"* at harvest time. Work on the plot was periodically inspected, and the *acordada* patrolled to ensure that not a gram of produce was removed from the fields before the day which the hacienda assigned for the harvest, which it carried out directly with squads of peons under *mayordomos.* In the case of ordinary *medieros,* the entire crop was removed to the warehouse, to which they went subsequently to "liquidate" their account. The final reckoning was carried out in terms of cash values, and in the presence of armed guards. The harvest was divided 50:50, but the value of all the advances was then deducted from the sharecropper's half.

In the absence of a free market in any of the items advanced as means of production or consumption, their overvaluation was almost guaranteed. But the problem was compounded by transparent acts of fraud on the part of the administration—the proceeds of which presumably did not accrue to the . Protest was obviously futile and indeed dangerous. What made the sharecropping system viable was not its economic return, but the alternative of work in the *cuadrillas,* with its constant supervision and, to use a recurrent theme of discourse on the hacienda by its ex-employees, humiliation. Failure to show "obedience," a concept to which many *mayordomos* gave a liberal interpretation, would at once be rewarded with a beating. A few of the ex-*peones* argued that work on the cane plantation was tolerable for those who showed "docility." More began their accounts of life on the hacienda by saying: "They beat us." Others added: "We were like the blacks in the United States, like slaves." "There was no respect for us, we were treated like animals, not men." Behaving in a way which ensured freedom from chastisement was, in itself, a form of humiliation, particularly for those who could lived in, or came from, communities which had known days of greater autonomy. As share-croppers, individuals probably worked harder than they did as field hands, perhaps in the hope of securing the elusive *"utilidad,"* perhaps simply to avoid a return to the *cuadrillas.* The hacienda gained the advantages of transferring part of the risks of temporal cultivation, reducing supervision costs, and gaining costless access to domestic labor. The hacienda itself used some female labor in the fields, and children were used for sowing and irrigating work from the age of seven onwards. A sharecropper's child suffered the double exploitation of and papá.

The specific economic form in which direct wage-labor based production was realized is also significant. Money wages in 1931 were 25 centavos a day, compared with a Michoacán average of 65 centavos, itself in turn 20% below the national average (Moreno 1980:146). Only a third of the wage was paid in cash, a third being imputed to the maize ration, and the remainder to the worker's account in the *tienda de raya*. Even the monetary third was sometimes paid in the form of a chit, half of which was to be redeemed in goods. The workers might have preferred their maize to its imputed money equivalent: the size of the ration was somewhat greater than its imputed value at 1931 prices. But it is difficult to see worker bargaining playing a significant role in shaping this system, which the hacienda was still defending against the attacks of a *sindicato* formed within its domain in 1932. Its primary function seems to have been to reduce the amount of cash advanced, and, along with sales of alcohol, to ensure that most of what the peons did earn flowed back to the enterprise. It is also worth noting that the estate was pricing cheap industrial manufactures which it shipped in by train at the same level as local artisan products. Many informants singled out the clothing which the hacienda imposed on them—another dimension of the living machine—as the prime symbol of their social humiliation.

The system was just flexible enough to ensure the workers a minimum level of security. They enjoyed free medical services, and could run up debts in the store, though only to very modest levels, and without prospect of cancellation. "The only thing the hacienda gave you was your coffin," as one ex-*peón* put it. Even so, the *raya* was not sufficient to cover family reproduction fully, and the hacienda supplemented it by continuing to permit its peons access to the subsistence plots called *ecuaros* in the hills. Worker self-provisioning on land which was of no commercial value offered obvious benefits. Functionally speaking, it seems equivalent to modern capitalist agriculture's use of "external" semi-proletarian labor (De Janvry 1981). But in the case of the *peones acasillados* of Guaracha it created a contradiction.

As I began to ask people about their cultivation of *ecuaros* in the days of the hacienda, I found that I was receiving two apparently contradictory accounts. The first ran as follows:

> We went to work in the *cerro* after finishing the *tarea*, in the afternoon. In this period, it rained more than it does now, and it was a help to sow in the hills, though we didn't use to sow much.

But others said that:

> We went to sow our *ecuaros* very early, before dawn, secretly. In the *cerro* we stripped off and worked naked, so that we [i.e. their clothes] didn't show up white against the hillside. The *acordada* didn't permit us to work, they forced us down, with really bad beatings [and in a few cases, gunfire].

Thus it seems that some of the peons used their *ecuaros* to practice a spontaneous form of "class struggle" against the hacienda. It is impossible to quantify the proportion of the workforce involved precisely at this remove, but it was substantial, and not confined to the minority which subsequently supported land reform. Resistance centered on the attempt to cultivate the *ecuaro* instead of performing their *tarea* in the cane. Despite the severity of the penalties, people persisted in this practice, for two reasons.

In the first place, the permanent workers of this hacienda did not enjoy any "slack season." Much of the land was permanently cultivated, even the fields of the sharecroppers were harvested with *peones*, and the rains also brought tasks of maintenance and repairing flood defenses. Guaracha was in danger of taking from the peon even that labor time essential to family subsistence, necessary labor which was not in practice covered by the *raya*. But the struggle went further. The peons could increase their real income by producing a marketable surplus in the *ecuaro*, which they might try to sell to small merchants from outside the hacienda who used Guarachita as a bridgehead for their penetration of the hacienda. Families with favorable consumer-worker ratios and cooperating kin strove to do this. Whatever the economic advantages, even necessity, of the *latifundio's* retention of the *ecuaro* system, its perpetuation of this peasant form of production gave the peons a practical means of contesting the division of the working day between necessary and surplus labor time. Some of the workers did steer clear of any act of disobedience, though it is difficult to know whether this was from lack of inclination or lack of necessity. It is, however, clear that the struggle over the *ecuaro* was wider than participation in *agrarismo*. The existence of this form of struggle seems to make the hostility to Cárdenas's offer of the land more of a puzzle, particularly since he took care to make no mention of collective ejidos on the occasion of his famous visit to the estate.

Perhaps the Guaracha peons were subject to the same ideological constraints as Luis González has reported for the case of San José de Gracia, and felt it shameful to receive a "gift" from the government of stolen land which they had not paid for (González 1968). There appears to have been some concern over this question, but also a means of resolving the issue: a number of older people with whom I discussed the philosophy of land reform referred spontaneously to the Spanish origin of the *hacendado* in contexts relating to the legitimacy of his property rights. There is much more to be said on the issue of why the peons refused Cárdenas, but we may begin from a false premise if we assume that the struggle to work the *ecuaro* represented a rejection of the principle of peonage, and that the peons really wanted to become independent peasant farmers. An alternative interpretation would be to view this form of struggle as the equivalent of a battle over wages, or more generally, an attempt to improve the balance between necessary and surplus labor. In seeking more time to sow their *ecuaros,* the *peones* may have been doing no more (and no less) than contesting the terms of an exploitation which was, or had become, extreme by relevant comparative and historical standards. The radical option of agrarian revolution may have been seen as something with quite different implications. Simon Miller suggests that "militancy" on the part of hacienda peons generally took the form of "economistic" strikes (Miller 1985: 83). Such economism was also characteristic of the Mexican industrial proletariat during the revolution, although, as Knight points out, it could hardly be seen as a "soft option" (Knight 1986a:137). The problem with this "all or nothing" distinction between radical and system-conserving options is that the actors seem to be able to change their orientations according to context. The collective labor system of the original ejido was rejected in favor of individual peasant cultivation. As we will see, the economic anxieties typically expressed by hacienda peons and sharecroppers who rejected land reform were concerned with the prospects of the peons' surviving economically as individual farmers without support, anxieties which were not without foundation, as events were to prove, and were, perhaps, already proving where ejidos were established in the 1920s. Had the collective ejido been run in a different way, the ex-peons might well have accepted it. Equally, they might have embraced the initial offer of the land with greater enthusiasm under different historical circumstances.

In order to understand the concrete forms of labor exploitation characteristic of Guaracha in the 1920s, it seems necessary to look at the enterprise as a whole, and in comparative terms. The profitability of the mill seems beyond question. But the separate technical assessments of the Ejidal Credit Bank (*Banco Nacional de Crédito Ejidal* 1937) and the Tarecuato Irrigation Project Commission (*Comisión Nacional de Irrigación* 1936) throw some doubt on cane cultivation. Ecological conditions were suboptimal. The Tarecuato Commission also recorded that regenerated cane which could no longer be processed economically was used as seed for new plantings in the early Thirties. This may have reflected the growing threat of agrarian reform, but cane cultivation could not have been as good business here as in the Tierra Caliente. Even if the returns from processing still justified the investment, the other branches of hacienda production must have been important for maintaining overall rates of profitability at an acceptable level. Furthermore, the margin raked off by the hacienda administration—which one assumes to be a normal feature of absentee landlord enterprise—might have had a direct impact on the comparative rate of exploitation if achievement of a normal profit rate was more difficult here than elsewhere.

In terms of Jeffery Paige's distinction between "pure" capital-based enterprises and the "commercial hacienda" (Paige 1975), Guaracha is still somewhat distant from the kind of enterprise represented by Grace or Gildenmeister in Peru. Such capitalist agro-industrial concerns could tolerate the formation of labor unions, or even the nationalization of their cane fields, with relative equanimity. In Mexico, a case such as Atencingo, where the mill remained in private hands after land reform under Cárdenas, offers a parallel with the Peruvian situation (Ronfeldt 1973). Guaracha's steam-driven mill, which required the expenditure of considerable man-power resources in maintaining the supply of wood, was in fact obsolescent technology by the 1940s. Certainly, the hacienda's cultivation of the plain was highly rational in terms of land use and management. Yields of wheat, maize and chickpea were most impressive. Yet this rationality has to be balanced against the fact that the labor force in the cane was disciplined in a most brutal manner, treated as quasi-servile, and often had to be driven to work by force. Certainly, the labor system was "modern," in its use of written contracts, the ubiquity of bookkeeping—albeit also a technique of exploitation—and in the systematization of the disciplinary machineries which schooled the worker in docility in field, mill and village. Both fieldhands and sharecroppers were sources of capitalist surplus-value, but the basic economic strategy of Guaracha's version of agrarian capitalism was the maximization of absolute surplus value by means of the mechanisms I have described. If this was in fact necessary for the enterprise to maintain rates of accumulation and secure an adequate rate of return (either in absolute terms or relative to alternative investments open to the *hacendado*), rather than simply an opportunistic response to the weak class position of the workers, then we are indeed at some distance from a "factory-in-the-field."

The peons and sharecroppers of Guaracha were not entirely passive in the face of capitalist exploitation and had good reasons for grievance. I doubt if many of its employees would have accepted the description of their lives given in the 1920s by Abraham Mejía in his beautifully illustrated guide to the tourist interested in the agricultural progress of Michoacán:

> In Guaracha there live several thousand happy men, who are given
> the greatest possible advantages as sharecroppers. (Mejía 1928: 63)

For its own part, the hacienda may not have been in a position to make significant concessions. Yet it was not the *peones* who destroyed Guaracha, if we should talk of destruction rather than receivership.

REVOLUTION, THE HACIENDA AND THE SOCIAL MOVEMENTS

There are a number of possible explanations for the peons' rejection of *Cardenismo*. The hacienda's repressive apparatus was certainly forbidding. Few peons had the means to acquire firearms, and those who tried to show they were not afraid risked assassination. The *acordada* was reinforced in the 1930s by a group of ex-*Cristero pistoleros* who killed several *agrarista* sympathizers. The Church also played its part. The priest not only threatened excommunication to those who petitioned for land, but also used the confessional as a source of intelligence for the *acordada*. The hacienda *cura* had always exercized vigilance in defending the prerogatives of private property.

As one of the villagers put it: "The life of a chicken was worth more than the life of a Christian in those days." But "crime" came to be seen as having even more menacing implications in the epoch of *agrarismo*. In one case, men who had been caught rustling cattle by the Guard were to be executed rather than sent to the chain-gang, because they refused to name their leader, who had not been apprehended. The good father secured the name, and the execution proceeded. When a relative tried to plead for mercy on behalf of one of the accused, he too was shot, for revealing himself a "politician."

One might therefore simply accept the interpretation of events offered by three of Moreno's informants, and repeated by many of those whom I interviewed on the subject:

> *La gente* didn't refuse the land. It was just that they were afraid
> because of the threats there were on the part of the *hacendados*;
> that they were going to be excommunicated.... (Moreno
> 1980:173)

Cárdenas armed the *agraristas*, but his guarantees remained of limited value, in Guaracha as elsewhere. Direct repression is therefore a factor to be considered seriously. Although neither "innate religiosity" nor the "ideological hegemony of the clergy" might be deemed adequate explanations of the peons' terror of excommunication, it is also worth recalling Friedrich's observations on the way impoverished Naranjeño Catholics refused to align with the agrarian cause. Other things being equal, peasants rebel when they perceive the power of the upper strata to have weakened, which is why agrarian revolutions are relatively rare events, and inter-class antagonisms more normally find other forms of expression, including cultural oppositional practices (Scott 1976). But there is evidence to suggest that physical repression alone is insufficient to explain the behavior of the peons of Guaracha. The widow of Pablo Canela, the principal agrarian leader, recalled to me how even her kin abandoned them utterly, refusing even a tortilla, when he declared himself for the cause. And even at the end, when the *hacendado* himself told his faithful servants to sign up for land, since the situation was beyond remedy, it proved difficult to *find* the 316 ejidatarios Don Lázaro decreed should exist in Guaracha.

Moreno's informants did in fact hint at additional reasons for the peons' rejection of Cárdenas's offer of the land:

> ...how were they going to work these lands, and afterwards there
> wouldn't be another person [like Don Lázaro] to look after them;
> that the government was only making promises.... (1980:173)

The implication of this second set of explanations seems rather different from the first, which imply no more than a fear of the immediate consequences of embracing the desirable: they might suggest a degree of confidence in the charismatic person of Lázaro Cárdenas, but there appears to be a general lack of confidence in both the economic future offered by land reform and the government. *Desconfianza* regarding the state was clearly not restricted to hacienda peons. But economic anxieties surrounding the proposed break-up of the haciendas on the part of peons have been widely reported throughout the Center-North, devastated by the impact of the revolution and Cristiada (Cross and Sandos 1981: 11-12). Some sharecroppers and non-*acasillado* hacienda workers might well have harbored similar fears about the prospects offered by the ejido: there was certainly significant opposition to *agrarismo* in communities like Las Zarquillas. One way of interpreting this factor in the opposition to land reform would be to see it as a reflection of a form of economic dependence particularly characteristic of hacienda peons.

A popular general explanation for the non-revolutionary behavior of resident peons bases itself on the greater security they supposedly enjoyed relative to other segments of the rural underclasses. Such considerations figured prominently in Hamnett's explanation of the role of *peones acasillados* during the Insurgency, quoted above: Hamnett defines the resident peons as a "relatively privileged" group in this period (Hamnett 1986:7). There were areas of Mexico on the eve of the revolution where the privilege of peons corresponded to a relative position of advantage in terms of income levels and positions of work (Knight, 1986a:86). But neither relative nor absolute material living or working standards seem a reliable guide to revolutionary potential: the *kulaks* who embraced agrarian struggle in Guarachita were certainly better off than most peons. As Knight points out, peon life might still retain the advantage of security at relatively low standards of living, and even with a strong dose of brutalization. There was always the chance to take refuge in the bottle, a solution to life's miseries which sugar estates like Guaracha tended to encourage, since sales of alcohol enabled the enterprise to recoup cash paid out in wages. The security factor is reinforced in the arguments of Hamnett and many others by an appeal to paternalism and patronage structures of hacienda social relations as a force limiting internal conflict, though not excluding it under unusual conditions.

Knight, however, argues that "personal, paternalistic bonds were loosening" by the later nineteenth century (Knight 1986a:85). His study places great emphasis on the way in which the revolutionary process produced a still more radical "decline of deference" among the underclasses (see, for example, Knight 1986b:519-520). For Knight, internal disciplinary practices and close supervision play a more important role than traditional paternalism in the internal social relations of the Porfirian hacienda. The plantations of the South represented the apogee of this tendency within the latifundist system, made possible by a specific kind of regional social environment: the South, Knight argues, was a land of "total social institutions" where, despite exploitative excesses and the sheer immiseration of workers reduced to a servile condition:

> ...the plantocracy had grown a carapace of social control and repression which, in defiance of concerted challenges from within, could only be dismantled by alien interlopers ... the peons, shipped into a strange malarial environment, lacked common origins, common traditions, even a common tongue, and the weakness and remoteness of free villages in the south made escape and resistance almost impossible. (Knight 1986a:88–9)

Though Guaracha also had something of the character of a total social institution, it was not, as I have stressed, a completely closed social world, and there is evidently something of a difference between the situation in Michoacán, where free villages had survived to fight another day even in the Ciénega, and the situation as Knight defines it in the South. One should therefore ask whether the "decline of deference" should not have insidiously undermined the structures of domination within Guaracha in the same way as it undermined the domination of the Noriegas over the encapsulated agrarian community of Naranja, and, indeed, that of Guaracha over its environs. Given that *agrarismo* did eventually emerge within Guaracha itself, albeit as a minoritarian movement, one might, of course, conclude that it did, although the appearance of *agrarismo* in Guaracha was fostered, of course, by the militancy of popular agrarian struggles elsewhere in the state, external political forces, and the rise of the CRMDT. But the isolation of the Guaracha *agraristas* from and *by* the community they sought to emancipate still requires explanation.

I will deal first with the evidence on the role of paternalism and patronage versus coercive disciplinary control in Guaracha. It is, of course, extremely difficult to work from the data provided by ethnography and oral historical recollections towards an assessment of the "mentalities" of people in the past. But I have already cited evidence which indicates that the practice of a certain style of disobedience towards hacienda authority was quite widespread. One might, indeed, argue that the elaboration and refinement of the disciplinary and coercive apparatuses of the hacienda in the later nineteenth century was a response to the fact that paternalism was incapable of stabilizing the relations between capital and labor characteristic of the Porfirian hacienda. Docility only needs to be inculcated in those who do not readily display it. Under the Porfirian peace, the Guaracha *acordada* had certainly become more of an instrument of internal control than a force to defend the hacienda against external threats, albeit partly because Guaracha had brought more or less everything "inside" its boundaries in the later nineteenth century. As far as patronage structures were concerned, it seems, first that prospects for mobility within Guaracha were not great. The division of the community into barrios today still reflects previous division in terms of ranks and offices within the hacienda workforce. The stratum of privileged *medieros* was largely hereditary, and in 1922, the *hacendado* removed most of these families to a new settlement at the foot of nearby Cerrito Cotijarán, to combat further petitions for land restitution from Guarachita. Labor relations remained personal and face-to-face, despite the use of force, and a degree of personal clientalism did exist. Occasional acts of patronage by the mighty did little to mitigate the negative aspects of peonage. But patronage did divide the *acomodados* from ordinary workers, preempting general solidarity to some extent, although the *agrarista* leaders did not come from the lowest ranks of the peons, and might themselves have enjoyed participation in the patronage system. On balance, it appears that the paternalistic element in hacienda social relations was undermined by the economic regime, disciplinary practices and style of the administration, coupled with Manuel Moreno's personal distaste for face-to-face contact with peons in the traditional fiesta rituals. Many ex-*peones* I interviewed maintained that fiestas were "only for the *acomodados*."

As for deference, there is an important distinction to be made between overt behavior and underlying attitudes. Much of the "decline of deference" after the revolution may have reflected a greater confidence in the overt expression of antagonism, accompanied by a greater confidence in the possibility of changing the world. One would certainly expect to see deferential behavior on the part of people who were beaten even for having the wrong sort of look in their eyes. But I was particularly struck by the lack of deference towards authority displayed in the spontaneous anecdotes related by the hacienda *acomodados* I interviewed. *Mayordomos* might earn respect— though rarely affection—as individuals. But they were not owed respect, and many, it seems, were secretly despised, even by their kin and persons who entered into patronage relations with them and could see merits in the hacienda's large-scale system of cultivation. *Mayordomos* who drove their men especially hard were seen as fools for imagining that trying to curry favor with the *patrón* in this manner would bring any real reward. The administrators knew less about agriculture than the *acomodados*, who were really the backbone of the estate. They understood that the world was unequal, unjust and ordered to the benefit of the *ricos,* but they could take pride in their honest and productive labors, which did not rest on the maltreatment of their fellow men. What was good about the hacienda was its organization and its system, which was as much their work as that of their masters.

The *peones acasillados* in general may, therefore, have harbored certain oppositional attitudes. But, as Knight suggests, what determines revolutionary commitment is not absolute class position, nor the objective form of class relation between the dominating and the dominated, but the dynamics of change in those relationships in a particular historical context (Knight 1986a:152–3). Escalating agrarian commercialization provided the general context for agrarian revolution in early twentieth century Mexico: it brought with it, if not for the first time in Mexican history, the movement of communities and persons across the thresholds of free peasant to tenant and tenant to wage-laborer which form the basis for Scott's analysis of the relationship between peasant rebellion and the colonial capitalist destruction of the "moral economy" of the Southeast Asian village (Scott 1976:55, Knight 1986a:166). The "moral economy" argument links the process of agrarian revolt to loss of subsistence guarantees, and it should be clear from the data already presented on the heterogeneity of the agrarian movements in Michoacán that this hypothesis is incapable of explaining all the instances of agrarian revolt which combine to constitute an agrarian revolutionary process. Leaving aside the problem of popular rural rebellions which are not class-based, nor primarily agrarian in content, the social forces which embark upon struggles for land are themselves heterogeneous. Revolts led by the upper strata of rural communities may enjoy the support of more humble families pushed to the subsistence margin, but the character and limits of the movement will reflect the contrasting motivations and grievances of leaders and followers and the differentiated impact of capitalist transformation on the community as a whole.

Such a conclusion reinforces, rather than diminishes, the need to look beyond mere "economic welfare" indicators to the subjective perceptions of the meaning of change in material conditions of life which mediate the relationship between structural economic transformations and social and political behavior. Guarachita's village elite resented the humiliation which their community suffered at the hands of the hacienda, which limited their possibilites for social advancement; the break-up of the hacienda also coincided with their immediate and long-term economic interests. The dehumanizing treatment which a hacienda like Guaracha meted out to its *peones acasillados* must be balanced against the argument for the security the hacienda regime provided. But we cannot assume that the latter automatically and invariably compensated for the former: peon restlessness was a source of mounting anxiety to the Mexican ruling class in the revolutionary period, and even in Guaracha some ordinary peons joined the *agraristas*, though they were invariably, and probably significantly, young, unmarried men. The moral offensiveness of their humiliation may often have struck former comuneros in a more intense and potentially explosive way because of the suddenness of its impact, but even families which had been resident hacienda workers for generations experienced changes in their conditions of life under the Porfirian form of commercial hacienda, with its written contracts, disciplinary violence and surveillance. We cannot evaluate the hypothesis that security took precedence over these experiences, and the changing social climate created by the revolution, without looking at the particular historical context in which subjective attitudes formed in greater detail. The *peons'* evaluation of the choice between hacienda and ejido was influenced by the way their social experience structured their view of the external world.

Since dispossession and poverty were a longstanding feature of life in the region, it seems immediately plausible to argue that considerations of subsistence security could have been an important determinant of peon unwillingness to reject the hacienda system here, particularly since the hacienda had survived the travails of the Insurgency to continue its own work of dispossession so triumphantly. The conditions of peon social life within the hacienda would reinforce anxieties on which the *latifundio* had already capitalized in making expulsion its ultimate sanction against workers who displeased it. *Agrarismo* faced an uphill struggle in overcoming such fears since known *agrarista* sympathizers were denied work. The evidence suggests that the peons did not view the hacienda in a positive way in the 1920s. But it seems possible to argue that in this region, the nature of the revolutionary process itself reinforced, rather than counteracted, the dominance of anxieties over aspirations for change.

As the events of the Revolution and the Cristiada had unfolded, experience had tended to confirm a belief that the world outside the hacienda was a wilderness of unemployment, chaos and desolation—or banditry and dishonor. However harsh the exploitation of the hacienda, it offered a minimum level of economic security and physical protection. The practice of agrarian reform as visible in other communities, including Guarachita, can scarcely have enhanced the credibility of the alternative future being promised by Cárdenas, since, as we will see, Guarachita replicated the history of violent "*agarista*" boss-rule so characteristic of Michoacán. Thus the hacienda's claim to be father to its children received a degree of legitimation, and its own coercive violence may have served to reinforce the peons' fear of an even greater and random violence without. Guaracha was at least a society in order, the only such society most of them had ever known.

Up to 1929, there had been an alternative: the United States, which in this period offered Mexicans employment in railroad construction and industry. Few of the early migrants were members of the poorest rural strata. Ciénega townsmen led the exodus, followed by children of kulak families from the villages which retained juridical independence from the hacienda. Many of the pioneers were literate. But as the migratory stream turned into a flood, a few Guaracha *peones* joined it, almost invariably unmarried boys of around fifteen years of age. By the 1930s the reflux was well under way. As I have already noted, returned migrants throughout Michoacán showed a distinct propensity to favor agrarian struggle, and this was clearly an important factor in its escalation. The same conclusion can be drawn from Craig's work in Lagos de Moreno (Craig 1983:91-94), although the agrarian movement there developed out of the organization, during the 1920s, of skilled artisans and laborers who had worked in the town's textile mill, and began with relatively advanced political ideas. Mexicans in "the North" interacted more freely with other social groups (especially European immigrants) in this epoch, and were directly exposed to the ideological currents of the international labor movement. Some of the *norteños* interviewed by Craig were profoundly influenced by contact with Protestantism (1983:180-181, 204), though what struck the responsive chord was less the positive message of Protestant doctrine than its critique of Catholicism: in Los Altos, as in Guaracha, the ultimate effect of *agrarista* activism seems to have been at the least a decline in formal religious observance. Though migrant peons and sharecroppers might be regarded as proletarians in Mexico in formal terms, the quality of the class position of free wage labor in the U.S. was quite different: the physically harsh and dangerous work in the foundries to which most of them aspired offered a different type of class socialization to peonage, as well as higher monetary rewards. If ex-migrants were more disposed to envisage the possibility of changing their conditions of life through organized working-class action, the experience of industrial capitalism in crisis increased the appeal of land reform as an alternative program for emancipation. Those who had stayed behind may simply have been reinforced in a conviction that the external world offered even less than the hacienda.

The revolutionary wars may also have played a crucial role in overdetermining the non-revolutionary stance of the peons. In Guarachita, the population suffered the double oppression of hacienda and government. Federal armies bore off food, animals and above all conscripts, most of whom failed to return. When the look-outs sighted the troopers, people fled in panic to the hills. But Guarachita, whose agrarian struggle long predated the revolution, retained an autonomous social order and consciousness of its own, like the Zapatistas and Villa's colonists. Its rebelliousness was founded on its latent capacity for self-organization, activated by the extremity of its conflict with the engulfing and intransigent hacienda. Organization was much more problematic in hacienda communities, and not only because of their repressive systems of social control: the majority of Guaracheño families had lived under the shadow of the casco for generations. To this day the ex-peons have difficulty defining their identity without reference to the hacienda.

It was, therefore, not simply the material dimensions of the security offered by peonage that mattered: the humiliated *peones* had a problem of social identity which may also have been a critical determinant of their religiosity. The hacienda was more than the *patrón*, his administrators, foremen and thugs. Much of the positive value which the peons attached to the hacienda may, in reality, have been constituted through the negative evaluation of peon status characteristic of the world outside the estate. Older men sometimes confided to me that they had been too embarrassed to walk the streets of Jiquilpan wearing the manta and sombrero of the hacienda. Their apparel marked them as men who were totally subjected to the alien power of a master. How could they endure the contempt of even of the poorest of urban artisans and peasants who retained some degree of economic and social autonomy, in particular peasants from the hill communities beyond the plain? Such "marking" served the ends of domination from the hacienda's point of view, but the meanings it encapsulated were just as much the work of the subordinated as of those who dominated them. To this day, the contrast between the hills as a domain of freedom and the plain as a site of domination remains a powerful and pervasive frame of explanation for Guaracheños when they reflect on their social and political situation. Pre-industrial discourses on the meaning of proletarianization clearly entered into the peons' feelings of humiliation and the practices of resistance. But insofar as a compensating identification with the hacienda could not efface an unconscious acceptance of the stigma attached to peonage in the eyes of others, emancipation became problematic: past subjugation of such long duration could not be too readily effaced from collective memory, and others might continue to contest an ex-peon's claims to social worth in terms of the values of the world beyond the *latifundio*. Although those who sought to escape the miseries or limitations of life in Guaracha through international migration were in a sense rootless, their interiorization of alternative class ideologies and political programs provided them with resources for ascribing meaning to history and change which were denied to the stay-at-homes, except through an act of faith.

Guarachita, despite its despoliation by the hacienda, remained socially differentiated. Apart from shopkeepers and a few professionals, it contained kulak families who rented land in the hills from the hacienda and employed wage-labor. The rest of the population sought work as *jornaleros* on the estate. An informant one of the better-off families described how his father had concealed his maize surpluses from the soldiers, before proceeding to recall how an abandoned woman and her daughter, who had come from another community to live from the skins of discarded melons they picked from the streets of Guarachita, had slowly died from starvation amid the poverty provoked by the revolution. Evidently a certain amount of "amoral familism" may have characterized Guarachita, although even the kulaks were scarcely affluent, and it was they who provided the staunchest support for the agrarian struggle. The same informant, who went for seven years to the U.S., returning to serve twice as ejidal commissar and as municipal president, explained that his father had to ship his maize to markets in Ocotlán and La Barca as contraband, loading the mules at night to elude the *acordada*. The hacienda's drive to monopolize everything therefore ensured it at least one type of rural opposition which had the organizational base to conduct a struggle. Given its relationship to the hacienda, there was a basis for the collective solidarity of the whole differentiated community against the hacienda. The commitment of the population to land reform was continuous, despite the fact that internal factional conflict proved a necessary means of distributing the resources won from the *latifundio* more equitably among the population, and the final results of this process were to prove less than perfect.

As the history of Guarachita shows, it required intervention from a higher political level for such struggles to bear fruit. The people of the village had little reason to feel enthusiasm for the government. It continued to oppress them even as it promised some support against Guaracha. Yet their lack of options was revealed during the Cristiada, when Guarachita, now renamed Villamar, remained loyal, and became a resettlement center for potential *Cristero* sympathizers expelled from the ranchitos in the hills.

While Guarachita, like the entire periphery of the hacienda, was suffering, the *peones acasillados* did enjoy a substantial degree of physical protection, though I did find a few people in the village who had left for other regions to escape the violence of the period of the Cristiada, and there may have been many more who never returned. Many people left the surrounding villages for the U.S. after 1926. The only serious damage to the people and the capital of the hacienda occurred in December 1917, when Inés Chávez García, "El Indio," sacked the annex of San Antonio. He could not penetrate the main hacienda, whose *acordada* was reinforced by sixty Carrancista troopers and enjoyed the further advantage of fortifications. But he did burn the mill, forcing a partial reconstruction. Chávez's force was not the only one to raid the Ciénega. Guaracha was actually occupied twice by groups operating under the banner of Villa, first in 1914 and again in 1916. These earlier invaders had done nothing to harm the hacienda, whose authorities summoned musicians from Guarachita to entertain them for days on end, an informant recalled. On the contrary, they paid for the hospitality offered by assaulting engineers attempting to implement land restitution to the *cabecera municipal* (Moreno 1980:121). The economic power of Guaracha was the key to many forms of alliance and compromise.

Chávez was different. He once fought as a Villista, but his basic program was rape, murder and pillage, of peasants as well as *ricos*. Yet the following he could muster was impressive: normally around 500 fighters. He sometimes achieved ten times that number (Olivera de Bonfil 1981:106). The forces in question were marginalized and landless village peasants from beyond the haciendas, who joined Chávez briefly and then returned to their homes, a pattern reminiscent of Zapatismo. Rationalizing the Chavistas is not easy, but perhaps that is exactly the point. Knight proposes that the distinction between "social banditry" and other forms of the phenomenon be made "relationally", in terms of the presence or absence of popular support, noting that former social bandits could become professionalized as a result of the autonomous "logic of the revolution" (Knight 1986a: 353-355). The problem posed by the Chavistas and their ilk is that they provoked both popular support and popular detestation in more or less equal measure. Violence itself may have a logic. Even assuming that political or social programs seemed meaningful to Chávez's men, given the concrete reality they faced, anti-social banditry might have achieved the same cultural value as the role of the murderous *hombre valiente* within the Michoacán villages: fear and loathing do not exclude respect. For many, Porfirian society had created a zero-sum game. It was easier for the losers to respect its moral order and turn on those who were weak.

After the armed revolution, the Cristiada landowners generally opposed the *Cristeros,* and Manuel Moreno had his personal connection with the *Jefe Máximo.* But the Cristiada was doubly advantageous to the hacienda. It maintained the violence and impoverishment of the external world and the *peones* identified with the Faith against *agrarismo.*

Not all of the heterogeneous rural rank-and-file who aligned themselves with the *Cristero* cause harbored a deeply rooted ideological opposition to the principle of agrarian reform—at least at the outset. In the days of Hidalgo and Morelos, Christian imagery had displayed its potential to encapsulate demands for social justice, although it is worth recalling that some of the greatest intellectual champions of social reform in the late colonial epoch, in particular Bishop Abad y Queipo, fell by the wayside when confronted with the actuality of the Insurgency. Jean Meyer has drawn our attention to the fact that "Social Catholicism" might express itself as a real critique of latifundism in the decade before the Revolution (Meyer 1976:9), and this current in the Church was to find a radical practical expression in the identification of parish priests with social confrontations between community, *cacique* and capital in some zones of Michoacán (Nava 1987:36). Due attention should also be paid to the role and position of leaders such as Ramón Aguilar. For their part, some *agraristas* remained deeply religious, retaining their personal faith despite hostility to the Church as an institution. Any potential *Cristero* identification with social programs was overridden by their association with secularization. Secularization was seen as the key to recentralization and modernization of the state by Mexico's rulers. But it was comprehended as a series of acts of sacrilege by people for whom the concepts of "state" and "nation" (and correspondingly universal conceptions of class identity) lacked their modern transcendent meanings: indeed, even words to express the idea of "the nation" were absent from the vocabularies of many rural Mexicans during the 1920s and 1930s (De la Peña 1986:34). To the extent that such transcendant meanings have been inculcated in subsequent decades, they are the products of the implantation of a secular educational system effected not by arbitrary fiat but through mass incorporation and the consolidation of a national state whose functions extended more deeply and comprehensively into the everyday lives of ordinary people.

The period of political turmoil and foreign intervention between the Insurgency and the Porfiriato did promote the development of a national consciousness at the higher levels of Mexican society, notwithstanding the exacerbated regionalism of caudillo politics brought about by the atrophy of central power.[3] But the mode of intervention of the government in the daily life of the provincial rural masses was that of an alien and, where it was distinguishable from local class repression, equally abusive form of arbitrary power. The social power of the Church had been consolidated in the space created by the comprehensive triumph of class power over state power after Independence. The Church emerged from the crisis of the Reforma with its temporal wealth relatively intact, escaping the encapsulation by the state which was Catholicism's fate in post-revolutionary France. This was undoubtedly a crucial determinant of the long drawn-out and violent nature of the Mexican revolutionary cycle and the vicissitudes of the national state formation process. Under the Porfirian settlement, the link between the Church and the landed oligarchy became, if anything, even more organic: members of landed families continued to enter Holy Orders, and the Church continued to dominate in the provision of financial and administrative services to the hacienda. Rejuvenating its organization and embarking on an aggressive campaign of evangelization to reconquer its mass base from the advancing wave of secular ideologies, the Church succeeded in serving agrarian capitalism while conserving much of its social power among the lower classes. It accomplished this notable feat in the name of a doctrinal orthodoxy counterposed to the heterodoxy of traditional "Folk Catholicism"—now deemed contaminated by magic and paganism—married to advocacy of a "third way" between capitalist possessive individualism and socialist collectivism (Tapia 1986). This calculated "anti-modernism" was perhaps the root element of Social Catholicism, although that movement was to replicate the long-established historical tendency of Christianity to develop simultaneously in socially critical and system-conserving directions.

The relative strength of particular positions and orientations within the Church as an institution was not the sole determinant of the course of events, since the symbolic meaning effects of the messages transmitted by clerical discourses were constituted through the reactions of their congregations in the particular historical circumstances in which they found themselves. In the past, the radical, classless ideology embedded in Christianity's janus-faced social cosmology had played a significant role in popular struggles against exploitation, but by the close of the Porfirian era even a Christian doctrine which defended the hierarchic order of the temporal world provided a sense of social identity and a message of salvation which was of more potent value to many segments of the fragmented provincial underclasses than appeals to class action and national sentiment (Gledhill 1987).

Agraristas may have had equal difficulty understanding the abstractions used to legitimize certain of the acts in which they were called upon to participate, but since they were forced to enlist the support of the renascent central state apparatus as their lever against class power, they were necessarily anti-*Cristero* in practice. As the *agrarista* army of Saturnino Cedillo swept the countryside in pursuit of *Cristeros, Cristeros* began to target local *agrarista* leaders in the villages wherever they could find them, and positions polarized in mutual bloodletting of unspeakable ferocity. In the end, revolutionary state-building from above found a sufficient popular social base to counteract a high degree of resistance from below, though a different attitude on the part of the government of the United States might have been sufficient to tip the balance in the other direction. The Guaracha *agraristas* were themselves put into the field, but too late to participate, except in the campaign against the Segunda: the son of one of the original leaders of the Guaracha movement was to witness the bloody extirpation of Ramón Aguilar, caught relaxing to guitar music in the house of some supporters and offered no opportunity to surrender. Few from Guaracha participated in the *Cristero* forces, though it appears that *peones acasillados* were recruited in significant numbers from the estates of the Tierra Caliente, and that in general the composition of the *Cristero* army cross-cut the different rural underclasses (Meyer 1976:90).

The *Cristero* movement was genuinely "popular," and all its elements might, individually, have been reacting against social pressures whose ultimate cause was capitalist expansion. But it was the mode in which the victors of the revolution sought to tackle the problem of consolidating state power which unified the disparate elements of disaffection around a common counterrevolutionary cause. It is unlikely that the rural clergymen of this region were beloved by the gente humilde, and Guaracheños had particular reason to loathe the hacienda's priest. It was the sacerdotal role and the sacrament itself which had meaning, in a world of repression, humiliation, insecurity and violence. The hacienda's own terrorism may have aided its struggle against *Cardenismo* because of this unintended ideological effect, which made the anti-Christ seem the worst of all evils: to lose even the immortal soul.... The *Cristeros* did not follow their priests, most of whom fled the villages, but their experience: they did not place credence in the possibility of a weak and alien secular state, whose roots lay in other social classes, ameliorating their condition. "Rationalist" or "Socialist" education had the same arbitrary thrust as the Porfirian recruiting sergeant and *jefe político* of recent memory. (And such perceptions of the project of the reforming state were scarcely dispelled by the subsequent experience of the Cárdenas presidency in Michoacán.) Worse, it seemed to strike at the one remaining guarantee of salvation in a shattered and increasingly inhuman world.

We should be careful not to over-rationalize or idealize the *Cristero* movement: attitudes were shaped by conditions of life overdetermined by the terrible insecurities which afflicted ordinary folk facing the successive shocks of massive social and political upheavals. All popular movements are capable of great brutality, and *Cristero* violence could be as much about settling local scores as *agrarista* violence. But the fact that subsequent experience acted to confirm the most pessimistic of expectations remains significant. In Guaracha the anxieties generated by the peons' cumulative experience, transposed into a model of hacienda versus external world, had crystallized into a stance: "No queremos tierra, queremos culto." The lived-in reality of emancipation hardly healed the divisions in the community, particularly after the closure of the mill created an employment crisis. Subsequently, as I noted in the previous chapter, more manipulative and reactionary heirs to the *Cristero* tradition were able to reap the harvest of resentment. Parish priests denounced individuals as "communists"—and they died.

AGRARISMO IN THE BOLSA DE GUARACHA

As for *agrarismo* itself, the case of Guarachita represented a pattern familiar from other communities. The movement was originally led by members of the *kulak* stratum. But after the outbreak of fighting in the region, travel to Mexico City became more difficult, the peasants became disheartened and leadership passed to Filiberto Ruíz, who was a shopkeeper with some education. Don Filiberto divided up the land he obtained for the community among those my informants described as "los primeros hombres *ricos* del pueblo." In 1931, Guarachita secured an amplification, only by the skin of its teeth against an *amparo* backed by the *acordada*. In 1935 Cárdenas assigned it still more land. The *agrarista* leadership each secured three or four *parcelas*, leaving the rest of the beneficiaries with tiny and uneconomic plots, against whose vestigial harvests no usurer would lend. Guarachita was ruled by the gun. Justly did Ramón Aguilar protest that *agrarismo* had become "agarrismo."

Popular power could achieve something. In 1938, ejidal elections saw a resounding defeat for the *caciques*. The community elected a returned migrant who promised a legal parcellization by lot. Dámaso Cárdenas and the Jiquilpan politicians intervened to try to overturn the election result, which seemed to threaten their political control by removing trusted clients. The result stood, thanks to popular pressure and the probity of the federal official in charge of the elections. But subsequently the *caciques* put their pistols to the temple of the engineer sent to make the parcellization. He left his bags in Jiquilpan and fled to Morelia under cover of darkness. Such were the limits of this "revolution from above."

In Guaracha, the *agraristas* did not become *caciques*. The nature of the leadership is quite predictable: they were men who had derived social and political experience outside Guaracha, though a few young *peones* disregarded the advice of their fathers and committed themselves to the struggle early on. Their number might have been greater had not others already left for the U.S. Pablo Canela's association with Cárdenas predated 1929: he was a man of conviction, who refused several attempts by the hacienda to buy him off. According to his son, the pretext for his revolt against the *patrón* had been a disgusto between himself and the administration while he had been working as a watchman, supposedly protecting the 's absolute proprietary rights. Marcelino Zarate, assassinated in 1931, and Federico Andrade were returned U.S. migrants. Federico had been particularly successful: he put a capital of several thousand pesos to work in usury and grain speculation. Maestro Abel Prado, a shoemaker with urban politicians as his matrikin, was an even more ambiguous figure: throughout the struggle he was busy improving ten hectare of hacienda land, enjoying the benefit of free loans of oxen. It eventually became his ejidal *parcela*. Abel was popular, demagogic, and no one displayed *envidia* towards him. But equally everyone agreed that he "shifted with the wind." Of the four original leaders, only Abel survived to see the ejido, in which he never held office.

Federico was killed by a comrade in a dispute about a loan, with under-tones of reaction to tendencies towards incipient *caciquismo*. Furthermore, neither Federico nor Abel were originally part of the Cardenista group. In 1932, Federico, then joined by Abel, formed a *sindicato*. They secured a dou-bling of the *raya*. The peons handed back the increase, almost certainly under duress. The *sindicato* tried to get the hacienda's contract declared illegal by Morelia, because of its use of payments in kind. They failed. That even reformism made little headway in Guaracha may, as we have seen, be signifi-cant. But so may be the fact that Federico was frequently labelled a "Serratista" by my informants. It is clear that a number of double games were being played in the period of Serrato's governorship, particularly in Guarachita, whose *agraristas* wanted to block petitions from Guaracha in order to take more land for themselves. The behavior of Don Dámaso—the senior Cardenista politician in Michoacán, still enjoying federal electoral office—also seems to have been profoundly ambiguous. Nevertheless, the Guaracha *agraristas* did eventually unify and organize themselves suffi-ciently to undertake direct action and seize land, albeit land immediately lost to the waters of Chapala. For more than a year there was a period of "dual power," as everyone waited for Don Lázaro. But it appears from my inter-views with the surviving ex-*agraristas* that he omitted to tell those who were dying for the cause that what they were waiting for was a collective ejido.

The fiasco of the collective was not quite the end of the *agrarista* party. They found a new, young and honest leader, again a returned U.S. migrant, to handle the transition to an individual ejido. But autonomous community lead-ers did not suit the plans of Don Dámaso and his friends. They found new community representatives, not ex-*agraristas*, who understood the new dis-pensation somewhat better. In practice, violent *caciquismo* was not needed to manage Emiliano Zapata. But there was a more subtle, and often murderous, settling of accounts. By 1945, a majority of the original *agrarista* group were either dead or gone, land rights were surrendered for a bottle of alcohol, and Guaracha remained—to adapt the famous aphorism ascribed to Porfirio Díaz—far from God but, for most of the increasingly impoverished ejidatar-ios, mercifully near to the United States.

CHAPTER 4

THE FAILURE OF THE COLLECTIVE EJIDO AND THE TWO PROJECTS OF *CARDENISMO* IN THE CIÉNEGA

Since the ejidatarios of Emiliano Zapata and Totolán were destined to receive not simply land but also the industrial part of the landlord's enterprise, the mill, the expropriation of the Guaracha *latifundio* was an event of national importance in Mexico at the time, and remains of some comparative interest even today. In theory everything that was Guaracha became the peasants,' and the Guaracheños were awarded the distinction of being selected to demonstrate the viability of a program of agricultural progress based on new collective forms of ejidal organization. Indeed, the wider significance of the creation of the Collective Ejidal Agricultural Industrial Society "Rafael Picazo" was very much in the minds of the officials of the Ejidal Bank appointed to administrate it. On August 6th, 1937, a general assembly of the Society published a printed booklet illustrated with photographs:

> With the effect of making known the operations of the Society to our comrades, the peasants of the Republic, taking to the agrarian communities our message of optimism and spirit, and at the same time making plain our profound regard for the efficient aid and cooperation received in our work.... (BNCE 1937:5)

The booklet is an extremely interesting text at a number of levels, not least for the literary and rhetorical devices it employs to express the "peasant point of view." The preamble both details the sufferings of the peasants under the hacienda and carries a subtext designed to emphasize the way in which Cárdenas's new measures would transform the position of ejidatarios. Consider, for example, the following two passages from page 8 of the document:

> Our children, with this harsh legacy suspended over their heads since their humble birth, saw their most sacred instincts of freedom suffocated since their infancy, in their eyes *the eternal sadness of the indian....* [*my emphasis*]
> What were we to do? Uncultivated, flooded lands, lack of implements of cultivation, without working animals to aid our feeble strength. The sad ejidal caravan, without food and clad in rags, began their poor and rachitic labors, but investing them with their unbreakable faith and all the love of the land which had also been watered by the sweat of their forebears, while the old overseers and peasants of little faith laughed and joked about our efforts.

But what is perhaps most intriguing is the admission of "problems" which surfaces beneath the rhetoric, problems related both to "adverse elements" within the community and malign private commercial interests without.

Perhaps the author subconsciously felt that it would shortly be time to present the case in a different way. The discussion of the events leading to the debacle of the collective experiment which follows is based on information from interviews with some individuals who were intimately concerned with the events insofar as they held ejidal offices, others who were ordinary ejidatarios or landless workers on the margin of decision making, and a reading between the lines of official statements, all put in the context of the wider pattern of political and economic events in the region. What needs explaining is how and why a policy which received the personal sponsorship of the President of the Republic could be allowed to experience such a failure. While the collective form of ejidal organization experienced difficulty in other contexts, the collapse of Cárdenas's project in Guaracha was unprecedentedly spectacular, rapid and total. Elsewhere it proved possible to deal with worker resistance and internal conflict within the emancipated peasant communities, at least for a time. The suggestion that some other force must have been acting in opposition to the project seems hard to resist.

THE FOUNDATION OF THE COLLECTIVE

The execution of Cárdenas's Presidential Resolution creating the ejido of Emiliano Zapata formally began in March 1936 with the arrival of the engineers to mark out the external boundaries of the ejido and the division between the ejidal terrain and 300 ha. of private property to be retained by the *hacendado* as owner of the sugar industry. As far as the *agraristas* were concerned, the ejido already existed, and had done so at least since the time of the Provisional Resolution and the spontaneous seizure of land in August 1933. The period of "dual power" which had developed in the aftermath of that event, notwithstanding Serrato's maneuvers, continued a while after the formalities of establishing an ejido had been carried out. Don Manuel remained proprietor of the mill. Though Moreno's suggestion that the hacienda administration was still running the mill at the time of the 1936-7 harvest is not confirmed either by the Bank's published account or my informants,[1] for the rest of 1936 his agents actively contested the legal status of cane standing in the fields which represented new or regenerated plantings predating the resolution of expropriation (Moreno 1980:193), and possibly continued paying wages to workers cultivating the remaining private land.

It was now clear to most of the hacienda's employees that the *agraristas* had finally won, but their leaders do not seem to have harbored any clear vision of the way in which the *latifundio* might be reorganized, beyond a presumption, confirmed by those I interviewed, that land would be allocated to individuals, other ejidos previously created in the region having all been individual. In the event, the new ejidal authorities waited to receive their instructions, and in due course a "representative of the government"—no one was totally clear on his name—arrived to organize the new agrarian regime.

THE TWO PROJECTS OF *CARDENISMO* IN THE CIÉNEGA

It was announced that work on the cane would be performed collectively, retaining the traditional organization by *cuadrillas,* though the ejidatarios would now chose *mayordomos* from their own ranks. They would continue to receive their *raya* as before, though now, as some of my informants put it, "we could work a little less hard for a little more money." Credits would also be provided to enable the ejidatarios to meet the other costs of sustaining cane cultivation, repairing equipment and so forth. As capital stock the ejidatarios received 400 mules, 28 heavy and 80 light plows, 20 carts and all necessary harness and tools. In addition to his share in the collective enterprise of the cane plantation, each ejidatario also received an individual one hectare plot located in one of the potreros of temporal land on the Villamar side of the ejido. This land could be sown in whatever crop the ejidatario wished: wheat, chickpea, beans. There was, therefore, from the start, an important concession to the principle of individual peasant farming. After the first land restitution to Villamar, a number of other ejidos had been created in the Ciénega during the 1920s: Pajacuaran and La Palma received land in 1923, San Pedro Caro and Vista Hermosa in the following two years. Emiliano Zapata itself was created as part of a much larger process of dismembering of the larger extension of the Guaracha *latifundio* in which other communities had finally taken precedence because of their greater activism. These other ejidos had all been organized on an individual basis, and this would, of course, be a factor at the forefront of the Emiliano Zapata ejidatarios' consciousness, though they would also have been aware of the illegalities, inequalities and *caciquismo* rife in the established ejidal communities. The instrument of Cárdenas's new credit policy, the Banco Nacional de Crédito Ejidal, had been inaugurated in 1935, though Moreno points out that during 1936 the Ciénega de Chapala was still assigned to the office of the Banco Nacional de Crédito Agrícola in La Barca, Jalisco, an organization which in principle still pursued strictly commercial criteria (Moreno 1980:194). The Bank's records for 1936 show that the ejido of Emiliano Zapata received a total of 78,675.60 pesos, or 49% of the total advanced to the thirteen ejidos of the Jiquilpan region that year, a degree of preferential treatment which might well suggest political pressure from the President rather than simply commercial considerations.

We might therefore postulate that a degree of rational forward planning was taking place at the moment of the collective ejido's creation, even if it was not being very fully communicated from the corridors of power in Mexico City to the ejidatarios in the village. It is, however, worth citing a more jaundiced evaluation of the innovations of 1935, dating from the early 1940s:

> In this period (1935–6), as a result of a strong tide of demagogy, (Local Ejidal Credit) Societies were organized in a disordered way, passing over elementary prerequisites such as purges of

> agrarian census rolls, study of the credit capacity of the soliciting
> units, complementary studies of the productivity of the land, etc.
> (Zaldivar Flores 1942:65)

A jaundiced view would not seem inappropriate in the light of the problems which arose in Emiliano Zapata, but before we confront such negative points, it should perhaps be conceded that the new credit policy was potentially a major advance given the vulnerability of the newly emancipated peasants to subsumption by private capital under twentieth-century economic conditions, a possibility soon to be realized as the effects of the abandonment of this policy made themselves felt in a spectacular fashion in this region later in the next decade. Furthermore, the fact that many of the problems under discussion in the past have proved equally endemic in the modern official credit systems of the 1970s and 1980s suggests that the speed of introduction of the reforms and demagogy were not the whole of the problem. In any event, it appears that more radical plans for the development of the ejidal system in the Bolsa de Guaracha were already being envisaged while this interim financial provision for support of a cane cultivating collective ejido was being arranged.

According to the Bank's booklet on the "Rafael Picazo" Society, the directorate of the Bank secured the President's enthusiastic agreement to commission a study of the "conditions and possibilities" of the ejidos around Guaracha in May 1936, and sent Ing. Guillermo Maqueo Castellanos, a sugar industry specialist, to Emiliano Zapata to carry out the necessary work. I did not encounter anyone who recalled the original purpose of Maqueo's arrival. He was simply remembered as the first Jefe to be sent to run the mill. According to the booklet, the "Rafael Picazo" Society was set up six months later, on December 18th, and on December 28th:

> On the basis of the study done the previous May, the Collective
> Agricultural Ejidal Industrial Society "Rafael Picazo," through
> preliminary negotiations on the part of the National Ejidal Credit
> Bank, S.A., and by unanimous assent of the membership of the
> Society, resolved to buy the ancient mill of "San Ignacio" in the
> ex-hacienda of Guaracha for the sum of $442,000, ... to be covered in four annual repayments, to the general astonishment of
> the birds of ill omen who affirmed the impossibility of fulfilling
> this, especially in the case of ejidatarios. (BNCE 1937:10)

The booklet goes on to tell us, and informants confirmed, that the mill was delivered in a "lamentable state of abandonment," requiring 35 days of repairs before it was in an operational condition, the first ejidal harvest beginning on February 8th, 1937, "with peasants performing all the work in the mill."

My informants remember the meeting at which the ejidatarios agreed to buy the mill. Several of them remarked that this was the last occasion on which the Bank administration in the mill gave information directly to a general assembly of ejidatarios. Henceforth the *modus operandi* of Maqueo and his successors was to deal only with the ejidal authorities and use them as intermediaries in their relationships with the mass of the peasantry. At one level this behavior might be intelligible in terms of purely personal motivations on the part of the administrators. Though men like Maqueo were certainly political and sympathetic to the Cardenista program, their social background seems to have made direct personal interactions with peasants like the Guaracheños uncomfortable, particularly given the revolution in status relations implied by the ejido. My informants recounted a number of anecdotes which exemplified this social distance, and indicated that some of the Bank Employees were much less adept at dealing with peasants than the local hacienda administrative stratum, with which the peasants identified the Cárdenases themselves.[2] The peasants' own lack of "preparation" (in terms of functional literacy and experience) was not the only factor which made the emergent state agrarian sector heavily dependent on the services of the old hacienda administrative stratum: technocrats and bureaucrats from the center often lacked the essential communicative and managerial skills—matters of competence in social sub-cultural idioms, personal style and simple sensitivity—for handling the state's provincial peasant clients. Nor should we underestimate the genuine physical dangers facing the new agrarian bureaucracy, especially in a context such as the Ciénega, where land reform had not received massive popular support and the installation of federal garrisons did not constitute as effective a means of social control as the repressive and disciplinary machineries of the haciendas. The charge that the peasants were savages was not, as we will see, wholly inappropriate, even if the nature, scope and causes of that savagery need closer investigation. The problem of interpersonal relations between peasant and bureaucrat must, however, be viewed as secondary to the more fundamental problem of the total lack of preparation or politicization which characterized this collectivist leap into the future. This was all the more disastrous given the fact that committed *agraristas* were only a minority among the ejidatarios, so many of whom had only signed up for land reluctantly at the eleventh hour. No attempt was made by the authorities at any level or at any stage to establish the basis for the development of democratic self-government within the ejidos of Emiliano Zapata and Totolán.

There is no evidence whatsoever to suggest that the ejidatarios of Emiliano Zapata and Totolán had any spontaneous conception of turning the mill into an ejidal cooperative: the most that might be claimed (by the politically committed) is that the project corresponded to the objective material interests and perhaps partially articulated wishes of the peasantry as a whole. It seems possible that Lázaro Cárdenas may have been in negotiation with the *Hacendado* via his personal contacts regarding the sale of the mill before December 1936, given that the latter made no attempt to preserve his asset in operational condition after the ejidatarios received their initial assignment of land. Maqueo's feasibility study certainly followed fairly hard on the heels of expropriation. The Bank's propaganda depicted the acquisition of the mill as a timely response by the President to anxieties manifested at grass roots level after the formation of the ejido:

> Nevertheless, the ill-omened bird of pessimism continued to sow the seeds of mistrust [*desconfianza*]. What will we do with our cane? Sell it at a derisory price to be processed by the proprietor of the mill? Abandon its cultivation, which brings better returns than that of other crops in the region? ... But there existed a man whose broad and humane gaze embraced the total panorama of the national territory.... (BNCE 1937:9)

Yet given that Cárdenas's government did not insist that all sugar mills be removed from the hands of their private owners, there seems to have been a gap between what might be considered desirable in principle and what was feasible in practice. It is possible that the President felt particularly strongly about Guaracha for personal reasons, but it may also have been a matter of finding an owner who was willing to do a deal, because the economic value of what was being sacrificed in Guaracha was not, in fact, as great as the effort to make it a showpiece of agrarian reform would imply. It is also conceivable that the higher authorities—the President or the Bank—took the view that the political problems with the Ciénega peasantry demanded a major effort. In any event, even the Bank's own propaganda makes it clear enough that problems experienced with the collective before the ejidatarios acquired the mill had not entirely disappeared.

INNOCENCE AND EXPERIENCE:
INTERNAL CAUSES OF THE FIASCO

The Bank begins by referring to "opposition based on *desconfianzas*" sown by merchants desiring to substitute themselves for the old "master" at the time of the creation of the first Credit Associations. There is, as we will see, an especially ironic sense in which this diagnosis is not too far from the mark, and it is also worth recalling that some of the local *agrarista* leaders in the countryside were petty grain speculators and usurers. But one suspects that the author's own intention was to suggest an external cause for a discontent which was mainly a spontaneous reaction to the imposed collective system from within the ranks of the ejidatarios. Later on, in the section entitled "Results Obtained," which includes the accounts for the year 1936–7, the author also remarks that:

> During this first ejidal harvest, ... the work was performed under
> the pessimism created by the labor of contrary elements, giving
> rise to a certain neglect of cultivation and irrigations, it being a
> meritorious group of ejidatarios who sustained their faith in
> favorable results and paid proper attention, within their possibili-
> ties, to the cultivation of the cane. (BNCE 1937:11)

The official account itself therefore concedes what is also conceded by living informants today when pressed. Though some people committed themselves totally, even during the first year of operation a proportion of the ejidatarios refused to participate in the collective work on the cane, but
dedicated themselves to their *ecuaros* or the hectare of temporal land which
they were free to sow as they pleased.

The collective principle had been imposed against the wishes of many, and
I could find little evidence of spontaneous enthusiasm for it even on the part
of dedicated ex-*agraristas*. Most informants from this group felt that this was
what Don Lázaro had really wanted and that it had therefore been their duty
to try to make a success of it. Their acceptance of collectivism was associated
more with the clientage relationship they held with Cárdenas than with ideological arguments about the "rationality" of collective production forms with
respect to national economic or social objectives. Furthermore, the technical
administrators of the Bank, resident in a housing complex symbolically set
apart from the village, next to the mill, seemed unable or unwilling to perform any effective supervisory role over the performance of work and the use
to which credits were put.

The cane for the first year's harvest had been sown by the hacienda, and so
the costs of the first year's operations were abnormally low, though losses
due to neglect might also need to be taken into account. In any event, each
ejidatario received a cash *utilidad* of 300 pesos in silver. The booklet
described the distribution ceremony as follows:

> ...our brothers, wide-eyed with wonder at the incredible, held out
> a trembling hand ... both hands and this still not being enough to
> hold what they were receiving, they brought up the old sombrero
> or the threadbare poncho to receive the $300.... (BNCE 1937:14)

Few ejidatarios today are willing to express themselves satisfied with the
300 pesos, though a few conceded that it was really a very large amount as a
lump sum for those days. It seems that Maqueo had made exaggerated
promises, and that the ejidatarios had agreed to forego immediate pay
increases in anticipation of a larger final pay-out. But the true roots of the
growing dissatisfaction lay elsewhere. Some ejidatarios had certainly committed themselves more energetically to the collective enterprise than others,
yet all shared equally in the rewards as *socios*. And more significantly, it had

rapidly become apparent that some ejidatarios were more equal than others in the eyes of the administration. The members of the ejido's *Mesa Directiva* had, one of its number explained to me, been offered double the normal daily wage from the very start. But that was only the start: those members of the *Mesas* who were closer to the *Jefes* had clearly come into money in a much bigger way. The peasant *Gerente* of the "Rafael Picazo" Society, an Emiliano Zapata ejidatario, has entered local folklore as the man who made a cigarette out of a hundred peso bill. Similar stories are told in Totolán about the behavior of their ejidal representatives, and it is clear that such good fortune was a reward for complicity in illicit operations being organized by the upper echelons of the administration, operations which involved unmarked lorries bearing off sugar and alcohol to unknown destinations in the night.

It is also clear that many ordinary ejidatarios lost their innocence, especially after the first year of the ejido's operation, abusing the credit system by, for example, taking money for *peones* who had not been hired. Such possibilities depended, of course, on the poor state of supervision, and in some cases there may not even have been conscious deception. Possibly, some of the new, uneducated and unpoliticized ejidatarios saw their role as "proprietors" of the land in succession to the *patrón* as giving them the right to an income without personal work: certainly many peasants today implicitly take the view that they should receive a *utilidad* in addition to a full payment for any work they personally put into the plot. In addition to influencing their evaluation of the cooperative, such a perspective could underlie some of the other abuses of the official credit system noted by Moreno, particularly the use of loans to sustain consumption on the model of the *Tienda de Raya* rather than to finance productive activity (Moreno 1980:197). But it was probably not simply or perhaps even predominantly a matter of miscognition, lack of preparation and inexperience. The ex-*peones* might be ignorant of many things, especially arithmetic and numbers, but they all understood the practice of fraud, so long-established a feature of hacienda routine. The ex-*peones* might have expected better of the government officials administering the mill, though it is difficult to think of any plausible reason why they should have done so. There may never have been any true innocence, simply a lack of scope for illiterate peasants to take much advantage of opportunities under normal circumstances, or to defend themselves from those who would sin at their expense. It is not really possible to assess the scale of the sin committed by the administration in 1936–7, beyond noting that the area harvested according to the published accounts does not tally with my informants' recollections, but the events of the following year speak for themselves.

After the first harvest, Ing. Maqueo asked to be transferred, and was awarded the management of the showcase ejidal industry at Zacatepec. His successor dealt only with official representatives of the ejidatarios, and rode about the countryside on horseback. The *utilidad* for the 1937–38 cycle was a mere 46 pesos, despite the fact that the propaganda booklet had promised double the previous year's harvest. Evidently costs had been higher in the second year of operation, and financial problems resulting from abuses and administrative failings in the credit system may also have been mounting. But even an unusually sober commentator, always loathe to point the finger at government officials or criticize the Cardenista party to which he was totally committed, the second comisariado, Don Rafael Vargas, proved unable to avoid references to "errors" in the "liquidation" following the 1938 harvest, and the absence of "straight accounts." The ejidatarios protested and demanded a public meeting at which the collective would have an opportunity to discuss the matter with the administration, but the Bank *Jefe de Zona* refused to countenance any public discussion and told them they could have 46 pesos or nothing.

After the second harvest, the system of collective work collapsed completely. An attempt was made subsequently to reorganize production on the basis of cooperating groups of ten ejidatarios, but abuse of the credit system was now the norm: a team leader would hire a few *peones* and pocket ten salaries. As Don Rafael puts it, after two years of collective ejido most ejidatarios had already "lost their love for the cane," some of which was dying in the fields, some being plowed up to give way to wheat, maize and other crops.

Dissensions within the community were mounting at all levels. Among ejidatarios, the argument was that the collective system was unjust because it gave an equal reward to people who had become totally lazy and were making no productive contribution at all. A *sindicato* had been formed in the mill, and as the crisis of cane production and credit repayment continued to escalate, there was mounting antagonism between the mill workers and ejidatarios, as well as between peasants and the Bank administrators, who continued to show a high rate of turnover in the job. The ejidatarios seemed anomalously privileged to the landless, who now had to serve them as *peones*, and the *agraristas* faced a degree of resentment from fellow ejidatarios. The *agraristas* also had their own reasons for feeling less than satisfied with the progress of the reform, since they had to put up with the sight of members of the ex-*hacendado's* administration (now resident in Jiquilpan) continuing to give orders in the hacienda mill, while only a few comrades were admitted to the inner circle of power and enrichment centered around the professional bureaucracy. From the ejidatarios' point of view, the only solution to the problem was a division of the ejido into individual *parcelas*, and there was a widespread, though not universal, feeling that it was time to be done with cane cultivation itself. This proposal constituted a direct threat to those families whose livelihoods depended on work in the mill, of course, and was probably seen as a general threat to employment by all the landless. The future of cane cultivation had not, however, been decided definitively when Rafael Vargas became commissar in the autumn of 1938, and he personally hoped that the cane would continue under an individualized system of cultivation.

Don Rafael, a young returned U.S. migrant and dedicated *agrarista,* was an individual who had office thrust upon him, and by general assent made an honest attempt to represent the constituency which elected him. His scope for action was not wide. Don Lázaro "was hard to reach" in this period, and it is more than likely that the Guaracha *agraristas* would not, by this stage, have regarded Don Dámaso as an acceptable substitute, since it was now evident that he enjoyed a very close working relationship with the Bank administration. Benjamin Zarate, son of the martyred *agrarista* Marcelino, and President of the Council of Vigilance during Rafael's administration, told me that he, together with another ejidatario who worked in the mill, did go to see Lázaro Cárdenas in Jiquilpan, and received a card which enabled them to see him subsequently in Mexico, after he had reflected on the issue of whether to parcellize the ejido. It is clear that the decision to abandon the collective experiment did come from the highest level, and the general belief of Guacheños that Don Lázaro took a long time to forgive them this latest failure may not be without substance, though there were a number of respects in which Cárdenas's personal patronage continued to seek ways to ameliorate the land and employment problem in the Bolsa de Guaracha, through offers of access to land elsewhere and help with job creation for those who migrated to Mexico City.

In a sense, then, the end of the collective ejido in Guaracha appears just as much of an act based on the personal power and role of Lázaro Cárdenas as its inception. Or perhaps, to an extent, it represents a further negation of the petty bourgeois revolutionary caudillo's power by a peasant community. Perhaps it represents a form of class struggle, against capitalism or at least the state capitalist substance behind the masquerade of "peasant coopera-tion," an extension of the disobedience so many *peones* had displayed against the hacienda when they went to sow their *ecuaros* in the morning. Their new *patrón* had no *acordada,* or perhaps rather could not use what was theoreti-cally a vastly greater coercive force to this end, in this political context. After an emancipation which would not be a total illusion in this respect at least, the peasants refused to work collectively, and collective work, and the cane, ended. But such an argument might be a little simplistic, even misleading. It ignores the possibility that the recalcitrant peasants might, indeed, have been "won" for cooperative and collective forms of production had circumstances been different. We have yet to give a complete account of what determined the actual circumstances of the case.

DON DÁMASO AND THE FRUITS OF REVOLUTION

With Don Lázaro now President of the Republic in Mexico, Dámaso Cárdenas and his younger brothers enjoyed even greater personal power in the region, without close supervision. They were active participants in every agrarian initiative. A photograph in the Banjidal booklet shows that the distri-bution of the first *utilidad* from the "Rafael Picazo" Society took place in the presence of Don Dámaso and Don José Raymundo Cárdenas. Though this fragment of evidence is trivial in itself, as part of a larger pattern of evidence to be detailed below, it is consistent with the view that the new agrarian bureaucracy did not function as an autonomous, center-orientated, force in the region, but became responsive to local interests and pressures channeled through the mediating role of Don Dámaso, who was already dedicating himself to "repairing the deep division between the *hilachentos* and cashmere plutocrats" (Ochoa n.d.:12). A crude reading of the evidence detailed below might suggest that Don Dámaso and the new Cardenista elite of Jiquilpan conspired with the Bank officials and the old hacienda-period economic elite of Jiquilpan to sabotage the sugar industry in Guaracha, in pursuit of the crudest forms of personal interest. Though the evidence does support the conclusion that public duty and ideology took a definite second place to private gain in the politics of Jiquilpan in the late 1930s and early 1940s, a conspiracy interpretation is neither necessary or desirable. If everything were explicable in terms of the perfidy of the President's brother, an interpretation which naturally appeals to many modern Cardenistas both outside and inside the ejidos, the events would be less revealing, and also less disturbing.

The first aspect of external influence on the development of the Emiliano Zapata ejido which requires examination relates directly to the issue of the political representation of the ejidatarios and the wider community. When the hacienda administration left in 1936, Guaracha received a new *Jefe de Tenencia,* a certain Don Rumaldo, who was a native of Tarecuato, but was known as an *amigo conocido* of Lázaro Cárdenas. Don Rumaldo had the good or bad fortune to bear a striking physical resemblance to Porfirio Díaz. The Guaracheños had the decidedly bad fortune to suffer a village government whose arbitrariness also retained a distinctly Porfirian face. Don Rumaldo was a comic-strip *cacique,* backed up by private hired guns and a detachment of federal soldiers whose tendencies to drunkenness and violence were to plague the community until the 1950s. In 1939, the Federal corporal arrested commissar Rafael for carrying a pistol. Don Rumaldo refused to intervene, despite the fact that the commissar was legally entitled to bear arms and had offended nobody, whereas the corporal had subsequently become a public menace, discharging the weapon at random in the street after imbibing heavily. Don Rumaldo accused the commissar personally of "lack of respect for the federal authority," and denounced the community in general for its repeated disloyalty to the government. Rafael replied that there was no problem of loyalty to the government of General Cárdenas in the village: the problem lay with a local authority which retained the style of Porfirio Díaz.

The commissar was eventually released after the intercession of the Banjidal Chief, who no doubt anticipated the popular reaction the incident did indeed provoke. Don Rafael himself stood against Don Rumaldo in the ensuing elections in the Tenencia and secured virtually all the votes cast. Yet the day after the elections he received a visit from Jiquilpan, in the person of the Diputado Federal, a pattern of events we encountered in the previous chapter in the context of ejidal elections in Villamar. On this occasion the election result was clearly beyond remedy, but the demand from Jiquilpan was that Rafael accept Don Rumaldo onto the village council as his secretary, a characteristic form of Mexican political compromise. Rafael refused, as a result of which Jiquilpan sought and subsequently found a pretext to have him removed from office.

Although Don Rumaldo packed his bags and left Guaracha, Rafael's removal was followed by a change in the type of person who acted as political representative of the village. The Villamar municipal archive shows that the office of *Jefe de Tenencia* was occupied in 1940 by a person who worked as a technical instructor in the Escuela Agrícola founded in 1938, and then, in 1942, by an ejidatario who had not been an *agrarista,* whom I will call by his nickname, "El Chiquitín." Though the ex-*agrarista* Benjamín Zarate's name appears on the record (which is incomplete) in 1949, El Chiquitín's name appears repeatedly as Jefe de Tenencia or Encargado de Orden in the early 1940s, and he was also to become ejidal commissar for the first time in 1944. As one of the more embittered ex-*agraristas* put it:

> The rich peasants, the *acomodados* and anti-*agraristas*, came into the ascendant then. El Chiquitín and his friends were in office all the time in the village, and then they took over the ejido too.

While ex-*agraristas* did, it seems, occasionally hold office subsequently, there is an apparently significant shift here. Its origin appears to be political, though El Chiquitín also advanced economically in the course of the 1940s, forming a partnership to buy machines for harvesting wheat with two friends who were not originally ejidatarios: one had been absent in the U.S., while the other had worked as a mechanic in the mill and tended to be seen as an *acomodado*, though he too was able to buy his way into the ejido after 1940, and eventually became ejidal commissar in the late 1960s. El Chiquitín was the president of the local branch of the PNR and subsequently the PRI, a shrewd pragmatist who represented the type of leadership which was best adapted to the new situation. Don Rafael had an ideological commitment and felt answerable to the ejidatarios, whereas El Chiquitín was willing to answer for them, and to carry out the instructions of the political bosses on whom his ascent ultimately depended.

If we review the events at a more abstract level, is the almost pathological obsession with pacification which characterized the Cárdenas epoch in Michoacán is striking. There would, of course, be reason to suspect the loyalty of the unrevolutionary peons of Guaracha, and it might not be unreasonable to have anxieties about the preservation of basic social order once the hacienda's disciplinary machinery was removed. Yet it is noteworthy that Cárdenas left the task of consolidating his regime to caciques like Don

Rumaldo in many parts of Michoacán, including zones where the social and political situation was very different from that in Guaracha. Though such a policy was hardly compatible with the rhetoric of Cárdenas's government, it was, as we have seen, perfectly consistent with the past practices of *Cardenismo*, and made obvious sense in terms of the guarantee of loyalty afforded by the personal relationship of patronage between caudillo and *cacique*. In purely practical terms, one of the major tasks confronting Cárdenas, as it confronted his predecessors, was that of creating more effective machineries of central state control, the means to effect macro-social change. But an explanation couched in terms of expedient means to more elevated ends may not be an adequate one.

If democracy and self-determination by the masses might be the ideal, and ultimate, objective, Cárdenas seemed unwilling to trust the unprepared and newly emancipated masses in the short or medium term. He did personally pay for the higher education of some of the *agraristas'* children, as well as sponsoring more general government provision of educational facilities such as the Escuela Práctica de Agricultura established in Guaracha. Since the peasants could not administrate their own ejidos properly because of their lack of technical preparation, and were equally unable to carry out the duties of public elected offices or bureaucratic posts effectively, it would be necessary to allow the old regime of hacienda administrators and Porfirian officialdom to continue to play their part in the public sector subject to political control. In the longer term, the peasants would be "prepared." But how significant it is that future self-determination actually depended on the peasantry being remodelled through education from above and how much weight was implicitly being placed on the supervisory role of a political vanguard in the whole conception. The peasants were not to be allowed the power to make those who acted in their name accountable. Mexico City was a long way off and Cárdenas's social program was not designed to socialize the urban economy or deprive the petty bourgeoisie from which it sprang of their opportunities for economic advance. Cárdenas himself had directed the struggle to emancipate the region's *peones* from a forty hectare ranch he had bought in Jiquilpan from the Villaseñor family, and subsequently acquired a larger property in Apatzingán. Genuinely representative peasant leaders were seen as a threat to political control, to be eliminated if they could not be effectively coopted. The Cardenista movement was disposed to tolerate *caciquismo* as a practical expedient for securing its control, though the strategy pursued varied according to the pragmatics of local circumstances, as indicated by the contrasting histories of Guaracha, politically marginal after the end of the ejidal agro-industry, and Villamar, always central to any strategy of political control as a *cabecera municipal*. Besides needing to respond practically to the task of consolidating state power under objective social and political conditions which were often adverse, and with limited central economic and coercive resources, *Cardenismo* was perhaps also inclined ideologically to see the masses as the objects rather than subjects of revolutionary action, thereby betraying the movement's true social class origin and orientation.

The political maneuverings of Jiquilpan politicians in Emiliano Zapata may have had more immediate objectives. When the ejido was formally parcellized on January 28th, 1940, some ejidatarios continued with sugar cane on their *parcelas,* but much of the cane was plowed up, and the level of production in the region had fallen to levels which made the operation of the mill quite uneconomic. In 1942, under the administration of Chema Inocencio, an agreement was signed to rent the mill's machinery to the ejido of Taretan in the Tierra Caliente, and it was dismantled. The ejidatario who was Vigilancia at the time, Pablo Quintero, told me that he had tried to oppose signature of the papers authorizing the removal of the machines, on the grounds that a full assembly of all the ejidatarios was required to approve the decision. What had happened was that the federal deputy and President of the Ligas Agrarias (CNC), Don Baltazar Gudiño, had arrived with an order to transfer the machines, presumably issued by Banjidal, and the ejidal officials were simply to countersign to permit the equipment's removal. Don Baltazar insisted that there was no alternative, because the mill could not continue operating at a loss; if the ejidatarios wished to grow cane again the mill could be reopened, and in the meantime the community would receive rental income from Taretan. Don Baltazar reinforced his argument by asserting that this was what Don Lázaro wanted. Don Pablo actually went to work in Taretan after the machinery was moved and maintained that what happened subsequently was that the ejidatarios of Taretan sent a commission to see Lázaro Cárdenas at his ranch in Apatzingán: they asked him to order the permanent sale of the machinery to them. Don Lázaro had replied that the equipment wasn't his to control, but belonged to the ejidatarios of Emiliano Zapata and Totolán. Subsequently, however, Don Dámaso and the Bank Jefe de Zona had agreed that the equipment should be sold. El Chiquitín was now commissar, and the sale was accomplished under his auspices in 1945. The Guaracha ejidatarios are convinced that their commissar participated in a massive fraud with the President's brother and the Banjidal chief. What does seem clear is that the commissar (perhaps understandably!) misled the ejidatarios when he cajoled them into signing a piece of paper (for the most part, of course, with their thumb prints), and that no clear explanation of the events surrounding the closing of the mill was ever provided. The ejidatarios were given to understand that they would receive money, but no money payments were ever made. It must be assumed that since the mill remained a Banjidal asset, and the industry had supposedly been operating at a loss, its value would be written off against the ejidatarios' debts, though this formal legal situation would abstract somewhat from contraband operations by the mill administration and other factors which might be set against what appeared in the enterprise account books. What is more interesting is that all the ejidatarios apparently believed that they were robbed of their birthright by their commissar and the

President's brother, but took no serious steps to avenge themselves on either. El Chiquitín was later to serve a second term as commissar. By that stage it was half the ejido itself which was up for sale.

With the sugar industry gone from Guaracha, the Emiliano Zapata and Totolán ejidos also lost their privileged rights to irrigation water, and the dam of the ex-hacienda now began to supply lands around Jiquilpan, lands in which both the old and new elite of Jiquilpan had a definite interest which again conflicted with that of the peasants. Here, however, the ejidatarios of Emiliano Zapata were not the injured parties and we might, in fairness, sympathize more with those who were, and are.

The community of Cerrito Cotijaran, made up of the sharecroppers the *patrón* moved from Guaracha in a bid to outflank *agrarismo,* received a grant of 88 hectares of land out of the 300 hectare of ejidal *ampliación* made possible by Manuel Moreno's sale of his residual private property in 1938. Although many in the Cerrito continued their rejection of land reform even at this stage, there were enough young men and returned migrants in Cotijaran to create a clear demand for more land. Between the town of Jiquilpan and the villages of Totolán and Cerrito Pelón lay a tract of land known as "La Beneficencia Pública," land left to the town by a rich and childless widow. Lázaro Cárdenas, whose own ranch was next to La Beneficencia, determined that the larger part of the latter, 208 hectare, should be distributed in *ampliación automática* to beneficiaries from Cerrito Cotijaran. In August 1941, his successor, Avila Camacho, signed the Presidential order putting this decision into effect. But both the order and the engineer were turned back to Mexico by Don Dámaso, on the grounds that the terrain of La Beneficencia had already been legally divided into small private properties. The new proprietors were an assortment of political and personal friends of the Cárdenas family. They included Don Baltazar Gudiño, whose role as president of the Ligas Agrarias hardly enhanced the possibility of the outrage of the ejidatarios of Cotijaran receiving an airing in official organs of peasant representation. Don Baltazar was a person of relatively humble, though not peasant, origin,[3] who had been working as a minor clerk when Cárdenas chose him as a political worker in the 1920s. But the new ranchers of La Beneficencia also included members of the Jiquilpan bourgeoisie who had supported "La Seda" and the brother of the parish priest in Totolán. The ranches of the Beneficencia mapped the end of ideology and the close political accommodation which had now been consummated between the old *ricos* and new political bourgeoisie of Jiquilpan in the most overt way possible. The *Jefe de Hacienda,* Enrique Bravo Valencia, another Cárdenas protegé who had originally worked as a photographer, must, as my Cotijaran informants claimed, have helped the proprietors draw up legal papers in full knowledge of the intention to distribute the land to their ejido.

The ejidatarios of Cotijaran had to wait for more than twenty years for a preliminary resolution of their land claim, and remain far from satisfied even today. It is in this community that peasant leaders today most frequently voice the desirability of achieving a truly independent peasant union. The problem for Cotijaran was that the same hands retained control of the peasant and state organizations over the years; they eventually sought to pursue their case via the CCI, but even this alternative channel of action promptly turned out to be capable of making back-stage accommodations with the old powers in Jiquilpan.

By 1940 Dámaso Cárdenas and friends had achieved an effective control of the offices of the agrarian agencies and the organs of peasant political representation in the region. Their power (and the wealth derived from it) had its origin, in the first instance, in the process of reform carried through by the national government and the enlargement of the bureaucratic apparatus and wealth-creating possibilities of public office. But the center made no attempt to exercise control over what it had created. Free of constraint, Dámaso Cárdenas and his friends now dedicated themselves to private enterprise, and thereby realized the kind of aspirations which motivated most of them to agitate for redistributive economic reform in the first place.

The reduction in cane production in Guaracha had been accompanied by an increase in wheat cultivation by the ejidatarios there, and wheat was the most significant ejidal crop after maize in terms of land area sown in the Ciénega as a whole until sorghum took off in the 1960s, as a facet of the general transformation of Mexican agriculture in this period (Table 2). At first the most important ultimate purchaser of the peasant product was the wheat mill in Jacona, which retained local agents resident in the Ciénega communities and entered into formal agreements with Banjidal on purchasing levels and prices when Guaracha was expropriated. (Thus, it appears, quite different considerations governed peasant dependence on private wheat mills to those which arose in the case of sugar.) In theory, the Bank itself should have both supervised the administration of credit during cultivation and collected the harvested grain. In practice, as in the case of cane cultivation, supervision and credit administration was imperfect, and private buyers began to capture an increasing proportion of the peasants' grain, partly because the Bank delayed payment for the harvest while it awaited notification of official prices. But this tendency was not the only factor tending to subvert the original plan to create an state-financed and regulated peasant wheat production system which would satisfy the twin objectives of maximizing peasant welfare and meeting the needs of the market in an economic manner.

While Emiliano Zapata was becoming an individual ejido, Don Dámaso Cárdenas was building himself a wheat mill in Jiquilpan. The Harinera de Jiquilpan S.A. was managed by none other than the last administrator of the hacienda of Guaracha, Don Manuel Robledo. Don Dámaso's mill offered the ejidatario its own system of credit. One went to the mill office and was offered a substantial cash advance to be repaid *a la dobla* in grain at harvest time. Don Manuel and his agents knew the individual peasants personally,

Table 2

PRINCIPAL CROPS SOWN IN THE CIÉNEGA
1950–1976

Principal Crops	Area Sown (in hectares)			
	1950	1960	1970	1976
Beans	1,943	675	487	358
Garbanzo [1]	582	2,565	4,760	1,903
Maize	16,267	7,086	9,595	3,735
Wheat	11,406	10,745	3,965	982
Sorghum	—	4,432	14,132	14,165
Cartamo [2]	—	—	6,432	1,330
Total Farm Land	30,693	26,015	42,015	26,925
Area Sown In These Crops	30,198	25,503	39,372	22,473
As Percentage of Total Farm Land	98.3	98.0	94.0	83.3

Source: Durán 1982. [1]Chickpea; [2]Safflower

and their credit system had none of the administrative defects of the Bank's: the individual's credit-worthiness (and exploitability) could be finely judged and the advance determined accordingly. In place of the bank inspectors, Don Dámaso's agents now walked among the *parcelas*. Few apparently resented Don Manuel's reemergence in the economic life of Guaracha, though the odd expression of violent animosity did occur. As one informant put it:

> Well, perhaps a few people felt bad about it inside, but he kept on
> good terms with most people. After all, it was a free choice, peo-
> ple weren't forced to take Don Dámaso's money....

True, Don Dámaso did not enjoy a monopoly of the peasant surplus, and in fact his mill did not have the capacity to absorb even the total wheat produc-tion of the ejidos. Perhaps he was simply responding in an entrepreneurial way to opportunities which were presenting themselves as a result of the col-lapse of the collective ejido in the Ciénega and policy changes at national level. At the time the Jiquilpan mill began to operate, many peasants were beginning to turn to dependence on private capital because of deficiencies in the Banjidal system, and the resources available to Banjidal were to diminish drastically during the 1940s as a result of the progressive abandonment of Cárdenas's policies. It is this, of course, which makes it necessary to qualify our conception of the "free choices" made by the peasantry in this period. Yet the timing alone belies a total disinterest on Dámaso Cárdenas's part. He was at the forefront of developments which contributed to the retreat of Banjidal and was promoting the replacement of official credit with private usury, at precisely the moment when the "correct" course for a loyal Cardenista would have been to call for a strengthening and reform of the Bank's operations. It is hard to resist the conclusion that Don Dámaso's interest in the state sector did not go much beyond the pecuniary opportunities new institutions offered. Now the collective sugar industry had collapsed, little money was to be made through official channels in Guaracha, except, perhaps, in the matter of liquidating the remaining capital assets of the agro-industry. Don Dámaso sold his mill to the Jacona company before becoming state governor in 1950. Merchant intermediaries who sold grain to the mill still bought peasants' wheat *al tiempo*, but the mill itself ceased to make usurious loans directly to the peasants under its new management. With the end of Don Dámaso's private business, and the virtual end of official credit from Banjidal, the economic exploitation of the peasantry was returned, for a while, to private interests whose political influence was a consequence of class position rather than the reverse. Indeed, despite the political basis for Don Dámaso's economic power, his own rise to the position of a *patrón* might be seen as simply a rather grotesque manifestation of a more general process: the closing of a phase of extended direct state intervention in the agrarian economy, and a cyclical return to the dominance of private capital.

Yet the process is not an entirely cyclical one, as if the Revolution had meant nothing at all. Although the economic power of the Old Porfirian elite had been far from broken by the events of the past twenty years, it was not the old landed oligarchy which returned to exercise their dominion over the campesinos, but a new, regional agrarian bourgeoisie. While many elements of this new bourgeoisie were members of families which belonged to the smaller landlord-hacienda administrator stratum of the latifundist epoch, there were also quite a number of "new men" whose fortunes were made in the post-land reform era.

THE GUARACHA COLLECTIVE AND CÁRDENAS'S AGRARIAN POLICY

The majority of the Guaracheños I spoke to who lived through these events felt that their community had suffered an enormous injustice in losing its mill and its monopoly over the waters of the San Antonio dam. Even today, the ruined mill is a powerful symbol. Ejidatarios in neighboring communities note this attitude, and hold it in contempt. Guaracheños have delusions of grandeur, an absurd pride in a heritage which was, is, and always will be, a complete illusion. If it was an illusion, however, then Cárdenas, among others, played his role in fostering it.

It is clear that there was considerable misadministration of the ejidal agro-industry by the professional bureaucracy, and it is also clear that the emergent coalition of old and new power holders in Jiquilpan benefited materially from the end of sugar in Guaracha. It also seems clear that the collective was prejudiced by the non-cooperation of many of the ejidatarios. As I noted earlier, it would be possible to describe this non-cooperation as a form of resistance to the imposition of state capitalist production relations, and to see it perhaps as a continuation and intensification of the earlier kind of struggle which some *peones* had undertaken against the total subsumption of their labor power by the hacienda. The ejidatarios did not wish to work collectively. They did not work on the cane. Cane production terminated. Yet it seemed probable that the struggle over the *ecuaro* did not, for the majority, constitute a complete rejection of the wage labor relationship, and was largely a struggle to win a necessary amelioration of family living standards. In the case of the ejidatarios' rejection of collective work, it seems even less clear how far this "resistance" can be seen positively, as a form of class struggle oriented towards some alternative system or conscious objective such as peasant self-sufficiency or self-management and independence in the labor process. Few ejidatarios in Guaracha succeeded in establishing themselves as independent farmers, and many were to abandon the land for migration and other forms of wage labor almost as soon as they received it. Some may simply have been exploiting the limited compulsion to work at all which characterized the collective. Some had a definite preference for individual peasant cultivation over wage-labor in any form, but for many the dominant consideration seems to have been negative: the rejection of the particular form of labor organization represented by the collective ejido in Guaracha.

Possibly, then, things might have been different had the collective been run in a different way or greater effort been put into politicization. The varying solutions which the ejidatarios have opted for in seeking their livelihoods under the individual ejido suggests that they were open to offers and negotiation at the time of expropriation.

On this view, then, the external forces making for fiasco would be decisive. The agrarian movement in the Ciénega had been the product of an alliance between educated urban petty bourgeois elements which had virtually no economic power and small and medium bourgeois who either saw their economic opportunities as restricted by the hacienda, or saw better opportunities for themselves following its destruction. Though the kind of provincial (rather than metropolitan) elite represented in the ranks of "La Seda" might have initially been fearful of the pandora's box which radicalism would open, the pacification and social control programs introduced after expropriation, and general absence of peasant militancy, calmed the situation and smoothed the way for a rapid accommodation with the Cardenista coalition of bakers, workshop owners, small landowners, functionaries, professionals and pedagogues. Their economic and political interests converged, and there was absolutely no reason why anyone in Jiquilpan should find anything very appealing in the proposal to replace a large-scale capitalist agro-industry in Guaracha with a more modest, but equally privileged, ejidal agro-industry. Yet the Cárdenas faction in Jiquilpan were more than a traditional "local oligarchy," since their power really depended on the national institutions *Cardenismo* created. It was because public administration now controlled the whole of the region, eliminating the remaining enclaves of juridical autonomy like the Guaracha fiefdom, and because peasant access to the political system was mediated through the CNC as an instrument of national political control, that Don Dámaso and his clique came to enjoy the type of power they did, as the group controlling the local branches of the national institutions of control and incorporation. The questions which seem the basic ones posed by this case are why the state bureaucracy displayed so little autonomy, why public policies were so rapidly and easily subverted, why the coercion of the peasantry did not take the form of more strenuous efforts to enforce the collective regime.

Abuses of power by the bureaucracy and the new political caciques created by agrarian reform and the expansion of the state were endemic to Cárdenas's Mexico. In some regions, peasants resisted abuses, and collective forms of production functioned in quite different, more participatory, ways. Conflicts over the imposition of collective forms of production usually took place in the context of factional struggles between supporters and opponents of collective organization among the ejidatarios.Though deep divisions within those ejidos where collective sugar cultivation was imposed from above were common and to be expected, in cases like Atencingo (Ronfeldt 1973) the struggles endured for decades, whereas Guaracha collapsed rapidly and totally, despite the fact that its industrial cooperative made it a showcase of national importance. And we should not forget that many collective enterprises were actually relatively successful, in terms of productivity as well as participation, during the Cárdenas years (Eckstein 1966, Hewitt 1980).

What seems a key variable in terms of regional comparisons is the development of autonomous peasant organizations, which is, as we have seen, in turn related to differences in pre-revolutionary agrarian social structures within broader regional historical contexts. Even if one of the central thrusts of *Cardenismo* was to incorporate such organizations and remove their capacity for autonomous action, the existence of effective peasant leadership and prior mass mobilization of substantial numbers of peasants and rural workers created a leverage on the balance of social forces quite different from the situation encountered in the Ciénega de Chapala. Functionaries could manipulate peasant organizations against local economic interests to their own advantage, and in turn be pressured themselves, at least to some extent, by local peasant organizations. In both senses, the effect of peasant activism would be to enhance the "autonomy" of the agrarian bureaucracy. Political control, the first priority of the regime, could thus be enforced without sacrificing the whole of its agrarian policy.

In all these events, the personal role of Lázaro Cárdenas remains shadowy and ambiguous. The personal acts and intentions of Don Lázaro versus the other *dramatis personae* are central to local historical recollections, and one should bear in mind that many in the region did have the opportunity to speak to Lázaro Cárdenas in person about these matters. Guaracheños feel that Don Lázaro finally lost patience with them after the sugar industry debacle, and it is certainly true that after 1940 he spent most of his time in Apatzingán, only renewing his personal links with Guaracha in the final year of his life. The Tierra Caliente offered the ex-president a new peasant clientele to work with in a double sense: they were new to him, and many were new colonists in a region where it seemed possible to form an economy and society *de novo*. Possibly the President's failure to intervene personally to correct the mounting débacle of his government's policies throughout the Ciénega might have reflected a shift in his own priorities and vision of a "Grand Design" for national development.

Not only had the Guaracha ejidatarios continued to demonstrate what Cárdenas would have seen as irresponsibility vis-à-vis their duty to the national economy, not to mention further evidence of their lack of political consciousness and incapacity for organization, but his desk was cluttered with unfavorable technical assessments of the Guaracha sugar industry. The quantitative economic performance of the agricultural sector remained salient to the Cárdenas administration's emphasis on the role of the agricultural surplus in rapid industrialization and modernization, while Cárdenas and the progressive agronomists who served him retained a commitment to the perfection of technical rationality even as they proclaimed its consistency with pursuit of social reform objectives. At the very least, the technical argument would have provided a post facto rationale for bowing to the pressure of an intractable circumstance, that circumstance being that in the last analysis Dámaso Cárdenas and company were the instruments of central political control in a region where the regime still lacked a solid popular base in the countryside. However much Don Dámaso depended on the national center, in the absence of such a base, the center in turn depended on the stratagems of the bosses. That consideration was probably a more important determinant of Lázaro Cárdenas's behavior than brotherly love or family reputation.

CHAPTER 5

FROM PEASANT AGRICULTURE TO
NEOLATIFUNDISMO

On the 28th of January 1940, at 10.00 a.m., C.C. Enrique Muñoz Franco, representative of the Departamento Agrario, assembled with the ejidal authorities, Rafael Vargas, President, Luis Manzo, Secretary, Genaro Jurado, Treasurer, and Benjamin Zarate, President of the *Consejo de Vigilancia*, to conduct the formal business which would divide the terrains of Emiliano Zapata among the ejidatarios on an individual basis. Six persons with potential rights to land were excluded in advance, one being in prison, another a widow who had remarried and moved to Mexico City, and the remainder absent. Three persons voluntarily renounced their rights, on the grounds that they had invested time and money preparing *ecuaros* and preferred to dedicate themselves to those. As for the rest of the eligible population, 321 persons could be accommodated on the 322 separate parcels into which the ejido's arable land had now been divided, since one 4 hectare plot had been set aside for instructional purposes and attached to the village's Federal School. The remainder of the 667 persons entitled to receive land according to the census of 1933 were of necessity to be excluded from immediate and direct benefit under the land reform program.

Such is the written historical record of the events of 28th of January 1940. Reality was naturally more complex. In the first place, Don Rafael managed to prevail upon the federal authorities to create a dozen extra "unofficial" *parcelas* in the *potrero* known as La Manga, land which has never been graced by the issue of formal titles. In the second place, a degree of discrimination was practiced in the selection of the ejidatarios. Several of those who failed to acquire land in the initial distribution claimed that they had wished to do so and been excluded by the agraristas as *acomodados*. There were a few exceptions to the norm of exclusion of those who had belonged to the ranks of "responsible" hacienda employees. One of the *parcelas* was given to the single son of a *mayordomo*, and another to an older man who had been a custodian of mules and oxen under the former *patrón*. The latter had a returned U.S. migrant son who enjoyed good relations with the *agraristas*, and prospered as an ejidatario, but the first soon abandoned his rights. It is also fairly clear that some positive discrimination was practiced in favor of widows and unmarried sons of *agraristas*, with the odd concession to personal friendship as well, as in the case of a friend of Isaac Canela who lived in Cerrito Cotijaran.

Those who were excluded at the time of parcellization did not in fact have to wait too long for another chance to get rights in the ejido. Leaving aside title holders who died and rights abandoned by widows of ejidatarios, more than 20% of those who received titles to land in 1940 had abandoned the land and given away or sold their rights by 1955. Many more *parcelas* lay uncultivated or were rented out by their owners. Significantly perhaps, some of the leading *agraristas* were among the first to abandon the land for which they had struggled. By the late 1950s a significant proportion of the ejido's best land was no longer being cultivated by its peasant holders but by a capitalist neolatifundist from another community.

This is one of several histories of the 1940s, 1950s and 1960s which requires a degree of reconstruction, though it is not the most suppressed in everyday consciousness or one where the shamefulness of the events in the collective memory seems to have resulted in a significant understatement of the facts. The other histories are more difficult to reconstruct on the basis of information supplied by living informants, because even those who lived in and through them are not the same people today. One set of histories is political, the continuing story of Church versus State in the peasant communities of the region, a new story of progressive incorporation—at least to a degree—of the recalcitrant ex-*peones*, into the institutions and control mechanisms of the national state. Its counter-point is the interplay of local power structures and larger forces, including perhaps, the relationship between the ex-President in Apatzingán and his brothers in Jiquilpan.

What makes this political history problematic is its relationship to an uncharted and unknown social and cognitive history. It is one thing to produce data on individuals' rental of their *parcelas*, experience of migration and so forth. It is another to ask people about their perceptions and motivations in the 1940s and 1950s, even assuming that one is not entering immediately problematic areas, such as the individual's contribution to the murder rate of the period. How can people talk about their past in a way which truly reflects its living reality, unreconstructed by subsequent experience? "We were savages then, arguments led to killings because we were too ignorant to exchange words and reason with each other...."

This applies to ordinary everyday experience as well as to the political events and epochs of policy change defined by the rhetoric of the ruling party, much of which has been interiorized and constitutes a mundane framework of discourse about ejidal affairs, however skeptical the individual remains about the final validity of the regimes's claims. The people the anthropologist interviews may be in no better position than he or she is to reconstruct the social history of a past era, and yet at least some understanding of this level seems necessary in order to assess alternative explanations of the economic trends.

The gap between the legal and political theory of land reform and actual practices which underlay this epoch of peasant subordination will require detailed analysis, but it would scarcely be just to dwell too much on minor irregularities in the actual process of parcellization in Guaracha, given the much more major irregularities which characterized the same process in neighboring communities. Guaracha followed the correct procedure of an assignment of parcels by lot, and Don Rafael surprised the official by refusing the ejidal president's usual privileged choice outside the lottery.

"Maestro" Abel was an exception to the norm of land assignment by lot, refusing, people concede, not unreasonably, to submit his existing ten hectare holding to the parcellization process. The difference between the ejido of Emiliano Zapata and its neighbors probably cannot be explained simply in terms of superior personal rectitude on the part of the leadership of the Guaracha ejido, though latent resentments over the fiasco of the collective ejido probably made it more risky for would-be *caciques* from the old *agrarista* faction to pursue overt self-serving behavior. Many of the old *agraristas* were far from being saints and even the more idealistic of them sometimes experienced personal tragedy through a momentary lapse of self-control. But it may also be significant that the group running the ejido were not trusted clients selected for their roles by superior political power-holders but men who enjoyed the confidence of those they represented and derived their authority from that, reflecting the extent to which the recalcitrant and divided community of Guaracha remained outside the practical orbit of *Cardenismo* even in 1940, despite the fact that the leadership itself thought it represented the General's party.

Many analyses of the 1940s treat this period as one of a retreat from, even betrayal of, an agrarian program uniquely associated with the Cárdenas epoch.[1] The villain of the piece is the State, or rather the faction which asserted, or reasserted, its dominance within it after Cárdenas left office. Yet as Hamilton (1983) has observed, the apparent reorientation of state policy may simply reflect the lack of objective autonomy enjoyed by the post-revolutionary state in the Cárdenas epoch itself: Cárdenas's room for maneuver was effectively circumscribed by the pragmatic social power of private capital, leaving aside any contradictions in *Cardenismo*'s relationship to the masses it represented or links between political factions within the state apparatuses and private class interests. Reality simply reasserted itself with increasing force as time went by. But we cannot, on the evidence assembled in the previous chapter, entirely ignore the internal limitations of *Cardenismo*. As Armando Bartra remarks:

> ...Cárdenas honored all the demands of agrarian radicalism, all except one: the independent political organization of the peasantry. Until 1940 this omission was not too noticeable, but in the following decades it proved decisive. (Bartra 1985:65)

The immediate form of the post-Cardenista state's alleged villainy lies in its progressive withdrawal of financial support for the development of land reform agriculture, increasing selectivity of credit provision from a hugely diminished global sum made available to the peasant sector, and reduction in finance available for capital projects and infrastructure investment directly benefiting associations of peasant producers. This withdrawal of positive support is then increasingly accompanied by a negative development: the subordination of agriculture to industry, and, as the 1940s gave way to the 1950s, an increasing emphasis on the use of agricultural tax and farm price policy to force peasants to provide resources to subsidize accelerated industrialization.

Such a policy relied on peasants' ability to survive in a deteriorating market by increasing rates of "self-exploitation",[2] lowering consumption standards, and increasing household participation in other labor markets. By the late 1960s, it reached its limits of viability in the Mexican case, since an increasingly commoditized peasant reproduction process could no longer sustain the surrender of such quantities of devalorized personal labor time in the form of a marketable surplus.

In short, the scenario is one not so much of progressive abandonment of the peasantry by the State, but of a tightening squeeze effected through fiscal and market intervention mechanisms, to the ultimate benefit of urban and industrial capital. Whether this "urban-industrial bias" was wholly the product of the post-Cardenista epoch is at least open to question, since, as Arturo Warman points out, it was the Cárdenas government which, in 1938, introduced the Regulatory Committee for Subsistence Markets, an agency which imported corn to depress internal prices (Warman 1980). As authors such as Vergopoulos (1978) have argued, such a policy might be seen as the culminating point of a project of agrarian revolution from an industrial capitalist (or state capitalist) "developmentalist" point of view, though a form of it was also advocated in the cause of "primitive socialist accumulation" by Preobrazhenski in the Soviet Union during the 1920s (Preobrazhenski 1965). The blockage on national development as a whole created by the mass of rent appropriated by the large landed estate sector in earlier epochs is removed. To the extent that peasants can be squeezed more than competitive capitalist farmers, and can live with price levels which are incapable of yielding an acceptable profit rate for capitalist enterprises, a land-reform agricultural regime appears to offer optimal conditions for rapid industrial advance—providing, that is, production levels and the marketable surplus can be sustained and indeed increased to meet rising urban needs. Such functionalist reasoning rather abstracts from the fact that peasant agriculture may not, in fact, be able to perform adequately in the long term, as well as from the fact that economically desirable situations can only be realized through the achievement of appropriate political conditions (Gledhill 1981). What happened in practice in the case of the Ciénega was that new forms of capitalist relations developed and became dominant in agriculture.

The great interest in the case, which is not, I believe, untypical of the irrigation districts in general in this respect, is that these relations ultimately involved the development of capitalist production through large-scale rental of peasant land, *neolatifundismo*. Though expropriation of the old *latifundios* had not been total even under Cárdenas, it is evidently debatable whether large-scale units of production are the "natural" tendency of agrarian capitalist development under free market conditions. As Djurfeldt (1982) has observed, the lesson to be drawn from European agricultural development since 1875 is that large-scale capitalist agriculture can only prosper where it obtains exceptionally high differential rents ("superprofits") from possession of land of unusually high natural fertility, or access to extremely cheap labor, unless it enjoys a domestic market protected from international competition. Whether it enjoys such protection or not will be a function of the relative political strength of industrial versus agricultural interests. If the latter cannot secure protection, Djurfeldt argues, then the normal form of capitalist development in agriculture is through the process Chayanov described as "vertical concentration": big capital invests in processing and marketing and leaves production to peasants, though it may, as Chayanov again pointed out, impose a considerable amount of control over the peasant production process in the form of technical control as well as credit-supply (Chayanov 1966:257-265). We have already seen how local merchant-usurer capital operating in the Ciénega in the 1940s was tied to larger capitalist processing interests in the case of the wheat mills. Don Dámaso's mill was surely an excellent parallel for what Chayanov described in the following passage:

> By developing oppressive credit conditions, [trading capitalism] converts the organization of agricultural production almost into a special form of distributive office based on a "sweatshop system." In this connection, it is enough to recall the examples of capitalist exploitation which Knop, the Moscow cotton firm, applied to the Saart cotton growers, buying up their harvest in the spring, giving out advances of food, and giving them credits for seeds and means of production. (Chayanov 1966: 257-258)

For the moment, however, a more promising line of inquiry with regard to the eventual development of neolatifundist agriculture in the Ciénega would seem to be that which invokes another of Djurfeldt's conditions favoring the development of large-scale capitalist agriculture: "a depressed wage level which may originate either from a big reserve army of labor or from a sizeable poor peasantry" (Djurfeldt 1982:154). But it will become apparent that it is still important to recognize the hierarchic and vertically-concentrated nature of the modern capitalist system in this context too, since the neolatifundist enterprise represented a specific type of investment strategy by a local entrepreneur who was located at a fairly low level in terms of larger interregional and national commercial structures.

We cannot, in any case, rely completely on general theory in discussing particular types of agrarian development. In particular, the form of peasant possession of the land guaranteed by the post-revolutionary state inevitably had an impact on possible trajectories of capitalist expansion in the Mexican countryside.

CAPITALIST DEVELOPMENT AND THE EJIDOS

Large-scale capitalist production would only be possible within the individual ejidos on the basis of the following two mechanisms of concentration of control over land. First, an ejidatario could exercise effective control over multiple *parcelas* by purchasing titles from the original holders, assigning the rights to children or relatives as proxies, while continuing to exercise real control of the land. There are evidently limits on the amount of land which could normally be brought under an individual's control by such a tactic, and to its durability as a mechanism of land concentration, unless the proxies were completely lacking in interest in their rights, seldom the case where young children's names are used as proxies unless they migrate or take up other occupations when they mature. In the case of the most vigorous peasant appropriator of ejidal rights in Emiliano Zapata, the second administrator of the *neolatifundio*, a certain degree of continuing cooperation between his sons has been preserved on a basis of mutual interest, but one son is conspicuously more entrepreneurial and ambitious than his brothers, and the family does not operate an integrated "business" together today.

The alternative mechanism, land rental, offers the apparent advantage of greater expandability in space, but an apparently even more limited stability in time. Rental rather than absolute ownership of land is clearly no barrier in itself to the development of capitalist farming: it might indeed be argued that the renter is pressured towards the path of accumulation by increasing relative surplus value more readily than the landowner (Brenner 1977). But rental of land in an individual ejido presents a number of apparently disfunctional features. Production organization is constrained by the physical and tenurial division of the land into plots. There is no guarantee that the capitalist renter will be able to acquire contiguous plots, and the physical infrastructure and communications characteristic of ejidos may be an additional constraint which becomes increasingly limiting as technological modernization occurs and machines replace animal traction and human manpower—hedges and ditches which impede the efficient use of machinery, tracks which are serviceable for burros but impassable to lorries or combine harvesters.

Worse, there is the problem of the legal status of the rental contract within the ejidal system. Theoretically, no long-term contract should be enforceable. In practice this does not appear to have been a problem in the Ciénega, for long-term contracts were made and observed. Heirs to land rented by deceased parents had to struggle, and in some cases are still struggling, to regain control, and they had to pay for premature termination where this was allowed. But stability did depend on a contract being made, and even here there remained the difficulty that not all peasants rented their land or wished to rent long-term. *Neolatifundismo* based on rental was therefore subject to certain limits as a form of direct capitalist production in agriculture, though its manifestation in the Ciénega may well have come close to being an optimal case from the capitalist point of view, at least with respect to the degree of predictability and stability in control over land which it offered.

An emphasis on the malign role and bad faith of the post-Cardenista state is not, however, a perfectly satisfactory starting-point for an analysis of the development of ejidos after 1940. It was scarcely the case that the Cardenista policy, as implemented in the Ciénega, had succeeded in justifying itself in terms of the criteria adopted by its own supporters, and the debates and conflicts over the way the ejidal sector should develop continued into the 1940s. Indeed, the picture of ejidal sector in the Ciénega which emerges from the study by the agronomist José Zaldivar Flores is not an inspiring one, even allowing for the author's distinct bias towards technocracy and contempt for peasant rejection of the eminent rationalities of cooperation.

Less than 50% of the money which the Banco Ejidal had loaned to local societies in the period 1936-1940 had been recovered, and it was hard to escape the conclusion that an improvement in the situation would require not only reorganization of the ejidos themselves, but a considerable expansion of both the funds and personnel of the Bank. The choice was not therefore one of continuing on the course set by Cárdenas versus abandoning the peasants (or the majority of the peasants) to their fate. It was really a choice between abandoning the peasants to market forces or revitalizing and reorientating the Cardenista reform. Commentators like Zaldivar Flores did not, of course, envisage a radical type of reform which would have orientated itself towards politicizing the peasantry. Along with technical improvements to methods of cultivation and mechanization, and a cultural campaign to convince the peasantry that their national duty lay in maximizing the marketable surplus, they proposed such unpalatable measures as general purges of unproductive and absent title holders from the ejidal rolls, coupled with the placing of administration in the hands of technical personnel, "who would act like hacienda administrators, that is, considering each ejido as a whole" (1942:75). The drift of this proposal was to increase direct supervision of the productive process and the global control of the bank over the harvest, allowing the individual peasant to conserve his or her individual plot, but preventing such undesirable practices as sales of grain *al tiempo* by carefully controlled cash advances.

It is easy to dismiss the proposals of a Zaldivar Flores as blatant technocracy and a betrayal of *Cardenismo*'s broader social conception of land reform. In fact the agronomist recognizes the social functions of the official credit system. He is simply pursuing the logic of *Cardenismo*'s own proposal that the ejidal system produce maximal commercial surpluses and provide the basis for agricultural modernization, realizing technical rationality alongside social justice. No such advances had been made or seemed likely to be made, in the Ciénega in 1942 without major reforms. Even technocratic reforms were not on the agenda financially or politically at any level at that time, and Cárdenas himself had dampened down the voices that advocated more radical courses. It can, as I suggested earlier, be argued that collectivism was more successful in other regions, and that the situation was all the more adverse here because of the absence of thoroughgoing popular mobilization in the Ciénega. But if the collectivist experiment was at least partly sabotaged by an emergent local oligarchy incorporating the Cardenista leadership itself, then it is difficult to argue that the root of the peasantry's problems after 1940 lay in the changing policies of the national state, or in a reassertion of their social power by elements of national or international capitalism. It lay in the peasantry's inability to reassert itself politically in the 1940s and 1950s, given the dual legacy of *Cardenismo*: a degree of economic failure, coupled with a greater degree of political success in terms of control of the masses. It would be some considerable time before large-scale grass roots pressure from the countryside would reemerge as a factor in Mexican politics. That it did reemerge was admittedly a function of the post-Cardenista agrarian policy, but the most interesting question, even today, remains the reasons for Mexico's apparent capacity to control and suppress its unresolved social contradictions.

As Zaldivar Flores conceded, individual peasants often chose to seek finance from the private merchants and usurers, the *particulares*, rather than from the Banco Ejidal, whose advances often failed to arrive opportunely and whose practices of repayment were inflexible. There was a spontaneous tendency on the part of many ejidatarios to withdraw from dependence on Bank finance before the availability of that finance was radically reduced in the mid-1940s. Even people who saw themselves as Cardenistas explained how they had found the official system "inconvenient" and turned to other sources of finance for their *parcelas*. Nor, of course, did recourse to *particulares* begin with the creation of an individual ejido. It was part of daily existence for peons working their *ecuaros* under the hacienda, and the ejidatarios had sown their hectare of wheat, chickpea or beans in their plot of temporal land in the collective phase of the ejido. The ranks of the *agraristas* themselves had contained several such *particulares*, the most notable being the distantly related Federico and Pablo Andrade, whose heirs remain ejidatarios of Emiliano Zapata and Villamar today.

In seeking to trace and explain the particular form of reexpansion of private capital characteristic of the Ciénega in the two decades after 1940, we should examine both the general features of peasant dependence on merchant-usurer capital and the specific factors which led this region in the direction of *neolatifundismo*, albeit *neolatifundismo* of a specific type. There is no doubt that the ejido of Emiliano Zapata was the core of the neolatifundist's domain—the community which was the basis for all his subsequent expansion—and it is therefore tempting to point to dependence as a micro-cultural characteristic of the ex-*peones*. This may, however, prove a somewhat facile correlation, as we will see.

MERCHANT CAPITALISM AS SOCIAL PROCESS

The term *"particular"* is the one most frequently used by the peasants themselves to refer to merchant capitalists with whom they have relationships. The expression *"prestamista"* might be used of some who regularly loaned money at interest within the village, but would not normally be applied to the relationship between ejidatario and merchant-money lender. The term *"acaparador"* is also part of the community's vocabulary, but it is more typically used to refer to large-scale grain traders to whom people sometimes sell their harvests today, without receiving more general financial support. When referring to the neolatifundist Guaracheños frequently use the term *"patrón,"* and some referred to relationships with other merchants financing their production in these terms. English terms like "usurer" or "merchant" are not well-suited to conveying the full import of the kinds of relationship we are about to analyze (see also Linck 1982). The first is morally loaded, but not loaded in quite the right way, while the second is too "economic." The advantage of the term *particular* is that it can convey various levels of significance, and presents the phenomenon we wish to analyze as a total social fact, which is precisely how it should be understood.

The individual ejido of Emiliano Zapata was a late addition to a system of individual peasant cultivation which was already well established in the larger region, and we have already noted one of the elements of private capital which was seeking to reorganize the new agricultural regime, namely the wheat mills. Now that it was necessary to deal with a plethora of peasant cultivators who were theoretically free to use the land as they wished, whole new problems of organization faced the mills, which had to ensure both that land continued to be sown in wheat, and that levels of production per hectare were maintained. They responded by appointing local agents, working on a commission basis, like Don Pancho in Villamar. Such representatives were commercial intermediaries, who continued to work on their own account in the maize market. Only Don Dámaso's mill adopted the radical strategy of offering large cash advances to clients who were supervised directly by its agents, a strategy which gave them advance control of the harvest and made it available at half the free market price. Other commercial intermediaries offered "help" with the direct costs of cultivation, and might loan a modest amount of cash as well as seed against a repayment *a la dobla* at harvest time, but with the exception of Don Dámaso, none sought a large-scale, systematic control by encouraging large-scale peasant indebtedness, until the future neolatifundist, whom I will call Don Gabriel, set to work in Guaracha.

All local commercial intermediaries perform a common function in a decentralized system of peasant agriculture. They articulate the peasant agricultural sector to the rest of society, and act as an instrument for intensifying peasant labor and increasing the level of peasant commercial production. Peasant agriculturalists might, in principle, use their *parcelas* as the basis for achieving a high degree of household economic self-sufficiency, particularly by combining the production of foodstuffs with animal husbandry. In practice, the configuration of the larger socio-economic system made it impossible for any peasant household to withdraw totally from the market, since all households needed cash income to meet some consumption needs, and few would have been satisfied with the quality of their consumption without enlarging their relations with the market beyond some notional minimum point which it might be possible to reconstruct were it not largely irrelevant to do so. Even today, there are households in the village which practice strategies which reduce market dependence at the price of a quality of consumption that earns them a significant social stigma as badly clothed and "unsociable" members of the community.

But beyond the consumption problem, which I will examine in more detail below, was the problem of *production* without cash. Many basic tasks remained labor intensive, and it was not easy for the ejidatarios to manage the complete cycle of cultivation without recourse to hired labor. Again, there were differences in degree between households in this respect, and in the very early days there was almost certainly more scope for deployment of family labor and reciprocal labor exchanges between households than in later periods. All that needs to be established at the outset is that the size of the marketed surplus of the peasant farm need not approach the maximum level attainable under given social and technological conditions, even if most farmers in a given community of cultivators are inclined to produce something for the market.

The *particular* not only "helped" the undercapitalized peasant farm find the resources it lacked in order to sustain production. The burden of debt and disguised interest increased the volume of product which the peasant had to produce to meet his obligations, and this process intensified if he was, in fact, unable to repay his debts fully at the end of the agricultural cycle. The particular was therefore at one level what Preobrazhenski (1925) termed a "transmission pump" for extracting the marketable surplus. To some extent, there might be competition and conflict of interest between different factions of capital with regard to which crops the peasants produced and how they used their land, and there might be conflicts of interest between local *particulares* and more powerful capitalists in the longer term. But in the most general sense, usury fulfills a vital function, and the local merchant capitalist is the key agent in the maintenance of commercial production in a decentralized peasant agricultural regime because he has the possibility of building a social network of personal clientage relations vital to establishing and deepening capitalist control over peasant surplus labor. Merchant capital does not simply find the peasant a passive victim and enslave him: it is not an abstract and impersonal force, but a personal and active form of capitalism, needing social skills and stratagems to maximize the advantage appropriated from the service offered. After all, the best clients are not the very poorest, those whose productive capacity is most exiguous, but those who can be guaranteed to cover both the debt and the interest due.

In the first years of the ejido, there were several *particulares* at work in the ejido besides the agents of the wheat mills, and they financed a range of crops. Don Daniel from San Antonio Guaracha retired in the early 1940s and went to live in Jiquilpan. From Jaripo came Don Reynaldo, "El Sordo," whose capital came from migration to the U.S. He bought cattle and a private property in his natal village and then began to expand into the commercial sphere. In Emiliano Zapata, Don Reynaldo encountered a poor but ambitious young man whom I will call Santiago, who subsequently became administrator of Don Gabriel's *neolatifundio*. Santiago's father was an ejidatario and had relatives in Jaripo. Santiago himself did not as yet even have a house of his own, but he had the reputation of being a hard worker, and Don Reynaldo advanced him money to sow rented *parcelas*. Santiago's cultivation went well, but it is said that he refused to repay his *patrón* when the time came to settle accounts. Don Reynaldo was illiterate, and had not drawn up a formal contract. There are various other stories about how people who subsequently became rich peasants got their start in life, all equally stereotypic examples of the kinds of dreams and frustrations poor people harbor. We should obviously treat them with skepticism. In Santiago's case, it is quite evident that the primary basis for his subsequent wealth was his relationship with Don Gabriel, which spanned the period of the apogee of the *neolatifundio*.

What is certainly clear is that the role of *particular* entailed a certain amount of physical as well as economic risk. The case of the *agrarista* leader Federico Andrade was admittedly entangled in politics, but Pablo Andrade of Villamar was killed in less ambiguous circumstances. He loaned maize to those who sowed *ecuaros*, and died at the hands of a client up in the hills while trying to collect his due at the time of the harvest. Yet such events were the exception rather than the rule. The *particular* enjoyed an ambiguous status within the community, and the relationship was conventionally described as "help" even as it was recognized as a type of exploitation arising from the fact that the *particular* had capital and the client had needs. Consider, for example, the following, at first sight surprising, assessment of Federico Andrade offered by Don Cleofas Prado, one of the few young non-migrant *peones* who joined the Cardenista *agraristas* at the outset of the struggle:

> [In the period of the collective, in the one ha. subsistence plots] people began to sow other crops—a hectare of wheat, chickpea or beans. We did all right and Federico Andrade was giving us credit: one hanega of maize repaid with two in the *ecuaros*. That's how we were living. He played it straight with us. My father or someone else would go to him and say: "Federico, I don't have maize for the family." And he'd say: "There's your maize, take an hanega or two." If that man had lasted longer, he'd have ended up as *patrón*, because he was there when you were sowing.

Federico was therefore seen as helping by guaranteeing family subsistence and providing the element of security previously secured through the hacienda *raya*. Though the notion of help is quite general throughout peasant communities in Michoacán and elsewhere, the equation between such help and the role of *patrón* does suggest that even those peasants most committed to emancipation from peonage were far from rejecting a notion of patronage based on a more freely contracted kind of personal dependence. The quotation also reveals the personal qualities required of a successful *patrón*. Federico "played it very straight." He showed a personal interest in his clients, and could be counted on. This aspect comes out even more forcefully in the accounts people gave me of the "nice personal style" of the man who did eventually become their "only *patrón*," the future neolatifundist, Don Gabriel. He was "very attentive," always asking about the family, remembering little details about individual members of one's household. His manner of speaking was cultured, but not in a way which emphasized social distance and humbled people. Many think, incorrectly, according to Don Gabriel himself, that he had studied to be a priest in the seminary in Zamora. Don Gabriel's easy manner was a point of no small significance in a world in which the peones experienced authoritarianism, abuse of power and corruption under the hacienda, and equally arbitrary, abusive and even more socially distanced exercise of authority by the representatives of the national state in the early days of the ejido. In Guaracha, the *particulares* may well have found an ideal ideological context for the rapid expansion of their control for the reasons already given. But Don Gabriel was able to drive out all external competitors, or at any rate reduce their competition to virtual insignificance, for a remarkably long period of time. A few Guaracheños did succeed in continuing to operate, on a very small scale, through the 1950s and 1960s, financing the cultivation of a few *parcelas*, buying a small proportion of the ejidal harvest. One of the most successful was an early U.S. migrant who had also worked in sugar mills in Guaracha and elsewhere, who specialized in financing ejidatarios from Cerrito Cotijaran and bought a warehouse in the center of Emiliano Zapata. But even Don Pancho from Villamar, former representative of the Zamoran wheat mills and now a major local purchaser of maize, remarked ruefully that Don Gabriel must indeed have been favored by the Almighty to corner such a share of the local business and virtually shut persons such as himself out of Emiliano Zapata.

To understand Don Gabriel's strategy we should examine the mechanisms of exploitation involved in the merchant capitalist's "help" to the peasant at a more abstract level, and relate the ature of a particular merchant capitalist strategy to the different positions in the larger hierarchy of regional and interregional commerce which different local *particulares* enjoyed. Evidently an operator like Federico Andrade was simply a local intermediary, selling either to peasant families, or to other merchants operating on a larger scale. His business was based on maize. Those large merchants who could amass large quantities of grain in their warehouses could make profits by speculating against interregional differential price movements, a source of profit denied to Federico. Even Don Gabriel started his business from virtually nothing, and while his staggering success in extending his control over Emiliano Zapata and neighboring ejidos enabled him to amass vastly greater quantities of grain than the likes of Federico in the warehouses he built in San Antonio, he has never been in quite the same league as the really big regional grain merchants. This may well have influenced his decision to concentrate on direct production rather than simply commercialization of a variety of crops.

The economic possibilities of *particulares* rest on the scale of their operations and level of capitalization (or terms under which they have access to external finance). The basic determinant of the rate of profit is the difference between cost price and final selling price on the grain they appropriate, assuming that loans in both money and kind are repaid in grain, as they invariably were in this context. Ignoring the possibility of merchants influencing the price of grain in final consumer markets by hoarding or other monopolistic practices, the key element in profit is the merchant's ability to use advances against the harvest to secure a greater proportion of the total peasant product at a favorable price, that is, a price which is favorable relative to the market rate ruling locally at the time of the harvest.

Assuming that all advances are repaid *a la dobla*, with a harvest of 100 hanegas and an advance of 10 hanegas, the *particular* collects 20 hanegas, and leaves the producer 80. Doubling the advance leaves the producer with 60 and the merchant with 40 hanegas. If the ultimate sale price per hanega is five pesos, and the purchase price for maize at the time of the harvest is three pesos, the profit in the second case also doubles, from 70 to 140 pesos. In money terms, for an investment which has increased 30 pesos, the profit has increased 70 pesos. From the producer's side, assuming he sells the "free" part of his harvest at the local price, the *utilidad* received is 240 pesos in the first case and 180 pesos in the second.

If the producer sells to the same merchant who made him the advance, then the merchant gains from this part of the transaction too, though his profit here arises solely from a monopolistic advantage in the sphere of circulation *vis-à-vis* the direct producer. Unless he enjoys another major source of income, the peasant cannot hoard his grain himself until the price improves later in the year in the same region, and it is even less likely that he could meet the costs of shipping it to a region where the local price is better. Both these factors give the merchant monopoly power as a commercial intermediary, though the second involves him in additional direct economic cost, and the economic return on hoarding to speculate against the price system should theoretically include a discount for any possible loss of income from capital tied up in stocks. Such considerations do not, however, affect the basic conclusions I wish to draw. To summarize the two cases in more detail:

1st Case

To the producer: 80 hanegas, value 240 pesos

To the merchant: 20 hanegas, value 100 pesos, less 30 pesos advanced, yields a profit of 70 pesos. Adding a further profit from the sale of the producer's "free" 80 anegas, of 160 pesos, yields a **total profit** of 230 pesos.

Total investment is 30 + 240 = 270, and **total value realized** is 500.

2nd Case

To the producer: 60 hanegas, value 180 pesos

To the merchant: 40 hanegas, value 200 pesos, less 60 pesos advanced, yields a profit of 140 pesos. Adding a further profit from the sale of the "free" 60 anegas, an additional 120 pesos, yields a **total profit** of 260 pesos.

Total investment is 60 + 180 = 240 and **total value realized** is again 500.

Assuming that all sales take place in the same region, the increase in the merchant's profit between the two cases is due to the increase in his advance, given the seasonal variability of prices, and the differential capacity of merchant and peasant to delay sale in order to realize the gains from speculation against the price system. Furthermore, it becomes clear that the circumstance which gives this more favorable result to the merchant at the same time leads the producer to suffer a loss of income which is greater than the merchant's gain in profit. True, the peasant has enjoyed the use or consumption of the larger advance, but at disproportionate longer term cost. And in fact, the merchant ended up laying out less money overall in the second case than the first, though it is true that he had to advance more at the beginning, and therefore had more capital tied up while he waited for the harvest.

There are thus two mechanisms of capital accumulation at work in this type of indirect control over peasant production by merchant capital. The first arises from the disguised interest charged on the advance returned *a la dobla*, and its basis is the peasant household's need for credit both to produce and to consume. The merchant's profit via the first mechanism is amplified by the second (price) mechanism based on commercial monopoly, which is the sole mechanism at work when the merchant profits from his purchase of the "free" part of the harvest. It is evident from the two cases above that the merchant's global profit on the same total volume of grain purchased increases as the contribution of the first mechanism is intensified. That is, other things being equal, the greater the size of the advance, the greater the merchant's profit.

Logically, this effect might be vitiated were there some alternative type of investment opportunity for the extra money tied up in the larger advance which paid a superior return. Under contemporary conditions this becomes a significant qualification, since there are innumerable speculative opportunities in formal and informal financial markets which yield good returns, along with real estate and other urban investments, though entry into most of these spheres requires substantial initial capital and such alternatives would not be relevant to the epoch we are discussing. The actual rate of return here is also heavily influenced by the extent of price differentials and the extent to which the merchant is in a position to exploit them by operating on an interregional scale himself rather than reselling to other intermediaries, for example. The proportion of the value difference realized between the crop leaving the *parcela* and reaching the final consumer which can be appropriated by a particular commercial intermediary depends on his place in the larger commercial hierarchy.

But it is, of course, the producer who ultimately pays the price for the increase in the merchant's profit based on increasing the size of the advance. In our numerical example, the producer loses 30 pesos of income in the second case which appear to have disappeared from the accounts, since the peasant loses 60 pesos overall, while the merchant only increases his profit by 30 pesos overall. These disappearing pesos represent an increased social cost of production, paid entirely by the producer in the form of an overall reduction in annual income. In the first case he received an advance in money or corn worth 30 pesos, to be added to an income of 240 pesos from the harvest, yielding total incomings of 270 pesos. In the second he was advanced 60 pesos, but only received 180 at harvest time, yielding a total of 240 pesos. What this calculation corresponds to in reality is a social process whereby producers met their immediate consumption needs at the cost of becoming even more dependent on their *patrón* in the next cycle. It contains the possibility of a cumulative process: as the size of the advance tends to creep up, so the "free" part of the harvest falls, creating a vicious circle of spiralling indebtedness, falling peasant income, and rising mercantile profit. Don Gabriel's genius was to realize that possibility, actively encouraging the ejidatarios to ask for larger advances, until the vast majority of them fell into a relationship of debt-peonage to a new *patrón*.

A NEW HACIENDA?

Like Daniel Ravelos, Don Gabriel came from San Antonio, where he still lives, though he also owns urban properties elsewhere. He was distantly related to the family of the ex-administrators of the San Antonio branch of the hacienda, but his parents had been relatively poor, and his father left for the U.S. in 1918, to return only in the year of his death, brought back by a son who was now a millionaire who could afford to take a vacation in the United States. It appears that Don Gabriel's father, like many long-term migrants, established a second family in the North, but he continued to remit money to Gabriel's mother, who opened a general store and put part of the income she received to work as a money-lender.

Female money-lenders are quite common in the Ciénega, as elsewhere, but their sphere of operations is generally restricted to purely monetary transactions within the villages. After the death of Pablo Andrade, for example, his widow became a major source of loans to would-be international labor migrants, a very risky business in which rates of interest are generally higher than the *a la dobla rate* normal in agriculture. Defaults were frequent, since some of those who went *al Norte* never returned. In addition to this type of business, the female money-lender will help out with family expenses, and women often take the initiative in soliciting small loans. Female *prestamistas* did not generally enter the agricultural sphere, but Don Gabriel's mother was willing to enlarge her sphere of operations, and her young son was eager to help her. Like many boys whose fathers had left for the North, Gabriel became notional "head of the family," but unlike most of the rest he had a precocious seriousness of mind and evident intellectual gifts which made him seem older than his years. From the age of ten he had enjoyed visiting the peasant farmers of Guaracha and observed other *particulares* at work. His mother sent him to study in Zamora, but he continued to visit the ejido whenever he had the opportunity and by the age of fifteen was already acting as her agent in arranging loans and buying grain. According to his own account, he decided, with mixed feelings, to abandon plans for a professional career, and set up business on his own in 1947, "helping" the ejidatarios and buying grain *al tiempo*.

Gabriel bought a truck and transported grain to Zamora, Guadalajara and Mexico, where he also bought clothing for resale locally. He would reach home at midnight, only to leave again at five in the morning. Even forty years later, Don Gabriel's dedication to work is grudgingly conceded by even his greatest detractors, and it is no trivial matter, since there are few rags to riches stories in the private sector in this part of the world which have not been based on a high degree of personal asceticism. Don Gabriel's entry into Emiliano Zapata was made somewhat easier by the fact that several of the leading *particulares* of the early 1940s retired or died in the course of the decade. But competition still existed, and what made Don Gabriel unusual was that he was determined to eliminate it as far as possible. The desirability of that objective from the point of view of maximizing profit is apparent enough, but Don Gabriel's genius lay in devising a "system" which made it possible to translate desire into reality.

I have already commented on Gabriel's personal charm, that "nice personal style" which was so vital to establishing a relation of *confianza* with the client. He himself ascribed much of his success to his "sagacity" in choosing the men who acted as his agents within the village. The first to serve him was an ejidatario who had been in charge of the hacienda dam and now worked in the same capacity for the SARH. Still alive at the time of my fieldwork, he had always had a reputation for honest dealing, and enjoyed the trust of his fellow ejidatarios. In retrospect, Gabriel felt that his agent's illiteracy militated against his administrative efficiency, but he was ideal as the initial bridge over which Gabriel entered the ejido. In any case, Gabriel needed someone to look to his affairs on a day-to-day basis, since he was often occupied transporting grain and dealing with the habadashery business.

At first, some forty ejidatarios received help from Gabriel, approximately the same number as sowed with Banjidal credits annually in the 1940s. In the space of a few years, Gabriel and his agent were able to offer their services to all who required them. But neither charm nor sagacity, however indispensible, were the real secret of Gabriel's success.

Gabriel fully appreciated the potential of deepening control of the harvest through extending the advances made to his clients. He never refused a loan. On the contrary, when he met someone, he would invariably inquire about the health of the family, the cost of a forthcoming wedding, the prospects of their building a new house or some other matter that invoked the need for cash, and asked whether one needed money. It was always there. A large proportion of Don Gabriel's day-to-day business was conducted through his administrator, but he regularly patrolled the village and ejido in person, to ensure that his personal style enticed as many clients as possible. No other source offered such ample lines of credit, and there were special factors in the social situation in Emiliano Zapata which increased the susceptibility of the ejidatarios to Don Gabriel's tactics.

The housing inherited from the hacienda was poor, and it, like the clothing in which the peons had traditionally dressed, carried the social stigmata of peonage. Recall the pervasive image which encapsulated their relationship with the hacienda: *humiliation*. Guaracheños wanted to improve their standards of consumption and credit offered that possibility. A former skilled mechanic on the hacienda opened a cinema. Though the electricity tended to fail at crucial moments, and cowboys rode the range upside down because someone had forgotten to rewind the reel after the previous showing, people took to this new form of diversion with a passion akin to madness. In this, and a myriad of other minor ways which rapidly added up in what remained a very poor community, the demand for cash crept upwards, and the temptation to sell an hanega *al tiempo* was frequently irresistible. The need for credit did, however, also respond to more immediate necessities. After the eruption of the Paracutín volcano in 1943, there were several years of drought and harvest failure in the region. The free medical services of the hacienda were a thing of the past. Rural-urban terms of trade deteriorated as the decade passed, an underlying secular rather than conjunctural process from which there was only an occasional respite as the new agrarian policy marched onwards with relative indifference to the mounting problems of peasant agriculture. But problems of peasant undercapitalization, lack of reserves and so forth were general throughout the peasant communities. Their effect on the peasants of Guaracha was heightened by the special legacy of deprivation which burdened the children of the hacienda.

The bottom-line of Don Gabriel's generosity was, of course, the apparently reassuring: "You can pay me at harvest time." People used to go to Don Gabriel's house in San Antonio to settle their accounts, at the crack of dawn on the Sunday after the harvest. At this point, those who sowed with the "help" of Don Gabriel begin to reprise the complaints of the old hacienda *medieros*. Don Gabriel made off with the whole harvest. Don Gabriel's books—for he restored the hacienda practice of keeping full written accounts and "made a paper" for every transaction—contained false accounting entries which the illiterate could not challenge. There were innumerable complaints against the *acaparador*'s use of non-standard measures. One old ejidatario described how Don Gabriel had come to his *parcela* with the sun going down, and brought out a candle to read the scales of a balance which had an unnatural propensity to turn its face away from his line of sight. Many described their ex-*patrón* as "Jewish." But in reality, most ejidatarios were going to end up in debt without any use of false measures or cheating in the accounts on Don Gabriel's part. The game was weighted against them when it was played strictly according to the rules, which were increasingly harsh in their effects on peasant income the greater the advance the client accepted. I asked all those who sowed with Gabriel to give me estimates of their best, normal and worst returns with him. The immediate response to the question of how much one got as *utilidad* with Don Gabriel was invariably "almost nothing," but it appears that we are talking of average returns to the producer ranging from five to twenty hanegas in the case of maize, beans and chickpeas, with harvests of up to 120 hanegas of beans, and more in the case of maize and chickpeas, from an eight hectare *parcela*. All spoke of years when they failed to pay, and had to carry over the previous year's debt onto their account for the next sowing. Yet despite the recriminations and accusations of fraud, people returned to seek Gabriel's aid again, year after year.

What Don Gabriel created was a system of debt-peonage in more than a purely metaphorical sense. His advances were the equivalent of the hacienda *raya*, covering the reproduction of the labor power of the peon-ejidatarios and the reproduction of their dependents, at least in the sense that Don Gabriel would not see a client's family go hungry or lack urgent medical care: in practice the income of many households was augmented by the earnings of migrant members. Would-be competitors were driven out by the simple tactic of offering more to those who were tempted to break away. If other merchants offered a better price for the "free" part of the harvest, Don Gabriel offered more, until the threat was gone. With the bulk of the ejidatarios drawn into the net, deepening levels of debt increased the proportion of the ejidal harvest which he controlled directly, and the "free" portion dwindled. Within a few years he became the peasants' "only *patrón*." But Don Gabriel was not content with simply intensifying the established system of indirect merchant capitalist control of peasant production. In retrospect, this was simply the groundwork for the more ambitious type of agrarian capitalist enterprise which was to become the dominant element in his business in the 1950s.

Rural capitalism based on usury and advance sales of grain has a number of possible drawbacks for the entrepreneur. Gabriel maintains that people frequently defaulted on loans. Sometimes they went to the U.S., and sometimes they managed to get credit from another source next year. Sometimes, he explained, he advanced them more money in the hope of recovering his initial investment, but they still refused to pay. Other informants conceded that defaults did occur from time to time, but when I raised the same issue with Don Pancho of Villamar, he maintained that defaults were relatively rare in his (long) experience. He put it down to religious scruples, but it seems equally clear that people generally had little practical choice but to repay and borrow more, since alternative sources of credit were limited in the period of Don Gabriel's dominance, and for many there was a genuine pressure of necessity. At least Don Gabriel would always lend one more. It is, of course, quite likely that some of Don Gabriel's clients got so deeply into debt that they had little hope of fully repaying what they owed. In any event, whatever the actual scale of default, Don Gabriel's strategy entailed acceptance of a proportion of bad risks, since the fact that "he never refused a loan" was one of the sources of his hold over the peasantry and his ability to keep competitors at bay.

Default was not the only problem. Even when he obtained control over the bulk of the peasant surplus, Don Gabriel's position was very different from that of the *hacendado*. The hydraulic infrastructure of the old *latifundio* had fallen into a degree of decay, while the ejidal system failed to realize economies of scale: then as now, individual holders failed to repair their section of roads or ditches serving several *parcelas*, for example, and the old hacienda system of sowing whole *potreros* in a single cultigen had also been abandoned. Don Gabriel enjoyed only a limited control over the intensity of peasant labor, and virtually none over the technical conditions of cultivation. Some of those who labored with Gabriel's help, especially those he financed to sow groups of rented *parcelas*, certainly worked themselves, their children and their *peones* extremely hard, in the hope of securing a decent *utilidad*, though none of those I interviewed expressed any satisfaction with their returns under Gabriel and all searched actively for other *patrones*. But many settled into a different frame of mind. Given that they received such a miserable share of the harvest, if any, they were really only working as peons. Don Gabriel was feeding them, but there was really no point in working at maximum intensity. "We were not really masters of our harvests," or in other words, free producers.

But neither was Don Gabriel master of the land, and this was the root of his problem. If he refused loans he lost his control of the harvest, and perhaps even money he had already advanced if the last harvest had been a disaster. The rate of exploitation of the peasantry under the indirect control system appears high, despite the risk factor, but the system could be defeated by falling peasant labor productivity. It had limited capacity to augment either absolute or relative surplus value in the long term. Under the hacienda, the sharecropper who refused to push himself was thrown off the land, and peon labor provided an additional incentive to make the best of a form of work which was generally unremunerative. Don Gabriel lacked these sources of compulsion and found himself in a contradictory position. Since he continued to finance independent peasant production despite complaints, and clearly made a significant amount of money in doing so, it seems clear that many of his clients did strive to make what they could from the relationship notwithstanding the limited final return. But the problem of those who were failing to cover their debts, or abandoning the land altogether, contained the seeds of its own solution. Don Gabriel began to take them on one side, pointed to the difficulties created by their mounting indebtedness, and suggested that their best course would be to allow him to sow their land in return for a fixed cash payment.

In a system of direct cultivation, based on direct exploitation of labor power in the sphere of production, the capitalist can exercise a much tighter control over the part of the gross product which covers the cost of labor power, and a complete control over the labor process and technical conditions of production. Some, and in certain cases, considerable, control over the peasant production process by external capital is possible, but it can never be as complete as it is under a direct production system. It may also be argued that an agrarian capitalist who does not own the land he cultivates is forced to seek to increase labor productivity in a competitive market, since the exploitation of labor power is the basic source of his profit. The issue of the effect of competition is, however, a complex one. As I noted above, there are strong general arguments against the idea that large-scale capitalist production of grains could be the "normal" form of capitalist development in agriculture in unprotected markets, arguments which are supported by European historical experience. Furthermore, capitalist farms based on rental of peasant land in the Mexican ejidal system should probably not be equated too readily with farms based on rental from private landlords. Ejidatarios are not the ultimate owners of their land, and they may not be in a position to extract any economically significant sum of rent for its use. In this case we are talking of a normal rent payment of 250 pesos per cycle, that is to say, a sum equivalent to less than 20% of the wages earned by a peon in this region over a six month period. Furthermore, this level of rental payment remained stable through the 1950s until well into the 1960s. In other regions, such as the Bajío, neolatifundist cultivation of crops such as sorghum in the 1960s was entirely speculative in character, based on short-term rentals of individual plots, and associated with substantial ecological damage (Díaz Polanco and Montandon 1977). Under the particular conditions created by the ejidal system, despoliation of the land was added to despoliation of the peasantry. There is at least less of a case for reproaching the forms of *neolatifundismo* which emerged in the Ciénega in this latter respect. A process of ecological degradation has indeed been taking place in this region, but it reflects the impact of the wider forces of capitalist technical "modernization" imposed through the mediation of the State on a peasant agriculture which remains undercapitalized. The cultivation practices of the capitalist renters arguably constitute a better husbandry of the land than that of the majority of peasant farmers, at least within the constraints of the technical practices imposed on modern agricultural systems by global market forces.

The replacement of a peasant cultivator regime dominated by merchant capital by a system of direct capitalist cultivation dedicated to the production of the same cultigens is not, therefore, a historical outcome which is unproblematic analytically. We cannot simply assume that capitalists will take over the land of any peasant community which is poorly equipped to resist such a takeover, but must examine the economics of the situation in more detail. Looking at the matter from the narrow perspective of the immediate choice which faced Don Gabriel in the late 1940s and early 1950s, it is clear that a switch from indirect to direct control implied disadvantages as well as advantages. Harvest failure on land farmed directly meant the loss of the entire sum advanced as wages, rent, and non-labor costs of production other than the retained value of fixed capital inputs. If an independent peasant client lost a harvest, he remained responsible for repaying the advance and might indeed repay it in time. The relative profitability of direct cultivation therefore depended on the possibility of increasing the value of surplus captured by increasing productivity or reducing costs.

In weighing up his options, Don Gabriel could derive no simple equations from past experience. He had to formulate expectations about the likely returns from direct cultivation versus the likely future trends in the economics of indirect control. There is no doubt that labor market conditions were as favorable to direct production as they could conceivably have been in the case of the Ciénega, always a relatively low wage area in comparison with surrounding regions. There was a substantial number of landless people, many poor ejidatarios, and many households partly sustained by seasonal international migration, which did not conflict with work on the *neolatifundio* at harvest time. Don Gabriel was not the first, nor the only, entrepreneur to interest himself in direct cultivation in the region, and direct cultivation had been an integral part of his plans from an early stage, if not from the very beginning. But not all successful merchant capitalists in western Michoacán chose the route of constructing neolatifundist enterprises producing grains, and we must therefore include another element in his overall calculations, namely his position in the larger hierarchy of grain traders enjoying profits from speculative commerce.

In comparison with the likes of Don José Pérez of Chavinda, for example, Don Gabriel remained a minnow, so I was assured by Don Pancho of Villamar, who trembled physically at the recollection of a past difficulty with Don José. In more recent years, even the by now vastly richer Don Gabriel has conceded defeat in attempts to enter the ranks of the merchants controlling the distribution of vegetables through the Guadalajara *Mercado de*

Abastos. As we will see repeatedly throughout this book, the limits of an individual's entrepreneurship are set by the monopolistic structures of Mexican capitalism. Don Gabriel's strategy was the one he judged the optimal route to increasing his wealth at the time. His calculations had to include estimates of the likely future productivity trends of peasant agriculturalists suffering progressive decapitalization as a result of their subordination to him. It would obviously not be possible to ask him whether he had consciously sought to impoverish his peasant clients in order to facilitate the creation of a *neolatifundio* on the most favorable terms, though that was evidently the effect, intended or not.

What is beyond question is that Don Gabriel was very content with the profits which he obtained from the *neolatifundio* in Emiliano Zapata, which subsequently expanded throughout the Bolsa de Guaracha, reaching a maximum area, according to its *patrón*, of some four to five thousand hectare, with a separate administrator in each of the ejidos. Nor would Don Gabriel contest the view that his success owed much to his choice of a new man to administrate his empire in Guaracha. His first administrator ended his association with Don Gabriel voluntarily around 1950. He had bought himself several additional ejidal *parcelas*, and still retained his post with the SARH. His aspirations satisfied, he preferred to dedicate himself to his own interests as an independent agent. His successor, Don Santiago, was a man of greater ambition, who combined a charismatic personality with an extraordinary organizational and managerial flair. The success of the enterprise in Guaracha laid the basis for everything else which followed, and while social conditions in this community may have created an ideal context for the emergence of such an enterprise in the first instance, the realization of the full possibilities of the neolatifundist form of production probably owed much to the talents of this individual.

Don Santiago was already active in sowing rented land, and had therefore proved himself as a capable organizer and hard worker, but lacked the financial resources necessary to realize his ambitions. Gabriel offered him a "partnership," expressed in the language of sharecropping arrangement. Gabriel would provide seed, money, and, in later years, agricultural machinery. These advances would be discounted from the value of the product, and Don Santiago would then receive a percentage on the net profit, Don Gabriel bearing any losses:

> I used to give them [Don Santiago and other administrators] a percentage, so that they too would have an incentive to work. Yes, they were very happy with the arrangement, because he who works, makes money. There are special people, and I was very sagacious. I looked for my man, like [Santiago]. He administrated for me, and he was a real worker, very honorable, and my *compadre* [later on]. I'd say, "Right, we're going to sow *a medias.*

We'll sow 500 hectares. You buy the *parcelas*." I gave him the money. He'd set about buying them. Then there'd be a tractor for him to plow with, to sow with. Day and night they used to work. Yes, the fact is that he got a percentage of fifty per cent of the profits. That's why these men are okay [financially] now. They didn't have money, I did have it, and I gave it to them so that they could advance themselves too.

It is, however, clear that in terms of capital accumulation, Don Gabriel's advance was disproportionate to that of his partner through the 1950s and 1960s. Don Santiago's sons also complain today that their percentage was not an adequate recompense for the long hours of overtime which they and their father worked on Don Gabriel's behalf. The older sons in fact have a personal reason for resentment, since their father had expected them to play a full role in supporting him from an early age, and drove them as hard as any peon, if not harder. The boys all ultimately benefited economically, rather more than those of Don Santiago's daughters who married landless men. But the older sons had several reasons to feel that this was an imperfect compensation for what they had lost in earlier years, in particular the chance of a decent education. Don Santiago was eventually to become the owner of tractors, trucks and a powerful combine harvester. But four of his sons participated in international migration like other peasants, and only the youngest was able to take up the kind of professional career which his brothers hope that their own children will attain. It becomes ironic that some of the poorer ejidatarios' have seen their aspirations for their children achieved more rapidly than the heirs of the community's most successful peasant entrepreneur.

Though Don Santiago was Don Gabriel's partner, and did better himself through the relationship, it remained an unequal one in social as well as economic terms. The transformation of a business relationship into one of *compadrazgo* was seen by Don Gabriel himself as a demonstration of his "respect" for his administrator, a public sign, but what was implicitly signalled by it was that the *patrón* honored the beneficiary of his trust. Furthermore, though Don Santiago's share of the profits of the *neolatifundio* helped him to buy more land, and a tractor of his own, his years of working for Don Gabriel were largely a stepping stone to the position which enabled him to accumulate the bulk of his ultimate wealth that of an independent capitalist renter of land, enjoying access to private bank credit as a person whose record of good management guaranteed solvency. Don Gabriel's claim that he provided the likes of Don Santiago with the opportunity to "progress" and an incentive to work hard is therefore valid, but so is the critique offered by the sons. Behind the partnership lay a type of class asymmetry which is masked by Don Santiago's role as a purchaser of labor power.

Don Santiago was not totally devoid of resources when he began working with Don Gabriel. He owned fifteen plow teams, though he had to hire additional teams as he began to sow more land. In the early years, cultivation remained almost totally unmechanized. The only machine-owners in the community were El Chiquitín and his two partners with their wheat harvesters and a couple of small gas-driven tractors. It was only in the second half of the 1950s that Don Santiago began to use tractors for preparing the land, a technical transformation which was largely made possible through Don Gabriel's money. Even when sorghum, a crop now harvested by machine, was introduced into the region at the very end of the 1950s, it was initially cut by hand. The *neolatifundio*'s demand for labor was therefore substantial. Of its principal crops during the 1950s—wheat, maize, chickpeas and beans—the former, which today absorbs less than 25 man/days per hectare, required 73 man/days in 1940, while even maize, which is still generally harvested by hand, required a 54% greater labor input in 1940 (Durán 1982:17).[3]

What Don Santiago brought to this labor-intensive system of cultivation was an efficiency based on a rationalized organization of the labor process itself. He sought out laborers with special skills. Those who were most effective with the spade, adze or other implements formed special squads, and the work was organized so that a single task could be performed on a sequence of plots in rotation within the minimum time. Furrows on the *neolatifundio* ran true and regularly spaced, because only the best drivers were assigned to the plow. This technical efficiency was complemented by a successful intensification of labor exploitation. Don Santiago paid 7.50 pesos for a working day which was theoretically nine hours (from 8 a.m. to 5 p.m.) but was frequently extended in practice. One of those who had worked with him regularly described him as "*muy acaparador de gente*," a person with whom you worked hard and gained little.

It is perhaps a tribute to Don Santiago's ability to manage people that few of his ex-workers expressed any real animosity towards him, despite the fact that some of them harbored a degree of *envidia* at his good fortune, remembering the days when he had been as poor or poorer than themselves. To judge from the performance of today's capitalist entrepreneurs, a successful manager of men can extract the last ounce of effort from a far from contented workforce by moving about the field unleashing a stream of badinage which creates a good atmosphere and creates a temporary sense of equal participation in a common enterprise. It is again a question of personal style and its symbolic effects, though in this context the metaphor of a chemical catalytic effect would also be appropriate. The workers respond to the energy transmitted through the *patrón*'s mastery of both words and the supervisory function, so that his intense application to the task becomes theirs. In this respect, Don Gabriel could not begin to match the skills of his partner, and it is interesting that he was, and is, to judge from comments made to me in San Antonio, seen quite negatively as a bad employer by his ordinary employees, notorious for levels of remuneration which are poor recompense for the hours worked.

Though the national minimum wage is a dead letter throughout the country-side of western Michoacán, Don Gabriel's rate for a cowman, for example—1000 pesos per week for seven days, 5 a.m to 8 p.m.—did not seem overgenerous when ejidatarios paid 200 pesos to field hands for an eight hour day.

Despite his defects, both as an employer of labor and an *acaparador* of land and harvests, Don Gabriel continued to enjoy the ambiguous popularity of the *particular*. Although he has loaned his support to candidates for the post of ejidal commissar from time to time, he has never enjoyed any real power of extra-economic coercion over the ejidatarios. When he himself wished to become an ejidatario of Emiliano Zapata, it appears that he obtained the consent and signatures of two-thirds of the ejidatarios without difficulty. What Gabriel offered, in contrast to the State which had briefly preceded him as *patrón*, was a certain *security*, even if people conceded that their condition was really only another form of peonage. The ejidatarios were quite clear in their own minds that they were the victims of a gross exploitation. But they also saw this period as one which gave them some limited stability and guarantees. The following statement, typical of many which were made to me, expresses the issue very clearly:

> He was a real bastard, he used to take all of the harvest, bought our grain really cheap and hardly gave you anything when you "passed" the *parcela*—250 pesos, just think of it!—but he never refused you. He had a really nice style. And he never refused. He made himself a big millionaire out of what he did here, but he was the only one who helped us in those days.

CHAPTER 6

PEASANT REPRODUCTION AND THE LAND

Neolatifundismo is only possible where a substantial number of peasants are willing to "pass" their land to an outsider. This chapter represents something of a shift of gear relative to its predecessors, since it examines the development of *neolatifundismo* in the Ciénega in terms of the vicissitudes of individual peasant household reproduction. I focus my analysis on the social facts which underlie the apparently idiosyncratic and contingent events of family histories. It will become apparent that certain types of generalization about the social processes of peasant reproduction stand in need of modification when they are confronted by empirical patterns. I also believe that data on the individual cases underlying those patterns have an intrinsic value in that they deepen our understanding of the concrete human realities we encapsulate in more abstract explanations of macro-social change.

Though the emphasis here is on factors which promoted disintegration of the ejidal system, we will also discern countervailing social processes which set limits on its decay during the neolatifundist period. Even during the period of the system's maximal degeneration, a degree of reconstitution was occurring, as new, active ejidatarios took over the land of older ejidatarios who died or chose to abandon their rights definitively. Earnings from migration played a significant role in this process of recomposition, but migration was also a process associated with the disintegration of peasant farming and the rise of the *neolatifundio*. Since migration, internal or international, has long been integral to the reproductive process of a majority of *campesino* households, rich and poor, ejidatario and landless, I give it an extended treatment in the chapters which follow, which also broaden the analysis out beyond the ranks of the ejidatarios. But I try, throughout, to avoid treating migration as "a thing in itself." Another advantage of using data on individual household reproduction processes is that it demonstrates the futility of treating migration processes in isolation from the total social processes of peasant reproduction. Individual migrant experiences were, and remain, very variable, particularly in the case of international migration: two people from the same village leaving for the same destination at the same time could earn very different amounts of money or evaluate the quality of their experience in very different ways. One cannot really say that people abandoned the cultivation of their land because they "developed the habit of migrating," as many people in Guaracha say. Not everyone who abandoned their *parcela* left the village; not everyone who migrated abandoned the land. Indeed, the possibility of sustaining a rural household by means of seasonal migration, often supplemented by income remittances by children working elsewhere, was what permitted the eventual resurrection of ejidal farming when the state intervened to change the conditions under which such farming was practiced. Migration is therefore a facet of a dialectical process of decomposition and recomposition which has marked the history of the peasantry as a social category.

As I suggested in the introduction, there are powerful reasons for wanting to analyze the processes which have continually transferred rural population more or less permanently to urban locations and occupations. But those who remain in the countryside have themselves been leading a mobile, betwixt and between existence, sustaining themselves from a web of income streams generated in different places and different forms of work. The place to start an analysis is with the ejidal land base, because whether or not a household retained its formal title to land, or invested subsequently in the acquisition of such a title, has inevitably played a crucial role in determining its long-term future in the countryside.

FROM *PEONES* TO PEASANTS: THE FIRST GENERATION

Mexico's *campesinos* were no more a homogeneous economic class in the 1940s than they are today. Even the small group of ejidatarios in Emiliano Zapata displayed a degree of social differentiation from the very beginning, reflecting both the forms of differentiation which had existed within the socioeconomic regime of the hacienda, and such extraneous factors as savings acquired from early U.S. migration.

Though it should certainly not be assumed that all ex-migrants, international or internal, had access to funds, a number of the Guaracha ejidatarios who succeeded in farming their land and educating their children over the years on the basis of their own resources without entering into relations with merchant capital do fall into that category. We have already seen how some local *agrarista* leaders set about pursuing careers as *particulares,* making loans *a la dobla* and buying grain *al tiempo.* Other ejidatarios would make loans to personal friends, a small circle of clients, without dedicating themselves systematically to a business of this kind.

Not all those who developed the reputation for "always having some money and maize in the house" had been to the U.S. Some of the hacienda's field workers were kin of local small property-owning families, urban and rural. Such networks might bring one an inheritance, loan or employment opportunity outside Guaracha which was the basis for subsequent success. *Envidias* give rise to many stories of how the petty rich of the community came by their money. As I noted in the previous chapter, one set of explanations involves enrichment through duplicity, but there are also innumerable variants on the theme of accidents of enrichment, many related to the revolution: rewards for rescuing injured soldiers, chance discoveries of hoards of wealth in the hills and so forth. There is a kind of reality behind these stereotyped tales. The revolution did offer some opportunities to make money, and there could be no better illustration of illicit enrichment than that provided by the patron-client relations between successful politicians and peasant leaders.

Someone like "Maestro" Abel Prado synthesized a number of the factors which produced "people who always had money" in the villages: the right kind of social background—kinship links to higher social strata—and an ability to hustle as a broker between peasants, hacienda and urban politicians, skills based on social experience as well as personal qualities. Some of the *agraristas* turned their cause too overtly into a business, and died for it. Others, like Abel, kept people's affection, though not their political trust, by moderating their spirit of enterprise to the levels needed to ensure their children a better tomorrow. Being an *agrarista* was not, however, a guarantee of immediate economic advancement, as those who expected such an outcome in the early years of the individual ejido were to discover, while not having been an *agrarista* was certainly no impediment to becoming a rich ejidatario.

The productive organization of the latifundio also played an important role in determining the economic position and technical knowledge of the new individual farmer ejidatarios. People who had worked as *medieros,* in their own right or as family labor with their fathers, were more used to both the technical and managerial requirements of the individual ejidal *parcela* sown in a crop like wheat. Although many of the hacienda's peons had experienced work as *medieros,* several of my informants spontaneously remarked that such and such a family were *azadoneros* and "not the sort of people who would have had experience with plows or carts." Since residence in the village's different barrios reflected occupational stratification, it is possible to see that there was a tendency for people from the latifundio's most humble occupational niches to fail to survive as ejidatarios, an impression confirmed by the total extinction of certain family surnames with the same association in the modern ejido. The scale of turnover in ejidal rights in the first decade of the individual ejido's existence had a quite marked effect on its social composition, in so far as it permitted the entry into the ejido of a greater number of better-off members of the workforce of the ex-hacienda who had either been excluded from obtaining land rights by the *agraristas* or had continued to refuse to request them during the Cárdenas presidency.

It is possible to refine these preliminary observations with a more detailed quantitative analysis based on data provided by the written records of the original assignment of *parcelas* and information collected directly and indirectly from informants in the field on subsequent changes in land tenure and the fate of original ejidatarios no longer present in the community.

Of the 321 persons to receive titles, one was a single girl aged 16 and fifteen were widows. Of the 305 men, 281 were married, with 11 recorded as widowers and 13 as single, though a few of the "widowers" may also, in reality, have been single men hoping to enhance their chances of receiving a *parcela.* At the time of the original agrarian census of August 1933, a mere thirty-four individuals had solicited land, and a number of ex-*agraristas* remarked ruefully that they had really had to struggle to make up a respectable number, first of solicitants, and then, later, of "acceptable" ejidatarios. My pro-*agrarista* informants estimated that even including the returned U.S. migrants sympathetic to *agrarismo* who had not been included in the original census, and other non-migrants who subsequently identified themselves with the cause and played important roles in the ejido, the numbers of those who had actively preferred an ejido to the hacienda in the late 1930s did not exceed seventy. Almost all the widows' husbands had been *agraristas,* and most of the single men also owed their land to their fathers' role in the struggle or family links of kinship, affinity or personal friendship with one of the *agraristas.* In some cases, though, it was the sons who were leading their fathers. At least one of the original thirty-four to petition for the land was forced to do so by his twenty-two year old son against his better judgement.

Of the original petitioners, ten did not receive ejidal *parcelas* in 1940. One, an ex-soldier without roots in Guaracha, who had only arrived the previous month, was presumably never a serious candidate. Three of the signatories died violent deaths and their widows received their *parcelas.* Another was absent in Mexico at the time of parcellization, but returned and bought land rights in the 1940s, from the son of a fellow *agrarista.* At least one of the others became an ejidatario in Villamar. A few people who had participated in *agrarismo* before 1933 did not sign the 1933 petition, presumably because of temporary absence, but subsequently became ejidatarios. Of those who signed and got land, two brothers were driven from the village in the late 1940s after committing murders, the second the killing of a much-loved client of the Cárdenas family in a treacherous and premeditated manner following a dispute about goats wandering onto the latter's land. Another of the signatories was himself murdered at about the same time. Two more of the petitioners had to leave Guaracha after killings.

Another was a failed ejidal commissar, who lived in Cerrito Cotijaran, hated farm work and maintained himself by acting as a *contrabandista* and charging *braceros* to have their names put on the lists, supplemented by "tips" received from the Cárdenas. His main proposed objective as commissar had been to take charge of the sale of all ejidal harvests. Another lost a harvest of beans after a heavy frost in 1942, went to Villamar for a beer, got on the bus for Mexico, and never returned. He too had been a failed commissar, serving for only twenty-four hours after announcing that "I intend to administrate from my bed." Another of the original petitioners simply abandoned his family and disappeared it is believed, to Jalisco. One sold his land after going to live in Villamar. Another rented his *parcela* from the moment he received it, and others were to rent their land subsequently. Two of the older men died shortly after receiving their land, and the widow of one of them immediately sold the rights. In all, only eight of the original petitioners who acquired land in 1940 were able to cultivate it into old age, and one of those finally sold his rights because he had no sons.

Those who had theoretically been most committed to land reform did not, therefore, necessarily thrive as ejidatarios, and a sample wider than the thirty-four petitioners of 1933 would include a number of other cases where active *agraristas* abandoned their land and sought an alternative livelihood in the cities. Ironically, several ejidatarios gave up the struggle to make a living from the *parcela* and went to work on the ranches of the Cárdenas brothers in Jiquilpan. Others took advantage of Don Lázaro's patronage in another form, through his arrangement of credit for Guaracheños to buy buses to operate the Mexico-Acapulco route. Although the scheme had originally been intended to help those who failed to receive land, several ejidatarios left to pursue new careers as owner-operators or more humble employees of the Line, depending on their standing in the patronage network. But these examples belong to a wider pattern of changes which cross-cut the earlier division between *agrarista* vanguard and the majority of reluctant beneficiaries of reform.

Some further points can be made specifically about the ex-*agraristas*. Some of the original signatories of 1933 were not, at the time, resident in Guaracha. This was in some cases simply because the hacienda had dismissed them and threatened their lives, but some had probably already begun to turn away from the kind of social horizons and lifestyle the individual ejido offered. Some, as at least one case described above suggests, were simply opportunists, who had no stomach for either the world of farming or the demands of commercial life: they saw *agrarismo* as a free meal ticket. Peasants who opposed *agrarismo* frequently accused some of the ex-*agraristas* of being lazy and not wanting to work, with justification in some cases, though certainly not in others. For a few of the ex-*agraristas* the problem was clearly one of a confounding of expectations, the failure to secure general, utopian objectives or their personal ones: they failed to receive the material rewards and public honor which their sacrifice and commitment deserved. Against this, should, however, be set the more positive attitude displayed by some of the other petitioners of 1933 and subsequent additions to the *agrarista* ranks, who set about coping with and responding to the opportunities open to them. Not all the ex-*agraristas* abandoned the ejido by any means, and their energies have ensured that the village's leading families today include people with backgrounds on both sides of the great divide of the 1930s.

What remains to be discussed is the way in which the *agrarista* camp seems to have attracted "men of violence." It would be wrong to point to the cases of violence on the part of *agraristas* without at once conceding that anti-*agraristas* could be and were equally murderous. Indeed, the minority status of the *agraristas* and the *envidias* and resentments which continued to smolder under the surface of social life for decades after land reform ensured them an unfavorable balance in the ledgers of violent death. Yet it is an important element nonetheless, for the violence of some *agraristas,* unacceptable in a community at peace when directed against the innocent, had a more positive function in the context of class struggles.

The "men of violence," *"valientes,"* were "the men who were not afraid of anyone"—in other contexts the folk heros of the community. *Caudillos* like

Lázaro Cárdenas knew the value of such men, and paid homage to the memory of those who died in the cause, like Erineo Manzo, one of a tribe of Manzos who worked as butchers in the village, and whose killings of each other and those who offended them make up a significant proportion of Guaracha's murder statistics in the 1940s and 1950s. A *valiente* might not be pro-*agrarismo,* but *agrarismo* not only attracted a proportion of men of this type, it needed them and needed to foster the qualities of aggression, pride and defiance which formed part of the *persona* of the *hombre valiente* in all its adherents, if they were to survive.

These were violent times, and violence touched the lives of many in the first three decades of the individual ejido. The roots of the intra-communal violence of the post-reform era should be sought in the pre-reform social conditions of the region. One other legacy of the hacienda *acordadas* was the symbolism of armed violence as an image of manhood. But it was not simply the end of the *acordadas* which made possible a wider social distribution of firearms, since economic factors had also limited the possession of guns. The renewed growth and extension of U.S. migration under the *bracero* program led to a massive increase in the number of firearms being carried on the streets and in the fields of regions like the Ciénega. The change in the technology of violence was significant: while peasants could (and did) kill each other by other means, the pistol made the killing surer and more frequent: a drunken quarrel, a momentary loss of control over some remark fueled by a brooding and unexpressed enmity. Whatever the immediate cause, many a life, including an otherwise virtuous life, was irremediably shifted from its natural course by this shift in the distribution of the means of interpersonal violence. Violence in its turn became a significant factor in the economic process: the reproduction of an otherwise viable peasant farm might be terminated by an act of violence perpetrated on or by the ejidatario.

Although the particular facts of the Guaracha case make a focus on the fate of the first *agraristas* intriguing and perhaps instructive, such an emphasis is really somewhat invidious. The original thirty-four signatories were not the whole of the pro-agrarian reform faction, though they included the early leaders. Furthermore, ex-*agraristas* were certainly not the only ejidatarios to fall by the wayside in the early years of the ejido, and since the great majority of ejidatarios had rejected *agrarismo,* we must look for other, more general explanations for the variable histories of individual peasant farmers in the ejido and the resultant evolution of the ejidal population over the succeeding years.

Some of the ejidatarios were already relatively old men when they received their *parcelas,* but sixty-four per cent of the male ejidatarios were under forty, and nearly eighty per cent were under fifty (Figure 1). All the original ejidatarios aged seventy years or over died during the 1940s, along with thirty-two per cent of those aged 60 or more years. The oldest of the fifteen widows to receive titles in their own right, aged fifty in 1940, also died shortly after

Figure 1
AGE COMPOSITION OF 305 ORIGINAL MALE EJIDATARIOS, 1940

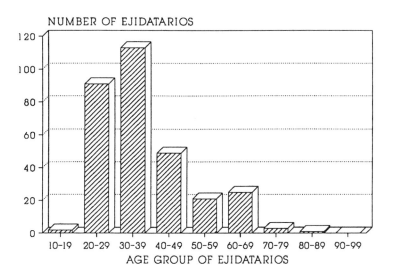

receiving the land. Some of the sexagenarians lived to a ripe old age. One survived until his ninety-sixth year, and five others lived on into the 1960s. A few continued to work in person on their *parcelas* until virtually the moment of their deaths, albeit with resident sons or other relatives doing the heavy work. Four of the older men had, however, left Guaracha early in the 1940s, abandoning their land, and one of the nine sexagenarians to die in that decade died by the bullet. Though a man of seventy might be seen working in the fields with his *azadón,* or following the plow, a significant number of much younger men either did not or could not continue as ejidatarios for very long after 1940.

Mortality accounts for 20 of the changes in the ranks of the Guaracha ejidatarios which occurred before 1945, and by 1950 a total of 39 *parcelas* had passed from an original male holder to an heir as a result of the holder's demise. Nearly 80% of the men's heirs were their widows. In seven cases, sons inherited, three of them minors who were unable to cultivate the land themselves. In two cases, the heir was a daughter. Three of the changes which occurred before 1945 were due to the murder of the holder, and violence accounts for at least 40% of the deaths of ejidatarios which occurred in the ensuing five years. Some of these deaths reflected latent *envidias.* In other cases, alcohol may have played the immediate causal role, given the context of prevailing social conditions, such as the death of an ejidatario at the hands

150

of a federal trooper, or a youth's killing of one of the widows who had succeeded to her late husband's ejidal rights. Alcoholism also made a more direct contribution to the deaths of at least two of the ejidatarios whose demise was not caused by the knife or the bullet in the years before 1950.

The number of female title holders in the ejido therefore increased during the 1940s. This was not solely through the mortality factor, since two men abandoned their families and simply disappeared.[1] A proportion of the women who succeeded to their husband's titles alienated them, as did one of the sons who inherited but chose to migrate. Table 3 summarizes the varying situations of the *parcelas* whose original holders died in the course of the 1940s, excluding the two cases where girls inherited. These patterns can be compared with the data in Table 4 on the fifteen widows and one single girl who received rights in the ejido at its inception.

Land alienation by widows and minors accounts for ten of the *parcelas* which became available for acquisition by persons who had not originally been ejidatarios during the 1940s, and four more of the women who inherited their husbands' rights in the 1940s were to sell them in the 1950s. Another 18

Table 3

STATUS OF 30 PARCELAS INHERITED BY WIDOWS
AND 7 PARCELAS INHERITED BY SONS, 1940–1950
(during the lifetime of the heir)

Widow migrated, alienated rights in 1940s	4
Widow migrated, alienated rights in 1950s	3
Widow migrated, alienated rights in 1960s	4
Widow migrated, rented land but retained rights	3
Widow remained resident, but alienated rights in 1940s	1
Widow remained resident, but alienated rights after 1950	1
Widow remained resident, rented land	6
Widow rented land in 1940s, later sown by son or son-in-law	2
Widow sometimes rented, sometimes gave land to son	1
Widow's land sown by son[1]	3
Widow's land initially sown by kin, later rented	2
Son sowed another parcela	3
Son inherited as a minor, land rented	3
Son inherited, but migrated and alienated land	1
Total	37

[1] One son died in the 1950s, and the land was then rented. One widow was killed c.1948, her only son left after her death and a daughter inherited the land.

PEASANT REPRODUCTION AND THE LAND

Table 4

STATUS OF PARCELAS ORIGINALLY ASSIGNED TO FEMALE
HOLDERS, 1940–1950

Holder migrated and alienated rights	1
Holder remarried, husband sowed land	1
Land sown by father	2
Land sown by uncle	1
Land sown by brother	1
Land sown by son	2
Rented land from the beginning	3
Rented land after early years	1
Holder died, rights passed to son	1
Total	16

parcelas became available for rental in the same period from this source, and one might consider some of the examples of relatives sowing land on behalf of female holders a form of land rental also: the terms under which the land of kin was cultivated might be identical (from the point of view of the share of the product obtained by the cultivator) to those obtaining in a rental agreement with non-kin based on the principle of payment with a share of the harvest, notionally a quarter of the total product, the traditional peasant rental arrangement known as sowing land *a la cuarta*. *A la cuarta* rental did, however, at least offer the possibility of a better return to the title holder than the fixed cash sum offered by the neolatifundist, though it also offered the risk of no return at all if the harvest was a total loss.[2] Furthermore, however we interpret its immediate substance, the help of an adult male relative did tend to ensure that the female holder retained her rights until a child was old enough to take over the land.

Of the new widows of the 1940s, two were childless (and finally sold their rights), and only eight had male children of working age at the time their husbands died. Of these, one saw her remaining son follow his father into the grave in a gunfight within a year, though she was able to bequeath her rights to a daughter's son. In two cases the sons had already migrated to Mexico and the U.S., respectively, at the time of their father's death, and did not wish to return. In one case the deceased father had himself never sown his land: he had worked as a poulterer on the hacienda and was remembered as "not really a *campesino*." Those whose sons did take over cultivation of the plot were not assured of a future either. One son without brothers died naturally in a few years, while another was jailed after a shooting incident, forcing his mother to sell the land to raise funds for his release. Another son subsequently went to Mexico and became rich as political boss of a *colonia popular*, but he has retained his ejidal rights and finances cultivation of his *parcela*. Women with dependent families who lacked economic support from other households in the village were clearly most likely to choose the migratory option; several of these widows worked with daughters in domestic service in Mexico. At least one, widow of an ex-*agrarista*, had not been born in Guaracha and returned, with her children, to her natal community. Those women who migrated but preserved their ejidal rights may not have committed themselves (or their children) so enduringly to the urban economy for several reasons: absence of the kind of kinship or patronage contacts which might have ensured them a better long-term future in Mexico might be as salient as the density of their social ties in their community of origin, but it might also be necessary to consider differing personal orientations to the prospects for a future in the countryside, or simply differing needs for cash. Though ejidal rights were worth little in cash terms in the 1940s and early 1950s, those who had a desperate need for money might have no alternative but to sell their ejidal rights to obtain it.

Women without working men, husband, son, or kinsman, faced formidable problems in continuing as active ejidatarios. Even under today's much less labor intensive conditions, a woman with the monetary resources to hire peones still generally uses a man, preferably a son or kinsman, as "administrator" if she does not rent the land. Even the most self-confident of women does not generally go alone to give orders directly in the fields. In the neighboring hill communities, however, where virtually all the men spend most of the year away in the U.S., women do play a more active role as farm managers and perform productive tasks in the fields generally restricted to men in Guaracha. This difference is acknowledged by people from the plain communities, who argue that hill practices are different because they evolved under the necessities imposed by almost universal annual male international migration. In places like Guaracha, where fewer families are so totally dependent on male migration, few women like to work in the fields, and few men would like them to do so. Or so it is argued. The argument does, of course, implicitly pose the issue of gender roles and hierarchization, suggesting that "normal" or "ideal" patterns are disturbed in the case of the hill communities by economic necessity. There is scarcely anything culturally universal about an absence of female farm management. There are a few women in Guaracha who work with their husbands or sons in the fields and enjoy doing so, and others who make the key decisions and manage the farm's finances, but this is not the same as taking on the full role of work supervisor in the fields during the entire cultivation period. In the hills, pastoral bias and less extensive use of hired labor perhaps diminishes the "problem" caused by peasant women issuing orders to men in the Guaracha context, the root, one assumes, of any female reluctance to assume the role of farm manager. And the need for female farm management was diminished on the plain by the high capitalist demand for rented land, the fact that the household's residual resources could be valorized to a degree without labor inputs. But if female title-holders faced special problems, they were far from being the only ejidatarios to migrate, or rent or sell their land in the 1940s.

THE LAND HAS NO VALUE

Twenty-two ejidatarios abandoned their rights to land in the first four years after 1940, and the number of living ex-ejidatarios increased by a further sixteen by the end of the decade. Thus, by 1950, a total of 38 of the *parcelas* assigned in 1940 were no longer held by either their original holders or their heirs. We have already accounted for 10 of those changes: six of them followed the death of the original holder (five male, one female), and four were sales by women who had received rights in 1940. The remaining 74% of cases, 28 transfers, therefore represent cases where an original male ejidatarios alienated his rights in the first decade of the ejido.

Today ejidal land rights constitute a type of commodity, albeit an "imperfect" one by the standards of true private property. Sales of rights are clearly defined and involve sums of money which are large by peasant standards. In the early years of the ejido, it is not always easy to decide whether rights to land were sold or given away. Individuals sometimes told me that they personally had paid a sum of money for their rights in the 1940s, but people also recalled cases where a transfer had been effected for a bottle of tequila and a pack of cigarettes, or the land was "given" in lieu of repayment of some earlier loan of money. The situation has been complicated by the fact that the land has now acquired a clear commercial and investment value to those possessed of capital. By 1982 a few heirs of ejidatarios who surrendered their rights in the early years had begun attempts to reclaim them by arguing that the change of title had never been properly implemented, though their claims naturally evoked little sympathy in the community.

Within the ejido, there is nevertheless a clear normative commitment to the principle of paying for that which one possesses. But agreement on payment between the parties immediately involved is not necessarily sufficient to gain the community approval which remains necessary for a transfer of rights to be ratified. In one case, discussed in more detail below, the ejidatarios frustrated an attempt by a merchant from another village to gain control of an ejidal *parcela* by paying the holder and appointing a proxy to hold it on his behalf. At least one early transfer which was subsequently challenged by a son of the original holder, returned from Mexico City, led to a substantial cash payment being made in the late 1960s or early 1970s. People also refused to acknowledge the validity of one early transfer of control: the holder migrated, but no arrangement had been made which validated the new cultivator's right to sow the land, which he was seen as usurping. In some cases the land was an explicit gift to a relative or friend, with no question of payment. Where the holder simply left with his family and abandoned the land without specifying any arrangement for its future use, an ejidal assembly could declare the *parcela* abandoned and assigned it to a new ejidatario, who would subsequently become the legal title holder. But I know of only two cases during the 1940s in Guaracha where it is certain that this, legally correct, procedure was followed.

In some cases, then, the distinction between a "gift" and "sale" of rights is not clear, and the number of formal reassignments of rights by the community (or, often, simply by the commissar) cannot be known with certainty. Up to 1950, I know of eight transfers which were certainly "free gifts." A number of ejidatarios also exchanged *parcelas* with each other, sometimes with an additional payment in cash or kind (such as a cow), where the exchange was, in fact, asymmetric, and involved an ejidatario acquiring land of superior quality from a *compañero* who might be poorer, temporarily in need of cash, or in a longer term clientage relationship of some kind. Many exchanges were not asymmetric, however, and the practice of exchanging *parcelas* long since seems to have fallen into abeyance, reflecting the rising value of the land and increasing commoditization of all social relationships. In the 1940s, fifteen *parcelas* were exchanged, the number falling to six in the next decade and then finally to two in the 1960s, the second of which, at the end of the decade, involved a poor ejidatario and the then ejidal commissar, and was subsequently revoked by the former.

In a few cases the purchase of rights to a new *parcela* by an existing ejidatario was the means by which better land was acquired, the holder's original land being sold in one case, or in a couple of cases ultimately given to a son, who had been the formal holder of the bought *parcela* since infancy (as the old ejidatario could not hold two *parcelas* himself). Despite these various mechanisms for redistributing land within the ejido, which were not, in the past, restricted only to the very richest peasants in the community, it nevertheless remains true that some ejidatarios retain possession of land whose fertility is low (because of salinity, for example) or plots on the lower slopes of the hills where stoney ground makes hiring mechanical implements problematic. Their economic possibilities as farmers are therefore limited, and their chances of changing the situation are probably even more limited today than they were in the past. What underlie changing conditions are the dual processes of the expansion of certain new forms of agrarian capitalism in the Ciénega during the early 1960s, and the reexpansion of the State's role in the region's agriculture, which began at the end of the decade. The differences between contemporary conditions and the agrarian world of the 1940s are clearly not simply technological, and it is important to try to reconstruct the early situation as accurately as possible in seeking to analyze the ejidatarios' behavior.

Without distinguishing sales from gifts or reassignment transfers, the thirty-eight transfers before 1950 can be broken down as shown in Table 5.

The predominance in these data of internal rural-urban migration as a cause of male alienation of land rights is fairly apparent. Some of the other categories may be less clear, but before we examine the individual and social causes of the observed pattern of permanent alienation during the 1940s in more detail, it is worthwhile conducting a similar statistical exercise for those *parcelas* which were rented but not permanently alienated in this period, so that both sets of data can be examined together. Some of the *parcelas* which were rented during the 1940s were to be sold subsequently by their original holders or their heirs, and a few were sold after only a few intervening years of rental in the early 1950s. Nevertheless, rental did not necessarily lead to alienation in the longer term, and the temporary surrender of control over the land by rental formed the basis for both the particular form of direct capitalist control over production associated with the ejidal system and the enlargement of the land resources available to individual peasant farmers within the ejido.

Table 5

CIRCUMSTANCES OF PERMANENT ALIENATION OF EJIDAL RIGHTS 1940–1950	
Holder died, widow migrated	4
Holder died, widow remained resident	1
Holder died, male heir migrated	1
Holder migrated to Mexico City	15
Holder migrated to Guadalajara	1
Holder migrated to another internal destination	4
Holder migrated permanently to the USA	1
Holder migrated seasonally to the USA	2
Holder preferred to sow ecuaros	1
Holder gave land away and worked with horses	1
Holder bought a better-quality parcela	1
Holder remained resident, did not work	4
No precise data on fate of holder, believed migrated	2
Total	38

A total of thirty-three *parcelas* was rented up to 1945, of which two were sold shortly afterwards and cultivated by their new holders in the second half of the decade. The number of *parcelas* being rented in whole or in part in the ejido more than doubled, to a total of seventy-three, by the end of the decade, and was in fact, as we will see, increasing at an accelerating rate into the 1950s, a process corresponding in large measure, though not completely, to the emergence of the capitalist *neolatifundio,* which reached its maximum extension during the 1960s.

Since data have already been provided on rental of land by female title holders included in the original group of 321 titled ejidatarios, together with that following inheritance of land by widows and children, I have excluded those rentals, which account for 37% of the total, from Table 6 and concentrated solely on those original male ejidatarios who passed their land to

Table 6

CIRCUMSTANCES OF RENTAL OF LAND
BY MALE TITLE HOLDERS ASSIGNED RIGHTS IN THE ORIGINAL
EJIDO
1940–1950

(1) Holder migrated internally to:

Mexico City	11
Guadalajara	0
Jiquilpan, Sahuayo or Villamar	4

(2) Holder migrated to the USA:

Permanently	0
Seasonally[1]	9

(3) Holder remained resident, but:

Did not work due to age or infirmity	2
Sowed ecuaros and worked as a peon	9
Sowed another parcela and/or had cows	2
Generally sowed half an 8 hectare parcela	2
Had other sources of livelihood[2]	5
Migrated after remaining resident in 1940s	2
Total	46

[1] One of these regular US migrants went to Mexico during the 1950s, and another worked as a peon in Guaracha, dedicating himself to drink after selling his land to his brother-in-law in the 1950s.

[2] One worked in a billiard hall owned by his brother, one of the leading figures in the ejido. Another lived mainly on money remitted by sons working in Mexico, two lived from casual non-farm work in the village, and one traded on his credentials as a former *agrarista.*

others. It is, however, worth remarking that three of the husbands of those widows who succeeded to their ejidal rights during the 1940s had not, in fact, been sowing their land prior to their deaths. One had cows and based his livelihood on them, and another had already left the village before his death. The third was an ex-*agrarista*. In all three cases, then, rental preceded the transfer of rights to the widow, and it will be seen that the behavior of these men does match the behavior of others in the sample who enjoyed a longer life span. Nor were the widows of these early renters necessarily the first to abandon their rights. One retained her rights in absentia, renting to a small merchant from the village for almost two decades before finally selling her title to him definitively. Rights to the cowman's land passed from widow to daughter and remain in the family until today, though the land continues to be rented, as it has been every year since 1940, along with eight other *parcelas* in the ejido. The other male ejidatarios who rented their land from the beginning are included in the table.

In the longer term, 39% of these *parcelas* were sold after a period of rental, four in the early 1950s, three later in the decade, nine in the following decade and two after 1970. Rights have therefore been retained by the original holder or a direct heir in more than half of these cases overall, but the proportion falls to only 27% in the case of Mexico City migrants, the most striking, but atypical, case being that of an original ejidatario who left in 1943 and returned to sow his land again in the late 1970s after being pensioned from his factory job.

A PRELIMINARY ANALYSIS OF SALES
AND RENTALS IN THE 1940s

If we combine the data on male rental with the preceding data on sales, it is clear that seeking work in the cities was, in fact, the predominant alternative economic option for men during the 1940s, though it only accounts for 24% of male rental, in contrast to the 35% of male land sales related to this type of migration in the 1940s. It is Mexico City which emerges as the main focus of migration in this period.

It should be conceded at the outset that some of this migration was not in any sense voluntary movement. Quite a few ejidatarios and non-ejidatarios left Guaracha temporarily or permanently because they had committed a killing (sometimes more than one), or felt threatened by violence as a result of some other *disgusto*. Sometimes people fled to escape official justice, as in the case of two brothers who spent two decades in continual migration to the States, returning only in secret, following a reprisal against truck drivers who drove dangerously through the village. Sometimes the village community at large would no longer tolerate their presence, but some acts of violence did not, it should be said, suffer much communal reproach. More typically it was a powerful sectional interest or supra-village power bloc which drove male-factors from their natal communities. Committing murder, or being held responsible for the act of a son or friend, may be said to account for the temporary rental of eight and permanent alienation of five *parcelas* during the 1940s and 1950s, a small, but not totally insignificant proportion of total rentals and permanent transfers. But although it is necessary to recognize the existence of this cause of individual migratory movements, the actual direction of those movements is determined by other factors which transcend individual circumstances and motivations.

Migration patterns are analyzed more fully in the next two chapters, but a few additional points should be made here. The other internal destinations in the permanent transfers data are diverse: one ejidatario went to Uruapan and became a policeman, another to the sugar mills of Los Reyes, one to Tamaulipas, another to Monterrey. Though each of these individual cases can be explained in terms of some personal contact which provided the new opportunity, the movement towards the Tierra Caliente sugar zone, zones of colonization and the northern industrial city all reflect larger social trends, though ones of lesser importance than the pull of the metropolis, some of special importance in this region, others of much wider significance. Here, of course, ejidatarios in possession of land are participating in population movements which are better represented in the behavior of the landless, though it is important to remember that sons of ejidatarios also belong to that category. There were, in fact, systematic attempts on the part of Cárdenas to find new outlets for the Ciénega's surplus rural population in other zones—in particular in the Tierra Caliente—aimed primarily at those who lacked ejidal rights, though quite a few ejidatarios tried out these possibilities too. Some of Guaracha's most resilient ejidatarios, men who farmed their own land throughout the period of the *neolatifundio,* were not averse to experimenting with other possibilities. A group went as far as Veracruz, to participate in the colonization program initiated under President Alemán, though the one who endured there longest in fact ended up working in the oil fields, abandoning his fifty hectares "when the money ran out." Although a few of the sons of the early ejidatarios did succeed in establishing themselves as farmers in other regions, the majority of those who experimented with other rural locations eventually returned to the village. The general retrospective explanation offered for this decision is that they had difficulty with the climate, though one might presume that relative material reward might also be a factor in the equation.

The fact that even people who did survive as peasant farmers in Guaracha in the long term were willing to experiment with alternative opportunities by the end of the 1940s seems to indicate a marked lack of enthusiasm for the results of the local process of peasantization or even, for some, the peasant life itself. Even ejidatarios who made a success of their own career as peasants were anxious that their children should not follow them. Relative income possibilities in different occupations were clearly important elements in perceptions and final choices, but even the qualitative elements in the choices seem to have been a matter of complex balances. City life, especially life in the industrializing metropolitan city of a peripheral country, has obvious disutilities. But "country life" is, we should remember, largely a conceptual creation of urbanized strata, and rather more congenial for a leisure class than for a pre-mechanization peasantry, half of whose long working day in the rainy season in the 1940s might be spent navigating their way through a wasteland of mud between village and *parcela*.

The other major migratory phenomenon of the 1940s, the renewed growth of international labor migration associated with the *bracero* program, figures much more prominently in the data on rentals than it does in the data on sales in the 1940s, and, indeed, in subsequent periods. Only 7% of permanent transfers are associated with international migration in the years 1940-1960, and only one of the migrants who abandoned the land in these two decades left Mexico permanently: the other cases were seasonal migrants who went yearly *al Norte*. In contrast, regular seasonal migration to the U.S. is associated with 20% of all long-term rentals of land by male holders during the first decade of the ejido, though even here it should be noted that the association between rental and internal migration, predominantly to Mexico city, is somewhat stronger.

The sale or rental of *parcelas* by U.S. migrants is seldom if ever a result of their encountering a better tomorrow in the land of opportunity. One of those who sold their rights in the 1940s may have been a victim of an unfulfilled American Dream. An extremely hard-working man both on his own *parcela* and on his yearly trips as a *bracero*, he was persuaded to sell, against his own inclinations and judgment, by his wife. Like most migrants, he spent some of his earnings on nice clothes, and had especially good sartorial sense. "You look like a doctor," his wife complained, "I don't like to see you getting filthy following the plow. Why don't you sell the *parcela?*" The poor man failed to maintain his earlier level of earnings as a *bracero* on future trips, and ended up seeking work as a peon for the next fifteen years, before finally leaving for Mexico, where he met a violent death at the hands of a juvenile street gang. Though it is true, as we will see, that individual fortunes in *bracero* migration did vary considerably, for most people the difference was one between saving enough to buy a cow or mule and build a house or simply meeting immediate household subsistence costs.

In 1982, seven holders of ejidal titles in Emiliano Zapata were *emigrados*. Permanent emigration to the U.S. does not necessarily lead to the abandonment of rights in the ejido, and a number of Guaracha's *emigrados* actually bought themselves into the ejido after establishing themselves in the U.S. labor market. I should stress that many legal U.S. migrants remain casual workers, but it is not simply this least secure group who have retained or purchased rights in the ejido. *Emigrados* may not have their families resident in the U.S. or see their future as lying in the country of which they have now become citizens. Some *emigrados* who obtained U.S. citizenship with the help of employers for whom they had originally worked as *braceros,* and have particularly stable employment in the northern labor market, with union representation and social security provisions, have become active ejidatarios, investing savings in agricultural fixed capital and renting other ejidal *parcelas*. Even one of the original ejidatarios of 1940 who emigrated in 1944, made his permanent home north of the border and never visits his natal community, retained his ejidal rights, leaving his land to be cultivated first by his father and subsequently by a sister and her husband.

If *emigrados* do not necessarily alienate their rights, then it seems even less surprising that seasonal migration as a *bracero* was more closely associated with rental than sale. It should, however, be stressed that working as a *bracero* did not necessarily force rental of the land. Some people combined short-term *bracero* contracts with farming, sowing the land and leaving kin or friends to look after the *parcela* in their absence, returning for the harvest. Even some of those who stayed longer in the North might have fathers or other relatives who could sow their land and look after the family in their absence. As I have already observed, the line between rental and kin cooperation sometimes seems a fine one, though the peasants themselves have a clear distinction between rental *a la cuarta,* where the holder of the rights plays no part in the production process, and "working *en unión*," with shared harvest. Generally fathers or fathers-in-law were simply helping their children's families survive, without making the terms of the arrangement too specific. But the content of the rental relationship at large was to change as the 1940s went on and were succeeded by the 1950s.

Much of the rental in the early years was rental by other peasants, ejidatarios or non-ejidatarios. The renters included some of the excluded *acomodados* who were later to buy their way into the ejido, and they also included some ambitious young peasants who wanted to better their social and economic position. Such rental was invariably *a la cuarta,* rather than in cash as was the norm in the case of rental by the neolatifundist, and most peasants clearly lacked the cash resources to pay rent in cash, even at the relatively low rate of 250 pesos a cycle which prevailed throughout the 1950s. But leaving aside this admittedly important difference between rental by "insiders" and "outsiders" in this period, it remains important to recognize that even the "peasant renter" category really was quite diverse. Apart from poor landless men who persuaded a relative or friend to "pass" them their land from time to time, some ejidatarios who have never been "small rural capitalists" by any stretch of the imagination were notably active in sowing rented land in years gone by.

Consider, for example, the case of a man I will call Cristobal, who was and has remained a single, working and sharing his harvests with a married brother and his father, who was the oldest surviving ejidatario in 1982. Cristobal obtained a *parcela* of his own as a gift from a friend, in return for a loan of 500 pesos to finance the friend's emigration to the U.S. In 1940-42 he had worked in Mexico "guarding the house and wife" of a General from

Jaripo, who was a friend of a *tío político* in Guaracha. He earned thirty pesos a month plus board and lodging. But the job ended, and he decided to return to the village. In 1943, he went with a brother who now works in a warehouse in Mexico to Santa Rosa, California, as a *bracero,* working a month in a brewery. But the two men ended up in jail, and were eventually released only after the intercession with the authorities of Don Manuel Robledo, the former hacienda administrator. The reason they had ended up in jail was that they had convinced themselves that the real objective of the *bracero* program was to send young Mexicans off to die in a foreign war, whose location remains a source of some confusion to many ex-*braceros*. Each cut a finger from the hand of the other to avoid this possibility. We are dealing, then, with a "simple peasant," an exemplar, that is, of the unnatural ignorance which the hacienda's tactics of control had imposed on its servants, who had nevertheless tried an alternative urban livelihood. His ex-patron still intervened in his life, and Cristobal's father, who had driven a cart under the hacienda, belonged to the non-*agrarista* majority.

Cristobal sowed up to five *parcelas ajenas* each year in the 1940s and 1950s—including some "passed" to him by members of the neighboring Sahuayo ejido—and owned four or five plow teams. He sowed wheat, and borrowed the seed (repaid *a la dobla*) from a particular, first Daniel Ravelos, then "almost all the time," from Don Gabriel, but he did not have recourse to borrowing money, and remained free of debt. He remarked that production costs were low in the late 1940s and 1950s, and he found it easy to make do on his own resources, since good harvests could be achieved without using fertilizers or machinery.

Cristobal was not the only peasant to cultivate alien *parcelas a la cuarta* borrowing from particulares. Cleofas Prado, the former *agrarista,* was even more active in the 1950s and 1960s, sowing up to 32 hectares of rented land. He in fact sowed some of the same *parcelas* that Cristobal had cultivated at other times, as well as the land of his father and father-in-law in their old age. Cleofas, however, did borrow cash to pay peones from particulares, and sowed with the "aid" of Don Gabriel from 1950 to 1958, recalling one year in which his utilidad at the end of the day amounted to six pesos. Clearly the fact that Cristobal was single made a considerable difference, since he did not have dependent consumers to support or face emergency needs for cash because of family health problems. While the case of Cleofas Prado indicates that ejidatarios with dependent children could also in some circumstances expand the scale of their cultivation and gross product, and at least remain solvent in their dealings with merchant capital, in neither case did the extension of cultivation ultimately serve as the basis for the creation of a "business." Cristobal consumed most of his income in transitory sensual pleasures, while Cleofas subsequently liquidated most of his stock of animals to raise cash to pay for the further education which he and his wife urged both sons and daughters to undertake. Cleofas made the boys work in the fields every day during the school holidays and at weekends, to ensure that they interiorized the lesson that a peasant farmer's life was "mucha chinga y nada de dinero," and his hours of toil in the 1950s and 1960s were really only finally rewarded by significant improvements in living standards when several professional children could make presents from their salaries later in the 1970s.

Forms of land rental and intensified productive activity which did not lead to the sustained expanded reproduction of the farming enterprise in the long term were the dominant phenomenon during the 1940s, and continued during the subsequent decade in which capitalist neolatifundist enterprise became dominant. Yet it is worth stressing that even the expanded peasant enterprise which did not accumulate capital might be critically dependent economically on merchant capital. Some of the 1940s renters had a little capital of their own (the ex-migrants, the ex-*acomodados*), though even the subsequent relative wealth of some of these families seems to be more fundamentally based on economic advance achieved through migration or education. Indeed, it seems extremely unlikely that peasant production could have served as the basis for any long-term capital accumulation by itself. There were ambitious young peasants who proved outstanding entrepreneurs, but their achievements nevertheless owed almost everything to the fact that the individuals concerned were selected for "promotion" as the internal agents of external capitalist control over ejidal production. Though the surviving brother of Don Santiago, for example, is, and always has been, an active ejidatario, sowing rented land and buying three *parcelas,* his lesser long-term economic achievement offers a strong indication of the importance of the "external link."

Cristobal argued that people "passed" him their land because "many people had no love of the land, and didn't want to work it." The data on people who rented without migrating suggest that such a conclusion might have an element of truth. As many ejidatarios dedicated themselves to their *ecuaros* and worked as *peones,* as rented while migrating seasonally to the U.S., and 43% of the cases of rental overall do not involve migration. A few of these individuals do not emerge from closer examination of the circumstances of their renting their land as men dedicated to honest toil and the support of their families. Most were, in fact, hard-working in their *ecuaros* and on other people's land. They simply failed to work their *parcelas.* A few of the plots were admittedly of a lower grade of fertility, though the subsequent purchaser of one made it more than a going concern in later years. But some were quite excellent pieces of land. Individual acts of renting by people who sowed in other years can be related to temporary phenomena such as enhanced needs for cash at particular moments of family crisis, just as the individuals themselves sometimes claimed in discussion of their decision. It could also be argued that mounting levels of general peasant indebtedness and poor returns from the *parcela* sowing with the particulares created a rising propensity to rent in the population at large. But if these structural phenomena seem more important in explaining general, long-term trends, it still seems probable that some of the early long-term rental simply reflects a lack of personal affinity for individual peasant farming on the part of some of the ex-*peones*.

Several people, including Don Santiago's eldest son, argued that the "custom" of abandoning the farm for *bracero* migration was what ultimately made the neolatifundist phenomenon possible. Evidently the statistical associations I have presented for the 1940s do not confirm that interpretation.[3] People who saw a direct causal linkage between rental of the *parcela* and international migration tended to be those who had themselves failed or suffered ill fortune as *braceros* and deprecated international migration in consequence. It is true that some people who planted their *parcela* before leaving for the North often did not succeed in making adequate arrangements for its care in their absence. Those who could not count on the full-time assistance of kin to tend their land might return to find their crops damaged by animals. Weeding and other tasks of cultivation, let alone work required for the long-term maintenance of the *parcela*'s productive potential, such as cleaning irrigation channels, were often inadequately done, if they were done at all. In some cases, poor farming practices linked to seasonal migration may have added to the growth of indebtedness despite the counterbalancing acquisition of dollar earnings. But the root cause of the malaise ran deeper, and was, indeed, responsible for recourse to the journey *al Norte* in the first place.

Neolatifundismo was a further stage in a process of subordination of the ejidatarios to private capital, a stage made possible by the mounting indebtedness of the 1940s and the inability of the majority of peasants to accumulate savings and reserves by retaining a significant share of any surpluses they produced. Peasants who had been producing in the 1940s rented in the 1950s and were equally, if not more, active as *braceros,* simply because their economic position was weaker than ever and their need for cash ever greater. A few fathers who proudly explained how they had stayed behind to care for the land others so carelessly abandoned for "the North" seemed to forget that their eldest sons had joined the ranks of the *braceros*. Some individuals might justly be accused of improvidence, but for the majority it was a matter of the mounting pressure of necessity. *Neolatifundismo* was ultimately a product of the overall trajectory of agrarian policy under Alemán and his successors. Though there is a case for arguing that the Guaracha ejidatarios may have been particularly susceptible to subsumption by merchant capital, it is important to see that capitalist interests were actively working to achieve their dominance in a situation in which many ejidatarios were ill-equipped to resist their tactics.

The analysis of the data in terms of temporal divisions into decades or half decades does not reflect diachronic trends and underlying processes with perfect accuracy. Plotting of the data against a continuous time-scale would indicate, for example, that there is a strong peaking of the outflow to Mexico City at the end of the 1940s and the start of the 1950s, a phenomenon of which the people themselves are very conscious. The rural-urban migratory process for the village as a whole reflected the way the collapse of the sugar industry played a specific role in determining the scale of the local relative surplus population at a particular moment in time. The closing of the mill increased the pressure to move, but migratory movements were not, of course, determined in a simple way. The growth of opportunities in Mexico City reflected the demand for labor generated by the post-war industrialization process (Arizpe 1980), which was itself the other side of the coin to what the ejidatarios were experiencing in terms of agrarian and agricultural policies. The reappearance of legal international migration represented, in the first instance, an effect of U.S. politico-economic hegemony, mediated by the interests of Mexico's rulers. Both of these macro-social processes superimposed themselves upon the local dynamic and were phenomena of such tidal significance that the curves for migration in Guaracha reflect them clearly enough, although it is still possible to demonstrate how the relative timing, proportion and composition of migration from different communities reflects local variables. In discussing the phenomenon of *neolatifundismo* in the Ciénega, it does indeed seem necessary to look at the specificities of the Guaracha situation, since Guaracha was the core of the new capitalist enterprise, the place where it began, and the community which turned over the greatest proportion of its land to the new *patrón*—who was in the fullness of time to join its ranks as an ejidatario.

INHERITANCE AND ALIENATION OF LAND RIGHTS, 1950–1960

Twenty-four *parcelas* passed into the hands of widows in the course of the 1950s. Three of these cases involved transmission of rights from a male holder who had not been their original bearer in 1940. All of these men died of violence, along with five others out of the twenty-four. Thus, a third of the sample consist of families whose lives were disrupted by the untimely murder of the male head of household. Interestingly, in half the cases, the son of the murdered man is now an active ejidatario, although only one was actually working the land at the time of his father's death, and did not inherit his father's rights but bought land of his own. And in three of the remaining four cases, the widow still retains her late husband's rights.

As the detailed presentation of data in Table 7 indicates, permanent alienation of rights from the family proves the exception rather than the rule in the case of widows who inherit rights in this period, and there is a contrast here with the pattern for the widows of the 1940s. This tendency to retain rights is not generally a consequence of the female holders having their land sown by coresident sons after their husbands' deaths. In fifteen cases the land was rented in the period immediately following the death of the holder, and in eleven of those it was rented to Don Gabriel. Women who sold after migration in this sample did generally have sons of working age, but these had either already migrated or went with their mothers and found work in the

Table 7

DISPOSITION OF RIGHTS TO 24 EJIDAL PARCELAS
INHERITED BY WIDOWS, 1950–1959

---

(1) 10 widows migrated to Mexico City

Sold land immediately	3
Rented land until sale in 1960s	1
Rented land until sale in 1970s[1]	2
Rights passed to son of husband's first marriage	1
Rented land until son returned to sow in 1980	1
Rented land until present (1983)	2

(2) 2 widows migrated to other internal destinations:

Guadalajara, rented until rights passed to son in 1960s	1
Tamaulipas, remarried and gave rights to daughter[2]	1

(3) 1 widow migrated to the USA:

Emigrated permanently, gave rights to daughter	1

(4) 11 widows remained resident:

Land sown by father[3]	2
Land sown by a son	1
Rented land until present[4]	4
Rented land until sown by son in 1960s	1
Rented land until sown by son in 1970s	3

Total	24

---

[1] One of these parcelas was sold to her step-son, already an ejidatario, by the original holder's second wife.

[2] The holder was absent, working in a hospital in Zacapu, at the time of his murder, and the parcela was already being cultivated by his son, who bought rights in another parcela.

[3] In one case, the widow later migrated to Sinaloa, accompanying her sons, who gained permanent jobs in the Costa Rica sugar mill; the rights passed to the sister of the present holder.

[4] In two cases, the original male holder was already renting before his death, and in one case rights have now passed to a daughter, though the land was still rented in 1983.

city. It did not necessarily follow, however, that women who took their sons with them to Mexico or Guadalajara relinquished their rights definitively, and the sample contains two examples of children returning to sow the *parcela* in later years. On the other hand, women who had sons of working age resident in the village did not necessarily allow them to sow the land. In one of the cases included below, the mother rented the land to the neolatifundist in preference to a younger landless son until the 1970s, when she finally allowed the latter to begin to sow it *a la cuarta*.

Most, but not all, such cases reflected the way the neolatifundist tried to establish long-term contracts with those who passed him their land wherever possible, contracts which seem to have been respected in this community, despite their lack of legal enforceability. Sons who had not been in a position to sow because of either youth or commitment to U.S. migration at the time when the rental began often had to wait some time before they could recover the land from Don Gabriel.[4] It is true that many ejidatarios were giving priority to *bracero* migration and renting their land in this period, as we will see. Some sons clearly did choose to migrate rather than work their mother's land. But some would have done both, and their access to land was not simply a matter of their own choices and preferences.

In some cases, of course, there were several possible heirs to the land, who might compete with each other for their mother's affections and the right to sow the land *a la cuarta*. In a few cases, the ultimate heir complained that his mother had behaved in an unjust and capricious manner by favoring a sibling who was better placed economically, or younger. In a few cases, the mother let other relatives sow the land in lieu of a son, which tended to provoke greater resentment than rental to Don Gabriel. The dynamics of intra-household, kin and patronage relations cannot be reduced to a series of static cultural norms. What seems to be the cardinal point throughout every aspect of this discussion is the effect on the life of the ejido and the family unit itself of a constant external capitalist demand for the use of the land, means of production which the peasantry controlled even if they were unable to valorize it effectively by themselves engaging in production, as a result of their undercapitalization. Neolatifundism, and its contribution to further increasing the centrality of various types of commodity relations in family reproduction, had created a whole complex of normative contradictions, even as it still participated in the various moral and social dimensions of the relationship between peasant and *patrón*. The extent of negotiation over rights to use land reflected that. General changes in social norms and expectations did occur over the long term, reflecting the structural tendencies and more basic shifts in the development of the situation over time. It remains important to acknowledge the persistently imperfect fit between practice and general norm, since this actually reflects the elements of conflict and negotiation through which norms and "typical" practices change and evolve.

In addition to the cases of inheritance by widows, mortality brought a change of title holder to a further 14 *parcelas* in the course of the 1950s, five of which involved inheritance due to the death of the widow of a holder who had died the previous decade. The data are summarized in Table 8.

Table 8

STATUS OF 14 PARCELAS INHERITED
BY HEIRS OTHER THAN THE WIDOW OF THE PREVIOUS HOLDER
1950–1960

---

(1) 7 sons inherited:

Sowed land[1]	2
Sowed land in the 1950s, rented it later	1
Rented land but remained resident	3
Sold land	1

(2) 4 daughters inherited:

Rented land to non-kin, but remained resident	3
Rented land *a la cuarta* to ejidatario brother	1

(3) 3 grandsons inherited:

Sowed at first, then migrated, rights passing to brother	1
Sowed at first, then migrated, land sown by ejidatario father	1
Land sown initially by ejidatario father, then sown by heir	1

Total	14

---

[1] In one case, the son had already been sowing the land of his father since the latter's migration to Guadalajara in the early 1940s.

There are certain idiosyncracies in these data, but several general points emerge on closer analysis. Daughters and grandchildren usually inherit because no male heir is available. It should be emphasized that a holder is under no legal obligation to make a son an heir in preference to a daughter. I know of at least one case where a father assigned rights in a *parcela* he bought to a single, teacher daughter, and quite deliberately excluded his sons, whom he regards as drunkards, idlers and ne'er-do-wells. In the case of the grandsons, two inherited because the original holder's son or sons had received *parcelas* of their own in 1940, and one of the daughters to inherit also did so because her only brother was already an ejidatario. In the latter case, the brother, a relatively prosperous pre-war U.S. migrant, whose father was one of the few of the hacienda's supervisory employees to seek and get a *parcela,* has effectively controlled his sister's land ever since, though he certainly has looked after her materially. Similarly, where rights are vested in grandchildren, it may be fathers who are already ejidatarios who become the real beneficiaries in the first instance. In one of the two cases where the new holder migrated subsequently, the father began to sow his absent eldest son's land in preference to his own *parcela,* which he rented to Don Gabriel, though he now sows both with the aid of a younger son who has become the formal successor to his brother. In the third of these cases rights passed to a son of the daughter of the original holder via her mother because his sons, like their father, had died violent deaths in a vendetta.

In one of the above cases, a daughter inherited because her only brother migrated (after his mother was murdered), but in another case a single eldest daughter holds the rights to the land in preference to a single younger brother, with whom she resides. Nor should the apparent uniform association between inheritance by daughters and rental present in the above data be taken too seriously, though there generally will be such an association for single daughters. In one of these cases, as in the previous sample of cases from the 1940s, rental finally stopped in the 1960s when the daughter's husband began to sow the *parcela* (at the end of a period of intensive *bracero* migration).

The data on sons' behavior also require some further elucidation if they are to be interpreted correctly. One renter became chronically sick, as did the wife of the childless ejidatario who began to rent the land he inherited from his father, along with another *parcela* he was given by his brother, during the 1960s. Another son who rented the land he inherited from a father who left the village shortly before his death was a chronic alcoholic, whose intention to sell the *parcela*, against the wishes of his brother, was only forestalled by his premature death. This gives us a clear indication of the extent to which even intense family opposition might have difficulty in preventing holders exercising their rights to dispose of the land as they saw fit.

Both one of the rentals and the sale were a result of the son's being imprisoned shortly after inheriting the title. The first, heir to a murdered father, had himself committed an (unconnected) killing in a drunken quarrel, but was finally released through the efforts of his father-in-law and was completely reintegrated into the community. The other, lacking the support of a larger family group, had to sell his land, but only to die while purportedly trying to escape two years later.

Each case therefore has a particular tale attached, which constitutes the immediate explanation for the fact that a man of working age failed to work his land. But these particular human tragedies correspond to manifest social ills of the time: the interconnected evils of alcohol and killing, and health problems associated with poor diet, poor sanitation and contaminated water. Illness could be either a direct cause of terminated peasant cultivation or an indirect one. Sickness of a wife or child was the most frequently cited reason why people who otherwise worked their land might be constrained to "pass" it for a short period, in order to secure cash. It is worth recalling that the ex-peones had become used to consulting doctors in the epoch of the hacienda. While some of them explicitly presented the doctor's function to me as an instrument of class control over the quality of the labor power the hacienda consumed, people in this region will consult orthodox medicine and pay what the doctors demand even if they also seek aid from other types of practitioner and consume herbal remedies.[5]

Forty-five *parcelas* were subject to a permanent transfer of rights during the 1950s, three of them changing hands twice during the decade. Four of the transfers were gifts. A single woman who had inherited the rights of her father, the ex-secretary of the "Rafael Picazo" Cooperative, after his disappearance, decided to enter domestic service in Mexico, and gave the land to her sister, whose husband now sows it. One of the widows to receive land in 1940 decided to give the rights formally to a son of her brother: in effect, she was persuaded to give the father of the boy even more secure control over land he had already been sowing, along with his own *parcela,* from the start. An ejidatario who had bought a second *parcela* in the 1940s gave it away to his childless brother (soon to inherit his father's land also) after he had killed someone and took himself off to Mexico. And later in the decade a new ejidatario who had purchased his land from a Mexico City migrant decided to seize an opportunity to emigrate permanently to the U.S. and gave his land to his brother.

It is clear from even these few examples that the principles determining the transmission of rights could hardly be relied on to guarantee a distribution of land according to household need. A single man could achieve effective control over several *parcelas* in the short to medium term, even if the different pieces of land were ultimately divided up among separate households in the longer term. But even within the ejido, other households of similar size and composition had to make do with less land in the earlier stages of their development cycle, and this must undoubtedly have made some difference to their longer term fortunes. Households that were not able or willing to sow the land might acquire title to it. No mechanism ensured an adjustment between demographic composition of households and the quantity of land in their possession.

It is true that concentration of control would tend to be diluted in the longer term if sons took over the cultivation of their *parcelas,* and gifts and sales of rights have often served to redistribute land to developing households equitably in the end. There were also mechanisms for redistributing access to land on a temporary basis, but possibilities of renting *a la cuarta* were affected by the alternative of renting for cash to outsiders, and a number of other variables affected the household's potential for increasing the acreage cultivated. In legal theory, of course, every transfer of rights was to be scrutinized by the community, under the watchful eye of the higher agrarian authorities. An ejidatario who wished to relinquish his rights might nominate a successor, but any transfer had to be approved by the community through the formal procedure of obtaining the signatures of the prescribed two-thirds majority of the ejidatarios. It would be unjust to say that considerations of social and individual equity have never figured in the community's decisions, and that the procedure has always been a rubber stamping exercise. In the period of my fieldwork, two disputes were finally resolved on the basis of arguments about which claimant could most justly claim that they wanted and needed the land in order to sow it to provide their main income for bringing up a family.

This is not, however, the only kind of argument which has arisen over the years. Among the sales which occurred in the 1950s, one involved an attempted purchase by an outsider, a corn merchant from Villamar. This was another case of an enforced flight to Mexico following a particularly unpleasant murder, and the vendor was eager to get cash in his hand as quickly as possible. The merchant had formed a partnership with one of the ejidatarios, and financed him to sow rented land, though on a tiny scale in comparison with what Don Gabriel achieved. He decided he would like to acquire permanent control of this 8 hectare *parcela,* and found a landless Guaracheño who was willing to act as a surrogate title holder. But the community rejected this arrangement, and the merchant felt (and still feels) himself to have been betrayed by his own partner, who subsequently acquired the rights for himself, even though it was the merchant who had actually put up the money.

Such events are probably best left in decent obscurity, but the case suggests that it is always difficult to decide whether a decision is made on ethical grounds by the "general will" of the community, or invariably reflects some degree of manipulation by an individual power broker. The merchant's partner did serve twice as ejidal commissar, though he belonged to the "better off" rather than "rich" stratum of ejidatarios. The fact that the neolatifundist was able to acquire ejidal rights in Emiliano Zapata during the next decade does at least demonstrate that the objection of being an outsider without legitimate rights under the Agrarian Law is not necessarily a barrier, either for the community, or for the supposedly supervising higher authorities. The community wished to remain on good terms with Don Gabriel (some may have felt grateful for his "help," though most had more ambivalent attitudes), and one may suppose that the higher authorities were paid off in a handsome fashion.

Out of the total of forty-eight transfers to take place during the 1950s, nine involved inheritance following the death of the holder. Excluding the gifts, of the remaining thirty-four transfers by sale, twelve had their roots in events in the 1940s in the sense that the holder had already migrated from the village or had not been cultivating the land, in the preceding decade. Most of these cases figured in the data given for rental of land in the 1940s. In at least one case, however, the holder had left for Mexico at the start of the individual ejido, and had simply left his *parcela* abandoned and uncultivated, until the undergrowth was cleared by the new purchaser, an energetic ex-*mediero* who worked with his brothers sowing rented land. One *parcela* had been rented until 1950, was then sold to a young landless son of an ejidatario, but almost immediately exchanged with another ejidatario who put it up for rental again. Most cases did, however, involve a transfer from people who did not want to sow the land to landless people who wished to work it, at least for the immediate future. The data for permanent sales not related to inheritance are summarized in Table 9.

Table 9

CIRCUMSTANCES OF PERMANENT ALIENATION OF EJIDAL RIGHTS
1950–1959
(excluding gifts and transfers by widows and other heirs)

---

(1) 30 holders migrated:

Mexico City	23
Guadalajara	1
Other internal destinations[1]	4
Seasonally to the USA[2]	2

(2) 4 holders remained resident

Sowed ecuaros and worked as a peon	3
Bought a better parcela	1

Total	34

---

[1] These were Jiqilpan, Sahuayo, Villamar and La Palma.

[2] One of these cases involves the sale of rights to 4 hectares of an 8 hectare parcela: in other words a division.

Two of those who at first stayed on working in agriculture in Emiliano Zapata after selling their rights to ejidal land, subsequently left for Mexico as well, one within a few years, another in the 1960s. Both the cases involving U.S. migration are somewhat peculiar. One represented a man selling to his brother-in-law, after he had abandoned the sister, who left to take up work in service in Guadalajara. He had never sown his land, was a heavy drinker and had a reputation for thieving. His son emigrated, and subsequently helped his uncle's brother do the same, using his now dead father's identity. Deprived of his absent brother's support in cultivation, and his health deteriorating, the new holder himself began to rent in the late 1960s. In this case, those who argue that international migration is the ruin of the peasant farm find an illustration of some of their favorite themes: vice, neglect of family, breaking of the bonds of kin cooperation. In the other case, only half of an 8 hectare *parcela* was sold, and this is a very special case, since ejidal land is not, by law, divisible. Here, therefore, it is not simply the payment of money which cannot be legally acknowledged but the result of the transaction itself. The original holder entered into the arrangement because he was short of money, but things were left very unclear on his death, and the heirs of the original parties to the transaction remain in dispute, with the son of the original holder still unable to recover control of the land.

Once these further details of the cases are recognized, the overwhelming importance of the migratory movement towards Mexico in this period becomes even more apparent. One of the cases is both startling, and perhaps indicative. A former commissar left and sold his rights in 1954, at the age of thirty-nine. Reynaldo was one of the single men to get ejidal rights in 1940. His father had left for the U.S. in the 1920s, not to return until his death was upon him in 1961. The father had not, apparently, continued to remit money after the early years, but Reynaldo's mother had cows, and his sisters worked in the fields. The family therefore had a little money, and Reynaldo was chosen as commissar because, unusually in those days, he was literate. The *agraristas* had also helped them: Reynaldo's brother Luis was educated as a doctor and now practices in Jiquilpan, though his sisters are in Mexico. Reynaldo ultimately became a brewery manager, and was apparently a man of ability as well as connections. But his departure suggests that migration was far from being the last resort of the totally impoverished, or of those who had never truly accepted the shift from hacienda to ejido.

If we look at the temporal distribution of these sales in a more fine-grained manner, even making due allowance for the possible inaccuracy in dates estimated by the informants from whom these data were elicited, it seems that the bulk of rural-urban migration was concentrated in the early 1950s or very late 1940s, though a minority of these 1950s sales were the delayed result of an initial exodus which took place right at the start of the individual ejido. Only fourteen of the total of forty-eight transfers of rights between 1950 and 1959 took place after 1954, and of these only two were associated with a male holder's migration to Mexico immediately prior to the sale. Before drawing any final conclusions about the causal processes at work, we should, however, examine the data on rental trends during the 1950s. The number of permanent transfers during the 1950s shows a modest increase over the 1940s, but the rates per decade are rather misleading indicators because of the concentration of sales due to migration in the early 1940s, and even more markedly in the early 1950s. But if we now turn to look at rental of land we find that there is a cumulative increase from the 1940s to the 1950s, since the vast majority of the *parcelas* rented during the 1940s continues to be rented on a long term basis into the following decade, while new *parcelas* are being added continually to the growing total of lands being "passed" by their title holders.

LAND RENTAL AND THE EXPANSION OF THE
NEOLATIFUNDIO, 1950–60

Fifty-nine *parcelas* whose rental began during the 1940s continued to be rented throughout the whole decade of the 1950s. This total includes the land rented by female holders and heirs who were minors and were treated separately in our original calculations, but it excludes land which was rented in the 1940s and sold in the early 1950s. The inclusion of these cases would increase the figure by 10% for the early 1950s.[6]

It is much more difficult to estimate the total number of people who periodically rented their land, sowing some years and "passing" others, perhaps staying longer in the North in those years. I have even excluded some particularly regular "on-and-off" renters in the data for rental during the 1950s, since there are undoubtedly some similar cases which I have not recorded. Many people feel ashamed of passing their land, and it is certain that more people passed their land a few times than volunteered this information to me, usually because those who did so felt they had a specific legitimate reason, like family illness. After causing several people a certain amount of pain by extracting information on this theme from them, I decided not to press the issue in subsequent interviews, since it was possible to approach the empirical question of the size of the *neolatifundio* from the other direction. Don Gabriel himself was happy to discuss the subject, as were his present administrators and the sons of Don Santiago. It is also more important to concentrate on the core of *parcelas* which were rented to Don Gabriel year-in, year-out, on long term contracts, since this long-term rental seems the key to the way this particular type of *neolatifundio* was operated. The figures given below are therefore biased throughout towards underestimating the proportion of *parcelas* being rented in any one year.

A snapshot of rental in January 1950 would give us a total of fifty-nine *parcelas* destined to continue in rental on long term contracts for the remainder of the decade. Another snapshot taken in the spring of 1955 adds a further thirty-five *parcelas* to this long-term group, and by the winter of 1959 the cumulative total reaches one hundred and twenty-one *parcelas*. In other words, since this figure is an underestimate of the actual number of *parcelas* being rented at that moment in time, upwards of 40% of the ejidatarios were passing their land by 1960. An analysis of the individual circumstances of the additional rentals emerging in the course of the 1950s is given in Table 10. On this occasion, it may be helpful to include all holders, in order to indicate more clearly the relative proportion of rental by healthy adult male holders in the overall total.

Though most of the categories included in this table are by now self-explanatory, and the majority of cases corresponds to circumstances already discussed, a few further points do emerge from these data. The temporary internal migration was one of the sad odysseys which resulted from an act of violence. One of the seasonal U.S. migrants listed was one of the commu-

CASI NADA

Table 10

CIRCUMSTANCES OF RENTAL OF EJIDAL LAND
1950–1960
(all holders)

---

(1) 18 holders migrated to Mexico City:

	Men	11
	Widows	7

(2) 3 holders migrated to Guadalajara:

	Men	2
	Widows	1

(3) 5 male holders migrated to other destinations:

Permanently to another internal destination	1
Temporarily to another internal destination	1
Seasonally to the USA	3

(4) 36 holders remained resident:

Widows	9
Other female holders	3
Suffered illness, excluding alcoholism	4
Alcoholic	3
Incapacitated by age	2
Physical disability	1
Sowed another parcela	4
Sowed ecuaros and worked as a peon	3
Concentrated on goat-herding	1
Children migrated	3
Other circumstances	3

Total	62

---

nity's most energetic procreators: married twice, he still had hopes of further issue in 1982, though his wife did not share these aspirations. With new children arriving more or less annually, his family lived in a permanent situation of crisis which absorbed all the cash he could earn as a *bracero*.

His brother also features in these data, but his case belongs to the group noted under "other circumstances" at the end of the non-migrant list. It is possible that this individual's renting was associated with his sons' committing themselves definitively to a future of life and work in Mexico City. Certainly in three of these cases it seems likely that the children's migration brought an end to the father's farming, either because the children provided their fathers—a widower in one case—with economic support on a long-term basis, or the parents decided that they could subsist on the small amount of cash obtained from renting, paid work and sowing an *ecuaro,* there being no point in continuing to husband land which would be passing to others in the future. But the fourth case is not totally clear cut, and the holder's final pre-mortem sale of his rights in the 1980s provoked much criticism: he was still in good health, his sons' commitment to the city had not been definitive when he first started renting, why had he never made the effort to sow in his later years when things improved...? So went the complaints of a diverse cross-section of older and not so old ejidatarios, indicating that their criteria of "legitimate cause" for an ejidatario to cease to be active had not been satisfied in this case.

These data include several previously more active ejidatarios, including an ex-commissar who had sown rented *parcelas,* and had bought rights in a second piece of land at the start of the 1950s. He belongs to the group of four ejidatarios who rented one piece of land while sowing another. In one case, the rental was to raise cash for children's educational expenses. In another case, as already noted above, a father gained effective control of land inherited by a son from his grandfather. But perhaps the most basic issue posed by a degree of retrenchment on the part of some previously active ejidatarios, the scale of rural-urban migration by ejidatarios, and those cases where abandonment of farming without migration is not readily explicable in terms of personal or family circumstances, is whether the trends observed do not reflect the way a process of decapitalization in the ejido was undermining morale as well as the material conditions of peasant reproduction. There seems little doubt that morale was not generally good, but such a conclusion would ignore the factor of indebtedness. People had been borrowing from Don Gabriel before they rented their land, and many began to rent to liquidate debts. This was, many felt, the intention behind Don Gabriel's strategy, and some of those who rented periodically while retaining residence certainly owed Don Gabriel money. Perhaps some of the permanent migrants left without repaying what they owed. In any event, the situation of the households of ejidatarios in the 1950s was clearly affected by a decade of association with particulares, as well as by demographic factors and changes in family fortunes and income levels related to the migration experiences of household members.

LAND RENTAL IN THE 1960s

The numbers of *parcelas* being rented by their holders either for the first time, or for a second time after a lapse of years, shows a significant fall in the course of the 1960s. In the first half of the decade twenty-five new cases are added to the cumulative total inherited from previous years, but a mere four additional cases occur between 1965 and 1969. Two of these were in fact controlled by the same ejidatario. One was his own, purchased from his brother-in-law in the previous decade, and the other the land of his hard-working, but now aged, father. Five new cases were added in the early 1970s, and five more, one very short-lived, in the later 1970s. A substantial number of *parcelas* whose rental began in earlier years continued into the 1960s, 1970s and even 1980s, so that the yearly proportion of ejidal land being rented did not fall as drastically as the rate of new rentals, but it becomes clear on closer analysis that the patterns underlying the rental of ejidal land in the previous decades were modified substantially by developments in the 1960s. In order to bring out the changing trend over time, I have summarized the circumstances of land rental for the first half decade of the 1960s separately, in Table 11, and then grouped the data for the remaining fifteen new rentals together in Table 12.

Table 11

CIRCUMSTANCES OF RENTAL OF EJIDAL LAND, 1960–1964

(1) 10 holders migrated:

Men to Mexico City	1
Newly widowed women to Mexico City	2
Single female holders to Mexico City	1
Men to Guadalajara	2
Newly widowed women to Guadalajara	1
Men to other internal destinations	2
Men migrating permanently to the USA	1

(2) 13 holders remained resident:

Widow holding rights in the ejido from the outset	1
Newly widowed women	2
Widow whose land had previously been sown by son	1
Men incapacitated by age or illness	6
Men sowing ecuaros and working as peons	2
Men faced with illness in the family[1]	1
Total	**23**

[1] This childless ejidatario also controlled the parcela of his absent brother, renting both of them when his wife fell ill. He subsequently spent some time in Mexico while his wife received hospital treatment there.

PEASANT REPRODUCTION AND THE LAND

Table 12

CIRCUMSTANCES OF RENTAL OF EJIDAL LAND, 1965-1980

---

(1) 2 holders migrated:

Men to Mexico	1
Men permanently to the USA[1]	1

(2) 12 holders remained resident:

Newly widowed women (unnatural causes)	1
Age and infirmity	5
Physical disability resulting from road accident	1
Male heir renting, co-worker brother migrated[2]	2
Cash needed for son's education	1
Cash needed for building a house or other expenses	2

Total	14

---

[1] A special case. This holder bought the parcela, but decided to emigrate a few years later. After a short period of rental, his landless father, an artisan sandal-maker, took it over and now sows it.

[2] One of these is the case to which reference was made above, where a son rented both his own (purchased) land and his father's parcela. As his father was still alive, it could be included under the 'age and infirmity' category, and the son's health was also poor when I interviewed him in 1982. But the emigration of the other son to the USA seems a crucial factor, and is worth stressing since the case demonstrates the mixed effects of international migration on peasant farming. The other case involves the permanent migration of one of a pair of cooperating brothers to the sugar mill in Sinaloa, this time after the death of their father.

A third of the new rentals in the early 1960s involve female title holders. An additional two widows inherited rights from husbands who had already been renting their *parcelas*, and are therefore excluded from this calculation. One went to Guadalajara after her husband's death. One of the original widows to hold rights in the ejido began to rent for the first time when her father, who had previously been sowing the land, died, her son being absent. A similar situation led to a period of renting by a widow who had inherited land which had been sown by a son. Rental began when he was killed, his younger brother, the present holder, being absent in Mexico. The 1965-80 sample also excludes seven cases where rental continued after rights passed to a widow or son who was absent following earlier migration, or to resident widows whose sons were absent.

Twenty one percent of rentals are associated with male migration within

Mexico in the early 1960s sample, approximately the same proportion as during the previous decade overall. Only two cases are directly linked to male migration in the 1965-80 data, though two others are related to this factor indirectly. Even in the larger 1960-64 sample, the absolute number of cases is quite low, and comparison of rates by decades would underestimate the proportion of total long-term rental whose origin lies in the two periods of peak male rural-urban migration in the first years of the individual ejido and the late 1940s and early 1950s. If we look at the 1960s sample in more detail, it also becomes apparent that male migration has somewhat different causes in this later period. The one ejidatario to go to Mexico and one of those to go to Guadalajara were following in the footsteps of children who had already established themselves in the cities. The parents were finally rejoining their absent families. The other Guadalajara migrant followed his wife to the city, as an indirect consequence of his own previous U.S. migration, and the case provides an exemplification of the peculiar stresses placed on family life by recurrent migration to the North, a theme I will explore in greater depth in Chapter Nine. The wife had an affair with another man during one of her husband's yearly absences as a *bracero,* a child was born of the union, and she left for the city in shame. But her husband forgave her, and they made a new start in Guadalajara.[7]

The two cases in the early 1960s where ejidatarios rented their land while working locally in agriculture are also instructive. In one case, the holder went to work seasonally in the sugar *zafra,* but this form of seasonal migration was also a symptom of his underlying problem, a constantly growing family. His wife's health has been bad for some time, largely in consequence of the reproductive demands placed on her. In the other case, the ejidatario worked in the hills with his *azadón* while his wife worked in the strawberry industry in Zamora, making good money by local standards for women. She also organized recruitment of younger women for the plant. Both families have remained relatively poor, and these cases demonstrate the way in which regular wage income and guaranteed rental income may be preferred to the uncertainties of farming by some families.[8]

A quarter of the new rentals of the early 1960s, and an even greater proportion of those in the 1965-80 group, were related to aging in the ejidatario population, though it is, of course, significant that sons were not available to take over the burden of cultivation from their fathers. In this sense, migration, generally to the cities, but sometimes in the form of emigration to the U.S., had a continuing impact which is not readily apparent in the immediate circumstances of the rental. In some cases, sons have returned subsequently to take over the paternal *parcela.* But this was less likely to happen when better economic opportunities were more readily available elsewhere, and the undercapitalized ejidal *parcela* was starved of financial and technical aid from the state. Even where ejidatarios had managed to sustain cultivation during the 1940s and 1950s, the difficulties of that epoch had created systems of household reproduction which promised further change in the future. Though the changes of the late 1960s and early 1970s did do something to reverse existing trends, they have created major new problems which leave the realization of the social aims of land reform perhaps even more problematic than in earlier years.

The most obvious structural change in the situation was the reexpansion of the state's role in the countryside. The official credit system offered ejidatarios who wished to sow their land the opportunity to do so at a vastly reduced real rate of interest, while the introduction of the official agricultural insurance scheme reduced the susceptibility of cultivators to debt as a result of harvest failure. The later 1960s and 1970s also saw significant techno-economic transformations of peasant agriculture, associated with changes in the mode of articulation of the peasant sector with the larger capitalist economy. Chapter Nine offers a more detailed discussion of the substance and impact of these changes, which must be understood in terms of the dynamics of the larger international capitalist system as mediated by political and economic developments within Mexico. At present we need only note the basic shift in the local political economy of the Emiliano Zapata. In the period between 1970 and the renewed onset of manifest crisis at the end of the López Portillo administration, direct capitalist control over land diminished (relatively) and peasant production expanded again, albeit in a very different form, both technologically and in terms of its social organization, from that which existed in the 1940s.

Even the nature of direct capitalist intervention in ejidal production itself had already begun to change in the course of the 1960s. Don Gabriel had never had a total monopoly of rented land in the ejido. Aside from the peasant renters, most, but not all of whom he had financed, a few other outsiders had always managed to secure control over a few rented *parcelas* from time to time. One example was a Teniente from Jiquilpan, reputedly an affine of the Cárdenases. He had offered better terms than Don Gabriel's standard cash rate of 250 pesos a cycle, and "made propaganda" against the neolatifundist's exploitation of the ejidatarios. Other merchant capitalists had tried to establish a bridgehead into Don Gabriel's domain from time to time, by setting up a clientage relation on preferential terms with individual ejidatarios of some standing or popularity in the community. But none of these outsiders made any real impact. Don Gabriel had made too great a proportion of the ejidatarios long-term clients, had offered too comprehensive a service, and had spun the web of debt, dependence and obligation too wide to be readily denied. He was a superlative tactician. Faced with a challenge, he improved his terms just sufficiently (for the moment) to dispose of potential competitors. Above all he knew how to manipulate the language of obligation and the qualitative social bond between himself and his clients, always reminding them that he would ultimately "guarantee" to see them through, to help, to support, come what may: others might not prove so reliable.

No entrepreneur of a similar type could ultimately make any headway against him. His control only finally began to disintegrate when he was faced with two other types of competitor. In the first place, his control of land was finally contested by more powerful capitalists, in particular the tomato growers from the Bajío and subsequently Zamora. The *jitomateros* pushed up the value of the land, and could afford to pay more. This influenced the economic balance sheets of Don Gabriel's enterprise, which had relied on a degree of insulation from this type of agrarian capitalism, now expanding spatially to supply the growing urban market of Guadalajara and the export trade. The tomato growers occupied a higher level in the monopolistic, hierarchized structures of Mexican commercial agriculture, and their arrival in the Ciénega finally revealed the structural limits placed on the enterprise of *acaparadores* of peasant land and grain harvests operating at the level of a single microregion like Don Gabriel.[9]

But a second factor was the growing wealth of some of Don Gabriel's own agents within the ejidos. Once Don Santiago was able to obtain finance from another source, the private banking sector which entrepreneurs like Don Gabriel had done much to create, he was in a position to set up independently, and could take a substantial proportion of his partner's former clientele, since he had been even closer to the peasant clients in social terms, and was directly in charge of the productive apparatus of the *neolatifundio*. It was also convenient for Don Santiago that his ex-*patrón* and ex-partner could serve to deflect the critical, resentful side of the ordinary ejidatarios' consciousness: Don Gabriel had become a millionaire at the expense of poor peasants, and Don Santiago had only shown himself to be a peasant who was clever enough to make the most of the opportunity Don Gabriel's patronage had offered.

In the course of the 1960s, then, the monolithic neolatifundism of Don Gabriel was progressively replaced by a more diversified set of capitalist enterprises operating on the terrain of the Emiliano Zapata ejido. At the end of the decade the state reemerged as an alternative *patrón,* and the physical space available for direct capitalist production was, for a time, gradually reduced, though far from eliminated. As time went by, the emphasis on extensive land rental and accumulation via direct production gave ground to an emphasis on other activities, in particular machine ownership. Rich peasants and small local capitalists came to see the intensive production of high-value vegetable crops as the optimal, if not necessarily feasible, type of production activity, following the model of the *jitomateros,* while recognizing that real competition with them was not a practical possibility and that it was necessary to settle for less ambitious forms of participation in the vegetable sector.

These structural changes in the political-economic context of peasant production are clearly the central factors in the changing pattern of land rental in the 1960s and subsequent years. But it is also worth considering the possible impact of the internal evolution of the ejidal population. On the one hand, surviving members of the original set of ejidatarios are aging: their families are growing up, and in many cases migrating. New ejidatarios have entered the ejido over the years through land purchases, and as time goes by a larger proportion of those new ejidatarios are younger men, including sons of existing ejidatarios whose fathers are still alive. Naturally, this last process biases land distribution towards the families in which the original title holders have survived as ejidatarios or bought their way in at an early stage as mature men. Some land purchasers cease to be active ejidatarios as they age, and others migrate, of course, but one might expect a certain degree of stabilization to arise as the economic possibilities of ejidatarios improved somewhat. Migration of potential heirs would become the primary factor in the dissolution of family farms, leaving an aging holder possessed of land which he or she cannot use productively.

A certain demographic renewal of active peasant farmers in the ejido took place in the 1960s and early 1970s, as young men from the less affluent families managed to buy land rights, but the possibility of this process repeating itself under contemporary conditions seems much reduced. The development of competing capitalist demands for land has pushed up land values enormously, and set up a bias towards purchasers who have sources of income outside agriculture—especially resident professionals. The processes of previous decades cannot therefore be repeated today. The gulf between theory and practice in the transmission of land rights in the 1940s, 1950s and 1960s was arguably not a cause for enormous concern, in the sense that it did not conflict totally with the social objectives of land reform. It is also undeniable that the partial commoditization of land did serve to permit peasants who were in a position to produce commercial surpluses to gain direct, long-term access to more than the minimum prescribed individual landholding. Ignoring considerations of social equity, it might therefore be argued that a degree of concentration of effective possession of ejidal land can serve the "national interest" in one sense, a sense that has often been central to official policy in its "agricultural" rather than "agrarian" phases. It is very dubious indeed whether either of these points can be made with equal force today. The sons of poor ejidatarios are increasingly restricted to that portion of the existing land base which will be transmitted by inheritance, while the stratum in whose hands possession is currently being concentrated may not be those likely to put it to the most effective productive use. They invest in an income and interest-generating capital asset rather than a means to sustain a dynamic agricultural enterprise.

The changing pattern of land rental can best be quantified and analyzed by returning to cumulative data. Figure 2 indicates the emergent pattern over the entire history of the ejido by grouping the data by five year intervals between 1940 and 1980. Long-term rentals peak, at 126, in the mid-1960s, but almost two-thirds of the *parcelas* being rented in 1965 had already been rented for a

decade or more. Only fourteen new *parcelas* come under rental after 1965, at
a rate of four or five per five year period, a marked change from the average
of thirty-two per five year interval observed in the previous decades, though
the figure also indicates a slight decline on previous levels after 1955. It must
be stressed that not all this rental was associated with *neolatifundismo*. A few
of the *parcelas* making up the aggregate picture were poorer quality land on
the hill sides or lands on the plain whose fertility was affected by salinity or
other problems. Don Gabriel was uninterested in the ejido's more marginal
lands, and favored *parcelas* which enjoyed better communications, good
access to water, or high productive potential in temporal crops. The 8 hectare
parcelas were particularly prized by Don Santiago and Don Gabriel, who
could sow virtually the whole of two of the temporal *potreros* as a unit for a
few years while the *neolatifundio* was at the apogee of its development.

Figure 2
CUMULATIVE DEVELOPMENT OF LAND RENTAL, 1940–1980

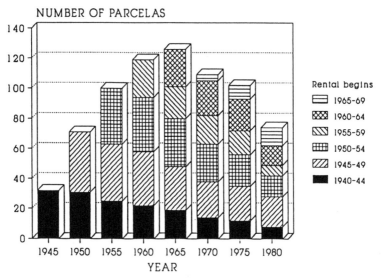

Note: excludes short-term rentals

Table 13 indicates the proportion of the land which Don Gabriel controlled, but here the calculation is much less exact, since all that can be indicated is the number of *parcelas* to which Don Gabriel enjoyed access at some
time. While a significant proportion were rented to him on long term contracts, many were "passed" to others either before or after he had control of
them. Nevertheless, in almost every case Don Gabriel did enjoy control over

Table 13

THE DEVELOPMENT OF THE LONG-TERM CORE OF THE CAPITALIST
NEOLATIFUNDIO IN THE EJIDO OF EMILIANO ZAPATA
IN RELATION TO THE OVERALL GROWTH OF LAND RENTAL

Period Rental Begins	Number of new rentals to the neolatifundist	As proportion of all new rentals in period (%)
1940–1944	17	53
1945–1949	31	78
1950–1954	31	84
1955–1959	18	72
1960–1964	14	54
1965–1969	2	40
1970–1974	2	40
1975–1979	0	0

---

parcelas which were rented to other people at other times throughout the 1950s and early 1960s. He was also financing the cultivation of ejidatarios who rented land in the 1950s and first half of the 1960s. His control began to disintegrate in the second half of the 1960s, and disintegrated more rapidly in the 1970s, as he faced modest competition from several ejidatarios with alternative sources of finance besides Don Santiago, in addition to the pressures created by the arrival of the *jitomateros*. It is, however, often difficult to be sure about which particular *parcelas* were taken over by Don Santiago when he became independent, and often the precise timing of Don Gabriel's loss of control of particular pieces of land to others is not known. Rather than provide data of dubious value for the later years, it is better to work from the estimates of land area cultivated by the different interests, and gauge their impact on Don Gabriel's enterprise from that. Don Santiago, for example, was sowing around 150 hectare—around twenty-five to thirty *parcelas* of four and 8 hectare—while the *jitomateros* regularly sowed a minimum of twelve of the very best irrigated *parcelas* annually. After Don Santiago's death, one of his sons became active, and a number of new ejidatario renters had also appeared on the scene by this stage, such as a son of "maestro" Abel who used his earnings from work in the oil industry to finance the cultivation of up to seventy *hectares* in the late 1970s and early 1980s. Several others sowed a few rented *parcelas,* including members of the agrarian bureaucracy and various other outsiders. By 1982, Don Gabriel had been reduced to sowing seven *parcelas* in Emiliano Zapata, two of them *parcelas* whose titles he had purchased in perpetuity.

Of the four *parcelas* to fall into Don Gabriel's hands after 1965, only one was a long-term rental, and even in this case he has only retained control of half an 8 hectare *parcela,* the remainder being rented to the *emigrado* son of one of the original group of ejidatarios, one of those who has always cultivated his land since receiving it. Bearing in mind that Don Gabriel had little competition during the 1950s and early 1960s, and that these data exclude cases where rental to him was short-term or periodic in early years, it does not seem unreasonable to conclude that at its apogee the *neolatifundio* included at least a third of the total number of *parcelas,* and a greater proportion of its lands of prime commercial quality.

Indeed, the total land area sown would be substantially more than a third of the total land area, since there was a strong concentration of rentals in the three *potreros* in the plain with 8 hectare *parcelas.* Figure 3 indicates the importance of the three notionally temporal *potreros* in the plain in Don Gabriel's enterprise. The 8 hectare *parcelas* high in the hills in the *potrero* known, appropriately, as "La Mesa," were of no interest to Don Gabriel because it was impossible to access them by truck, quite aside from considerations of fertility.

Though the extent of Don Gabriel's control was greatest in Los Pirules, he controlled 60% and sometimes more of Cerrito del Buey in the heyday of the *neolatifundio,* and the total for all three *potreros* from these figures shows him in long-term control over forty-one of the total number of seventy-nine *parcelas,* or just over half these 8 hectare *parcelas.* Of these, four did not come into his possession until the 1960s, and new acquisitions more or less balanced the few which left his control in the early years of the decade. Allowing for people who rented their land to Don Gabriel occasionally, or for shorter periods, it becomes clear that informants' statements that Don Gabriel sowed "half the ejido" were not exaggerated in the case of this part of it from the mid-1950s through well into the 1960s. These lands were not of interest to the tomato-growers, though they were of great interest to the independent Don Santiago and other competitors who emerged later on and gradually wrested control of the land which remained available for rental from Don Gabriel. Even so, several holders have only recently succeeded in extricating themselves totally from long-term contracts made with their ex-patron. A staggering 67% of Los Pirules was leased to Don Gabriel for periods of 15 to 20 years or more.

In five cases it was generally only half the 8 hectare *parcela* which was rented each year, at least in more recent years. The effect of this on the *neolatifundio* is marginal, though it is important for understanding the economic strategy of the individual ejidatario. The possibility of acquiring such extensive control of a series of neighboring *parcelas* in a *potrero* permitted the realization of some economies of scale in the organization of cultivation and

Figure 3
RENTAL OF 8 HECTARE PARCELAS

POTRERO CERRITO DEL BUEY

(20 parcelas)

Proportions of land rented by
neolatifundist and other renters

Long-term rental
to neolatifundist

POTRERO LOS PIRULES

(21 parcelas)

Proportions of land rented by
neolatifundist and other renters

Long-term rental
to neolatifundist

POTRERO LA LOBERA

(38 parcelas)

Proportions of land rented by
neolatifundist and other renters

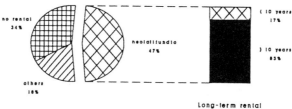

Long-term rental
to neolatifundist

transport, to which Don Santiago added his highly rationalized labor organization. A visit to the *neolatifundio* in the 1950s would therefore have revealed a landscape dominated by a fine capitalist farm, recreating some of the past glories of the hacienda, along with a passable replica of its relatively low wage economy and extended working day. What remained absent from the enterprise, at every level, was the system of physical coercive power and absolute control of land. With the emergence of effective competition for rented land, followed by a change in the economic possibilities of the peasant farmer, the *neolatifundio* melted away, to be replaced by a more untidy pattern of various smaller rental domains representing enterprises of different levels of capitalization and market power, alongside a much increased proportion of "peasant" farms. But this shift also accompanied major changes in the larger system of capital accumulation in agriculture, and their role in the transformations in question will be examined in Chapter Nine.

CHAPTER 7

PEASANT REPRODUCTION
AND MIGRATION

Thus far migration has figured in my analysis primarily as a factor of dissolution within the ejidal community. Excluding inheritance by widows and focusing solely on male holders and male heirs, fifty-four migrant ejidatarios abandoned their rights during the years 1940 to 1960. The vast majority of cases of permanent alienation of rights, 78%, were ones where the holder left for Mexico City or Guadalajara; 15% of transfers involved migration to another internal destination, generally other communities in the local region. International migration was only associated with 7% of the permanent transfers and only one of the U.S. migrants who abandoned the land in these two decades left Mexico permanently: the others were seasonal migrants who went yearly *al Norte*. Regular seasonal U.S. migration was more closely associated with long-term rental of the *parcela* than definitive abandonment of rights.

The contradictions between peasant farming and U.S. migration should not, therefore, be overstated, and it may be more appropriate to stress the positive, conserving effects of international migration on peasant agriculture than to dwell on its negative effects. U.S. migration has served as a means of securing family reproduction for existing ejidatarios and it has also permitted previously landless people—some of them sons of ejidatarios—to secure rights in the ejido. It is important to note the operation of certain negative tendencies in the long-term: the possibility of children of poor families becoming ejidatarios on the basis of migrant earnings has diminished as land values have risen, while land-holding by *emigrados* is frequently resented by the children of poorer ejidatarios who remain landless. Nor should the extent to which international migrant earnings have been invested in land be exaggerated: of the one hundred and eighty-two persons cultivating ejidal land whom I interviewed in 1982–83, only twenty-one sowed land bought with U.S. migrant earnings. Only three of these were *emigrados*, leaving aside a case where a son had bought the *parcela* before deciding to emigrate and left it to his landless father. Although my interview sample did not, for practical reasons, include all *emigrado* holders, a few of whom belong to the ranks of the original ejidatarios, no more than eight other current title-holders bought their land with U.S. migrant earnings. Several people did suggest to me that they had considered buying into the ejido with savings accumulated *al Norte*, but had not done so through "lack of interest," preferring to work as *jornaleros* and sow their *ecuaros*, or wait to reap the benefits of investments made in their children's education. Nevertheless, despite the fact that internal migration also plays a central role in the processes of peasant reproduction, international migration has been of special significance precisely because it has been conducive, on balance, to the reproduction of households as *rural* households. Even where earnings from a sustained, long-term, commitment to international migration help the next generation to achieve social mobility through education, it is not uncommon for part of that generation to opt for a continuation of the migrant-rural way of life, as sons follow their fathers to the North.

It is therefore necessary to analyze the long-term dynamics of the international movement in depth, not least in order to judge whether its character is changing in a secular manner which might entail new consequences for rural society in the future. But analysis should start with the processes of internal migration, not merely in order to put international migration into its proper context, but in order to provide further material on one of the central issues I posed in the introduction to this study: the relationship between the processes of peasant reproduction and the larger processes of class formation associated with Mexico's development since 1940.

INTERNAL MIGRATION, SOCIAL NETWORKS AND STATE POLICY

We have seen that more than 10% of the original male title holders in the Emiliano Zapata ejido abandoned their rights in each of the first two decades of individual land reform farming, and that Mexico City was the principal destination of those who left the community, the proportion of Mexico City migrants increasing in the second decade. Although the early migratory stream included both ejidatarios and their children, the closure of the sugar industry had an even greater impact on totally landless families, and I have already noted how Lázaro Cárdenas intervened personally to secure new sources of urban employment for the unrooted population in urban as well as other rural contexts. But political patronage was only one dimension of the processes which mediated the rural-urban movement.

In the last analysis, rural-urban migration was the other side of the coin of the import-substituting phase of Mexico's industrialization, since that model of development produced rural impoverishment. It was not the only other side of the coin: some elements of the rural population remained *in situ* as a rural proletariat or semi-proletariat servicing the various forms of private land holding and neolatifundist capitalist agriculture that prospered and expanded in the countryside in the post-Cárdenas era. And it might even be argued, adopting some of the logic of the classical "dual economy" thesis, that the transformations in question represented a painful, but in the longer term desirable, "shake-out" of relatively unproductive rural surplus labor into other employments with a higher marginal product per worker. The demand for labor on the part of the industrial sector in the first two decades of post-war industrialization was reinforced by protectionism and the contribution of agricultural policy to the control of urban wage levels. But the *bracero* program would scarcely have been necessary if the rural surplus population being released had not been of quite unmanageable proportions—even allowing for the normalcy of a "reserve army of labor"—and the long-term conse-

quences of the processes in question were not adjustment and the establishment of a new equilibrium state through tendencies towards the equalization
of rural and urban earnings, but problems of urban employment coupled with
escalating problems in the provision of a marketable surplus of basic foodstuffs. The state's various interventions to deal with the problems of both
employment and agricultural production from the mid-1960s onwards have
all reflected the legacy of constraints imposed by their starting-point, though
it would be naive to suggest that leaving everything to "the market" would
have produced more beneficial consequences: Mexico's process of development reflects both the political influence of powerful capitalist interests
domestically and the fundamental inequalities of economic power which
underlie the structure of the international market system.

The local effects of the national development strategy which evolved under
Alemán and his successors varied in line with local factors. An obvious
source of variation in "push" factors is the productive resources and sources
of employment possessed by individual communities (Arizpe 1978), but the
distribution of local resources among the population is just as significant as
their overall quantity: communities where social relations were of a kind
which permitted the landless poor to retain some form of access to productive
resources or stable employment, even on relatively unfavorable terms, might
display lower rates of outmigration than communities which were better
endowed with land and other resources per capita but had different distributive relations, other things being equal (Arroyo Alejandre 1986:15-16). In the
case of Guaracha, the relationship between local employment and the sugar
industry created a strong "push" early in the post-war period, but relatively
easy access to *ecuaros* and the development of neolatifundism should have
helped make a semi-proletarian local rural adaptation more viable here than
in some other contexts. It remains important, however, to emphasize that not
all "push" factors in individual migratory strategies were economic, as has
already been demonstrated by the case studies detailed in the previous chapter, and that these other social causes of migration were not of entirely negligible quantitative significance.

"Pull" factors also varied locally, since certain sectors of rural society were
better placed to find niches in the urban labor market than others. Migration
is not a wholly costless operation, and access to savings or loans plays some
role in variations in migratory behavior between households and communities. Besides favors dispensed through the channels of political patronage,
and bonds between individual peasants and bureaucrats and other people with
urban backgrounds entering the region from without, patrons born in the
community could exert a substantial influence on the employment prospects
of their *paisanos*: in the case of Guaracha, the role of professionals is particularly notable in the long-term, an especially influential example being a son
of "Maestro" Abel Prado who became a hospital doctor in Mexico City. The
patronage of professionals gave uneducated members of the community

access to unskilled public sector jobs, and has given rise to a ramifying and ever-expanding chain of help relationships. The role of professionals in the Guaracha case was an indirect consequence of the Cardenista patronage of the community in the form of the Escuela Agrícola (Pardo Galván 1982), and some of the school's in-migrant educated employees were also an important source of practical help to the first generation. Others sought help from the family of their ex-*patrón*: a number of current residents of the community are retired household servants of the Moreno family, though I must record that their present economic position seldom seems particularly enviable. No significant role is attributable to the ex-*hacendado* with respect to Guaracheños' access to industrial employment in the cities in the data at my disposal, although these data are biased by the fact that they only include households which retain residence in Guaracha.

Patronage relations between persons of distinct statuses are not the sum total of the social relationships which mediate the flow of migrants from rural to urban locations, though access to patronage must play a significant role in determining some of the selectivity found in migration patterns. Once migrant communities are established in new locations, horizontal relations of kinship, friendship and *compadrazgo* can play an increasing role in channelling the flow of people, although the *compadrazgo* relation is often associated with inequality of social position and vertical patronage relations continue to figure prominently in the process of finding work among contemporary Guaracheño households, particularly in the public sector. In the longer term, the social process of movement acquires a certain momentum of its own: younger children may, for example, go to live with siblings or aunts or uncles in the cities, receiving their secondary education there rather than in the village. Sometimes the existence of a resident household in the city might be seen as a determinant factor in whether a young daughter would be sent or permitted to work in the urban environment outside domestic service,[1] though in other cases such movements constitute an act of rebellion against parental authority: migratory movements provide ways of resolving tensions in domestic relations, but they can also add to them.

In the context of the ejidal system, it is particularly important to recognize that rural-urban movements are not simply one-way. Men of different ages can return from the cities to reclaim ejidal rights: some, like the former propietor of a small clothing workshop in Mexico City, return to Guaracha with some capital accumulated in urban enterprises to invest, others return to retire to the land with their pension, and still others, younger men, return to see whether the land can offer them a better life than a dead-end manual job in the capital. Another factor in urban-rural movements, exemplified by some of the cases discussed in the previous chapter, is the way in which the access of sons to the land can be determined by the domestic politics of households headed by urban-resident female title-holders preoccupied with a calculus of the degree of responsibility and filial devotion displayed by different offspring. But much more important as a structural consideration is the extent to which a majority of rural households are directly linked to the urban economy through income remissions from internal migrant children.[2]

Due concern for varying local circumstances and the social mechanisms underlying individual migratory movements should not distract our attention completely from the impact of larger processes of secular structural change at regional and national level. Guaracheños recall the end of the 1940s and the start of the 1950s as a period of intensified rural-urban exodus. But from the perspective of western Mexico as a whole, the local upsurge marked the beginning of a continuous upward movement in rates of rural emigration. In the period 1950–1960, the average rate of net emigration for persons between the ages of twenty and forty for all the municipios in western Mexico[3] was sixteen persons per hundred, rising to twenty per cent in the following decade and up to almost fifty per cent in the 1970s (Arroyo Alejandre 1986:17, and Tables 1–3, pp.iv–vi). Although these gross figures include a proportion of students, housewives and non-working men, the rising proportion of rural municipios with relatively high rates of net out-migration in the total figures—and the virtually vanishing proportion of rural communities experiencing net in-migration—leaves the overall significance of the processes in question beyond doubt. The only major complication to the gross trend of increasing rural-urban movement over time is the fact that larger, "less rural," communities also begin to display rising rates of net out-migration over time, a reflection, at least in part, of the growing concentration of capital and resources in metropolitan urban centers. Certain rural areas in states like Nayarit and Sinaloa do contain municipios which have attracted population in recent years as a result of colonization schemes and the establishment of agro-industries. But the particularities in the patterns seem less striking than their underlying uniformities (Arroyo Alejandre 1986:18).

Analysis of the age patterns of migrants also presents a relatively homogeneous picture of massive emigration on the part of younger people (aged twenty to twenty-nine) from rural municipios, at a steadily and strongly increasing rate over time. In the case of those who are slightly older (thirty to thirty-four), the same rising trend afflicts semi-rural municipios.[4] Throughout the entire thirty year period, the one exceptional group remains those in the thirty-five to forty age range. This category is marked by relatively low rates of net emigration, and the rates show no tendency towards increase over time. Arroyo suggests that such persons are in fact the least mobile overall, being those who have achieved a certain stability of employment and perhaps a certain accumulation of capital in their places of origin (Arroyo Alejandre 1986: 19). He also notes, however, that a relatively large number of rural and semi-rural communities show net in-migration of persons in this age-group, a fact which seems likely to reflect processes of urban-rural return migration as well as rural-rural movements.

Figures for total net migratory movements of persons aged between twenty and forty for the municipio of Villamar are given in Table 14, along with comparative data for the neighboring municipios of San Pedro (Venustiano Carranza), Jiquilpan and Sahuayo, and for the municipios of Zamora, Apatzingán, Uruapan and Morelia. Morelia's growth during the 1970s is striking in comparison with the net outflow of population of working age from the other municipios except Uruapan, a reflection both of the expanding role of the public sector in this period, and of the relative debility of the larger regional economy.

Table 14

TOTAL NET MIGRATION AND NET MIGRATION RATES FOR EIGHT MICHOACAN MUNICIPIOS, 1950–1980

Municipio	Total 1950s	Total 1960s	Total 1970s	Rate[1] 1950s	Rate[1] 1960s	Rate[1] 1970s
Villamar	-592	-2537	-4600	-10.2	-33.7	-56
San Pedro	-662	-2395	-2802	-12.8	-37.2	-43.5
Jiquilpan	-1952	-3441	-2944	-20.8	-32.3	-26
Sahuayo	1616	-2936	-156	34	-30.1	-1.4
Zamora	209	865	-2620	1.5	4.4	-8.6
Apatzingan	2705	5276	-5598	41.2	45.2	-23.5
Uruapan	-4568	11925	155	-22.5	71.7	0.4
Morelia	591	-1925	12137	1.5	-3.5	15.4

[1] Net Rate of in- or outmigration is measured in number of persons per thousand and expressed as a positive or negative percentage.

Source: Arroyo Alejandre (1982: xlii–xliv)

The table provides a striking indication of the way the development of Apatzingán as a zone of colonization and agro-industrial center through the 1950s and 1960s went into reverse during the 1970s. Despite the significant investments in transport infrastructure made under the Cárdenas administration and the concomitant development of commercial agriculture and agro-industries, including the resin industry (Espín 1986:164-165), after a phase of significant urban growth in the late 1930s and early 1940s, the municipio of Uruapan experienced net outmigration in the 1950s.[5] Further agro-industrial development and Uruapan's increasingly nodal position in its larger regional context produced a phase of substantial net in-migration during the 1960s, but this levelled off to virtually zero in the 1970s. Sahuayo, a center for both commerce and small-scale industry, expanded during the 1950s, but lost population of working age at a similar rate during the 1960s, before recovering to more modest levels of net outflow in the 1970s. The municipio of Zamora never displayed high rates of in-migration during the 1950s and 1960s, and began to experience net out-migration in the 1970s—though at a more modest rate than the municipios of the Ciénega—despite the development of the strawberry agro-industry during the second two decades. In interpreting these data it is certainly necessary to remember that rural Michoacán was experiencing high rates of rural population growth over the period in question, but the inability of even the more dynamic sectors of the regional economy to absorb a growing rural surplus population in the long-term remains striking.

The municipio of Villamar not only had the greatest net out-migration during the 1970s within this sample: it has the highest rate in the state in this period with the exception of the municipio of Melchor Ocampo del Balsas (on the border with the state of Mexico). Its rates were also high in earlier periods, though exceeded by those of Venustiano Carranza. Villamar has higher rates of net outmigration than Venustiano Carranza in all age categories during the 1970s, and an unusually high rate of outmigration by people in the highest (35-39) age category by state-wide standards,[6] suggesting that no age-specific factors play a role in determining its loss of population. It is difficult to draw any more precise conclusions from the municipal data on net balances of migration, since the figures are the product of a large number of possible variables. In turning to the more detailed data on Guaracha, it will not be possible to reconstruct the entire post-war pattern of internal migration with any precision, although the data provided in the previous chapter on migration of ejidatarios seem broadly consistent with more general patterns in the community. Nor can the data on Guaracha be assumed representative of all the other communities of the municipio of Villamar, given their different resource endowments and social characteristics.[7] But given the degree of similarity observed in the migratory patterns of the rural communities of the Ciénega, it seems unlikely that Guaracha will be totally unrepresentative.

OFF-FARM EMPLOYMENT AND INTERNAL MIGRATION IN GUARACHA

The community of Guaracha had 631 constituent households in 1983, of which 259 were headed by holders of ejidal rights. A further 104 households could be described as "ejidal families," in that they were headed by resident children of ejidatarios who currently lacked rights in the ejido, but might inherit them. The remaining 268 households—42% of the total—were landless in the full sense: the parental house from which they sprang also lacked ejidal rights. 217 of the non-ejidal landless households, 81% of the total, were theoretically headed by men.[8] Three others were households containing single, childless women, and 36 those of widows. Five percent of the landless households were female-headed as a result of divorce or separation. In the case of ejidatario households, the proportion of separated or divorced persons was half that found in landless houses, and there was only one household headed by a single woman. The proportion of widows was only slightly lower, at 11.2% in comparison with 13.4% for the landless, though it should be noted that the average age of ejidatario household heads is higher than that of landless houses. There were only three households headed by widows within the category of resident children of ejidatarios, and an equally small number of cases of divorce or separation.

Excluding two deceased persons, and an elderly ejidatario who was resident in Jalisco, but no longer working, 104 households in the village, 16.5% of the total, had male heads whose primary work was outside Guaracha in the local region or other parts of Mexico. Two persons held rights to land in other local communities. One was an ejidatario in Cerrito Cotijaran who had married into Guaracha, and the other had inherited private land in Jaripo from a father who had also married in; the son bought rights to ejidal land in Guaracha in the late 1960s, and dedicated himself to commercial cattle-raising. Of the remainder, one was a return migrant factory worker from Mexico City receiving a pension, and eight were either formally divorced or had effectively abandoned their families,[9] leaving a total of 94 households, just over 15% of the total, receiving income from a male head currently working outside the community in some form of salaried or self-employment other than ejidal or private agriculture. A further 49 households, almost 8%, were headed by men working in the United States on a regular basis, excluding four cases of abandonment, but including a case in which the male head of the house died in tragic circumstances in Los Angeles during the course of my fieldwork. Of those whose main source of livelihood lay outside Guaracha, but not in the U.S., forty six percent were heads of landless families, with ejidatarios and their sons making up roughly equal proportions of the remaining 54% from ejidal houses. In the case of male heads working in the United States, the pattern is somewhat different: a majority (57%) are from landless households, and heads of households holding ejidal rights constitute only 14% of the total. These patterns reflect differences in the age groups most active in the various labor markets concerned, although it is also necessary to take into account variations in the opportunities available to different sectors of the village population in particular historical periods.[10] In order to explore the underlying meaning of the figures, it is necessary to examine the actual occupations and economic activities in which the individuals concerned are engaged outside the community.

Of the ejidatarios with work outside the community within Mexico, one worked as a plumber in Guadalajara and generally rented his land: a widower, he no longer had any dependants to support in the village, and had previously been a long-term international migrant. Another who was mainly resident in Guadalajara suffered health problems, and it was his wife's work there, as a playgroup supervisor, which provided the basic source of income derived from the city. The only ejidatario with a family resident in the village who was deriving his primary income from work in Guadalajara—in a cantina—had abandoned his family. In the case of those holders of ejidal rights who were currently working in Mexico City, all kept their primary residence there, along with their families. The main significance of work in metropolitan centers on the part of resident male ejidatario household heads lies, therefore, in the modest number of return migrants found in this section of the community. One of the main ejidal entrepreneurs, a son of "Maestro Abel," was still working in the oil industry in Campeche in 1982, but like a brother who had previously run a small clothing enterprise in Mexico City, subsequently abandoned his work outside Guaracha to dedicate himself full-time to agriculture. Of the remainder, only three had employments in the private sector to supplement income derived from farming: one worked as an itinerant salesman in Tamaulipas, one was a professional *mariachi* player, and one worked as a freelance trucker in Ciudad Lázaro Cárdenas on the coast.[11] In all the remaining cases, 57% of the total, the additional source of income obtained by the ejidatario derived from public employment. Three were fully qualified teachers, two working in neighboring communities, and one in Zacapu. One was an engineer, working in the agrarian bureaucracy in Jalisco. One was a teaching assistant, and another four worked in skilled or technical capacities within the region in the educational or agrobureaucratic sectors. The remainder (40%) of the ejidatarios in public employment had manual jobs, mostly local, with the SARH, SEP and SAHOP.

In the case of sons of ejidatarios, public employment accounts for nearly 60% of the cases: within this group, a higher proportion (50%) of those in public employment belong to the skilled-technical category, 31% holding manual jobs, and a rather larger number work outside the Ciénega in more distant regions of Michoacán and neighboring states. Of the three persons with higher educational qualifications in the group, one, who bought rights in the ejido after 1983, worked as an inspector for the ANAGSA in Jalisco, one lectured at the Tecnológico in Jiquilpan, and the third was a school-teacher in Villamar. Public sector employment was again almost equally divided between the educational and agro-bureaucratic sectors, and kinship and patronage relations with educated *paisanos* played a crucial role in providing the individuals concerned with access to this work. In the case of the 40% in private sector employment, three were working in Mexico City while their families remained in Guaracha: two brothers worked as a bus driver and ticket collector respectively, while the third person worked in a factory. Another person was working in a factory in Guadalajara, having previously been employed in a hotel there, and a fifth person worked driving a delivery van for a snack food company in Zamora. Those working in the Ciénega towns provide a representative sample of local private sector opportunities in the region: there is another musician, one worked in a small soap factory in Sahuayo, one drove a bus, and one was a mechanic. Two brothers worked in the Liconsa milk processing plant in Jiquilpan, an enterprise which straddles the border between the private and public sectors, having been brought into public ownership after operating under the management of Nestlé in earlier years.

Excluding the six cases of divorce or abandonment found in this group, the pattern for landless households appears superficially similar to that found for ejidatarios, in that, excluding those working in the Liconsa plant, 5 persons, or 11% of the total—public employment accounts for 45% of the cases. But the breakdown of public sector employment shows a much stronger bias towards manual occupations than that characteristic of ejidal households in the broader sense of ejidatario parental households combined with the households of resident children. Sixty five percent of landless household heads with public sector employment are manual workers, and the inclusion of employment in the Liconsa plant in this category would reinforce this contrast between the two groups. Only two heads of resident landless households belonged to the upper stratum of professional public employees: one was a school teacher in Cerrito Colorado, the other a hospital doctor, working in Mexico City in 1983. Overall there is a clear difference between landless and ejidal households in terms of both levels of access to, and average income obtained from, public sector employment.

At least one of the manual workers in public sector employment in the landless households group was a returned migrant from Mexico City, and of those working in the private sector in this group, two were factory workers in the capital and one a construction worker. Another ex-factory worker in Mexico had established himself as a travelling salesman in the region with savings from his previous employment, and two others worked in factories in Guadalajara, although one of them had found a new, and somewhat better paid, job as a mechanic in the year of the survey. The landless group included another professional musician, and a self-employed contract painter who worked with an unmarried son in Morelia. Two others had found artisan occupations in the Ciénega towns, and a further two worked as caretakers in Sahuayo and Zamora respectively, a type of occupation to which relatively uneducated rural men might aspire in the public as well as private sectors, and one which accounts for 5% of cases where the primary income source of the male household head lay in work outside the village in the overall sample. In the case of the landless households, however, we have a small group of men whose income from work outside the community derived from internal migrant earnings in agriculture: one worked as a day-laborer in Apatzingán, while three worked as cane-cutters in Los Reyes. Another worked seasonally as an itinerant fruit vendor with some cousins resident in Guerrero. If the occupations of men who had abandoned their families were included, the proportion of families dependent on employment of this kind would increase, since of the six cases of separated or divorced internal migrant heads found among the landless households, one worked cutting cane in Sinaloa, and another worked variably as a street sweeper and agricultural laborer in Zamora. Within the very restricted framework of employment opportunities offered by the local regional economy, therefore, landless households were more prominent in the lower paid and more unstable private sector employments, while those who obtained better jobs tended to have a background in past migration to the cities. Whether employment was in the public or private sector, manual work predominated in the case of landless households.

Overall, however, the most striking pattern in the data for all strata within the village population is the role of public employment. Excluding employment in the Liconsa plant, public sector jobs accounted for 55% of the cases where male household heads derived their principal source of income from employment outside the village in 1983, and the proportion rises to 62% including employment in the Liconsa. This was a situation pregnant with implications in a period when pressures for the reduction of public expenditures and employment were already beginning to make themselves felt in the form of layoffs at the Liconsa plant and reductions in the employment of both manual and middle-ranking technical employees on the part of the main branches of the agro-bureaucracy.[12] Since the village economy itself was dependent on the state in so far as it was dependent on an ejidal farming system receiving credits and subsidies from government sources, reductions in public expenditure could only work to increase what were already high rates of net out-migration in the years after 1983.

The large negative balance of net in- and out-migration observed for the rural communities of the Ciénega is primarily determined by the departure of children born in the villages to seek a livelihood elsewhere. Excluding return migrants and a few children of Guaracheños who were born elsewhere during the past migration of their parents, but have subsequently returned to live in the village, a mere twenty male heads of household were in-marrying men from other communities. Twelve of them came from communities in the immediate region, and fourteen were Michoacanos. One, an army officer born in Guanajuato, now deceased, met his wife while he was stationed locally. All of the remaining five in-marrying men came from Mexico City, meeting their wives there while the women were migrating. The association between in-marriage and female migration can also be extended to some of the cases of marriage between persons from different local communities: one of the Michoacanos initiated his relationship with his future spouse while both were in the U.S. Only two of the Mexico City-born husbands were actually resident in the village in 1983, a federal employee and a house painter: two had died, and one had abandoned his family. These cases are therefore not ones of real in-migration, but of the return of women without husbands to their natal communities in search of the support of their kin. Three of the women married to non-Guaracheños from Michoacán were also widows, and one was separated. Two of the women held titles to ejidal land in their own right: one was one of the widows, while the husband of the other was not working as a result of illness. One of the younger in-marrying men is the step-son of an ejidatario who had married out, and had been brought up in his step-father's house. Another, older, man was an ejidatario in Cerrito Cotijaran. The twenty in-marrying men do not therefore represent any significant process of labor migration into the community. Indeed, less than half of them were actually working within the village in 1983. One of the regional migrants, from Apatzingán, makes a living as a locksmith, one drives tractors and trucks for a son of Don Santiago, there is one other federal employee, a manual worker, and three are *jornaleros*. But the two remaining in-marrying men whose origins are regional actually work in the U.S., one of them being an *emigrado* factory worker from Chavinda.

Past migration of community members is also central to the movement of women born outside Guaracha into the community. Forty-three wives of male heads of household had married into Guaracha, 58% of them from other communities in the state, mostly local, 30% from other states, and 12% from Mexico City. A full 35% of these cases of in-marriage concerned the families of professionals: in many cases the wife was herself professionally qualified, and the couple had generally met while the husband was studying or working outside the village.[13] A further 40% of the cases were related to the past labor migration of the male partner, leaving only a minority of cases related to other forms of social intercourse between communities in the immediate vicinity of Guaracha. Of the in-marrying women, six (14%) were still working in professional, federal employments, one worked as a nurse in Guadalajara, leaving her children in the care of kin, one was an *emigrada* accompanying her husband to the U.S., and one, abandoned, was working in the *congeladoras* in Zamora. The remainder were no longer working, although at least five of those without professional qualifications had worked in the past in the cities or in the U.S.

Against this very modest in-flow of labor power must be set the exodus of 1,101 younger people summarized in Figure 4. Seventy one percent of ejidatario households have migrant children, as compared with 50% of landless households and 24% of the households of resident sons of ejidatarios. But these differences mainly reflect differences in the average ages of the household heads and the maturity of the average household in the different categories: the proportions of children to have left school in the three categories are 69%, 53% and 25% respectively. Figure 4 adjusts for this factor by excluding those children who were still in school in the village or not yet old enough to attend school, and shows the proportions of migrant children in different locations against the proportions of children who had left school remaining resident. Table 15 shows the breakdown of this data in terms of sex and marital status categories.

Migrant children who were in continuing higher or vocational education in their place of destination have not been excluded from the figures on migration. Many of these children were working as well as studying, and in some

PEASANT REPRODUCTION AND MIGRATION

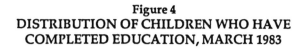

Figure 4
DISTRIBUTION OF CHILDREN WHO HAVE
COMPLETED EDUCATION, MARCH 1983

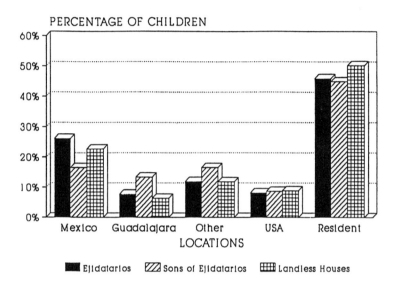

cases making significant income remissions to their parents. Furthermore, that some village children have the opportunity to go to live with urban-resident relatives and pursue further vocational or higher educational studies is an important aspect of the long-term social process of rural-urban migration. Older children who have completed their studies may help to subsidize the further education costs of younger siblings by offering them free or cheap board and lodging, and cities provide greater opportunities to combine further study with part-time work. A number of today's working migrants went to the cities to study in the first instance, though not all who leave to study enjoy sufficient support from their parents or kin to complete their courses of study, and some fall by the wayside and turn to full time work even without the pressure of economic necessity, often to the considerable disappointment of their parents. Nevertheless, whether a given household has internal migrant children who are willing or able to help their siblings progress in life may play an important role in the long-term destiny of the family concerned and have a socially differentiating effect. Many of the younger unmarried children who go to stay with urban kin after leaving school in the village do not, of course, go on to further training or education. Indeed, as I noted earlier, some rural children enter the urban labor market—in particular domestic service—in their early teens. Sometimes what started off as merely a visit culminates in a long-term work commitment in a relatively unplanned way.

Table 15

LOCATION OF MIGRANT HOUSEHOLD MEMBERS
BY SEX AND MARITAL STATUS
(as percentages of all graduates)

	% of Houses[1]	Married Men (%)	Married Women (%)	Single Men (%)	Single Women (%)
(1) MEXICO CITY					
Ejidatarios	57.84	27.85	34.26	17.68	15.10
Sons	37.84	5.56	30.30	4.65	24.24
Landless	44.85	30.57	33.65	13.69	8.79
All Houses	50.74	28.19	33.86	14.67	13.02
(2) GUADALAJARA					
Ejidatarios	20.10	8.61	10.08	4.55	4.17
Sons	13.51	16.67	15.15	6.98	18.18
Landless	20.61	7.42	8.17	2.98	6.04
All Houses	19.70	8.41	9.72	4.16	6.14
(3) OTHER					
Ejidatarios	42.16	13.67	10.83	12.12	10.42
Sons	35.14	27.78	24.24	16.28	3.03
Landless	35.15	13.54	16.83	9.52	6.04
All Houses	38.67	14.02	13.48	11.49	7.86
(4) USA					
Ejidatarios	27.94	11.90	4.79	13.13	2.60
Sons	21.62	33.33	3.03	9.30	0.00
Landless	27.88	11.79	4.33	18.45	1.65
All Houses	27.34	12.46	4.55	14.91	1.97
(5) RESIDENT					
Ejidatarios	90.20	37.97	40.05	52.53	67.71
Sons	81.08	16.67	27.27	62.79	54.55
Landless	86.67	36.68	37.02	55.36	77.47
All Houses	87.93	36.92	38.40	54.77	71.01

[1]The figures in this column measure the number of houses with children in the location as a percentage of all houses in the category which have children who have graduated.

But in general it would be most appropriate to view the movement of younger children to the households of migrant kin as a reflection of the imbalance between parental income and family reproduction costs in rural areas: the sites of family reproduction are extended in order to take advantage of any contributions working children are disposed or able to make towards the reproduction costs of their own natal family.

There is only a small difference between ejidatario households and the landless with respect to the overall propensity of children who leave school to migrate, and it is the households of ejidatarios and their resident sons which have the highest migration rates in the community: only 46% of the children of ejidatario households and 45% of the children of their resident sons remained in Guaracha, as against 50% of the children of landless households. Differences are, however, somewhat more apparent at the level of household units, as Table 15 demonstrates.

A significantly greater proportion of ejidatario households with children of graduate age (58%) have migrant children in Mexico than is the case with landless households (45%), and there is also a somewhat smaller difference (42% versus 35%) in the case of migration to other internal destinations besides Guadalajara. At the same time, the proportion of ejidatario households which have resident children is higher than for the other two categories, though only marginally higher than that of landless houses. A smaller proportion of the households of resident sons of ejidatarios is involved in migration to all destinations than is the case with landless households, with the exception of internal destinations other than Guadalajara, where the percentages are equal.

Data on the sex and marital status composition of the residents shows a similar pattern between ejidatario and landless households as far as married men are concerned: 38% of the married sons of ejidatarios remain resident, as against 36.7% of the married sons of the landless. Ejidatario households have the highest proportion of resident married women of any category, though the difference between ejidatario and landless households is not great. Single men, and more significantly, single women from landless households are, however, more likely to remain resident than those from ejidatario households, and it is differences in these categories which account for the differences in aggregate rates of migration between landless and ejidatario households. Compared with ejidatario households, landless households display lower rates of migration for single men to all destinations with the exception of the United States, and their rates of migration for single women are lower to all destinations except Guadalajara. Their migration rates for married women are also lower than those for ejidatario households in the case of international migration and movement to the metropolitan cities. A much higher proportion of the migration of landless families in general, and of married women in particular, to these other internal destinations is, in fact, movement to local rural communities or to other destinations within the state of Michoacán than is the case with ejidatario households and those of their resident sons. As we will see, these differences correspond to differences in the socio-economic status of the migrants themselves, and that of their families and of the men they marry.

It is apparent from Table 15 that patterns in international migration differ significantly from those found in internal migration. Just over a quarter of the community's households with graduated children have children resident in the North, though a much greater number contain children who have been to the North temporarily, and a few of the urban migrants continue to spend part of the year there. With the exception of Guadalajara, internal destinations attract a greater proportion of households. The proportion of married women involved in international migration is substantially less for all three categories of household than for any kind of internal migration, and the proportion of female migrants who are single working women is even lower. Although female migration to the U.S., even in the company of husbands or brothers, was rarer in the past than in more recent years, it still remains the exception rather than the rule. International migration is also the sphere in which there are the most striking differences between types of household with regard to patterns of male migration. Resident sons of ejidatarios are much more likely to have married sons in the U.S. than either landless or ejidatario households, though the absolute number of persons in this group is in fact very small. More significantly, migration rates for single men from landless families only exceed those of both the other categories in the case of international migration, and are significantly below the rates for ejidatario households in all forms of internal migration. It is entirely the greater propensity of single men from landless houses to migrate to the U.S. which accounts for the fact that the highest proportion of U.S. migrants overall comes from the landless household category. That single men comprise the highest proportion of international migrants from landless families, 44% of the total in contrast to 27% and 36% respectively for children of ejidatarios and children of resident sons of ejidatarios, suggests that *el Norte* is increasingly becoming the first resort for children of poor families in the 1980s. But we will see that these results must be set in the context of a general deterioration of the migratory possibilities open to the least educated stratum of the village population, people who generally belong to the poorest landless households.

The data on the sex and marital status composition of migrants from the different household categories reveals one further apparent anomaly behind the aggregate figures: the propensity to migrate on the part of the married children of sons of ejidatarios seems unusually high, only 16.7% of married men (three persons out of twenty-one) remaining resident. Because of the relative immaturity of the majority of households concerned, the proportion of married children in these families is in fact substantially less than in the other two categories: 40% as against 67% and 56% respectively for the ejidatario and landless households. The fact that this group also has a higher proportion of resident single men than the other categories is clearly also a reflection of their households' relative immaturity: a number of these young people would, in reality, be on the threshold of a migratory career. There is also a particular bias in the case of the resident sons of ejidatarios in the sense that married men constitute only 14% of the total of graduates and only just over half the number of married women in this group of households, whereas male and female married children occur in roughly equal proportions in the other categories. Nevertheless, it may be significant that the migrant married male children of these younger families have pursued rather different patterns of migration to the older generation, being concentrated in the U.S. and in internal destinations other than Mexico City.

The overall data on the migration of children certainly do confirm the fact that it is Mexico City which has attracted the greatest proportion of migrants historically. A total of 206 households have children resident in Mexico, as compared with 111 with children in the U.S., 157 with children in other internal locations—mainly within the state—and only 80 with children in Guadalajara. But the absolute numbers of persons involved do not match these proportions exactly: Mexico remains the primary migrant destination in an overwhelming manner, with a total of 510 migrants, other internal locations account for a further 255 persons, but the U.S. and Guadalajara are not too far apart in terms of numbers of people, accounting for 178 and 158 migrants respectively. Although the absolute numbers of people involved are very small, the relative diminution of migration to Mexico in favor of movement to Guadalajara on the part of the (younger) male children of the resident sons of ejidatarios may provide an indication of the impact of that city's development in more recent years, and it is noticeable that the proportions of households with children in Mexico City declines in line with the relative maturity of the households found in the three categories. Since, however, migratory movements are mediated to a considerable extent by established social networks, as younger people seek help and hospitality from kin and patrons already established in the place of destination, it is no surprise that patterns established in the past display considerable resilience in the face of changing labor market structures; the "opportunities" which theoretically exist in the impersonal structures of the free market are no secure guide to likely migratory behavior, at least in the medium term.

SOCIAL DIFFERENTIATION IN MIGRATION PATTERNS

Although there are differences in patterns and rates of migration between landless and ejidal households, the close similarities in the migration patterns of married men from these two categories of household seem more striking than any of the differences in the data surveyed thus far. Clearly, however, the social consequences of migration depend crucially on the occupations and incomes obtained by the migrants in the different destinations, with one important proviso. The benefit to a given rural household of the activities of its migrant children will clearly be dependent on the extent to which the children concerned remit income to their parental family or aid its members in other ways. Whatever formal norms may be stated, there is considerable variation in the extent to which single working children contribute to parental income (as they are theoretically morally obliged to do), and also in the extent to which married sons (or daughters) may continue to help their parents out (something which they are not, in principle, obligated to do). In the case of Mexico City migrants, for example, ejidatario households reported that 39% of their married sons, 17% of their married daughters, 43% of their single sons, and 45% of their single daughters made some form of income remission to their parents; as might be expected, contributions from married children tended to be more irregular and gift-like than those from single children. In the case of landless households with children in Mexico, the proportions were comparable for single daughters, but slightly higher, at 43% and 20% respectively, for married children, and higher still for single sons, at 65%. This is despite the fact that the landless households contain smaller proportions of professional migrants and public employees, who proved somewhat more likely to remit income than other migrants in the case of ejidatario (but not landless) households.

In some cases it is clear that single children are having a hard time making ends meet or even finding regular work (particularly in the U.S.), but I encountered a number of concrete cases in which an ability to help was not matched by a willingness to do so. In some cases, this reflects the fact that the actual decision to migrate on the part of a child may be the cause of a rupture in family relations. Although some children migrate with the specific intention of helping their parental families, in other cases the motivation is primarily the child's own search for personal economic betterment and produces an immediate conflict with parental expectations regarding his or her role: a son might have been expected to aid his father with the cows, a daughter to make a contribution to the care of her siblings and to help mother with her general domestic burdens. More frequently, particularly in the case of men, the parents accept the child's departure as an unavoidable necessity or even as desirable, things being as they are. The tensions emerge subsequently, when the child returns as a person socially transformed. Such criticism or even rejection of the migrant on the part of their rural families of origin seems to be particularly acute in the case of female migrants who have taken up non-traditional occupations such as work in the *maquila* plants in the border region.[14] Socio-economic transformation of the country is therefore producing social transformations of the family and its internal relations, mediated through perceptions of social transformation of the person rooted in a peasant culture evolving under conditions of virtually incessant crisis. In many cases, of course, it is the children who reject their parents, though I should stress that my research in Guaracha also uncovered a great many cases of filial self-sacrifice and solid commitment under difficult circumstances.[15] The apparent amorality of some children with regard to family obligations is, in a general way, a reflection of the commodification of social life. But it is in these mediated forms, which poison what might previously have been close affective relationships, that the social consequences of commodification reveal their darkest side.

Figures 5 through 9 summarize the occupations pursued by internal migrants. The categories used to classify the individual data have been modified slightly for different types of migration, in order to adjust for differences in the range of occupations available in different locations and for differences related to gender. I will outline their significance for the analysis of Mexico City migration before proceeding with any further analysis, commenting on variations which occur in the case of other migrant destinations as need arises. The basic distinctions drawn relate to income levels, with a subsidiary

Figure 5
OCCUPATIONS OF MEXICO CITY MIGRANTS
MALE CHILDREN OF LANDLESS AND EJIDAL HOUSES

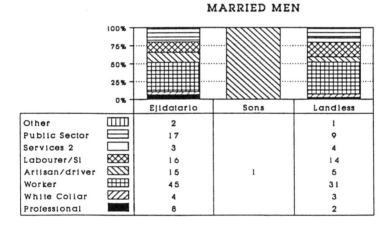

MARRIED MEN

		Ejidatario	Sons	Landless
Other	⊞	2		1
Public Sector	☰	17		9
Services 2	☐	3		4
Labourer/Sl	✕	16		14
Artisan/driver	⧄	15	1	6
Worker	⊞	45		31
White Collar	⧄	4		3
Professional	■	8		2

SINGLE MEN

		Ejidatario	Sons	Landless
Other	⊞	7	1	4
Public Sector	☰	3		3
Services 2	☐	1		
Labourer/Sl	✕	4		3
Artisan/driver	⧄	1		
Worker	⊞	11	1	12
Professional	■	4		1

emphasis on security of employment, though I must stress at the outset that correlations between broad occupational categories and relative income levels can only be approximate.[16] A key category, which also corresponds to a distinction emphasized within the community, is that of professionals (doctors, veterinarians, teachers, engineers, lawyers, etc.), whether they work in the public or private sector. I distinguish "professionals" from a category defined as "white collar workers" in the private sector, which includes, for example, men working as bookkeepers, clerks and bank employees, and women working as secretaries. "Workers" include people defined explicitly as "factory workers," and those defined more vaguely as *obreros*. Even the term "factory worker" as it used in the village might cover employment in enterprises of radically different scale, with different implications in terms of earnings, stability of employment and conditions of work. Many factory workers in fact work in the food and drink manufacturing sector (breweries and snack-producing companies are prominent), but the category also includes workers in the pharmaceutical, automotive, industrial manufacturing and capital goods sectors (where the role of foreign capital is more significant). It also includes some workers in small-scale manufacturing enterprises and workshops: in some cases, this type of employment was identifiable from the data, in other cases not.[17] In a few cases it was possible to determine that the person concerned had moved from a job in a large factory to work in the "small-scale sector." As I noted in the introduction, research in Mexico City and Guadalajara has shown that there is substantial movement of men from (both "formal" and "informal") manufacturing to "services" in the course of the family development cycle, and it is natives of the city rather than rural migrants who predominate in the small-scale manufacturing sector in Guadalajara (González de la Rocha 1986:151, 227-228). It is quite clear from my own data that a number of Guaracheño migrants entered the metropolitan labor market as construction or factory workers and subsequently proceeded to other, generally more remunerative, activities, including forms of self-employment. Given these patterns of mobility, it does not seem meaningful to analyze the processes of urban class formation in terms of a distinction between "formal" and "informal" sectors, even if we restrict analysis to patterns of male employment.

I have separated out three other categories to give an indication of what are potentially significant variations in the current labor market position of rural migrants, bearing in mind the qualifications already made regarding occupational mobility, relative income levels and variations in working conditions and risks to health. The "artisan-driver" category includes mechanics, electricians and various craft trades such as master mason. It also includes bus drivers, people driving delivery vehicles and taxi drivers. "Laborer/S(ervices)1" includes shop-workers, grave-diggers, casual workers in construction, and night-watchmen and caretakers in the private sector, as well as men working in warehouses and as porters in hotels and hospitals. In the case of women, this category is particularly important, since it includes domestic service, although this is not, it should be stressed, an exclusively female preserve for peasant children. Men from rural areas are as likely to work as gardeners as chauffeurs. Furthermore, women are also a significant element in the industrial work-force, as these data indicate. The category "Services 2" deals with another stratum of the service sector, with the emphasis on self-employment or contract work within the commercial sector: within it are included shop-keepers and stall-holders, sales agents, car salesmen and street traders, and a few proprietors of small workshops.[18]

With the exception of professionals, I have distinguished between private and public sector employment. In the case of Mexico City, the category "public employees" essentially denotes federal employees, although a larger proportion of Guadalajara public sector workers is employed by the state and civic authorities. It is vital to stress that this gross category includes clerical, semi-skilled and technical workers as well as manual workers, policemen and soldiers. Only professionals such as university-trained engineers and teachers are excluded. The amalgamation of people enjoying widely differing salaries and conditions of employment—and also stability of employment—serves to highlight the role of the public sector as a source of jobs for rural migrants: indeed, public sector employment is a major factor in promoting migration to some destinations. But it will prove necessary to give more detailed breakdowns of the composition of public sector employment, since closer analysis reveals that this is a significant source of differentiation in the life chances enjoyed by the children of ejidatarios and landless families. This leaves one final category, which is generally labelled as a residual "other" in the charts: the exceptions are where the entire residual population not included under the other categories are housewives, students or not yet working. In the case of the married male migrants to Mexico City, the "other" category includes a person from a landless family incapacitated by an industrial accident. It also includes two children of ejidatarios who have achieved unusual careers: one is a successful singer, the other a sports referee. The "others" in the figures for single migrants are mostly full-time students, predominantly from ejidatario households, and particularly so in the field of university education, where landless families only had two representatives in the capital in 1983. One of the single men from a landless household was unemployed, a single woman studying to be a secretary from the household of a resident son of an ejidatario was working to finance her own studies, and three single daughters of ejidatario houses pursuing vocational education were also declared to be undertaking paid employment part-time by their parents.

Taking into account differences in the relative maturity of the average household in the three categories being compared, the imbalance between ejidatario households and those of their resident sons, on the one hand, and landless households, on the other, in terms of children pursuing higher educational studies in the capital seems totally consistent with the broader picture

Figure 6
OCCUPATIONS OF MEXICO CITY MIGRANTS
FEMALE CHILDREN OF LANDLESS AND EJIDAL HOUSES

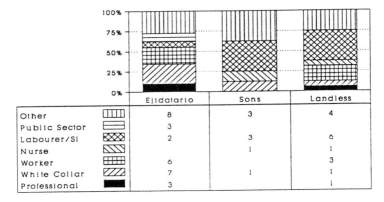

MARRIED WOMEN

		Ejidatario	Sons	Landless
Housewife		113	9	63
Public Sector		1	0	1
Services 2		0	0	1
Labourer/SI		4	0	4
Owns Workshop		1	0	0
Worker		5	0	1
White Collar		6	1	0
Professional		5	0	0

SINGLE WOMEN

		Ejidatario	Sons	Landless
Other		8	3	4
Public Sector		3		
Labourer/SI		2	3	6
Nurse			1	1
Worker		6		3
White Collar		7	1	1
Professional		3		1

suggested by Figure 5. Ejidal families either have, or will in the future achieve, a higher proportion of professional children moving into the middle class than landless families, and the ejidal sector of Guaracha as a whole enjoys a superior position on the metropolitan labor market. This is not to ignore the fact that many individual ejidatario households remain poor, or that the children of such households are to be found in the less well-paid sectors of the Mexico City labor market, working as casual laborers, domestic servants or grave-diggers. By the same token, landless households have also produced successful professionals. But the aggregate figures do indicate one of the central paradoxes of land reform in Mexico: possession of land rights has done little to promote a prosperous peasant agriculture, but it seems to have conferred a selective advantage on those who seek to escape peasant status.

The superior position of the aggregate of ejidal households with regard to access to professional, white collar and public sector jobs is apparent for all sex and marital status categories of Mexico City migrants, including married women, though the vast majority of married women in Mexico City are, in fact, housewives. More than half the married women of landless households who were working were in domestic service, and only one was a public employee. Only one married woman from an ejidatario household was a domestic servant, though three other women were fulfilling menial roles in hospitals, and a small number worked in factories or workshops—two of them widows. But although the presence of a significant proportion of secretaries, bookkeepers and professional married daughters in the ranks of working married daughters from ejidatario families does differentiate the group quite sharply on aggregate from the corresponding group in the landless category, it is also necessary to consider past patterns of work on the part of married women. A number of married women from ejidatario as well as landless households worked in domestic service before marriage, going to the capital while they were still single and marrying there, rather than migrating with their husbands after marriage. Others worked in factories; one girl from a landless family married the son of the boss. In a few of the cases of which I have detailed knowledge, women who worked in service subsequently returned to the village to marry and have remained resident, but the more general pattern seems to be one of definitive movement to the cities, even if the woman in question was originally encouraged to seek urban work in order to contribute to rural family income. It is difficult to draw firm conclusions about the extent to which the employment patterns of migrant single women from ejidatario and landless households might have differed in the past, but the proportion of single women currently employed in domestic service in Mexico City is higher for landless than for ejidatario families. (The proportions of factory workers in the total are similar for both groups.) Migration rates for single women to Mexico are, of course, lower for landless than for ejidatario households (Table 15), but the data for migration to Guadalajara and other internal destinations provide stronger reinforcement for the conclusion that those single women from landless households who do migrate tend to be concentrated in the more menial sectors of the labor market (Figures 7 and 9).

In the case of Guadalajara, no married women were reported to be still working from either landless houses or from the houses of sons of ejidatarios, though a number of the women from landless houses are known to have worked in domestic service, factories and hotels or restaurants in the past. Two married women from ejidatario families were still working in domestic service, one—a widow—worked in a factory, one ran a diner in a working-class district, one kept a shop, and the remaining two were secretaries. Even in the context of Mexico City's more differentiated pattern, it is worth

Figure 7
OCCUPATIONS OF GUADALAJARA MIGRANTS
Married Males and Single Men and Women

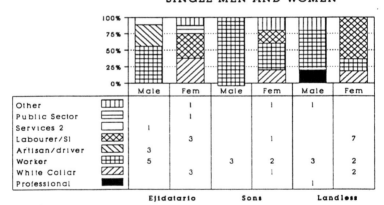

MARRIED MEN

		Ejidatario	Sons	Landless
Other	▥	1		1
Public Sector	▤	6		2
Services 2	▢	3		
Labourer/Sl	▨	4		2
Artisan/driver	▨	6		6
Worker	▦	7	3	5
Agro-pastoral	▧	1		1
Professional	■	4		

SINGLE MEN AND WOMEN

		Male	Fem	Male	Fem	Male	Fem
Other	▥		1		1	1	
Public Sector	▤		1				
Services 2	▢	1					
Labourer/Sl	▨		3		1		7
Artisan/driver	▨	3					
Worker	▦	5		3	2	3	2
White Collar	▧		3		1		2
Professional	■					1	

| Ejidatario | Sons | Landless |

emphasizing that the majority of all married female migrants are married to working-class men, and that those peasant women who have achieved the status of professionals have often done so through their own unaided efforts. Two doctors in this group started working as nurses, and financed their own further education.

The married sons of ejidatarios in Mexico City have a slight advantage over the sons of the landless with regard to access to public employment, but there is a more striking contrast between the two groups in terms of the types of public employment in which their members are engaged. Forty percent of the public employees from landless households are in the police and the military, and only one is a professional. Only one single man from a landless household enjoys a job in PEMEX. The children of ejidatarios are concentrated in a range of state sector jobs which enjoy notably superior levels of pay or security of employment. In the case of Guadalajara, ejidatario houses have both a higher overall proportion of married male public employees and a complete monopoly on both public and private sector married male professionals, though the sole single male professional, a lawyer working in a private administrative capacity, comes from a landless household. Within the Mexico City private sector there is also a clear pattern of relative weighting towards less stable or less remunerative forms of employment in the aggregate data on married men from landless households. In the case of Guadalajara, it is necessary to introduce the occupational category "agro-pastoral" in order to accommodate the existence of an ejidatario's son working as a cowherd, and a man from a landless family who is working as foreman on a ranch on the outskirts of the city. Both ejidatario and landless houses in Guadalajara also include married men who are still studying while working. But abstracting from the existence of two persons in the "services 2" category among the married male children of ejidatario houses in Guadalajara, there is a less marked differentiation in private sector employment between landless and ejidal houses than is the case in Mexico City among married men, and the total number of landless single men, a mere five as against the ejidatario houses' nine, is too small to draw any strong comparative conclusion other than that it is public sector employment and incidence of professionals which provides the chief differentiating factor between married men from different categories, overall differentiation being less marked than in Mexico City.

In the case of migration to other internal destinations, differentiation between categories in terms of proportions of professionals is particularly marked for both married men and single children. Ejidatario households are overwhelmingly preponderant in the production of professionals of both sexes, over 30% of their married, and 50% of their single male migrants falling into this category. Landless houses actually possess a marginally higher percentage of public employees, taking professionals into consideration as well as other types of public employee, though once again we find that the ratio of professional to non-professional employees in the public sector favors the ejidatario houses (48% non-professional, as against 60% in the case of the landless). Furthermore, a higher proportion of the married children of landless households become migrant agricultural workers—*jornaleros*—in the cane or agribusiness enterprises of the Tierra Caliente.[19] Of the agro-pastoral workers among the married sons of ejidatarios, two (a third of the total) are actually themselves ejidatarios, having obtained ejidal rights in Sinaloa after migrating there to cut cane. Of the ejidatario married male "others" two more are former U.S. migrants who have settled in the border region, engaging in activities which are the subject of intense, and malign,

Figure 8
MIGRATION TO OTHER INTERNAL DESTINATIONS
Occupations of Male Children

MARRIED MEN

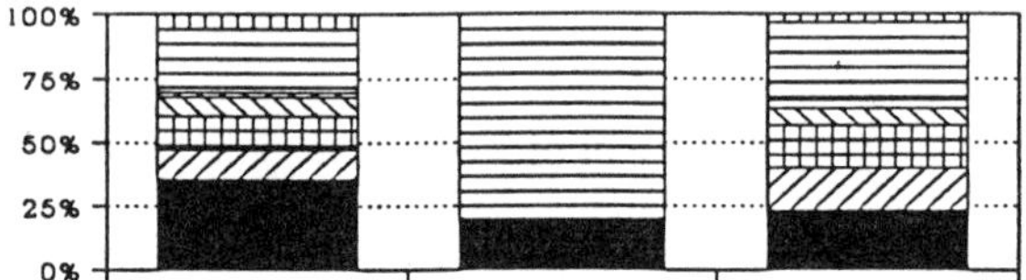

	Ejidatario	Sons	Landless
Other	3		1
Public Sector	1 2	4	9
Services 2	1		1
Labourer/Sl	1		
Artisan/driver	4		2
Worker	7		5
Agro-pastoral	6		5
Professional	1 9	1	7

SINGLE MEN

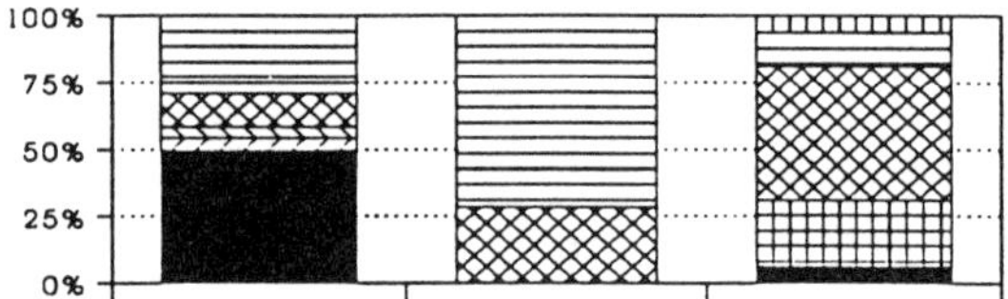

	Ejidatario	Sons	Landless
Not yet working			1
Students	6	5	2
Priest	1		
Public Sector	3	2	8
Artisan/driver	1		
Agro-Pastoral			4
White Collar	1		
Professional	1 2		1

local gossip. In general terms, the married sons of ejidatarios tend to enjoy somewhat better types of private sector employment or self-employment than the landless in these other forms of internal migration, though the data for all groups confirm the dismal picture with regard to local urban employment opportunities which we surveyed in discussing the off-farm work of household heads. But what is most striking about the picture as a whole is the very great importance of public sector employment: all of the married sons of resident sons of ejidatarios are public employees, and the national state is, in fact, responsible for providing a livelihood to virtually 50% of the total number of

Figure 9
MIGRATION TO OTHER INTERNAL DESTINATIONS
Occupations of Single Women

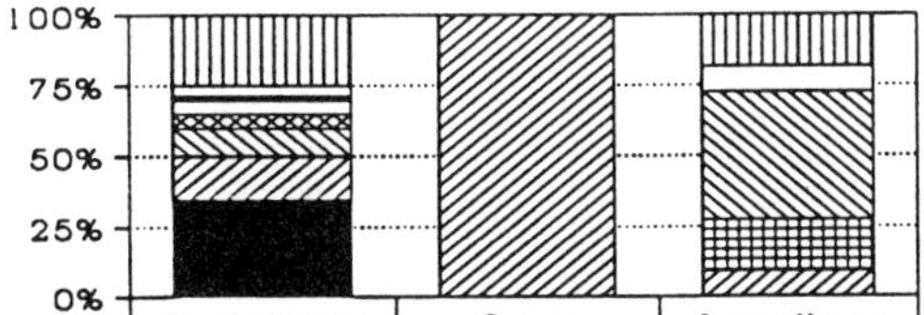

		Ejidatario	Sons	Landless
Students	▥	5		2
Public sector	▤	1		
Nun	▢	1		1
Nurse	▨	1		
Domestic Service	▧	2		5
Factory workers	▦			2
Secretary/cashier	▨	3	1	1
Professional	■	7		

married men engaged in migration to destinations other than Mexico City and Guadalajara from both landless and ejidatario households.

I present no graphical data on married female migrants to other internal destinations, for the usual reason that the numbers are very small. There is, however, a marked pattern of differentiation between ejidatario and landless households in this category. Of the forty-three married daughters of ejidatario households, 70% are housewives, but 70% of the remainder are professionals, mostly teachers, and 15% secretaries; one co-owns and runs a craft workshop with her husband, and only one, a domestic home-worker, represents a low-income worker. Only three of the married women from landless households (8.5% of the total) were recorded as working by their parents, and of these, one is a teacher, one a social worker (in Oaxaca), and one an agricultural worker. In the case of single women migrating to other internal destinations, the predominance of domestic service (and absence of both professionals and federal employees) among landless households is striking. And while public sector work is highly significant to single men from landless households, the preponderance of professionals among single sons of ejidatario houses is, in fact, largely a preponderance of professional public employees. Three of the single sons of landless families are, in fact, technical auxiliaries working for the SARH, and one is an instructor in a *Centro de Capacitación*: in comparative terms, this group represents the best educated group from landless households overall, and also contains three men working for PEMEX. Nevertheless, the occupational advantages of the sons of ejidatarios remain marked, particularly when we add the four farm workers in the landless group into the balance against the mechanic and bank clerk from the ejidatario households.[20]

Landless households also differ greatly from ejidatario households in the terms of the actual geographical range of their migration to other internal destinations besides Mexico City and Guadalajara, as Figure 10, which also breaks the data down by sex and marital status categories, demonstrates. Only 29% of migrants from landless houses move beyond the borders of Michoacán, as against 48% in the case of ejidatario households, and 57% in the case of the children of their resident sons. A greater proportion of their movement is, in fact, purely local, reflecting the greater involvement of their men and married women and sons-in-law in the agricultural sector and small-scale industries of the region, as well as domestic service. The relative dearth of professionals in landless houses is, of course, in large measure responsible for the more restricted range of their migration.

Figure 10
INTERNAL MIGRANT DESTINATIONS
Other than Mexico City and Guadalajara

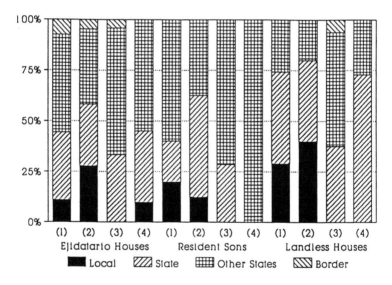

Key: (1) MM, (2) MF, (3) SM, (4) SF

CAUSES OF DIFFERENTIATION

While it is clear from these data taken as a whole that the destiny of the majority of rural-urban migrants is that of joining the "urban working classes," whether they come from ejidatario or landless families, the children of landless families do seem to suffer from a clear pattern of disadvantage in the kinds of private sector employments they obtain. Furthermore, the state has played a major role as a provider of employment, and here too the greater benefits have accrued to the children of ejidal houses. There are three factors which might create differences in the patterns of employment of migrants from landless and ejidatario families: economic differentiation between rural households, differences with regard to the social networks offering aid to new migrants in their various places of destination, and differences in educational levels.

I will only deal briefly with the first factor at this stage in the discussion. If obtaining a given type of employment, or moving to a particular destination, involves cash expenditure, then one might expect ejidatario households to enjoy an advantage over landless households. This is not so much because their absolute levels of income are necessarily higher, but because the possession of land, particularly when accompanied by the expectation of a harvest, gives ejidatarios superior access to credit, which may be used to finance the migration of children. There is no doubt that this was a crucial factor in ensuring that ejidatarios would participate in international migration during the *bracero* period in larger numbers than the landless men to whose problems the program was theoretically addressed, and the extra-legal payments extorted in a highly systematic way by the Mexican officials running the *bracero* program have their parallels in certain types of internal migration today. Obtaining the post of a school-teacher in another state, for example, will routinely involve the candidate in a payment to the head teacher, and union officials play an important role in controlling access to the more attractive forms of urban public and private employment: patronage has its price in many spheres of Mexican society.

The second factor which might create differential patterns of migrant employment between landless and ejidatario households is differences in the aid available from kin who abandoned the countryside for the city in earlier decades. It is important to stress that the present comparison is one between migrants from existing rural households: those landless families which migrated *en masse* at an early stage in the history of agrarian reform, along with the many ejidatarios who abandoned the land for the cities in the early decades, entered the urban labor market under more favorable general circumstances than those who have entered in more recent decades, particularly after the large upsurge in labor supply which accompanied the end of the *bracero* program. As I remarked earlier in the discussion, the impact of general labor market conditions is mediated by a given community's past history of migration and the kind of social networks this establishes: villages which were relative late-comers to the mass rural-urban migration process were undoubtedly disadvantaged. As a community, Guaracha does not fall into this category. But it is still possible that segments of the community were disadvantaged through late entry into migration.

Overall, a marginally higher proportion (77%) of landless households resident in the village today reported the existence of kin based in the metropolitan cities than was the case with ejidatario families (73%). Of houses with graduates, 78% of ejidatario houses reported having kin the cities, compared with 79% of landless houses. These gross figures include migrant children, and in a few cases, migrant parents or parents-in-law. It is more revealing to compare the help which different households might potentially receive from migrant siblings and their children, and from parents' siblings and cousins.[21] The results of the comparison are shown in Figure 11. The percentages of households reporting kin in each category were quite strikingly similar between landless and ejidatario households. A rather higher proportion (21%) of landless households reported uncles in Mexico than was the case with ejidatario households (14%), and the figures were virtually equal for aunts (12% and 13% repectively). There was no other category in which the percentage of landless households reporting relatives was lower than that of ejidatario houses, each type of relative being reported by between 28% and 33% of the houses in question, with a maximum difference between ejidatarios and landless of 3%. In the case of Guadalajara, figures were equally close, though here ejidatario houses were marginally ahead in terms of uncles (7% versus 6%) and cousins (14% versus 11%), while a rather greater percentage of landless houses had siblings in the city, 16% to 11% in the case of sisters,

Figure 11
KIN RESIDENT IN MEXICO CITY AND GUADALAJARA
Ejidatario and Landless Families

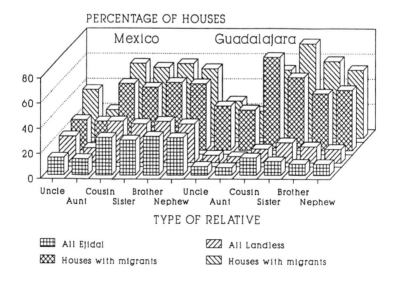

Note: nephew = nephews and nieces

13% to 9% in the case of brothers. These percentages rise across the board if the analysis is restricted to houses which actually have migrant children in the destination in question, almost a quarter of the ejidatario houses with migrants in Mexico reporting uncles or aunts, and over just over half reporting cousins or siblings. Again the percentages are still higher for landless houses, at 38% for uncles and close on 60% for brothers and cousins. In the case of Guadalajara, the landless again report higher numbers of siblings and lower numbers of uncles and aunts, and the differences are more marked. Sixty one percent of landless households with migrants report brothers resident in the city, as against 45% of the ejidatario houses with children there, while the figures for uncles, aunts and cousins put the ejidatario houses in the lead, 35% as against 29% in the case of uncles, 32% as against 21% in the case of aunts, and 74% as against 54% in the case of cousins.

These results confirm that migration to a given destination is more likely if kin are already there, though the effect is much more marked in the case of Guadalajara than Mexico. The comparative figures on the overall incidence of kin in the two cities reflect the legacy of the past concentration of Guaracheño urban-rural migration on the capital, but the differences in percentages for households which do have migrant children in the destination and those which do not would seem to suggest the importance of kinship networks in the migratory process itself. Yet in the case of Mexico, only 46% of ejidatario households and 36% of landless households with migrant children there responded affirmatively to a series of questions regarding the receipt of aid in migration, either in the form of direct help finding work or more indirectly in the form of hospitality. In the case of Guadalajara, the percentages were even lower, at 19% for ejidatarios and 25% for landless houses, despite the apparently stronger association between the presence of children there and the presence of siblings in the case of individual households. It is true that what aid was reported came overwhelmingly from kin rather than family or personal "friends" and patrons, particularly in the case of the landless. Aid from kin in migration may, and indeed frequently does, take the form of aid from one's own siblings established in a destination, though it should be noted that a higher percentage of ejidatario than landless houses which had migrant children lacked kin apart from those children in the cities—11% as distinct from 7%. Much of the past temporary internal migration of currently resident household heads is clearly linked to the presence of close kin in other destinations. In the case of the United States, there is a clear tendency not just for kin but for people from the same community to cluster in specific "colonies" north of the border.[22] Mutual aid and support can take many different forms, including "one off" economic or moral aid in crisis circumstances, and people may simply wish to be close to people they know for reasons of psychological security and sociability. Migrant kin may also be a primary source of information regarding job opportunities even if they do not do anything more concrete to help their relatives obtain work or support their entry into the city. In a few cases, however, people explicitly stated that their relations with migrant kin were distant or even strained, and even if mutual aid networks in the more general sense do play a significant role in promoting the concentration of kin in a particular urban destination, it remains possible that such concentration is also at least partly determined by an underlying similarity between closely related people with respect to other factors which govern their life chances and occupational patterns.

Education is one of these factors, and it may be not only a relatively persistent source of differentiation, but actually promoting increasing social polarization within rural communities because of its relationship to opportunities in migration. It is evident that the level of education a given household's children may be able to attain is not unrelated to its economic circumstances. Access to loans may again play a role here, and I also noted some cases in which ejidatarios decided to rent their *parcelas* with the specific objective of financing their children's further education in the previous chapter. Another consideration is the extent to which young children may be encouraged to neglect their studies in order to undertake some casual paid work in the fields or village. Even where the parents favor education in principle as an investment in the future, actual budgetary crisis may lead them to take an indulgent attitude towards truancy, though I also encountered cases where the children themselves defied parental authority and played truant with the intention of retaining their modest earnings as long as their absence from school went unreported.[23] There is, however, a more obvious and direct relationship between a family's economic position and the educational attainments of its children, since the costs of education rise sharply once a child must study outside the village.[24]

Guaracha has possessed its own secondary school since 1970, and the long hoped-for establishment of a *Preparatoria* to replace the *Escuela Práctica de Agrícultura* which closed in 1958 came to fruition in 1988. In 1983, however, studying *prepa* entailed—at the least—daily journeys to Sahuayo or Jiquilpan, which also offers courses at a higher level at its *Tecnológico*.[25] Most higher study is, however, undertaken in Morelia, other educational centers in the neighboring Bajío states, the famous agricultural college at Chapingo, or in higher educational institutions in Mexico City and Guadalajara. To some extent, children of poor families may be able to obtain higher education through the help of working migrant siblings, supplemented by their own efforts. Simply having kin to stay with—even if they live in a shanty town—reduces costs. There are some families in both the ejidatario and landless categories where one child has achieved higher education while his or her siblings have only the most minimal schooling. There are also families where the children are polarized in terms of educational achievement in a more balanced way, for a variety of reasons. In some cases, resources will not stretch to the education of all from the outset, and some leave school and pursue migrant careers with the explicit intention of contributing to the collective betterment of the larger unit. In others, the academic inclination (and perhaps, though not necessarily, ability) of the children differs. To take but one example, a long-term *bracero* migrant decided to emigrate in 1963, with the explicit intention of using his earnings from the North to educate his children. The daughters generally responded enthusiastically to this opportunity, but two of the sons chose to follow their father as migrant agribusiness workers after completing secondary school. There is, therefore, sometimes an element of choice, albeit a choice structured by circumstances which are themselves structural: in an epoch in which even some of the best educated rural people are to be found doing manual work in the United States, education can no longer be represented as "the peasant's best way out." Nevertheless, despite these and other complications, certain clear patterns of variation do emerge from comparisons between landless and ejidatario households in terms of overall educational levels, on the one hand, and migratory and occupational patterns, on the other.

Table 16 compares the average proportions of children from different categories of household who have attained a hierarchically ranked series of levels

Table 16

AVERAGE EDUCATIONAL LEVELS OF CHILDREN FROM HOUSEHOLDS WITH GRADUATES
(as percentage of graduates)

Group	Level 1	Level 2	Level 3	Level 4	Level 5	Level 6
Ejidatarios						
Mature (F)	7.8	18.2	42.1	16.1	3.7	12.2
Developing (M)	10.3	25.7	46.0	9.8	2.8	5.5
Developing (M)	1.1	4.4	23.8	49.1	8.4	13.2
Developing (F)	2.3	9.1	43.8	28.5	6.9	9.4
Landless						
Mature (F)	13.1	24.1	39.2	15.1	2.3	6.1
Developing (M)	16.5	31.0	41.2	5.4	3.4	2.4
Developing (M)	6.6	10.0	40.0	34.5	4.4	4.5
Developing (F)	11.8	23.4	44.7	13.7	2.2	4.1
Sons						
Mature (M)	0.0	6.7	39.3	14.0	40.0	0.0
Mature (F)	10.0	6.7	30.0	53.0	0.0	0.0
Developing (M)	0.0	15.4	35.3	40.4	7.7	1.3
Developing (F)	0.0	15.0	48.6	25.6	6.4	4.4

Key: Level 1 = illiterate; Level 2 = did not finish primary; Level 3 = finished primary; Level 4 = finished secondary; Level 5 = finished preparatory; Level 6 = completed course in higher education; (M) = male; (F) = female.

of education as a percentage of all graduates. In addition to the normal division between ejidatario households, those of their resident sons and those of landless households, for the purposes of comparison of educational levels I also subdivide the figures in accordance with gender and a simple measure of the relative maturity of households. Households in which the youngest child is aged fifteen years or older are classified as "mature," whereas the remainder are classified as "intermediate," since while they have at least one child who has completed his or her education, the vast majority still have children in school.[26] Since potential access to education locally has improved in more recent years, this subdivision provides some indication of its consequences, although it should be emphasized that the *quality* of education provided by the old *Escuela Agrícola* may have compensated for the fact that children who attended it may have done so for a shorter period of time than present-day children who complete their studies up to *secundaria* level.[27] The table shows percentages of graduates in each category, level 1 representing the illiterate, level 2 children with some schooling who did not complete primary education, and levels 3 through 6 children who have completed primary, secondary, preparatory and some form of higher education, respectively. Higher education includes both teacher training (Normal) and university or polytechnic courses leading to other professional qualifications.

Comparing the relative educational attainments of mature and developing households across the categories reveals a clear pattern of rising average levels of education over time in the case of ejidatario households. The proportion of children in higher categories increases for both men and women. The proportion of children who are either illiterate or did not complete primary school falls drastically, and the fall in the figures for children completing primary school reflects the extent to which more children are proceeding to higher levels. Though women, on average, remain less well educated than men, and the proportion of women who terminate their education with primary school does not fall much in the case of developing households, their relative advance in the top two levels of education is actually greater than that of the men. In the case of landless households there is also a significant fall in levels of illiteracy and failure to complete primary school between mature and developing households, but it is a much smaller relative fall than that which characterizes the ejidatario households, and the difference is more marked in the case of male children than daughters. Indeed, the average proportion of illiterate daughters remains higher in *developing* landless households than it was in *mature* ejidatario households. The proportion of children of both genders in these categories has always been substantially higher in landless households than in ejidatario households, but the relative gap between them has apparently widened over time, despite the significant reduction in the average proportion of male children from landless households in the first two categories in the case of developing households. In general, the picture for landless households is one of inferior average educational attainment across the board, greater proportions of children completing primary school in landless developing households in comparison with ejidatario households simply reflecting such households' lower average proportions of children completing secondary and higher levels. The data for the households of sons of ejidatarios show a pattern of relatively high educational attainment for the small group of mature households, and an average performance somewhat between that of landless and ejidatario households in the case of developing households, rather low rates of graduation from higher education being matched by a very small incidence of illiteracy. Since, however, these households are, on average, the least mature in the total population being surveyed, they have a higher proportion of children yet to complete their education, among whom there will be a significant number of graduates from higher education.

There seems to be a *prima facie* case for arguing that the differences in aggregate occupational patterns between the migrant children of ejidatario and landless households reflect differences in educational background. To take the analysis further, I will employ an index of household educational levels constructed by awarding each level of education a cumulative score and calculating the mean score per household separately for men and women. A household of total illiterates would therefore score one, the minimum, whereas a household whose children were all university graduates would score six. The average score for men for all ejidatario households is 3.5 utilizing this index, the average for mature households is lower, at 3.3, and that for developing households higher, at 4.0. This contrasts with average male scores for landless households of 2.9 for mature households and 3.3 for developing households, only slightly less than the average for developing households of resident sons of ejidatarios. Average scores for female children are predictably lower, 2.9 and 3.6 for ejidatario houses, and only 2.6 and 2.8 for mature and developing landless houses respectively, a reflection of the relatively severe continuing educational disadvantage of many women in landless houses. If houses which do not contain any migrants in the relevant gender category are excluded, average scores rise a little for all categories except women from landless houses. The proportion of women who are migrant from landless houses is also relatively high for those houses which have relatively low scores (between 2 and 3) in comparison with ejidatario houses. The latter have higher proportions of women migrants from houses with relatively higher scores than their landless counterparts. No household with the minimal mean score has any single migrant children of either sex, but developing landless houses have higher proportions of single women in all destinations, including the U.S., than developing ejidatario houses in households with average scores of 4 or below, a reflection of the fact that landless houses continue to produce far fewer highly educated women.

In the case of ejidatario households, the houses with higher mean scores—in the range 4 to 6—have higher average proportions of migrant men than those with lower mean scores, though an average of 40% of men are migrant in mature ejidatario houses with mean scores less than 2, and 50% of men are migrant in the case of developing houses with mean scores of less than 3. The relationship between high levels of education and migration is particularly marked in the case of developing ejidatario households. In the case of landless houses, the highest proportions of male migrants are found in houses with scores in the range of 4 to 5, and the average proportions for households scoring 6 are lower than those for ejidatario houses. 50% or more of the men from the lower scoring houses were migrant in the case of mature landless houses, rather more on average than is the case with ejidatario houses, but the proportion falls to considerably less than 50% in the case of developing landless houses. Thus, from a situation of relative equality in overall male migration rates, despite relatively lower levels of education, younger landless households have fallen behind ejidatario households in rates of migration, and a higher proportion of those who stay in the countryside belong to less well educated households. Those landless households which lack any migrant men are also characterized by below-average levels of education.

The final question which should be posed on the basis of these data is that of the relationship between educational attainment and migrant destination. The highest average proportions of married male migrants are located in Mexico City in the case of mature households in both the ejidatario and landless groups: in the case of the ejidatarios, the highest proportions come from households scoring 1 or 3 overall, with Guadalajara in second place for the least educated households, followed by the U.S.. Other internal destinations attract a higher average proportion of migrants than Guadalajara for households in the intermediate, 3 to 4 range, and the U.S. achieves its highest average proportion (15.3%) in the case of households whose average score is 4, though it is also high (over 11%) for households in the bottom two categories. Disaggregating these figures, we find that in only 30% of the households in question are the U.S. migrants men who had failed to complete primary education, and in the case of developing ejidatario households, there are no married male U.S. migrants who fall into this category; indeed, two-thirds of the men concerned had completed secondary education. The United States is therefore less and less a migrant destination for the uneducated, and its labor market is receiving a hidden subsidy from the Mexican public education system. Two out of the seven mature ejidatario houses with single children in the United States had sent sons who were not educated to primary level, but two more had also supplied graduates of secondary school, and all but 20% of the single male U.S. migrants of developing ejidatario houses had completed secondary school, the remainder having finished primary education. The few women to have migrated permanently to the U.S. in recent years are also relatively well educated.

Guadalajara migration on the part of single men is only really significant in the case of developing ejidatario households dominated by children who terminated their education at primary level. Slightly more educated single men concentrate on the U.S., and the very educated on Mexico City and other internal destinations, something which reflects the role of public employment in their careers. At least one of the Guadalajara male migrants is also a periodic migrant to the U.S. from his residence in the city, and it is evident from the breakdown of occupational data on single male migrants in Guadalajara presented in Figure 10 that single children from ejidatario households are concentrated in the "worker" and "artisan-driver" categories. Guadalajara's urban and industrial expansion has sustained a demand for workers in manual occupations which are constructed as "unskilled," even on the part of large enterprises which also employ a sector of "skilled" workers (Escobar 1986:188), making it a pole of attraction for rural migrants who have no more than a basic education, the slightly better educated continuing to prefer Mexico City or the U.S.

Turning to the mature landless households, we find the married male migrants from the least educated households concentrated in Guadalajara and single men in the U.S.,[28] with only a small proportion of married men in Mexico City. A much higher average proportion of married men from households with mean scores of 2 is to be found in Mexico, with the U.S. in second place for married men, figures for single male migrants becoming comparable with those for mature ejidatario households. Guadalajara again takes second place for married migrants to Mexico City for mature households with an average score of 3, falling behind other internal destinations and the United States again for households at the next level. Once again, we find a relatively high proportion of single male migrants to the U.S. in households with a mean educational score of 4, a pattern repeated in the case of developing households, where there are no single male U.S. migrants from households with scores less than 3; though the United States is only just in second place to Mexico City for married male migrants from developing landless houses, households in this category scoring means of 4 and 5 also have relatively high proportions of married international migrants. In the case of landless men from mature households, almost half those in the U.S. failed to complete *primaria*, but this proportion falls to under 18% in the case of developing households. Thus, while the relatively high rate of international migration on the part of single men from landless households does reflect a peculiar tendency on the part of illiterate males from these households to seek their fortunes in the North, accompanied by a tendency for married men from developing landless houses with a mean score of 2 to do likewise, over time the pattern for landless houses seems to be falling into line with the educational selectivity in international migration already noted for ejidatario households. All this must be set in the context of the overall decline in male migration rates observed for developing landless households. There is little diversity in migration patterns for men from the least educated of these households: it seems to be simply a matter of Mexico City, the U.S., or nothing. Their future does not seem promising.

Relatively high proportions of uneducated single women from developing landless households are to be found in Guadalajara, which also attracted an unusually high percentage of married women from uneducated mature landless households, though less than other internal destinations. The pattern manifested by Figure 10 reflects the fact that a very high proportion of these women have worked in domestic service or the hotel sector, though Guadalajara's relative popularity as a destination for single women from developing landless households extends up the ladder of household educational attainment in a manner reflected by the proportion of single women from landless households who hold jobs in the "white collar" category there. Nevertheless, the contrasts in aggregate employment patterns for single women from the different types of households are apparent, and reflect the educational differentiation of households by gender. The developing landless household category does have the distinction of containing the highest proportion of single women working in the U.S.; one is a factory worker in Los Angeles and entered the United States as a student with her father, who subsequently acquired legal migratory status, while the others, less well educated, accompanied married brothers and sisters and remain undocumented. At least one of these lost her work in the factory in which she was employed and was forced to turn to casual farm work. Thus, while remitted international migrant earnings may help some landless families acquire improved educational standards for some of the next generation at home, the educational disadvantages with which some migrants enter the U.S. labor market are unlikely to be transcended. Furthermore, a particularly disturbing feature of the current crisis pertains to the role of some of the more highly qualified male children of peasant households, particularly those who work as teachers in local rural communities.

Faced with an increasing gap between the aspirations generated by education and the real values of their salaries, in the years since 1983 a number of local teachers with whom I am personally acquainted have embarked upon a new career as semi-skilled migrant workers in factories and the construction sector in the North, using their educational qualifications to facilitate their entry.[29] Some have already decided on the course of long-term emigration. The ultimate irony may therefore be that the internal labor market advantages secured through education, particularly on the part of ejidatario households, may increasingly be translated into a new form of social polarization in which the chief value of the education lies in its facilitation of emigration, and entry into a quite different type of working career in the North. Clearly, landless households will continue to suffer a relative disadvantage in pursuit of this new strategy, and its consequences, should it become entrenched, may be socially divisive, leaving aside its impact on the quality of rural education. To the extent to which the educated migrants are successful—within the terms of what the U.S. labor market offers them—they may invest in the acquisition of local assets and add to the proportion of the rural patrimony of

Michoacán which has fallen into the hands of *emigrados*. The new basis for their superior economic position relative to the poor may provoke greater resentment, since it will no longer be legitimized by their provision of a social service, and the relatively privileged position of the educated as migrants in comparison with the less educated undocumented worker seeking increasingly scarce casual work may itself be a cause of resentment. It is, however, difficult to abstract the possibility of such an "objective" socio-economic tendency from the possible political impact of a generalized frustration of peasant aspirations to secure social mobility in the national society through education. Emigration is only one type of response to crisis on the part of rural professionals, and it has uncertain political implications in the larger picture.[30]

TEMPORARY INTERNAL MIGRATION: RETURN OF THE PRODIGAL SON?

The discussion thus far has focused on what appear to be permanent movements of people from the village. But 75% of household heads in Guaracha have some history of migration. Much of this temporary movement concerns the relationship between the region and the United States and, though not invariably, has a primarily seasonal character. But there is also some movement within Mexico, and such internal peregrinations may be of more extended duration.

Just over 22% of ejidatario household heads have some past internal migratory experience; in the case of the landless, the percentage falls to 16%, that of the resident sons of ejidatarios being similar, at 17%, though it is necessary to bear in mind the possible influence of the lower average age of the latter category. Only 27% of the past internal migration of the sons of ejidatarios was seasonal in nature, whereas just under half of it was seasonal in the case of the other two groups. As far as ejidatarios are concerned, internal migration is generally not a substitute for international migration. Only 24% of the ejidatario internal migrants had no experience of the United States, and although a majority of those who went (77%) had only been to the U.S. as *braceros*,[31] the mean number of trips per person, 4.5, does not represent a gross distortion of the typical individual's number of visits to the North, despite the presence of four long-term U.S. migrants in the sample. In the case of the landless men, however, 53% had never been to the U.S., and the percentage who had only been after 1964 was more than twice that of the ejidatario houses, at 24% of all U.S. migrants in the sample. But three quarters of those who went from landless households had only made three trips or less to the North. Three were long-term migrants, one turning to the North after a spell of internal migration working on the roads, the others turning to cutting cane in Jalisco in the 1960s after going to the U.S.A. as undocumented entrants during the period of the *bracero* accords, though one of these returned twice to the North subsequently. That ejidatarios and their children have enjoyed superior possibilities of access to the international labor market is reflected in the fact that a rather higher proportion (66%) of the resident sons of ejidatarios with internal migrant experience had been to the United States, though this group, being younger, naturally has the highest proportion of persons whose migration is restricted to the period after 1964, half of the total migrants in the group, while more than half of the remainder had been to the United States both before and after the end of the *Bracero* program.

It might be assumed that rural people would have turned to alternative internal migratory strategies after the possibility of legal entry into the United States was terminated for the majority in 1964. Although this pattern is exemplified in the data currently under discussion, it is by no means uncommon for people in this category to proceed to the United States after a period of internal migration, or to combine both types of migration on an intermittent basis. Some individuals, particularly in the landless group, substituted internal for international migration when they failed to secure a place on the *bracero* list for a given year, and some disliked going *al Norte*, made one or two reluctant visits because the alternative of internal seasonal migration was less remunerative and their families put pressure on them. Where people substituted internal migration for past *bracero* migration, most followed the path of a more permanent move from countryside to city.

Just over half the ejidatario internal migrants worked in agriculture, and one other had worked as a gardener in Mexico City, although two of those who worked in the agro-pastoral sector returned to it after a period of work in industrial occupations. A majority of the agricultural migrants sought work in the sugar sector: most of these cases relate to the early decades of the ejido, though there are some more recent examples. Most of the agricultural migrants were simply making seasonal trips, though one of them was the chief recruiter for the Sinaloa sugar mill. But some had more extended sojourns outside the village. Two of the present ejidatarios went to Apatzingán and worked there virtually full-time as that region's demand for labor increased during the 1960s, having kin there with whom they could lodge, and there are four highly idiosyncratic cases where personal calamity—in one case imprisonment—produced an unusual destination or migratory career. A quarter of the persons concerned had at least some experience of industrial work, one, already mentioned earlier, operated a garment workshop, and one worked in construction in Mexico City. Their return sometimes reflected a distaste for city life, though it might also be motivated by an improvement in prospects back in the village linked to inheritance or marriage. In the case of the ejidatarios, some cases of return migration are based directly on a decision to invest urban savings in ejidal assets, but the mere fact of belonging to an ejidal family must clearly increase the probability of return on the part of those who migrate as landless sons, though some of the returnees were already in possession of rights in the ejido when they experimented with migration. In some cases, movement was simply a reflection of economic difficulties, a not uncommon non-economic "push" factor in migration was acts of violence perpetrated in the community, and in at least two cases, return was the result of a similar misfortune in the city. One of the ejidatario returnees is a teacher, and four had enjoyed temporary manual jobs in the public sector. Another had worked on the roads and one on the railway. Two became policemen, one in Zamora and one in Mexico, and another, who also worked in the agro-pastoral sector, spent some time in the Civil Guard. Three had played more entrepreneurial roles in the cities, two of them, brothers, earning a somewhat colourful reputation as a result of their seemingly extraordinary success in the activities in question. There is therefore considerable variety in individual cases within this larger group.

A smaller proportion of resident sons of ejidatarios to have worked outside the community has worked in urban industry than is found among the ranks of the ejidatarios themselves, though it is still higher than in the case of landless families. Another of the urban migrants worked in a jeweller's shop after returning from a trip to the U.S., one is a teacher, and another worked briefly in the police force in the region. Only a third of this group worked in agriculture, half of these in locations in the Tierra Caliente where siblings or other relatives had settled, though these men also went to the U.S. The remaining agricultural workers worked seasonally as cane cutters in Los Reyes, two of them men from very poor ejidatario families who worked in the domestic sugar industry in lieu of *bracero* migration to the U.S.

In the case of the households which remain landless, factors relating return to purchase or inheritance of ejidal rights are no longer relevant. Again half the past internal migrants worked in agriculture, virtually all of them as seasonal cane-cutters. The involvement of landless houses in seasonal agricultural migration was also sometimes linked to the presence of kin who had moved permanently to the new destination and could provide accommodation, or even help in the search for work, though this was by no means a general situation. Only 12% of migrants from landless houses had any experience of industrial work in Mexico City. Two had worked as street traders in Guadalajara and one had worked on the roads. Three were teachers, one worked for the post office and one had worked as a mechanic in the sugar mill in Taretan for fifteen years, following in the footsteps of his father on the hacienda. Divorced and living alone, he now works repairing electrical appliances in the village. There are comparatively few real return migrants in the landless group, and the overall picture is one of restricted opportunities short of definitive emigration from Guaracha.

Although the analysis of temporary internal migration could be extended to children currently residing in the village and from male to female migrants, such an extension would add little to the information already presented through the analysis of longer-term movements and the conclusions which have been drawn from it regarding the relationship between migration and intra-household socio-economic differentiation. It might even be misleading to place too much emphasis on the continuity of historic patterns in evaluating the prospects for the children of the current generation. IMF pressure and domestic neo-liberalism are producing a radical shift in the opportunities offered by the public sector. The market for male labor power demands higher qualifications from new entrants. Women with some education can find industrial work, but the experience of dynamic sectors such as electronics is that these enterprises consume such labor-power on a short term basis only—if they do not consume it totally by crippling the body of the worker.[32] Work in the urban services sector still exists for uneducated women, but the evidence suggests that a prime characteristic of this region in recent years has been its relative retention of labor power of this type. When I completed fieldwork in 1983, people were still prone to remark on how different the scene in the village in the early morning was now that the *congeladoras* in Zamora had cut back so much on the number of women they were willing to employ and one no longer saw a line of buses coming to collect them for work. By the time of my visit in the summer of 1988, things had changed considerably. Much more ejidal land was being rented, and the women were going back to work on the trucks of a new group of agricultural entrepreneurs engaged in the international vegetable trade. Male *jornaleros* were beginning to complain that their labor was being displaced by that of women. Ejidatario fathers sat in their houses anxiously scrutinizing the most recent letter received from their son in the U.S.: friends speculated that over a thousand of the young men of the community were now in the North, and the letters were full of stories about the difficulties of getting work. Two young men in a souped-up VW Beetle who had arrived from Los Angeles were extremely cheerful, but that image was offset by the obvious trepidation in the eyes of a sixteen year old whose precipitous marriage to a pregnant sweetheart was to be followed in short order by a hasty exit to the United States to seek the means to support his new family.

Mexico's political discourse often centers around a debate about whether *"la crisis"* is "conjunctural" or "structural." I have argued that the structural conditions for the reproduction of rural households through the combination of rural activities and labor migration are undergoing major, and worrying, changes. In the past, expansion of the domestic urban economy, combined with international migration as a "safety-valve," have permitted the continuation of a form of "development" in both social and material terms from the national point of view, though a large segment of the country's population has been deprived of any real share in the fruits of this process. Rural crisis, as manifest in a growing tide of rural unrest during the Echeverría period, was eventually moderated—though scarcely eliminated—by state intervention. The Mexican urban middle class convinces itself that at least there is no *hunger* in the countryside today. They are not correct in this assertion, either in terms of international standards of minimum adequate nutritional levels or in terms of families simply going hungry several days a week, even if the number of households to which this applies is very small in a community like Guaracha. But this assessment of the sustainability of life in rural Mexico misses the real issues behind the current crisis. Those issues are work, the growing difficulties of securing access to it on a regular basis anywhere in the system, and the potential additional social polarization stemming from these changes. When asked whether they thought the future in the village would be better, worse or the same in the future, Guaracheños tended to stress two things: the hope of progress through education, and the lack of local employment opportunities. Hope lies in escape, and pessimism resides in remaining immobile. The were more inclined to the pessimistic than optimistic view, even in 1983. In a sense, the renewed expansion of labor-intensive agribusiness in the region offers a new element of hope, despite its low wages, since it does at least offer more work. But this is only one dimension of a larger, and more contradictory, process of internationalization of the peripheral rural economy. In turning to the historical role of the international labor market in the reproduction of Guaracha's peasantry, it is not sufficient simply to emphasize the differences between earlier and more recent economic conditions, even in the broader sense which takes into account the technological transformation and geographical relocation of agricultural production systems tied to the global agro-industrial complex. It is also necessary to evaluate the social costs of this dimension of peasant reproduction in the past, and point to the way these may escalate if present trends are allowed to pursue their course. Indeed, even an assessment of the significance of the international migratory movement in terms of the quality of the social life of the migrants and their families is inadequate. International migration has always had a political dimension and domestic political implications. American restrictions on migration have presaged political difficulties for several régimes, even if the "safety-valve" procedure of selling one's population as an ethnic underclass to a foreign country played a major role in calming the crisis which followed the Cárdenas era. Not for nothing, perhaps, do the modern Cardenistas seem as capable of putting their people on the streets in Los Angeles as they do in Mexico City.

CHAPTER 8
EL NORTE

There is a real danger of producing a distorted understanding of the role of Mexican migration to the United States if we attempt to generalize the experience of Michoacán to the country as a whole. The countryside of Michoacán has experienced high rates of net out-migration to a variety of destinations, but it is also marked, along with neighboring Jalisco and the Bajío, by a particularly extensive and long-standing commitment to migration to the United States. Even the locals themselves speak self-reflexively of their "custom" of going to the North as a cultural feature of the area.

Elsewhere in the country the balance of internal and international migration has been very different historically, and not all parts of rural Mexico are places from which people leave. De la Peña notes that the relatively late incorporation of the Altos of Morelos into the *bracero* program at first sight appears anomalous, given the close proximity of a *Centro de Contratación* to their homes, a factor which is often cited in order to explain the weight of the *bracero* migration from Guanajuato, Michoacán and Jalisco (De la Peña n.d.). But Morelos lacked a tradition of migration in the earlier years of the century, had a different—if scarcely satisfactory—experience of agrarian revolution and reform, and developed its agriculture along different lines in the ensuing decades. The neolatifundist phenomenon encountered in the irrigated zones of Michaocán, Jalisco and the Bajío cannot, however, be treated as a discrete "determinant" of migration: it was the product of a complex conjuncture of socio-economic and political conditions of regional agrarian development which included the already established flow of people to the North. Opportunities to go to the United States as a *bracero* were dispensed to ejidatarios by the politicians of the region as a means of managing menacing social and political problems (and building careers on patronage), in a context where those politicians enjoyed close ties with various segments of a regional agrarian bourgeoisie intent on inserting itself into the space created by the destruction of a particular form of *latifundismo*. Furthermore, the conditions under which agrarian reform occurred here were determined by the nature of the preceding phase of revolutionary violence and counter-violence, factors which combined with the nature of the Porfirian social and economic order in the region to produce the early commitment to the United States. This in turn, through the creation of colonies in the North and development of migratory social networks, canalized subsequent events.

From this perspective, the seamless web of history appears—with hindsight—strongly teleological, but there were moments when alternative patterns of development would have been possible, and new factors played a role at different stages. The population of Morelos was particularly well-positioned to take up opportunities provided by the Mexico City labor market during the first decade of the *bracero* program, and the salience of this factor (given local agrarian conditions) is equally evident from differential patterns in Michoacán. In municipios around Morelia, for example, *jornaleros* work seasonally in construction in Mexico City (or Morelia itself) as an alternative to work in the United States, just as do peasants from the Altos of Morelos: wage rates[1] are much lower than in the United States, but one avoids the debts required to meet the costs of travel, and payments to *coyotes* (Trigueros and Rodríguez Piña 1988:207). Here we also are dealing with the factors of social selection in migration discussed in the previous chapter, and even so a majority, especially of young people, from these Michoacano communities prefer to run the risks and bear the costs of visits to the United States because of the earnings differential. This reflects the additional secular forces which canalize the flow of people north from the "traditional" migratory states.

Even in Michoacán there has always been a substratum of the rural population which has pursued a strategy of recurrent seasonal migration to work as laborers in cities or as workers in domestic commercial agriculture. International migration opportunities were unequally distributed in the *bracero* period, and today's poorer and less educated men are again being seriously disadvantaged. In terms of definitive movement, the major migratory phenomenon of the past was that to the cities. Nevertheless, international migration has left an indelible stamp on the economy of the region, manifested in the type of commercial agriculture and agro-industry which has developed there, and in the particular role played by female labor locked in the villages, which now extends to such activities as garment making as well as agriculture and food processing (Arizpe and Aranda 1981; De la Peña n.d.). Still more significantly, perhaps, it has had a profound impact on the social, cultural and political life of the area. Michoacán is not Mexico. But without those millions of rural people moving to the North, and the one to three billion dollars of migrant remissions flowing in annually during the early 1980s,[2] Mexico as a whole would be a very different place.

TIES THAT BIND, STRUCTURES THAT DIVIDE

An obvious difference between international and internal migration is the fact that the predominant tendency since 1929 has been for American capitalism to absorb male Mexican labor power divorced from the family unit left behind in Mexico. Although the vast majority of those who went to the North before the Great Depression were males without families, at least some of those who did emigrate definitively from Guaracha in the 1920s seem to have married women from the village who followed them to the United States The very name of the *bracero* program reveals its different presuppositions: the achievement of citizenship, though still very much a practical possibility, was formally separated from the process of drawing off surplus labor from the Mexican countryside.

In signing the *bracero* accords, the government of Mexico conceded the premise that those of its workers who escaped American control should justly be expelled while those who entered with contracts should nevertheless possess restricted civil rights (Bustamante 1983b). It thereby provided the entrepreneurs of the North not only with cheap and relatively powerless labor, but also with the means to use Mexico as a labor reserve external to national responsibilities in accordance with the economic cycle. Indeed, in this latter sense the ending of the *bracero* program and the corresponding sharp increase in the proportion[3] of "undocumented" workers in the annual migrant labor force was not necessarily a disadvantage to employers: providing the state was sufficiently lax in the implementation of control when American demand for labor was high to prevent acute shortages emerging, the "illegality" of the migrant made his or her counter-cyclical expulsion that much the easier. Wage rates and earnings did drift upwards over the decade after 1964, and most of the long-term undocumented migrants I interviewed in Guaracha stated that they increased sufficiently, at least until the 1980s, to more than compensate for increases in costs. But as Bustamante has pointed out, levels of vigilance on the part of the authorities and stimulation of "public awareness" of the "problem" of undocumented migration display a remarkable cyclical correlation with economic conditions (Bustamante 1983b).

There was certainly a reaction to the end of the *bracero* program on the part of agribusiness, particularly in California, in the form of an accelerated drive towards mechanization, and it has been argued that this produced a process of decasualization and a resultant preference on the part of employers for a stable work-force of "green card" holders by the 1970s (Cross and Sandos 1981). But though this is true of larger enterprises in California, Arizona and New Mexico, it must be noted that "illegals" may hold permanent jobs, particularly in smaller concerns, and may also belong to trade unions, while "legal" migrants may be restricted to non-unionized casual employment, particularly as they become older. Furthermore, the expansion of the employment of undocumented workers in other sectors over the years is at least in part related to the ease with which the employer can dispense with both his own legal responsibilities and the workers' services. To date, despite the anxieties created by such developments as the Simpson-Rodino Law, the problem has never been one of undersupply of migrant labor power of the right quality to the American labor market as a whole, but on the contrary, the advantageous situation of increasing oversupply.

The United States government's direct intervention with regard to the conditions under which Mexican migrant workers might be employed in the North was merely the culmination of a series of official and informal processes which had been subtly transforming the position of Mexicans in the United States even before the crisis and mass expulsions of the depression years. Indeed, the *bracero* program was another expression of the geo-political hegemony which the United States had claimed over all its southern neighbors for a century, subtle in the symbols of domination displayed when the contract workers made the transition across the border, less subtle in their treatment at work, and finally brutal when, in 1954, economic downturn produced the mass deportations of illegal entrants known as "Operation Wetback".[4] Government action which disadvantages Mexican workers in the United States has, however, also been accompanied by widely-diffused social practices of discrimination against incoming Mexicans by their hosts.

One significant example is the way the United States's internal stratification system has promoted anxieties on the part of Chicano Americans towards their Mexican cousins. Guaracheños seem universally agreed that it was always the Chicano foremen with whom they had most trouble, and relatively recent long-term migrants to the U.S. often singled out their lack of social acceptance by fellow "Hispanics" as one of the most painful dimensions of their experience. But the increasing antipathy towards undocumented Mexican migration shown by some other sections of U.S. society in recent years does not seem explicable simply in terms of divisions provoked by social and labor market inequalities; through their numbers and cultural distinctiveness the Hispanics have all become "aliens" in a more radical sense. In the 1980s they manifested a difference that could no longer be tolerated within the revivalist totalizing ideologies of national identity and destiny promoted by the New Right.

Such demands for the radical exclusion of Mexicans and suppression of Hispanic identity should be distinguished both from everyday practices of social discrimination and from the type of opposition to the entry of Mexicans manifested throughout the *bracero* period by organized labor in the North. Although the U.S. decision to terminate the program in 1964 was made in the context of belated Mexican government attempts to renegotiate its terms in response to mounting public pressure, it also reflected the fact that the opposition from American labor had reached a new pitch of intensity. Cézar Chávez's new United Farm Workers Union now added its voice to the long-standing protests of the Teamsters and AFL-CIO in the face of its failure to make a break-through in organizing the *braceros* (Solkoff 1985:150-152). Some UFW organizers were themselves the children of an earlier generation of Mexican migrants, and though union opposition sometimes helped to legitimize maltreatment of Mexican co-workers, it did constitute a genuine problem from the point-of-view of the employers, because it not only threatened to disrupt the supply of Mexican labor but raised arguments which challenged the entire rationale of denying such labor its "normal" rights. More pragmatically, the unions saw that it would not be as easy for employers to use undocumented migrants to break strikes as it had been for them to use the *braceros* for this purpose. In the longer term, however, the ending of the *bracero* program created problems for the unions, at least in Californian agribusiness. It was not simply the increasing cost of undocumented migrant labor but fear of even worse consequences in the face of increasingly extensive and effective unionization which produced the rapid acceleration of investment in mechanization after 1963, much of which had already come to fruition by the end of the decade.[5] Over the decade fewer and fewer citizen workers sought employment in agribusiness, and the unions faced severe losses of members. Although César Chávez was still talking about the need for strict border control and expulsion of undocumented workers as late as 1974, both the UFW (now an affiliate of the AFL-CIO) and the Teamsters had abandoned this stance by 1976: not only did their officials begin to declare publicly that they were uninterested in the migratory status of those they represented, but both unions began to recruit members inside Mexico and set up offices and clinics there (Solkoff 1985). For the moment at least, their antagonism to undocumented Mexican migration ended.

Both concerted state policy and a variety of different forces within North American civil society have acted together or independently over the years to filter the flux and reflux of migrants from the South. But none of these filters has prevented either a growth in temporary movement or a more permanent cumulative transfer of population over the years. The *bracero* program was designed to enable the United States to draw on reserves of Mexican labor power without being forced to accept the permanent immigration of its bearers and their dependent families. In the longer term it actually stimulated a new round of emigration, although a majority have used their green cards as a work permit for annual entry rather than as a means of taking up permanent residence in the United States (Massey *et al.* 1987:177). Though the establishment of networks of kin and *paisanos* was always the key factor in obtaining papers—leaving aside those whose real status in the United States is that of an "*emigrado* chueco" bearing a false identity—on more than one occasion, a *bracero* migrant from Guaracha obtained his papers through the aid of an employer. New restrictions were imposed on access to green cards after 1964, albeit moderated by periodic amnesties for illegal entrants. But the ranks of the *emigrados* in the village are still increasing even in the crisis-ridden 1980s, a reflection of the continuing importance of the social infrastructure of migration created by the migrants themselves in the period since 1918. Over the decades, a substantial number of Guaracheños have committed themselves permanently, or at least semi-permanently, to the kind of life the United States offers them, in the sense that they regard the North as their home for the time being and have their families there. And although absolute numbers remain relatively low, the data from Guaracha on more recent migrants presents a picture which is consistent with that observed elsewhere in western Mexico (Massey *et al.* 1987:76-103): during the 1970s, a larger proportion of undocumented as well as documented migrants began to take wives and children with them to the North, at least on a temporary basis. Furthermore, although male employment has become increasingly problematic, as more and more people compete for jobs in sectors where labor-saving technical change has occurred, scope for employment of women has been expanding on both sides of the border.

A LAND OF OPPORTUNITY?

The waged employment of women (and children) is certainly nothing new: one third of the factory work-force within Mexico was female in the early decades of the country's industrialization and domestic service has always played a significant role in the reproduction of rural households. But today's patterns are more complex and variegated, involve much larger numbers of people and households, and reflect the processes of uneven and combined development characteristic of Mexico's post-war economic transformation— processes which rest on the economic hegemony of the United States mediated in critical respects through the actions of the Mexican national state. It is, however, vital to re-emphasize the fact that changing employment patterns do not really correspond to significant enhancements of economic opportunity, since the new labor market opportunities tend to be unstable and short-term. We are dealing not with the creation of new occupations for people, but a transitory consumption of a certain kind of labor-power, which is, in many cases, actually destructive of the long-term working capacity of the worker. Furthermore, these developments must be set in the context of overall wage-levels (on both sides of the border, and in all sectors of the economy) and need to be considered in relation to the problem of global family income. Not only are individual earnings generally absolutely low throughout the total system, but the problem of household reproduction is complicated by the impact of socio-economic change on the internal distributive relations of the household and by the reciprocal impact of tensions over distribution of earnings on the social fabric of peasant life.

Despite these complications, international migration continues to divide family units in the majority of cases. Only the *emigrados* technically possess the opportunity to commit themselves fully to life in the United States, even if, to date at any rate, many "illegal" migrants have found it possible to stay for extended periods and come and go more or less as they please. But by denying the Mexicans whose labor power it consumes full social incorporation, American society has ensured that many of those who could stay continue to focus their dreams on Mexico. This is perhaps more true today then it was in the earliest period of emigration from the Ciénega, which resulted in a substantial colonization of certain centers of the United States by families from the region, many of which continue to interact with their kith and kin to the south. And the impact of social discrimination has been reinforced by the increasing economic polarization of the sending and receiving regions, which favors the expenditure of dollar earnings in Mexico and siting of the basic family reproduction process south of the border. The cost of the situation in terms of disruption of family life and psychological pressure is not inconsiderable, and may help to explain why a growing minority are taking their families with them despite the possible disadvantages of such a strategy. Most of those who remain residents of the village are not habitual international migrants, but for regular and sometime international migrants alike it remains true that the bulk of the dollar remittances which have passed south across the border over the post-war period has been absorbed by the consumption expenses of the migrants' families in Emiliano Zapata.

It is important to define "consumption" in its historically and socially concrete form, rather than to treat it in universalistic terms as an embodiment of "basic needs," even though this is how many of the migrants themselves would define the use to which they put their earnings. In this particular case it is essential to remember how little the peasants of Guaracha had inherited from their former *patrón* in the sphere of consumption standards and domestic capital. The hacienda's housing stock was scarcely much of a legacy, and building a more permanent and comfortable dwelling was high on the list of priorities of those who set off as married men to the United States in the early years of *bracero* migration. Building one's own house has naturally remained a priority for younger migrants up to the present day, and remains a major financial commitment. Several of the young ejidatarios of the 1980s were renting their land precisely for this purpose. The house is, of course, more than a roof over the head: in the early days it was a critical arena of what one might term the "emancipatory consumption" of the post-hacienda epoch, and to "have one's own house" has remained an important element in the establishment of adult male identity. People emphasized the "rags to riches" achievement of Don Santiago by stressing the fact that he was originally "so poor he didn't have his own house," and it is quite normal for sons to build themselves new houses even though the parental home only contains a widower father. Sixteen percent of the ejidatario migrants I interviewed defined the building of their houses as the chief asset acquired by migrant earnings, and a much higher proportion used dollar earnings to buy furniture or make improvements to their dwellings. Men have also been preoccupied with clothing and relatively costly guns, for reasons which are equally clearly socially defined. Other types of expenditure whose significance bears some initial comment are family education, where U.S. migration, or even emigration, is sometimes consciously chosen as a strategy likely to optimize the chances of children or siblings achieving social mobility, and medical costs.

Some of the younger long-term U.S. migrants I interviewed had been meeting the medical costs of their parents as well as the needs of their own families, and others played an important role in enabling a sibling to achieve a professional career through higher education. Here it becomes apparent that the social unit being "reproduced" on the basis of an individual's migrant earnings is variable. Some migrants are single, supporting aged or sick parents or younger siblings in a family whose head has died prematurely, some are supporting two families, while at the other end of the spectrum, we have migrants without major responsibilities, and those who, like the internal migrants surveyed in the previous chapter, fail to live up to them. Older people in Emiliano Zapata frequently argued that today's young U.S. migrants were less inclined to obey what they defined as "norms" of remittance to parents. In some cases, married migrants in the U. S. have actually abandoned their families in Mexico, though the effective end of a conjugal union does not necessarily lead to the termination of remittances, and "shacking up with another woman." Even having a new family in the United States, does not invariably lead to a permanent marriage break-up. This is not a new phenomenon historically, but there seems to be truth in the assertion that today's children—particularly male children—are withholding a greater proportion of their earnings for themselves and even defaulting on remittances to parents more frequently than in the past. In part reduced remissions reflect rising costs and difficulties in obtaining work, but they are also symptomatic of the more general social process of distributive atomization within household units and the growing commoditization of social relationships.

We must recognize that spending money on drink and whores, for example, is a social fact rather than a purely individual one. Men often spontaneously seek to justify such expenditures as necessary on grounds of "natural" male needs, thereby highlighting their constructed nature. In some cases, relatively high male migrant earnings may have been less significant to a family's real economic reproduction process than the largely unacknowledged and unquantified sacrifices of the migrant's wife, although the fact that the wives of U.S. migrants in Michoacán villages often make direct contributions to family income by seeking paid work generally simply reflects the fact that the earnings of casual field workers in the North today are too unstable to provide a secure basis for family survival.[6] A few of the men I interviewed did undertake a certain amount of retrospective self-criticism of the way they spent what they earned, albeit with something of a gleam still left in the eyes. But the problems created for women by their husbands' "diversions" are certainly too serious to pass over without comment. While it is true that the men in the North face a labor regime which places a great physical, and in many cases emotional, burden upon them, women have few symmetrical compensations for their burdens. Those few who have sought respite in passion did so on terms largely determined by men, and paid for it in another currency.

The contribution of U.S. migration to the reproduction of the Guaracha ejido can hardly be overstated. Besides the more dramatic instance of use of migrant earnings to buy an ejidal *parcela*, dollar income participated more generally in the reproduction of farming livelihood and basic social reproduction: ejidatarios acquired traction animals and plows, and cows and goats which provided a reserve to defray some of the major regular costs which occur in the peasant life-cycle, such as marriages, as well as the unexpected, such as medical bills. For many, as is already clear, such additional income was not sufficient to enable them to avoid debts, and the absolute amount of income generated by migrant work in the United States was also very variable, for reasons which will be examined in more detail below. But a full appreciation of the impact of international migration on the social reproduction process in Emiliano Zapata and neighboring communities requires more than a simple quantification of income streams arising from different forms of work and productive activity.

THE REALITY OF THE FRONTIER

International migration from the Ciénega to the United States is a process of long duration which amounts to much more in sociological terms than a simple movement of working people from one location to another. Migration is simply the most obvious manifestation of a series of social nexuses which transcend the boundaries between the politically-defined societies of the United States and Mexico. The bulk of Mexican migrants to arrive in the United States during the 1920s and 1930s came from the states of Guanajuato, Jalisco and Michoacán (Ramos Arizpe 1983:36). People from particular communities tended to cluster in particular locations in the United States where the early pioneers had settled, and this clustering of emigrants naturally tended to canalize later migratory streams to some extent. Though the more centralized organization of labor allocation on the American side during the *bracero* program disrupted the established patterns somewhat, and created new ones as some temporary migrants found stable employment, a continuing process of permanent or semi-permanent emigration reinforced the tendency to produce colonies of people with a common local origin in Mexico across the border. By no means everyone who has gone from Emiliano Zapata to the United States *al alambre* since 1964 has found work through the intervention of emigrant relatives or even the *contratistas* and *coyotes* who come from the Ciénega communities. Nevertheless, much of the migrant stream is socially organized, by Mexicans, through chains of particularistic relationships which transcend the political boundary between states and the interventions of governments and interest groups.

Yet the frontier is far from becoming an irrelevance. Thanks to the political boundary, the use of Mexican migrant workers by American capitalism offers advantages which could not be secured in the employment of a domestic ethnically-defined laboring underclass. This fact of political economy needs to be stressed, since one might otherwise argue from an analysis of the integration of the two national economic systems that the frontier has progressively become less meaningful from the point of view of the dynamics of world system relationships. But this is not the only consideration. Neither increasing economic integration nor the ramification of cross-border social networks have diminished the cultural bifurcation of the system.

Long-term migrants may display superficial indices of identification with the North, in styles of dress and other patterns of consumption, and certainly tend to mark their identities in obvious ways such as the way they improve their houses—bronze metal window frames seem particularly popular, for example. But there is little trace of emulation of *anglo* patterns even at this superficial level of consumption and display of commodities: in consumer culture we are talking about a *sui generis* Norteño syncretism or California Hispanic, and it is worth noting the extent to which small-scale non-agricultural production in Michoacán and Jalisco itself is orientated towards satisfying the export market created by *paisanos* resident in the United States. There is a kind of valorization of the experience of the North here, but at a more profound level of subjectivity such valorization seems increasingly ambiguous and contradictory. In part this is a consequence of the experiences of rejection suffered by so many Mexicans in the North. Some habitual migrants whom I came to know particularly well found me the ideal medium for expressing their feelings:

> Here you can live with us amicably (*convivir*), we accept you and we are friends. But it's not like that there, we don't get treated like we treat others. People don't want to live together. It's hard, Juan, it's hard.

Even in the case of *emigrados*, conditions of life across the border seldom seem to promote feelings of "belonging" or assimilation into American society, but on the contrary pose a sharp and regretful contrast between "life" in Mexico and what enduring work in the United States can offer, money without a real life.

In what is in many respects an exemplary discussion of international migration from western Mexico, Massey and his collaborators speak of the "integration" of long-term migrants into American life in terms of their acquisition of certain kinds of competences in dealing with bureaucratic procedures and understanding how things work (Massey *et al.* 1987:254-270). Yet it is a strange kind of integration.[7] People who have spent virtually their entire working lives in the North may come to understand the drift of conversations between *gringos* in English, but they cannot speak the language beyond possessing a working knowledge of a few terms directly connected with the work situation and search for work, and the expletives and terms of domination and abuse of which they themselves are habitual victims.[8] Though they may speak warmly of particular *patrones* or other individuals who offered them some aid, this is not the dominant theme of their discourse, which is largely about difference:

> "*There* everything has its owner, you're not *free* like here."

> "The government of the United States is very civilized, if you obey its laws. Everything is very regulated."

> "They have different customs, and I never liked the food."

> "Working under a foreman, for a boss, is okay because the money's good, and I'd accept that here if the work and the money

were guaranteed and the same, though it's better to be your own
master really, if it weren't for the poverty ... but we don't have to
work here, it's free."

And, of course, from undocumented migrants:

"You can never feel totally comfortable, the fear of the *Migra* is
always there."

As some of these remarks suggest, experience of the difference represented
by the North in turn creates reflection of the nature of Mexico itself, a process
of reconstruction of the meaning of "Mexico" as a total system of social life.
In particular, Mexico and the United States are constructed in their mutual
oppositions as political economies and as juridical systems, each with its positive and negative attributes. It is important to understand the concrete experiences underlying these paradigmatic conceptions. When, for example, I asked
about whether deportees had been fairly or badly treated by the American
immigration authorities and border patrols, it became apparent that experiences were variable but that it was not unusual to be beaten and robbed by the
Mexican police on being repatriated. The victims of such treatment naturally
tended to place particular emphasis on American "legalism" versus Mexican
arbitrariness and lack of "justice." But this is only one small facet of the total
matrix of concrete experience which it is the objective of this book as a
whole to portray. At this juncture it is preferable to summarize the factors
underlying the "unhappy consciousness" of the migrant in more abstract terms.

The international migration situation entails a series of contradictory processes of identity construction. First, capitalist enterprises impose the disciplines of wage labor on peasants. Despite the fact that the Guaracheños had,
in a sense, already experienced proletarianization, they had not received the
same kind of capitalist socialization under the hacienda as they were to
receive in the United States, and land reform and the existence of the
Mexican alternative complicated the process after 1940. Although the evidence suggests that Guaracheños make good workers, they have the problematic quality of being drawn into a continual reflection on alternative working
regimes and modes of livelihood which prevents their being "normalized" as
proletarians. Indeed, the peculiar conditions under which the majority are
employed as undocumented migrants forecloses on the possibility of normal-
ization. Hence the ambiguities and discontents of their subjectivities as workers. At the same time, the U.S. state apparatus must impose the disciplines of
a different kind of society on people who were still weakly integrated into a
modern type of national society in the 1940s, and whose situation reproduces
problems of political integration even if it tends to consolidate identification
with "the nation" under modern conditions. While migrants are being subjected to these processes of domination abroad, stay-at-home neighbors (and

less successful fellow migrants) are constructing the more successful Norteños as a different type of person. Migrants have to attempt to reconstruct themselves as human beings in a situation which has a significant number of distinctly dehumanizing facets—being in an alien cultural milieu, often experiencing poor living conditions, being abused by foremen of different social and ethnic backgrounds, and suffering intensive surveillance by police and migration authorities. To speak of long-term migrants becoming more integrated into the society of the North is therefore somewhat misleading: the real problem, even for the most economically successful and secure *emigrado* migrants, is that their integration becomes problematic everywhere in the system. The divided selves produced by the experience of the recurrent migrant life-style receive only partial recognition in both the socio-cultural spheres in which they operate and yet experience difficulty in establishing an autonomous identity of their own. This is why the long-term nexuses between the Ciénega and the North had a political as well as a social, economic and cultural impact on the region's development in the past, and may do so again in the future.

The frontier is neither an irrelevance nor a datum. It is something that is reproduced and recreated both by the action of states and the subjective reactions of people to their experience. This is not to deny that there are areas of analysis where a fixation with the boundary constituted by the border is unhelpful. I do not believe that the "problem" of Mexican international migration, however defined, or from whatever perspective, has a "solution," precisely because we are not dealing with a flow of people between two utterly discrete societies, but an integrated system of social interaction within a single, economically bipolar system. The level of unequal development within this system is so great as to constitute an apparently irreversible phenomenon. It may well be the case that international migration flows could be reduced by new models of economic development within Mexico, though the possibility of such models actually being implemented seems dubious, and it seems somewhat naive to suggest that American aid or greater American investment could play a positive role in improving the rural situation south of the border. In the wake of the transition from incorporation of the Mexican countryside into American agriculture as a source of labor power to its more direct incorporation as a production zone for the U.S. agro-industrial complex, the economic relationship with the United States seems to be exacerbating rather than ameliorating the rural "push" factors in migration. But international migration is not, in any case, sustained simply by either poverty in Mexico or the promise of superior economic opportunities in the United States, as envisaged by the traditional kind of "push-pull" distinction.

As Massey and his collaborators have observed, the existence of long-standing migrant traditions and the creation of social networks give the flow of people to the North a certain momentum of its own, independent of purely economic determinants (Massey *et al.*, 1987:312-314). As we have seen, not all individual cases of migration are determined by economic factors. But more significantly, the "adventure" of going to the North has become a regular test of manhood and a feature of growing up in Michaoacán. Given that the infrastructure for getting people across the border exists, it can be used for many purposes. The economic links with the North established from the Mexican side of the border are not purely concerned with labor migration. Without wishing to exaggerate this dimension unduly, I note that they include currency speculation and drug trafficking as well as a number of entirely "legitimate" forms of local enterprise which are dependent on the part of Michoacano society which resides in the U.S. If migration itself is seen as a more "total" socio-cultural phenomenon, then it becomes less clear whether it would be totally responsive to purely economic measures or certainly measures directed at agricultural development. But perhaps this argument is also somewhat misleading.

The Ciénega de Chapala and regions like it have experienced plenty of agricultural development. It is the forms taken by capitalist development in Mexico which are the problem, and these processes are indeed systemic. To say that the migratory phenomenon has acquired an independent momentum of its own is not to say that the interdependent economic development processes taking place on both sides of the border have not played the major systemic role in determining the shape and extent of migration over the decades. To talk of the way the "migrant adventure" has become ingrained in local culture as if it were a factor in the long-term reproduction of mass recurrent migration is particularly unsatisfactory. Many young people, especially today, neither enjoy nor profit from their first experience of migration, and yet more are returning to try their luck again. The role played by the social infrastructure and migrant tradition of the region is to make a key contribution to sustaining the conditions under which U.S. migration remains a leading strategy in local solutions to the problem of securing a livelihood and to perpetuating the various other dimensions of economic dependency between North and South.

Changing conditions in the United States also influence the conditions for the reproduction of the migratory strategy. It may well be the case that the capacity of the U.S. economy to absorb the presently available pool of migrant laborers from Mexico (and its southern neighbors) is diminishing for structural reasons, and that jobs in agriculture will be sharply reduced, not simply through continuing mechanization, but because much of the irrigated agriculture in which migrants work may not be ecologically sustainable (Solkoff 1985). To some extent the endlessly expanding supply of Mexican undocumented labor may create its own demand in other sectors or even be responsible for the development of new sectors: the fact that a number of Guaracheño migrants of both sexes have found work in small-scale urban industrial enterprises in California in recent years may reflect tendencies of this kind. But the limits to such adaptations may already have been reached.

The northern labor market tends to restructure itself in ways which create downward pressure on the occupations available to Mexicans, a corollary, perhaps, of the way the employment prospects of other segments of the American working class have been affected by deindustrialization and the transfer of U.S. manufacturing production to offshore locations.[9] It is not simply a matter of the absolute number of jobs, but of the way changing labor market conditions redistribute opportunities and above all, diminish the prospects of the lower substrata of the Mexican rural population obtaining any sort of livelihood from recurrent international migration. Combined with the possible impact of American "nativism," labor-market trends in the North may add yet further dimensions to Mexico's domestic social and economic crisis, and as Walker (1985) emphasizes, one cannot abstract policy changes in the North from their direct and indirect political repercussions in Mexico. The final results of the present trend towards militarization of the frontier remain uncertain for reasons of pure logistics, leaving aside the role of the employers of migrant labor in shaping the practice of official policy. But it is evident enough that political considerations have quite rationally underlain the Mexican state's long-term commitment to fostering international migration as a safety-valve for venting its rural surplus population.

Further deterioration of prospects in the North will not "solve" the migratory problem but bring it to a new pitch of intensity, from both the American and Mexican points of view. It is not simply a matter of reducing the economic bipolarity of the system but of dismantling an entire social system and the integrated and multi-faceted political economy which has developed across the line represented by the political border. It is hard to see how the contradictions inherent in this situation can ever be resolved. Mexican migrants in the United States do not feel they fully "belong," and in most cases do not want to belong permanently to North American society. But part of their own society is entrenched behind the line, and cannot be shifted from that position after several generations of movement *al Norte*. Because of this, a situation has developed in which the North offers many the best of a generally unattractive set of options, and the government of their country is scarcely unaware of this fact in considering the implications of the limited series of policy options available to it in an epoch of crisis.

INTERNATIONAL MIGRATION BY EJIDAL CULTIVATORS

Of the 182 cultivators of ejidal *parcelas* whom I interviewed in Emiliano Zapata, almost 80% had been to the United States to work at some time in their lives. Since the sample was selected on the basis of identifying the effective current cultivators of the land, it does not correspond precisely to the current title-holders of *parcelas*. Some land is sown by husbands of women who hold the formal title. In other cases, a son is sowing the land of a father or mother who is still alive, in the absence of a formal pre-mortem transfer of rights. Sometimes use of land is vested in a brother, nephew or other relative. The sample excludes cases where the holder is renting out his or her land, but it includes cultivators who enjoyed effective control over multiple *parcelas*, either through rental or by virtue of having bought rights to additional land placed in the name of non-adult or absent children.

Since the situations underlying the current rental of *parcelas* have already been analyzed, it is more appropriate to look at the migration histories of the current cultivators of land in examining the relationship between migration and the reproduction of the ejidal system. It is this picture which is most revealing from the point of view of understanding the processes which have sustained peasant agriculture in the past, and the likely future implications of contemporary economic, social and political trends. The picture does not, however, emerge with total clarity and in its entirety from the bare statistical data on migration histories. Nor are the processes of social reproduction fully intelligible in terms of the situations of individual family units extracted from what is in effect simply a cross-sectional "snapshot" of a longer term process of social reproduction, at an arbitrary moment in time. It is often necessary to know something about the history of the parental family of the current culti-vator, and in some cases, of the generation prior to that, to unravel the full set of circumstances underlying his existence as an ejidal cultivator. This is not simply a matter of recognizing the importance of kinship and other types of social networks such as friendship and *compadrazgo*, in determining an indi-vidual's life chances. Sometimes these networks are of the essence, but it also turns out that they may *not* be in a particular case. The most effective way of bringing out this and other dimensions of variability is to take some examples of long-term processes of family reproduction and analyze them in depth, in a more holistic way, so that the role of migration can be placed in its context in individual and collective life histories. It is also important to bring out further qualitative detail on the international migration experience itself, both to indi-cate the factors which come to bear on individual economic strategies and to highlight the general tendencies which have operated to canalize choice in particular periods. To this end I supplemented the qualitative data obtained in my interviews in Emiliano Zapata with further information collected in surrounding communities, from persons whose life situations present certain significant variations from the Guaracheño norm. Nevertheless, I will begin by examining the migratory behavior of my sample of ejidal cultivators, and then proceed to compare the migration patterns of landless and ejidal house-holds on the same basis.

Forty persons in the cultivator interview sample, 22%, had never been to the United States as migrant workers. (One of them had toured U.S. cities as a member of a mariachi, but is obviously best counted as a non-migrant for this purpose.) I summarize the international migration history of the remain-ing 78% in Table 17; equivalent data on ejidatario household heads not included in this sample are provided in Table 19 below, which compares the

CASI NADA

Table 17

INTERNATIONAL MIGRATION HISTORY OF 142 EJIDAL CULTIVATORS
By number and period of visits to the U.S.A

Number of Trips	Number of Persons	Period of Migration					
		I	II	III	IV	V	VI
1	21	2	0	12	0	7	0
2	26	1	3	18	1	3	0
3	19	0	2	13	2	2	0
4–5	31	0	3	22	2	4	0
6–10	27	0	3	17	7	0	0
11–15	4	0	0	0	4	0	0
16+	14	0	0	4	9	0	1
Totals	142	3	11	86	25	16	1

migratory behavior of ejidatario household heads with that of their resident sons and heads of landless houses.

The data in the tables are grouped by years in which an individual migrated. Period I represents cases where an individual migrated only in the period prior to the introduction of the *bracero* program. Period II represents persons who migrated both prior to and during the *bracero* period. Period III represents those who went only during the *bracero* period, and Period IV those who went both before and after the close of the *bracero* contracts system, whether they went legally or illegally after 1964.[10] Period V represents those cases where persons have only been post-1964, all of whom are "undocumented" in this sample. It must be stressed that some of those who went to the United States during the *bracero* period did not do so as legal contracted workers on every trip. Though the end of the *bracero* program was a significant event, and many people abandoned U.S. migration because they did not wish to go *al alambre*, the distinction between legal and illegal entry to the U.S. is not as clear-cut as it might seem. Period VI represents the single person in the sample, one of the original ejidatarios, who rounded off a career of U.S. migration which began in the 1920s with a single trip as an illegal after 1964. Involvement in migration is measured by number of "trips." It must be stressed that, particularly (but not exclusively) in the pre-*bracero* period and in the case of recent undocumented migration by younger men, trips may be counted in years rather than months, so that low numbers of trips give an imperfect measure of the significance of international migration in these cases.

Four percent of the total interview sample were over 80 years old, 21% over 70, 22% over 60, 30% between 50 and 60, 42% between 40 and 50, and 22% between 30 and 40. Only three persons were in their twenties. These proportions accurately reflect the paucity of very young farmers in the ejido as a whole, though the most elderly ejidatarios are underrepresented in the sample in the sense that they tend to figure most prominently among those who have rented their land. Nevertheless, those interviewed included old men who are now helped in cultivation by sons or other younger men. While some do little more than visit their *parcelas* to escape the confines of the house, some men in their seventies still perform various tasks of cultivation as well as a supervisory function, and it is therefore often difficult to determine when a person ceases to be an active cultivator. Since many elderly ejidatarios do not have any resident sons, there are a number of old ejidatarios who simply supervise work performed by hired labor. More significantly the sample data understate the importance of undocumented migration to the United States from the point of view of the future reproduction of peasant farming in the ejido, since many of the sons of those interviewed are presently going regularly to the North *al alambre*, and they also obscure the extent to which remittances sent by single (or in some cases married) migrant children are making a significant contribution to current parental household income following the end of their father's migration career.

Data on the U.S. migration of all resident sons of ejidatarios who head independent households but are themselves landless are provided in Table 19, but these data still do not provide an exhaustive picture of the potential contribution of U.S. migration to the reproduction of the cultivator households in the interview sample, since they do not include the contributions of children who remain members of the parental household or who are now resident elsewhere, including the United States itself. For the moment I will postpone discussion of the cases of the forty non-migrants in the sample, and also exclude those households where a contribution from U.S. migration on the part of the next generation is already known since a U.S. migrant son is included in the sample as an ejidal cultivator in his own right. Twenty-seven of the remaining cultivator households do not have sons of migratory age,[11] leaving ninety-three cases for which there is a potential contribution from U.S. migration by children of the present male household head. Of these, almost half (46%) have sons who have been to the United States. This is a minimal estimate, based on direct data, and the true proportion of those with a son who has made a migrant journey to the United States probably lies between 60% and 70%.[12] Most of those recorded by the minimal estimate were still engaged in active migration in 1982, a majority as undocumented migrants. It is also worth repeating that an exclusive concern for male migration is less appropriate for the period after 1964 than for earlier periods. Though most of the women from Guaracha have moved to the U.S. with husbands from the village, some have married there after working. This was the case, for example, with a daughter of one of the non-migrant ejidal cultivators, all of whose children were female. Though domestic service within Mexico and other forms of female employment within the country still constitute the predominant activity of single women of peasant origin, the existence of similar opportunities for women across the border are significant in the sense that they may not be declining in parallel with casual male jobs in agriculture and industry, and are the least susceptible of all occupations to the effects of unionization in restricting access to newcomers to the American labor market.

The data on long-term migrants are particularly interesting. Twenty-three subjects in the sample went *al Norte* in ten or more different years. Excluding two whose children are too young, fifteen (71%) have sons who have been to the North, and eleven of the sons themselves have children who are currently in the North. Only three of the twenty-three are *emigrados*, though the eldest son of one of the others is *emigrado*, one of the long-term migrants whose children have not been to the United States has an *emigrada* sister there, and three others have *emigrado* relatives—an uncle in one case and brothers in the other two—one an ejidatario not included in my interviews because he was still in the North. Of the three *emigrados* I was able to interview, two had encouraged their children to study, and counted professional sons and daughters in their families: even so, some of their sons had chosen to follow them to the United States rather than study. This was also true of some of the non-emigrant long-term migrants, and in five of the six cases where no child had followed the father to the United States, this was because the children had chosen to study for a professional career. In the other case, the father had migrated to the U. S. in the course of a career as a factory worker in Mexico City, returning to the ejido only on retirement, and his older children had found work in the capital. There is therefore a tendency for particular families to become locked into international migration generation after generation, as children whose fathers have a long association with the U.S. labor market follow in their footsteps, unless the cycle is definitively broken by social mobility associated with education. For a number of these long-term migrants the primary purpose of their long periods of absence in the North has been to offer their children that option.

We should now consider the circumstances of the non-migrants in the interview sample, summarized in Table 18. At least one subject falls into two separate categories in the table. Two of the interview subjects had fathers who were particularly successful pre-war migrants: both dedicated themselves to the business of loaning money and died violent deaths, but left their heirs well-provided for. Two of the partners in the Mora-Moreno-El Chiquitín machine owning partnership are also included among the non-migrants, though Manuel Mora himself had been a long-term migrant in the pre-*bracero* period, and one of El Chiquitín's sons was to spend some time in the United States. The partners came from the better paid stratum of the hacienda work-force, and possessed their particular skills as mechanics, though it should be stressed that an origin in the ranks of the hacienda *acomodados* was not incompatible with U.S. migration in all cases. At least one of the hacienda *mayordomos* of the late 1920s was himself a *Norteño*, and despite its antipathy to married workers leaving for the North, the hacienda was happy enough to employ returnees who had acquired useful skills there.

Table 18

ANALYSIS OF 40 EJIDAL CULTIVATORS WITH NO U.S. MIGRATION
EXPERIENCE

Engaged in other migration within Mexico	7
Long-term seasonal migration to cut cane	1
Other regular off-farm work within the region [1]	5
Had other assets or income sources [2]	3
Physically disabled	1
Single man	1
Attempted entry to USA, but fell ill	1
Inherited land, siblings rural-urban migrants	3
All children daughters [3]	1
Siblings migrated to USA (emigrados)	2
Siblings migrated to the USA (undocumented)	4
Sons migrated to the USA	12
No US migration by either subject or close kin	2

---

[1] Includes a Mariachi player whose work takes him across national boundaries, and a primary school headmaster whose agrarista father made money in the U.S.A in the 1920s.

[2] Includes another case of prosperity linked to assets partly acquired from a father's U.S. migration in the 1920s.

[3] But one of the daughters currently works in the U.S.A..

Nor did being single necessary free one from the need to migrate, though in this particular case the single man did not have to support a parental family or siblings at the stage in his life cycle when international migration would have been on the agenda, and also suffered rather poor health.

It is clear that U.S. migration did touch the lives of most ejidatario families in Emiliano Zapata. In 42% of cases, children or siblings of these non-migrants went to the North. Only three subjects with families appear to have been devoid of contact with the U.S. labor market without enjoying some additional or alternative source of income to farming: one inherited the *parcela* when he was single and had no siblings to support, another is the son of an independent herdsman and *ecuarero* in the hacienda period who has combined subsistence cultivation with work as a peon around the ejido, and the last made the attempt to go to the North, but was struck by illness in Tijuana. Internal migration was another option. Eighteen percent of the non-U.S. migrant cultivators in the sample were long-term internal rural-urban migrants, and many of the title-holders excluded from the sample were currently engaged in some form of long term urban employment, either in the local towns or metropolitan centers. Scarcely a single family in the sample with adult children lacks members who are working in urban areas, and 17% of the cultivators who had been to the United States had also worked in Mexico or Guadalajara at some point in their lives, 70% of them for more than two years.

Though one of the non-migrants in the sample was a single man, three of the migrants had also remained single, and U.S. migration before marriage is not uncommon. Fifty-four (38%) of the migrant cultivators first went to the North as single men, twelve in the pre-*bracero* period, thirty-eight as *braceros* and four as illegals. The hacienda's custom of evicting the unproductive dependants of married workers who went to the North clearly influenced the early patterns of movement, and some people even said that they would not have gone had their parents been elderly, since they might have suffered the same fate. Though several of those I interviewed did remit money to fathers working on the hacienda, it is clear that most of the men who accumulated a certain amount of capital in pre-*bracero* migration did so because they were able to retain their earnings for their own use, remitting to neither wives nor parents nor siblings. Most of them did not become "rich" even in a relative sense, but absence of obligations might at least be sufficient to invest in some mules, for example, and become an *arriero* in lieu of a hacienda peon. Pre-*bracero* migration certainly provided a foundation for a number of ejidatario families which survived and prospered subsequently, by giving them some modest cash reserves in the difficult early years, though it is clear from the data presented above that a great number of early migrants returned to the United States a second or more times as *braceros* after they married and had children to support. A more detailed discussion of case histories is provided below. Most of the single migrants in my sample who went as *braceros* did remit money to parents or siblings, and some of the long-term migrants continued to do so after their own marriages. There are, however, a few notable exceptional cases where men whose fathers had no real need of their economic support retained their earnings to acquire assets to improve their personal prospects, a strategy which on occasion provoked a certain amount of bad feeling between father and son.

DIFFERENTIATION BETWEEN LANDLESS AND EJIDAL HOUSES

The differential pattern of international migration on the part of ejidatario and landless houses discussed previously in the context of the migration of children emerges with even greater clarity when we consider the past migratory behavior of household heads. Table 19 provides a direct comparison between landless household heads, ejidatario household heads and resident sons of ejidatarios who head separate households, in terms of numbers of trips and periods of migration, and it also expresses both the total numbers of migrants in each group and the numbers of migrants per period for each group as percentages of the community totals in the salient categories. There are slightly more landless household heads than ejidatario household heads, but the former constitute a much smaller proportion of the total ex-migrant population than the latter. Ejidatarios are also seen to have enjoyed a strong advantage in terms of access to international migration in the *bracero* period,

Table 19

INTERNATIONAL MIGRATION HISTORY OF MALE HOUSEHOLD HEADS
By number and period of visits to the U.S.A

Number of Trips	Number of Persons	Period of Migration					
		I	II	III	IV	V	VI
(a) LANDLESS HOUSES							
1	35	1	0	18	0	16	0
2	30	0	1	14	1	14	0
3	17	0	0	11	2	4	0
4–5	15	0	0	1	8	6	0
6–10	20	0	0	7	9	4	0
11–15	3	0	0	0	2	1	0
16+	4	0	0	0	4	0	0
Totals	124	1	1	51	26	45	0
As % of all migrants	32	14	8	30	33	41	0
(b) EJIDATARIO HOUSES							
1	30	4	0	17	0	9	0
2	35	2	3	23	1	6	0
3	21	0	1	16	3	1	0
4–5	41	0	4	30	3	4	0
6–10	28	0	3	14	10	1	0
11–15	11	0	0	5	6	0	0
16+	18	0	0	3	14	0	1
Totals	184	6	11	108	37	21	1
As % of all migrants	49	86	92	64	47	19	100
(c) RESIDENT SONS OF EJIDATARIOS							
1	18	0	0	2	0	16	0
2	13	0	0	2	1	10	0
3	19	0	0	5	4	10	0
4–5	11	0	0	2	6	3	0
6–10	9	0	0	0	3	6	0
11–15	1	0	0	0	1	0	0
16+	0	0	0	0	0	0	0
Totals	71	0	0	11	15	45	0
As % of all migrants	19	0	0	6	19	41	0

heads of landless houses having their highest relative share of total migrants in the category of persons who have only been to the United States as undocumented migrants since 1964. Furthermore, as the table demonstrates, the ejidatario group contains much higher numbers of long-term, recurrent migrants, largely because many more men from ejidatario families were able to go regularly as *braceros*.

The essential factor underlying this pattern of differentiation was the fact that ejidatarios could raise the money required to gain access to a *bracero* contract more easily than landless men. The great irony of the *bracero* program was that it was theoretically designed to help landless people: ejidatarios were technically excluded from participation. Yet it worked in precisely the opposite way: more ejidatarios than landless peasants went to the United States during the *bracero* period, and many more ejidatarios than landless men went legally (Cross and Sandos 1981).

It is important to stress that even ejidatarios sometimes found the costs of *bracero* migration prohibitive: many of those I interviewed made a point of drawing my attention to the years when they had to go *al contrabando*. In the country as a whole, at least as many people went without documents as obtained a contract, and many of those who entered according to the rules stayed on without ever securing a formal renewal of their contract. As we will see in the discussion of case histories which follows, borrowing money to pay intermediaries acting as labor recruiters and facilitating passage across the border has always been a feature of going to the North, on top of travel and subsistence costs. But the scandal of the *bracero* period was that the program was supposedly intended to eliminate much of this cost and facilitate the entry of the truly needy. The fact that the Mexican state tolerated the access of ejidatarios to the program might be regarded as a purely pragmatic, if not shrewdly political, calculation, given what was happening to the ejidos at the time. The existing land reform beneficiaries were those most likely to continue to support the regime if they were given some respite. But such rational considerations were not the sole determinants of what happened.

The peasants were not surprised when the recruiting officers working for the *licenciados* in the *Centros de Contratación* started coming to the villages to demand *anticipos* for people to be "put on the list." Nor were they surprised when they were asked to pay again at the *Centros*. It was a matter of "business as usual." It was a very lucrative business, and as I remarked earlier, a very political one. Political careers were made or broken by the ability of people from state governors downward to obtain *bracero* places for their *gente*. At least one local notable and protegé of Dámaso Cárdenas, Enrique Bravo Valencia, failed in the contest of calling in markers and of endless telephone calls to higher officialdom. On the Mexican side, the *bracero* program was a market, on which both wealth and political power were accumulated by selling people. Even the local priest in Guaracha came in on the act of manipulating his contacts to secure *bracero* places, dispensing them free to the faithful who promised to put part of their earnings towards the cost of building a church primary school in the community.[13] This too was, in reality, a highly political intervention—by an aggressively anti-communist priest—rather than simply an act of charity. Father Emiliano showed that the Church could still get things done perpetuated ideological combat with the forces of secularism in state education.

By virtue of the factors creating selectivity, the advantages accruing to ejidatarios in the *bracero* period extended to their sons. Indeed, many of those who are currently ejidatarios were not the title-holders of their *parcelas* at the time of their participation in *bracero* migration. Given the age differences between the groups being compared, some adjustment for this factor is necessary to provide a convincing demonstration of the correctness of these interpretations of the patterns observed in the table.[14] Figure 12 provides a breakdown by age groups, including deceased persons. This confirms the relative disadvantage of the landless households, and the degree of involvement in international migration of sons of ejidatarios is comparable to that of their fathers, once one allows for age differences. Figure 13, which relates numbers of trips to age groups in a two-way comparison between landless and ejidatario houses serves as further confirmation of the difference in access to the U.S. labor market enjoyed by members of ejidal houses during the *bracero* years.

Figure 12
INCIDENCE OF U.S. MIGRATION BY AGE GROUPS
Landless and Ejidal Households

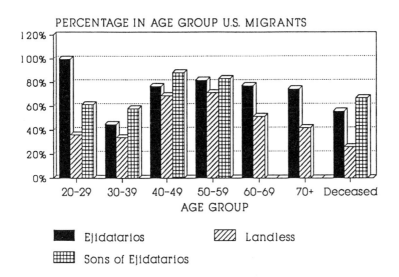

Figure 13
FREQUENCY OF U.S. MIGRATION BY AGE GROUPS
Landless and Ejidatario Households

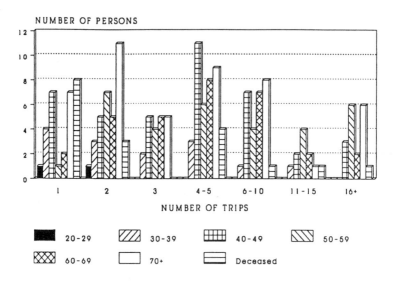

EJIDATARIOS

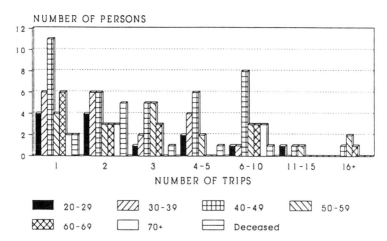

LANDLESS

As Table 19 shows, a larger absolute number of landless household heads went to the United States after the end of the contract labor system than ejidatario household heads, and there is only a comparatively small difference in the numbers of landless going before and after 1964, although it is equally evident that resident sons of ejidatarios were much more likely to go than other landless people. But the data on the relationship between age group and incidence on migration indicate that the decade after the end of the *bracero* program was something of a leveller: now most Guaracheños who went were undocumented, as the majority of landless men had always been, and while it was still necessary to make payments to *coyotes* for services rendered in "crossing the line" and to *contratistas* for aid in securing access to work, it is, perhaps, something of a reflection on the extent of the surcharge the Mexican bureaucracy levied on some of its poorest citizens that this should be the case. Unless one was particularly unlucky, a trip in the second half of the 1960s or first half of the 1970s was almost certain to pay better than a trip as a *bracero*, and the region's private sector labor brokers were well placed to secure their customers work in the North.

Most of the undocumented migrants I interviewed expressed themselves satisfied with the "service" they received from these intermediaries, whatever their origin, though a few had experienced problems of bouncing checks or unsatisfactory working conditions when they had turned to operators who were not "*conocidos*" belonging to the regional migratory network. Since retrospective judgments on the migrant experience focused almost exclusively on whether one benefited financially relative to staying in Mexico, short of a disastrous encounter with the *Migra*, serious illness or a failure to find work, the criteria for judging the situation "satisfactory" were not too demanding. It would be naive to paint too positive a picture of the role of these private intermediaries in a structural sense, let alone of the undocumented migrant experience in general, even in the period when unskilled and uneducated undocumented migrants still had relatively good prospects of finding work. Some of the migrants themselves are far from unreflective about these structural considerations. But the more significant negative factor is that few of the landless men who went in this period succeeded in transforming their families' situations in a radical way. Already bearing the weight of past disadvantage, the landless could not advance significantly under the new conditions, which were rapidly to become even less favorable.

Of the seventy-one heads of landless families who have been to the United States since the end of the *bracero* program, 75% have worked exclusively in agriculture, more than half of them having no previous experience as *braceros*. Eight began their migrant careers as factory workers in California.[15] The oldest in this group, who works in a furniture factory, was fifty-two in 1983, and entered for the first time as an undocumented migrant, but succeeded in emigrating almost immediately. He, like all the other factory workers among the landless migrants, had kin who were already permanently resident in California. Two of the other factory workers are in their early forties, and the remainder in their twenties or thirties. None of them had been to the United States during the *bracero* years. One of the youngest was forced to turn to farm work on his last two visits, and three were not engaged in recurrent migration at the time of the survey, having made one trip of up to a year and returned. One of the others had abandoned his family after leaving for the North in 1977, and his current occupation and whereabouts were not known by his brother. One former farm worker, aged forty, had made one trip as a *bracero*. He secured work in a steel plant in Dallas, Texas, on the last of his five visits, in 1980, through the good offices of a friend who is an ejidatario's son. Another had passed from casual farm work to a restaurant, another in the opposite direction, and a third had spent his single migrant year as a waiter in Long Beach. Two other former field workers had secured jobs in the Los Angeles airport, where there is a certain concentration of people of Guaracheño origin.

One of the remaining two *emigrados* in the landless group had worked for over a decade as a manual worker in the Los Angeles olympic stadium. The son of the former postman of the hacienda, still resident in the village, Roberto was an unusually popular man, as I discovered in the tragic circumstances of his funeral, following his murder in 1982. Aged forty-seven at the time of his death, he first left in 1968. He probably received some initial assistance from an uncle and aunt already established in Monte, California, but much of his success as a migrant was clearly due to his own initiative. "Success" is a relative term, even abstracting from any additional motives besides robbery which might have underlain Roberto's death by the hands of a teenage gang. His widow and daughter live in Los Angeles, the daughter having become a factory worker. His other child, who remains in Guaracha, was able to receive higher education and works as a *técnico* in Jiquilpan. Roberto's popularity arose both from his personality and from his eternal readiness to offer any aid he could to fellow Guaracheños seeking work in the Los Angeles region— something to which my collection of individual migrant histories eloquently attests. Since his father had been a notable foe of the *agrarista* cause, the scene at Roberto's funeral, where the children of both sides of the intra-communal divide forgot any past differences in a genuine shared grief, demonstrated the strength of the moral community which can be generated by networks of mutual aid and solidarity in the North. In such an emotional context it is too easy to forget that not everyone receives such help, that the journey to the North sunders as well as creates moral bonds, and that the entire edifice rests on other structures which have little to do with considerations of morality.

Of the remaining landless men not working in agriculture, one works on piece-rates in a workshop in Los Angeles, and the other has obtained a service sector job in the city's main post office. Another, who works as a tailor in Guaracha, has also worked in the garment trade in the North as well as in agriculture. But few of these men have any stable situation in the North. One of the farm workers, the last *emigrado*, has twenty-five visits to the United States behind him over the course of his fifty-one years, including eight as a *bracero*. He works for a lettuce company in Salinas. Another has become a foreman in Merced. But the majority has depended on the demand for casual labor in the fields of California, the Los Angeles region, Stockton, Merced, San José, Santa Ana and Santa Rosa being the most popular destinations. Oregon and Washington State have become increasingly popular in recent years as shortage of work forces people to look further afield, beyond the existing areas of Guaracheño colonization. Few of those who have found work outside agriculture have achieved any permanent place in the economy of the North, and as the data indicate, comparatively few have actually become long-term or recurrent migrants. For more than half of the farm workers too, at least up to 1983, involvement with the North had gone no further than a couple of visits, generally of less than a year. The most that such men seem to have gained from the experience is a few consumer durables and some new clothes: many declared that everything had been absorbed by family subsistence needs. The sample excludes two divorced women and a widow from landless households who have sought a solution to their economic problems by entering domestic service in the United States

In the case of the ejidatarios, the proportion of those with experience of U.S. migration after 1964 who had only worked in the agricultural sector was marginally lower than in the case of the landless, at 68%, and a higher proportion of these men, 80%, had been to the United States as *braceros* previously. One of the ejidatario household heads with experience of undocumented migration is a widow who worked for two years in domestic service in Los Angeles. Five men began their migrant careers in urban factories, but only one, aged thirty-eight, became a long-term migrant, making ten trips over as many years. He, however, left factory work in Los Angeles for the fields of Merced. His wife accompanied him and also worked in the fields in 1981. Three men moved from field to factory, and another into construction after emigrating during the *bracero* period. In all, five out the fifty-nine men in the group are *emigrados*. One of the recurrent migrants was able to find work in an agribusiness factory rather than the fields thanks to the help of a permanently resident sibling: he stayed two years on one of his four trips, and took his wife and small children with him on his last visit in 1978. Interestingly, he was one of those who confessed that he could never feel comfortable in California because of the constant feeling of rejection by other elements of the local society. Three ejidatario migrants have experience of work in restaurants; two of them worked in the kitchens, and one stayed four years in the North since a killing made his return problematic.

Although the ejidatario group contains a higher proportion of long-term and recurrent migrants overall than the landless group, it is evident that the roots of this difference lie in the past rather than in the more recent period of undocumented migration. The prime result of this pattern has been to enable the individuals concerned to remain or become ejidatarios. Only 25% of the ejidatario household heads with migration experience after 1964 reported the presence of kin in the regions to which they went, in contrast to 44% in the case of the landless migrants (and 33% in the case of the resident sons of eji-datarios with migration in the period.) Although subjects sometimes denied that they had received any substantial aid from their kin, this difference seems to be consistent with an emphasis on *bracero* migration as a major differentiating factor. It is the resident sons of ejidatarios who have the highest proportion permanently engaged in factory work of all three groups (15%) and these men also seem to be those who are enduring longest in these non-farm occupations. Although the ranks of the sons of ejidal houses include a typical handful of other occupations—airport worker, construction, kitchen staff and work in the garment trade—the proportion of those working in agriculture remains at 68%, even though more than three quarters of this relatively young group of migrant agricultural laborers have no experience of work in the *bracero* period. Thus, sons of ejidatarios have greater possibilities of access to the North than sons of landless houses, their position in the northern labor market is more or less comparable.

It is clear that international labor migration from rural Michoacán must be analyzed as a process of long duration. The prospects of the present generation are determined by a number of factors which represent changes at the northern end of the system, both economic and non-economic. Since factors such as oversupply of casual labor in the United States and changes in its agricultural technology cannot easily be divorced from the dynamic interrelation of the two "poles" of the system, it is often meaningless to make a distinction between local and global phenomena and between recent changes and systemic trends. But migration flows are shaped by past history and the internal history of migration itself as a social process has had an identifiable impact. Past processes shape the present distribution of migratory opportunities within regions, albeit in a complex way which is mediated through such factors as educational opportunities, themselves related to the underlying patterns of socio-economic differentiation to the point where they tend to create a vicious circle of deprivation and polarization of life chances. The "international migratory tradition" of Michoacán as the cumulative development of a social infrastructure ranging from mutual assistance between kin to the business of labor contracting has strengthened a particular kind of regional response to crisis. My analysis thus far does not suggest that the North has offered the majority of rural Mexicans a way out of their problems, though it may have ameliorated their situation somewhat in purely material terms. But the best way to draw out a fuller qualitative picture is to let the migrants speak for themselves a little more. In the remainder of this chapter I will examine the process of long duration which has locked rural communities like Guaracha into their relationship with the North in terms of the testimony and understandings of people who lived the experience.

THE RIVER'S JUST FULL OF DEAD MEN

As Mexicans themselves are only too aware, there is a certain irony in describing the start of "Mexican emigration to the United States" as beginning at the end of the 19th century, since the destinations of most of these emigrants had previously been part of Mexico's post-independence national territory. Nevertheless, the rapid acceleration of cross-border population movement after 1910 does correspond to the conjunction of two separate social dynamics: on the one hand, a rapid growth of demand for types of labor power which Mexican migrants were well suited to filling, and on the other hand, the effects of the dynamic of the armed phase of the Revolution, both economic and social. (Some of those who migrated managed to make money from both). Around 370,000 Mexicans entered the United States legally between 1910 and 1916, with perhaps a million more crossing the border without documents in the same period (Ramos Arizpe 1983: 36). Some 43% of all legal immigrants into the United States came from Mexico by 1919, and what had been a gathering wave of migration up to 1920 became a flood during the years up to 1929, a period during which 10% of all Mexican emigration to the United States to date took place, only exceeded in intensity by the 1950s and 1960s. Between 1920 and the crisis of 1929, 436,733 Mexicans emigrated legally to the United States predominantly from Michoacán, Jalisco and Guanajuato, and concentrating within the United States in Texas, California and Arizona (Ramos Arizpe 1983:50). Thus, the destination of 82% of this first wave of emigration was to regions which had formerly been Mexican.

After 1929, the tide turned dramatically, though movement never ceased entirely: two of the ejidatarios I interviewed went as undocumented migrants in the 1930s. Faced with depression, the United States embarked on a program of repatriating Mexican workers. It is tempting, therefore, to see this first round of cross-border migration as a sort of informal rehearsal for the later and formalized bilateral arrangement of the *bracero* program. But beyond considerations relating to the role of the Mexican state and the political economy of migration already discussed, there are other reasons for avoiding too ready an equation between the two periods.

In the first place, Mexicans filled different niches in the U.S. labor market during this early phase. As I emphasized in earlier chapters, many people of rural origin did not work in agriculture or even on railroad construction (*El Trake*) a major element in U.S. demand for Mexican labor, but in the foundries of car factories and other steel plants. Some of those who started on the farm or the railways moved on to industrial work later. Chicago and Indiana were the favored destinations of Guaracheños, though a few made their way north to Buffalo and New York subsequently, and recalled the pleasures of drinking whiskey legally across the border in Canada. Those who did work on the farm mostly did so because they were too young to fool the industrial plants into hiring them, and generally did not give up their ambition to work in the industrial sector. Factory work was not generally more physically attractive than farm labor: it was both stiflingly hot and dangerous in the foundries. (The hacienda's sugar mill was also prone to industrial accidents, but certainly could not compete with the blast-furnaces). The former *campesino* migrants I interviewed preferred the relatively superior monetary rewards of industrial wage-labor to both the labor-gang on the railroad and farm work, which in some cases consisted of a relatively relaxed and unregimented, albeit menial, position working for a *ranchero*. It is interesting that so many made a comparatively smooth transition to industrial work at its physically harshest, most disciplined and rationalized from agrarian peonage, or for that matter, the much less capitalistically disciplined life of a sharecropper from one of the neighboring pueblos.

The contrast between the sectoral allocation of Mexican labor before and after the Great Depression has implications which extend beyond the sphere of economics. Whether the migrant worked on the track, on the farm, or in a car plant or steel mill, his social and class position differed from the pattern which was to emerge subsequently. The stratification system was a different one: Mexicans interacted much more freely with other ethnic groups. In particular, their relations with blacks were very different from those of more recent years. Consider, for example, the following piece of testimony:

> I worked for 4 years on the Rock Island and then the Santa Fe. I was only 15 then, and they didn't want to give me work. The *mayordomo* said I was too small to do some of the *tareas*, but the older men used to help me. All races worked side by side —there were Italians and blacks and so forth— and we made friends among ourselves. There was this black who wanted to learn how we swear in Mexico, so he came to me for coaching and I taught him to say *chinga su madre* and all that. Then the blacks wanted to work, it's not like today where the government pays them for not working and Mexicans there don't get the same benefits. Now there's all those drugs there, and the blacks are all tied up with that...[16]

But there were certain qualifications to this picture, perhaps:

> I worked with all the other races blacks, Polacks they're almost all Polacks in Indiana, you know Romans [Italians], and then there were the Jews, with their shops, they're very rich, right? Millions of foreigners there were there. Relations between us were pretty good on the whole. Everyone looked well on us even the blacks. But the blacks was separate, apart from us, on the edge of the town, while we were in the center, with the white folks.

Mexicans in this period could easily identify with other immigrants, and found themselves in the midst of people in a like civil situation within American society. A number of them could also identify, to a degree, with the historical situation of blacks in America, and several people made the comparison to me spontaneously in trying to express their feelings about the hacienda: "We were like the blacks in the North, slaves...." But even in this early period, as the second quotation suggests, a certain degree of social distance separated blacks and Mexicans. Individuals interacted across this divide, and perhaps a measure of the strength of the interaction is provided by the fact that people are still willing to tell such anecdotes today, and express a kind of solidarity with respect to earlier periods, despite the deterioration in relationships which has taken place since and the overt racism which is often manifest in everyday conversation—made somewhat ironic by the African genetic element in much of the Guaracha population itself, often phenotypically very marked in the very people making the comments. Mexicans and other European white immigrants seemed on an equal footing, as refugees from lands without opportunity participating together as in the formation of an industrial working class of a "classic" type. As such, they were also exposed to the ideological currents within the international labor movement of the time in a quite direct way. Thus the social and cultural context of migrant participation in American society was rather different from what it was to become in the later periods.

This was reflected in the political impact of the *Norteños* in the era of repatriation, their serving as a catalyst for heightened radical activity in Michoacán.[17] They had seen a vision of the future which had not entirely delivered what it promised. Many had clearly become convinced of the potential of working-class self-organization, but now saw *agrarismo* as the strategy which would offer them a more secure future. The distinction between agrarianism and other forms of working class struggle in terms of "backward" versus "forward-looking" objectives is particularly inappropriate in this context, since many of the lower class promoters of *agrarismo* were manifestly aware of the various forms of alternative working-class program. Nor is the well-known argument of Martínez Alier (1977), that the choice between "land" and "work" must be seen in terms of the returns to each option offered in particular historical contexts, an adequate account of the problem presented here, since it reduces to the mundanely pragmatic and non-reflective something which, for the activists at least, may in fact entail quite long-term judgments about the developmental possibilities of total socio-economic systems.

The first migrants to leave the Ciénega for the North belonged to families which had occupied relatively secure and prosperous niches in the pre-revolutionary socio-economic system. They were urban people from Jiquilpan and Sahuayo, who had operated as muleteers or plied other trades which had been disrupted by military action. These pioneers provided a bridgehead for a larger exodus from 1918 onwards, sometimes sending money for relatives to make the journey after them, or helping them find work when they arrived. The migration phenomenon was socially selective for a number of reasons, the chief of them being that a straightforward legal crossing of the border required proof of the ability to read and write. The children of independent sharecroppers who worked land in Jiquilpan and of Villamar's *kulaks* were prominent in the movement after 1918 because they too tended to have some level of literacy. But even in the early 1920s, the movement north was becoming more generalized and involving persons who were not literate, including peons from Guaracha. Since children of *acomodados* on the hacienda were often forced to do their stint as *peones*, and were not immune to the positive attractions which U.S. migration seemed to offer in the early 1920s, an increasingly diverse range of persons began to participate in what most described as the "adventure" of going North, those from an uneducated rural background going illegally. I will develop this theme by quoting in extended fashion from the testimonies of a selection of migrants with rural origins, beginning with two non-Guaracheños, born in Villamar and Totolán respectively, who were to become relatively prosperous in later years.

Case One. Don Luis C., Villamar

Don Luis's father was one of the Villamar farmers who rented hill land from the hacienda and produced a commercial surplus for sale in Jalisco. His own family has maintained and extended the links he forged with the United States in his years of migration, and now has a Californian branch. He is a brilliant *raconteur*, and his story loses a little in a purely literary transcription, but remains worth quoting in an extended fashion. Don Luis had given a graphic description of the effects of armed revolution on the people of Villamar. So I asked him directly whether the beginnings of U.S. migration were linked to this:

> Exactly. It was in this period that people started going to the States, in the year after that war [a reference to Celaya and subsequent confrontations between Villista forces and Obregón's troops in Michoacán]. They went to Texas. There was a lot of work then in Texas, because it still wasn't developed then, there was a lot of desert and it was when the U.S. began to develop its industry, its communications. They began to build railway lines and highways, and Texas was where there was work clearing and levelling ground. So this is when a few people started going from round here. Let's see. From Nicolas Romero there was a man called Camilo Tolento. Anastacio Ceja was from Las Zarquillas. They were living here, but they began to go to and fro to work, they went two or three times, and they'd come back really well dressed. So people began to widen their horizons, and that's

when the situation here began to get better. I got to know part of the United States. I worked there for eight years, real years of sweat and toil.

I went in 1923 with a group of friends. Three of us from Villamar and eighteen from Las Zarquillas went on the train. Emigration to the U.S. was easy then. They just paid eight dollars, and the only requirement was knowing how to read. But I was taking two good friends with me who couldn't read. Then the *contrabandista* used to charge four dollars for getting people across the river, and so that I could go with the two friends who couldn't read, I too went *de contrabando*, and from Las Zarquillas six of the eighteen who went could read, and we all crossed the border illegally in order to go together. Ignorance, that's all there was to it. Anyway, that *contrabandista* charged four dollars, with the condition that he'd get us across again with the same money. They kept us shut up in a house. They took us out at dusk, walking across the desert it was as if we were walking from here to El Platanal up to where the boats were to take us over the river, and they took us across three at a time. Twenty-five of us altogether went across. Then the *contrabandista* says to us: "I'll send you a guide to take you on from the side of the river." Well, we'd have walked about a thousand meters, and then he said to us: "Right boys, now I've fulfilled what I'm supposed to do. If you want me to guide you any further, then I'll need you to help me." "So how much do you want?" "Well, how about a dollar from each of you?" So we each gave him a dollar, and he guided us on. It would have been about four kilometers, like from here to Emiliano Zapata. Then he said: "This is as far as I go now, because I've got to get back." There we stayed to sleep out in the middle of the desert. It was in June, you see. So in the morning we asked them what was the right route to the North. They told us, and we went on walking through the desert, but by eleven o'clock we hadn't found any water to drink, and we began to say perhaps we can find a railway line which is going some place, in order to find water. We saw a line in the distance, and went straight to it, and by good luck straight away came across some tanks with water for cattle. It was all desert, and now we were drinking water. We'd brought some rolls of bread and we ate them now, because we couldn't eat them without water.

Then I said to my two friends from Villamar: "Let's go boys, let's split off from this crowd of people, because we're going *de contrabando*." So we split off, just we three, and went off to rest apart from the others under some trees, and when the sun was very low, we set off again. The others had already gone but at dusk we caught up with them again, at a tank where they supplied the railway engines with water, and when we got there we said: "Fine compañeros you are, now you don't want to go with us." "No," they replied, "it's you who are the bad compañeros. We didn't want to split up. On seeing you hadn't got here, we stopped to see if you'd arrive." So we joined together again. In the morning, we set off walking again, and came to a little town, with a railway station, and sat down, the whole crowd of us, on the highway about a hundred meters from the track, and there we were, happy as sandboys, chatting away on the side of the road, when a car arrived, with a sheriff in it. There were two of them. "Good morning, gentlemen," we said. "Good morning, how are you, where are you going to, my friends?", replied the sheriff. "Well, we're here looking for work. We come from Mexico, and we're eager to go to work." "Well then, let's all go over here by the station, everything's fine boys." We all went voluntarily and straight away one of them said: "You must be hungry, right?" "Well yes, we're hungry." They served us rabbit. There weren't many houses, it was pure desert and hills around the houses. There was a shop, and many began to go to buy cigarettes, and some didn't come back, you see there were hills behind the shop and so a few made their escape that way. Well, you see as it was mid-day, and time for lunch, they left us free there so we could get away. Just ignorance, or fear, perhaps... Then one of the men asked me if we were all there, and I said I didn't know, perhaps six were missing, they'd gone to the shop. As six had escaped, they didn't leave us alone after that. When I saw that, I moved up close to the sheriff and said: "Please don't think I'm being disrespectful to you with a question, I mean no disrespect at all." "Please tell me what do you want?" "Why don't they give us the chance to leave with the others? We come in search of a livelihood. We want work. We have families in Mexico, and so we've come to seek a livelihood for our families." "Look", he replied, "it's not possible. What you're saying's fine, but it's not allowed. But the governor's going to pass by here later on. Talk to him. I think he'll let you go if you explain that to him." He convinced us, and there they had us with the thought of the governor to console us. Later on a police truck arrived. He says: "Boys, the governor didn't pass by, get into this truck." We got into the truck and it took us off to the frontier, to the *Migración*.

They handed us over to the *Migración* in Nuevo Laredo. "You don't have papers?" "Well, no sir." "You crossed the river illegally?" "Yes sir." They took us to a hall, and there were three barbers there. They cut our hair. So I asked the barber: "Look here, why are you cutting our hair so short?" "So that if you enter the U.S. again we'll know what you are." Then they cut our hair and handed us over to the Mexican immigration authorities. They put us in a big stockade where there were some two hundred others. Then the migration officers gave us a real dressing-down: "Asses, thick-heads, why don't you go to school so you can write your names and then go to the United States?" They scolded us and then they set us free. We went off to sleep and then another day my other two friends crossed the border in the same place and weren't charged for it. But of the people from Las Zarquillas there were six who could read, and myself the seventh. So they went to emigrate in the morning. The requirement was to pay eight dollars and they gave you a card to read and that was all there was to it. They crossed the line in the morning, and I went off to the market in the center. That's the simple truth, I went off on my own, and they used to shut the office at 12 o'clock, and so when I went, it was already closed, and I didn't manage to emigrate. So there I was after one o'clock when it reopened and then I passed over the border.

The others were waiting for me on the other side, and said: "Man, you're always hiding yourself, wanting to leave us." "Well, I was looking for you before, I went to have breakfast in the market, and you lot left." "Okay, that's the very reason we're here waiting for you." "It's okay." "We're also waiting to see how you're off for money, with what we've paid I've only got two dollars left, he's got five, he's got one-fifty..." and so on. The most any of them carried was five dollars, but I still had twenty-eight dollars. You see, my grandfather gave me some money, and then he said: "I don't have another cent" and went to see Don Moncelado, and asked him for money. He gave my grandfather more money because he held him in great esteem. So that I shouldn't suffer, my grandfather borrowed money for me. So as I've said, I still had twenty-eight dollars. You see, I'd lied to the others, not telling them how much I'd really got, so I said to them: "Right, boys, I've got seven dollars left."

We left in the afternoon, and followed the railway line in the direction of San Antonio, when it was dark, and later took the highway around eight o'clock at night. We spent the night by the side of the road, and set off walking again at dawn, outside a town called Ario. I remember there were a lot of watermelon there, an orchard of watermelon, and it was very hot. They gave us a couple of melons for the journey. Before reaching the town, two cars driven by Mexicans caught up with us, and they asked where we were going. We explained we were going to San

Antonio and they asked if we were going on foot, and then offered us a ride. One was the owner of the cars, the other the driver: "Some of you get in with him, and the rest of you with me." They gave us a ride to the town, and we got there as dusk was falling. Then he said: "Right boys, now we've given you a lift, we're going to have dinner." They went off to eat, and I said to the others: "There's the money we've got with us, right, so perhaps they'll take us to San Antonio if we give them what we have when they come back." "Listen, boys, we want to know if you'll help us. We've got few centavos here." "How much have you got?" "Well, between all of us we've got 10 dollars." "Give us them then." So we gave them the ten dollars and they took us to San Antonio. We arrived in the early hours, it was a long way away. The owner of the cars asked if we were going to look for a labor contractor (*enganchito*) in the city. We said yes, and he said: "I'm going to take you to the house of a really good contractor. Perhaps he'll send you off the very next day."

He said there was this contractor called Alcantar, very famous, who came from Monterrey—he'd been repatriated by the revolution. Well, we came to a big hall. They told us to bed down there. They look for people who come to be contracted there. Well we searched around in the dark and bedded down there and woke up shortly to find that the people who were there were going to leave at 10 o'clock on the train for Wilson Forge. So they were all over us in the morning with the contractor: "When did you arrive, boys?" "In the night." And the contractor said: "These people are going to leave on the train now. Have you got money to pay for the *chance*?"—that's what they called it. They charged two dollars. Well, the others said they hadn't got it. Yes, I'd got it, but they wanted to fleece me, so we all said we hadn't got any money. So the contractor said: "Okay, if you want I'll send you to work where you can earn money to pay for the *chance* of a contract." "Okay then, if you send us somewhere round here that'll be fine." "Right then, come and have some breakfast," the contractor said, "They haven't got any money." They gave us something to eat, and at about ten or eleven a truck arrived. The contractor said: "You're going to go and work about fourteen miles from here in San Antonio. Later on, when you've got the money for the contract, come back and I'll send you to the North." Well we believed him when he said fourteen miles, but they sent us to Corpus Christi, right next to the line of the frontier. It took all day, and then from Corpus Christi they sent us to a place called Rogerstown, to pick cotton. We were fed up, it was very far away. We were to go to work for a farmer, and we worked for a week there. They paid us a dollar for each hundred pounds of cotton, and we made tortillas of wheat flour.

We worked another two weeks down there and then we went on to Fort Worth, and it was there I met the late Jesús C., who was my father's brother. It had been five years since we'd heard anything from him. We went to a restaurant to eat and there were some benches out front and we went outside again to eat. My uncle worked in a tortilleria and went to take tortillas to the restaurant. So I said to one of my friends that this gentleman I saw go in there looked like one of my uncles whom we hadn't seen or heard from in five years. So when he came out we'd go up to him. He said hello, and it turned out he was working with a lady in a restaurant and they made tortillas. There he was, quite content, because he was working with eight women and he was the foreman in charge of the mills. He had good reason to be enchanted, since there he was working with nothing but women.

Anyway, there in Fort Worth there was an office contracting workers, and so we signed up to go to this place called Lawrence. There was another office in San Antonio and we left in two cars from Fort Worth and two from San Antonio. There were few Mexicans there in 1923. When we arrived it was about eight o'clock in the morning, and there were about two or three hundred people waiting because they'd put an advertisement in the paper saying that they were going to contract Mexicans, so there were two or three hundred people waiting for the arrival of the train. Lots of people didn't know anything about Mexicans then, and were just coming along to take a look at them, but all of us were going because of the rough time we'd had, just humble people. Later on we spent a few days having a good time, and I bought a Texan hat. Well you see the American army used a khaki-colored hat like the Migration Service has, and that was the type of hat I bought in Texas. It was just a joke, that hat marked me out, right? Anyway, we arrived on the train, and the interpreter said to me: "Form up in a line there." There were restaurants in the factory and they took some of us to where the restaurant in the entrance was and there we formed up in the restaurant. It was very big, and thirty-eight people used to work in it. There they gave us a meal and from there they took us to the work office and began to distribute us by name to the departments.

I worked there for eight years. During the eight years I came back home three times to my house here. I was very happy working there. I worked in the department where they made railway track. Well, they made the rails in one department but passed it on to another straighten it out, where they aligned it and flattened it at the end and perforated it to make the joins to put it together. I worked there for eight years, as I've said, and I returned to Mexico in 1931. At the time I went to the North, in '23, it was when they killed Pancho Villa, and as I wore the big hat, they all used to rib me and say I was Pancho Villa, they all made a big joke of it and wanted me to say I was a Villista, well it was because of the hat, right, I really looked a dreadful sight with that hat.

Well, as I've said, we were off on this adventure during this period, but I returned in 1931 because I became sick. I got this illness which makes the skin go yellow, the face and everything, and I had a friend who is from El Platanal, we used to work in the same department and went around together every day, and he said to me: "Go home, you're going to die"' You see I didn't have any appetite, my diet was fruit, milk and bananas. That got me worried, so I went to a specialist and he told me that he'd cure me but it would cost me two hundred dollars, and I'd need a rest of sixty days. Luckily at that time I had the two hundred dollars in the bank. I lived with an Italian, and the Italian said to me: "Well then, cure yourself. Don't worry about it if it's a month or two or three years, you've got your meals here with us." They were good sorts. I lived with them eight years. Then I went to see another doctor. The Italian said to me: "I know a doctor who looks after my family," and I went to see him. He said: "Look, it's the climate which is making your illness so difficult, it's because the climate is very hot. It's a bit difficult, but I can cure you, but you need a rest of two or three months." "So how much will it cost me, doctor?" "Well it'll cost you two hundred dollars." Then he asked: "You're from Mexico? From what part of Mexico?" "From a state called Michoacán." "What's the climate like there?" "It's pretty temperate." "Well then, you'll get better easily there. Here the climate makes it difficult to cure you. In a temperate cold climate you'll cure yourself easily. I'd recommend you to go back to your village. Look, I've got a son getting treatment in Mexico, because I think the climate helps." So I thanked him and paid his consultation fee. His surgery was above a bank, and the general labor offices were right opposite. So I simply left the surgery and reported my work-time, and at two o'clock they paid me off and at night I took the train and came home. It was when that guy who'd lost an arm, Librado Ramírez, came back. He'd been many years in California. I came back with him, it was July, and very wet. We reached Querétaro and there in Querétaro we changed trains and I ate a meal there. I'd been more than a month without eating to my satisfaction, and there in Querétaro I drank a beer and ate perfectly well, and came home to my house.

In Zamora there were some doctors called Guerra, who I'm sure had studied in Chicago, they were really well qualified. On the third day I went to Zamora to consult them. The doctor examined me and said I'd get better soon. He gave me medicine, it cost me ten dollars, that's twenty pesos. He gave me medicine for eight days and told me to come back when it was finished so he could see how I was. When I came back I felt better, my color had returned to normal. He gave me more medicine and charged me ten pesos. I recovered right away. Then I stayed on here until the end of the year. Now the crisis was on in the States. When I came home from working there, when I went to the office in which they signed the check to pay us, the general overseer asked: "You're going back to Mexico?" "Yes, I'm going back because I'm ill," I explained. "When you return you can have your job back," he said. Because I'd been back three times and returned to work, and they'd given it to me right away, I thought it would be fine. At the turn of the year, I did go back with the aim of entering at the frontier, and they didn't allow me to enter. It was when they began to repatriate the Mexicans. Now it was the crisis of unemployment. Here the President was Obregón, and he put trains on the frontier to receive the Mexicans who were being repatriated, and now they wouldn't allow me to enter again. I didn't go back until 1943, when I went to California, and by chance I spent another eight years there before I came back in '51. That's why I can tell you something of this adventure I lived through in the United States and also know about agrarian matters here in Villamar.

After his return from his first trip to the North Don Luis became ejidal commissar, and led the campaign to achieve a fair distribution of land in his community against the preceding generation of *caciques* supported by Jiquilpan. He was ejidal commissar a second time, and has also served as municipal president.

Case 2. Don Antonio G., Totolán

Antonio's father was a *mediero* who sowed land belonging to *ricos* in Jiquilpan rather than the Guaracha hacienda, though Antonio himself had worked for the hacienda as a child. He has a large family, 10 sons and 2 daughters, and his sons have also worked in the North. Antonio has bought a number of ejidal *parcelas*, and owns a tractor. He has been *Jefe de Tenencia*, but is less of a political animal than Don Luis, devoting most of his energy to his directly economic interests.

I don't know much about the agrarian movement because I was in the United States when they distributed the land. I worked in Saguillon, Michigan. I was 11 years working there in a foundry, and when I returned they were distributing the land. But I was with a friend in a place they call Pueblo Viejo, in Veracruz, and I had a relative in the body guard of Don Lázaro, who was the captain and right hand man of the General and was in his confidence, so I came and sat down outside where Don Lázaro was dining, and then my relative brought me inside and said: "Look, my General, here I present a fellow countryman to you." "Where are you from?," he asked, and I said I was from Totolán. We were chatting there and he asked: "Wouldn't you like to go to work the land where you live?," and I said that of course I would... He gave me a note and I presented it to the Municipal President of the community and they gave me land and I worked it and am still working it. So I got this piece of land as an *agrarista*. It was waste-land, covered with scrub, and I put people to work clearing it. Good luck favored me, and I began to buy land, because when I returned from Saguillon I bought a taxi and it helped me a lot. I bought *parcelas* and now I've got some 30 hectares more which I've bought.

I went to the United States in 1927 via the frontier in Texas. I had a letter from an uncle of mine who lived in Houston, Texas, and this letter favored me and they let me enter. If I hadn't had it they still wouldn't have let me in because I went when I was fourteen years old and they wouldn't have admitted me until I was twenty-one. Those who were emigrants were from here and from Sahuayo, and there they were on the side of Don Lázaro. I showed them [the migration officials] the letter and passed, paying them eighteen dollars. It was very hard work in the foundry. I worked from eight in the morning until four in the afternoon. From four o'clock to midnight were hours of overtime. They paid us two dollars an hour, and four for overtime. All the time I was there I worked overtime and that was a great help. There was insurance against accidents. In 1942 I went again as a contract worker, and got sent to Merced, California. I have a boy who's a soldier there. He fought in Korea, and was wounded. But he got better and he's a veteran now. I knew he was wounded from a letter he sent. So I asked permission to go and find him. He was in San Francisco. I went there but I didn't find him. Then they told me he was in San Francisco in a government concentration camp [sic]. He got better and now he's in Glenton and pensioned. I think he works in a bakery now, but I'm not sure.

1942 was the first time I went as a *bracero*. I returned for another little trip in 1946, and returned at the end of 1948. Then I stayed put, but later I went again in 1955. I didn't go again.

When I went to the United States in 1927 it was when there was the *Cristero* Revolution here. I decided to leave because it said in the paper that they would burn Jiquilpan and cut Totolán to pieces. It was a lot of fuss about nothing really. A brother-in-law of mine is buried in Saguillon. We were together there and he stayed on and died there. At that time very few people went to the North. The Americans didn't care much for one in that period. When I went there I enslaved myself to work in that foundry and didn't go out much. They used to treat us badly. Nowadays there are more Mexicans than Americans there, at least in California.

Do you know the river which divides Mexico from the United States? There was a crowd of guys who invited me to cross the river into Texas. I sailed around a lot there. I couldn't enter, but it was because I was a fool, I didn't show the letter I carried. Afterwards we were talking with the employees of the emigration service there, and they said that they were going to get me transport to send me off back to my own country. I said to them: "Gentlemen, don't get me the transport. When you know that I'm dead, get it for me so they can bury me, but I'm not going home." "Where are you from?," asked the emigration officer. "I'm from the furthest corner of the world, in the state of Michoacán," I replied. And then one of them said, "I know Michoacán. Perhaps I also know where you come from." When I said I was from Totolán he said: "Heavens, they're all assassins there, is that why you want to die?" "No," I said, "that's not why I prefer death. It's because when I left home I made my father make a big sacrifice to get me money to come on this adventure. I prefer to die than come home alive skinned." Then he asks if I know people in Jiquilpan and what I think of the Cárdenas, and then he goes on to Sahuayo and begins with those ones who used to be there who were millionaires and good friends of Don Lázaro. So when I said the Picazos, I told him yes, I know Don Rafael Picazo and Felipe Picazo, I tell him virtually all the Picazos. Then he says: "Fancy that! We're from Sahuayo and think of us not letting through a miserable poor person who's come in search of a livelihood. But the thing is it's not like in Mexico here. If you kill someone down there, all you do is give a peso to the *Ministerio Público,* and then you're free. Here no, here the laws are very hard. If you've got some sort of document for us to see who we're dealing with, then we'll give you your passport, but otherwise no." I knew what that letter said and that my uncle was called Jesús Inocencio and lived in Houston, Texas. "With that

272

you'd have crossed right away," the emigration officer said.

I tell you, one of those boys got into the river and he was going along treading very carefully, and the river was full of dead people. He came out really frightened because he lowered his hand and took hold of the hair of a dead man. "No," he said, "the river's just full of dead men."

Case 3. Don Alfredo H., Cerrito Cotijaran

Alfredo was born in 1900. His father was a hacienda *mediero*, who also worked as a baker. An uncle was a *mayordomo* and *Juez* of the *Acordada*. Alfredo was told to leave the hacienda after an altercation with this man, supposedly over a minor breach of work discipline. He spent some time working on the land of smaller proprietors around San Pedro, and though he was readmitted to the hacienda subsequently, decided to leave for the United States. His brother also went to the North, but disappeared, leaving Alfredo working alone with his father.[18]

Alfredo went to the United States earlier and stayed longer than any of the other people I interviewed. He too returned as a *bracero*, and in his sixties embarked on a new round of internal migration, getting a job as a painter in the Buenavista railway station in Mexico through his sister-in-law. Still a vigorous man in his eighties, Alfredo is strongly committed to the work ethic, and repeatedly argued that acceptance of an employer's contract, whether on the hacienda or in the United States, placed one under the obligation to perform the work entailed. Though he was scathingly critical of the hacienda administration's abuse of its authority, he insisted that the problem did not lie with the hacienda system as such, and that those who complained about the work regime were not willing to accept their responsibilities and commit themselves to mastering work. It is evident, however, that Alfredo's long working life has not placed him in as advantageous social and economic situation as some other *Norteños*, though he has always been able to sow his land with his own resources, and has been ejidal commissar. Cerrito Cotijaran has a notable proportion of "new" ejidatarios who work in the United States on a permanent basis, either as foremen or *contratistas*.

I began to work when I was twelve. I didn't spend long in school, just some four or five years, and then they took me out to work. I did learn to read, but only a little, and in 1920 I went to the United States I worked in the Chevrolet, the Pontiac and the Ford. I worked in many places. I worked in Indiana in the steel sheet plant, in Pennsylvania where they made helmets, bullets and cannons. I used to change jobs because one went around seeing where pay was best. I entered in 1920 when they were paying 18 cents an hour in Texas, while they paid 50 cents up there in the foundries. It just cost five dollars to pass over then. One didn't need a passport. One just paid five dollars there on the bridge, and passed on to San Antonio where there were contracts for the foundries. I worked in Chicago. We turned out the line from Plainsville, Illinois up to Kansas City. I worked making cylinder blocks, pistons and munitions. We made good money, it was contracted work in those days. We made about 300 pesos every two weeks, a hell of a lot of money. That was in 1924. Yes, the work was hard, but anyone who takes a job takes it upon themselves to work hard at it. After three days you start getting in the swing of it, and then the work isn't hard for anyone. I spent sixteen years there. I only came back once. I had my work there, you see. Work was hard in the foundries, and on the railway too, but people used to take work as a duty then.

I went to the North because we could see that those who went there made a few cents more. You see, at that time the dollar was worth two pesos. If I sent a hundred dollars from up there, my father could buy two hundred *hanegas* of maize with it. Everything was cheap here then, you see. That was why we were interested in going. We didn't worry about clothes. They gave us 50 centavos a week in wages on the hacienda for the whole week. So we were drawn to leave to work outside.

This was the time when a lot of people began to go to the United States There was no *Migración* or anything at that time. The first time we went we all went together. I went to San Antonio with all the Orozcos [pseudonym for Alfredo's paternal family name]. We walked all day along the railway track. Sometimes the train drivers would stop the train in order for us to get on. José Orozco said: "Damn them, who knows where they're going to take us." But no, it wasn't like that. Three days they gave us food. They met up with us again and gave us things. The only train that came to Nuevo Laredo was the one for New York City. It was the fastest train there was in those days... Later, when Manuel Robledo was hacienda administrator, I sent my father money and he sowed wheat. That time my father was robbed of the whole harvest. That's why I tell you the hacienda was good, but sometimes bad.

I went back to the States as a *bracero* from 1943 to 1955. I couldn't go back there [before] because they wouldn't let me enter. When I went as a *bracero* in 1943, I deposited a thousand pesos in the consulate to see if I could sort out the billiard hall. I left a billiard hall, my car and a house behind there in Salem. But no, when I came back, the guy who'd had the billiard hall had died—can't remember his name, but he'd been left with it. So I went home. But the United States was good. The first time I returned, in 1924, I stayed here only 8 days and went back. Well, you've got to keep your eye on the money whatever way you look at it. Yes, the U.S. was really good. When we went at that time, they and we were as one. I mean you left work and there were a lot of girls there who wanted nothing better than to go to the cinema or some place with you. Later on they began to make fun of girls who went with Mexicans and really started screwing the Mexican. But at first, they didn't want us to associate with the blacks. There were times when we did join up with a black and then they'd even jail us sometimes. In Indiana they jailed a lot of people because of the blacks. They didn't want the Mexican and the black to associate. That's why I say that the relationship between Mexico and the U.S. was good in those days. There wasn't so much dissipation then. People did start to behave badly later, around '24 or '25. That's when the Americans began to think badly of Mexicans too. There was this big foundry in Gettysburg, Pennsylvania. We got work there, and there were these baths where we used to go, like the one in Guadalajara. The white girls (hueras) used to come in and bathe, and we did too. Then one day a notice appeared: "No Mexicans Here." It was our fault. It's the same anywhere, a man gets treated as he treats others.

Alfredo was invited to return by the leaders of the new ejido of Cerrito Cotijaran, who were friends of his. He did so, though his heart was still set on returning to the North, and he did not manage to get land in the initial distribution in 1936, though he subsequently obtained land in the *ampliación*. He was commissar in 1947, and drew some acid comparisons between that era and the possibilities for self-enrichment through office in the epoch of BAN-RURAL. He himself left 42,000 pesos in the ejidal chest on leaving office. I then asked him why he had gone to Mexico:

The titles (to our *parcelas*) say we can't sell or rent our land. But that's what they do here anyway. Look at X and Y [in Guaracha]. They were people who said they didn't believe in work. You've got to work to maintain your family. I dragged myself away from here to work and left for Mexico. I got work on the railway, and got pensioned off there. I went in 1960, and stayed nineteen years. I was pensioned off and I came back here to work. I worked my bit of land. What they pay me there is better. If I'm here I just don't have enough. Now I've got a pass on the railway, to go anywhere the trains go. I worked for two years as a painter and five as a plumber, in Buenavista. Normally they take on people between thirty and sixty years old, but I got in at sixty-one years of age through the Station Master. You see they gave me my pension according to my age. I left at seventy-seven years old. I earned 8000 pesos a month and now I get 16,000. I get along happily with that, along with my son who studied the *prepa*. He's got bad lungs. He qualified as a teacher but didn't want to take up the job. So we both get by on the money. Another boy bought his own bit of land, it cost him 50,000 pesos. We sow the land and so we get by. I have a little house in Mexico, and three children living there. I get 3000 pesos in rent and that helps me to live... I tell you here people want to earn little and go home early. The right thing to do is work in order to have things. He who doesn't work, doesn't get.

Alfredo's years of toil have left him in a position which could be described as "comfortable" but which clearly does not compare with the situation of Don Luis, in his California-style house in Villamar, or Don Antonio in Totolán, dedicating himself to providing land for all his sons. Dollar earnings in the pre-war period could only provide foundations for subsequent prosperity. In Alfredo's case the situation was complicated by the fact that Cerrito Cotijaran was an ejido which lacked resources, but the real difference is more likely to lie in the way he managed the resources he did have once he returned home, and perhaps in the contribution made by his own sons. Alfredo did, of course, have to support his aged father, but that was not the whole of the story. As the text of the interview indicates, he invested in assets in the United States, and might, had he not returned to survey the prospects created by *agrarismo* and then been refused reentry, losing his investments in the process, have decided to base his future in the North. As things turned out, his migrant labor ended up being essentially reproductive. Don Luis pursued the path of politics in a particularly notable way, becoming one of the municipio's most respected figures, and subsequently developed a family enterprise of some scope. Don Antonio bought his taxi, tractor and chicken farm in Michoacán, and sowed a considerable amount of additional land. He enjoyed the aid of his numerous sons. Alfredo could sow his land *sin compromisos*, but did not create any kind of self-expanding economic enterprise.

Interestingly, Alfredo was quite scathing about the "new" Cotijaran ejidatarios whose careers were based on the U.S. in a quite different way to his own. What he had to say draws our attention to the negative dimensions of the social networks which underpin the migratory process:

There are some people from here who serve as *mayordomos* in the North. They kill the people there, the poor who only go for trips up there. Yes, they work them there all right, they earn money from bringing people to work and then the *Migra* comes and throws them out and they put others to work in their place. That's how they become naturalized.

These three accounts do, however, have much in common. All concern people who were literate and emigrated legally to the United States, following in the footsteps of older relatives who had already gone, though this was only a direct help to Don Antonio, and then only in a limited way, since his uncle did not assist him to find work. It is, however, striking in both Don Luis's and Don Antonio's accounts of their "adventures" that they did not immediately exploit this advantage, but at first preferred to try to cross illegally with friends who failed to meet the requirements for a legal passage. Don Luis's story gives a particularly graphic illustration of the dilemmas posed by the bonds of friendships which cross-cut the stratification system within the rural underclasses. He had money, but he kept some of it on one side, probably as much to avoid being seen as someone who was better placed than for more directly self-serving interests. And behind the talk of "adventures," a much harsher and darker reality is clearly visible. Don Luis's group's wanderings in the desert could have had a much less happy outcome than deportation, and as border control became stricter in the late 1920s, many more were to die in the river.

The individual histories also reveal more of the social environment into which this type of migrant stepped. Alfredo's comments are perhaps the most illuminating here, since his migration spanned the longest period. In this account we see the same evidence for a freer interaction between the old black American underclass and the new immigrants in the old days, but an even sharper delineation of the forces which were rapidly foreclosing on the possibilities of continuing easy interaction. From the beginning, the blacks and the Mexicans occupied discrete social worlds, which were increasingly forced apart. Alfredo also describes the way in which Mexicans themselves became the subjects of discrimination in the mid-1920s, even though he adopts a perspective of self-blame in interpreting these events. There was no doubt some variation in this phenomenon between regions. Don Luis's account recalls how Mexican migrants were still a novelty in the early Twenties in some areas. The accounts mention specific acts of kindness shown towards migrants by both Americans and immigrants of other nationalities, though money also changes hands regularly along the line. While it would be unwise to read too much in to these individual experiences, particularly since much more recent migrants have sometimes received the hand of friendship from *gringos*, it does seem that harder and harsher lines of stratification have emerged in the period after the Great Depression, paralleling the increasing segregation of Mexican migrant workers within the labor market structure of the North.

All these men were recruited by contractors specializing in channelling Mexican labor towards the foundries. Recourse to such self-serving agencies of recruitment is therefore something with a long history. But not all early migrants passed through such formalized channels. In Guaracha itself I was able to interview a number of men who belonged to the flow of undocumented workers who found their way into the U.S. labor market in a more informal way, and it is time to examine their experiences in a little more detail, beginning with those whose experiences most closely parallel the cases already examined.

Case 4. Don Juan V., Guaracha

Juan was born in 1908, and began work at the age of seven. He started off working in the fields sowing like other children: "*Muchachillos que nos agarraban, vamos a la chinga.*" Later he was sent to work in the mill, stoking a furnace with wood, a job which involved three to five hours very hard work on a Sunday, cleaning out the furnace and preparing it for relighting. He said he went to the United States to escape all this, with four or five friends, at the age of sixteen.

As he had only spent a couple of weeks in school, it was important that he had gone with a friend who knew how to read. This had got them all across at Nuevo Laredo. He went to the office hiring workers for the Chevrolet foundry. When they asked his age, he said he was twenty, but they didn't believe him and told him that he would present a risk for them if they hired him and he had an accident. He kept coming back to the office, doing casual farm jobs in the vicinity to keep him going. Eventually, the man who was in charge of hiring workers seems to have taken pity on him, and took him to meet a friend of his who was a farmer. Unlike the Chevrolet man, the farmer didn't speak any Spanish, but he was able to use signs to show Juan the work he was to do. Juan tended the chickens and ducks and did other jobs, including helping with the preparations for family parties. The farmer had a wine cellar. The farmer was a kindly man, and paid him two dollars a day. This was obviously not particularly good pay, even for agricultural work, in this region in this period, though it compared favorably with the 75 centavos he had earned per week in the hacienda mill. But after eighteen months he tired of life on the farm, not least because it was singularly lacking in the kind of diversions teenage migrants had hoped to encounter in the North.

So he decided to try the foundry again, but this time with a new stratagem. He had found out the number assigned to a worker from Guaracha who had already been contracted to work at the foundry, and presented himself in his place. Unfortunately, the man whose identity he had borrowed arrived from Mexico a few days later, and was rather surprised to be told that "his number was already working." Juan was working alongside a German immigrant in the plant, wearing a pair of goggles. A plant official tapped him on the shoulder, took away the goggles and his protective clothing, and told him to come back in two years time when he was old enough to work there. But Juan did now succeed in getting a job in his own right in the Pontiac plant, and stayed there for two years, before briefly moving on to the Ford works in Detroit. After the Ford plant, he moved on to a steel works in New York, where he spent the next three years. He lived with three friends from Guaracha, in nice rented rooms, and was now earning two dollars an hour for an eight hour day. Life was now full of diversions, but he decided to move to Buffalo in search of still better wages. But when he got there he received news from his kin in Guaracha that the land was to be redistributed and decided to return "*para buscar un pedazo de tierra.*" Once he had the land he decided to finish with the United States. His only daughter, however, married a man who became an emigrant worker in the San Francisco construction industry. Most of Juan's sons studied and have pursued careers outside Guaracha.

Case 5. Don Miguel M., Guaracha

Miguel was born in 1900. He left for the U.S. in 1918, and did not return until 1932. A member of the *Mesa Directiva* of the first ejidal administration, he returned as a *bracero* in 1943, and again in the period 1951 to 1955. His eldest son, Tiburcio, who now works for the SARH, went as a *bracero* in the three years following his father's last visit, and one of his sons, aged twenty-four, is *emigrado* through his wife. Two of Don Miguel's sons are educated, a deputy-headmaster and doctor respectively, and the remaining two work in Mexico as a carpenter and a driver. Like Don Alfredo, Don Miguel has always managed to sow his land *sin compromisos*, and he used to rent a small amount of additional land in the past, sowing it with the aid of Tiburcio. Migrant earnings were used to purchase cows and mules as well as to finance cultivation itself.

In his early period of migration, Miguel covered a range of different types of work, though always in Indiana. He did some farm work, and also worked on the railway, for the Santa Fe. Pay on the railway was 30 cents an hour, compared with the 50 cents paid by the foundry. He eventually went to work for a foundry in Chicago, and stayed there for the last seven years before his return to Emiliano Zapata. Here is his description of that work:

> It was harder than working here on the hacienda. It wasn't just hot, but dangerous too. There was the risk you'd fall, and your body would just be cut off, like this... But whenever anyone was killed at work there, the company paid. There was a regulation then in the United States, and the lawyer would see to it that if some poor person lost a leg, the company would see to it, put him in hospital and pay him. But there were some ignorant persons who started law suits, put lawyers to work, so that person would get paid more. If the lawyer won, the company was obliged to pay more. So the company would pension the man off, even though there was an agreement that anyone who was injured at work would have work in the plant for the rest of their life if they remained in good health. If you put a lawyer on the case, clearly the lawyer would get money from the company, and so later the company would retire that individual. Here it was quite different.

Here in our country, in the mill, there were also a lot of people working. And there was this boy. He lost an arm in a big gear wheel, and they didn't pay him. The owner of the factory had the responsibility to pay out, because the boy was now only half a person, he couldn't work with one arm, how was he going to work? They didn't give anything when someone died at work either. Here. With the *patrón*.

Employers here and in the United States were more or less the same. There were good and bad there. Some forced people to work really hard, it's still the same now. Now when a person goes as an illegal to the States, without papers, passport, they give them work, but they've got them like this...you see what I mean? The *Migra* arrives, "let's see, where are your papers?"— and off we go to Mexico. In the United States it suits them better to have people entering illegally, because they pay them less, right? And he who's there properly naturalized, those who are there with all their papers and know the law, they get sick and don't go to work and report they're sick... Not many people knew their rights under the law in the old days, that's the way it was.

A lot of people who went in the 1920s stayed in the North. There are people from Guaracha all over the United States, in Chicago, Pennsylvania, Ohio, Michigan, New York, in all the states really. People went young, some unmarried, some with their families. Some emigrated, some went al contrabando. But a lot of people came back, like me. There was a crisis there in 1929, it was really hard. The foundries came to a standstill. Roosevelt was President, right? [Miguel probably witnessed the elections of 1932, though Roosevelt did not enter office until after he returned to Mexico.] Yes, everything stopped, the factories, the foundries, because of the crisis. The government sent provisions to each house where there was a family, all they needed for meals, right. For single people, they provided a house like a restaurant, where they could get something to eat, though I didn't use it myself. Anyway, they put out an announcement that for anyone who wanted to go back to his own country, there was a train leaving at such and such a time, engine number whatever. So I went and put my name down, and came home. The American government paid everything, or rather the American train brought us here. It suited the American government to repatriate people because it couldn't afford to maintain them, because there were millions of Mexicans, laid off, and millions of foreigners as well, whites, from all nations... I don't know whether they went home to their countries, but we Mexicans, we came back. Those of us who wanted to. The rest stayed there.

I thought there was a better chance living in Mexico. The temperature here gives a helping hand. For example, the mesquite puts out a pod, and people eat it. The nopal gives prickly pears. People eat it, and no one bothers them. In the United States there was no work. There was snow in winter, the hardest season. In spring one went about looking for work, but there wasn't any. The railways were cutting back on the camps they used to have. They left behind a certain number of people they called a section, one to look after a stretch of track, like from, say, here to Zamora, four or five people. But there'd been camps in which there'd been up to two hundred people, repairing the line, opening ditches for oil and gas to run through. As the gas came from here in Mexico, we gave it them cheap, it was virtually stolen. Give him two dollars, and the President of Mexico would make them a gas source. We'd give the gas and take ... what? That's how it was then.

THE MIGRANT TRADITION AND FAMILY FORTUNES

The significant variability in the subsequent fortunes of the families founded by the early international migrants is brought into much sharper focus when we consider the family histories of the some of the other early Guaracheño migrants who still live in the village.

Several other people I interviewed in Emiliano Zapata had worked, like Don Miguel, in the Chicago Steel Plants. Don Rafael, the second ejidal commissar, went at the age of twenty, before marriage, before returning to resume work in the cane. He too recalled the onset of the crisis in the United States. People who had their money in the banks began to panic, except, that is, for the Mexicans. He had seen fellow countrymen march up to the cashiers and demand their money at gun point! Like many of his fellows, Rafael drew a sharp contrast between the capitalist work regime in the North and the alternative which land reform produced in Mexico, in the context of a disparaging reference to the poor standard of cultivation evident in one of the neighboring *parcelas*: "Here one works in a natural way, I mean people don't carry out their work properly" (*Aquí no se cumple*). There is no doubt that for men like Rafael the promise of land reform was the creation of a system of independent peasant farming, the promise of de-proletarianization, though his strong political commitment inhibited him from openly opposing the original collectivist regime, and he remained convinced that the continuation of the sugar industry was essential to the prosperity of the community. But like many of the ex-migrants, he did not see his children's future as lying on the land but in education and social mobility. Although not all Don Rafael's children have achieved social mobility, his eldest son, Diego, a senior national official in the ANAGSA, has advanced further up the status ladder than most people of peasant origin, on the basis of self-evident talent. Diego's education required sacrifices on the part of his siblings initially, though he has since made a substantial contribution to the family's development.

A similar pattern of social mobility through education for part of the next generation characterizes the case of Don Antonio O., who left a job in the mill (which he described as somewhat less demanding than fieldwork) to go to work for the Steel Company of Indiana in Chicago at the age of seventeen, in 1924. He worked there for seven years, sending 50 dollars home to his parental family every month.[19] Antonio had begun work in the cane at the age of nine, and received his schooling in the United States rather than in Guaracha. Several of the men who had gone young to the United States explained that they had been sent to government financed night-schools two nights a week for a year, where they had received a free basic education. Teaching was in English, but they were able to achieve some basic literacy. Though workers contracted for the foundries were in principle supposed to be aged twenty-one and literate before they could be signed on, the massive emigration from Mexico in the Twenties was still insufficient to match the demand for labor of the foundries in the earlier boom years: not only were the regulations relaxed during this period, but the American state itself was willing to provide a certain subsidy towards the creation of new Mexican-American workers.

Antonio returned three times to the United States subsequently as a *bracero*, staying eighteen months on his first *bracero* trip in 1950. He had accumulated savings from his original trip, and used to loan small amounts of money to fellow ejidatarios. But his second son, now a school inspector who has acquired land in the ejido with his professional earnings, was studying in Mexico City and Tlaxcala during this period, so that Antonio's *bracero* migration was specifically targeted towards meeting the additional expenses created by his son's education and living costs. His eldest son did not study. He became a manual laborer in the *Secundaria* in 1969, following a spell of migration to Stockton in the period 1959-67, and bought rights to a cerrile *parcela* shortly afterwards. Thus, in the Guaracheño cases we have considered thus far, there is no simple correlation between U.S. migrant earnings and children's social mobility: these families contain a mixture of professionals and *campesinos*, and pioneer U.S. migration was not the direct key to the families' subsequent fortunes. It probably was of some indirect significance in that ejidatarios who had been to the North prior to the formation of the ejido were potentially better placed to survive the economic tribulations of the 1940s and 1950s than those who had not. Even so, it should be noted that other kinds of tribulations—in particular those arising from intra-communal violence—sometimes struck such families in subsequent years: being better placed initially was no guarantee of ultimate survival as a peasant farmer.

It would be misleading to suggest that this pattern of pre-*bracero* migration linked to subsequent social mobility for at least part of the next generation was a norm, though various other cases where this was so have been noted already. Two of the pioneer migrants in my sample had only worked in agriculture. One, Don Antonio C., had gone to Texas in 1922, aged twelve, and spent a mere two months picking cotton, before returning. He received 15 cents a pound for the cotton he picked, and in fact spent several weeks without pay. Given his age, there was clearly no hope of his getting work in the better paid sectors of the U.S. labor market. Though such very young illegal migrants did sometimes manage to sustain themselves for long enough in farm work across the border to make a new life for themselves in the longer term, this was clearly a marginal case, and Antonio's second trip as a *bracero* in the late 1940s was also a comparative failure. It is with some justification that people in Michoacán speak of "luck" as a major determinant of the fortunes of an international migrant, particularly in the *bracero* epoch. Agricultural earnings varied according to the region and the crop, and even according to the particular task one was assigned: a strong worker often earned much more when paid *"por contrato"* on a piece-work basis rather than on an hourly rate. Cotton-picking in Arizona paid much less than picking fruit in California, though living costs were higher in California. Earnings were also affected by the weather: if the harvest to which one was assigned failed, so did the trip unless one could find other work. Such variations were absolutely critical, since although real wage rates were substantially higher than in Mexico, they remained absolutely low and more or less constant throughout the *bracero* period, and actual earnings were highly variable. But personality also played a significant role at the individual level. The "docility" which was so prized by the hacienda was not necessarily a virtue in the North. Furthermore, despite the emphasis on "luck," and the dangers of *envidia* facing the "excessively" successful, a certain social stigma might be attached to "failure" as a migrant, whatever its actual cause, provoking shame in the individual and discouraging him from going again. Antonio's eldest son did acquire an education, and is now the director of a Technical School elsewhere in the state, where he has been able to offer his younger, uneducated, brother a manual job. In this case, however, there is no link at all between the father's migration and the educational attainment of his son.

Another purely agricultural migrant, Don Alfonso V., fared somewhat better, though he only stayed two years. He was older, aged eighteen, and his parents were already dead when he went in 1926. Alfonso worked in St. Louis, Missouri, earning between 40 and 50 cents an hour. He had been given a cart to drive by the hacienda, and used it to make his escape, just dumping the vehicle at the boundary of the estate. Despite this minor crime, he had no difficulty getting work on the labor-hungry hacienda again when he returned. The trip was pre-planned, and he had borrowed money to get himself to the frontier. Alfonso laughed when I asked him what he had done with the money he earned from this first trip. Most of it had apparently been spent on the pleasures of life. He returned eight times as a *bracero* in the years 1944 to 1951, working first on the railway in Boston, and then in various types of farm work. His pay was only marginally better in dollar terms than it had been in the Twenties, at 60 cents an hour, but on these trips he said that he both remitted money to his own family and saved enough to buy himself an ejidal *parcela* for 5,000 pesos in the 1950s.

He had four children. His eldest son Alfonso Jr. died in 1980, but went annually to the United States as a *bracero* between 1956 and 1962. He returned *al alambre* for a final visit to Merced in 1975, and in the interim spent six years from 1962 onwards cutting cane in Sinaloa, taking his wife and family with him. The wife cooked for the unaccompanied men who went to El Dorado, but is also the eldest sister of one of the younger long-term U.S. migrants in my sample, Pedro C., who spent the years between 1966 and 1978 working as an undocumented migrant for the unionized Productos Manzano company in Santa Rosa. Even before Alfonso Jr. died—he was a heavy drinker—some of their children, two boys and two girls, began to gravitate towards the fields of California in a way which reflected this connection. First one son left for Santa Rosa in 1972, then a second followed five years later, together with a sister, though her work destination was different from her brother's. Finally the last daughter left to join her sister in 1981: all found work in agriculture, according to their grandmother, and have remained in the U.S. since their departure. The mother is also in Tijuana with one of her daughters, and for this family, the U.S. has clearly provided a strategy for coping with the premature loss of the earning capacity of the male household head, though not in circumstances which are intimately connected with the migrant behavior of a the parental generation constituted by Alfonso Sr. and his daughter-in-law's father, an original ejidatario who dedicated himself to sowing his land and herding goats while his sons migrated to the United States. Alfonso's surviving son now works for the SAHOP. He obtained this job through his father-in-law after returning from a series of trips to Stockton between 1958 and 1963, undertaken after he married. He also now cultivates an ejidal *parcela* which his wife inherited after the death of her brother. His own eldest, single, son, is also in the U.S., working as a cashier. In this case, then, there is quite heavy family involvement with the U.S. in the post-war years, but it represents strategies adopted individually by autonomous households in the next generation, with *affinal* connections playing the dominant role in shaping the opportunities and choices of the units concerned.

Alfonso had five siblings, three of whom are also ejidatarios. Don Enrique, the youngest, is married but childless, though he has raised his wife's sister's daughter as his own. He acquired a *parcela* which had been abandoned at the beginning of the individual ejido. He went to the U.S. as a *bracero* three times, and earned better money than Alfonso, first because he obtained a rather hourly rate on his first trip, to New Mexico, and then obtained *por contrato* work for three months in Stockton, earning $25 a day in the asparagus. His final trip, to the cotton pick in Arizona in 1951, brought him up to $28 a day, because he found he had a particular aptitude for the work, and with experience managed to pick up to 1,500 lbs a day, albeit working twelve to fourteen hours.

Don Cenón, born in 1912, married in 1933. His only surviving child, a daughter, married a particularly hard-working landless long-term migrant, Alberto S., who bought two *parcelas* with his migrant earnings and has secured an education for the majority of his large family. Alberto now works for the SARH in Zamora, and forms a joint household with his father-in-law. Cenón received one of the untitled *parcelas* created in La Manga, and the two men work together on their joint holdings, with Cenón taking special responsibility for tending their joint herd of eleven cows. Cenón's migrant career in the United States is an unusual one. He went only once as a legally contracted *bracero* migrant, in 1943, working on the track in Los Angeles. But he had already been to the United States, *al alambre*, in 1938.

He first went, already married, to Michigan, working in the sugar beet fields, earning $2.50 a day working very long hours. From Michigan, he moved to Indiana, where he got work on the railway, where his earnings improved to $3.50 for an eight hour day. He had been in the United States for twenty-two months when he was caught by the *Migra*. Conditions in 1938 were very different from those of the early Twenties, when even a young migrant who lacked the formal prerequisites for emigration might get across the border and remain unmolested. Cenón spent two months in prison and said that he was subjected to very harsh treatment by the *Migra*. Mexico's surplus rural population was no longer needed nor welcome across the border during the 1930s, and would never be welcomed again on quite the same terms as before. Cenón returned again as an illegal in 1952, spending a month hiding from the *Migra* working in the grape harvest in Indio, California, where he earned between ten and twelve dollars a day. In between his first and second trips to the United States, he worked for two years as a gardener in Mexico City, earning 2.50 pesos a day. The migrant trail was not, therefore, restricted to those households with high ratios of consumers to workers, nor to those without interest in the land, though it should be said that Don Cenón's land is of rather poor quality, and it is important to stress that married men often decided to migrate in order to earn some money to help support the family they expected to have rather than in response to the needs created by children already born.

The eldest brother in the family, Don Antonio V., went to the U.S. twice in the *bracero* period, in 1943 and 1944, earning what was comparatively good money for the period in a peach cannery in Merced on his first trip of six months. He acquired his land in *potrero* Guarachita in the 1950s. His eldest three children are daughters, one of whom lives in Mexico with her factory-worker husband. His eldest son, Luis, though now blind, works a *parcela* inherited by his wife which he began to sow originally in the late 1960s, and also works with others as a peon. Luis went four times to the U.S. between

1956 and 1960, staying there for virtually the whole year on each occasion, and working in a cannery as well as in the fields. Carrying on what seems to have been something of a tradition in this relatively poor family, he made some of these trips as an illegal rather than a formally contracted worker. He then spent a year working in a soft drinks bottling plant in Mexico City. The next son, Salvador, aged forty-five, also went to Mexico City to work in a factory in 1960, but started combining this work with singing, from which he gradually built a successful career. Brother Jesús, aged forty-one, also went to Mexico in 1961, to be followed in turn by Roberto and then Mario, who found work in a furniture store. But Roberto found work in a factory in Los Angeles in the early 1970s, and Mario subsequently followed him across the border. Jesús also left for Los Angeles in 1979, but returned after a year, and now works on the Metro in Mexico. Roberto has not returned for some years, and Mario returned only to marry, his new wife then following him back to the United States. Salvador, the singer, obtained his father a passport, and he and his daughter-in-law were able to travel legally to Los Angeles as tourists, while Mario reentered illegally. These two sons have, therefore, apparently decided to make their futures in the North: though they have no legal status there, their families are with them and they have permanent jobs outside the agricultural sector.

In this last case, the minor U.S. migration of the father, and the much more extensive international migration of the eldest son, seem at first sight to be less significant than internal rural-urban migration in the reproductive dynamics of the family as a whole. But the case illustrates the important principle that rural-urban migration may be a stepping-stone to further, and more permanent, forms of international migration, in which the problem of undocumented status is weighed against the superiority of urban wage-levels on the two sides of the border. Sometimes rural-urban migration creates a new social contact which provides an opportunity to find work in the North. If one looks, therefore, at the larger picture which embraces the reproduction of the children of the peasantry, it becomes apparent that a simple opposition between internal and international migration as mutually exclusive alternative strategies would not, in the last analysis, be appropriate.

There is no necessary correlation between the level of parental involvement in the U.S. labor market and that of the children. Once children have their own families, they are likely to pursue autonomous strategies, and migration by single or newly married sons may, of course, be sustaining nonmigrant parents, though in some cases, the older generation was staying behind cultivating the land while a son or sons supplemented family income with work in the North. It would seem likely that possession of land would make the *bracero* migration option more attractive than definitive rural-urban migration, but this was clearly not invariably the case, given the relatively high rate of abandonment of *parcelas* correlated with rural-urban migration in the 1940s and 1950s. These variations cannot, however, be seen in terms of simple voluntary "choices" of livelihood strategy. This principle is well exemplified by the case of the family of another of those I interviewed who went to the United States both in the Twenties and as a *bracero* migrant.

Don Juan F.'s father, Antonio, had been chofer to the hacendado. He had five brothers, two of whom also received land as original ejidatarios. Jesús was a hard-working man, who always sowed his land, despite the fact that he was a habitual *bracero* migrant, using some of his earnings to ensure that he was always smartly dressed. I have already related the tragic story of how his wife persuaded him to sell his *parcela,* because she considered it demeaning for her husband to be seen toiling in the fields. Jesús spent a period working as a *jornalero* before migrating to Mexico. Another brother, Enrique, was involved in a killing, and forced to leave for Mexico. The three landless brothers left to find work elsewhere, two going to the cities and one to Sinaloa, where he works in agriculture. Don Juan went to the U.S. for the first time in 1926, to Chicago, staying nearly five years. Like Antonio O., he received some limited schooling there, though his level of literacy remains low. Throughout his time away he remitted money to his parental family, marrying on his return. He then returned during the first three years of the *bracero* program.

Juan's eldest son, Benjamin, was fifteen when he made his final trip North in 1945. Benjamin himself did not go until after his marriage, but stayed for two years in Moor Park, California, working in fruit picking for between $60 and $80 a week, and then for eight months with a chicken-farmer, work which was both unattractive in itself and brought inferior pay, at 30 cents an hour. He made one further, 45 day trip in 1962, earning quite good money by *bracero* standards in the tomato harvest. Juan's third son, Luis, was a much longer term migrant, entering the United States yearly between 1955 and 1977, mostly going to California. Luis stayed for nine months on his first trip, which was one of two undertaken before his marriage, but generally just went for the three month temporada. Both these sons have become ejidatarios. Father Juan bought the *parcela* to which Benjamin now has title in the mid-1950s. His early migration may have left him with a little in the way of cash savings, since he exchanged his original *parcela* for a better piece of land. He might, however, have also been able to use some of Benjamin's migrant earnings for the transaction. Benjamin also now enjoys control of an eight hectare *parcela* in La Lobera inherited by his wife. He has a large family of thirteen children, of whom six were still studying in 1982: his eldest son works for the SARH in Tepic, but he has five single educated daughters at work. A younger son, aged twenty-two, was just marrying, and had remained a *jornalero*. Luis has sown an eight hectare *parcela* inherited by his wife Guadalupe since the end of his U.S. migration period. Rights in the land had passed to his wife's sister, after their father, the famous secretary of the "Rafael Picazo" cooperative, disappeared, and were then given by her to Guadalupe around 1974. Luis's older brother Felipe had sown the land *a la cuarta* for the few years when Luis was still migrating. Luis's educated eldest son works in a laboratory in Mexico, and another daughter is studying to become a teacher.

Brother Felipe had been only twice to the United States, after marriage, though he stayed a year on one occasion, but his wife spent six months working as a domestic in Los Angeles in 1979: her access to this opportunity was mediated not only by some relatives living in the city, but by other kin involved in the people trade across the border. Felipe has always worked as a *peón* and *ecuarero,* and is now enjoying the fruits of encouraging his children to study, as two single children who have qualified as teachers are able to contribute regularly to the income of the parental household. His wife's visit to the United States was a means of helping with the costs of graduation of these first family professionals, though it was also a stage in the break-up of their marriage.

The two youngest brothers, Juan, who sows an *ecuaro* and keeps a shop, and Carlos, a *jornalero* and *ecuarero*, aged thirty-eight and thirty-six respectively, both also went to the U.S. Juan went five times to California, once as a *bracero*, and four times *al alambre* between 1963 and 1975, staying up to a year across the border. Much of his migration was before marriage, in contrast to Carlos's two trips after marriage as an illegal in 1978 and 1979. Juan bought his house and set up his small business on the proceeds of his migration. Felipe and Carlos's migrant earnings were probably more directly orientated towards helping with the costs of family maintenance, though both also possess their own houses. Juan also has three daughters, the eldest of whom is in Mexico. The other two live in Cerrito Cotijaran and Zamora respectively.

Father Juan continues to sow his *parcela,* often using the labor of some of his innumerable resident grandchildren. At various points in his life he has received remittances from single sons engaged in international migration, though three of his sons were already married when they went *al Norte.* He could, of course, also draw on the labor of the single sons who did not migrate. He did not, however, accumulate sufficient resources from his own international migration to sow his land *sin compromisos* in the epoch of the particulares, and while his sons have remained resident in the village, they have pursued autonomous economic strategies after marriage, and have all decided that education is the way forward for the next generation. As Felipe once said to me: "What luck that my two eldest kids were girls and wanted to study. I can say goodbye to all that chinga now."

The pattern represented by Don Juan F.'s case is not that unusual, though in most of the other similar cases in my sample, the father had been absent for a somewhat shorter period. One man who spent a total of eight years in the North, first in Indiana Steel Company Foundry, and subsequently in the Chevrolet engine plant, had four daughters but no sons. Migrant earnings provided him with a pleasant house, but he was never to be a particularly active ejidatario. More reminiscent of Juan's case is Don Ceberiano F., who left for Chicago in 1924, before marriage, working eight months on the Track: his father had been killed when he was small, and he grew up in his grandfather's house. He returned for another eight month stint, this time to a foundry in Michigan, after marriage in 1928, and migrant earnings provided him with enough money to set up as a muleteer. His two married sons have remained in Guaracha, working as *jornaleros* and helping their father. The eldest, aged forty-eight, went four times to the U.S. as a *bracero*, followed in turn by his own eldest, single son, who went to Stockton for over a year in 1980. The rest of the family are, however, studying for professional careers. Don Ceberiano's second son, aged thirty-eight, went once as a *bracero*, and twice *al alambre*, staying eighteen months on one occasion, after marriage. His eldest son is now studying *prepa* in Chapingo. Two further cases in the sample are essentially similar, though the father only made one relatively short trip. For some, of course, conditions in the foundries proved intolerable, despite the higher earnings.

Three further cases will bear some specific further comment. One is that of Don Chema B., the one ejidatario to have been to the United States in each of the major phases of United States migration. Chema first went as a single man at the age of eighteen, in 1928, and stayed three years across the border. He experienced no difficulty in entering, and stressed its low financial cost. He went first to Michigan, working on the Track and in a factory making pipes, and then got into the Chevrolet plant. On his return he committed himself to the *agrarista* cause, and participated in the Andrade-Prado *sindicato*. But at the start of the *bracero* period, he began to make his way north again, going yearly to California, often renewing his contracts and staying on occasion up to nine months in the North, remitting between $50 and $100 every two weeks. He continued going to the North up to 1960, but had already effectively shifted his residence to Guadalajara during the 1950s, where he worked as a plumber, renting his land to Don Gabriel. He made his final trip North in 1968, working in the strawberry harvest for two months, earning up to $15 a day, though he felt that the slightly improved pay did not really compensate for the increased difficulties of entry. Furthermore, the need to make the effort was reducing, and not simply because he had found an adequate mode of livelihood in Guadalajara.

His eldest son, Abram, born in 1932, became a priest, and began to help his father financially. His second son works as a brewery delivery man, another in a plastics factory, and two others in the public sector as manual workers, in Guadalajara, where they were brought up. His youngest son, Alberto, aged twenty-nine, is a lawyer in a government office. One of his four daughters is in the U.S., having followed her migrant Guaracheño husband, who now works in a cannery. Chema's migration, both internal and international, therefore became his basic mode of livelihood, coupled with subventions from his educated children. He did return to sowing his land briefly in 1979, but had already decided to rent again in 1982. He insisted, with some emotion, that he would never sell the title to his land, since the struggle to attain it represented the part of his life he could look back on with most pride. But the ejido had never really been his life nor the basis for his children's future.

Many of the *Norteños* who returned to the Ciénega in the 1930s did so because they found themselves without work. Those who were there illegally were naturally the most vulnerable, but even legal emigrants were not immune from the forces of capitalist crisis. Nevertheless, this was not true of everyone, and it is clear that a number of those whom I interviewed had relatively good prospects in the North despite the depression, returning, not from economic necessity, but in order to take up the new opportunity created by land reform. A significant number of ejidal commissars were to be recruited from the ranks of the returned Norteños.

In the early days this probably did reflect their tendency to identify ideologically with *agrarismo* and orientation towards political action, but in the longer term it was more likely to be a reflection of the fact that many of the *Norteños* remained a little more prosperous than their peers. Not only were they willing to take on an office which was normally less economically rewarding from the personal point of view in earlier years than it has become in the epoch of BANRURAL; having a little money in hand tends to ensure one a certain degree of personal popularity in the community, since it enables one to build up personal clientship and friendship networks more readily through commonplace social transactions. In the case of Emiliano Zapata most of these *Norteño* office holders do not seem to have been notably political, nor to have pursued a concerted strategy of personal advancement through occupancy of an office.[20]

We will look in more detail at two families in which the pre-war migrant father became a substantial member of the community and occupied public office. At first sight one might expect such families to consolidate their roots in the community, or at any rate break with the United States and achieve social mobility within Mexico in the next generation. These examples indicate that this is by no means necessarily the case. Education is the main route to significant social mobility out of Mexican peasant society and if that course is not followed, the next generation may see the North as an attractive alternative.

Don Carlos A. was born in 1905. He was one of two brothers, and their father had been a hacienda mediero who enjoyed a position of relative privilege. He was in charge of the cultivation of ten tierras held by the aged *Tenedor de Libros*, Marcelino Rodríguez. This patronage relationship ensured that their father obtained a reasonable return on the cultivation of the lands assigned to him as a sharecropper, and according to Carlos's brother Antonio, provoked a certain amount of envidia amongst those who were less fortunate. Despite this, both brothers obtained land in the original ejido.

Carlos, the elder brother, left for the U.S. when he was fifteen years old, entering by Texas. He went to Houston and Dallas, and then to Kansas City and Chicago, working on the Track, for the Rock Island Line and then the Santa Fé. An illegal entrant, he managed to get work despite his evident youth and the foremen's doubts about whether he was physically capable of doing what was required of him. He earned $2.08 for an eight hour day, and stayed four years. His brother remained behind, working with his father, and Carlos joined him on his return. I should stress that both men had followed the normal "career" of peonage as children, despite their father's relatively privileged status, which was quite informal. Neither expressed any nostalgia for the days of the *patrón*. Carlos returned to the United States around 1950, after he had served as ejidal commissar in succession to El Chiquitín, spending six months in California picking oranges. Don Antonio began to go as a *bracero* at about the same time, though independently of his brother. He entered five times in consecutive years, staying for three or four months and remitting money to his wife and only child, a daughter. He told me what little surplus money he had was spent on beer and clothes, and gleefully observed that he'd bought the Levis he was wearing on his last trip in 1955.

Antonio's *parcela* is unsuitable for mechanization. He now sows it as a joint enterprise, *a medias,* with his forty-one year old son-in-law, whose father was a long-term recurrent *bracero* migrant for reasons which were not primarily economic. Antonio's life has therefore been spent in a process of simple reproduction based on his land, *ecuaro* and animals, his circumstances supplying neither the conditions nor motivation for any other strategy. Don Carlos, in contrast, has been considerably more active. In addition to being ejidal commissar and subsequently *Jefe de Tenencia* in the period 1960-62, Carlos entered into a partnership with the Villamar comerciante Don Pancho. Don Pancho was unable to compete effectively with Don Gabriel, but he continued to operate as a source of credit for a few ejidatarios and has concentrated his mercantile activities on the maize trade since the end of his period as intermediary for the wheat mills. Although Carlos also sowed with Don Gabriel "many times," he entered into a special form of partnership with Don Pancho, sowing land for him on an *a medias* basis which offered much more attractive returns than those associated with Don Gabriel's finance.

Carlos has four sons and two daughters. Both the daughters are married to *jornaleros*. His eldest son, Roberto, has worked full-time for the SARH as an *auxiliar de asistencia técnica* since 1960. Prior to that, he made three trips to the U.S. as a *bracero*, during the formative stages of his large family of thirteen children, whom he has encouraged to study. He stayed a year in 1956, and made shorter trips in 1958 and 1959. A second *parcela* bought by his father was originally put in the name of his second son, but Roberto began sowing it in 1979, having rented another *parcela* previously. The formal title holder decided to pursue a migrant career in California, though his family remains in Emiliano Zapata. Don Carlos's third son has been in California since the mid-1960s. Whereas his elder brother Carlos works in agriculture, José has a factory job, and has his family in the United States, though he still returns to the village on visits. José is an *emigrado*. He has been joined there by the youngest son, Ramón, aged twenty-two, who also has his family north of the border, though his status in the United States remains that of an undocumented entrant.

Most of Carlos's sons have therefore chosen the North, and Roberto might conceivably have made the same choice had he not secured his post with the SARH. Their father has remained a "solid" member of the community, though because of his youth and his failure to obtain the most rewarding type of work in the North, he cannot have accumulated very substantial savings in his four years there. He was not, apparently, able to sow extensively *sin compromisos*. At one point he had a herd of thirty cows, but sold them in the early 1960s. Furthermore, being a relatively successful ejidatario in terms of keeping one's head above water enhanced the chances of one's sons achieving a foothold in the North, by making it easier for them to borrow the money required to participate in the *bracero* program and subsequent illegal movement.

Carlos's career illustrates something of the limitations on peasant differentiation within the community. Being "active" and sowing rented *parcelas*, accumulating a stock of animals, even filling public offices, was not sufficient to turn peasants into even minor capitalists. Such outcomes were restricted to those who had much more substantial sources of capitalization, and even more substantial off-farm or migrant earnings accumulated over many years generally did not result in the creation of an expansionary enterprise. Though one of Abel Prado's sons has become an ejidal entrepreneur with the help of a year in Chicago, earnings in the oil industry (and a professional brother), his father remained simply a relatively prosperous member of the community (whose prosperity owed much initially to his role as an *agrarista* and political contacts). Abel's main interest in life was in providing his sons with an education if they wanted it. The partnership of Manuel Mora, El Chiquitín and Rafael Moreno owed something to the savings Manuel accumulated in the U.S., but all the partners started with a little capital and were, in effect, simply developing an economic strategy appropriate to their background and skills as mechanics and drivers. Whether or not El Chiquitín also raised capital through his political relationship with Dámaso Cárdenas and role in the dismantling of the old hacienda infrastructure enjoyed by the ejido, this kind of enterprise would probably have remained viable. The most spectacular case of capitalist entrepreneurship amongst the ejidatarios, Don Santiago, was, of course, the product of promotion via a relationship with an entrepreneur from outside the ejido, but such outcomes were, as the case of Don Carlos demonstrates, dependent on a major direct capitalist penetration of ejidal agriculture. One of the current *emigrados* is cultivating a small amount of rented land and owns a tractor, but his main interest in life has been in securing his children an education rather than building a "business." As we will see in the next chapter, modern conditions are probably even more inimical to the development of "entrepreneurs" among the ranks of ordinary ejidatarios than those of the past.

The case of one of the *emigrado* ejidatarios I was able to interview, Pedro B., will be instructive in this regard. His family's history is of particular interest, since his late father Amado was also an ejidal commissar who had emigrated to the U.S. in the pre-war period. Unlike the other pioneer migrants I have discussed, Amado had subsequently taken his wife with him to the U.S., so that his older children were born there rather than in Mexico. Don Amado's father had worked in the hacienda mill, and his brother Aurelio also became an ejidatario, who has dedicated himself over many hard years to improving an untitled *parcela* carved out of uncultivated land in *potrero* Frutyales. Aurelio encouraged all his children to study, and the majority of both the boys and the girls have done so. He went twice to the U.S. as a *bracero*, staying a year in 1943, and his second son, Ernesto, now a psychology professor in Mexico, also apparently made a trip *al alambre*, presumably to help with the family's education costs. But Aurelio did not care for life in the North. Brother Amado, however, left for the first time in 1920, when he would have been eighteen, and was to return definitively in 1961, to end his days in Los Angeles. He married young, and it appears that his wife either accompanied him on this first journey or followed shortly afterwards. Amado went to Colorado, where he worked in agriculture rather than the better paid industrial work enjoyed by most of these early migrants.

Amado did not become a naturalized American until 1960, when he was able to emigrate though the sons who had been born there and chose to return earlier.[21] Amado's eldest son is dead, but Pedro has six siblings living in Los Angeles, Tijuana and San José. Pedro, aged seven in 1940, was the third youngest of the family and was born in Mexico. His father must therefore have returned by 1933. Pedro's own account would put his return in 1928, but this seems rather too early given that, like many others, he came back to get land. In any event, he received a *parcela* in El Monte.

Don Amado was elected commissar in the mid-1950s. He is remembered with great affection in this role. He apparently told the ejidal assembly after his election that: "You appointed me as a joke, and a joke I'm going to turn out." (*De burla me pusieron, y de burla voy a salir.*) In fact, Amado was rather conscientious, going on foot to Jiquilpan to negotiate with officialdom, and leading a successful campaign for the provision of an irrigation canal in *potrero* El Carrizo. If Amado's original comment reveals what a number of living informants said explicitly, that few people actively sought the post of commissar in those days and that the collective life of the ejido was at a particularly low ebb, it is also clear that a commissar who was thus inclined could do something to benefit his fellow ejidatarios, however slight the personal rewards. Amado was certainly not a rich man, and it is perhaps not surprising that his older, American born sons, decided to return to the North to seek their livelihoods, though all Amado's children married in Emiliano

Zapata. Pedro himself first went to the United States at the start of the 1950s, going to Fresno. In the interview he said that he went *al alambre* rather than as a legal contracted worker. His brother Wilfredo went to live in Los Angeles, working in agriculture, and he sent Amado his *cartas* to emigrate first, before helping Pedro the following year.

Since 1961, Pedro has spent six months of every year in the United States. Unlike some *emigrados*, he does not have a regular job with a single employer, but works as a casual laborer hired through *contratistas*. His work is not unionized, which Pedro himself regarded as an advantage, since he argued that one still had to pay one's union dues whether one worked or not, and he sometimes didn't find work for several weeks on end. How could the unions guarantee work for all the people who were arriving in California these days? Unlike some of those I spoke to, he regarded the insurance schemes offered by the *contratistas* as satisfactory, though he admitted that this "insurance" does not, in fact, cover illness or accident outside working hours: it is therefore scarcely comparable to a full social insurance scheme. In effect, Pedro's status as an *emigrado* does not place him in a particularly advantageous position relative to some undocumented workers. During his months in the North—May to October—he lives in government-run camps set up for legal seasonal workers, and has nothing to fear from the *Migra*. This latter is the chief benefit of emigrant status in Pedro's case. In essence, his situation is similar to that of an old-time *bracero*, although his earnings are considerably better in absolute terms, at between 30 and 50 dollars a day in 1982.

Pedro did not work in agriculture in the first two years after he emigrated, but in a restaurant. The pay was little better, and he did not take to the regime of clocking on and off: he felt "*más encerrado.*" It is significant that the rest of the family, father, brothers and brothers-in-law, were also fieldworkers. Though the family had all eventually returned to the North, all seem to have been reluctant to sever their links with the ejido totally. Amado rented his land after he went to Los Angeles, and after his death Pedro and an older brother disputed who should inherit the rights to it. Pedro finally prevailed, and rights have been assigned to one of his daughters, since Pedro himself had already bought another *parcela*, a large piece of land in need of considerable clearance and improvement before it would yield a reasonable harvest. Pedro himself expressed a definite preference for life in Mexico. Of course, the money was better in the North, and the cost of living was already rising more rapidly in Mexico than in the U.S. when I interviewed him late in 1982.

But there was more to it than just economics. Familiar themes emerged. Everything in America had its owner, and the police were everywhere. California was full of drugs: the government maintained too many young, strong men in idleness, with nothing to do all day except turn to crime at night. In Mexico, you could sleep if you wanted to. Furthermore, for Pedro as an individual, the seasonal migrant life *al Norte* was becoming ever less attractive for reasons simply of age. Now he was fifty, everything was becoming harder for him physically, and he got tired easily. Where work was *por contrato*, there came a point where experience couldn't compensate for declining strength. Of course, his earnings were also threatened by the increasing imbalance between supply and demand for labor: more and more people were going to find work there (mostly, of course, *al alambre*), and mechanization was taking away more jobs every year. As a casual worker, Pedro enjoyed no advantage in the labor market over anyone else. He remarked, rather bitterly, on how his inability to speak any English kept him out of the best jobs: "It's the same in the United States as it is here for a *campesino*, you earn to eat." On balance, he thought that his years in the North had delivered him and his family a rather better standard of living than he could possibly have achieved as an ejidatario in Mexico. But he thought it likely that he would stay permanently in Emiliano Zapata after one more year in the North.

Though Pedro emigrated through the good offices of his older brother, he made his own way to Stockton after he decided to give up on work in the restaurant, and Wilfredo himself subsequently moved there. Because the family's labor power has always been dedicated to casual agricultural labor, it has not, in practice, been able to acquire as much economic security as its apparent initial advantage in terms of possibilities for naturalization would suggest. In a very real sense, Pedro remains just as much an uprooted Mexican peasant in a foreign land as his father had been in Colorado in the 1920s. His children are also *emigrados*, and his son, aged twenty-five, made his first trip north with his father aged seventeen. He is now working in Manteca, having married in the United States. His other five children are all daughters, three of them married, and to Guaracheños. In Pedro's absence, a son-in-law looks after the *parcelas*, having given up his own (undocumented) migration after marriage. He, interestingly enough, found work through non-*emigrado* friends as a plumber for five months in Bernais, and in a foundry in Chicago, where he spent ten months of 1979. Pedro's other two married daughters are both married to men who are regular migrants to Stockton like their father: but the women of Pedro's family appear to have visited Stockton for a couple of months yearly in the years since 1973, and also worked in the fields on these occasions, according to the data given in the village census by Pedro's wife.

In this case, then, legal emigration to the North has not led to a definitive breaking of a family's links with the countryside of Michoacán nor to a fundamental transformation of the socio-economic status of the migrants. A third generation is now reproducing the pattern of casual work in North American agriculture established by their grandfather in the 1920s. Though Amado's U.S. born children chose to base their futures north of the border, and Pedro's resumption of his father's role as an ejidatario may not be replicated by his own son, now that he has his own family in the U.S., the North may yet find these modern emigrant workers as surplus to its current requirements as their forebears were in the era of the deportations. What is certainly clear enough from this case is that a combined peasant-proletarian socio-economic system of great complexity has developed across the divide represented by the border over a long time period, and that the migration process may not engender any great transformation in the social situation of *campesino* families which have participated in it for all those decades.

CHAPTER 9

PEASANT AGRICULTURE
IN THE EPOCH OF BANRURAL

As the 1960s gave way to the 1970s, the international labor migration processes discussed in the previous chapter became merely a facet of a broader process of internationalization of capital which was transforming rural production systems within Mexico itself in an increasingly profound way. As Sanderson has emphasized, the new global division of labor being created in the 1970s was fundamentally different from the military imperialisms and trade-based export economies of earlier eras (1986:14-28). Both labor and capital became increasingly mobile, and the capitalist production process, in both agriculture and industry, became a global one in the sense that the accumulation and valorization of capital became dependent on the integration of labor processes distributed across different national units. This kind of integration is most obvious in the case of transnational industrial production which sources components from a number of different production facilities scattered about the globe and offers its international consumers a standardized product differentiated only by cosmetic appearance. But modern agro-industry shares much of this emphasis on standardization of both technical production process and quality of intermediate and final products, and it also displays another dimension of the new global division of labor in a paradigmatic way: the increasing "vertical concentration" of agricultural production systems on a global scale through transnationals' dominance of input supply, packaging and marketing.

Standardization of production and consumption patterns on a global scale inevitably encounters some resistance from social and cultural variation, although cultural factors can scarcely be treated as pristine essences unaffected by these transformations in the conditions of life of the world's population. But what is potentially most important in the recent pattern of development of the global system is the increasing diffuseness of the networks of economic power and the changing relations between capitalism and national state machineries it engenders. Marxist arguments about the nature of imperialism in the late Sixties and early Seventies tended to focus on the role of the transnational corporation and the extent to which transnational corporations in reality maintained a "national" identity (leading either to the global "super-imperialist" domination of the United States or to a continuing or even intensifying competition between rival blocs). Some continued to stress the ultimate interdependence of military-political hegemonies and economic hegemonies, and the political impossibility of a global centralization of capital based on the genuinely multinational *ownership* of transnational corporations, in opposition to the "ultra-imperialist" thesis that the internationalization of capital was developing to a point where the power of the national state would wane in the face of the power of the transnationals (Mandel 1972:325-338). More significantly, as Poulantzas emphasized, "state" and "nation" are not interchangeable terms: if the specific terms of the dominant class fraction's hegemony and the nature of the state itself reflect the historical balance of forces in a social formation, while class conflicts retain particular national political and ideological dimensions, then it is hard to see how the functions of the national state in capitalist reproduction could be fulfilled by any supranational organization (1975:78-84). Seen from the perspective of the Mexican *campo*, neither the political nor economic hegemony of the United States seems questionable, whatever nicer issues might be raised about equity ownership or the implications of transnational corporate policies for the domestic economy of the North. Nevertheless, it remains worth emphasizing what most of these older debates focussing on the power of the transnational corporations versus the state obscure: the unplanned and spontaneous nature of much of the process of transformation which has been taking place, and its more insidious contributions to the disarticulation of national societies.

THE LOGIC OF CAPITALISM AND THE LOGIC OF INTERNATIONALIZATION

The global integration of commodity production systems is promoted by the historical legacy of uneven development. Poor peasants use chemical herbicides because they are cheaper than paid labor working with *machetes*. Entrepreneurs on the periphery respond to market incentives to produce export crops the profitability of which is premised on gross international differences in real incomes. Corporate planners shape their plans to relocate production and investment not simply in line with costs in a purely quantitative sense, but in relation to particular qualities of local labor forces which are the product of specific patterns of local development and adjustment to changing global conditions (Pearson 1986). Yet the conditions which have made the global integration of production systems possible are at the same time political. We have seen how the Mexican state mediated the conditions of labor migration to the North. Its interventions have been equally significant in the development of the *maquila* industries (Bustamante 1983a) and of the contract farming systems established by transnational companies south of the border (Feder 1977; Burbach and Flynn 1980): one example of this mediation found in both contexts is the "guarantees" offered to foreign capital by the official labor organizations.

Much of this chapter will be concerned with the national state's so-called "refunctionalization" of the disintegrating ejidal system as a producer of low-value raw materials for the agro-industrial complex. But the nature of this more extensive, and expensive, state intervention seems to reflect both a response to mounting internal social and political crisis and an approach which was, and is, highly constrained by the distribution of economic power in the global economy. Since 1982, the state's room to maneuver has visibly diminished: production and welfare subsidies have been removed at the behest of the IMF, programs designed to ameliorate the nutritional disadvantages of present patterns of agricultural development have been abandoned, and foreign control of the domestic economy has increased in unprecedentedly overt ways. Present expressions of concern for environmental issues by the governments of metropolitan countries, in response to middle-class mobilization, might suggest the continuing significance of national state power as a counter-weight to unregulated capitalist development at the more affluent center of the global system. But this tardy response to potentially catastrophic global phenomena is constrained by "practical" considerations which amount to an implicit concession that the logic of the economy as it has developed over the past decades is beyond question. No serious consideration is given to the idea of compensating Third World countries for the costs of *their* adopting "greener" policies, and radical policies of a kind which would imply fundamental shifts in northern life-styles are not discussed in "serious" political circles. It is true that the costs of radical solutions would be unacceptable for "ordinary people" in the North, but the *impasse* imposed by the legacy of our past development reinforces the principle that structural considerations limit the scope of state regulatory power.

The same principle applies to the state's response to political pressures emanating from farmers or industrial workers affected by the restructuring of the global division of labor; despite some concessions to protectionism, the characteristic response of the metropolitan state seems to be one of adjustment to global trends by forcing disadvantaged sections of the population into new and inferior occupational niches, reducing public expenditure on welfare services and increasing the means of internal repressive power. In both contexts—"center" and "periphery"—the state may be increasing its levels of social regulation in many spheres (even where there are increasing symptoms of public antagonism to the process), but in a way which facilitates the continuation of processes of capital accumulation. This is not, however, something which should be seen as confirming the purely instrumental nature of the "bourgeois" state. The international mobility of capital does pose problems of regulation, and national political regimes today are as dependent as they were in the mercantilist era on maintaining accumulation of wealth in the civil societies within their national boundaries. Their interventions are orientated towards securing a distribution of wealth which is politically sustainable under local conditions. Even if they could secure internal unity, the underclasses face the problem that they have a much reduced potential to organize across nation state boundaries and can only act directly on particular local agencies of transnational private enterprise or through pressure on their national state machines. It is difficult to negotiate with more than some isolated limb of the global capitalist system: local producers might, for example, achieve improved pricing terms with the local agents of some transnational contracting firm, only to find the firm selling out its local assets and moving off to control their market more indirectly at some higher level of the international agro-industrial system of vertical concentration (or simply moving out of their region altogether).

But the capitalist system itself is more (or less) than a collection of large corporations with office blocks and financial institutions dealing in money which never exists as cash and trading commitments to buy commodities which have yet to be produced. While consumer demand (for organically-grown vegetables, for example) may influence patterns of commodity production for markets where the consumers have disposable income to allocate between different uses, the primary logic of the economic process must be the valorization of capital. This is hardly a process which can rely on the ambiguous signals of the market in terms of post-hoc expressions of "consumer choice." The "affluence" of advanced capitalism is based on the cheapening of the real production costs of items of mass consumption combined with the synthesization of tastes and demand. Anthropologists who have emphasized the way consumption of commodities participates in the construction of self and social identities in capitalist societies wilfully ignore the particular form of dependence of consumption on accumulation characteristic of capitalist production—the reasons for Marx's (relative) underscoring of the significance of use values in favor of a relentless critique of the reification which impedes understanding of the runaway nature of capitalism as a class process (Fine and Harris 1979:8-12; Rosdolsky 1980:437-443).

The argument of this study is opposed to the idea that the manner in which Mexico's *campesinos* are inserted into the modern class process of capitalism is determined by a purely economic "logic of capitalist accumulation." But the analysis of the preceding chapters suggests that, even abstracting from the subsumption of the peasant production process by capital, a "study of the peasant farm from the organizational point of view" in the manner of Chayanov would be meaningless without recognition of the way farming activity today is related to patterns of wage labor, migration and income remissions from household members not working on the land. Indeed, as Chayanov himself clearly appreciated, regular labor migration (in the Central Industrial Districts of Russia) created an entirely different situation from that on which he centered his theory of farm organization. The role of the national state in peasant agriculture, as a supplier of credit and infrastructural investment, is equally evident in modern Mexico, and was not entirely insignificant even in the era of *neolatifundismo*, though its negative role (as the promoter of industrialization at the expense of the peasant) is more evident in this period than its positive role, which was mainly concentrated on certain spheres and regions of private hydro-agricultural enterprise (Durán 1988: 55-61). But the more recent development (and after 1983, renewed decay) of peasant farming in the Ciénega provides a striking exemplification of the impact of an industrialization of the agricultural production process itself, under the aegis of the domestic state, within the context of the growing internationalization of the agricultural economy. Its analysis poses particular problems, since a simple distinction between local and global factors in change (and peasant strategies for coping with or responding to change), simply replicates the dangerous assumption that change can be analyzed adequately in terms of a hierarchy of spatial units (village, region, country) within national units which are the constituent elements of the global system. The analysis of international migration has already suggested ways in which such an assumption may be problematic. The migrant experience is not just about being "there" or "here," but about being "betwixt and between," in a distinct and problematic identity. Migrant social and economic networks have a specifically transnational quality: the existence of national boundaries is central to their functioning, but much of the way they function depends on the way they transcend and manipulate the regulatory activities of states.

Capitalism can do that too, and the institutional order of economic power under late capitalist conditions is infinitely harder to pin down to some kind of human or spatial locus. Although monopsonist or oligopsonist conditions frequently characterize the market conditions facing Mexican producers north of the border, export trades in vegetables or fruit involve a multitude of different kinds of economic agents, ranging from small peasant producers through larger growers and a hierarchy of commercial intermediaries. Such markets are ones of mutual economic adjustment in which shifts in one sector may influence others, and have unexpected implications for other areas of rural policy.[1] The agro-industrial pattern of development is promoted by domestic entrepreneurs and state agencies to serve domestic markets. While different markets often demand different kinds of products, as is the case with fresh tomatoes grown in the Ciénega, some products, particularly those subject to processing, may be variably assigned to domestic or export markets in accordance with price fluctuations. It is therefore inadequate to treat world market forces as purely external trade-related phenomena linking national economies, to be analyzed at a "macro" level of analysis requiring simply empirical qualification in the light of the impact of local factors of variation. Micro-analyses of the peasant reproduction process, including the farming process, are still worthwhile precisely because peasant adaptations, along with domestic state adaptations, themselves play a significant role in promoting the internationalization of production (and consumption) processes. Agribusiness development based on female labor reserves is, for example, linked in a systematic way to patterns of farming and male migration in Michoacán (Arizpe and Aranda 1982:469-471). But internationalization does not necessarily involve the direct intervention of transnational corporations or international trade. Peasant production of sorghum in the Ciénega, and their children's consumption of potato chips and *refrescos* in place of tortillas, milk and fresh fruit drinks, are just as much facets of the process as the famed "strawberry imperialism" centered on the Zamora region.

Micro-analyses of the peasantry are, however, also important in another sense. Even in their present decaying form, peasant production systems provide reminders that there are alternative possible modes of rural social and economic organization. Analysis of the social costs of agricultural modernization and of the failures of state policy in the context of internationalization of capital reveals the starkness of the real issues in contemporary rural development. The crux of what continuing sense of *campesino* identity exists in the Ciénega lies in a collective sense of victimization: "We are always at the bottom." This is not an unreasonable view in a context where policy "success" in official terms is defined by the provision of a "basic subsistence basket." *Campesino* status is something to be escaped, and villagers rich and poor are victims of official banditry and periodic violence on the part of elements of the *Policía Judicial*. The only alternative to the processes described in this chapter is a radically new concept of the social role of rural people (and by implication, of modern urban civilization as well). A reconstitution of the social position of the peasantry in practice would have to go a long way beyond what may already seem the utopian objective of providing farmers with a minimal material livelihood.

WHO ARE THE REAL EJIDATARIOS?

It is not, of course, entirely unproblematic to assume that an ejido can be defined as a community of peasant farmers. During the period of my original field study in 1982-83, seventy-five of those who held formal titles to land in the ejido of Emiliano Zapata—almost a quarter of the total— were renting their *parcelas*.[2] Nineteen of those who were not renting their land were not resident in the community. These included an *emigrado* whose family was resident in California, and a few people who ran small urban businesses. One of the latter, resident in Mexico City, regularly visited Guaracha and exercised a good deal of personal supervision over his crops. Non-residence is perfectly compatible with securing credits from BANRURAL, although some of the absentees preferred to sow with their own money. Two of the absentees were widows who retained their titles, and all appointed administrators to look after their interests on a day-to-day basis. Absentees might shift from the cash or *a la cuarta* forms of rental to the "administration" mode and back again, and the possibility of securing a *utilidad* by cultivating with BANRURAL credit—perhaps supplemented by additional private finance—was one of the factors which underlay their levels of interest in their land. One of the more notable non-resident ejidatarios was the former neolatifundist, who bought a third ejidal *parcela* after 1983.

The ranks of the absentees would be increased if one included persons who were engaged in recurrent annual migration to the United States but whose families remained resident in the village. But for our present purposes, the problem is one of identifying the "real" ejidatarios, that is, members of the ejido who are active farmers. Some of Michoacán's *emigrados* are particularly active, extending their area of cultivation by rental, buying additional ejidal titles, and investing in agricultural machinery. It is important to bear in mind that not all *emigrados* are sufficiently affluent to become agricultural entrepreneurs on even a modest scale. The years of deepening agrarian crisis since 1983 have produced a number of new land sales to *emigrados* in Guaracha. Recurrent international migrants with stable employment and a few of the better-paid internal migrants whose families remain in the villages—such as people working in the oil industry—are the kinds of persons who have the financial resources to sow a *parcela* independently. But many remain "small-scale cultivators."

By the same token, rental of one or two *parcelas* by a permanently resident ejidatario is no automatic symptom of rural capitalism in the Ciénega, although rental of alien land cannot be explained in terms of a direct correlation with the peasant family development cycle on the lines of Chayanov's theory of demographic differentiation. "Peasant renters" may continue to sow extra land using hired labor after their families have grown up and moved out, but more significantly, the possibilities of renting additional land are, under contemporary conditions of relatively high land values, more closely related to disposable money income than to traditional factors such as availability of family labor and possession of working animals. The phenomenon of rental of land is a complex one: in a few cases at least, it was clear that the title-holder had decided to forego a potentially higher money return and rent *a la cuarta* to a peasant kinsman as a favor to the person concerned, though such favors depend on the holders being relatively comfortable economically. But despite such exceptions, the power of money as a means of securing control over land is clearly paramount today, to the point where holders may deny poorer kin or even a son access to their land in pursuit of a higher money return. Since not all ejidal land in Guaracha is of a quality which offers an adequate commercial profit, the scope for peasant forms of renting is greater at the margins of the ejidal system, and a few of the cerrile *parcelas* have been divided into what are, in effect, a series of *ecuaros* distributed among kinsmen or friends of the holder. Poor communications reduce the commercial value of some of the irrigated *parcelas*. Nevertheless, the potential for concentration of control over ejidal land via rental by holders of capital both within and from outside the land reform community is strong and it is strong irrespective of the current returns to peasant farming. The extent of migration is such that elderly men or widows may not have any resident sons eager to take over the land.

Land concentration is not, however, simply a product of rental. Although individuals may acquire effective control over more than one *parcela* by means other than purchase of the title, purchase of titles to additional land by existing ejidatarios is the most common cause of enduring concentration of control. In some cases, sons who were minors when the title was acquired do take over the land and farm it independently in the fullness of time, though in other cases the children study for a career or migrate to the United States or urban industrial sector, and the father sells or rents the surplus land in his old age. Sometimes, however, the land is bought and put in the name of a child who has already embarked on a career outside the village, as an explicit technique of land engrossment. There are also cases where fathers and adult sons cultivate two or more *parcelas* as an integrated unit, with subsistence and forage crops on one piece of land, and crops sold to provide cash income on another. Here acquisition of multiple *parcelas* leads to the development of a form of household economy which would at least have been more problematic on the basis of a single landholding or supplementation of holdings by rental.[3] Taking a purely formal view of concentration of effective control over land by means of acquisition of multiple titles, 11% of the ejidatarios controlled 24% of the land of the ejido in 1982. But the implications of control over multiple *parcelas* differed widely in terms of the substance of the farming enterprises and farm organization associated with the practice. In only a few cases does land concentration form part of a sustained strategy of capital accumulation.

We could readily rank ejidatarios into "rich," "middle" and "poor" strata in terms of absolute levels of income and of the extent to which returns achieved from farming fall below minimal subsistence requirements. But only a small minority of families could live from their farming income alone, and it is important to recognize that the solid type of "middle peasant" whose family lives reasonably comfortably without either conspicuous accumulation of wealth or periodic bouts of crisis may only be in this position because of income supplements obtained from migrant or professional children. The question of how many "real ejidatarios" exist in an agrarian community can only be answered by identifying the people who actually cultivate the land.[4] In addition to the seventy-five rented *parcelas* and those cultivated by absentees, an additional forty-five *parcelas* were held by ejidatarios with one or more additional pieces of land, and so the one hundred and sixty-eight resident cultivators I interviewed in 1982 represented 87% of the resident ejidatarios active at that time.[5] Socio-economically, they ranged from the most entrepreneurial children of Don Santiago and "Maestro" Abel and some of the village's resident professionals through to people who strove to minimize their relations with the market, possessed few if any modern consumer durables, and sometimes went hungry. But we should not attempt to analyze the functioning of peasant farming systems under land reform by attempting to exclude certain categories of cultivator in search of "authentic" peasants. The activities of rich, middle and poor farmers within the ejido are interdependent in various respects in economic terms, and the implications of their differentiation are central to the dynamic and future of the system.

It is important to know that some active ejidatarios are school teachers and agrarian bureaucrats in order to understand the circumstances which might underlie the continued production of particular types of crops within the ejidal system. Those who buy land purely as an investment are more likely to cease cultivating it if economic circumstances change, even if they are better placed financially to secure optimal yields per hectare or to change to crops which command better returns at a given moment. Other ejidatarios trying to survive by farming alone observed that a teacher showed himself to be a person who was not a "real" *campesino* when he rented his land after a couple of bad harvests. But it by no means follows that someone who has an alternative source of livelihood will not be an active and persistent farmer. One of my interview subjects, a headmaster (in another community), active in the teachers' union and a member of the municipal cabinet, acknowledged that he did not have sufficient free time to supervise cultivation of several different pieces of land in two different ejidos in an agronomically optimal manner. Nevertheless, it would be wrong to assume that such people invariably simply treat the land as an investment; in this particular case, a family background in *agrarismo* and personal political orientations made farming the land something meaningful in more than economic terms. Agrobureaucrats constitute a special category, since they may be able to divert public resources to their private benefit, and not all agrobureaucrat purchasers of ejidal titles are natives of the community in which they come to acquire land. Nevertheless, those who are the children of ejidatarios often have the strongest of ideological commitments to keeping family land producing, and such individuals may also play a positive role in the ejido in other respects. Besides offering patronage in the form of openings in public sector employment, they can be a source of advice on agronomic matters,[6] and on issues relating to the community's negotiations with the state apparatus. But much of their support is directed selectively towards kin and friends, and while a community's "organic intellectuals" can play a role in fostering peasant self-organization, there are obvious contradictions in the situation of those who become ejidatarios—starting with their lack of juridical entitlement to land—which may militate against their adopting a high profile in this area. Some, indeed, attempt to protect their economic position by conspicuous devotion to the PRI.

The existence of ejidatarios with professional careers influences the process of peasant differentiation by inhibiting the take-over of ejidal land by more conventional capitalist interests, although it does not inhibit the process of proletarianization. Where land rights become concentrated in the hands of "rich" ejidatarios—who often describe themselves as "running a business"— we seem to have a pattern more closely resembling the Leninist paradigm. Such people accumulate capital within the ejidos on the basis of land concentration, use of hired labor, and ownership of agricultural machinery. But even here, matters are not completely straightforward. Where the state conserves a peasantry in an undercapitalized and semi-proletarian condition, the impact of the activities of rich farmers is not exclusively one of undermining the existence of their poorer fellows. Rich ejidatarios use more wage labor per hectare than other ejidatarios, and some younger ejidatarios have regular jobs with them—as tractor drivers, for example. They also provide other facilities which help poorer cultivators to deal with a perennial shortage of cash.

Village residents who own tractors tend to wait for payment for their hire, something which was important for ejidatarios cultivating with BANRURAL credit, since the payments to cover the cash costs of preparation of the land were almost invariably delayed until well into the cultivation cycle. While certain traditional sources of loans, in particular Don Gabriel, continue to play a role, the socio-economic differentiation of the children of the ex-*peones* has created many more sources of short-term finance, generally on more moderate terms than in past decades.[7]

Since inequalities between ejidatarios lead to land concentration, there is a tendency for the number of households securing benefits even under the existing land reform to be reduced through time. This is potentially the most negative implication of differentiation, since the effect may become cumulative. It is true that land concentration by ejidal entrepreneurs may increase the likelihood that a given *parcela* will pass into the hands of a person with a professional source of livelihood. Rich ejidatarios generally wish to invest in higher education for their children, and though juridical mechanisms for removing land rights from those who no longer need to enjoy them are never activated, the educated child may not replicate the father's activism within the ejido. There is, however, a strong possibility that at least one child will replicate the career of the father, and while the father's land holdings are likely to be divided in the next generation, other advantages are cumulative. Only one of the sons of Don Santiago has become a professional, and his eldest son has remained a peasant of relatively modest ambitions. But all the children have benefited indirectly from the stock of agricultural machinery left by their father, and a younger son has become the major ejidal entrepreneur of his generation, buying further land titles for his own sons. The results of past processes of land concentration in Guaracha have therefore been to extend the dominance of the families of Don Santiago and "Maestro Abel" in the agrarian community.

Some of those who cultivate land in the ejido do not belong to the agrarian community juridically, socially or culturally. Don Gabriel is a rather special kind of outsider, and he does possess land rights in the ejido. But his social integration into the community can only be of a peculiar and incomplete character, and he deliberately adopts and manipulates an ambiguous cultural identity—priest-like and cultivated one moment, a man of the *campo* the next. He also belongs to a different socio-economic stratum relative to even the richest ejidatarios, although it is his position in the market which makes his class position different rather than his ownership of private land *per se*. Another ejidatario born and raised in the village has a (40 hectare) *pequeña propiedad* in Jaripo, inherited from his in-marrying father, and as I noted earlier, Don Santiago at one time acquired a *pequeña propiedad* from an aunt in the same community. But although place of birth is theoretically of the cardinal importance in defining a "real" ejidatario in the juridical sense, outsiders cultivating rented ejidal land may *not* differ socio-economically in radical ways from ejidatarios born in the village. One of the outsiders renting land (including the *Parcela Escolar*) in 1982, a native of Cojumatlán, had begun his career in the latter half of the 1970s with savings from three year's work in a restaurant in Los Angeles, and possessed rather less capital than the richest of the Guaracha ejidatarios.[8]

There is a sense in which all the different types of cultivators, including the large-scale commercial vegetable growers, form integral and interdependent parts of the ejidal farming system, whether or not they are ejidatarios. In addition to being the employers of the greatest quantities of labor per hectare, and of female as well as male labor, the *jitomateros* buy and sell agricultural inputs on the village black market, and their activities affect, and are affected by, the ecosystemic base of the system as fertilizers are added to the land, chemicals circulate along irrigation channels, and pests find new habitats to colonize. They are a distinct type of economic agent, commanding much greater economic power than the "rich" ejidatarios of the community. The big vegetable growers are not tied to a single agrarian community, sowing land in and drawing labor from a much wider area than the Ciénega, and they are also capable of making direct sales into the export market. But the economics of their operations represent one side of a system of bipolar mutual adjustment which also includes peasant farming, gravitating around values of land and labor which are being drawn apart by the coexistence of peasant impoverishment and capitalist access to high profit activities.

As we will see in the next stage of the discussion, "peasant economy" in Guaracha is to some extent amenable to analysis in terms of classical approaches to the micro-economics of the family farm. The economic strategies of many ejidatarios are based on the substitution of personal labor time for commoditized inputs and the use of unpaid or low-cost family labor. Like peasants throughout the world, many ejidatarios have to make choices about the desirability of growing crops which can be eaten by the family as against those that can only provide a monetary income. Economic strategies are varied, and this variation cannot be explained in terms of differences in disposable cash incomes alone. But we cannot answer the question of where the ejidal system is going without looking at the system as a whole, which ultimately means talking about modes of *campesino* livelihood—including its urban dimension—and forms of capital reproduction in the countryside in a much broader way.

The question of where the system might be going is becoming an increasingly urgent one. In the rainy season of 1980 and 1981, 68% of the ejidatarios I interviewed sowed a small range of crops with official credits from BANRURAL. In 1982, only 53% were *socios* of the Bank. This change was partly a reflection of the fact that a number of ejidatarios in *temporal* potreros had chosen to sow garbanzo earlier than the date authorized by the Bank, though in some cases they have remained outside the official credit system since that time, and their decision was equivalent to the more explicit voluntary withdrawal of others who said they had decided to sow "with their own money" that year. Some had, in fact, failed to repay their debt to the Bank the previous year and been deprived of future credit, as had some of those who had not sown with the Bank in 1980 and 1981 at an earlier stage. The main underlying trend in the changes observed between 1981 and 1982 was that operation with the Bank was becoming increasingly non-viable for people with more marginal land, but as time has gone by more producers have become marginal in a variety of locations in the ejido. By the 1986 rainy season cycle, no more than eighty ejidatarios were still sowing with the Bank, by which point the number of rented *parcelas* in Emiliano Zapata had risen to at least one hundred and twenty-one, more than a third of the ejido, and in effect a return to the situation of the early 1960s. The trend has continued: several hard-working men with irrigated land have lost access to credit since 1986 after refusing to accept the Bank's terms for liquidating accounts on poor harvests, and a number of the middle-aged ejidatarios who were capable of producing significant surpluses in 1982 have chosen to renew a career of U.S. migration in pursuit of higher returns to their labor.

In principle, the reexpansion of the state in the Mexican *campo* was intended to halt the decline of basic grains production by poorer ejidatarios and stem abandonment of land and flight to the cities.[9] The new credit system established under BANRURAL and the ANAGSA in the Ciénega did get more ejidatarios back in their fields as active producers, but it did so only because peasants adapted themselves to the system and because the system itself was adapted to the changing nature of capitalism in the countryside. In both cases the adaptation was marginal, and crisis has destroyed what semblance of equilibrium existed in earlier years.

PATTERNS OF PEASANT FARMING: THE ROLE OF THE BANK

The credit system managed from BANRURAL's office in Jiquilpan in 1982 had certain peculiarities arising from the fact that a proportion of BANRURAL's staff owed their position to the past patronage of the Cárdenas family, and local political interests continued to exercise some influence over the local implementation of national norms. Nevertheless, the *modus operandi* of the official system and its agricultural and agrarian implications are paralleled across the country (Rello 1986:143-144). The system aims to provide ejidatarios with sufficient credit to cover the basic costs of production of their crops under average conditions of production. Cost levels are calculated on the assumption that the ejidatario will possess working animals. There is also an implicit presumption that the ejidatario will engage in a degree of self-exploitation to reduce cash costs of cultivation, and that those on more marginal land will either have to supplement the financial credits from other sources or use non-commodity based peasant strategies of sharing human and animal resources to get by. To a limited extent these presuppositions are realized in practice, though wider economic conditions limit the extent of their realization, and some aspects of peasant adaptation to the system are undesirable from both an agricultural and fiscal point of view.

I will deal with the fiscal dimension first. The credit system administered by BANRURAL differs from earlier systems of official credit in its limited recognition of the problem posed by harvest failure and inability to repay. The farm security agency (ANAGSA) indemnifies BANRURAL against loss of its investment by repaying the whole or a proportion of the loan on the ejidatario's behalf in the event of loss of the harvest. The standing crop is inspected by ANAGSA officials, its potential sale value (if any) estimated, and the ejidatario is informed of the size of repayment due (if any), though not necessarily in any official manner at the time of the inspection, a major source of subsequent difficulties. Ejidatarios frequently complain of discrepancies between the ANAGSA assessment of how much they should repay and the sum finally demanded in the BANRURAL office. Little reflection is required to appreciate that creative book keeping by BANRURAL can record the ejidatarios as having repaid only the amount not covered by payments from the ANAGSA, the excess charges disappearing into the pockets of the Bank officials. The sanction the officials command is denial of credit for the next cycle. The force of this sanction lies in the fact that many ejidal commissars are loath to make trouble because they themselves are overtly or implicitly encouraged to engage in maladministration by the agrobureaucracy. Those ejidatarios who are illiterate are not in a good position to check the precise meaning of the different items charged to their accounts. Each *socio* receives a notebook for recording credits received, but it is the ejidal officials who record their data on official papers, and commissars enjoy extensive opportunities to abuse those whom they represent, since they collect the credit money from the Bank's offices for redistribution within the ejido. The power of paper within this heavily bureaucratized system is pervasive: those who antagonize the *comisariado* may find they have been excluded from the lists of ejidatarios requesting irrigation water, for example. Some acts of maladministration have no economic motivation but are simply motivated by particularistic grudges. Peasant office holders within the ejido have, however, found their own ways of profiting economically from the insurance system. Severe drought led to widespread losses in the maize harvests of 1982, and the ANAGSA inspectors had no choice but to award "total losses" in the majority of cases: yet the secretary of the outgoing ejidal administration who accompanied them daily on the *parcelas* was asking the ejidatarios affected to pay him two thousand pesos to "ensure the settlement was satisfactory." Many did pay, a reflection of the extent to which they doubted that justice would otherwise be done on the basis of past experience.

The entangling of peasant leaders in the web of corruption surrounding the state agencies has insidious implications for the power structures which weigh down on the Mexican countryside today, though it is only one facet of a broader process of individualization of the peasantry as social agents which was central to the new systems of intervention and bureaucratic domination introduced in the final years of the Díaz Ordaz administration and the early years of Echeverría's presidency and extended thereafter, Echeverría's moment of "agrarian populism" notwithstanding (Martínez Saldaña 1980; Sanderson 1981). It is not only the leaders who are entangled in frauds surrounding the administration of agricultural insurance. In 1981, a former U.S. migrant son temporarily in charge of the cultivation of his absentee widowed mother's *parcela* in *potrero* Cerrito del Buey borrowed 10,000 pesos to bribe the ANAGSA inspector to award a "total loss" on a harvest of 36 tons. He did the same thing with the twenty tons of sorghum he harvested from four hectares he rented in Los Pirules. He paid 5,000 pesos to the inspector and sold at a price of 3,900 pesos a ton, without making any payment to the Bank. On a *cartamo* (safflower) harvest, a bribe of 15,000 pesos brought a net money return of 60,000 pesos. An ejidatario in El Monte, who also controls two other *parcelas*, only paid BANRURAL 3,800 pesos (equivalent to a ton of sorghum at the time) in return for a harvest of thirteen tons. Such practices clearly benefit the ejidatarios themselves, assuming they can raise the sums required for the *mordida*. (Ironically, acquisition of a "total loss" indemnity by this means is actually rather easier when the real harvest is reasonably good.) Such frauds require complicity between the officials of the ANAGSA and those of BANRURAL,[10] and they were pervasive in fairer economic weather: in 1980 the whole of *potreros* Cerrito del Buey and Los Pirules (a total of 328 hectares) was awarded a "total loss" by means of these payments, at a probable cost to the Mexican treasury in excess of four million pesos. In so far as peasants became the accomplices of the agrobureaucracy in such "*cosas cochinas*"—whether voluntarily or, as was often the case, under threat of victimization—their power to challenge such self-serving interests or to press for reforms in agrarian policy is correspondingly reduced. Most people took the view that the agricultural insurance system was what made sowing with the Bank today an advance on sowing with the *particulares*. But even when the system is operated honestly—and I should stress that I have witnessed inspections carried out in a highly professional manner—it does not indemnify the ejidatario against the bulk of the loss of income incurred as a result of harvest failure. In this and a variety of other senses, the ejidatarios are essentially correct in complaining that the insurance is for the Bank and not for themselves.

BANRURAL credit policy has functioned as an agent of "agricultural modernization" in the sense that levels of credit provided encourage the use of chemical herbicides in place of (more expensive) manual cutting of grasses, and levels of credit were woefully inadequate for those forced to prepare their land without tractors. Most ejidatarios complained about the inadequacy of the credits given for the *escarda* (cultivation of the developing crop for weed control). Even people who possessed their own plow team ideally wished to hire other animals in order to finish the work in optimal time from the point of view of soil humidity and minimizing damage, but the implication of the credits offered was that they should all be thinking about using a tractor instead, as a few did. Tractors are, however, less suitable for this task than animal drawn plows when the land is soaked from heavy rains.[11] But the most significant implication of the credit policy for agricultural modernization lay in the kinds of crops for which credit was available. The Bank would finance the sowing of traditional staples, maize and irrigated (though not the riskier *temporal*) beans, as well as garbanzos. But it also financed the cultivation of sorghum and *cartamo*, products which are central to the industrialization of modern Mexican agriculture, and which are raw materials in larger agro-industrial complexes. Sorghum is a product for the pasture mill, where it is transformed into feedstuffs for the commercial dairy and beef cattle industries and for the pig industry whose most important local center is La Piedad. To some extent, those with dairy herds or other animals can make direct use of sorghum within the ejido, though alfalfa (not financed by the bank in the 1980s) was the preferred feed for dairy cows. But for the majority, sorghum represents only cash in the pocket.

The BANRURAL credit system biased ejidatarios lacking capital or off-farm sources of cash income towards the production of sorghum and *cartamo* simply because the proportion of real production costs covered by the credits was greater than for maize or beans. Many of those who possessed land suitable for growing sorghum had sown nothing else for more than a decade. The bias towards sorghum was not, however, restricted to the less affluent ejidatarios. One of the major ejidal entrepreneurs, a thirty-eight years old son of "Maestro" Abel nicknamed "Tito," remarked that he felt that sorghum cultivation was damaging to the land, but that Bank policy effectively constrained him to sow large areas of the crop in place of the maize and beans he would have preferred to sow (along with the vegetables he cultivated on a smaller scale).

In adopting this policy, albeit in the larger context of national policies on the pricing of food grains, the Bank promoted the deeper incorporation of the producers into the global agro-industrial production process: not only did what they produce serve as an input into the larger production complex, but the absorption of chemical and mechanical inputs was also maximized. At the same time, the returns to machine ownership were increased within the region, and rich ejidatarios and elements of the regional agrarian bourgeoisie outside the region benefited accordingly. In this regard Tito had less reason to complain about the policy of the Bank: the annual income from his Massey Ferguson combine harvester was 75% of its capital cost a few years earlier, although the rapidly escalating purchase price of machinery was encouraging him to renovate an older machine he had bought in 1972. In addition to the use of tractors for sowing (and to some extent applying fertilizer) and the relative ease with which sorghum and *cartamo* can be harvested by machine, agro-industrial crops create a demand for bulk transport over longer distances than maize, though the economic difference between prosperous ejidatarios and major regional *acaparadores* is physically manifest in the enormous size of the latters' trucks.[12]

To some extent, geography and ecology conspire to limit the triumph of mechanized cultivation and harvesting. Tractor costs are much higher in the *parcelas* located off the plain: charges are generally by the hour rather than by area, and the presence of large stones and unevenness of terrain damages the equipment. In many cerrile *parcelas* mechanical preparation of the land is out of the question, and mechanical harvesting even more so. The few who experimented with sorghum on cerrile land tended to return to maize and garbanzo, despite the crop's other advantage of greater physical resilience in the face of lack of rain and weed infestation. Nevertheless, the fact that people had tried to cultivate sorghum at all under such unpromising conditions provides a preliminary indication that money costs and peasant conditions of production may be more determinant of "choice" than the relative prices of different crops. The relative prices of grains reflected a high degree of state intervention in the market through the purchase and importation programs of the CONASUPO throughout the 1970s and early 1980s. Although the CONASUPO's role was redefined as that of fortifying peasant production to restore food self-sufficiency in the period of Echeverría, and its role in the sorghum market has tended to be one of depressing harvest period prices, emphasis shifted decisively to agro-industrial modernization and management of urban prices and distribution under López Portillo, generally to the disadvantage of the peasant producer. But it is noteworthy that the one divergent moment in this administration's policy, the major improvement in the relative price of maize brought about by the *Sistema Alimentario Mexicano* in 1980-82 stimulated production by commercial farmers but was more limited in its impact on less capitalized peasant producers: price improvements must be matched by credit policies which can overcome the barrier of higher monetary costs in a commoditized and industrialized countryside. As relative price deteriorates, maize becomes the crop of the marginal or infra-subsistence farmer again (Barkin and Suárez 1985:176-189).

The local credit policies adopted by any branch of BANRURAL must mesh with wider policy considerations. Much of the reluctance of the bank to provide credits (or appropriate varieties of seed) for sowing wheat was premised on the argument that other regions had a comparative advantage in this crop. Recent years have seen some revision in this policy as wheat production levels have failed to keep pace with national needs, in part because of displacement of wheat by other crops in the northern irrigation districts discussed further below. Levels of risk are also central to BANRURAL thinking on what it is appropriate for peasants to grow. Credit was made available to a few ejidatarios to sow strawberries in 1968, but good harvests were not matched by good prices, and it was decided to concentrate public aid in this sector on ejidos which had higher levels of infrastructure and organization. Some form of long-term planning over a wider area is clearly essential, and it would be unfair to deny the official sector all claims to rational behavior within its broader policy remit. Nevertheless, it would be naive to ignore the fact that private interests have considerable informal influence over public policy, and wilfully obtuse to pretend that BANRURAL has implemented its policies in ways which have maximized their success even in their own (official) terms. Before embarking on a more detailed discussion of the pathologies of the system implemented in the Bolsa de Guaracha, it is, however, important to stress that BANRURAL is not the only arm of the state implicated in these processes, even if it is the most detested by peasants. Besides the ANAGSA, two other state agencies played an important role in determining agricultural patterns at ejido level in 1982: the SARH, responsible for the irrigation infrastructure, technical assistance and the supply of heavy machinery used to improve the quality of the land, whose local offices are in Sahuayo, and the PRONASE (*Productora Nacional de Semillas*), whose regional headquarters are in Briseñas, on the Jalisco border.

The desirability of concentrating development effort on irrigated agriculture can be questioned from different standpoints both in Mexico (Durán 1988) and in other contexts (Richards 1986). From the ejidatarios' point of view, the primary problem in Guaracha is one of supply: the irrigation system is gravity-fed from the San Antonio and Jaripo dams, and therefore remains dependent on rainfall. Not only do some ejidatarios lack any access to irrigation water, but a second group is disadvantaged in years when there is a shortage, and SARH allocation of water at the wider regional level is not immune to informal pressures from vested interests outside the ejidos.[13] Excluding two *potreros* (Guarachita and La Mesa) where no water is available to any cultivator, just over half the remaining ejidal cultivators received irrigation water in the rainy season of 1982, a particularly dry year, and only fifty-two per cent of cultivators sowed anything in the previous winter.

SARH technical assistance is also a subject of considerable complaint: not only did the engineers from Sahuayo seem loath to visit the *parcelas*, but the contribution of younger *técnicos* with a secondary education employed as extension workers provoked much dissatisfaction. As one old ejidatario put it, their main contribution to the national economy appeared to be one of sustaining distilleries making brandy that most peasants could no longer afford to buy. The lack of supervision underlying the behavior of the *técnicos* was merely one of a number of evident dysfunctions in the operation of the SARH: the easiest way to get one's *parcela* levelled appeared to be to rent it for a year to one of the *ingenieros*, who would then bring in the machinery for his own immediate benefit. But despite a list of shortcomings which could be extended considerably, the SARH did play a role in shaping the policies of BANRURAL with regard to patterns of land use, and on occasion played an autonomous role as the agency sponsoring particular types of development schemes within the ejido, as will be exemplified in a case discussed below. But since 1983, its role has become central in a more negative sense; although an initial attempt to remove subsidies from irrigation water and hike the cost was defeated by a mobilization of the ejidatarios led by some of the region's most experienced and influential *priista* peasant leaders early in 1983, the escalation of charges did begin the following year. Between 1982 and 1986, the proportion of water costs in total production costs for a crop requiring a single irrigation had increased from just over 1.5% to over 7%. One could certainly argue that the extent of the subsidies given to water users in the past were inconsistent with the federal water law's stipulation that charges cover the costs of maintenance and conservation of this vital natural resource (Sanderson 1986:204). But it is equally clear that the benefits of such subsidies have accrued primarily to the private sector, and to the private sector in the northern irrigation districts in particular, in parallel with the proportions of direct public investment in hydraulic infrastructure they have received (Durán 1988:56-60). Input subsidies to the farm sector offered the Mexican state the advantage—particularly in the case of petroleum-based products—of minimizing the consumer price effects of programs to stimulate production by more marginal cultivators at a cost which would be partly transferred to future generations in so far as destruction of non-renewable resources was concerned. But they were neither crop specific, nor easily targeted at particular types of producer. Market forces determined what the private sector would grow. Subsidies on water benefited all producers. And as we will see, some subsidized inputs delivered directly to the *campesino* end up on the fields of large private sector growers. On the other hand, reduction of input subsidies has a disproportionate effect on the viability of the peasant farm. The problem lies in the structure of the system as a whole.

BANRURAL policy locally was also modified in accordance with programs sponsored by other agencies. In the dry season of 1982, the Bank was making rebates to those who chose to sow irrigated beans, a reflection of the implementation, albeit limited, of the *Sistema Alimentario Mexicano*. Although beans always command a relatively good price, their costs are the highest of all the basic cultigens, and the promise of rebates did bring forth rather more production than normal. Nevertheless, receipt of the cash was characteristically delayed, and such schemes could only bear limited fruit, given that the major disincentive to sowing beans was one of lacking the cash to pay peons during the cultivation cycle itself. Rebates may be attractive to accountants, but they are less attractive to peasants who have to borrow money from private sources to supplement bank credits. The intervention of PRONASE did, however, have a quite noticeable impact on patterns of cultivation, tipping the balance of advantage away from sorghum in the minds of a significant number of ejidatarios in 1982.

It is immediately apparent from the data presented in Table 20 that the relative increase in maize production observed in the ejido in 1982 was largely

Table 20

CROPS SOWN IN THE TEMPORAL CYCLE, 1980–82
Number of cultivators per crop by potreros
and percentage of all cultivators sowing each crop

1980	Mze	Pro	M/O	Srg	S/O	Grb	Pas	Veg	Mix
La Manga	1			11					0
Casa del Trigo			1	2	1				
Paso de la Arena	3			2	2				
El Camiche	2	1		10					
El Monte	6	2		15	3				1
El Salitre	2	1		7	1				1
Frutyales				9					
Guarachita	6	2	1						
El Carrizo	6		3	5					
La Mesa	1					2			
Los Pirules	1			6					
La Lobera		1		14	1		2		
Cerrito del Buey	3			9	1	1			1
Totals (%)	**21**	**5**	**3**	**60**	**6**	**2**	**1**	**0**	**3**
1981									
La Manga					14		1		
Casa del Trigo	1	1		1					
Paso de la Arena	2	1	1	2	1				
El Camiche	4	1		11			1		
El Monte	5	2		17	4				1
El Salitre	3	2		3	2	1			1
Frutyales	1			9					
Guarachita	2	3	1		2	1			
El Carrizo	7		2	4	1			1	
La Mesa	2			2					
Los Pirules	1			6	1				
La Lobera		1		11	2	1	2		1
Cerrito del Buey	1			12	1				
Totals (%)	**19**	**6**	**3**	**57**	**9**	**2**	**2**	**1**	**2**
1982									
La Manga	2		1	11			1	1	
Casa del Trigo	1	1	1					1	
Paso de la Arena	2	2		1	2	1			
El Camiche	6	3		6			1		
El Monte	4	5		14	4	2			1
El Salitre	2	2	1	3	3			1	1
Frutyales	1			9					
Guarachita	1		1	1		5		1	
El Carrizo	8		3	1				1	
La Mesa	1					3			
Los Pirules				7	2				
La Lobera	7	1		4	7		1		1
Cerrito del Buey	1	10		1	2				
Totals (%)	**21**	**14**	**4**	**36**	**12**	**7**	**2**	**3**	**1**

Key: Mze = Maize only; Pro = PRONASE maize; M/O = Maize the primary crop with another crop also sown; Srg = Sorghum only; S/O = Sorghum the primary crop with another crop also sown; Grb = Garbanzo; Pas = Pasture crop (alfalfa or meadow grass) the primary crop; Veg = Vegetables sown on whole parcela; Mix = Parcela sown in a mixture of cultigens due to an increased cultivation of PRONASE maize, concentrated particularly on the *potrero* of eight hectare *parcelas* most distant from the center of the ejido, Cerrito del Buey. The table shows the relative proportions of maize, sorghum, garbanzo and other crops sown in the ejido in the rainy season cycles of 1980, 1981 and 1982 on the *primary parcelas* of each of the resident ejidal cultivators interviewed who was cultivating in the year in question. That is, in the case of persons who cultivate multiple *parcelas*, only the land to which they actually hold the title is included. Just under 30% of the interview subjects in fact cultivated more than one *parcela*: of these 62% had only one additional piece of land under cultivation, and only five were cultivating four or more *parcelas* on their own account in 1982. The vast majority of ejidatarios therefore only farm one piece of land. The ejidal entrepreneurs who cultivate larger numbers of rented *parcelas* in addition to those they control in a more permanent fashion are clearly making economic calculations of a more complex kind, depending on the nature of their "business" as a whole. These complications are best treated separately, since excluding all the ejidatarios who sow multiple *parcelas* from these preliminary data would distort the picture as much as including the few individuals who sow a great deal of additional land. Indeed, while the two wealthiest ejidatarios did sow some vegetables in 1982, they sowed much more sorghum and maize, and were subject to the same basic external market conditions as other ejidatarios in deciding what to plant. The ejidatario who sowed the largest land area in vegetables in 1982 was the out-going *comisariado ejidal*, and the means by which he did this will be discussed below.

The data in the table are broken down by *potreros*, since what can realistically be sown varies with differences in land quality and factors of location in a manner which correlates in an admittedly approximate way with the division into *potreros*. This is an important consideration given that the proportions of maize and garbanzo sown in the ejido overall are influenced by the non-viability of alternatives on some land as well as by socio-economic differences between cultivators, and the lack of viable alternatives in its turn plays a role in determining the socio-economic position of the *dueños* and the strategies of farm organization they adopt.

The *Productora Nacional de Semillas* was established so Mexico could play an autonomous role in the development of the "Green Revolution" technology inaugurated on its national territory and offer some counterweight to the power of the transnational seed stock companies. In the Ciénega, PRONASE is primarily associated with improved strains of maize, though it is also a provider of sorghum and wheat hybrids.[14] PRONASE exports its high-yielding variety of seed corn throughout the world, and it differs from some of the products of the "Green Revolution" in providing a superior product to the final consumer. Like the maize peasants normally grow for subsistence, and unlike the imported corn many are forced to buy during the year, it is a white corn ideal for making tortillas, and one of the attractions of the crop is that the harvest is divided into two parts: the *hembra*, delivered direct to the PRONASE, has a good price, guaranteed before planting, while the *macho* is left to the producer, for private sale or use in feeding the family and animals. Maize will always offer the advantage over sorghum, particularly in an era of rampant consumer price inflation, of being capable of direct consumption, but it is the possibility of having maize to eat and a good cash return which is PRONASE maize's special attraction. In 1982, the price being offered looked particularly good, even from a purely commercial perspective.

This was certainly the view of Don Santiago's most active son, whom I will call Julián. In August 1982, he had 30 hectares under cultivation in grains, 10 hectares of it sorghum and 20 hectares *maíz productora*.[15] Although he had sown PRONASE maize for seven years, this represented an increase on the proportion of land he normally dedicated to the crop. With PRONASE, there were no freight costs, and relative to ordinary maize there was a 2000 peso differential per hectare in the credits received for sowing, with a further 3000 pesos per hectare for the special process of *quitando espiga* required to produce the *hembra*. There was also a rebate of 25% of fertilizers and pesticides to be deducted from the final account with BANRURAL after the harvest, as in the case of irrigated beans mentioned earlier. And finally, there was a 300 pesos per ton premium on the already good price for yields of more than three tons per hectare. Julián controlled and rented land in Cerrito del Buey where yields of 7.5 tons per hectare were possible. This was the only crop which he sowed with the Bank, since he was able to secure credit—at an interest rate of 12%—from the private sector bank *Bancomer* to sow his other crops, an advantage which he alone of the ejidatarios possessed and a legacy of his father's success. Like any other ejidatario, he complained about the BANRURAL's tardiness in supplying credit, and observed that with private bank credit he could afford to apply double the amount of fertilizer offered by BANRURAL. Although the credit offered to sow PRONASE maize was administered through BANRURAL, from Julián's point of view the special terms offered for this crop made direct participation in the public credit system attractive in this case.

Julián had, in fact, played a leading role in promoting the cultivation of *maíz productora* in the ejido, during his period of office as ejidal commissar, at the end of the 1970s. At first, other informants told me, no special financial facilities had been available to meet the extra costs of sowing this type of corn: indeed, the PRONASE expected people to pay for a contract. Julián had made a list of people who wanted to sow *productora*, and took it himself to Briseñas.[16] When PRONASE agreed to offer extra aid from its own funds, more people agreed to participate. Although, as Table 20 shows, PRONASE maize was sown by isolated ejidatarios in various *potreros*, it is preferable to cultivate single *potreros* in the same crop as far as possible for a variety of reasons. Sorghum seed scattered by the wind can affect maize yields seriously in neighboring *parcelas*, and chemical herbicides carried in irrigation water can also do damage, particularly to squash or beans intercropped with the maize. In the case of distant Cerrito del Buey, peons will be reluctant to go to work for a single maize cultivator unless he can provide transport. Although people who live as *jornaleros* are unemployed for much of the year unless they migrate, there is no labor surplus in the countryside at the seasonal peaks of demand like the time of the *temporal* maize harvest, since people are harvesting *ecuaros* as well as responding to the demand for harvest labor in the ejidal *parcelas*. I observed poorer ejidatarios experiencing difficulty finding adult male laborers at other points in the cycle when U.S. demand for field labor was at its height. Even Julián said that he had difficulty finding more than ten individuals a day to work in his maize.[17] Where many ejidatarios sow maize together, these problems are eased. There are, however, significant structural reasons for the absence of such rationalization of ejidal farming practices—source of regret though this is to "enterprising" ejidal leaders of different backgrounds and ideological orientations. On this occasion, the economics of the situation seemed particularly favorable, and were reinforced by active promotion on the part of officials of the PRONASE.

PRONASE officials were the only representatives of the local agrarian bureaucracy whom I regularly observed dirtying their shoes in the fields talking to peasants about farming, and I was sufficiently intrigued by this departure from the agrobureaucratic norm in the region to pay a visit to Briseñas. Interviews with staff there confirmed my initial impression that this agency was imbued with a quite different form of populist ethos to the other branches of the agrobureaucracy with which I came into contact. PRONASE officials were interested in talking to rather than at *campesinos* and in understanding why things so frequently went wrong, despite their use of highly effective formal instructional techniques and frequent inspections of the progress of the cultivation cycle. Briseñas was a useful reminder to an increasingly jaundiced researcher that the shape of rural development in Mexico is still being contested by different factions within the state apparatus, and on political terrain that has a long and resilient history in Mexico. The structural limits of such developments are, however, severe, and while this chapter concentrates on the limits imposed by the situation, in the countryside, a depressing reminder of the constraints imposed by the political system was provided by the following letter from Roberto Velázquez Coutiño, General Secretary of the PRONASE union, which published in the weekly political magazine *Proceso* in March 1983. It would lose something of its rhetorical effect translated from the Spanish:

> Sr. Director:
> En una carta enviada al presidente Miguel de la Madrid, los integrantes del Sindicato Nacional de Trabajadores de Productora Nacional de Semillas, denunciamos el hecho de que el exsecre-

tario de Agricultura y Recursos Hidráulicos, Francisco Merino Rábago—actual director de Pronase—, "acepte en la empresa a individuos que no son congruentes con la política moralizadora del gobierno actual."

Es el caso, sostiene el sindicato, del "técnico publicista Miguel Angel Ortega Aguilera, jefe de la Unidad de Información y Relaciones Públicas, Publicidad y Promoción de Pronase, quien se ha convertido en un sátrapa de la clase trabajadora, a la que explota y se sirve de sus servicios para fines estrictamente personales."

En la misma, el Sindicato pide a De la Madrid que "investigadores de la nueva Secretaría de la Controlaría General de la República, sepan que el ingeniero Luis Alonso Mcginnis Moreno, gerente de comercialización de esa institución, "se ha dedicado desde hace más de tres años a realizar actividades muy productivas para su persona, teniendo como coparticipante al mismo Ortega Aguilera, en diversos negocios que son de sobra conocidos por los trabajadores de Pronase..."

Don Francisco Merino Rábago, a close confidant and protegé of Lázaro Cárdenas in his later years in Michoacán, was remembered by one of my older interview subjects as the man who had ordered him thrown out of a meeting in Zamora for attempting to denounce "irregularities" associated with an ill-fated Ejidal Cattle Cooperative administered by the Bank at the end of the 1960s. One interesting facet of this episode is that the ejidatarios complained that they were forced to sell their milk to the local Nestlé plant (now the LICONSA) at a price which was lower than that in the free market. The then-*gerente* of the Bank subsequently became *gerente* of the Nestlé. *Plus ça change*, perhaps. But even where local representatives of a state agency genuinely try to help ordinary *campesinos* to benefit from the development process, the best will in the world has difficulty overcoming the basic limitations of peasant resources. Don Julián, possessor of tractors, working animals and ample reserves of cash, could pride himself on his optimization of productive inputs. Less well-endowed producers of PRONASE maize frequently had difficulty producing grain which met PRONASE's quality standards.

Consider, for example, the experience of one of the ejidatarios who sowed *maíz productora* in *potrero* Guarachita in 1981. Francisco was thirty-eight, with seven children, all in school except the eldest, aged seventeen, who had finished secundaria and was now working as a *jornalero*. Francisco worked at weekends for the SARH, as a caretaker, earning 7000 pesos every two weeks in 1982. Two of his brothers were casual manual workers with the SARH in Zamora and Sahuayo. He had begun cultivating the land with BAN-RURAL in 1979, receiving a *carta de poder* from his widowed mother, who remained *dueña* but did not insist on receiving any fixed share of the harvest. The *parcela* is cerrile and had previously been worked in *pedacitos* by Francisco and his older *jornalero* brother Joaquín, who sows an *ecuaro* and had been a regular seasonal migrant to the cane fields of the Tierra Caliente for decades.[18] All preparation must be done with animals, and Francisco did not, at this time, possess his own plow team. Like all the ejidatarios cultivating cerrile land, including those who did have a *tronco*, he argued that BANRURAL credit only covered half the costs of preparation.

In some contexts, what ejidatarios mean by this kind of statement is that the levels of credit do not cover the full costs of their personal labor, when it is assigned an imputed value equivalent to the costs of hiring non-family labor and *troncos*. To explore the full significance of this proposition, we should return to some of the issues raised earlier. As I remarked in the Introduction, non-commoditized systems of labor exchange (known locally as *días prestados*) began to atrophy during the 1950s. Although such practices have not disappeared entirely, their decline was clearly an effect of the widespread participation of Guaracha's peasants in neolatifundist agriculture and labor migration, and we can now see that this is simply one reflection of the way the process of capitalist valorization of peasant labor power creates a situation in which the cost of personal labor inputs are not measured merely in subjective terms as Chayanovian "drudgery," since unpaid work usually has a real (cash) opportunity cost. Yet BANRURAL's credit system implicitly assumes that the countryside remains a Chayanovian world as far as the economic rationality of their poorer clients is concerned. It accordingly suffers from a lack of legitimacy in the eyes of ejidatarios, whose logic is that they should receive a "labor payment" which covers the imputed market value of their personal work with an additional *utilidad* at harvest time, conceived, in peasant terms, as society's payment of rent to them by virtue of their position as *dueños* of the land.

But, to develop another issue raised earlier, undercapitalized ejidatarios may not be able realize any form of rent under prevailing market and credit conditions, and even their own hours of work may be devalorized by their lower than average productivity. Neo-Marxist analyses have emphasized the elimination, reduction or displacement of capitalist ground rent as a key factor in the "conservation" of the peasantry. The existence of peasant producers at the margin of a branch of production lowers the differential rents accruing to capitalist producers operating in the same market. Where an entire national commodity-market is dominated by peasant producers cultivating land of differing quality, the ability of more favored producers to capture differential rents depends on price, which may be set at international levels reflecting the costs of more productive farmers abroad, and directly and indirectly on the credit system: credit is the means by which most peasants augment their productivity while interest payments determine the share of the surplus generated which the peasant retains. Absolute rent in the Marxian sense pertains to the relationship between agriculture and other sectors, and its significance lies in the possible unfavorable effects on the overall rate of accumulation of valorization of capital in the agricultural sphere, through the determination of average rates of profit and prices of production. These effects can also be reduced, in theory, by use of private or public credit to sustain peasant farming (Gutiérrez and Trapaga 1986:93-112, 181-183). Nevertheless, the actual levels of productivity attained by peasants influence the functionality of the system from the standpoint of the national economy as a whole, and even if the average rate of return on capital is not relevant to the majority of ejidal cultivators, under modern conditions it cannot be assumed that peasant economic rationality is unaffected by the wider process of the valorization of capital.[19]

BANRURAL is charged with maintaining peasant production of commodities: assuming that levels of credit are adequate to secure surplus production, its ability to perform this function depends on the size of the net income the system leaves to the farmer in relation to alternative uses of his time and the land. One might assume that the lower limit of acceptable net income is represented by the case where six months' work with a harvest at the end of it does not yield a "labor payment" equivalent to the rural wage for the same period, bearing in mind that most *jornaleros* who remain in the village obtain the equivalent of no more than twenty-four weeks of work annually, but the situation is complicated by the effects of capitalist rental of land and access to other forms of employment. The general implication of the existence of alternative modes of valorizing land and labor time must be to increase the size of the minimum acceptable net return to farming, but where the ejidatario enjoys some additional source of livelihood or income which does not conflict with working the *parcela* and cannot readily valorize the land other than by farming it, it is possible that any positive net return, in cash or kind, may be deemed worthwhile—if it is possible to achieve it. Francisco's case in fact illustrates the limits of BANRURAL's ability to incorporate the marginal producer via this kind of logic and the tendency of such producers to withdraw from the system and underutilize their land.

The essential problem facing producers like Francisco is the commoditization of the production process. In the case of cerrile *parcelas* the statement that BANRURAL credit does not cover the full costs of cultivation must generally be taken literally. Agricultural production has limited seasons, and "self-exploitation" working alone with one's own animals is unlikely to get a *temporal* crop sown on time. Francisco had sometimes managed to borrow a team of animals from a friend, and there are still a few individuals who practice exchanges of work on these *parcelas*. But thirty-five per cent of the active cultivators interviewed in 1982 did not possess working animals, cash did generally change hands where additional teams had to be hired, and the owner of the animals normally insisted on being hired to drive them. Francisco hired eight *peones ajenos* to perform the *despigue* on his

PRONASE maize, in addition to family labor. He harvested just over 3 tons from the whole of his four hectares, in comparison with Don Julián's results of 4.5 tons per hectare of *hembra* alone. None of his harvest was acceptable for delivery to PRONASE.

One possible reason for this, as in other cases of failure to meet PRONASE quality standards even on the part of less marginal farmers on the plain, is that the timing of the *quitando espigas* process is crucial: those who are struggling to pay alien labor are unlikely to keep on schedule even if they perform the manual process properly. One of the ejidatarios who sowed *productora* in Cerrito del Buey in 1982, Santiago, told me that he had been unable to find enough peons to do the work in the recommended three days and had been forced to take longer. But many simply abandoned any attempt to perform the operation properly, hoping to salvage enough of a surplus for sale elsewhere to avoid ending up in deficit on their credit accounts. Whatever problems exist on the labor supply side, cash flow is a major problem because BANRURAL credits invariably arrive late. Santiago waited two months before receiving the money to cover preparation of the land and sowing.[20] This may be more than a symptom of inefficiency. Fertilizer is delivered in kind, from stocks held by the bank itself. But the freight charges are payable on delivery, and it is a common practice for the official making the delivery to suggest that they be dealt with by "returning" a bag or two to his care. In this manner, BANRURAL officials have become active black marketeers in fertilizer which is in short supply to producers in all sectors as a result of other inefficiencies in the operation of the state monopoly producer FERTIMEX and the BANRURAL's preferential control over supplies. Some ejidatarios who could afford to sow their crops privately said that it was the guarantee of supplies of fertilizer which kept them within the credit system, and even the *jitomateros* were known to resort to the black market on occasions.[21] The other side of this coin is that poorer ejidatarios economize on fertilizer application. Part of the stock received from the bank is diverted to their *ecuaros*, part are sold to raise cash to pay for labor and *troncos*, and the agronomic results are only too apparent in the yield differences between *parcelas* of similar quality. Whether or not the credits received ultimately cover costs actually incurred in cash, delays in receipt create problems for the producers which are sometimes resolved through borrowing and sometimes by abandoning cultivation standards on the *parcela*. The diversion of fertilizer and other chemical inputs to the *ecuaros* is, in a sense, a spontaneous peasant adaptation, but it is also a response to a deteriorating ecosystem and part of a larger complex of processes associated with the market for industrial inputs in which all producers and the agrobureaucracy are enmeshed.

Whatever the reasons for Francisco's poor harvest of PRONASE maize in 1981, the consequences of harvest failure proved catastrophic. The ANAGSA inspected the *parcela* and informed him that he would only have to repay the credits on 400 kilos. This should, he thought, have amounted to 1200 pesos, but when he arrived at the office, a repayment of 8,000 pesos was demanded. He did repay the PRONASE what he owed them, but he refused to repay BANRURAL, and was deprived of future entitlement to credit. He had decided to go it alone with his own resources, and now bought himself a *tronco* with the money he had obtained from the harvest. But his family expenses were high: his wife said she had spent 10,000 pesos on clothes for the children in 1981, and education costs were running at 1700 pesos a month. His SARH salary was absorbed by family consumption, and he borrowed 38,000 pesos, with interest payments on top, from a *compañero* at the SARH in 1982. The most he could manage to sow from his own resources in 1982 was a single hectare of garbanzo. He was working building a house for his niece, a kind of work he had done before, in an effort to deal with his debts. In the course of the interview I discovered that he had used chemical herbicides in the maize field in the past, despite the fact that he had intercropped beans with the maize and they were inevitably damaged. Although in theory he commanded the unpaid labor of a son, and talked of the whole family turning out to weed with *machetes* in the past, Francisco was already a marginal farmer.

Carlos, aged forty-two, who also farms a *parcela* in Guarachita, along with two *ecuaros*, one cultivated by *azadón*, provides a case to compare with that of Francisco. He has some regular cash income, since he drives a tractor for Tito, having previously worked for Julián. At the end of 1982 he was earning 300 pesos a day, though he does not earn money throughout the year. He had four single sons still working with him on the land when he sowed *productora*, one of whom had also begun to work for Tito in 1982. Like Francisco, Carlos lacked his own working animals, but he did have the advantages of a strong family labor force and a *parcela* which could be prepared by tractor, which he could drive himself.[22] In 1980, he had delivered 7 tons to PRONASE, and retained 6.5 tons of *macho*. His yields per hectare were even higher in 1981, at 4.4 tons per hectare overall, though the PRONASE rejected part of his *hembra* on this occasion, and there was still a substantial productivity gap between Carlos's best results and those of Don Julián—who could buy or rent the very best land. Nevertheless, his 9,000 peso net money returns per hectare were similar to those a cultivator like Don Julián achieved with sorghum, and Carlos fed some of the maize he harvested to his pigs. Indeed, for those who are not in immediate need of cash, maize and beans provide an additional advantage even as a commercial crop, since they have a ready market within the village. Those who sell enough to repay the bank and then store their surpluses in the house for sale later in the year can take advantage of the rise in prices which inevitably occurs as supplies harvested from *ecuaros* run out. For Carlos, then, *maíz productora* did seem a suitable crop for the less affluent and he sowed it for a number of consecutive years before 1982, when he turned to garbanzo. One of the sons had left, to seek factory work in Mexico. Although he remitted money, the loss of labor was, Carlos argued, a crucial factor in his decision to change crops. A man who is certainly willing to engage in self-exploitation, Carlos has continued sowing over the more recent crisis years, but it was ordinary *temporal* corn he sowed in 1985 and sorghum in the following year, a reflection, no doubt, of the increasing dispersal of his family labor force and the rising cost of both purchased inputs and BANRURAL credit itself.

Carlos' persistence with PRONASE maize certainly cannot be attributed simply to the fact that he is a hard-working man, and it is also important to stress that traditional strategies of non-commodity transactions in labor and working animals at most offer only an amelioration of the problems posed by basic shortages of cash. Manuel, another ejidatario in Guarachita, was the one person in my interview sample sowing sorghum alone in Guarachita in 1982. He had generally sown more sorghum than maize, partly because of bad relations with the *dueño* of the neighboring *parcela*, who also sowed sorghum and did not preoccupy himself with any contamination of Manuel's crops caused by his own rather careless practices of cultivation.[23] Sixty-five years old, Manuel had lost his only son, and this tragedy had left him responsible for a widow and three small children. His only resident single child was a daughter, just about to complete her training as a teacher, but already working. Manuel did have his own *tronco*, and still worked on the land of others with his animals, being one of the few who still practiced labor exchange with friends. He had always sown his land, with or without state aid, and was willing to intensify his personal labor time to levels that would have embarrassed a much younger man. He did sow *temporal* maize in 1980, achieving a respectable harvest of 16 tons, but the following year planted half the *parcela* in sorghum again. Manuel's two resident sons-in-law—one of whom he could only describe as *un campesino de botella*—would only work on the *parcela* as paid labor. He had tried *productora* once, when Don Julián first promoted it, but he could only meet the costs by selling animals (liquidating savings) and additional borrowing, something he had to do fairly regularly, he said. The additional complexities of cultivating the crop and its many *requisitos* worried him, and the problem had been compounded by a *seguro* settlement which he regarded as less than just when the time came to liquidate his debt to BANRURAL. Manuel's 1981 maize harvest was poor, at four tons from two hectares, but his ten ton harvest had been sufficient to repay the Bank and leave him with some cash income. In general, he adopted the strategy of relying on his *ecuaros*, cultivated by *tronco* in alternate years, to supply him with maize and beans for subsistence. For him, sowing an *ecuaro* "always gave a return," because he did almost all the work alone, only hiring a son-in-law when absolutely essential, and paying harvest labor in grain when he had no money to hand.[24] He fed his animals maize when they were working, and used his sorghum harvests as a source of cash income, once again only hiring labor for applying fertilizer. Manuel enjoyed the advantage of having one of the few *parcelas* in this *potrero* which was suitable for mechanized cultivation and harvesting, though he lacked irrigation water, and never sowed in winter. But his consumer-worker ratio remained poor even in his mature years, and he lacked significant remittances of cash income from migrant children. He maintained himself as a cultivator, working only with other peasants, and he too has continued to sow his land in the years since 1982, in sorghum alone.

Despite its active promotion, excellent technical backup, and potential ability to provide a good cash return and a subsistence reserve of basic food-stuffs, PRONASE maize has not become the crop of preference for ordinary ejidatarios. In the end 1982 was an extremely bad year because of the severity of the drought, and most of those in Cerrito del Buey who had put their collective trust in PRONASE suffered heavy losses. As we have seen, part of the reason for the crop's limited success lies in the administrative deficiencies and corruption of BANRURAL. But much more would need to be done than offer supplementary finance and rebates on credits to cope with the underlying structural limitations in peasant conditions of production which have limited take-up of the crop. To take the analysis of those conditions further, we need to examine the rest of the agricultural pattern in the ejido and the full variety of peasant adaptations to the environment which capitalism and the state have imposed upon those whose livelihood is rooted in the countryside.

STRATEGIES OF HOUSEHOLD ECONOMY AND FORMS OF COOPERATION

It may seem paradoxical that some ejidatarios assert that they sow sorghum because they cannot afford to sow maize and others argue that "maize is a better crop for the poor," because sowing it ensures that there is at least food in the house. As Manuel's case suggests, part of the answer to this paradox might lie in the *ecuaros*. Albeit at a considerable cost in terms of effort, ejidatarios can often meet their maize requirements in the *cerro*, providing they have working animals and are willing to invest the labor required in the long term to prepare an *ecuaro* for *tronco* cultivation by terracing.[25] Just under half of the cultivators interviewed in 1982 (48%) sowed an *ecuaro*, and the proportion rises slightly, to 51%, if we exclude persons controlling more than one *parcela*. Nevertheless, while 55% of those sowing sorghum alone in 1982 also sowed a maize *ecuaro*, the proportion actually falls to 46% in the case of those only controlling one *parcela*. While a few people in this group formed parts of larger cooperating family units and shared in harvests of subsistence crops sown by a brother or father on another *parcela*, no real correlation exists between sorghum cultivation and sowing *ecuaros*.

Sorghum is sown by a diverse group of people. It is the crop of choice for the majority of ejidatarios who lack family labor or a source of cash income external to the farm. On the other hand, despite their defection to maize in 1982, sorghum has also been sown in quantity by the ejidal entrepreneurs and the likes of Don Gabriel, since it offers a stable return despite vagaries of climate, low costs of labor supervision, and is economical for the owners of machines. It is also sown, particularly in its *puntillado*, irrigated form, by ejidatarios of the middle rank. Many of these ejidatarios are able to sow one piece of land in subsistence staples and another in sorghum. But since sorghum has given a better average monetary return per hectare sown than maize in recent years, is drought resistant and still gives a harvest if less than optimal cultivation techniques are applied, even people controlling two *parcelas* often prefer to sow both in sorghum. Excluding the cases of Tito and Julián, a third of those controlling more than one ejidal *parcela* in 1982 sowed nothing but sorghum, and a third of them sowed sorghum on three separate *parcelas*. One of these extensive sorghum cultivators was a tractor owner and the community's leading *emigrado* cultivator, one was to become the next ejidal commissar, and a third, also owner of a tractor along with a herd of twenty dairy cows, was a son-in-law of Don Santiago who had worked as a trucker earlier in his career. The fourth was a resident professional of the community and the fifth an old ejidatario whose activity was not of a particularly entrepreneurial type.[26] A further eleven people, 24% of the total, sowed maize on one *parcela* and sorghum on another. Only one of this group controlled three *parcelas*, and two out of the eleven had only a *pedacito* of maize on one of their fields for subsistence purposes.

Of the remainder, fourteen, 31%, sowed some sorghum along with other crops. One had a *parcela* in garbanzo, another, controlling three *parcelas*, sowed sorghum, garbanzo and maize, and another had sorghum, maize and *temporal* beans. Three sowed some alfalfa for their cows, two of them with some maize for family consumption as well. One, an old ejidatario's son who sowed tomatoes on one piece of land, along with two other *parcelas* sown in sorghum, had had an extensive migratory career and help from a brother who was a priest. The ejidal commissar had sown one piece of land in sorghum, along with twenty hectares of onions sown with a partner from another community. Another, much less affluent, ejidatario had sown 1.5 hectares of cucumbers, along with some other vegetables and maize. His sorghum was not a new planting but regenerated from the previous year's sowing: around 8% of all the sorghum in the ejido was regenerated. Three other ejidatarios, one a leading community professional with an old ejidatario father who remained active in his own right but supervised much of his son's cultivation during his frequent absences, planted some land in sorghum while dedicating their main *parcelas* to a quite different type of organization, combining cows stabled on the land, alfalfa, maize, fruit trees, sugar cane and *pedacitos* of vegetables. This strategy, described as a "mix" in Table 20, represents the polar opposite to a strategy based on sorghum monocultivation, but it is important to see that it is not necessarily an alternative to it. The diversity represented by the "mix" strategy may perhaps be seen simply as the end of a continuum, since maize is often sown intercalated with beans along with squash, some plant a hectare of subsistence crops in the same field as sorghum—though this pattern has agronomic disadvantages—and a few sow *pedacitos* of chiles and have a few fruit trees as well. But very few of those who only farm one *parcela* achieve any great level of diversity, and this is only partly because such pleasurable gardens in the countryside are difficult to protect from stray animals and those with scant respect for proprietary rights in more distant parts of the ejido. To a considerable extent, diversity in the *parcela* is related to the possession of money rather than simply the existence of kin cooperation which permits the pooling of land and labor.

Only 12% of the ejidatarios sowing multiple *parcelas* sowed maize alone in 1982, and even this situation was an exceptional one, since two of the five individuals concerned were sowing *productora* in place of sorghum sown in the previous year on one of their *parcelas*. There is some acknowledgement, at least in principle, that rotation of crops would be desirable, and monocropping of sorghum is generally recognized to bring declining yields in the long term. There is much talk of "resting the land" from the sorghum regime. Nevertheless, inclusion of additional *parcelas* sown by the active ejidatarios has served to confirm sorghum's dominance in the fields of Emiliano Zapata. The question to pose is therefore not: "why do people grow sorghum?", to which the answers are already apparent, but: "why do some people *not* grow sorghum?"

Two *potreros* have a consistently high proportion of maize producers: El Carrizo and El Camiche. In the case of El Carrizo, the proportion hovers around fifty per cent of ejidal cultivators annually. Carrizo is, in fact, a *potrero* of mixed land quality, including some cerrile land which cannot be irrigated. *Potreros* La Mesa and Guarachita are also beyond the range of the irrigation system, and their inconsistent proportions of maize farmers are, in fact, merely a reflection of the fact that people farming land there often alternate garbanzo and maize in the rainy season cycle, whereas those with irrigation generally sow garbanzo in the dry season as a second crop. There is strong evidence to suggest that yields of garbanzo in the plain have fallen[27] as a result of pests which have multiplied under the sorghum monocropping regime, but it is a cheap crop to sow with mechanized cultivation and threshing. Garbanzo too is a crop which enters the agro-industrial complex as an animal foodstuff: merchants from Sahuayo, as well as Don Gabriel, buy it from the *parcela*, and Don Gabriel sometimes spoke to people personally to "animate" them to sow it. But it is also fed directly to animals in the village, and garbanzo is most popular with those who have animals, since even a poor harvest will leave a useful amount of feed. A number of farmers chose to sow garbanzo without BANRURAL credit on the plain, but the proportion sowing "particular" increased in the more marginal *temporal potreros*, particularly where preparation by machine was impractical. As one farmer in Guarachita, whose primary activity was goat-herding, put it: "Money returns from sowing garbanzo here are seldom sufficient to repay the credits, but it is worthwhile for the animals if you can use family labor in place of hired hands." Here, of course, the logic of peasant economy is partly simply a question of the limits imposed by the land itself and the communications infrastructure. But it is not wholly that. Those who have proved enduring cultivators of land in La Mesa have generally been people who combined their farming with animal husbandry and had resident sons of working age willing to aid them both directly in the form of work and by sharing migrant earnings.[28]

The same environmental limitations which prompt farmers to alternate maize and garbanzo cultivation in La Mesa and Guarachita are also a factor in the case of Carrizo, but the Carrizo data confirm the overdetermining role played by the structure of the productive unit and kin cooperation. A relatively straightforward example would be the case of Francisco. His land is cerrile, and is divided into three corrals, on two of which he pastures his five cows and other animals. He has two *troncos*. His annual maize crop, supplemented by the output of a *tronco ecuaro*, is rotated between the corrals, so that he sows 1 hectare or 2 hectares depending on the year. He has two resident single sons, aged twenty-five and fifteen respectively, one of whom works as a *jornalero*, as, indeed, does Francisco himself. Francisco is unusual in having never attempted any form of labor migration, working instead for the local *patrones*. He does not sow with the bank because he does not need to do so; the intensity of his cultivation is determined solely by what he can manage without recourse to paid labor. His harvest is used for autoconsumption, any surplus being sold in the village. Francisco does not participate much in modern consumer society and belongs to the category of villagers who are not noted for their sociability. This is the price of a stubborn adherence to the limits of peasant economy. The reward, aided by a little patronage, was that his second son was studying agronomy and had already secured work with the SARH in Guanajuato.

Francisco's cultivation and animal husbandry are clearly not sufficient to sustain his family by itself, and it is never going to make a significant contribution to feeding the landless of Mexican society. The case of another poor Carrizo *dueño*, Juan, aged fifty-two, is somewhat different. Juan does farm land of commercial quality. Irrigation is available for a winter sowing, and his aged father had rented the *parcela* to both Don Gabriel and the Bajío *jitomateros* in his final (and expensive) years of infirmity. Juan's eldest brother is an *emigrado*, but he never returns nor maintains any contact with the family. Juan only went once to the North, in 1950, because his own family consists solely of a daughter, married to a *jornalero*, Ramón. Yet the *parcela* has never been sown in sorghum nor even garbanzo. It is always maize and beans. But it is only 1.5 hectares of beans, and none of the crops is sown with BANRURAL. Although Juan has inherited the land, it is in fact sown by a cooperating unit of three men; himself, his younger brother, Raul, and son-in-law, Ramón. They work together, with help from the women of the family and Raul's younger children. Raul, like his brother, only went once to the

United States, though he has some financial aid from a married daughter in Mexico and two single daughters residing in Guadalajara. He also has a twenty-one year old resident single son who is a *jornalero*. Off-farm income is not, however, of the essence in this case (and the educational level of the next generation is low). The only labor hired is for harvests, and it is paid in kind on the *parcela* (though not in the *ecuaros*), since cash is scarce. The cooperating kin do all the *tronco* work themselves, and so pay only for machinery, fertilizer and the pesticides used for beans. Yields are relatively good for beans, which are irrigated—around two tons per hectare—but less good—one ton per hectare—for maize, sown *temporal*; but they are not particularly variable, since the land in this part of the ejido is excellent for these crops. A part of the harvest must be sold to finance cultivation, and the hoarding of beans for subsequent sale within the village was a particularly attractive strategy given the constant pressure on an already relatively high price exerted by constant local shortages.[29] Even with high levels of self-exploitation of family labor, the land cannot be fully utilized, and the extended family unit's independence is premised on at least two of the men working regularly as *jornaleros*. Juan has effectively incorporated his son-in-law into his household, but Raul's share of the harvests is based on the idea that he has his own *pedacito* to sow. In this case, the kinsmen enjoyed harmonious personal relations, and all saw themselves very explicitly as poor people who had to help each other to survive.

But such arrangements are fragile. Even as things were, more of the harvest would be sold if there was any financial emergency. Were Juan or his wife to become seriously ill, the temptation to rent the land again would be great. Though the most taxing phase of his family development cycle was passing, brother Raul still had heavier domestic commitments, and son-in-law Ramón's family might grow beyond the two small children he had in 1982. The entire nature of the farm had been made possible in the first place by Juan's small family. This is not a typical situation, but it does represent one possible direction of development of peasant economy: a retreat into "sowing what one can" for family subsistence without the aid of BANRURAL. A few ejidatarios have pursued this option since 1983, but they are likely to remain a minority simply because it depends on substitution of some form of family labor for cash. The majority of younger ejidatarios would not be satisfied with the living standards and levels of cash income enjoyed by Juan and his kin, and the same principle draws potentially available family labor into migration.

Other maize cultivators in Carrizo do, in fact, enjoy some additional sources of income. One has a son who is a *licenciado*, though he still engages in high levels of self-exploitation and confessed to still selling a few hanegas "*al tiempo*" to make ends meet. After 1982 he switched to sorghum. Another, with a much more prosperous resident professional brother and a father whose "solidity" as a peasant cultivator dated back to U.S. migration in the 1920s, has persisted with maize in a totally cerrile *parcela*, despite the costs of *tronco* cultivation, by dint of doing much of the work himself, labor inputs from four single sons, and a job as a *manual* in the *secundaria*. There is one ejidatario in Carrizo who combines sowing a *parcela* with herding goats, sowing maize and sorghum, part of which is fed to the animals, without benefit of family labor. His land is mostly unsuitable for machine cultivation, and he borrows within the village to help finance his crops. But his father-in-law, one of the village *particulares* of the previous generation, had sown tomatoes on this *parcela*: land quality is an economic rather than a natural category. With sufficient money capital to sow a labor-intensive crop, returns from the *parcela* can be transformed. But perhaps the two most significant habitual cultivators of maize and beans in Carrizo are two original ejidatarios who sow these subsistence staples in combination with a small (1-1.5 hectares) planting of alfalfa for their cattle, with the continuing participation of resident married sons in a family enterprise. Both enjoy two harvests a year, but they are the relatively exceptional embodiments of the model Lázaro Cárdenas is supposed to have commended to the peons when he originally tried to win them to the agrarian reform cause with the promise of individual tenure: a self-sustaining agro-pastoral subsistence enterprise.

And the self-sufficiency is more apparent than real. In the case of Don José, aged eighty, two of the sons who work with him are *jornaleros* sowing their own *ecuaros*, but one is another secondary school *manual*, while one works in a *brigada* in Guanajuato. The son who works outside the village makes the largest financial contribution, although the older of the *jornalero* children is the nominal owner of nine of the family's eleven cows. For eighteen years the father, from a *mayordomo* family, has steered clear of any entanglements with the bank, and as far as possible with the external market. Much of the produce is retained for autoconsumption, and it is again a question of sale of surplus maize, beans and milk within the village to meet the cash costs of production. Essentially, the joint family constituted by the parents and their sons' families is feeding itself, but it has not been immune, despite hard work and the highest standards of husbandry, to the migratory processes and search for wage-work characteristic of other households. The sons went to the United States in order to build their houses. Andrés may own nine cows, but his daughters, like the daughter of Francisco, have worked in the *fresa*. Seen from this wider perspective, even an attractively shady peasant plot, with its mango trees, small shelter for the cows and meticulously weeded crops, is a functional part of the same political economy as the sea of sorghum further up the road. There are differences: this agricultural regime will do less damage to the land, and the absorption of chemical herbicides is likely to be less, though few now sow without pesticides or observe any precautions when handling them. In terms of farming practice, the difference in paradigm could, of course, be developed further—in a different world. Under present conditions, even these modest variations on the sorghum monocropping regime depend on particular qualities of family leadership and kin cooperation which the contradictions of living in a world dominated by capital tend to undermine in the majority of cases.

The other case of an agro-pastoral cooperative unit in Carrizo is the family of Don Pablo, whom we met in Chapter Four as the *Jefe de Vigilancia* who refused to put his signature to the document authorizing the transfer of the mill machinery to Taretan. As a result of Pablo's contacts there, his eldest son settled in the sugar fields of the Tierra Caliente, leaving him to build the future around his three remaining resident sons. Both father and the two middle sons paid a few visits to the United States, but Pablo made an excellent investment in acquiring the rights to a fertile *parcela* in Carrizo in addition to his original land in La Manga, which had been sown in sorghum and garbanzo for twelve years in 1982. La Manga is sown with BANRURAL credit, and yielded an average annual net money return of 40-50,000 pesos in the early Eighties. Pablo had experimented with other cash crops there in the past, including *fresa* in the year when the bank offered aid for it. Carrizo is self-financed and it gives the family consistent returns of just under three tons per hectare of maize and over two tons per hectare of beans, with an additional 1.5 hectares of alfalfa. The maize harvest was split between Pablo and the three sons, and the by-products of these crops also provide supplementary forage for their animals, which included eight milk-yielding cows in 1982. Surplus milk is sold in a shop owned by Pablo's step-daughter. Yet even two *parcelas* cannot sustain this number of people. Although Pablo's sons give priority to the family land in allocating their working time, all work independently. In 1982, one worked as a *jornalero* cutting alfalfa for another ejidatario and as cow-man to the ejidatario in Cerrito del Buey who owns a *pequeña propiedad* in Jaripo and has a much larger scale agro-pastoral enterprise. Another works as a house-builder. The youngest son, title-holder of the Carrizo *parcela*, also works as a *jornalero* regularly. The sons have their own animals, but none would think of himself as in any way affluent. None finished primary school, and only one of their children has finished *secundaria* to date. Some of the third generation are drifting off towards Guadalajara, and one grandchild was in the U.S. in 1982. This is a "solid" *campesino* family which has always sown its land and husbanded it well. But the returns to self-exploitation are not great, and the reproduction of such patterns of farming in the future seems far from secure.

There were six other integrated cattle-raising and farming units in the ejido in 1982-3 which could be described as enterprises of family reproduction not orientated towards capital accumulation. As Figure 14 demonstrates, only 32% of the ejidal cultivators interviewed had any cattle, and the numbers keeping more than a couple of cows were not substantial.[30] For most, cows simply represent a domestic convenience and a form of savings. All these agro-pastoral units were based upon the cooperation of fathers and resident sons or cooperating kin of the same generation, but two of them are favored by financial assistance from professional children, and they could be further

Figure 14
CATTLE OWNERSHIP BY EJIDAL CULTIVATORS, 1982

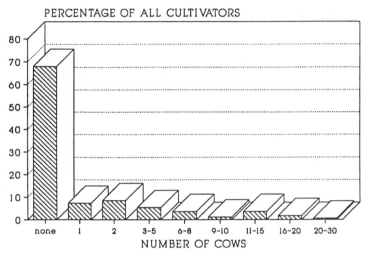

Note: Includes mature animals only

differentiated in terms of the emphasis placed upon the cattle as the primary activity and the extent to which sorghum and garbanzo are favored as crops. Two of the units concerned pursue the "mixed" cultivation strategy on multiple *parcelas*. Among the cases where only two cows were being kept in 1982, there is one example, in potrero El Salitre, of cooperation between brothers which is an equally salient example of the non-expansionary family enterprise, and it has the additional value of illustrating some more of the factors which may sustain and limit such forms of cooperation.

The elder brother, Rafael, acquired the rights to the land neighboring that of his father with his own international migrant earnings. He cultivated about a hectare as an orchard and vegetable garden, with a *pedazo* of alfalfa, and had 3.5 hectares of grains sown on the land behind. Younger brother Rogelio sowed beans followed by garbanzo and then maize with a *pedazo* of cucumber between 1981 and 1982. Rogelio had one resident *campesino* son who finished secondary school and younger children to help with the work, while Rafael's children helped financially: three had accountancy qualifications, and a single daughter working in Mexico in this profession was a particularly important source of financial aid. Another son was an undocumented migrant in Los Angeles, working in the urban industrial sector: he also remitted income. Rafael sold part of his small harvests—which have included strawberries and other fruits as well as every conceivable variety of vegetable—direct to the Jiquilpan market on occasion, but could also sell direct to passing truckers, since his land is adjacent to the road. In 1988, he built a roadside shop, from which he could sell cigarettes and drinks to those who stopped for a snack of cucumbers or other products from the *parcela*. The brothers also sold maize and beans to *particulares*. But Rafael estimated his cash income from the *huertita* in 1981 as 15,000 pesos net for 20,000 pesos costs; the bulk of the produce was consumed by their families (and innumerable friends), and the cost of producing it in terms of personal labor time was substantial, since much of the land was not susceptible to mechanical cultivation. The brothers each had a plow team and did all the work together without recourse to hired labor: indeed, they hired themselves regularly to neighbors who required *tronco* work done. By pooling their resources, they were able to adapt their cultivation practices optimally to the limitations of their land and shortage of capital, and were, at the time when I first met them, also benefiting from the meshing of the different stages of their respective family development cycles. But family circumstances change, and with them the need for cash income. In 1982, Rogelio's children were available as family labor and none was involved in the more costly stages of higher education, but he subsequently turned to work as a housebuilder, leaving Rafael to continue cultivating his garden alone.

The regular cultivators of maize and beans in El Camiche also include a case of cooperation between brothers, one of whom is the single man called Cristobal whose early activism as a renter of *tierras ajenas* I described in Chapter Six. One of his two married brothers was still cultivating a rented *parcela* "*a la cuarta*" in 1982, and while the family also planted some sorghum in most years, they invariably maintained their subsistence base on at least one of the *parcelas* they farmed. Their original ejidatario father—reputed to be approaching the centenary of his birth—was too infirm to take an active role in directing operations, but the unit of kin cooperation also incorporated their brother-in-law, Emilio, whose own land in La Manga was generally sown in sorghum. He regularly worked as a peon with others, and still sometimes borrowed from Don Gabriel for farming his own land. The data at my disposal for years after 1983 suggest the progressive diminution of farming activity on the part of this group of relatively poor ejidatarios. Camiche does, however, also contain examples of farmers who generally shun sorghum without drawing on the resources of kin cooperation between families. The best example is perhaps Don Carlos, as he is nicknamed by his friends, an ejidatario aged fifty-seven in 1982, who has never migrated to the United States, nor engaged in any form of internal migration.

In 1981, Carlos harvested twenty-eight tons of maize from his four hectares, and was justly awarded a prize by the SARH for his achievement. He had sown beans in the winter of 1980-81, but more recently sowed *cartamo*, with which he obtained a relatively poor result of seven tons, and garbanzo, with which his results were better than average. One of his sons was studying to be a veterinarian in Mexico, but it is a measure of the limited return secured even from good harvests that Carlos had been unable to support him for more than two years of full-time education, forcing him to seek paid work while studying. While he received some financial help from his married son in Mexico and another single son working in a laboratory in Guadalajara, and his eldest daughter had worked in domestic service in Guadalajara before marriage, Carlos was in fact still facing an adverse consumer-worker ratio. He not only had two of his own eleven children—a son and a daughter—still in school, but was also maintaining the three children of his eldest daughter who had been widowed and had now remarried. He did, however, have the unpaid labor of an eighteen years old *campesino* son, and the rest of the family were much in evidence working with *machetes*—Carlos also shunned herbicides—and at harvest time.

Carlos evaluated different crops in terms of their money returns as a percentage of harvest value: beans produced a return, he estimated, of 30-40% of a high harvest value, whereas garbanzo produced a higher rate of return, 50%, on a lower harvest value than maize. He described garbanzo, like sorghum, as "a crop for the lazy," because of its low levels of labor input. But he also observed that BANRURAL credit only covered 60% of his production costs for maize and beans. Carlos did have to hire labor for beans, since he preferred to sow by *estaca*, the manual planting of seeds in a prepared bed.[31] He applied the pesticides aided only by his son, and performed all the work with the plow alone, but non-family labor was also needed for the harvest, the children being in school. As the costs of family education had risen, he had been forced to turn to garbanzo and *cartamo* as more economical alternatives, though he continued to resist substituting sorghum for maize on the grounds that it exhausted the land. Like most cultivators, Carlos was forced to economize on money costs, but he never economized on his own working time. He possessed two vast *tronco ecuaros*, capable of producing two tons per hectare of maize and 600 kilos of *temporal* beans per hectare in a good year. These were worked exclusively with family labor. In 1982 he experimented with sowing garbanzo in one of them, but his primary purpose in investing so much energy in his *ecuaros* was to ensure that he could sell the bulk of what his *parcela* produced while meeting his family's still substantial consumption needs.

It is noteworthy that cultivators like Carlos who pride themselves on their farming standards, and explain the logic of their farming decisions in terms of highly rationalized form of economic calculus, have an antipathy to sorghum, but are at the same time drawn from sheer considerations of money cost versus necessary money income to look for alternative crops to beans for the winter cycle. Table 21 summarizes the pattern of land use characteristic of those cultivators who sowed in winter in the 1981-82 cycle by *potrero*, excluding those (5% of the total) who have alfalfa and other pasture crops, mixed cultivation patterns in all seasons, Don Julián's winter onions, a winter sowing of irrigated sorghum and a sowing of maize *elotes*, sweet corn. Sweet

Table 21

CULTIVATION OF WINTER CROPS, 1981–82

Potrero	Number of Cultivators of:		
	Garbanzo	Cartamo	Beans
La Manga	6	1	
Casa del Trigo	1	1	1
Paso de la Arena	2		6
El Camiche	1	1	4
El Monte	7	2	1
El Salitre	1	1	7
El Carrizo	3		7
Los Pirules	3	3	
La Lobera	4	8	1
Cerrito del Buey	3	9	
Totals	31	26	23
As percentage of all winter sowings (%)	36	31	27
Percentages adjusted for multiple parcelas (%)	34	31	30

corn is an essentially commercial venture, with which a few have experimented over the past few years. In this case two hectares were sown by an aged but active ejidatario, who was given some fertilizer as a favor by the Jacona *jitomatero* whose onions he cultivated with his tronco and who also employed one of his sons as a foreman. The eldest son of Don Santiago also sowed half his 8 hectares *parcela* in sweet corn (along with garbanzo) in the previous cycle. Some *potreros*, of course, have no winter cultivators, though the land can be used for grazing.

As the table demonstrates, beans are a minority crop in winter sowing; although the percentage of beans rises to virtual parity with *cartamo* when the sowing of additional land is taken into account, two cultivators sowed more than one *parcela* in beans. One of them was Manuel C., at that time administrator of the land owned or rented by Don Gabriel in the ejido, and the other an ejidatario mentioned earlier who experimented with tomatoes in one of his *parcelas* in the next cycle. In the 1981-82 cycle, one might have expected to see some increase in sowings of beans relative to earlier years, because of the rebate scheme in operation. In 1980 and 1981, including multiple cultivation in the calculations, sowings of garbanzo outnumbered sowings of beans by 7:4 and 3:2 respectively. The absolute number of sowings of winter beans in the ejido in 1982 showed an increase of fifty per cent relative to 1980. But the number of *parcelas* sown in *cartamo* had increased over the same period from a mere nine to thirty-one, with a strong concentration on irrigable *parcelas* of eight hectares. *Cartamo* represented a substantially greater total volume and value of production than garbanzo, and the apparent proportion of beans production in the output of the ejido must be adjusted for the fact that many cultivators sowed only half their land or less in this more costly crop.[32] Although *cartamo* cultivation is highly mechanized, as Don Julián observed, possession of capital is important for securing optimal yields because of the quantity and quality of fertilizer required. Less affluent ejidatarios who turned to *cartamo* often secured much lower returns than the entrepreneurs. But as I noted earlier, Julián and Tito also benefited from the extension of *cartamo* cultivation in a different way. By selling direct to the Guadalajara cooking oil factories, they improved on the local price by some twelve per cent, an indication of the margins available even to local intermediaries in the agro-industrial system.

On the evidence presented so far, the ejidatarios of Emiliano Zapata are not making a huge contribution to feeding Mexicans who do not farm. Maize today is the food of the countryside, whereas wheat has become the staple of the urban working class, in consequence of a heavily-subsidized, price controlled urban market and massive investment in irrigation infrastructure in the north of the country (Sanderson 1986:184-185). Even wheat cultivation by large-scale enterprises in the North is threatened by the profitability not only of winter vegetables, but of garbanzo sown for export and animal consumption and safflower. Safflower is destined for culinary oil which is consumed by the urban middle and upper income groups rather than the working class: as Sanderson observes, its growing popularity reflects the "double marginalization" of the rural producer (1986: 211). The wheat peasants sowed in earlier years in Guaracha was a cash crop,[33] but relatively few of even their urban migrant children consume safflower oil. Table 21 demonstrates that the dominance of the culinary oil and animal foodstuff industries over human nutritional needs is as apparent in the winter cycle cultivation in the Ciénega as it is in the northern irrigation districts. Bean producers are relatively few even in the winter cycle on irrigated land. Some sow with an eye to the cash return, and some sell to commercial intermediaries from Sahuayo: the commercial trade in beans must have an adverse impact on prices from the rural consumers' point of view. Some prefer to hoard their surplus to sell at better prices in the village later in the year, but such surpluses are often exiguous, and the village market may be shrinking. In Guaracha, "to live on *frijoles*" is a synonym for poverty, and beans remain a more economical source of protein to the poor than meat: in the summer of 1986, a kilo of meat cost 1000 pesos, whereas the same weight of beans cost 380 pesos. As real incomes fall, some households will consume more beans and less meat, but in 1982-3 the price of beans was a constant cause of complaint and at least some households were cutting back on their consumption.

To some extent the poor of this rural community, unlike the urban poor, can meet their needs from their own production on *ecuaros*, although yields of rain-fed beans are generally very low in the *ecuaros*, and some yield no beans at all. Seventy percent of landless heads of households who work as *jornaleros* in the village sow *ecuaros*, including sons who work with ejidatario fathers, some regular international migrants, and persons with other manual occupations, like housebuilders. Excluding the resident sons of ejidatarios increases the percentage slightly, to three quarters of the total. But at times of financial crisis, any "surplus" sold from the *ecuaros* may in fact be food the family might otherwise have consumed before the next harvest. The widespread practice of applying fertilizer to the *ecuaros* (along with seeds originating in BANRURAL stocks) not only indicates that even this marginal peasant production is subsumed by the industrial framework of an internationalized agriculture, but is also a symptom of secularly declining yields. Furthermore, the *ecuaros* ultimately serve the same purpose under modern conditions as they did under the hacienda: they facilitate the continued depression of rural wages—and indirectly, those of more distant labor markets—by drawing on the reserves of peasant economy. But the general retreat of non-commodity labor relationships has left its mark even in the *ecuaros*. Although labor exchange is more likely to occur in *ecuaro* cultivation than in the cultivation of ejidal *parcelas*, those without family labor resources within their immediate households often have to pay *peones*. Where no cash is available, harvest labor may be paid in kind, but as everyone recognizes, this amounts to paying labor more than the cash wage for the day in real terms. It is also interesting to note that people forced to resort to hired labor often preferred to employ their own kin or friends, despite the fact that it offered no advantage in terms of cash costs. Michoacán possesses a low wage economy which everyone consciously sees as a low wage economy (in terms of either urban or international wage levels). Peons adapt to this situation by demanding reductions in working hours and other compensations[34] for their relatively poor remuneration. Such reactions are just as visible in the tomato harvests of the big *jitomateros* as in the fields of peasant cultivators, but the latter sometimes seek to moderate their effect by seeking out persons of *confianza* to work for them in the hope of at least improving the quality and intensity of the labor performed over whatever working day is the current norm. Though cash rates are generally non-negotiable, the persistence of labor-intensive forms of production and seasonal labor shortages in a local regime of high labor underemployment creates another type of system of mutual adjustment which ultimately links the fields and factories of California to the Ciénega through the mediation of Mexico's domestic agrarian policies.

It is evident, that undercapitalized peasant farms adapt to the economic environment in which they operate through a sequence of adjustments. Kin cooperation and substitution of family labor and personal labor time for cash can, to a limited extent, enable farmers to grow the basic peasant staples, but at the cost of a very low cash income. Less labor-intensive agro-industrial crops may still be grown even where brothers farm together or some unpaid labor is available if higher levels of disposable cash income are required, education being high on the list for many families, particularly relatively immature ones. Food security is abandoned under this strategy, which becomes problematic if food prices rise more rapidly than farm prices. Nevertheless, cash income can be an overriding consideration even for cultivators who would otherwise prefer to sow maize and beans, as the case of "Don Carlos" illustrates. Kin cooperation and substitution of family and personal labor time for cash may remain central even in the case of sorghum cultivators. The more one puts in, the further the aid of BANRURAL is spread, and the greater net money return at the end of the day. Implicitly, this is the effect the system is intended to produce. Some cultivators regularly supplement BANRURAL credits to ensure high standards of cultivation even when they attempt to maximize their own work inputs, even if it means borrowing.

Such was the case, for example, with two brothers in El Monte. The younger, Joaquín was married with young children. His elder brother Felipe was single. He had driven buses in Guadalajara earlier in his life and used savings from his urban migration to buy land next to that of his father, who had a reputation for hard-work and frugality.[35] They farmed their two *parcelas* together, rotating them in sorghum and maize, with occasional winter sowings of garbanzo, and also treated their animals as joint property. A large *tronco ecuaro* sown in maize alone produced feed for the mules and pigs, as well as subsistence resources for the family, and they generally sold some maize from the *ecuaro* in the village, or less frequently, to merchants from Sahuayo. The brothers hired additional *troncos* to supplement their own labor, hired some additional labor for manual weeding, and spent a considerable amount beyond BANRURAL's allowance of 700 pesos per hectare on the rockets used to discourage birds from eating sorghum grains over the three month period when such vigilance was required daily. Since the fields were adjacent, the conditions for joint cultivation of two *parcelas* were optimized from the labor-time allocation point of view, but Joaquín still maintained that they supplemented BANRURAL credits by a sum of 15-20,000 pesos. The use of additional *troncos* on their own land wiped out their earnings from working for others. Joaquín had been obtaining contract work as a peon from the SARH in Sahuayo between 1980 and February 1982, but cuts in public employment were already under way, and it was apparent that there would be no more work of this kind in the future. Despite the major asset of Felipe's cooperation, unencumbered by responsibilities to children, Joaquín spoke of "selling an animal" and "selling a bag" (of fertilizer on the black market) as their habitual means of acquiring the cash to optimize cultivation in a combined sorghum and maize regime. Their recent maize yields were good in comparison with the district average of 3.9 tons per hectare: the last harvest on Joaquín's *parcela* had produced 5 tons per hectare and that on

Felipe's almost 7 tons per hectare in a year when the other maize cultivators in the same *potrero* averaged 3.5 tons, and only one other cultivator apart from the brothers achieved a yield (slightly) above the district average.

But if even this farm might resort to sale of fertilizer to achieve a good standard of cultivation in other respects, it is only too obvious that others suffering a greater thirst for cash are tempted to push the adaptation to the next stage and economize on preparation of the land, weeding and fertilizer application in order to use the money eventually received from BANRURAL for other, more pressing purposes. As I explained earlier, the delay in receipt of credit fosters "economizing," but even without the delay some might continue to skip stages of preparation and sell some of their fertilizer. The extent to which this is possible clearly depends on the losses incurred at the end of the cycle in terms of harvest value, but a thousand pesos in September may have a greater utility than a thousand pesos in November, and with sorghum, risk-taking is not always totally disastrous. Since the defects in the bank's administration of the credit system are sufficient in themselves to generate sub-optimal cultivation practices on the part of those who have no family labor resources and little ready cash, we should not exaggerate what is a secondary phenomenon. The achievement of optimal yields depends primarily on the resources available to the producer beyond those provided by the bank, be they other income sources or traditional peasant resources for substituting labor for capital, and the latter form of adaptation is no longer normally sufficient to reproduce a "traditional" peasant economy, as we have seen. Nevertheless, it is worth ending this phase of the discussion with a little more data on the purely quantitative implications of all the problems I have described. Variations in yields are related to a multitude of factors: there are micro-variations in land quality, drainage, salinity and access to irrigation channels. Damage to crops may be caused by animals breaking through a hedge, or by neighboring cultivators who fail to keep irrigation ditches clear. Sometimes a tractor operator performs the work of preparation badly. Sometimes the cultivator simply falls ill in the course of the cycle. It is often difficult to decide whether a factor affecting yields is "beyond a cultivator's control" or a consequence of his approach to farming—animals find it harder to penetrate a well-maintained hedge, for example. But the figures bespeak not particular deficiencies or misfortunes, but a more global malaise which is systemic.

Potrero La Manga had the highest proportion of sorghum monocultivators in 1981. Excluding two total losses and one vestigial harvest owing to inundation after late irrigation, yields per hectare ranged from 1.25 tons on the part of an ejidatario who admitted to me that he had economized on the second two stages of tractor preparation, to a maximum of 4.25 tons per hectare. Half the cultivators achieved less than 3 tons per hectare. In El Camiche, where almost all the land is irrigated, only a third of the cultivators achieved 5 tons per hectare, and over half failed to achieve 4 tons per hectare. In El Monte, where twenty ejidatarios (73% of the total) sowed some sorghum in

1981, yields again ranged from just over 1 ton per hectare to 6 tons per hectare. Three achieved over 5 tons per hectare: one was Don Gabriel's administrator and another a long-term U.S. migrant with a large family but substantial savings. He also sowed the land of his mother and possessed an *ecuaro* on the slopes of Cerrito Cotijaran capable of preparation by tractor. The third was a poorer ejidatario who habitually borrowed money at interest to maintain cultivation standards. Forty-five percent of the El Monte cultivators failed to achieve 3 tons per hectare. In Cerrito del Buey, 86% of the 1981 cultivators sowed a primary *parcela* in sorghum alone. Their yields were conspicuously better on average, despite two total losses. Of the remaining nine cultivators, only one failed to achieve 4 tons per hectare, three achieved between 5 and 6 tons, and one, an *emigrado*, over 6.

The good harvests in Cerrito del Buey were mostly achieved by better-off ejidatarios. But one of the best results was obtained by Benjamin, an ejidatario aged thirty-nine who was caretaker in the secondary school.[36] In 1982 he was also sowing his father's land in El Monte and his uncle's land in Frutyales (*a la cuarta*). Benjamin had devised a complex system of personal time scheduling and organized his cultivation so as to minimize market-dependence. He irrigated each *parcela* in turn, so as to be able to do all the work himself, and scheduled the harvests so that the proceeds of his sorghum sales would cover the higher cash costs of a maize harvest. He kept his two cows and horses corralled in El Monte, with 1 hectare sown as pasture there, along with some maize and sorghum or garbanzo, and beans in the winter. He produced most of the forage consumed by his animals on his own land, and only hired a peon to work with the cows for the equivalent of two months a year, to free himself for cultivation work. He used chemical herbicides in his sorghum, but had to hire about sixty-five man-days of paid labor a year, since the whole purpose of his cultivation strategy was that his children should dedicate themselves to their studies and therefore only work on the land at weekends and in the school holidays. A succession of harvests and daily income from milk sales gave him a regular flow of cash income over the year, but he still had to plan carefully to be in a position to buy the children text-books and meet other elements of the rising education costs associated with their progress.[37] Sale of calves was an important means of meeting the costs of books. Benjamin devoted most of his cash income to his children's education, leaving himself and his wife only the barest necessities after meeting the costs of cultivation. Every aspect of his farming strategy was the subject of careful economic reflection in his evening hours in the school, and the day was filled with "self-exploitation." Yet he was quite conscious of the fact that no amount of personal sacrifice nor planning would enable him to meet the higher education costs of his family, and was waiting for help from his two educated brothers, one a vet in Guanajuato with a second teaching job, the other a bank employee in Sonora.

His brothers were, in fact, already giving him some aid, not inappropriately, since Benjamin had become the main bread-winner of the family in his early teens, when his father first became ill: he went four times to the U.S.A. as a bracero, and when the program ended, spent five years working in first a foundry and then a print-shop in Mexico City. The money he remitted from his migrant earnings financed his sibling's education.[38] He returned when his brother left for Sonora, to care for his father (who was still alive in 1982).

Benjamin's circumstances as a cultivator have their favorable dimensions, though his life has been a hard one. But his story is worth telling, however inadequately, because it provides a very clear example of the complexity of the historical factors which underlie the productive performance of an individual ejidal farmer. Benjamin had some external financial aid, but had himself played a major role in making that aid possible by earlier labor migration. His strategy was dependent on his controlling more than a single *parcela*, and his uncle allowed him a strict *a la cuarta* rental arrangement because his own primary interest was in goat-herding. On his return from Mexico, Benjamin and his uncle had collaborated in the management of a herd of forty cows for a period of four or five years. But despite the past benefits of kin cooperation, once he started cultivating alone, Benjamin had to sell grain *"al tiempo"* to keep going before he obtained his modestly paid job in the school. Even a supremely "rational" peasant adaptation has its obvious limitations when the margin between sufficiency and deficit in cash income is so narrow, and it was not, by 1982, sufficient to guarantee social mobility to the next generation. The widespread orientation of peasant farmers to raising the cash to provide their children with prospects of social mobility may, as in Benjamin's case, be favorable to physical yields, though it is much less favorable to the production of basic foodstuffs. But the dismal evidence I have presented on physical yields of sorghum on some of the best land in the ejido suggests that such a motivation can only yield results where something more than the willingness of the individual to work is involved. Given the returns to labor offered by the system, even Benjamin would have to ask himself whether he might not do better to rent some of the land as his children progressed at school.

ON DIFFERENTIATION, WEALTH AND CAPITAL

I have already identified most of the ejidatarios who would readily be identified as "rich" by poorer members of the community and it is evident that peasant differentiation in the past has largely been a product of the ejido's articulation to the larger capitalist system and, in the first instance, to the new regional bourgeoisie which emerged after land reform. Modern forms of state intervention in the countryside have created new avenues of capital accumulation at various levels and in various forms. The accumulation of wealth by public office-holding is scarcely anything unprecedented in the Hispanic-American world, but there are certain innovations worth emphasizing. To a certain extent, the modern agro-bureaucracy constitutes a specific "quasi-class" interest, in so far as its opportunities for capital accumulation depend on the existence of a land reform sector which can be plundered. Like the Chinese mandarins, these modern *literati* must ultimately invest their spoils in private sector assets, but they could scarcely view the wholesale dismantling of the ejidal system with equanimity. To large-scale capitalist entrepreneurs like the *jitomateros*, state intervention in agriculture has both its positive and negative dimensions. To some extent, they benefit from input subsidies justified by the need to support the peasantry, they acquire rented land cheaply, and they have even been known to become ejidatarios in order to participate in fraudulent transactions in cattle managed by BANRURAL. On the other hand, their access to peasant land is impeded by competition on the part of agrobureaucrat renters, and they not only have to pay to "normalize" their use of ejidal resources officially, but must also pay back at least part of the subsidies flowing from the state to the bureaucracy in order to guarantee preferential access to water.

But despite moments of antagonism, private enterprise and bureaucracy seem to have achieved a working relationship which is fostered by the general directions of public agricultural policy. Initiatives aimed at "integrated rural development," restoring lost production of basic foods and improving nutritional standards are visible as projects in the Ciénega but have had only the most marginal impact. One significant alternative to programs aimed at supporting basic grains cultivation is schemes which envisage a greater role for the pastoral economy in the region, and the promotion of cattle raising bears further discussion because it synthesizes all the different issues which are the concern of this chapter: the nature and significance of socio-economic differentiation within the ejido, the effects of state intervention and bureaucratic domination of the peasantry, and the impact of urbanization, industrialization and the internationalization of capital on rural production processes.[39]

I have already mentioned the ill-fated Cattle Cooperative scheme of 1968. It had received the personal sponsorship of Lázaro Cárdenas as part of a package of measures he promoted in his final round of personal interventions in the region, which included the building of the secondary school in Guaracha. Run from a main center in Zacapu, the scheme involved the creation of similar cooperatives in Villamar, El Platanal and Venustiano Carranza, of which only the latter survived. Approximately forty ejidatarios wished to participate in the ownership of cows, while others agreed to sow alfalfa, which in this context did receive credit from the Bank, though opinions differed as to its adequacy. The cows themselves were delicate Canadian beasts which had to be stabled, and the old mill was refurbished for the purpose. Besides the milk price difficulty, the episode was marked by a familiar pattern of private transactions in stock by Bank officials. Those *socios* who had actually received cows were ordered to return them to the bank, with the addition of any calves born in the interim, since the operating losses on the entire scheme now constituted yet another debt charged against the ejido.

Those who complied did not receive a receipt.

This second failure in large-scale cooperation under public auspices has left an indelible impression on the minds of Guaracheños. It was followed by a more modest scheme, run by the SARH, to promote smaller private associations between ejidatarios. Four *socios* with land in La Lobera agreed to sow the *parcelas* in meadow grass, and were equipped with a pasture cutting machine of Italian manufacture. The project was, in fact, part of a national program, and the ejidatarios received unprecedented levels of technical and veterinary advice from specialists who were not local men. But private cooperation proved no more successful. Two of the partners wanted to make a road around their *parcelas*, but their neighbors protested to the *Reforma Agraria* in Morelia on the grounds that their own lands would be invaded. Then two of the other *socios* refused to cooperate in producing the pasture grass on the grounds that one of the partners, Miguel, was receiving the lion's share of the profits by virtue of his personal patronage relationship with the SARH engineer responsible for the project in Sahuayo. They plowed up their land and withdrew. Miguel continued alone with both the pasture cutting machine and a herd of fourteen cows stalled behind his house, of stock which he relentlessly sought to improve. He was the only dairy farmer in the village to sell to the LICONSA plant in Jiquilpan. His eldest son works in the Ford plant in Mexico City, and Miguel said that his gifts and income remissions had played an important role in improving his standard of living. His next four children, all girls, are married to factory workers, and his thirty year old son Marcos, who had previously worked with the cows and was a specialist in artificial insemination, also left for Mexico in 1983.[40] Miguel estimated that his herd, with the stable and the machine, represented a capital value of a million pesos in 1982. He had also recently bought a truck for transporting his pasture. He was left with a certain bitterness towards other ejidatarios and their *envidia*, described BANRURAL as "a mafia," but at least had the satisfaction of seeing his youngest son graduate as an agronomist from Chapingo. Nevertheless, with his family gone, he decided to sell the herd a few years later, sowed his *parcela* in sorghum, and dedicated his energies to politics, becoming a leading local member of the neo-Cardenista PRD.

Miguel had certain personal qualities which may have recommended him for patronage in a scheme of this kind: his father had been in the *acordada*, and he had therefore received more education than most. He must have seemed an appropriate leader for a scheme based on technological progress, and is undoubtedly a serious man in every respect. The same seriousness marked the other ejidatarios who had the larger herds in Guaracha. One is the ejidatario with the *pequeña propiedad* in Jaripo mentioned earlier. The owner of the largest herd in 1982 was Don Gabriel's administrator, Manuel, whose father Marcos was a former *acomodado* of the hacienda epoch.[41] All of these people are "comfortable" and business-like, but their own personal energies are the core of their enterprises, which possess no very strong dynamic of expansion. Another ejidatario who pursues a cattle-orientated strategy is Abelito, an elder brother of Tito. He is the return migrant from Mexico City who used to run a garment workshop mentioned in Chapter Seven. Since 1983, he has benefited from new BANRURAL schemes to foster cattle-raising which seem designed primarily to help those with some capital, and would certainly threaten any poorer recipients with serious financial difficulties given the present value of the cattle and the costs of pasture to those who do not control significant areas of land. But Abelito is more interested in gaining a secure livelihood with a decent standard of living without the grime of city life than in taking over the ejido, and was, in fact, rebuilding his herd after selling most of his animals to build a new house in 1982. As far as Abelito was concerned, the great merit of cows was that they brought in a stable and regular income, whereas farming was *"muy eventual."* This view was shared by another dedicated cow-man and former ejidal commissar who had a herd of twenty animals which he valued at 400,000 pesos in 1982.

Manuel was one of the young men who received an untitled *parcela* in La Manga at the beginning of the individual ejido. One of his sons was a migrant farm worker in California, and others were in Mexico: only two of his younger children were continuing to study beyond secondary level. Manuel too was "business-like," calculating in terms of yields per hectare and differential net money returns. Much of his preoccupation was, however, with the scheduling of his own managerial time, since he had two *parcelas* to cultivate as well as the herd to manage. He had begun his career with goats, herded with his brothers, and had changed to cows, on a small scale at first, when his kin migrated. He owned a pick-up, and expressed interest in taking on ejidal office a second time, but he was certainly not thinking of expansion: he told me rather bitterly that with one son seemingly committed to the United States, only his seventeen year old son Fernando now showed any interest in the herd, and unless he saw more signs of interest from the children, he intended to liquidate it. This he in fact did, and after his second bid for ejidal office failed, he left for the United States himself.

At first sight, it might have appeared that the larger cattle-owners registered in Figure 14 above constituted an archetypical "rich peasant" stratum. In a sense, and in varying degrees, they did, though each had a different background and became a larger-scale cattle raiser by a quite different route. But the most striking characteristic of such enterprises is their transitory nature. The extent to which the next generation is advancing socially as a result of pastoral accumulation is very variable. Ejidatarios of this type are in a good position to aim for the office of ejidal commisssar, but it is equally common for acquisition of cattle to follow rather than precede occupancy of office for obvious reasons. The economic impact of these enterprises on the rest of the ejido is relatively marginal, since they aim at self-sufficiency in pasture production. Were there to be an increase in the number or scale of pastoral enterprises this might well lead to further increases in land concentration, but there was a clear limit to the amount of agricultural land which could be managed by an ejidatario who was personally involved in the management of a herd. At least one active son was virtually indispensible. Furthermore, it is more difficult to build a commercial dairy herd today than in the past, promotion by state agencies notwithstanding.

The situation was summarized with characteristic lucidity by ex-commissar Manuel. There were fewer cows in the village today than in earlier decades because the purchase price of a cow was now much higher in real terms, and the supply of pasture was reduced. Over-grazing had reduced pasture yields on the hill behind the village, and garbanzo yields had fallen on the plain. The costs of transport, seeds and purchased pasture, including balanced foodstuffs, had also increased, but the price of milk in the countryside was declining relative to its price in the cities. As far as Manuel was concerned, the return on his personal work input—the "labor payment" received—was deteriorating. All this is, of course, a reflection of larger structural tendencies, and again represents the "double marginalization" of the rural producer. The bulk of the region's production of the dominant crop, sorghum, is destined for pig producers in La Piedad, who supply urban upper income and export markets. Some cattle-owners mill their own sorghum, though one, the ejidatario with the *pequeña propiedad* also sells part of his output direct to La Piedad. Most, however, only feed it to their animals after it has been processed into balanced feed by agro-industry as a purchased input. Sorghum cultivation does not displace garbanzo directly to a great extent, but the extension of its cultivation does correlate strikingly with the decline in garbanzo yields, and the fresh pasture crop of choice for peasant dairy-farmers, alfalfa, was deprived of BANRURAL finance[42] and therefore suffered an indirect displacement. Part of the ejido's garbanzo production is itself commercialized for subsequent industrialization, and fresh milk production in the urban context is centered on a packaged and refrigerated pasteurized product. Meat production for export and upper income groups distorts the whole of the domestic agro-pastoral sector in complex ways, but it will prove extremely difficult to establish a new balance to satisfy urban demand for dairy products on the basis of promoting peasant production of milk by offering credit for cows, even with additional measures to promote pasture production, without tackling the problem of the milk price, and thereby further marginalizing lower income consumers. The only logic which one could see in giving the likes of Manuel a better "labor payment" without radical change in the other dimensions of the system would be the political one of striving to retain support for the PRI among the upper stratum of the peasantry in an increasingly socially polarized rural situation, and such a strategy might not, as I will argue in my concluding chapter, be guaranteed success.

As we have seen, the highest returns within the ejido accrue to those who are owners of agricultural machinery. In the cases of Tito and Julián, profits from hiring machines and sowing rented *parcelas* have been increased, at least on occasion, by their adoption of a direct sales strategy to agro-industrial consumers, by-passing the region's professional intermediaries. But despite these sporadic developments within the ejido, there is no doubting the continuing and expanding power of larger scale commercial intermediaries. During the period of my fieldwork, the intervention of CONASUPO as a purchasing agency was little in evidence, though this might have been expected, since the free market price was high. But the lack of intervention continued under different circumstances: by 1986 farmers in the Bajío were blockading roads in protest at the CONASUPO's refusal to buy at the guaranteed price, and by 1989, the contrast between the abandoned appearance of the CONASUPO *bodegas* in the Ciénega and the flourishing look of private installations in Sahuayo and Briseñas was only too apparent. But in the case of Guaracha, the only form of positive action of which I have knowledge was a protest in 1984, not against the CONASUPO's refusal to buy grain, but its refusal to sell villagers subsidized maize, a reflection of the fact that the majority occupies a radically different position in the market structure to the farmers of the Bajío. Even in fairer times, many ejidatarios had been loath to sell sorghum to the CONASUPO because its staff were more rigorous about quality standards and humidity than the *acaparadores*, and payments were often delayed as well as discounted. But though it was not simply price to which they were sensitive, only a minority never sold to CONASUPO as a matter of principle. Some of them were given food for thought in 1981 when they sold to a new *acaparador* operating from Sahuayo, who, it transpired, built up his business with little starting capital on the basis of delaying payments to peasant farmers in order finance fresh purchases. But such speculative ventures are of their nature ephemeral, since most of the *acaparadores* have a long-term interest in building up a reputation for reliability with their peasant clients in order to protect their market share. The role of regional intermediaries today is clearly markedly different from their previous role as sources of seed and production credit. In essence they are mediating between the industrial and growing side of the agro-industrial system, gathering up the output of small farms into the most cost effective loads for bulk transport—in a state where even the Lázaro Cárdenas steel works ships out most of its product to the interior by road—and in many cases distributing industrialized inputs flowing in the opposite direction. Even the richest of ejidatarios are unlikely to offer very substantial competition to these operators, though the continuing existence of a hierarchy of intermediaries of different scale remains a necessary dimension of the larger system: transactions with peasants still demand operators adept at face-to-face contact and possessed of local knowledge.

The cases of Don Julián and Tito also suggest that those enjoying profits from machine ownership are likely to turn their thoughts to sowing crops with higher returns. In the case of the vegetable market, however, the structures of intermediation are even more complex and monopolistic. Julián, characteristically self-confident, had taken onions to Guadalajara in his own truck, but still had to sell to a wholesaler after making appropriate enquiries. The big commercial growers who operate in the ejido are the only sowers of vegetables who belong to the circle of *bodegeros* who run the regional wholesale trade and produce for export.[43] Given the internationalization of the vegetable trade, and the power of U.S. distribution companies, even they cannot be price-makers in the larger market, and as Arturo, a *jitomatero* from Jacona, explained, the essence of his growing business was to make informed guesses about the future states of the different markets for which he could produce. Different markets required different types of tomatoes and it was generally not possible simply to divert produce from one market to another in accordance with prices. Each field was committed at planting time to a given destination, and even the packaging, performed on the *parcela*, was a variable. The *jitomatero* operation was therefore an exercise in risk management, and the stability of the growers' accumulation of capital depended on the sheer scale of the operation. They planted in different zones to reduce the impact of physical losses from climatic factors and ran a recruitment and transport infrastructure to ensure adequate supplies of appropriately skilled manpower. Although the tomato harvest and other phases of vegetable cultivation drew in both adult and juvenile labor of both sexes from the village, the female labor Arturo used for weeding his irrigated onions was a squad of young women from San Antonio working under the unyielding eye of a more mature female supervisor. Plantings were staggered, and different varieties sown to hedge against market fluctuations. At the level of the individual ejido, the results appeared quite *eventual*. Arturo lost an entire field of produce, and harvested another at a time of low prices. But this was normal: profits from a third field proved highly satisfactory, and this was only a fraction of his total production. The reason he decided to harvest one of the fields on a particular day was simply that he had a truck going north to Monterrey and needed some more cases to fill it to capacity. No expense was spared in either the quality or quantity of chemical inputs, and Arturo constantly drew my attention to the technical innovations he was already introducing in his cultivation in the Zamora region. His ideal was technical parity with the United States, and he did not regard the way forward as one of substituting cheap labor for physical technology. This is not to say that low labor costs were not of the utmost concern: Arturo's personal presence on the *parcelas* was mostly aimed at reinforcing his peasant foreman's control over a sometimes recalcitrant workforce. Large both physically and in personality, he used humor in place of the whips of the hacienda, secure in the knowledge that his peons were not in California and today, at least, had no other place to go.

By virtue of their international migratory experience, ordinary ejidatarios are often well-versed in the techniques of vegetable cultivation. A few speculate with a private sowing of tomatoes from time to time, though there are few if any success stories here. The market is too differentiated—even Sahuayo and the metropolitan cities have different tastes—and too volatile to make small-scale production viable, since profits one year are likely to be wiped out the next. Onions, potatoes and cucumbers are somewhat preferable in this respect, and also have lower, though still relatively high production costs. Even so, fewer and fewer ejidatarios seem willing or able to speculate. Possession of multiple *parcelas* and family labor is virtually a *sine qua non* for sowing even a modest quantity of vegetables on a regular basis without some additional source of capital. Such was the case with Pedro, who cultivated the neighboring *parcela* of his uncle in maize and beans, while sowing his own land in a combination of sorghum and 1.5 hectares of cucumber. In the decade up to 1966, Pedro had been annually to the United States, staying for six to eight months each year. On his return he had sown rented land and also built up a herd of thirty-six cows.[44] He decided that continuing with the cows would require a greater investment in planting alfalfa and building a pasture store than would be justified by the returns, and turned to goat herding on a smaller scale: in 1982 he had fifteen animals, which were being herded by another *chivero* in return for money payments and pasture from Pedro's *parcela*. Pedro had one single working son to aid him, two others having left for factory jobs in Mexico. One absentee son was a professional, but a son who had previously worked in the LICONSA plant in Jiquilpan had been laid off after sustaining an injury for which he had received no compensation. He was, however, able to draw on the labor of daughters, nephews and nieces, and his wife, at harvest time, though he perceived his family labor situation as close to the margin.

Pedro had withdrawn from the official credit system, but had achieved self-sufficiency in meeting his pasture needs. Excluding the harvest, he calculated the cost of his cucumber at 50,000 pesos in labor, seed, fertilizer and pesticide, with an additional 15,000 for the harvest, of which there were two per year. The harvest value of the crop in 1982 was 120,000 pesos, and it was sold to a Sahuayan merchant who also dealt with the brothers Rafael and Rogelio whose land was located further up the main highway to Jiquilpan. The merchant, Antonio, had provided the transport, and the price had been agreed before the harvest began. In Pedro's view, cucumber offered little real risk. The ratio of years of good prices to years of bad prices was around 3:2, and the only physical risks were from caterpillars or the excessive application of pesticides in unusually dry conditions. There were many different buyers operating in the region. Prices were more stable, but less attractive, in the markets of Mexico City and Guadalajara, where the big monopolists held sway, but they tended to be high in Sahuayo when they were relatively low in the metropolitan markets.

Tomatoes were, he agreed, a quite different matter, and his only experiments with tomatoes had been small and unprofitable sowings for sale in the village. Even with cucumbers, increased scale of cultivation would be preferable, since he could then sell the standing crop and avoid harvest costs. This had been possible sometimes when more of his neighbors had sown vegetables in earlier years. Pedro's suggested solution to the scale dilemma was the kind of system of contract farming which the American companies had introduced in Apatzingán. He would produce at a fixed, guaranteed, price, and receive the finance required for technically optimal cultivation. Under such a system, he would not hesitate to sow tomatoes. As it was, his skill was wasted by his lack of capital.

Pedro's scenario for agrarian progress would evidently have radical implications for the future development of the Ciénega, but is an alternative way in which ejidatarios might acquire the resources to sow vegetables on larger scale, though it does not contain the important element of price guarantees. In 1982, the then ejidal commissar, Alfredo, was entering a second year of partnership with Abel, a native of the community of Nicolas Romero, on the Zamora side of Villamar, who also rented some land in the ejido. The crop they chose to cultivate was onions, sown *temporal* on twenty hectares, all but four of them on land controlled or rented by Alfredo in the Emiliano Zapata ejido. Alfredo regarded his partnership with Abel as a pioneering development in showing his fellow ejidatarios the way to break out of the cycle of underproduction and perpetual debt. Partnership not only overcame the problem of lack of capital, but also offered the chance of increasing scale of cultivation to a level which spread risks effectively. In the previous year they had sown only one piece of land, in Nicolas Romero, and the profit had been a mere 70,000 pesos, because of low harvest time prices, but twenty hectares of onions would, Alfredo believed, guarantee better returns.

Temporal onions only provide one harvest, but offer the advantage that there is still time to sow garbanzo after them. Alfredo and Abel used children for sowing, reducing their sowing costs by approximately 26%. The children were paid by the row. As I watched the first planting of two hectares taking place in Nicolas Romero, Alfredo was complaining that they needed more *gente* and that the trouble was that parents didn't encourage their children to work any more or discipline them into turning up on time for the truck. Alfredo had his own tractor, which was adequate for preparation of the land, though limited in other respects. The partners were subsequently to argue over the relative merits of using tractors or *troncos* for the *escarda*. They did, however, agree from the outset that the standing crop would be sold to truckers in order to save harvest costs. Alfredo worked tirelessly in the onions, in between working with his animals in a large *tronco ecuaro* and relieving his brother from the duties of herding his two hundred goats. He also found time to enter into an "*a medias*" agreement to sow yet more onions with a fellow ejidatario and friend to which reference was made earlier: the two men planned to do all the *tronco* work themselves. Alfredo did hire peons—in quantity—to weed his *ecuaro* with machetes, but as well as his farming work he also had to devote some time to his role as ejidal commissar. In addition to the normal duties of commissar with regard to questions of land rights, credit and other agricultural matters, 1982 was a presidential election year, and commissars were expected to promote the cause of the PRI. Though the election of his successor as commissar took place in late October, Alfredo was active in the campaign, and had to defend himself publicly against charges of maladministration on a number of occasions once the new administration had taken office. It is difficult to know how far Alfredo's numerous preoccupations influenced his physical returns in onion cultivation, but the partners also found prices at harvest time relatively unfavorable for a second year.

Alfredo gives the appearance of being a highly acquisitive person. There was no shortage of fingers pointing accusingly at the correlation between his becoming *comisariado* and the escalating level of his economic activity. It is, however, important to place him in structural context, both as an economic agent and as a social type. Alfredo was another ejidatario who had been forced into international migration at any early age on the death of his father. He had been to the North annually between 1961 and 1967, buying his land with savings from his final visit, but remitting money to his mother and siblings in the earlier years. Two of his brothers are themselves now in Los Angeles, but three siblings are in Mexico, where an educated brother works as a civil engineer. The younger brother who still lives in the village complains that Alfredo displays little generosity towards him financially, but the roots of Alfredo's carefulness do not lie in meanness of spirit. Talking to him, I realized that his father's sickness and early death weighed heavily upon him: accumulation was a hedge against an insecure future, a means of preparing for bad times which were always waiting around the corner. Alfredo regarded most of his fellow ejidatarios as lazy and thriftless, but he saw hard work and saving as an adaptation to the darkness of the world: fertilizers had brought declining yields, epidemic diseases threatened the village's pigs, the government offered the *campesino* no real aid.... Alfredo's pessimism did sometimes border on paranoia, and there might be a case for arguing that an element of suppressed guilt entered his psychological makeup. But it might also be seen simply as an extreme form of a general pessimism of the spirit characteristic of so many ejidatarios, enhanced by past personal suffering. Alfredo differed simply in his unflinching determination to turn ceaseless work and frugal living into iron-clad reserves against bad times. Both objectively and subjectively he belonged to a different social category from Julián and Tito and he was not destined to become one of the ejido's dominating entrepreneurial figures.

DEVELOPMENT AND MATERIAL LIFE IN THE COUNTRYSIDE

Despite the vicissitudes of their history, in terms of the standards of welfare enshrined in the notion of a "minimum subsistence basket" and the more obvious immiseration of other segments of the rural population, the Guaracha ejidatarios might be deemed relatively privileged. But it is worth concluding this discussion of the impact of the state's renewed patronage of ejidal agriculture by taking stock of the absolute level of this privilege as reflected in general standards of material consumption.

Over 10% of households resident in Guaracha whose heads hold an ejidal title reported that they did not eat either any meat or chicken regularly in 1982 (in comparison with just over 16% of landless households). Although this group included a number of elderly women renting their land, less than half the ejidatario households ate meat or chicken more than three days a week. Bearing in mind that people tend to exaggerate their levels of welfare in response to questions of this type, and that such enquiries tell us nothing about how food is distributed at meal times among different members of the family, these results do not seem particularly impressive for a community of "privileged" peasant food-producers in a period of relative prosperity by the standards of recent years,[45] though they are admittedly superior to those of landless households, only just over half of which reported consuming meat or chicken more than two days a week. The top 10% of the ejidatario houses in terms of per capita spending on clothes spent between five and sixteen thousand pesos in 1981, but over 61% spent less than the average of fifteen hundred pesos. The average spending of ejidatarios on clothes was higher than that of landless households, of whom only 27% per cent spent over fifteen hundred pesos per capita, but it is not a very marked pattern of differentiation, even allowing for differences in the age distributions of the two populations and the fact that older people are less likely to be preoccupied with their wardrobes and are more likely to be given clothes by their children. In absolute terms the expenditures on clothes of the majority of ejidatario houses were scarcely extravagant, and we have yet to consider how far patterns of consumption are dependent on migrant remissions rather than farm income.

Farming is, as many ejidatarios themselves stress, a very uncertain source of livelihood. As we have seen, in some cases, the primary significance of the *parcela* is as a source of subsistence provisioning rather than cash income, and in others part of the harvest is retained for consumption while part is sold. But many farmers in Guaracha only sow cash crops, and in any given year some failed to secure any net cash return at all from sowing their *parcelas* with BANRURAL. In the 1980 rainy-season cycle, of those sowing only one *parcela* who reported positive net cash returns, almost 45% reported a figure which was less than the wage income received in twenty-four weeks by a *jornalero*; the proportion improved somewhat in the next year's figures, to 32%, though the average return in both years was similar, at double the *jornal* equivalent. Such calculations cannot give a very precise indication of the real income from farming achieved within the ejido as a whole, nor of the long-term fortunes of particular households. If the differences between the net money incomes received by different ejidatarios in a given year are very substantial, so are the year-on-year fluctuations in the incomes of many farmers. The maximum net income secured from sowing a single *parcela* in the rains during these two years was four times the average, but these were exceptional results achieved by single individuals, neither of whom secured more than the average net return in the other year: twice the average would be an exceptional result for most people. All that one can reasonably conclude from consideration of monetary returns is that there would be scope for improving the farm incomes of the majority of ejidatarios within the existing agricultural regime, and that a proportion of the farmers capable of producing a surplus will not obtain a cash return from farming superior to the wage of a *jornalero* in any given year.

Another way of assessing the economic welfare of ejidatarios which provides a better index of their long-term fortunes is to examine their possession of consumer capital. Ownership of pickups and cars is so restricted among the ejidatarios as to make its analysis pointless: off-farm or migrant income, gifts from children working outside Guaracha, occupancy of ejidal office or membership of one of the entrepreneurial families are the factors associated with vehicle ownership by ejidal cultivators, and in most cases the vehicle is used in connection with the owner's work.[46] Teachers and doctors are the main recreational users of motorized transport in the community. For most ejidatarios, the main item of consumer capital in which they will invest in the course of their lives is their house, and some people with whom I discussed the subject explicitly said that they preferred to spend their money on improving their dwelling than on achieving a richer and more varied diet. Expenditure on the house and its furniture is, as we already know, a major destination of migrant incomes, along with a range of other consumer durables. People who have nicer houses also tend to own a greater range of consumer durables, but items like refrigerators and washing machines still belong to the category of luxuries as far as most Guaracheños are concerned, along with hot running water, decent sanitation and separate bedrooms for mature children of different sexes. Only 15% of all households in the village possess a washing machine, a fact which may admittedly also reflect a certain male bias in spending patterns, and just over a quarter a refrigerator. Fifty-two percent of all refrigerator owners are ejidatarios, but the use of a refrigerator is not necessarily simply or even primarily domestic: some owners are butchers or shop-keepers, while others sell cold drinks to their neighbors. A majority of both ejidatario and landless families possess a black-and-white television (76% and 64% respectively), including a few who do not possess a gas stove: few owned a color television in 1982, and all of them were purchased from professional salaries or earnings from migration.

Figure 15 provides a summary of the community's consumption of these and a range of other items: radios, cassette players, record players, stereos, typewriters and sowing machines. The index of consumption created from the data is a crude one, based on alloting the luxury items—refrigerators, washing machines and color televisions—double the score of the more mundane. But the figure does indicate the relative deprivation of a substantial number of ejidatario households as well as the relatively greater proportion of land-

Figure 15
CONSUMER DURABLES CONSUMPTION, 1983

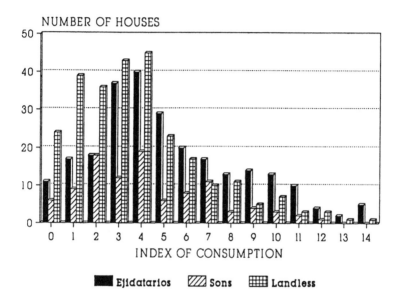

less families possessing little in the way of modern consumer durables. A large proportion of the houses of sons of ejidatarios which are poor in consumer durables are in fact of fairly recent formation, and the poorest categories again include some elderly widows and abandoned women. But 76% of the ejidatario household heads whose houses score one or two are men over the age of thirty, as against 57% of the relatively greater proportion of landless household heads in this category. Most of the landless men are *jornaleros* who receive little income from migrant children and are not themselves regular migrants. As one moves up the scale, whether one is dealing with ejidatario or landless households, higher levels of possession of consumer goods of this type are increasingly associated either with greater income from migration—either of the head himself or of his children—or with possession of some other form of livelihood. The upper levels of consumption found among the landless households predictably reflect the existence of professionals and people with better-paid public and private sector jobs in this category, as well as a few *emigrados*. The block of underprivileged landless households is, in effect, the rural laboring underclass. Yet the better-off members of the ejido in terms of possession of consumer durables are better off for the same reasons as the landless and the standard of living of the majority of ejidatarios is not particularly enviable in terms of this measure.

It would be possible to develop this kind of analysis in other directions. The average expenditure of ejidatario houses on education was predictably somewhat higher than that of landless houses, for example. But even this very limited discussion indicates the relative deprivation of these privileged peasants in terms of the criteria of modern capitalist consumer culture and the dependence of "advances" in this sense on urban-rural ties and international migration. There is no doubt that a significant minority of families in Guaracha is poor in terms of the most minimalist definitions of basic needs, including a few households within the ejido itself. A much larger number find themselves periodically short of cash to meet day-to-day expenses, and even more perceive themselves to be disadvantaged by the standards of a consumer culture which shapes their aspirations to an increasing degree. Since 1983, new items, in particular videocassettes, have entered the village, extending the tendency already present in the widespread use of televisions: through the cheapening of industrial commodities, capitalism has become increasingly even-handed in distributing access to the worlds of its imagination, but leaves its implicit promise of access to so many other dimensions of material welfare—quality of diet, living and working conditions—out of reach.

Although there are marked, and resented, differences in wealth within the ejido, it ultimately makes very little analytical sense to talk about "the development of capitalist relations" within the community. Capitalist relations are everywhere, but different households are inserted into the system in different—and generally multiple—ways, in a manner which is determined by a complex combination of both local and global factors. It is evident that even the most prosperous and enterprising of the ejidatarios occupy a relatively lowly position in the transnational agro-industrial system and that they belong to the majority that sees progress in terms of education and social mobility. This is as much a product of the forms of political domination as of the unequal distribution of economic power, though these two dimensions of the modern peasant condition should not be divorced. The "refunctionalization" of the ejidos in the 1970s was based on a strengthening of bureaucratic modes of domination, and forms of *caciquismo* associated with that mode of domination, which today's neo-liberal regime finds it convenient to critique, but generally in abstraction from the issue of the objective power of capital in the civil society which it seeks to strengthen *vis-à-vis* the state. Nevertheless, current attempts to reform the state have a real content, and are a reflection of the structural crisis of the established forms of post-revolutionary hegemony—a crisis to which renewed, if disparate, strivings on the part of the peasants themselves for land, livelihood and real freedom from dominatory incorporation have made a significant contribution through the Seventies and Eighties. To assess the prospects for the future I return, in conclusion, to a more holistic analysis of the dynamics of the hegemonic process.

CHAPTER 10

MEMORIES OF UNDERDEVELOPMENT, HOPES OF EMANCIPATION

As I stressed at the beginning of this study, Guaracha is not rural Mexico in microcosm. In many respects it cannot be considered a representative community even in its own region. The landscape of the Ciénega de Chapala is less homogeneous than it appears at first sight, and there are substantial historical differences between the region dominated by the Guaracha hacienda and other zones in terms of systems of land tenure and patterns of economic organization (Moreno 1989; Boehm de Lameiras 1989). Some aspects of the articulation of the region with the larger world—in particular patterns of emigration—have continued to produce variations in the social structures of different communities in the period following land reform. But the processes discussed in the previous chapter have produced a strong convergence in contemporary agricultural patterns throughout the Ciénega, and as Boehm de Lameiras concludes, the nature of this regime has little to do with local social needs or concern with the health of what was once an exceptionally rich ecosystem (1989:76). Up to a point a majority of the peasants in the Ciénega today faces common social and economic problems, and have a similar experience of political incorporation into national society, an experience which is, in its broad outlines, certainly not unique to this region. In the years since 1982, it has become increasingly apparent that the experiences which divided the first generation of ejidatarios in this zone are being effaced with the passage of time, and that the current crisis is producing a new type of response, which is both more political and more unified than anything seen in the past. It is still too early to make any firm predictions about the likely future course of events, but it is appropriate to conclude this study with a discussion of how local developments might be related to wider tendencies. Events in the Ciénega today seem to be closing a cycle which began in the era of Cárdenas, but in a way that suggests the possibility of a new beginning. There is some danger of allowing hope to triumph over realism in evaluating these developments, and I am conscious that my own role as a witness has become increasingly affected by partisan sympathies. Nevertheless, there does seem to be a case for arguing that, whatever the short-term outcome of contemporary struggles, they signify something which is significant in terms of broader national trends.

In terms of the problem of the place of peasant agriculture in the larger rural economy of Mexico, the majority of the ejidatarios of Guaracha belongs to the category of land reform farmers who theoretically possess the means to produce a surplus of food over their household subsistence requirements. In Central Mexico, a substantial proportion of the land reform was completed prior to the period of Cárdenas, and produced a different kind of ejido, the ejido *pegujal*, where the grant of a tiny *parcela* was conceived from the outset as a complement to a wage and the creation of ejidos itself was conceived as a transitional measure on the road to a modernized and efficient private enterprise agriculture (Rello 1986:112-118). In practice, Cardenista land reform in Michoacán produced its own share of minifundists and some gross inequities in the distribution of land within ejidos. But as we have seen, land distribution in the Guaracha ejido was performed in as exemplary a manner as one could hope to encounter. Since the pre-Cardenista regimes generally insisted on distributing land to agrarian communities as a *dotación* rather than a *restitución*, even in Morelos (1986:119), the ex-*peones* were no more juridically subordinated to the state than many who had pursued an active struggle for the land. Guaracha's significance for an evaluation of the Cardenista project of land reform must turn on the fiasco of the collective ejido, but collective cultivation was the exception rather than the rule even in the agrarian reform of the Cárdenas period in the Ciénega, and the community's subsequent history rejoins that of the majority of its neighbours in centering on the individual type of ejido. In contrast to many other zones, the peasants of the Bolsa de Guaracha enjoyed the central position in the local system of land-tenure, since private property was restricted to the periphery of their microregion and the majority obtained land of high quality. While it is true that the ejido lost its commanding position in terms of control of hydraulic resources—and land quality is also influenced by the communications infrastructure—it has remained a richly endowed proof of the proposition that even a radical redistribution of physical means of production cannot produce a flourishing peasant commercial agriculture in the absence of the money capital and market conditions required to valorize those resources.

This study has suggested that the problem facing those ejidatarios whose resource endowments permit the production of a surplus is not simply one of protecting that surplus from appropriation by commercial intermediaries, industrial capital, and the state and its bureaucracy. There is also a problem of producing the level of surplus which is technically feasible in the first place. This second problem should be distinguished analytically, since the grain and other crops which are not produced in the ejidos provide the real, use-value, measure of the cost to society as a whole of present patterns of agrarian organization, but it is not independent of the first: underproduction reflects the domination of peasant farming by wider social forces rather than an irremediable weakness of the ejidal system. One might therefore expect any form of peasant mobilization which emerged in Guaracha to center on attempts to retain and expand the peasant share of the surplus combined with demands to improve peasant access to the means of valorizing the land and labor in their possession. But the situation is complicated by additional contradictions.

In the first place, the bureaucratization process through which the state effected its "refunctionalization" of the ejidal system in regions like the Ciénega proved so pathological that it itself became a focus of discontent and opposition, though in criticizing the effects of what the Mexican literature now labels the "statization" of peasant agriculture we should be careful not to forget the dismal agrarian situation which preceded the epoch of BAN-RURAL. Escaping the negative aspects of state intervention in the ejidos implies struggling for greater autonomy against bureaucratic domination and representation through official organizations, in particular the CNC. In the 1980s it has become increasingly evident, not least to the *campesinos* themselves, that the subordination of ejidal agriculture to BANRURAL is itself a mechanism of surplus appropriation which ensures that ejidos never dispose of their own fund of accumulation. In some contexts ejidatarios have conducted relatively successful campaigns to free themselves from the dead hand of economic control exercised by the bank in favor of new systems of self-management through reconstituted ejidal organizations (Rello 1986; Gordillo 1988).

But many of these struggles for peasant appropriation of their productive processes have taken place in new ejidos created during the expropriations of the Echeverría period or under the terms of legislation introduced by that administration (Rello 1986:90), under the auspices of leaderships born in a recent moment of agrarian struggle. In the case of the *Coalition of Collective Ejidos of the Yaqui and Mayo Valleys* (CECVYM) analyzed by Gustavo Gordillo, formerly one of the organization's principal technical advisers and a functionary of the SARH under the Salinas de Gortari administration, we are dealing with a trajectory of recent agrarian struggle culminating in collective cultivation in the highly "modernized" agricultural environment of Sonora. In the case of the Huastecas of San Luis Potosí, Veracruz, Hidalgo, and Tamaulipas, discussed by Rello, the panorama is more varied, in consequence of differences in local historical backgrounds, the types of ejidal organizations produced by land reform and the relationships between the new ejidos and the other social forces with which they were articulated in their local area. In the case of the *Occidente* of Mexico, as I noted in the previous chapter, ejidatarios have frequently been incorporated into regional producer organizations dominated by private capital, in their turn subordinated to transnational capital. Under the provisions of the Ley de Fomento Agropecuario of the López Portillo administration, a few new forms of producer associations uniting ejidatarios with private capital were created, but the formation of unions of ejidos in the period 1977-1982 was primarily associated with the increasing penetration of the state into the countryside, and many of the developments which did not involve the participation of private capital were located in zones of more marginal resources (Rello 1986:107-109). In this kind of context, the problem facing ejidal organizations is twofold: faced with the dominance of private capital over the best resources and most profitable activities in the regional economic space, state economic intervention is essential for the development of the ejidal sector, but the form taken by this intervention has seldom maximized efficiency or social justice in practice, creating a need to reconquer organizational autonomy from the state and its bureaucracy. Yet in many cases, ejidal organizations are weakened by the fact that they already have a long history of internal disarticulation and differentiation linked to the prior penetration of private capital and forms of *caciquismo* associated with that process.

Looking at the issue through the optic provided by the history of the Ciénega might suggest that if a general decentralization of control to self-managing ejidos is to produce a new era of prosperity and social justice in the entire Mexican countryside, it will require a revolution in terms of the empowerment of poorer ejidatarios: not only *vis-à-vis* the state, but in the face of the entrenched social power of external capitalism and richer neighbours and community *caciques*. The problem of maintaining relative equality within ejidal communities has been posed explicitly and with some realism in Sonora (Gordillo 1988:180), and the leadership of the CECVYM seems under no illusions about the extent to which improving the position of peasant producers in an era of crisis demands a wider (and not exclusively rural) unity both to improve the terms of the peasantry's incorporation into the national economy and to redefine the substance of justice and democracy for the rural milieu (1988: 164-168). But the social and political base from which these issues are being posed in the Sonoran context is different from that of the individual ejidos of the Ciénega, despite the fact that the problems generated by the "modernization" and "statization" of agriculture in the two regions are not wholly dissimilar. The question is clearly political, social and economic, and to achieve democratic and efficient self-managing ejidos functioning autonomously for the benefit of all throughout the country as a whole might require not only a major new economic investment in many cases, but a much *broader* and more radical kind of state intervention in civil society. A peaceful realization of peasant demands for greater social justice in the countryside means, at the very least, changing the existing balance of the structures of social power in ways which would prevent the newly autonomous agrarian communities disintegrating under the impact of internal and external inequalities.

This brings us to a second major contradiction: it is not only the ejidos but also the larger rural communities of which they are a component which are internally differentiated, and this complicates the problem of defining social justice, including its formulation in actual peasant demands. As we have seen, a major demand in Guaracha is for the creation of local sources of employment, and this demand is not restricted to the landless. One can again see both a parallel and a difference between the cases of the Ciénega and the Sonoran ejidos, where the collective nature of the cultivation process and the distribution of *utilidades* in proportion to days worked make an assessment of ejidatario incomes from farming more straightforward. In 1981, farming supplied ejidatarios working in the collectives with around seventy-five days of work a year, for which they received an income equivalent to that which would be gained working all year round as a *jornalero* at the minimum wage: this was, in fact, superior to the average level of income achieved in the individual ejidos in the region, but it remained insufficient to maintain a family of six members, and forced a search for work outside the ejido which promoted social differentiation within it (Gordillo 1988:29). Like the Guaracheños, the ejidatarios of the Yaqui and Mayo valleys see the creation of local agro-industries as a major demand in terms of securing a long-term solution to their employment and income problems (1988:176). But given the widely different structures of regional economies, different strategies for developing particular ejidos—which might include replacing some of them with labor-intensive forms of large-scale farming—would have different effects on local employment and income distribution. An emphasis on the desirability of peasant organizational autonomy and self-management should not be allowed to obscure the need to produce forms of peasant enterprise which satisfy local needs in the broader sense and which also correspond to some consistent project for national development.[1] These issues cannot be discussed in abstraction from the question of the role and power of private capital within the larger system, and they are issues which ultimately transcend regional structures of power. But it is clear that local struggles centered on the defense and extension of peasant appropriation of surplus cannot be divorced from patterns of differentiation within agrarian communities: optimal results in terms of generating income and employment in the larger rural community, other things being equal, may imply a case for radical reorganization of existing patterns of farming. Reorganizing an individual ejido which is already highly differentiated is clearly a harder task in terms of forging consent than preventing differentiation within an ejido which is collective.

The last, but by no means least, of the contradictions to be resolved is the fact that the question of improving rural incomes cannot be divorced from the larger problem of Mexico's development process. Improving farm prices for basic grains has an immediate impact on the food costs of both rural and urban consumers, and both food price subsidies and the increased aid to producers which would be required to translate better prices into increased commercial production by undercapitalized farmers, entail inter-sectoral transfers of resources. Since part of the incomes of many rural households is generated in other areas of the economy, the policy dilemmas posed by the notion of "greater social justice for the countryside" have been progressively exacerbated with the passage of time. Differential guaranteed prices and differential consumer price subsidies aimed at supporting poorer producers and consumers could play some role in moderating these contradictions, but the general direction of state intervention under the Salinas de Gortari administration seems, to date, to be in a different direction, with the beginnings of privatization of CONASUPO. Although undertakings have been given with regard to the maintenance of guaranteed prices for maize and beans, the prices of wheat, sorghum, soya, safflower and rice are to be left to market regulation. The argument that sale of CONASUPO industrial plants and retail outlets would free the organization to target provision of subsidized goods to the poorest strata of the population seems less than plausible given the limited achievements of the CONASUPO-COPLAMAR[2] program of the López Portillo administration and the tendency for the private sector to be the prime beneficiary of subsidization of final products (Barkin and Suárez 1985:180-181). Nor, it seems, are demands from urban community organizations that CONASUPO retail outlets be turned over to them to be run as cooperatives receiving a sympathetic hearing. Once again, the withdrawal of the state from economic regulation seems unlikely to serve the needs of social justice: what is required is a change in the nature of state intervention, which implies, in the last analysis, a change in the nature of the state itself of a quite different kind from that which is occurring at the present time.

The agrarian question is therefore also an urban question, or more precisely, a question which involves consideration of the relations between town and country, the urbanization and industrialization process, and ultimately the entire class structure. The underlying integration of the socio-economic process of development is also reflected in the ebb and flow of modern social movements in various respects: the upsurges of peasant mobilization which have provoked concessions to the countryside on the part of the state in recent years have been accompanied by pressures from urban and industrial struggles, and the leaders of peasant movements are often—though not always—people with experience of urban migration. But it is also necessary to recognize the heterogeneous and to some extent contradictory nature of these diverse movements at the base of Mexican society. Even in the case of rural mobilizations, it is still as true today as it was in the nineteeenth century that it is the larger conjuncture which lends unity to diverse struggles to recover or obtain land and to improve the position of the peasant producer *vis-à-vis* capitalism and the state, and past history is replete with examples of the disintegration of temporary solidarities formed on the basis of confrontation of a common enemy. It is, furthermore, necessary to question how far certain forms of struggle actually constitute fundamental challenges to the structures which they are confronting rather than processes which act to reproduce them.

The particular problems of Guaracha, and the type of responses they have provoked on the part of the ejidatarios, certainly cannot guide us very far in understanding the dynamics of the larger hegemonic processes which will determine the future shape of rural society in Mexico. But recent developments in the region do have a broader significance in two respects. First, any evidences of peasant mobilization in a region previously noted for its passivity are worth examining, and second, the process of mobilization has escalated with the rise of neo-*Cardenismo*.

Although we have seen that "development" has brought only limited material benefit to the majority of Guaracheños, and that what has been achieved by the ejidatarios owes more to their own or their children's migration than to farming, this study has already provided ample confirmation of the fact that there are no simple correlations to be made between material deprivation, absolute or relative, and social conflict and political orientations. It is true that peasants have a well-developed sense of social justice, and their conceptions of what is just and what is to blame are also modernized by cumulative experience. Although possession of land has been advantageous in significant respects historically, it has never, in itself, offered economic security. I have stressed the way in which harsh experience has reinforced a negative view of rural life and provoked investment in education: one of the effects of the crisis since 1982 has been to reduce the prospects of recently qualified young people, provoking considerable anger and frustration. Perhaps such trends may have a salutary effect, if they help return the question of valorizing rural life onto the agenda, and they certainly contribute significantly to the practical meaning of crisis. All has never been well in the ejidos and villages of the Bolsa de Guaracha, and it is getting worse once again for the majority. Some of the ejidatarios and their children have resorted to traditional methods and are striving to solve their problems and frustrations by international migration.[3] But this time there is another response, manifest in the banners of the PRD draped over the occupied municipal *presidencias* of the Ciénega. As their exits are blocked or become less attractive, even the ex-peons seem, at last, to be becoming Cardenistas. But there may be another, more positive, dimension to this new activism. As Göran Therborn has argued, all ideologies provide human subjects with three orientations: towards what exists, what is good or just, and what is possible (Therborn 1987:15-16). The third orientation is crucial in analyzing social action because it is possible for people to harbor profound antagonisms towards the existing order without acting to challenge it simply because of fear of repression or resignation to the practical impossibility of change. The significance of neo-*Cardenismo* may lie precisely in that it makes the possibility of change thinkable to those previously characterized by resignation.

In the light of Guaracha's past history there is a certain irony in the fact that so many Guaracheños now regard themselves as a vanguard in a revitalized Cardenista revolution, but there is no doubting the force of the movement in the rural communities of the Ciénega. At both regional and national level, the social forces articulated by neo-*Cardenismo* are clearly diverse, and it is noticeable that a number of PRD candidates in Michoacán's municipal elections of 1989 were *comerciantes*: the candidate in Jiquilpan, the owner of a substantial hardware business, had achieved a notable, if unrecognized, victory for the PAN in the town on a previous occasion (after being denied the PRI nomination). The participation of elements of the regional bourgeoisie alongside peasants and urban workers in populist movements is scarcely unusual, but neo-*Cardenismo* does not seem to represent the standard kind of populism with which Mexico has long been familiar. The caudillistic dimension of the movement in general is undeniable (Tamayo n.d.), and particularly evident in Michoacán, but it does not seem to reflect Cuauhtémoc's personal charisma or capacity as a leader[4] but his peculiar structural position as a symbol and the embodiment of an idea—a *Cardenismo* revitalized, recreated and reappropriated by its mass base. The movement seems to depend little on his direction, which remains unclear and ambiguous. Reconstructed in a regretful popular consciousness formed in the years after 1940, neo-*Cardenismo*'s power is not based on what was actually achieved historically during Lázaro Cárdenas's presidency,[5] but in its myth—the unfulfilled but conceivable possibility of constituting an alternative outcome to the social revolutionary process. Legitimate bearer of the more egalitarian and democratic discourses of the Mexican revolution, and able to appropriate the mantle of a nationalism which neoliberalism is perceived to have abandoned, the new *Cardenismo* has succeeded, for a while at least, in lending political unity to fragmented and heterogeneous popular social movements. It is, therefore, also a child of neoliberalism, gaining part of its force from the fact that a determined effort is being made to change the nature of the hegemonic process.

It is important to distinguish the question of the post-revolutionary hegemonic process from the narrower question of the political power of the PRI. In the Gramscian sense,[6] "hegemony" is a dynamic process of "establishment of unstable equilibria," which is shaped in a significant manner by the actions and reactions of subaltern classes (Forgacs 1988:205-206). Hegemony includes the cultural, moral and ideological leadership of allied and subaltern groups, and is a combination of practices, including symbolic practices, which present the hegemonic group's dominance in a universalizing manner, as the motive force behind the development of the whole society. Gramsci insists that the class exercising hegemony must also exercise a decisive direction over the economy, but that no hegemony can be based purely on the narrow "economic-corporate" interest of the dominant class, and that all hegemonies have an ideological-cultural dimension. In the case of Mexico, the bourgeoisie's hegemony has been expressed through the "institutional revolution": a mediating state stands above "civil society," maintaining a balance between different sectors—seen as separate corporate interests—and protecting this "national" arrangement from external forces which would undermine it. Neoliberal ideology posits an *open* civil society of citizens and associations whose mutual relations are to be regulated *through* government. But the dynamics of hegemony do not rest entirely on discursive dimensions of power. One dimension of the power of the PRI clearly arises from the non-discursive realm—through control of repressive apparatuses, electoral fraud and the purchase of loyalties. The longevity of the official party's rule through successive crises has depended on its ability to reappropriate the universalizing discourse of the Mexican revolution, but this has in its turn been endlessly recreated through processes of social struggle which are determined by non-discursive factors, conjunctures of socio-economic crisis and political balance of force, the ossification of agencies of control such as the CNC, and secular processes of social change.

As rampant inflation and social crisis affected large segments of the Mexican population, the De la Madrid adminstration sought to cope with the mounting crisis of economic management by conceding the inexorable logic of transnationalization while simultaneously beginning the process of privatization of the state sector. This created the space in which an alternative political force could appropriate the broader discourse of the revolution, but the realization of this possibility rested, in the last analysis, on the fact that the post-revolutionary hegemony was not entirely the patrimony of the PRI, and that a particular alternative project had retained its force in mass consciousness—because it corresponded to unsatisfied social needs and aspirations. Although Salinas de Gortari has displayed considerably greater adeptness in terms of political management than his predecessor, retrieving some of the additional ground lost by the fact that popular opinion held the PRI's victory in the presidential elections of 1988 to be fraudulent, his determination to press forward with "modernization" by continuing further on the same course of sacrificing the "national autonomy" dimension of the old post-revolutionary hegemony and reducing the direct economic role of the state, has so far depended on the use of the same non-discursive methods for retaining power. Large segments of Mexican society remain to be convinced that the present course of economic policy will improve their material lot, and attempts by the administration to appeal to anti-statist sentiments are hampered both by the fact that its practices with regard to political democracy remain suspect and by a more general fear that existing social inequalities are likely to be magnified. In distinction from its predecessors, the present crisis is now seen as one which is irrevocably concerned with the question of reestablishing and redefining the broader hegemonic process in a fundamental sense.[7]

The argument that neo-*Cardenismo*'s force lies in its ability to focus and unify disparate kinds of existing anti-systemic forces receives a certain amount of support from the particular sequence of events in Guaracha. The first stirrings of resistance to the established order of things occurred while Cuauhtémoc was still the PRI governor of Michoacán and López Portillo was still President of the Republic, enjoying a short-lived moment of popular acclaim for the bank nationalization—which Guaracheños symptomatically compared with Cárdenas's nationalization of the oil industry—and they were led by the same individuals who were subsequently to become the leading figures in the *Frente Democrático Nacional*—equally symptomatically referred to as the "Frente Cardenista" locally—and the PRD. Initially, however, all that was involved was a modest plan for a revitalization of the ejido based on an attempt to mobilize the ejidatarios to defend themselves against bureaucratic domination.

INTIMATIONS OF RESISTANCE

The institutional setting of this precursor movement was the election of new ejidal authorities, and its rhetoric turned on the issue of *caciquismo* within the agrarian community. In the discourses which were developed in the campaign to persuade people to support the movement, the particular form of *caciquismo* in Guaracha was linked to the experience of the neolatifundist period, and sometimes to the earlier conflict between *agraristas* and anti-*agraristas*, but a link was also made at the outset between the continuity in the power of a certain family and its allies in the ejido and the community's lack of ability to challenge the bureaucracy.

As an analytical category *caciquismo* is somewhat imprecise, since its ubiquity in popular as well as scholarly usage in Mexico has made it a catch-all for a variety of distinct contemporary and historical situations. In Guaracha, it was often used to refer to people who were relatively rich by village standards and opposed land reform, such as a former mechanic in the hacienda mill who opened a shop and built a small cinema in the village: such *acomodados* did not necessarily have significant political power, let alone coercive power, nor did they necessarily seek nor obtain key roles of intermediation between the local community and the power structure. It is the last characteristic, intermediation, which is most significant from the point-of-view of posing the question of the ubiquity of the *cacique* in Mexican society, and whether performance of the role of *cacique* involves violence depends on contextual and conjunctural factors.[8] In the case of Guaracha we are talking about a *caciquismo* which was essentially pacific, and involved a continuity in the group holding representative offices based on wealth. Continuity in control of offices implies continuity in the group exercising functions of intermediation—and in the appropriation of any pertinent spoils of office—but the nature of the intermediation function changes as the relationship between community and the powers dominating it changes.

The family labelled *caciques* was, unsurprisingly, that of Don Santiago. As a consequence of his economic position within the community and the clientage relations that position made possible, Don Santiago had exercised considerable influence over the selection of ejidal commissars, as, indeed, in an earlier period, had Don Gabriel. Alfredo had not, however, been Don Santiago's candidate of choice, but emerged as a compromise because the candidate Don Santiago had favored was challenged by one of the peasant sons of the second ejidal commissar, Don Rafael. In the elections of 1982, Don Rafael's son, Salvador, stood again, and on this occasion stood against the eldest son of the now deceased Don Santiago, who was more or less dragooned into a role he did not find congenial by his brother Julián. Salvador argued that the ejido needed an administration which sought radical improvements to its infrastructure, for the benefit of all its members, and that it was particularly crucial that an administration be elected which was willing to challenge the way BANRURAL in Jiquilpan operated. The old guard was too preoccupied with its own private interests, and even with the best will in the world, the long and cozy association it had enjoyed with the authorities in Jiquilpan made it far too complacent.

Although Alfredo had not been Don Santiago's candidate, he maintained cordial relations with the family. For his own reasons, he attempted to persuade people to vote against Salvador's group, and this scarcely helped the other party. Like many before him, Alfredo had demanded private payments for "expenses" he incurred in pursuing land disputes with the authorities in Morelia. He had made an influential enemy in the form of Don Santiago's brother Cecilio, who accused him of actively encouraging his father's third wife to contest Cecilio's son's right to inherit the land after Cecilio refused to pay him the sum demanded to "arrange things." In consequence, Cecilio sided with Salvador against his nephews. Alfredo was also accused of having conspired with the private machine owners to allow two heavy tractors supplied to the community by BANRURAL to fall into a state of disrepair, and of having profited at every turn from the kind of irregularities in the administration of credit, irrigation water and agricultural insurance mentioned in the previous chapter. With the exception of the tractors, the charges ranged against Alfredo were accusations made against most commissars throughout the region, and entirely symptomatic of the way the commissar's role as intermediary between BANRURAL and its peasant clients had developed nationally. But Alfredo's particular brand of economic activism combined with a deteriorating national economic situation to create a particularly favorable conjuncture for a political shift within the ejido.

Salvador did not have a significant migratory career, but he was a member of a highly political family. His eldest brother was a highly placed figure in the agrarian bureaucracy at national level, and very much on the left of the PRI with regard to social issues. He also had the support of a younger professional brother working for ANAGSA resident in the village, and his father was deeply respected. His slate included a number of other ejidatarios who were well-liked individuals, mostly of *agrarista* background from "solid" community families. His opponents, however, enjoyed the active support of the officials of BANRURAL, though this was to prove counter-productive in the climate prevailing in 1982, and both veiled threats and quite open offers of money for votes came into play during the campaign. Salvador's platform offered an unusually comprehensive and broad-ranging plan to wrest new resources from the state by challenging BANRURAL Jiquilpan's policies with the authorities in Zamora, and it also suggested a quite pragmatic set of measures for improving conditions in the ejido through self-help and cooperation at *potrero* level. It was also somewhat more ideological in tone than was normal in the ejido, but at that time the majority of the electorate was probably more dubious about such matters. Over the years, the PRI's use of rhetoric had devalued almost every possible mode of political argument, which is why the subsequent splitting of *Cardenismo* from the PRI is so significant, creating as it does a greater space to oppose the "authenticity" of the Cardenista national revolution to the official hegemony. Favorable comment was, however, made about the way the regular campaign meetings held by

Salvador's faction were organized.[9] They were both democratic and *dignifying* for the participants, and it is clear that the aspiration that community affairs should be run in this way is very important for most ejidatarios: empowerment, both as individuals and collectivities, was something peasants in Guaracha clearly wanted and appreciated. But there was still some skepticism about how things would be run after the elections, and in 1982 most people simply wanted to try out leadership by a new faction.

I cannot offer a detailed account of the new administration's tenure of office, since I did not witness day-to-day events after the first five months personally. Shortly after he became commissar, Salvador and some of his associates attempted to renovate the ejidal tractors, though the damage, caused by what looked suspiciously like deliberate running of the machines without lubricants, was severe. I was told of an interview with the *gerente* of the Bank (long since replaced) in which it was intimated that in the event of the tractors being returned to BANRURAL, some benefit from the proceeds of their sale would accrue to the *comisariado*. In response, Salvador convened an ejidal assembly at which the authorities in Jiquilpan were, in effect, forced to give a public account of the terms on which the tractors had been assigned to the ejido, in the presence of senior colleagues from Zamora. It became apparent—to understate the matter—that the procedures adopted were not entirely consistent with modern legislation on ejidal credit societies. In adopting a strategy of manipulating his personal contacts within the bureaucratic apparatus, Salvador did manage to free the ejido from a further burden of public debt, but the process of winning concessions was kept within clearly defined bounds. There was a marked increase in cooperation between ejidatarios in collective work on the infrastructure of the ejido— applauded by Don Gabriel, among others—though it became increasingly apparent that cooperation was limited in scope to particular nuclei of ejidatarios in individual *potreros*. As the economic climate deteriorated further, a certain disillusion seems to have set in. By the time of my return in 1986, there had been new elections, there was much talk of people selling themselves, and the defeated candidate of the previous round was in office. Ejidal meetings once again became rare events. Towards the end of the new commissar's period of office, however, the community as a whole was to receive a salutory reminder of the relative powerlessness of all its official representatives, irrespective of their background and alliances, when faced with superior relations of force in the vertical structure of power.

The village finally achieved its long-standing ambition to have a *preparatoria* constructed in the old hacienda *casco*. The new institution needed farm land for its agricultural courses, and the *secundaria* appeared to have land to spare. Furthermore, it was a frequent cause of complaint that the terrains of the *secundaria* were run as a business by the teachers, particularly on the part of the children, who labored unremunerated for little apparent educational reward. Both the ejidal authorities and the *Jefe de Tenencia* supported the idea of transferring some land from the *secundaria* to the *prepa*, but the newly appointed headmaster and his staff mounted a vigorous campaign of resistance, with, it seems, the support of an ejidatario who is also a school inspector with his own political connections in Morelia. The confrontation culminated in the arrival of the *Policía Judicial*, the arrest of most of the community authorities, and the application of some extra-legal techniques of persuasion. The *prepa* subsequently received some land of lower economic value which had not been incorporated into the ejido, and the *secundaria* was left to continue as before. The incident seems to have caused little permanent animosity between the teachers and the rest of the community, and the use of arbitrary power effected through patron-client ties is scarcely a revelatory experience for any Mexican; but the incident does provide a paradigmatic example of the informal mechanisms of domination which it would be necessary to eradicate in order to secure an empowerment of the peasantry *vis-à-vis* urban society, and of the way the existence of vertical relations can accentuate divisions and interest conflicts within socially differentiated communities.

The ejido is itself differentiated, and attempts to mobilize around a platform of honest administration and securing benefits for all do not inhibit all of the processes that produce differentiation. After he left office in 1985, Salvador and three key members of his *mesa directiva*[10] formed a private association to collaborate in cultivation, dubbing themselves the "*Grupo Contadora.*" By February 1986, they were cultivating four rented *parcelas* in addition to their own land, and had obtained a five year loan from BAN-RURAL to buy themselves a tractor.[11] It must be stressed that Salvador encouraged others to do this while he was in office, and organized deputations to the offices of BANRURAL in Zamora, Briseñas and even Uruapan as well as Jiquilpan. This campaign resulted in at least one other tractor's being delivered to a group which included a number of equally "solid" but far from "rich" ejidatarios who had supported Salvador in the election campaign. Credits were also made available for the purchase of draft animals and plows. Nevertheless, the sum that was to be repaid on the tractors was twelve million pesos excluding interest payments, with penalties should the group fail to repay within the term of the loan. While in theory such schemes should free middle ranking ejidatarios from dependence on a small number of private machine owners and enhance their incomes, they still serve to fragment the ejido and there is a clear additional danger that the benefits of joint machine ownership will not accrue equally to all members of the group even where they are all actually farming their land.

The reform movement therefore led to a modest improvement in the economic position of some members of the reforming faction, but did little to disturb the basic structures of inequality within the ejido. In the 1988 elections Salvador and his associates supported the candidacy of Tito, largely one suspects, in an attempt to continue the struggle against Don Santiago's family in another form, although some of their supporters of 1982 expressed disquiet at this move. Tito won. But by this stage Salvador himself had become the leader of the PRD in the village, and was nominated as the party's candidate for *síndico* in the municipal elections of December 1989. This new platform proved a more than adequate basis for rallying his followers.

This brief history does not suggest that latent antagonisms between different socio-economic strata within the ejido are likely to produce confrontations corresponding to class conflict. Indeed, it might be tempting to attribute the alignments observed to the rather different kind of division between the old *agrarista* families and the new *ricos* who emerged after land reform. But there was some cross-cutting of these divisions in 1982, and while Don Santiago's family continues to occupy a special position by virtue of its wealth, the rise of the PRD has brought further unity to other people who were previously divided by memories of the previous generation's stance and social position at the time of land reform. It should therefore in principle be easier to pose the issue of the future of the ejido in terms of the problem socio-economic differentiation today, though such elements as clerical discourses on "communism" continue to play a role in the hegemonic processes in which struggles concerned with social questions are embedded, just as they did at the time of the first *Cardenismo*. But the main objective of Salvador's original reform program was not in essence very radical: he proposed a renegotiation of some of the terms of the ejido's clientage relation with the state and its bureaucracy for the benefit of a greater number of ejidatarios. Other things being equal, the result of such efforts, though certainly worthwhile, might in the long term reinforce the very forms of domination they seek to confront.

The edifice of bureaucratic domination was designed to limit the possibility of ejidal leaders forming horizontal alliances to demand radical change. To remain popular, a commissar had to provide some tangible benefit to those he represented, and the source of such benefits was the state. As resources become more limited, the power to give or withhold will, at least for a time, remain a potent one, unless resources fall to such a critically low level that maintaining any significant rural clientele becomes impossible. As I noted previously, since 1983 resources have tended to be targeted to a minority in a relatively privileged economic position. Such a "wager on the strong" can produce a backlash effect on the part of those who are left behind, but it could also further the internal disarticulation of the ejidos, particularly if the policy were accompanied by further promotion of mutually beneficial associations between private capital and an ejidal elite. In a carefully engineered policy, "the strong" would include persons below the top socio-economic stratum who might otherwise be tempted to espouse more radical causes. One might assume that people who drive tractors would be likely, in the last instance, to look after their own business. Much depends, however, on the extent to which the state withdraws from a direct economic role in agriculture and what kind of balance is maintained between private (including transnational) capital and the ejidos. Even better-off ejidatarios are scarcely yet "the strong" in terms of this larger context, and the experience of the United States and Europe demonstrates the vulnerability of even relatively highly capitalized family farming enterprises: the price of raising productivity has been a mounting burden of debt to the banks, farm prices have failed to keep pace with the cost of servicing that debt, and governments have proved unwilling to meet the full costs of agricultural stabilization. Furthermore, one could envisage an alternative strategy in which the state withdrew almost entirely from the irrigation districts, on the assumption that a majority of peasants would abandon their land, leaving market forces and direct capitalist penetration of the ejidal system to secure the reproduction of a small ejidal elite on the basis of existing patterns of differentiation thereby securing the benefits of privatization without confronting the question of land tenure head-on. This would free resources for some continuing state support for *temporal* agriculture beyond the margin of capitalist production—a measure which would subsidize reproduction of labor power in the name of "social policy"— although private sector demand for reconversion of arable into grazing land on grounds of "economic rationality" might complicate the implementation of such a strategy.

Assuming that the first scenario were pursued, one might infer that its beneficiaries would feel some residual attachment to a "system" which remains their bulwark against total subsumption by vastly more powerful capitalist forces or the uncertain future of an agrarian radicalism of the landless. A reduction in state support for the ejidos generally would also reduce the opportunities for leaders to profit from the innumerable illicit opportunities for personal advancement which the "statization" of peasant agriculture previously offered them, and the further the process of private capital accumulation is allowed to dominate the ejidos, the more uncertain will be the political consequences. Corruption in Mexico is neither an essential cultural condition nor a pathology but the product of a highly contradictory system which has been held together through perpetual crisis by this redistributive cement for more than four decades, as the state's formal role in regulating capitalist accumulation has shifted in different directions. Given the bipolar structure of Mexican agriculture, and the limitations of the formal policies of state economic support for the ejidos even in those periods when support has been strongest, informal distribution of resources to ejidal leaders has undoubtedly played an important role in maintaining the system. At the same time, it is the very lack of empowerment of the majority of ejidatarios which maintains high levels of official corruption.

Yet while the web of corruption encompasses even the lowly on occasion, this is not in itself sufficient to prevent negative reactions on the part of the disadvantaged, and it is almost impossible to establish an equilibrium, since the balance in the effective distribution of resources is determined within

local contexts as well as by the global effects of official policy. More significant is the capacity of a system of bureaucratic domination to divide and fragment communities through the process of individualization. In the case of the
Ciénega, with its absence of a past tradition of peasant self-organization, the
structures of domination of the 1970s and early 1980s not only proved relatively effective in preventing the formation of horizontal alliances between
leaders of ejidos—since given the extent of their dependence on the state, dissident ejidos could easily be victimized—but the same logic thwarted collective action within single agrarian communities.

Among the many meetings I attended in Guaracha, one of the most memo-
rable was one in which the outgoing administration of Alfredo was to render
its final accounts to the assembly of the agrarian community, an event which
had taken place with an illegal, but for the Ciénega typical, lack of regularity
over the past three years. A representative of the CNC made a quite impas-
sioned speech to the ejidatarios on the need for each to display *"valor civil"*
and denounce any irregularities or wrong-doings on the part of their leaders.
Though it was, at one level, structured around the highly conventionalized
discourse of the institutional revolution, the passion of the performance lent it
authenticity and elements of the audience seemed to be taking its content
seriously. Alfredo rather nervously proceeded to his accounts. "Visit to the
Reforma Agraria in Morelia, to render a *compañero* assistance in a matter
relating to his land rights: *refrescos*, 4000 pesos." On a visit to Mexico, it
seemed that Alfredo must have stayed at the María Isabel Sheraton rather
than in his mother's house to judge from the level of his expenses. From
Alfredo's point of view the accounts were merely a vehicle for his attempting
to persuade the community to reimburse him for the many days on which he
had been unable to attend to his own affairs, and he continued to press (in
vain) for the community to vote him more money at the first meeting after the
new administration took office, which was attended by the BANRURAL officials from Jiquilpan. As accounts in the conventional sense they were an
absurdity and given the general view of Alfredo's administration, laughter
soon turned to hostility. Once again the CNC man encouraged the ejidatarios
to do their duty. An old and poor ejidatario from La Manga stood up with his
fist clenched and embarked upon what would have been a lengthy catalogue
of Alfredo's alleged sins. He was interrupted. What was his name? "We must
get all the facts written down clearly and make a scrupulous investigation." The
problem was that it was left systematically unclear *who* was to be investigated.

The ejidatarios of Guaracha are not really Marx's potatoes in a sack, isolated from each other by their conditions of production. They have always
valued unity and cooperation as ideals and simply tended to despair of attain-
ing them after attending a school of harsh historical experiences. The
hacienda, commoditization and the post-revolutionary state made them what
they are,[12] and the instruments of politico-economic domination were re-
engineered to increase their individuation and powerlessness. Individuals, not

ejidos, were deprived of credits and water. Individuals were protected and rewarded for their cooperation. By official edict, representation of ejidatarios was increasingly concentrated in the person of the commissar. One could send delegations to the offices, but not for the day-to-day work. How could one trust one's leader when he entered the office of the *gerente* alone? There have never been functioning Vigilance Committees in this region, and even if a faction of poor ejidatarios were to back a candidate for commissar, they would need to find a functionally literate representative if he were to have any hope of furthering their cause through bureaucratic channels. In days gone by, commissars had little to do and even less to read. Today one needs a person who understands both the numbers and the documents, the ever more arcane technology of modern forms of domination. The root of this dilemma lies in the fact that, for all its deficiencies as a patron, the state apparatus is the poor peasant's only means of defense in a capitalist society. Those who sow without its financial aid on the basis of one of the forms of peasant adaptation I described in the previous chapter may have no interest in participation in ejidal assemblies nor care who is commissar, but even they may recall that it is the state which guarantees their right to land and might be persuaded to improve the price of maize and subsidize their fertilizer. Attempts at withdrawal or grudging resignation to powerlessness have the same ultimate implications.

In the last analysis, those ejidos which have mounted successful campaigns to secure greater autonomy in the management of their own affairs have nevertheless had to pursue their ends through negotiation with the state, and, as the demands of the Sonoran ejidos suggest, defending and enhancing their gains depends, to a considerable extent, on continuing to pressure the state to create the conditions for sustaining processes of peasant accumulation through market intervention and the provision of new resources for investment. In a context like the Ciénega, the possibilities of breaking out of the structure of bureaucratic domination through a process of peasant resistance and self-organization were probably more limited: the events described for Guaracha indicate the difficulties of sustaining such movements in this region. Nevertheless, the economic contradictions of the 1970s process of "statization" have proved decisive, and as the dominant factions of Mexican capitalism have exercised an increasing influence over state policy, the situation has changed radically. As the material basis for reproduction of bureaucratic domination has decayed, and with it the micro-mechanisms for inhibiting peasant commitment, the rise of neo-*Cardenismo* has provided an alternative to resignation as a response.

DEMOCRACY, SERVICE AND CLEAR ACCOUNTS

One of the most significant dimensions of neo-*Cardenismo* from the Guaracheño point of view is that it implies a change of government and a change of style of government. That such a result seems possible is a consequence of the fact that *Cardenismo* has a natural association with power. Ironically, it was Lázaro Cárdenas's role as President of the Republic which has made it possible for *Cardenismo* to become what it was not in the days when it first emerged as a regional movement: an organic movement which can be presented as the common patrimony of all Michoacanos. One dimension of the movement's power in Michoacán lies precisely in the fact that it can be appropriated as a regional movement, lending it a unificatory quality other forms of political opposition would lack. But there is also considerable emphasis, in the spontaneous comments of rank-and-file affliates of the PRD, on the fact that their struggles form part of an alliance of forces at national level. Certain solidarities, in particular with Guerrero, receive particular emphasis, but there can be no doubt that *Cardenismo* has enhanced confidence in the viability of collective action.

As I have already argued, neo-*Cardenismo* derives much of its force from its ability to confront neoliberalism on the ideological terrain of the foundations of post-revolutionary hegemony, thereby embodying a multi-class project. In 1988, the national movement succeeded in mobilizing the normally non-participant segments of Mexican society and bringing people who did not normally vote to the *casillas*, but its strength in rural areas like the Ciénega also lies in the fact that natural community leaders like Salvador Vargas have committed themselves to a course of opposition to the regime, along with elements of the regional urban petty (and in some cases, not so petty) bourgeoisie and intellectuals.[13] There seems little doubt that much of the leadership perceives neo-*Cardenismo* as a vehicle for improving the terms of their insertion into national society at the expense of the upper echelons of the national elite and the interests of foreign capital: their commitment to social and political transformation, though in many cases undoubtedly sincere, is therefore premised on the assumption that any radicalism will be at someone else's expense, and that such policies will be implemented through a reformed national state machine dominated by a political movement led by their strata. Neoliberalism has brought them into an antagonistic relationship with the PRI, and the success of the Cardenista alternative in July 1988 suggests the possibility of achieving a reorientation of the national regime, but this is only part of the process which sustains the PRD as a mass movement, and there may be limits to the kind of confrontation with the regime which parts of the movement are willing to undertake in the event of a peaceful conquest of power proving impossible. Nevertheless, one should not discount the prospect of an alliance of forces such as is represented in neo-*Cardenismo* proving the vehicle for radical social change, since the prospects of such change may depend rather more on whether the existing apparatuses of power can continue to function coherently than on the animus or intentions of any of the individual groups of actors involved in social and political conflict.

In practice, even the PRD's alternative social and economic program remains extremely vaguely defined, partly, one assumes, as an attempt by the leadership to avoid alienating the elements from higher social strata included in its popular base. The following extracts from the PRD's manifesto for the local elections of 1989 provide an indication of the kind of balances which are currently being struck:

> ...We Cardenistas have a clear *compromiso* with the citizens of Michoacán: to achieve the changes which our State requires to achieve development with democracy and improve the standard of living of Michoacán's families.
>
> We do not promise to do everything, we undertake to do that which the community considers indispensable, giving preference at all times to the zones with greater needs.
>
> We will be rigorous guardians of respect for the labor rights of all the workers and in defense of the peasants.
>
> We propose an economic development which generates employment and just earnings for our population. Private enterprise will be fully respected and we will create investment programs in the cities and the countryside.

Other aspects of the manifesto, which stressed the desirability of municipal autonomy in terms of decision-making regarding the use of resources allocated to local government by the state government, emphasized the style of administration to be expected from the PRD: open meetings, permanent consultation of public opinion, and vigorous action against corruption. These pretensions to democratize municipal life should not be undervalued as an aspect of the PRD's message, and it is worth stressing that the PRD did make a serious attempt to ensure that members of the municipal government would be drawn from different communities rather than simply the *cabecera*. Guaracheños have long complained about their lack of representation in the municipal government of Villamar, and the *cabecera*'s persistent refusal to distribute resources equitably among the *tenencias*. There was therefore a potential radical democratic project embedded in the manifesto, and it is also important to emphasize that the oral propaganda of the PRD on social questions tends to be considerably more radical than the written version, particularly when it is entrusted to some of the intellectuals who participate in the movement.

Nor should one understate the step represented by the occupation of *presidencias* and the sense of their potential power that people acquire through collective action. The ambiguities of the PRD's official social program may not at the present time constitute much of an impediment to its securing the active support of poorer elements of the population, in so far as the symbolic force of *Cardenismo* lies in its promise of empowerment and dignity, and to some extent action itself provides that.[14] Yet if a dream of freedom and dignity is the basis for the movement's appeal to the poor, and such dreams are not irrelevant even to the less poor in a society in which power is as unequally distributed as it is in Mexico, one must question the extent to which its impetus can be sustained as Salinas's sexennial proceeds. The PRI has, after all, retained control of the state apparatus at national level, and denied the PRD control of the state government of Michoacán in July 1989. Neither the government nor national policies can therefore be changed directly by democratic means, which implies not only deepening crisis for poorer families, but a space for the PRI to rebuild its own power after the disaster of the 6th of July 1988, if only by default and the negative process of securing a consensus of resignation. In the municipal elections of 1989, rates of abstentionism were high in most of the state, and although the PRD vote was undoubtedly reduced by the selective non-delivery of voting cards, this must indicate some degree of disanimation of the rank-and-file.

Nevertheless, the elections were scarcely a triumph for the PRI, which conspicuously failed to honor its pledge to eschew fraud, but did concede defeat to the PRD in the state capital, Morelia, seven of the other seventeen major population centers and over forty smaller *municipios*. With three *muncipios* falling to the PAN, and one to the PARM, the PRI was left in control of under half the town halls in the state. Even so, the PRD refused to accept the legitimacy of a number of the PRI victories confirmed by the State Electoral Committee. On the Sunday after the elections, the *Perredistas* in Jacona had held a large public meeting in the plaza and proceeded to add yet another town hall to the seventy or so from a total of one hundred and thirteen already physically in their power. Opposition to the PRI in Jacona had previously been centered on the PAN, which won in Zamora, and all three parties had run with strong candidates who enjoyed personal popularity in the community. The PRI enjoyed the advantage of an opposition vote split between two strong parties. Yet it seems its local agents were unwilling to risk democracy. The PRD's complaints of malpractice were legion, but one in particular—the manipulation of electoral lists—was typical of the state at large in these and earlier elections: certain addresses in Jacona were registered as the domicile of an extraordinarily large number of electors, many *Priistas* had more than one vote, since they held more than one voting card, and many PRD supporters were disenfranchized through non-delivery of their voting cards. The PRD had clearly done extremely well in Jacona, and it seems likely that a considerable proportion of former PAN voters had defected to it, but its occupation of the town hall was designed to force new elections rather than to attempt to wrest victory from official defeat. Nevertheless, the party announced that it would not accept a fraudulently elected PRI administration, and that its candidates would form a "parallel popular power" in the event of their demands not being met.

The PRI proved equally unwilling to play the game democratically in the case of the *municipio* of Villamar: here its tactic of desperation in the *cabecera* was to employ such overt fraud—including providing minors with the facilities to vote—that the opposition would be forced to protest and provide grounds for annulling results from polling stations where the PRD would certainly have obtained a majority in clean elections. Annulment of *casillas* with strong PRD majorities was to prove important in other contexts: the PRI's claim to a narrow victory in Apatzingán was based on the invalidation of results from a polling station where the PRD majority was seventy-nine (*El Universal*, 14th December 1989). In Guaracha, the PRD won handsomely in an atmosphere of total tranquility and rectitude on all sides, the PRI drawing much of its residual support from federal employees and other persons with a *compromiso* with the regime, and the margin in Jaripo was also substantial, though things went more positively for the PRI in the remaining larger population center, San Antonio. Nevertheless, as the polls closed in Guaracha and the substantial size of the PRD majority in one of the two *casillas* became evident, the PRI unexpectedly placed a protest against PRD menacing of voters on the table for inclusion in the packet to be returned to the municipal electoral committee: besides being spurious on the evidence of my own observations, according to the electoral law (and common sense) such a protest should have been made at the time of the alleged events, and was evidently a pre-meditated tactic. The following Sunday the meeting of the PRI-dominated electoral committee in Villamar declared the PRI the victors. More significantly, a group of *Priistas* was carrying arms, though the PRD forces retired in a disciplined fashion from the streets to the captured municipal palace to avoid any possibility of provocations, and took their case to the state committee in Morelia, optimistic of being awarded their triumph. They were disappointed, but proceeded to press for referral of their case to the state congress, confident that they did, in fact, have the support of the majority of the *municipio*'s population.

There was even less sign that the PRD star was waning in the Meseta Tarasca, where the PRD's militants had shown themselves willing to go to considerably greater lengths in terms of violent confrontation to defend respect for their votes than the occupation of *presidencias*.[15] On balance, therefore, despite the dual problems of fraud[16] and abstentionism, the PRD continues to enjoy ascendency in Michoacán, and the PRI's stock has yet to recuperate significantly. Nevertheless, the dilemmas facing the *Perredistas* are substantial. As municipal authorities under a state government still controlled by the PRI both their powers and resources are limited, threatening a further process of disillusion, particularly if decisions have to be made with regard to the use of available resources which entail addressing the social questions. Although discipline has so far been remarkable, the PRI had orientated its attack on the PRD around the question of violence, and frustration alone may lead the movement into a situation of greater confrontation, which might result in some defections. Yet at least some elements of the PRD's base are likely to demand greater radicalism in the movement's stance on social questions, and expect its backing for direct action on, for example, agrarian issues.

In essence, the PRD has so far failed to formulate a completely coherent hegemonic project of its own, defining the exact terms upon which an alliance of diverse social forces is to be based and interests and aspirations reconciled. It centers its strategy on the objective of taking political power through a sustained struggle to win electoral victories rather than the strengthening of its bases through the direct organization and initiation of social struggles. To adopt the latter strategy would, of course, imply a more specific project on fundamental questions of social policy, including redistribution of resources, which would not be without political risk. But to fail to respond adequately to the possibility of mass mobilization created by the triumph of the 6th of July would be to risk instead a slow fragmentation of the movement, converting the PRD into another political party. The situation is already complicated by the break-up of the political coalition which supported Cuauhtémoc's candidacy in 1988, and the appearance of other political rivals for the mantle of *Cardenismo*, in particular the PFCRN (Partido del Frente Cardenista de Reconstrucción Nacional). If the PRD is to sustain, let alone strengthen, its mobilization of a mass base in Michoacán, it will have to keep the alternative it offers, the image of "the possible," alive, in concrete forms which transcend caudillistic loyalties. One positive possibility offered by the capture of municipal government does lie in the prospect of changing the style of the latter towards more participatory and democratic practices: a genuinely popular and imaginative form of local government might be able to mobilize resources from the community which could compensate for the reduction in funding to be expected from the levels of government still controlled by the PRI.

As I stressed at the outset, it is important to be realistic about the magnitude of the barriers in the way of the realization of an alternative hegemony in Mexico in the sense of a fundamental shift in the relations of forces which have shaped post-revolutionary national development. Even in the comparatively heady political atmosphere of Michoacán, the contradictions of the situation are apparent enough as one surveys the panorama of social inequality which characterizes the state and ponders on what needs to be done and what could conceivably be done to change the situation. Even at its lowest ebb, the PRI continues to command not only the macro-mechanisms of power, but a considerable number of effective micro-mechanisms, and the questions of social power which the political process has yet to address in a decisive manner are formidable. All these propositions seem even more valid at the national level.

AGRARIAN STRUGGLES AND HEGEMONY

Although it has experienced its ebbs and flows, agrarian radicalism has proved persistent in Mexico's history: once there has been an agrarian reform in theory, it is hard to banish the idea that agrarian revolution might be consummated in practice from popular consciousness. Despite repeated declarations from the presidential chair that there is no longer any land to redistribute, peasants have found an expanding number of *latifundios* to invade over the decades (Paré 1988). At the outset, López Portillo's administration was particularly insistent that the state's role would no longer encompass regulation of land tenure and would henceforth be restricted to the provision of economic support to existing ejidos: "distribution of the product, not the land." Despite the damage this pronouncement inflicted on the legitimacy of the regime in the eyes of the rural poor, López Portillo underscored the definitive nature of his position by making Toledo Corro, cattle farmer, latifundist and Mexican representative of the John Deere agricultural machinery company, his secretary of Agrarian Reform in 1978 (Bartra 1985:135). The CNC leadership had agreed to abandon the struggle over tenure, and some CTM leaders even began to demand the privatization of ejidal land (1985:140). During the first two years of López Portillo's presidency, levels of state repression escalated continuously—sometimes extending to the physical destruction of communities—while a renewed confidence in the wisdom of violence was apparent on the part of private *guardias blancas*: the average number of *campesinos* dying per month in the agrarian cause had reached twenty by 1978. But by the end of that year, faced with mounting rather than diminishing rural resistance, the CNC was again denouncing *latifundios* and Toledo Corro was talking of "the initiation of a historic moment" as he began to implement new orders of expropriation (Bartra 1985:136).

Even so, López Portillo's administration continued to preserve some elements of its initial orientation. Besides its promotion of associations between private capital and the ejidos, the *Ley de Fomento Agropecuario* sought to legalize the practice of rental of ejidal land, and gave new guarantees to private property and private investment (Gordillo 1988:267). Although the consequences of this piece of legislation were not as profound as many expected, it could be seen as a step towards a covert process of privatization of the ejidos. But the other major initiative of the second half of López Portillo's sexennial, the SAM, led in a different and contradictory direction: while it emphasized "integrated rural development" and the use of price and credit policy to redistribute income within an unchanging agrarian structure, there was an implicit suggestion in the program's proposals with regard to achievement of food self-sufficiency that a condition for success would be a reversal of the "pastoralization" of agriculture—in turn implying the possibility of further land redistribution. Although the SAM's successors in the De la Madrid sexennial, the *Programa Nacional de Alimentos* (PRONAL) and *Programa Nacional de Desarrollo Rural* (PRONADRI), were pale imitations of an already flawed prototype, it seems impossible to pose the issue of the basic foods problem in Mexico without raising the issue of the structure of rural land tenure, and despite a vigorous propaganda offensive mounted by cattle ranchers early in the Salinas de Gortari administration against the "irrational" arable use of land that would be better employed for grazing by infrasubsistence peasant farmers, it will prove difficult to suppress peasant action against the pastoral *latifundio*. Nor will it be easy to ignore the broader social issues connected with the pastoralization process discussed in the previous chapter. In modern industrialized societies, animals "eat men" in a multiple sense. A "pastoralized" countryside maximizes neither rural employment nor society's potential production of protein for human consumption; free market forces will continue to give urban and foreign consumers of meat commanding higher incomes precedence over Mexico's poor, consigning those whom pastoralization displaces from the countryside to an increasingly undernourished urban future.

Given the fact that capitalism has proved so deficient in providing alternative livelihoods for rural people, and given the institutionalization of *agrarismo* in the structure of the state apparatus and in legislation which sets limits on private landholding, it will be no easy task to end the agrarian side of the Mexican revolution. Furthermore, while the urbanization process has shaped the problems of the countryside, the limitations of the urban alternative to rural existence must, to an extent at least, encourage agrarian resistance. Difficult and often bloody though such struggles have proved, independent agrarian organizations like the *Unión de Comuneros Emiliano Zapata* in Michoacán have continued to exploit the contradictions of the postrevolutionary hegemony by focussing direct action on cases where the legal situation was favorable, with some success in the early 1980s. But the pattern of action became increasingly defensive after 1983 (Zepeda 1986: 366-367), the phenomenon of internal factionalism which dogged the movements in the *Meseta Tarasca* in the 1920s has reappeared in a violent form in some of the communities affiliated to the UCEZ in the last few years, and the situation is complicated by a variety of other forms of mobilization focussed exclusively on ethnic politics. Furthermore, even if we take an optimistic view about the potential for solidarity between the different types of social actors found in the countryside and the levels of commitment to fundamental change on the part of peasant leaders and footsoldiers in the mid-1980s, the age of agrarian revolution *as such* has now passed. This is not to say that urbanized, industrialized Mexico has no further need of agrarian reform, but simply to recognize that Mexico is no longer a peasant country. Tackling the social question in the context of a vastly more complex modern class structure represents an infinitely harder task conceptually than the one which confronted Lázaro Cárdenas in 1934, and it is certainly much harder to see what configuration of existing social forces might succeed in establishing an alternative hegemony and pattern of development in the country.

Keeping the discussion at a very abstract level for the moment, it might be possible to conceive of a hegemonic project which would unite the urban working classes, peasantry and elements of the domestic bourgeoisie in an economic nationalist reaction to the existing thrust of neoliberal policy, given a conjuncture of circumstances unfavorable to maintenance of economic stability. Yet it remains very uncertain how much economic nationalism would be possible under modern conditions, and what the consequences of an extreme version of economic nationalism—such as the "war economy" advocated on a number of occasions by David Barkin—would actually be. After all, quite lowly segments of the economy of Michoacán, for example, are highly integrated into the U.S.-Mexico economic network, not simply in terms of labor migration, but in terms of various spheres of commerce and domestic production. To some extent at least, one could argue that these networks have acted to moderate the impact of crisis in the national economy (Zepeda 1987). Admittedly, the increasing internationalization of the economy has some highly problematic implications for industry as well as agriculture. Levels of direct U.S. control of the domestic economy have increased substantially, and while this is presented as a positive process of "investment" in official circles, much of the growth generated thus far has been in the form of *maquiladoras*, a type of industrial development which has little commitment to permanence. Since Mexico's entry into the GATT shops have filled with cheap imported consumer goods of low quality—often, no doubt, manufactured by Mexican hands—and even products such as sweets are now as likely to come from American as from national factories. Nevertheless, it is by no means certain that this model of development is incapable of producing at least a kind of economic dynamism benefiting a significant minority of the population, nor, more significantly, is it entirely clear what kind of alternatives are open.

Let us suppose that a determined effort were to be made tomorrow to eliminate Mexico's problems of poverty. How much redistribution of income and resources would be required? What kinds of social and economic reorganization would be required to meet that objective? How much of a sacrifice would such a program involve for the middle strata of society, particularly if there were an aggressive reaction on the part of the United States? These are not questions I am equipped to answer, but they are not questions which many people seem anxious to pose. As the experience of the government of Salvador Allende in Chile demonstrates, they are questions which need to be posed. There are some impressive environmental as well as social and economic arguments for transforming the nature of Third World development processes via a transformation of the relation between town and country. In the framework of a radical redistribution of rural resources and major changes in lifestyles, it is possible to conceive of the possibility of a process of de-urbanization which could have a major impact on the quality of life as well as constituting a more "sustainable" pattern of development (Redclift

1987). But this kind of transformation would involve levels of coercive (and presumably centralized) intervention not only in the market but in terms of property relations without precedent in Mexican history: and it might not simply be the dominant class who would need to be coerced. Indeed, as we have seen, one of the major contradictions of Mexico's development process is the fact that "urban bias" is partly associated with the problem of ameliorating the problems of the urban working classes, whose real incomes are also relevant to the welfare of their rural kin. It is one thing to revolutionize an agrarian society, quite another to dismantle the complex social legacy of an advanced process of industrialization and urbanization.

It has become fashionable in the West to declare socialism an established historical failure on the grounds that socialist countries are now abandoning planning in favor of "the market" and are convulsed by demands for political democracy. Such arguments choose to ignore the fact that the existing socialist societies, while certainly not egalitarian, liberated from alienation in the workplace, nor free from the bureaucratic form of domination, are not actually societies the basic structure of which is determined by economic class relations (Giddens 1980). Mexico is a class-based society, and one in which a very small economic elite has exercised a substantial influence over the policies adopted by a patently undemocratic form of government. This is not to say that mass reactions to the effects of those policies have not influenced the course of Mexican post-revolutionary history in a significant way. Nevertheless, the hegemonic apparatus established in post-revolutionary Mexico has canalized the process of class struggle in a way which has promoted capital accumulation by the few at the expense of the many and at the same time made the state a necessary intermediary in the subordinated classes' attempts to negotiate the terms of their exploitation. There is no denying the extent to which the particular rhetoric of the Mexican national revolution has been interiorized by the subordinated classes, even in their radical moments, and one line of interpretation of neo-*Cardenismo* would be to highlight the "third way" quality of the Cardenista paradigm—in a sense a "socialism," but a Mexican socialism that leaves the extent to which private property is to be eliminated open, a program in which the "social question" is paramount (poverty and misery must be eliminated), but in which the root causes of poverty and misery are left without the kind of definitive definition offered by Marxist versions of socialism.

It has also now become fashionable—if not very original—to argue that class-based politics are increasingly irrelevant to the advanced capitalist societies and to see the so-called "new social movements" as the agents of a global struggle against bureaucratization, massification and commodification in search of more decentralized, participatory forms of democratic political order (Gledhill 1988b). The anti-statism and lack of a "totalizing" social project characteristic of the new social movements is seen as a symptom of their newness and liberating potential, although it is conceded that the processes underlying the production of the antagonisms expressed in the individual movements can lead them, through the contingent articulation of social and political discourses, in what are, in traditional terms, rightist as well as leftist directions (Laclau 1985:33). But the experience of neo-*Cardenismo* seems to suggest that the long-term potential of a plurality of heterogeneous social movements to transform the structures of social power depends entirely on their subsumption within a broader, universalizing, hegemonic project, and the enormous weakness of this whole line of analysis is its refusal to recognize that the social question can only ultimately be resolved by addressing the issue of state power. Neoliberalism in Mexico proposes to strengthen "civil society" *vis-à-vis* the state, and it is undeniable that this discourse can have some appeal to weaker groups in civil society which are struggling to emancipate themselves from bureaucratic domination—including peasant organizations striving to achieve autonomous management of their own process of production. Yet, as we have seen, even the most aggressive protagonists in this kind of struggle have made demands on the state which relate to the non-discursive conditions of the hegemonic process and the unequal distribution of economic power in particular. Leaving aside the fact that the implementation of the neoliberal project has thus far been dependent on a denial of respect for the political votes of a majority of the citizenry, the market does not even correspond in principle to a democracy in which every voice is of equal value.

Up to a point, perhaps, the creation of democratic institutions from below can be a vehicle in a struggle to transform the larger political system, though as Zepeda's analysis of the UCEZ demonstrates, fomenting participatory democratic organization in communities in which vertical caudillistic relations have previously predominated is by no means easy (Zepeda 1986:359-360). But the state apparatus remains the lever by which mobilization is translated into a shift in the balance of social power, into the appropriation of real resources claimed by other elements of civil society and into changes in the broader economic conditions which govern the value of those resources as a basis for livelihood. Advances by independent movements are related to the fact that the responses of higher agencies of power are determined by the balance of all the diverse forces which impact on those agencies' behavior: what appears as the work of a faction conjuncturally dominant in the state apparatus or the result of internal struggles within the apparatus, is, in fact, conditioned by relations of force at the level of the whole social formation. While the new social movements may play a significant role in a Gramscian "war of position" against the existing order, to the extent that they can actually install democratic practices at the base, they also reflect the way the mechanisms of the existing hegemony tend to fragment and disarticulate popular struggles. If negotiation with the state apparatus remains the ultimate focus of social action, then rearticulating those struggles, and creating the social conditions for the realization of their goals, must entail the conquest of the state itself.[17]

Even if this is not the sole factor involved in present changes, neoliberalism reflects the extent to which the model of accumulation established from the 1940s onwards has proved increasingly deficient from the point-of-view of the private sector. If we assume that resolving the social question in Mexico requires a new (and radically different) model of development, one possible way in which such a change might come about might be through a radical failure of the neoliberal project, which is heavily dependent on the future health of the U.S. and world economy. Should the economic situation of the country deteriorate significantly, exacerbating what remains a substantial social and political crisis, the capacity of the existing political apparatus to control the situation might well prove inadequate, since the strain to which it is already subject is evident enough. This is the risk inherent in any attempt to introduce any fundamental change in the hegemonic process "from above."

The classical social revolutionary scenarios were all premised on the radical disorganization of existing state apparatuses, and while the content of any modern cataclysm in a developed society like Mexico would certainly be different, it is not impossible to envisage such a scenario, notwithstanding the greater efficiency of modern technologies of repressive power. As Therborn has suggested, following the lead of Barrington-Moore and Skocpol, just as feudalism was not destroyed by its fundamental form of class conflict, that between lord and peasant, there is no real theoretical reason to imagine that the normal form of transformation of capitalist societies would be through its fundamental form of class-struggle (Therborn 1987:89). Class relations and their associated ideologies are important in the sense that they are the principal vehicle through which alternative possible social forms are defined, but there is no reason to think that new social worlds will not continue to be created by complex coalitions of social forces, just as they were in the past. Classical forms of working class organization—trade unions and political representation through social democratic parties—may be judged the normal mode of class struggle under capitalism in the sense that they entail forms of conflict (from the perspective of the bourgeoisie), but forms which secure the reproduction rather than the transformation of the fundamental relations of the system (Therborn 1987:54; Gledhill 1988b:263-264). But the ideologies of "the possible" which achieve an organized form under a capitalist regime remain vital, since the collapse of an existing hegemonic apparatus cannot lead to social transformation unless there exists an organized alternative, even if the actual shape of the future society is negotiated over a long period through the readjustment of the social forces involved in the initial destruction of the old order and may be different from that originally propounded at the ideological level. Some of these considerations are clearly equally pertinent to a less catastrophic scenario for Mexico's future.

As far as the situation in the countryside is concerned, the broad panorama of post-revolutionary agrarian history suggests the ebb and flow of a continuous agrarian struggle whose counter-point is renewed state intervention, renewed cooptation and incorporation of independent peasant leaderships, and transformations in the nature of an equally enduring rural *caciquismo*. The equilibria achieved are evidently unstable, and despite profound socio-economic changes, the agrarian issue seems to remain an important element in the formulation of alternative possible social worlds in the Mexican case. But it is necessary to pose the issue of whether we are really dealing with the same question or the same kinds of peasant organizations today as in the past.

Gordillo has suggested that there is a significant difference even between the situation of the Echeverría period and that which accompanied López Portillo's precipitate change of emphasis, in that in the earlier period change of state policy was directly related to generalized peasant mobilization, with factional conflict within the governing apparatus playing a secondary role, whereas in the later period, intra-state conflict (as reflected in the simultaneous formulation of the SAM and the *Ley de Fomento Agropecuario*) was intense and profound, and agrarian mobilizations were regionalized (1988:267-268). It is clear that the early forms of rejection of the official apparatus of incorporation, the CNC, corresponded to attempts to form independent organizations replicating the CNC's structure as a "central"—the *Unión General de Obreros y Campesinos de México* (UGOCM) and the *Central Campesina Independiente* (CCI) being obvious examples of this process. But by the time of the crisis of the Echeverría period, there is an apparent parallel with the situation prior to the Cárdenas regime: a proliferation of independent organizations operating at state level, a few of which are attempting to extend their influence into neighboring regions (Bartra 1985:110-111). Some regional struggles are still formally conducted under the auspices of the official centrals, though they generally lack any organic links with the leaderships of those organizations (Gordillo 1988:263). But the general tendency is towards an increasing rejection of centralized structures of organization towards umbrella organizations which attempt to escape the bureaucratization and cooptation characteristic of the early model: the most important of these is the *Coordinadora Nacional Plan de Ayala* (CNPA), established in 1978, of which the UCEZ in Michoacán was a founder member.

The Echeverría reform had, however, also changed the context in which future agrarian mobilizations could operate, Gordillo suggests, in two ways. In the first place, statization restored a situation in which the primary basis for the regime's legitimacy in the countryside was to be its support for peasants already in possession of land, and a corollary of this was the "rise of a new peasant social actor"—the peasant producer organization. From an initial basis in regional Unions of Ejidos, this development eventually produced its own national coordinating body, the *Unión Nacional de Organizaciones Regionales Campesinas Autónomas* (UNORCA), at the end of 1984. At the same time, Echeverría's reforms raised the stakes for any further process of land redistribution: conceding any significant further advance to the cause of agrarian radicalism from this new base would "risk breaking the basic pacts of the state with the dominant classes," and this promoted the increasing regionalization of the struggle for the land (Gordillo 1988:264-266).

The natural predisposition of the forces represented by UNORCA must, as I have already indicated, be towards negotiation with the state rather than total confrontation, although this process may involve intense and even violent forms of conflict in particular regional settings. Given that the economic problems facing producers in different regions are not identical, it is unsurprising that UNORCA favors mobilization on a regional level. Furthermore, a majority of producer organizations continue to be affiliated to the CNC. The problems facing the CNPA as an organization are somewhat different: its *agrarismo* is associated with much greater levels of confrontation and repression, but where demands for the land were realized, the new ejidatarios frequently entered, or reentered one of the officially recognized organizations, the CNC or CCI, since they now faced different problems. In 1983, 60% of the base organizations of the CNPA were groups seeking land rather than established ejidos or communities, half of the regional organizations affiliated to it had a predominantly indigenous base, and most of its current demands concerned land tenure (Bartra 1985:152). In an attempt to expand its base, the CNPA reformulated its program to embrace the problems of *jornaleros* and ejidal producers in 1984, the year in which it led a highly successful march of peasant militants from the four quarters of the republic to the capital in collaboration with the UGOCM *Roja* and the *Central Independiente de Obreros Agrícolas y Campesinos* (CIOAC), the latter founded as the peasant arm of the Mexican Communist Party, though its primary regional base is in Veracruz. Standing in the Zócalo on the 10th of April 1984, it may well have seemed as if the forces of Zapata had returned to reoccupy Mexico City. But this triumph was shortly followed by divisions: some sections of the CNPA sought to pursue the struggle through explicit alliance with the parties of the Left, and others, including the UCEZ, argued that this represented a betrayal of the movement's autonomy, while the CIOAC had already entered into certain compromises with the state at the time of the SAM (Gordillo 1988:276-277). At the time of the presidential elections of 1988, the CNC's power to engineer a successful outcome for the PRI in many rural areas of the country was still evident, and abstentionism remains, as I have already noted, a significant factor even in Michoacán in the new situation created by the rise of neo-*Cardenismo*.

The structures of incorporation which have sustained the post-revolutionary hegemony are far from defunct: although the PRI governor of Michoacán, Genovevo Figueroa Zamudio, will, from the beginning of 1990, look out on a state capital governed by the PRD, his party's campaign had benefited from its continuing control over large sections of the population employed directly by the state or represented through the official trade unions, and these tentacles run deep into the social fabric of the country. There seems to be no question of "modernization" leading to the abandonment of these bases of power.

For Gordillo, the root of crisis in the countryside in the long term has never been the state's non-provision of resources, but the post-revolutionary state's tutelage of the *campesinos*, their reduction to the status of a "rural infant." Eschewing what he presents as the two poles of "privatization" and "statization," he proposes greater peasant control over productive processes as a "third way" which would leave the state in control of global policy within the framework of a new "social pact" to share out the burdens of austerity, all premised on the revitalization of the ejido as organ of peasant representation and respect for the peasant vote (Gordillo 1988:281-282). The empowerment of ejidatarios is essential, but one can see fairly readily how such proposals might be manipulated in a populist rhetoric as accompaniment to one of the neoliberal scenarios for resolving the problem of the countryside discussed earlier. If change were to consist solely in turning ejidos into autonomous economic actors, rural communities would be still more profoundly subordinated to the polarizing logic of the fundamental relations of the economic system. Isolation of the ejido from the other elements of rural and urban society which are the victims of Mexico's model of development is the first step along a path which could culminate in the internal decomposition of the ejidos themselves. The broader process of politicization and alliance between disparate social forces associated with neo-*Cardenismo* and the PRD can embrace the kind of project espoused by Gordillo, but on much broader social terrain. If the forces congealed in the PRD continue to define the PRI's surrender of power as the only acceptable form of victory—and it is by no means certain that the political leadership of the party will not prove willing to compromise that objective—there is a continuing possibility that a more fundamental shift will eventually occur on the terrain of those "pacts" with capital that maintain large sections of the population in a permanent condition of crisis and poverty.

Justice does not entail that people be equal in all respects, but the injustice of capitalist society is that wealth remains the primary determinant of life chances in other spheres. Misery is to be found in both rural and urban places. But rural society suffers the additional injustice of being devalued in an urban world, despite its role as the producer of the most basic material conditions of life. Rural people have both interiorized and resisted the condition which has been imposed on them, but it is certain that a solution to the national social problem must entail the delivery of the promise of the revolution: full social emancipation. Economic security and absence of material deprivation for all are necessary but not sufficient conditions for the emancipation of the countryside, and emancipation cannot ultimately be delivered from on high. In their continuing struggles for dignity and self-organization rural people are achieving the other dimension of emancipation, but they cannot achieve it alone. The traditional Marxist prescriptions of alliances between poorer elements of the peasantry and the urban proletariat seem to have little practical meaning in modern Mexico: the urban and rural popula-

NOTES

CHAPTER 1

[1] But since such transactions are extra-legal, the land cannot become a commodity in a full sense, and remains cheaper than it would be if it were actually private rather than state property.

[2] It must be said, however, that some renters of land from outside the ejido who sow grains do not necessarily produce particularly splendid harvests, often because they are too busy with other interests and contented with a small profit on what by their standards are low costs. And when the renters are agrarian bureaucrats the bulk of their costs may, in fact, be met from the public purse without reimbursement.

[3] To some extent, intensified policing of the border assists the situation of people who have the most entrenched and rooted migratory networks, since those who do not are less likely to succeed in crossing.

[4] The key differentiating factor is level of education, but this is in part related to past differentiation in migration possibilities between different strata in the community.

CHAPTER 2

[1] Don Victorino operated eighty mulepacks plying the northern trade from Tangancícuaro, owned by Spanish merchants (Hamnett 1986:25-26).

[2] It is important to emphasize that there were substantial variations in the effectiveness of the attempts of liberal "modernizers" to "reform" colonial systems of land tenure throughout Latin America. Even where communal land was eventually transformed into private property, the past existence of village-level institutions for regulating access to land or other communal resources might influence subsequent developments and patterns of social conflict. Communities like Guaracha which were founded by haciendas clearly had a different micro-institutional history from their beginnings, but additional distinctions could be drawn between "indigenous" communities—like Villamar—which were encapsulated by haciendas at any early stage and communities of the kind found in the Meseta Tarasca. These considerations may be significant for placing the post-revolutionary developments recounted in this book into comparative perspective, though it is interesting that, as we will see, even the Guaracheños recount their myths of dispossession and talk about their historical experience in terms of ethnic models of power and stratification.

CHAPTER 3

[1] See Alonso (1988) for further discussion of this issue in the context of northern Mexico.

[2] San Antonio's land was entirely given over to sharecroppers, though the community was also the prime source of the additional seasonal labor which was required by Guaracha.

[3] I should stress that despite the increased bureaucratization of the epoch, the Porifirato did not displace the *caudillo* system, but on the contrary transformed it into a mode of centralized state power based on personalistic ties between Díaz and regional bosses: to this extent at least the Porifiran state was "*caudillo* politics writ large" and structurally compromised (Gledhill 1987, 1988a).

CHAPTER 4

[1] It is, however, true that former members of the hacienda administration continued to be employed in the mill after it passed into public ownership.

2 The last administrator of Guaracha, Manuel Robledo, came from a Guaracheño family, and was related to a few of the new ejidatarios by ties of kinship or affinity.

3 The structure of peasant representation through the CNC becomes increasingly hierarchical as one moves upwards from the ejidos towards the national leadership, which is appointed directly by the current presidential administration, but the fact that even regional leaders are not persons of peasant background is a cause of particular complaint at the grass roots.

CHAPTER 5

1 See, for example, Hewitt (1980) for a particularly trenchant exposition of the qualitative difference between the agrarian policy of Cárdenas and the policies of subsequent regimes. I would not wish to deny the existence of a difference, but I see it more in terms of potential rather than accomplishment, since I take a more jaundiced view than Hewitt on the internal historical limitations of *Cardenismo*. Any attempt to revive the Cardenista project of "integrated rural development" under modern conditions would have to grapple with both the external and internal, political, conditions for the successful pursuit of such a strategy. But it is certainly true that the kind of "agrarian populism" which emerged under Echeverría, for example, differed fundamentally from the original *Cardenismo*, despite its occasional rhetorical appeals to that tradition. Echeverría's administration not only abandoned all idea of further radical land redistribution and applied strict technocratic managerial principles to the new collective enterprises it established (Sanderson 1981), but showed no practical concern for the principle of the social empowerment of *campesinos* which was at least present as a *project* in the original Cardenista movement.

2 The expression "self-exploitation" describes the form of the peasant adaptation to deteriorating market circumstances accurately, but is not a valid description of its substance, since peasants are forced to augment their labour inputs and receive a lower rate of payment for that labor by the control other classes exercise over the social process we call "the national economy."

3 Though mechanical preparation is now universal in the agriculture of the plain, use of animal traction continues to dominate up to the present day for cultivation of standing crops during the rains, and a few still prefer to sow manually with animals rather than use a tractor and mechanical seeder.

CHAPTER 6

1 Their wives are treated as widows here, though their situation was arguably worse, since they had no prospect of remarriage.

2 It is certainly significant that Don Gabriel only once rented a *parcela a la cuarta* rather than for cash, the land in question being held by an ex-*agrarista* who refused any other arrangement as a matter of pride.

3 The *neolatifundio* was, of course, still in its formative stages in the 1940s, but the data on long-term rentals during the 1950s presented in Table 10 below seem even less supportive of this hypothesis, though there was an increase in the proportion of ejidatarios involved in seasonal U.S. migration in the 1950s, and it is probable that more people were "passing" their *parcelas* for short periods at this time.

4 This effect of long-term contracts becomes most apparent in the 1970s, when a number of male heirs anxious to return to the land after the introduction of the new credit policy found themselves in difficulty.

5 Which is the "insurance" is not always clear, but it seems from stories recounted to me in other contexts that members of the local political elite were as likely to consult the curers and herbalists as the poor. Since they tended to assume that their illnesses had unnatural political causes, this is perhaps not surprising.

[6] The calculation also excludes a number of cases where I know that the holder of a *parcela* rented for a couple of years because of some family crisis and then resumed sowing it.

[7] The case of one of the internal migrants was more conventional and unconnected with economic factors or family development: he shifted his residence to Jiquilpan following a killing and the period of rental was very brief in this case, a matter of letting tempers cool.

[8] The *congeladora* in which the wife, Consuelo, had worked from December to July for eight years was unionized, and offered its workers social security benefits, bonuses and paid vacations. Payments were on a piece-rate, and it should be stressed that even the strongest, most adept and experienced female workers would only earn between one and two thousand pesos a week in the peak season *before deductions*, at a time when the rural male day wage was 200 pesos. Many women found the cramped working conditions unbearable, and some scarcely covered their travel costs. Women like Consuelo did, however, probably achieve more paid days of work a year than the average *jornalero* working only in Guaracha. Before she worked in the *congeladora*, Consuelo had worked as a field-worker for the *jitomateros* in Guaracha: here women earned only half the male rate, the male preserve of carrying the tomatoes from the field to the packing area being constructed as heavier work impossible for women. The family had resumed cultivation of the *parcela* again by 1982, and this is one of the few cases where husband and wife worked together on the land. Two single sons remained resident in the village, one working as a domestic outworker sewing jeans, and a single daughter worked in domestic service in Mexico City. In 1986 the *parcela* was again rented to a *jitomatero*, though by this stage it is probable that more of the children had married and were no longer contributing either labor or income to the parental household.

[9] Although Don Gabriel has himself sown some vegetables in more recent years, both on his private land and rented ejidal *parcelas*, much of the land he rents continues to be sown in grains: the enterprises of the *jitomateros*, analyzed in more detail in Chapter Nine, are much larger scale operations, based on the integration of production located in different micro-regions and the process of commercialization.

CHAPTER 7

[1] Daughters sometimes enter domestic service in their early teens, and residence with kin in cities may be a significant factor in the entry of young women of rural origin into other sectors of the urban workforce.

[2] Most urbanized Guaracheños display a marked enthusiasm for returning to their rural place of origin. Even people who have achieved substantial social mobility generally keep up some form of contact with their poorer relatives. The economic nexus between them ranges from regular financial aid to family outings which terminate in the car driving off laden with pumpkins and white maize that the relatives could scarcely afford to give away, but while few receive substantial financial aid from migrant siblings, the rural-urban parent-migrant children link tends to be central to the processes of household reproduction, irrespective of the economic position achieved by children in the urban economy and the marked patterns of socio-economic differentiation which may emerge between them.

[3] Western Mexico is defined here as the states of Zacatecas, Nayarit, Sinaloa, Colima, Aguascalientes, Guanajuato, Jalisco and Michoacán. Arroyo Alejandre's study calculates rates for age groups between twenty and forty years, each group spanning a range of five years.

[4] Defined as those where twenty-one to sixty per cent of the population live in communities of 2,500 inhabitants or less.

[5] Agrarian reform and state intervention in the exploitation of the forest resources of the region had a restraining effect on out-migration from the communities of the Meseta

Tarasca in the Cárdenas years. *Comuneros* who had previously engaged in seasonal migration to the haciendas of the Tierra Caliente turned to the exploitation of forest resources, despite the manner in which the rationality of the state's policy, and the continuing disguised dominance of private sector interests, impeded small-scale exploitation (Espín 1986:168-169). From 1973 onwards, however, the abolition of traditional controls accelerated rates of exploitation of the forests by private companies, and other forms of capitalist expansion—tourism, cattle-raising and avocado production—have added to pressures increasing levels of both migration and agrarian conflict (Zepeda 1986:326-331).

6 Arroyo Alejandre 1986:lxxx-lxxxii. Guaracha's relatively high levels of participation in higher education may not have a great impact on the municipal figures. The education factor could, however, also influence rates of out-migration in the higher age groups, since educated people are also likely to move to other regions.

7 Guaracha's resident population may not be substantially less than that of the *cabecera*. My own census recorded a resident population in Guaracha of 3,460 persons in 1983, and some people whose main residence is urban do maintain a house in the village and return regularly to attend to land or other assets they continue to control. One thousand, one hundred five children of resident families were engaged in migration. Villamar's population is estimated officially as being over 5,000, but Guaracheños observe that Villamar contains a much larger proportion of *emigrados*. The official census apparently failed to survey a significant proportion of houses in Guaracha.

8 The notion that men are "heads of households" in some natural sense is not simply androcentric, even allowing for consistency of such an assumption with local cultural values ostensibly shared by both sexes—itself a problematic formulation. It may also be analytically misleading where the "male head" plays a less significant role in the household's reproduction than his wife. I use the formulation here only to distinguish households which are headed by widowed, separated or divorced women from those where a senior resident man contributes regularly to household income: in a few cases, couples are not legally married.

9 In one case, the abandoned wife was working in the United States.

10 The latter factor is especially important in the sphere of international migration, since landless households had much reduced possibilities of entering the United States as *braceros*. Nevertheless, the effect of this past difference in the structure of opportunities on the population resident in the village in the 1980s may be influenced by the fact that those who enjoyed reduced opportunities for international migration were more likely to opt for permanent internal rural-urban migration.

11 A son-in-law of Don Santiago, the ex-administrator of the neolatifundist Don Gabriel, he had received help from his father-in-law in establishing himself in this occupation.

12 Four male heads of household had recently been laid off from public employment at the time of the census and are not included in these figures, but the numbers of Guaracheños whose livelihoods had already been affected by the policies of Mexico's international creditors by early 1983 was substantially greater, since unmarried people tended to be dismissed first.

13 In a very few cases, the couple had met because the wife had come to the community to teach, and in one of these cases the male partner was not himself professionally qualified, though he was both relatively educated and relatively affluent.

14 See, for example, the moving interview with a *maquiladora* worker published by Bustamante (1983:252-254), and the even more traumatic extended case-history provided by Arenal (1986).

15 It is difficult to place precise figures on the incidence of one type of behavior over the other, and current "normality" in practices probably lies somewhere between the polar situations of great self-sacrifice and total disengagement. Parents may claim that they receive more aid from their children than they actually do because they feel a sense of

shame, but were often explicit about the absence or unreliability of those income remissions which were normatively expected of single children. Parents were asked to specify whether income was received regularly or sporadically, as well as its quantity. It would be idle to pretend that such data can ever be totally reliable, but I was able to supplement many of the questionnaire responses with more direct knowledge of the family's circumstances.

[16] Manual workers employed to unload trucks in the Guadalajara *Mercado de Abastos*, for example, enjoy monetary earnings which are the envy not only of other types of manual workers, but of many non-manual employees: the need for speed and intensive application of labor power at peak moments in the daily cycle of operations in this highly profitable sector justifies the cost from the employers' point of view, while the workers who succeed in obtaining this type of employment often compare it favorably with the U.S. migratory option. In comparing the returns from different types of employment it is also necessary to take into account the nature of the work itself, its long-term impact on the health of the worker, and the kind of non-monetary benefits and security it offers. The "neo-liberal" policies pursued by the state in the years after these data were collected have tended to depress salaries in some areas of public sector employment demanding relatively high qualifications.

[17] Parents are not always very precise about the kind of employment their children enjoy. A major reason for imprecision is the variability in the extent to which the children continue to contribute to parental income. It is equally clear that the parents sometimes simply do not know how much the children are earning because the children in question are careful not to give them precise information on this matter. And in a few cases the child's real occupation is not a matter for public disclosure.

[18] There are only three unambiguous cases in this last category, all of which are enterprises operated by a married couple.

[19] It is important to remember that a number of other Guaracheños moved to and settled in the cane-producing regions of Michoacán, Jalisco and more distant states in the past, rather than to the cities, and that the migration of some professionals is also to other rural places.

[20] One of the latter is, in fact, another person of locally contested occupational categorization in the border region.

[21] Cousins, especially male cousins, constitute an important category of kin to Guaracheños, and individuals may well be able to activate useful relationships with both parallel and cross-cousins in the context of migration, even if they have never met before: indeed, the term *primo* is sometimes applied beyond the range of parents' siblings' children, where a more distant kinship is recognized as further support for aid between persons with a common community of origin (*paisanos*). But while *primos* often enjoy warm relationships, divisions dating to the agrarian reform period, more recent feuds between different lines of kin, or a reputation for violence or anti-social behavior on the part of a particular line may all militate against acknowledgement of kinship in practice. There is only a weak normative expectation that cousins *might* help each other, since this is a context where responsibilities to one's own children within the individual family unit take precedence even over aid to parents.

[22] In the case of the United States, and of some forms of internal migration within Mexico, such as the movement to the cane-growing regions of Sinaloa on the part of agricultural migrants, part of the clustering phenomenon is related to the activities of *coyotes*, contractors and recruiting agents of local origin whose primary clients are their *paisanos*. Nevertheless, even here concentration also results from the operation of more diffuse and spontaneous social networks operating at the household level.

[23] Both capitalist and ejidal agriculture employ child labor on a paid basis; ejidatarios sometimes have to "make do" with inexperienced and ill-disciplined young children as peons for scattering fertilizer and other relatively light tasks in the production cycle sim-

ply because adult men are not available in the season when the greatest number of workers are absent in the North.

[24] No stage of education is entirely free of costs, though it is true that costs rise progressively as one proceeds up the educational ladder. Primary education in Mexico is theoretically provided free by the state. In practice, parents have always been surcharged illicitly in a number of ways at the state primary school, and some prefer to send their children to the Catholic primary school in the village for ideological reasons, thereby incurring greater costs. Landless families may have been more inclined to pursue the latter course to the extent that they included the highest number of persons with long-standing ideological antagonism towards the secularizing state and land reform.

[25] Some students studied at this level in Zamora, though they generally lodged with relatives there, and a few attended the *prepa* in San José de Gracia. Others went as far as Morelia, Mexico and Guadalajara, though they might also be working in those locations.

[26] The number of households in the "mature" category is naturally relatively small in the case of the households of resident sons of ejidatarios: five, in contrast to 118 in the case of ejidatarios, and 72 in the case of landless households.

[27] The local community is full of praise for the old federally-recruited teachers, and full of censure for the present pedagogic generation, some of whose appointments are without doubt nepotistic in character. The results obtained by the old *Escuela Práctica de Agricultura* were certainly impressive, to judge both from the migrant generation and those of its alumni who remained *campesinos*. For further discussion of the *Escuela Práctica*, see Pardo Galván (1982).

[28] There are no married male migrants in this category in the United States.

[29] One is not simply a teacher, but headteacher of a primary school and secretary of the local branch of the teachers' union.

[30] Many rural teachers of peasant origin in this region have at least sympathized with the "left" of the ruling party in the past, the role of school-teachers in past episodes of radicalism in Mexican history is obvious enough, and militant teachers have played a key role in development of neo-*Cardenismo* in Michoacán. On the other hand, as public employees teachers can be subjected to pressure by the state, and it is also apparent from earlier remarks that teachers may buy ejidal titles and use their earnings and the institutional resources they control in other self-serving ways. The policies of the government of Salinas de Gortari with respect to the teaching profession seem unlikely to promote quiescence on the part of those who continue in the profession. But while there is no particular reason to think that those who embark on a career of emigration will applaud the regime for bringing them to this pass, their choice of migration looks like an alternative to the course of political resistance. Such a judgment on their future potential as rural political leaders might, however, prove premature given the uncertainties inherent in their situation in the North and the drastic nature of the socio-economic changes which neo-liberal policies might provoke in regions like the Ciénega.

[31] 10% had only been to the U.S. since the end of the *bracero* program, and 7% had made trips both before and after 1964.

[32] See, for example, the evidence presented in Arenal (1986) on the *maquiladoras*. Their stratagems for disposing of those workers who retain their health—in the interests of thwarting worker self-organization and avoiding their legal obligations as employers—include offering "vacations" to those innocent enough not to realize that they will not be re-hired when they return. It might be argued that the border enterprises represent an extreme case, but temporary absorption followed by expulsion of single women is just as characteristic of the industrial structure of Guadalajara, where it is also clear that women factory workers are relatively well-educated in comparison with male workers in the same sector (González de la Rocha, 1986:207). Indeed, in the second half of the 1980s it is increasing apparent that the *maquila* system itself is proliferating to other zones of Mexico as the domestic economy becomes increasingly internationalized.

CHAPTER 8

[1] In 1981, the weekly wage of these migrant construction workers was around 2,800 pesos, while a peón earned between 100 and 150 pesos a day, and could only find the equivalent of two or three days work a week. Higher living costs in the cities have to be offset from this favorable balance, along with travel and the dangers of an industrial injury in this sector, but workers could return regularly to their homes. Their net earnings were not, however, generally sufficient to invest in improvements to the house, or buy consumer durables like furniture, stoves and record players (Trigueros and Rodríguez Piña 1988:207). Those were the aspirations of those who went to the North. "Unskilled" work in construction is one of the principal entry-points into other sectors of the urban labor market for migrants who settle in the cities, and workers in construction who are classified as "skilled" enjoy larger relative pay differentials than those characteristic of many other sectors (Escobar 1986:174-175), but this reflects the way the association of "unskilled" construction work with rural migrants is self-reinforcing: this segment of the labor market is open because pay and conditions are unattractive in urban terms, a situation which is perpetuated by the fact that it is open to rural migrants.

[2] See Walker (1985) for a discussion of this figure. As will become apparent in later stages of the discussion, migrant remissions are only one facet of a complex of economic flows produced by the establishment of stable networks of cross-border social interaction.

[3] It is vital that we never lose sight of the fact that at least as many people entered the United States illegally during the period of the *bracero* program as entered as contract labor. The change after 1964 is simply relative, though certainly far from insignificant.

[4] Again, Bustamante is to be applauded for emphasizing the complicity of the Mexican state in these processes. Although the experience of César Chávez in the early 1960s did demonstrate the unwillingness of *bracero* migrants to embrace unionization, their behavior must be put into context: their own government had accepted American proposals for further reduction in the degree of legal protection to which they were entitled in the 1950s, and insisted that they could secure legal representation in the United States only through Mexican consular officials, many of whom were also deeply involved in the "business" side of the *bracero* program described below.

[5] Machines harvested 1.5% of California's tomatoes in 1963. By 1968 they harvested 95% (Solkoff 1985:151). Mechanization had begun earlier in other sectors, such as cotton. Though the *bracero* program reduced the pressure for technical innovation, its low labor costs also, ironically, made it easier to finance where other considerations made this desirable (Cross and Sandos 1981).

[6] Even if the trip eventually produces earnings sufficient to meet the family's basic needs and leaves a small surplus for luxuries, the danger of losing work prematurely through harvest failure, capture by the *Migra*, or the sudden collapse of an economically fragile urban enterprise, place the family economy in a permanently precarious position which encourages women to seek additional sources of income.

[7] Paying taxes and knowing how to claim social security benefits do not guarantee success in claiming one's entitlement, and the fact that so many regular migrants are not unionized clearly does not help. Many take the view that union dues are a luxury they cannot afford and prefer the "insurance" offered by *contratistas*, despite its limited practical benefits. Undocumented migrants may join unions where they obtain regular work in an enterprise with a substantial union presence.

[8] International migration has, however, had a readily apparent effect on local vernacular Spanish in the form of loan words. One hideous but revealing example is the ubiquity of the word "chance" (opportunity), which is used in innumerable contexts both to inquire about possibilities and to make direct requests. In other words, its usage derives from the migrants' repeated need to inquire whether there was any work going and then to ask that they, individually, be given the "chance" to do it.

[9] Since these locations extend to many other zones of the world economy besides Mexico, there can be no question of this process having any substantial impact on rates of migration from Mexico. In any case, the offshore plants favor the employment of women, and the *maquiladoras* have not only failed to have any impact on male migration, but have actually stimulated female movements from the plants across the border (Bustamante 1983b).

[10] Only three persons are in fact *emigrado* in this sample.

[11] Three subjects are single, and one childless.

[12] In the detailed interviews, I could not record total migration histories for every member of each subject's family in view of the numbers involved and the fact that many children were currently working in the cities, but this information was obtained from the questionnaire data provided by my total census of the population.

[13] A number of people only went "cuando Padre Emiliano," in 1951 and 1952, because they lacked the wherewithal to raise the normal costs and the stomach to try their luck *al alambre*.

[14] The average age of landless migrants is forty-seven, that of ejidatario migrants fifty-seven, and that of migrant resident sons thirty-nine.

[15] So did the sister of one of the long-term migrant farm workers. Single women are as likely to be employed in this sector as men, although female migrants may also work in agriculture, particularly when they accompany farm worker husbands, and domestic service inevitably figures strongly in female employment patterns in the North. Of the nine wives who are known to have accompanied their landless migrant husbands, five worked in the fields, and two in domestic service, while another, an *emigrada* through her father from another community, has worked in both domestic service and factories. Divorced or widowed women generally seem to concentrate in domestic service.

[16] At the time of the interview this old ejidatario had three sons in the U.S., only one of whom was there legally.

[17] Armando Bartra has suggested a similar correlation between an upsurge of agrarian struggle and the mass deportations of 1954 and 1955; he estimates that one in every four rural workers was a repatriated *bracero* in the mid-1950s (Bartra 1985:80). But the regional impact of the process would reflect differential patterns of development after land reform: in the neolatifundist environment of Guaracha, the primary economic significance of the repatriations was probably a reinforcement of the depression of real rural wages. Nationally the demand for rural wage-labor did not increase in line with its supply during the 1950s, and the average number of days worked by *jornaleros* fell as well as the average rural real wage rate, but the continuing replacement of peasant farming by neolatifundist agriculture would tend to mitigate the local effects of population growth on employment, though not on real income.

[18] Alfredo reiterated the point that the *acordada* evicted the dependent families of migrants: it was important that he was the unmarried son of a man who remained a productive worker.

[19] His father belonged to the category of hacienda workers with special responsibilities, but received land as an original ejidatario, almost certainly because his *Norteño* son was on good terms with his fellow *Norteños* among the *agraristas*.

[20] Office-holding might bring a few personal benefits, but for some at least, it seems to have been largely a question of wishing to enjoy a degree of public esteem. The functions of *Jefe de Tenencia* were not very extensive in the 1940s, 1950s and 1960s. Only the most minor juridical matters were handled at the level of the *Tenencia*, and little in the way of public money flowed into the village in an era in which official sources invested little in infrastructural improvements. The post of commissar was also neither onerous nor lucrative by contemporary standards. Only a handful of people sowed with BANJIDAL, and the commissar's main function was to coordinate with the SARH in the distribution of water. Even the commissar's chief legitimate perk, a 25% cut of the pro-

ceeds of all sales of pasture, was not introduced until the later 1960s. Villamar was a very different matter, since it enjoyed control of resources flowing through political channels as municipal cabecera, and was not subject to quite the same degree of domination by outside capital as the neolatifundist core in Guaracha. The quantity of both public and 'free floating' private economic resources to be struggled over was therefore rather greater in Villamar.

21 It is quite common today for older men to retire to Michoacán from a life-time's career in the North. There is little doubt that the vast majority of the children they bring back with them have serious difficulties adjusting to life in what is now a vastly more alien cultural milieu relative to their birthplace in the North.

CHAPTER 9

1 See, for example, Sanderson's discussion of the ramifications of agribusiness vegetable and citrus fruit processing with regard to the nutritional objectives of the *Sistema Alimentario Mexicano* and cereal production (Sanderson 1986:96-109).

2 As noted earlier, a further twelve *parcelas* created during the formation of the individual ejido have never been assigned formal titles, though their *dueños* have the rights of ejidatarios and may receive BANRURAL credits. A similar proportion of this land was rented in 1982.

3 Again, however, this type of development is not immune to secular changes in land values. A young or middle-aged man could acquire a second *parcela* very cheaply in the early days of the ejido. Those who wish to pursue a subsistence-orientated strategy based on a combination of crop and livestock raising today would be least likely to be able to afford to buy prime quality land, and even the costs of buying cows has escalated relative to *campesino* incomes. Having a sorghum harvest to sell annually and a daily income from milk sales may provide sufficient cash to meet the costs of sowing half a hectare of alfalfa, providing cash needed for consumption and maintaining the herd. But starting from scratch would be a quite different matter.

4 Official documents are often very misleading in this regard. BANRURAL credits, for example, may be secured in the name of the legal title holder for use by persons renting the land. In one list, from 1986, one finds an elderly ejidatario who had supposedly achieved the notable coup of securing BANRURAL credits for sowing tomatoes: the real cultivator was the *gerente* of BANRURAL in Jiquilpan himself. Many titles remain vested in absentees, and it is not unusual to find the names of the long dead as well as the long gone in official documents, since decades pass without any definitive revision of titles.

5 This calculation rests on the assumption that the few cerrile *parcelas* which have been permanently divided between multiple cultivators should continue to be treated as a unit. Excluding them would reduce the number of resident cultivators of ejidal land in 1982 to one hundred and ninety. Only three persons refused to be interviewed, and the other cultivators not interviewed represented cases where the land was being sown by a professional person or the cultivator was absent at the time of the interview program.

6 This depends, of course, on the kind of professional training they have received and the branch of the agrobureaucracy for which they work. Many of the ejidatarios' problems lie in the area of defending themselves from abuse through official manipulation of accounting systems and the provisions of agrarian legislation, and any kind of agrobureaucrat ally in the community is potentially useful. Since, however, useful agronomic advice is singularly hard to obtain from those officially charged with providing it in the Ciénega, other than in the form of pamphlets and "special relationships" with SARH personnel established at some cost in terms of food, drink and other inducements, the potential value of having professionally competent personnel within the ejido is substantial. People frequently remarked that it would be nice if the SARH engineers lived in the *campo* rather

than the towns, and it might also be said that their characteristic vision of rural development reflects the same kind of urban bias that determines their choice of place of residence.

[7] Cultivators I interviewed in 1982-83 spoke of borrowing money from various patrons at
rates of 10%, repaid in cash, to meet money costs of cultivation not covered by official
credits. In some cases, loans are secured free of charges, though the relationships
involved may not be entirely disinterested in other respects, and debts are still used as a
lever for securing land for rental.

[8] He finally withdrew from the ejido, after suffering a series of losses, in 1986, and had,
indeed, only had one really successful harvest prior to my interview with him early in
1983. His sowings in 1982-83 were financed from a 1,400,000 peso profit (on costs of
300,000 pesos) made on a 4.5 ton onion harvest in 1981, and he failed to repeat the success in the following cycle. In the course of the interview, it became clear that he saw
himself as a quite different sort of person than the "ricos" of Cojumatlán, for whom he
had earlier worked as a *peón*, and to whom he generally sold at least part of his own produce for onward shipment to the *Mercado de Abastos* in Guadalajara and other national or
international markets. His self-assessment of his identity was validated by the ejidatarios'
lack of *envidia* towards him and the easy relations he enjoyed with many of them.

[9] This preliminary statement is not intended to encapsulate the entire substance and determinants of the changes provoked in official policy by the crisis of the early 1970s. While
the structural base of the crisis lay in the long-term effects of the configuration of rural
production systems, its conjunctural force was amplified and spread throughout the economy by changes in Mexico's international trade position, provoking a dramatic intensification of rural social conflict—now more closely articulated to urban social movements
(Bartra 1985:100-102). Mounting socio-political crisis forced the Echeverría administration to abandon its earlier refusal to make any *agrarian* concessions, and 1973 also
marked the beginning of a period in which there was a significant increase in the flow of
resources destined for the rural sector (Rello 1986:57).

[10] Another variant which is internal to the workings of the bureaucracy is where the
ANAGSA indemnity to the Bank is greater than the actual amount of credits paid. This
scheme requires someone to sign for the spurious credits within the ejido, but an obvious
candidate is the commissar. Forgery of signatures is commonplace, and particularly easy
where peasants cannot actually sign their names.

[11] Standards of tractor driving in the community were also somewhat variable, skill and
attention being a distinct pre-requisite in the case of a mechanical *escarda*. People often
complained that they had suffered problems of seed regeneration from the previous
year's sowing or unevenness of plant germination because of poor handling of tractors,
though it must be said that in at least some cases this was more evidently a result of the
dueño's having "economized" on some of the stages of mechanical preparation to save
the money for other purposes.

[12] The small size, irregular shapes, uneven surfaces and poor access routes characteristic of
many ejidal *parcelas* do create suboptimal technical and economic conditions from the
point of view of mechanized harvesting and bulk transport, and the fact that adjacent
parcelas may be sown in different crops adds to these limitations. Machine harvesting of
maize was still in its infancy in the ejido in 1982. Although the machine of Don
Santiago's widow was equipped to harvest maize, labor still had to be hired to cope with
a substantial number of flattened stalks and there was considerable spillage, again a
reflection of the problems of applying a North American technology to a radically different farming system.

[13] These "informal" processes lead to discrimination even within the private sector itself in
crisis years. Both Don Gabriel, with potatoes sown on his ranch in Jiquilpan, and the *jitomateros* spent a considerable amount of money on maintaining their water supplies in
the drought of 1982. But Don Gabriel suffered the indignity of seeing a politically pow-

erful neighbor securing water to plant supposedly prohibited strawberries, while his own yields were reduced. There are sound technical reasons for the SARH's reluctance to drill artesian wells to supplement the output of the dams—though permission has, in fact been granted to some private users to sink wells. An extension of pump-fed irrigation would accelerate depletion of underground supplies, exacerbating an already critical situation produced by competing industrial demand (and contamination) in the Lerma-Chapala basin. But the politics of water at regional level are determined by the relative informal power of different types of users and the contradictory nature of national development policy: pump-fed irrigation systems have already been allowed to produce catastrophic saline infiltration elsewhere (Sanderson 1986:196).

[14] One ejidatario, the village postman, who is a relatively comfortably off member of the community able to risk experiment, sowed PRONASE wheat in the dry-season cycle of 1980-81. He obtained a profit of 28,000 pesos on 16,000 costs, less than his returns from sorghum and beans in the following cycles, with a 9 ton harvest from 3.5 hectares and a price of 4,800 pesos a ton, though in this case the harvest was sold to the mill in Jiquilpan rather than to the PRONASE itself.

[15] Tito also experimented with sowing more maize in 1982, planting 15 hectares of maize to 10 hectares of sorghum, though his maize was of the ordinary commercial variety, 12 hectares irrigated and the rest *temporal*. This reflected the general improvement in maize prices, although drought caused heavy losses in maize, and the price of sorghum rocketed at the end of the year as animal feedstuffs became in short supply in the commercial sector. Tito was also the ejidatario sowing vegetables in Casa del Trigo in 1982, planting tomatoes and onions, along with 1 hectare of beans which were intended purely for family consumption. All these crops were sown privately, since BANRURAL does not offer credit for any of them, including *temporal* beans, on grounds of risk.

[16] This may not have been an entirely disinterested act, since Julián also offered to transport harvests to Briseñas in the early days. In the 1981-82 winter cycle, he and Tito had combined to buy *cartamo* harvests from other ejidatarios and sold them direct to the oil factories in Guadalajara. This is another reflection of the way agro-industrial integration creates opportunities for "rich" ejidatarios to insert themselves into the chain as intermediaries and thereby pull further away in economic terms from their fellow producers. But the appearance of such intermediaries selling direct to the market within the ejidos has further implications: in the previous year the Bank had apparently instructed producers to sell their *cartamo* harvests to Don Gabriel.

[17] Julián blamed the shortage on the fact that "everyone wants to study now," implying that adolescents were a significant source of harvest labor for him. He also noted, in the context of a discussion of his plans to expand his production of onions—which he had already sown in one *parcela* in the winter cycle with good results—and other medium cost and risk vegetables in the future that increases in labor costs associated with the greater labor intensity of these cultigens was mitigated somewhat by the fact that a proportion of this labor would be female, and therefore cheaper and more readily available on demand than adult male labor.

[18] Francisco also worked in the cane both in Michoacán and Sinaloa during the 1960s, and then spent a disastrous year in a unionized electrical factory in Mexico City, injuring a finger and hating every moment of city life. He obtained his work with the SARH a few years later, and paid his only (unremunerative) visit to the U.S. in 1976, with a guarantee that from his employers he would be able to return to his job. He described the labor contractors he worked for in the North as "*puros pinches metegentes.*"

[19] A striking indication of the existence of such influences is provided by the fact that a number of ejidatarios in the Ciénega decided to sell their land titles during the period of spectacularly high bank interest rates in the final years of the De la Madrid administration, although the decision subsequently proved to be a poor one.

[20] The normal BANRURAL credit for 8 hectares of maize, to which PRONASE added sup-

plementary credits for later stages of the process and rebates, was 16,000 pesos in 1982. This informant had already spent 16,900 pesos before receiving the credits, made up of: plowing, 6,400 pesos; sowing the *hembra*, 2,850 pesos; pesticide against caterpillars, 1,400 pesos; freight for fertilizer and seed from Jiquilpan, 1,050 pesos; and furrowing and sowing the *macho*, 5,900 pesos. He did not possess his own plow team for the *escarda*, and anticipated hiring sixty to seventy man-days of harvest labor.

21 Don Julián said that he did not experience serious difficulties securing fertilizer for those crops he sowed with private sector credit, though he did have to go to Zamora and Guadalajara to obtain it, and did not pass up offers of sales through less formal channels.

22 Carlos only went once to the United States, in 1973, with the specific purpose of earning enough money to buy his own house. But he stayed two years, working in a factory in Bernais, and then in the fields in Merced.

23 Manuel hinted that the antagonism arose from the fact that he had himself received rights in the original ejido whereas the neighbor had bought his way in from an anti-*agrarista* background.

24 People generally prefer to pay in money if they can, since the real value of maize payments tends to be higher than the *jornal*. Manuel did sometimes sell corn from the *ecuaro "por cualquier necesidad."*

25 A few have *ecuaros* which can be prepared by tractor, though such a resource commands a relatively high price if it is purchased.

26 One of his sons is also an ejidatario, who bought his land in the 1960s. He entered into an *a medias* arrangement with the then ejidal commissar to sow onions on his *parcela* in La Manga in 1982. But the fact that the son put up the land and the commissar the capital is an index of the fact that this entire family belong to the "solid" stratum of *campesinos* who have managed to reproduce themselves through a generation without any significant accumulation of capital. The other sons are relatively uneducated Mexico City migrants, and it is only the next generation which is achieving mobility towards the middle class. It is, however, noticeable that the families which form this "solid" stratum in the community also form a series of clusters of closely related people.

27 This fact was not only evident in the data provided by cultivators on present versus past yields, but in the testimony of some of the larger herders of cattle, who emphasized the impact of reduced pasture yields on the costs facing potential new entrants into cattle-raising.

28 Although La Mesa is unattractive to capitalist entrepreneurs, a considerable proportion of its land has been rented to people from the *ranchos* behind Guaracha who are primarily interested in growing pasture for their herds. All the "solid" cultivators in this *potrero* are people who have either had more than one resident son working with them—in between trips to the United States and independent work as *jornaleros* and *ecuareros*—or have enjoyed income remissions from absent children who were long-term U.S. migrants or achieved some professional qualification. Even in the latter cases there were resident sons to aid in cultivation as well. In the case of one other ejidatario in La Mesa who had no son, and whose working life was terminated by a car accident, the family labor was supplied by an unmarried co-resident half-brother.

29 A number of other beans cultivators explicitly stressed this point. But maize prices in the village did rise further and faster than beans prices in 1986, at 46% and 27% between February and August, the only period for which I have complete data. The monetary value of a kilo of beans remained 300% higher than that for maize, an important consideration in evaluating the real returns from production of small areas of beans using minimal commoditized inputs: Juan estimated his cash costs at only 3000 pesos for 1.5 hectares, sowing with animals and hiring no non-family labor. But the significance of the lower inflation rate for beans prices may be that poorer Guaracheños were being forced to lower their consumption, an issue discussed further below.

30 The proportion of ejidatarios keeping goats is even smaller. Only twelve of the cultiva-

tors interviewed in 1982 had any goats, and seven of these possessed less than ten. Two had herds of between ten and fifty animals, and three others had herds of eighty, one hundred and thirty and two hundred respectively. Since goats breed rapidly, it would be appropriate to say that all five with more than ten animals took goats seriously, and at least one ejidatario renting his land to a kinsman was also a serious *chivero*. The owner of the largest herd was the ejidal commissar, whose *jornalero* brother was charged with their care when the cultivation of the commissar's onions took priority.

[31] The majority of cultivators I interviewed regarded this as the optimal technique, though it was less frequently practiced than sowing in a furrow created by a *tronco*, since it more than doubled sowing costs if peons were hired, and some people complained that today's *jornaleros* were inadequately skilled in the technique.

[32] Poor garbanzo crops are sometimes sold "green" to merchant intermediaries, and a number of cultivators reported poor results in each of these years, making no attempt to sell their produce but feeding it direct to their animals or even selling the crop on the *parcela* for grazing. But even allowing for the fact that garbanzo may have some value as feed where it is technically cultivated at a substantial loss, the tonage of *cartamo* harvested in 1982 must have been at least four times greater than that of garbanzo, much more than compensating most who sowed it for the difference in costs per hectare of up to 100%, depending on standards of cultivation and quality and quantity of fertilizer applied, an effect then reinforced by its higher market price.

[33] Winter wheat cultivation enjoyed a shortlived revival after 1983 in Guaracha, as the state began to respond to the displacement of wheat in other regions. A SARH technical booklet on its cultivation issued from Sahuayo was revised to correspond to the new realities, beginning: "El trigo es un cultivo que se adapta bien a esta región y es necesario incrementar su explotación para evitar que México importe del extranjero." As in the case of PRONASE maize, rather more than promotion and technical advice will be required to effect a permanent shift in cropping patterns, but another major limitation has been scarcity of irrigation water.

[34] One elderly ejidatario in El Salitre who habitually sowed beans—with financial aid from a daughter in the United States—appeared one day full of indignation because a peon had demanded he supply new batteries for his ghetto blaster! "*Ahora los peones son los dueños*," he complained. Like many older men, he often had the relatively young children of other people working for him, sometimes truant from school. Faced with an elderly, and rather kindly, peasant *patrón*, such workers tended to be much less cooperative than they would have been on the land of one of the ejidal entrepreneurs or in a commercial tomato harvest, and I sometimes wondered whether the low quality of the labor provided did not wipe out any cost saving in the long-term, though it eased the immediate problem of scarcity of cash for production.

[35] He also always had a resident son to help him farm and his wife was a sister of the last hacienda administrator, which may have helped him to continue sowing his land independently through the difficult years. Two of his sons are professionals. Nevertheless, one of them—now an engineer in Puebla—had also been to the United States, like Felipe and Joaquín, as had another son who remains an urban bus operator in Guadalajara. There were few real silver spoons in the mouths of the first generation of ejidatarios, and Joaquín complained that his wealthier urban siblings never helped them financially but simply helped themselves to their produce on visits, something he attributed to the high-spending habits of their non-Guaracheña wives.

[36] His salary, paid by the municipio, was only 100 pesos a day, but this job left him with a day free for other work.

[37] The eldest of his four children, aged eighteen, had just completed prepa.

[38] His sister also studied agronomy. During his time in Mexico, in the second half of the 1960s, living costs were lower, and by working a twelve hour day, he latterly managed to send 270 pesos a week back home while maintaining himself—modestly one sus-

pects—on 150 a week. On weekends he played baseball.

[39] The agricultural regime of the Ciénega is, of course, a reflection of the "ganaderización" of Mexican agriculture, in turn a facet of the internationalization of capital (Barkin and Suárez 1985:221-224) and changing urban consumption patterns (Rello 1986:50). One might argue that in the absence of any attempt to control the tendency at the level of the national economy, greater participation of the ejidatarios in the raising of diary and beef cattle would be desirable, although schemes to increase cattle ownership promoted by BANRURAL since 1983 have been very clearly targeted at better-off ejidatarios.

[40] Miguel still enjoyed the help of a (paid) worker de confianza—his son-in-law—who is also an ejidatario, though he subsequently joined the ranks of the ejidatarios returning to U.S. migration, in this case after a lapse of many years.

[41] Manuel himself, however, had a significant career of bracero migration in terms of the duration of his early trips, and invested migrant earnings in cultivating tierras ajenas as well as buying a parcela of his own.

[42] In one case, an ejidatario of limited means in El Camiche sowed his parcela in alfalfa for four years by entering into a private partnership with an agrobureaucrat working for the SARH Rehabilitación branch in Jiquilpan. Otherwise, only those who have cattle themselves now sow it, and generally in limited quantities with another crop.

[43] It is important to emphasize the pyramidal and monopolistic organization of the production of high-value crops. The production of crops such as tomatoes, strawberries, melons and avocados is organized through Uniones Agrícolas Regionales, in turn controlled by the Unión Nacional de Productores de Hortalizas (Rello 1986:100-103). The grower associations were formed to improve the position of Mexican producers vis-à-vis the U.S. transnationals, but even where ejidatarios form a numerical majority in such organizations, they are dominated by the most powerful private growers and a handful of ejidal caciques, and the commercial elite who control the UNPH in turn exercise a decisive control over the activities of the UARs, particularly in the field of exports. Nevertheless, as Durán demonstrates, American distribution companies continue to exercise another, decisive, level of control over the grower associations, despite the fact that processing and packaging are left to local capital in some branches of the food industry (Durán 1988:101-107).

[44] Pedro was given his parcela by its original holder, his step-father, who migrated to Uruapan.

[45] I make no pretence that these data are significant from the point of view of analyzing nutritional welfare, an issue which would involve a much broader consideration of diets and intra-household distribution of food, accompanied by the use of biometric techniques quite beyond my resources and competence. Nor, for the same reasons, can I attempt any assessment of the negative welfare effects produced by alcoholism in the community.

[46] Many of the region's rural vehicles are brought back from the United States, and may be sold relatively cheaply locally, since, unless the new owner meets the expense of importation procedures and re-registration, they are likely to be confiscated by the police. But most families in Guaracha cannot afford the running costs of a vehicle.

CHAPTER 10

[1] While it is certainly necessary to criticize the results of the process of "statization," part of those results has been determined by the scope allotted to the logic of international market forces by the nature and limitations of state intervention. As is again recognized in the proposals of the Sonoran ejidos, development of the internal national market is a condition for significant advances in terms of the employment prospects and welfare of the rural (and urban) poor (Gordillo 1988:168), and such a pattern of development is scarcely conceivable without further resource redistribution.

2 COPLAMAR (*Plan Nacional de Zonas Deprimidas y Grupos Marginados*) was established in 1976, and represented, *inter alia*, one of the Mexican state's few significant interventions in the field of distribution of basic goods. It was brought into the ambit of CONASUPO with a view to strengthening the program's effectiveness as a vehicle for guaranteeing the lowest-income consumers access to basic goods at subsidized prices.

3 By the end of the De la Madrid administration, it was becoming clear that a "neo-*bracero*" arrangement was evolving, as U.S. employers responded to the changing situation created by the Simpson-Rodino law and the impact of crisis in Mexico by taking on more Mexicans as legal (short-term) contracted labor. Under the new dispensation, new migrants are effectively on probation, and subject to close scrutiny. Many have had to travel outside the traditional areas of Guaracheño settlement to find regular work, and earn little and spend much in the period in which they are establishing themselves. Undocumented migration, however, typically does not show any signs of diminution, despite the fact that only 10% of the H2A entry visas for agricultural laborers authorized for 1989 were utilized (*La Trilla*, Number 6, October 1989: 32). Many who entered with visas for farm labor in fact sought other kinds of work. The CNC has begun to advocate Mexican administration of a formalized legal system of labor contracts as part of its contribution to moderating the political effects of deepening agricultural crisis, demanding that access to the U.S. labor market be restricted to "real peasants" (rather than school-teachers and other "less needy" persons). It is difficult to imagine such a proposal could lead to any more beneficial results than the original *bracero* program, and it indicates the official *central*'s complicity in the present drift of state policy.

4 As PRI governor of Michoacán, Cuauhtémoc Cárdenas was not, as far as I could discern, particularly well-liked by the peasantry of the Ciénega, though it must be admitted that the abysmal record of his successor, Martínez Villacaña, forced to resign before completing his period in consequence of scandalous personal conduct and his marked lack of affinity with political modernization, would have retrospectively enhanced the reputation of almost any predecessor.

5 In his later years the old *caudillo* did, of course, adopt a more explicitly favorable posture towards socialism, sought to protect the Left from persecution, and expressed his support for the formation of new independent mass organizations, in particular the CCI. Whether one should interpret any of his actions as a commitment to the idea of a fundamental transformation of Mexican society must be open to question: see, for example, Armando Bartra's commentary on the significance of Cárdenas's patronage of the CCI (Bartra 1985:92). It does, however, seem plausible to argue that Cárdenas's actions reflected his frustration with the turn taken by social policy under Alemán and his successors, and his increasing recognition that the hegemonic apparatus of the institutional revolution was ossifying. As Enrique Krauze has remarked, once out of power, Cárdenas began to understand the problems of concentration of power—to which he had himself made a signal contribution (Krause 1987:181).

6 In his earlier writings, Gramsci's discussion of "hegemony" concerns the conditions for the proletariat's establishing its leadership of a revolutionary class alliance. In the prison writings, it is broadened into a theory of bourgeois power which transcends utilitarian and instrumental conceptions of the state, and indeed, extends the concept of the state and its hegemonic apparatuses well beyond the domain of political institutions and agencies of government (Buci-Glucksmann 1978).

7 To some extent, Salinas could be said to have appropriated the program of the PAN, and cooperation between the PAN and the PRI could be mutually beneficial in the sense that the former are unlikely ever to win national power in their own right while the latter would benefit from moderated opposition from this quarter. Nevertheless, the concession of the state governorship of Baja California to the PAN and subsequent promises of greater access to power were followed by a refusal to recognize some PAN victories in Sinaloa in municipal elections in 1989, suggesting that it may not be so easy for the cen-

ter to impose its will on the local forces controlling the party apparatus at regional level.

[8] *Caciques* who must habitually resort to violence to implement their control under modern conditions are likely to lose the backing of their patrons in higher circles, and the optimal form of *caciquismo* is one where the *cacique* provides enough benefits to his clients to retain their support both for himself and the power structure without resort to coercive or repressive violence. It is not hard to find examples of other styles of *caciquismo* even today in Michoacán, and both use of violence and monetary purchases of votes and loyalty are indices of the weaknesses of the hegemonic apparatus of the state and the decentralization and segmentation of power which persists despite extreme administrative centralization and an autocratic form of presidential government. For a discussion of the relationships between these apparent paradoxes of the Mexican power structure, see De la Peña (1986).

[9] I was invited to attend these and did so. The other party did not, as far as I am aware, campaign by means of open public meetings, preferring to solicit support on the basis of approaching individuals.

[10] One of them was "Don Carlos" in El Camiche, one the single son of an old ejidatario, and the other an ejidatario sowing the lands of his grandfather and great-grandfather, who had also worked driving combines and tractors for one of the leading ejidal entrepreneurs of Villamar. All are close friends. Though the group has mainly cultivated sorghum, Salvador's agrobureaucrat younger brother also came to play an increasingly active role in the enterprise, and his earnings helped finance additional capital investments and some diversification of the crops the group planted, which included a modest sowing of tomatoes in 1989, although, as so often happens, the experiment was unprofitable because the price proved very low at harvest time.

[11] In order to do this, they had to produce a "society" of ten cooperating ejidatarios, and among the names appearing on the list were elderly kin who held ejidal titles, including a widowed aunt and absentee uncle of Salvador. The typical existence of "phantom ejidatarios" in these associations places a question mark over their effectiveness as a means of creating greater equality: it is difficult for poorer ejidatarios to participate in them and it is also difficult to find ten individuals who have sufficient *"confianza"* in each other to agree to manage a joint asset of such value in the first place, let alone to succeed in managing it—hence the need for the phantoms.

[12] The people themselves often offer a quite different sort of explanation for the absence of cooperation between non-kin: the mixture of their races. As well as reflecting the power of the European forms of racial stratification imposed by the colonial reconstitution of society in the Americas, the self-blame at the heart of this model is an index of the power of the hegemonic socio-cultural structures to which they are subjected.

[13] Although it must be stressed that some elements of the regional professional classes remain activists of the PRI, including teachers, the rise of a dissident and militant teachers' movement in Michoacán has played an important part in the mobilization of other elements of the population, and militant teachers played an important role in the PRD campaign in the Ciénega.

[14] In any assessment of the historical role of Lázaro Cárdenas, the one factor which appears to survive most critiques, whether from the Right or the Left, is that when rural people met the General they came away feeling that they had some value as human beings.

[15] In the weeks before the elections a large group of armed PRD militants from the indigenous town of Cherán had blockaded all exit roads from neighboring Nahuatzen with a view to apprehending, and presumably assassinating, the PRI local deputy imposed on them in the state elections (Salud Maldonado, personal communication).

[16] To some extent, of course, fraud is counter-productive under present circumstances, though it seems that some elements of the party organization in Michoacán are congenitally incapable of democratic practices even where honesty would be a better political policy. The PAN's triumph in Sahuayo was all the more resounding because the internal

party elections to select the PRI candidates had been characterized by levels of chicanery of almost comic proportions.

[17] The Leninist conception of revolution was flawed by its focus on the question of capturing the state at the expense of consideration of the post-revolutionary hegemonic process required to transform society socially and democratically. Gramsci's mature concept of hegemony improves substantially on the Leninist vision of the *praxis* of the revolutionary process, but also entails abandoning faith in the the inevitability of human emancipation through the direct effects of class conflict between proletariat and bourgeoisie. For this reason, he can be appropriated as the Marxist precursor of the new "post-Marxist" theory of social movements. It is possible to read Gramsci in either a voluntarist or structuralist manner, and this no doubt reflects real ambiguities and contradictions in his thought. But in my reading, Gramsci did not relinquish a commitment to a totalizing view of the social question: he simply accepted its growing complexity under more developed capitalist conditions. Nor did he abandon the idea that the social development of capitalist societies is shaped in a fundamental way by the class and capital accumulation process.

GLOSSARY

1. SPANISH WORDS USED FREQUENTLY IN THE TEXT

Acaparador Normally a large-scale commercial intermediary, though also sometimes used to refer to people who engross large numbers of ejidal plots and in other contexts where exploitation is implied.

Acomodado The better-off people in the hacienda labor force and specifically those who sided with the landlord interest.

Acordada The "white guard" of armed agents of coercion employed by a hacienda.

Agraristas Partisans of the struggle for land.

Agricultor A farmer, but with different social connotations to the word *campesino*.

Al alambre "By the wire". To cross the U.S. border as an undocumented migrant. An alternative common idiom is *al contrabando*.

A la cuarta (rental) Rental of land on the basis of offering the title-holder a percentage of the crop rather than a cash payment paid in advance.

(Amigo) concocido Sometimes simply refers to a "friend" in whom a person has confidence (often as a patron), but more normally here refers to a trustworthy *lieutenant*, a person of confidence chosen by a political leader.

Amparo A juridical restraining order.

Arriero A muleteer.

Azadón A hoe. Many of the *ecuaros* can only be cultivated by hoe and those who sow them are termed *azadoneros*, but work with the hoe also represented the lowest grade in the labor hierarchy on the hacienda.

Baldío Land not being cultivated.

Barrio In this book generally a "quarter", a residential subdivision of a village.

Bodegero The proprietor of a wholesale warehouse in a *Mercado de Abastos*.

Bracero The laborer as an "arm": used to refer to the contract workers who went to the U.S. under the inter-governmental accords of 1943–64, though it is also sometimes used of more recent migrants.

Brigada A brigade: refers to public sector and social service work organized on the basis of teams or work groups.

Cabecera municipal The "head-town" of a municipality: its official politico-administrative center.

Cacique In this book generally used in the modern sense of a "boss," though the issue of *caciquismo* is given more detailed and specific discussion at various stages of the analysis.

Campesino The generic term equivalent to the English "peasant," a "country person." It applies to people who are landless and, as I suggest in the book, should not be seen as a purely "socio-economic" category, nor a "traditional" one, since other kinds of status categorizations characterized the estamental society of the colonial era. Ideologically speaking, it might be said that the *campesino* is a product of urban society, though the fact that rural people of differing socio-economic status continue, in many contexts, to define *themselves* as *campesinos* is also worth reflecting upon as a theoretical issue.

Caporal Another word for foreman used on the hacienda to refer to specific posts of responsibility of lower rank.

Casco The "Great House" of a hacienda, used by the absentee owners only on visits.

Caudillo A major political leader with a clientele, often a military strong-man.

Cerro A larger hill or small mountain. The diminutive *cerrito* is used of the small volcanic hillocks which dot the plain. "Sowing in the *cerro*" refers to cultivation of hill land (see *ecuaro*).

Chivero A goat-herder.

Comisariado Ejidal Should denote the entire ejidal administration, but has come to denote the commissar himself in this region.

Comuneros Generally refers to members of an "indigenous" village community here.

(Des)confianza Presence or absence of trust regarding others.

Contrabandista A smuggler, but also used to refer to people who make money in shady ways in other contexts by exploitaing the venal possibilities in Mexican bureaucratic procedures.

Contratista A labor contractor acting as recruiter and intermediary between undocumented labor migrants and U.S. employers.

Coyote A person who facilitates undocumented entry into the U.S. for a fee.

Cristeros Supporters of the Cristero rebellion of 1926–29.

Cuadrilla A squad of workers. Still in use to refer to work gangs.

Cura A parish priest.

Disgusto A quarrel.

Dueño The owner or master of something. Although ejidatarios only enjoy usufruct rights over their land, the aspiration to feel oneself a real *dueño* is very marked.

Ecuaro Plots of land located in the hills which were originally distributed to hacienda peons for self-provisioning and today constitute a form of private land-holding within the village community. People who live by agricultural wage-work locally and sowing ecuaros are often referred to as *ecuareros*.

Ejidatario A member of a land reform community (ejido) whose rights are officially recognized: not necessarily the *de facto* cultivator of the land.

Emigrado The local term for persons with legal rights to residence in the U.S., though those whose papers are false may be distinguished as *emigrados chuecos* ("bent" or "crooked" emigrants) by the community.

Envidia Envy.

Escarda Cultivation of the standing crop, usually done with a *tronco*.

Eventual Used of casual labor and in other contexts where activities are subject to chance and uncertainty.

Fresa Strawberry.

Frijol(es) Beans.

Ganadero A cattle-man, rancher.

Gente humilde "The humble people": often a term of self-ascription by the rural poor.

Hacendado The owner of a hacienda.

Hacienda Although the term has become the principal word used to denote a landed estate, its original meaning was broader, denoting any form of moveable property, and it retains the broader sense in its meaning of "finance".

Hanega An alternate spelling of *fanega*, the Spanish bushel (1.58 American bushels).

Hombre valiente Literally "a man of courage," but with the implication of "man of violence."

Huerta (Huertita) An orchard or commercial avocado or fruit farm.

Jefe de Vigilancia Theoretically the senior figure in the "Vigilance Council" of an ejido, which should represent a parallel structure to the commissar of the agrarian community and his administration, though the system does not function in this way in the Ciénega.

Jefe de Tenencia The senior elected authority in a community below the level of *cabecera municipal*.

Jefe político Literally a "political chief" and a significant element in the power structure created by Porfirio Díaz (1876–1910).

Jitomatero A large-scale commercial tomato grower.

Jornalero A day-laborer, though the term *peón* is still used to denote hired labor in the region.

Latifundio A great estate.

Licenciado A lawyer in this context, though the first undergraduate degree in Mexico is the *licenciatura*, so *licenciados* may be found in many professions.

Manta A coarse-cloth blanket which was obligatory dress for peons.

Manual A manual grade employee.

Mayordomo A foreman: the term is still in use and is used to describe foremen and supervisors in the U.S.

Mediero The local term most commonly used for sharecroppers.

Mercado de Abastos An urban wholesale food market.

Mesa directiva The "executive," referring to the elected officials of an ejido.

Neolatifundio In the context of this book, the term refers to an agrarian enterprise based on the rental of land reform land.

Paisano A "fellow countryman": normally used to denote people from the same village, though it can be extended according to social context.

Parcela The individual fields into which ejidos cultivated on an individual tenure basis are divided.

Particular A merchant-usurer.

Pedazo A piece or "bit" of land. The diminutive *pedacito* is also commonly used, and this is the normal way to describe cultivation based on dividing up the *parcela* between different crops or cultivators.

Peones acasillados Permanent workers resident on the hacienda.

Peones ajenos Non-family hired labor.

Pequeña propiedad A "small private property": in reality covers everything from infra-subsistence small-holdings to illegally large landed estates.

Pistoleros Hired gunmen.

(Policía) Judicial The investigative branch of the Mexican police.

Potrero Literally "fenced-in pasture land," but used in Guaracha to refer to divisions between different areas of land in the hacienda which have continued in use following the subdivision of the land into individual plots.

Preparatoria Preparatory school: the level of education beyond the secondary school prior to entrance into university or polytechnic education.

Primaria Primary school.

Pueblo Normally refers to a village in this book.

Puntillado A rainy-season crop which is given one irrigation.

Rancheros In the pre-revolutionary Mexican context denotes private small farmers as distinct from latifundists, though the precise socio-economic significance of the category requires further analysis in any particular regional context.

Ranchito A hamlet: diminutive of *rancho*.

Raya The wage of a peon, still used, for example, by younger children to refer to any payments made to them by their fathers as "pocket money" when they are working for them.

Refresco Soft drinks such as Coca Cola.

Reparto A distribution of land (both division of former communal land into private lots and agrarian reform distribution).

Secundaria Secondary school.

Seguro Insurance.

Sembrar a medias To "go halves" (usually not in a literal sense): a sharecropping arrangement between two individuals.

Sinarqistas Partisans of a social movement of the right which succeeded the *Cristeros* as a major problem for the post-revolutionary state in the 1930s and early 1940s.

Sindicato A trade union.

Socios Partners or members of an association. *Sociedad* denotes either a partnership or a cooperative association depending on the context.

Tarea "A task." Agricultural labor processes were generally broken down in terms of *tareas* in the hacienda period, and the *tarea* is still sometimes used as a measure of labor needed in cultivation today.

Temporal Unirrigated.

Tienda de raya The "company store" of the hacienda.

Tronco A plough-team of horses or mules, which replaced oxen after land reform.

Utilidad A "return" or "profit": used in various senses discussed in more detail in the text.

Vecino A neighbor.

Ventas al tiempo Sales of grain to a merchant prior to the harvest in return for a loan.

2. ACRONYMS

ANAGSA Aseguradora Nacional Agrícola y Ganadera

BANRURAL Banco Rural

BNCE Banco Nacional de Crédito Ejidal

CCI Central Campesina Independiente

CECVYM Coalición de Ejidos Colectivos de los Valles de Yaqui y Mayo

CIOAC Central Independiente de Obreros Agrícolas y Campesinos

CNC Confederación Nacional Campesina

CNPA Coordinadora Nacional Plan de Ayala

COPLAMAR Coordinación General del Plan Nacional de Zonas Deprimidas y Grupos Marginados

CONASUPO Compañía Nacional de Subsistencias Populares

CRMDT Confederación Revolucionaria Michoacana del Trabajo

CROM Confederación Regional Obrera Mexicana

CTM Conferederación de Trabajadores Mexicanos

DAAC Departamento de Asuntos Agrarios y Colonización

PAN Partido de Acción Nacional

PDM Partido Demócrata Mexicana

PNR Partido Nacional Revolucionario

PRD Partido de la Revolución Democrática

PRI Partido Revolucionario Institucional

PRM Partido de la Revolución Mexicana

PRONAL Programa Nacional de Alimentos

PRONASE Productora Nacional de Semillas

SAM Sistema Alimentario Mexicano

SARH Secretaría de Agricultura y Recursos Hidráulicos

SEP Secretaría de Educación Pública

SRA Secretaría de Reforma Agraria

UAR Unión Agrícola Regional

UCEZ Unión de Comuneros 'Emiliano Zapata'

UGOCM Unión General de Obreros y Campesinos de México

UNORCA Unión Nacional de Organizaciones Regionales Campesinas Autónomas

UNPH Unión Nacional de Productores de Hortalizas

REFERENCES CITED

Aguilar, Rosalía, Beatriz Cervantes, Ma. de los Angeles Colunga, Ana Ma.
Crespo and Raúl Vargas
    1981 El Movimiento Sinarquista en el Estado de Guanajuato. In *Jornados de Historia de Occidente: Movimientos Populares en el Occidente de México, Siglos XIX y XX*, pp. 153–168. Centro de Estudios de la Revolución Mexicana "Lázaro Cárdenas," A.C., Jiquilpan.

Alonso, Ana Ma.
    1988 "Progress" as Disorder and Dishonor: Discourses of Serrano Resistance. *Critique of Anthropology* 8(1):13–33.

Alonso, Jorge, Alfonso Corcuera Garza, and Roberto Melville
    1974 *Los Campesinos de la Tierra de Zapata. II: Subsistencia y Explotación*. SEP-INAH, México, D.F.

Ankerson, Dudley
    1980 Saturnino Cedillo: a Traditional Caudillo in San Luis Potosí, 1890–1938. *Caudillo and Peasant in the Mexican Revolution*, edited by David A. Brading, pp. 140–168. Cambridge University Press, Cambridge.

Appendini, Kirsten A. de and Vania Almeida Salles
    1979 Algunas Consideraciones sobre los Precios de Garantía y la Crisis de Producción de Alimentos Básicos, *Foro Internacional* (El Colegio de México) XIX(3):402–428.

Arenal, Sandra
    1986 *Sangre Joven: Las Maquilidoras por Dentro*. Editorial Nueva Imagen, México, D.F.

Arizpe, Lourdes
    1978 *Migración, Etnicismo y Cambio Económico*. El Colegio de México, México, D.F.
    1980 Cultural Change and Ethnicity in Rural Mexico. In *Environment, Society and Rural Change in Latin America*, edited by David Preston, pp. 123–134. John Wiley, Chichester.
    1985 The State and Uneven Agrarian Development in Mexico. In *Politics in Mexico*, edited by George Philip, pp. 206–220. Croom Helm, Beckenham.

Arizpe, Lourdes and Josefina Aranda
    1981 The "Comparative Advantages" of Women's Disadvantages: Women Workers in the Strawberry Export Agribusiness in Mexico. *Signs* 5:453-473.

Arroyo Alejandre, Jesús
    1986 *Emigración Rural de Fuerza de Trabajo en el Occidente-Centro de México: Una Contribución de Información Básica para su Análisis*. Cuadernos de Difusión Científica 6. Universidad de Guadalajara, Guadalajara.

Banco Nacional de Credito Ejidal
   1937 *Sociedad Colectiva Agrícola Ejidal Industrial "Rafael Picazo"*.
   DAAP, México, D.F.
Barkin, David and Blanca Suárez
   1985 *El Fin de la Autosuficiencia Alimentaria*. Centro de
   Ecodesarrollo/Ediciones Océano, S.A., México, D.F.
Bartra, Armando
   1985 *Los Herederos de Zapata: Movimientos Campesinos
   Posrevolucionarios en México*. Ediciones Era, México, D.F.
Bazant, Jan
   1977 *A Concise History of Mexico from Hidalgo to Cárdenas,
   1805–1940*. Cambridge University Press, Cambridge.
Benítez, Fernando
   1977 *Lázaro Cárdenas y la Revolución Mexicana*, Vol. 1. Fondo de
   Cultura Económica, México, D.F.
Boehm de Lameiras, Brigitte
   1989 Peasants and Entrepreneurs in the Ciénega de Chapala, Michoacán,
   Mexico. *Agricultural History* 63(2):62–76.
Brading, David A.
   1978 *Haciendas and Ranchos in the Mexican Bajío: León 1700–1860*.
   Cambridge University Press, Cambridge.
Brenner, Robert
   1977 The Origins of Capitalist Development: a Critique of Neo-Smithian
   Marxism. *New Left Review* 104:25–92.
Buci-Glucksmann, Cristine
   1978 *Gramsci y el Estado (Hacia una Teoría Materialista de la
   Filosofía)*. Siglo XXI Editores, México, D.F.
Burbach, Roger and Patricia Flynn
   1980 *Agribusiness in the Americas*. Monthly Review Press, New York.
Bustamante, Jorge
   1983a Maquiladoras, a New Face of International Capitalism on
   Mexico's Northern Frontier. In *Women, Men and the International
   Division of Labor*, edited by June Nash and María Patricia Fernández-
   Kelly, pp. 224-56. SUNY Press, Albany.
   1983b Mexican Migration: The Political Dynamics of Perceptions. In
   U.S.-Mexico Relations: Economic and Social Aspects, edited by Clark
   W. Reynolds and Charles Tello, pp. 259-276. Stanford University
   Press, Stanford.
Chayanov, A.V.
   1966 *The Theory of Peasant Economy*, edited by Daniel Thorner, Basile
   Kerblay and R.E.F. Smith. R.D. Irving, Homewood, Illinois.
Comision Nacional de Irrigación
   1936 *Estudio Agroeconómico Preliminar del Proyecto Río Tarecuato,
   Michoacán*. CNI, México, D.F.

REFERENCES CITED

Connolly, Priscilla
  1985 The Politics of the Informal Sector: A Critique, in *Beyond Employment: Household, Gender and Subsistence*, edited by N. Redclift and E. Mingione. Basil Blackwell, Oxford.
Craig, Ann L.
  1983 *The First Agraristas: An Oral History of a Mexican Agrarian Reform Movement*. University of California Press, Berkeley.
Cross, Henry E. and Jorge A. Sandos
  1981 *Across the Border: Rural Development in Mexico and Recent Migration to the United States*. Institute of Government Studies, University of California, Berkeley.
De Janvry, Alain
  1981 *The Agrarian Question and Reformism in Latin America*. Johns Hopkins University Press, Baltimore.
De la Peña, Guillermo
  1978 Empresarios en el Sur de Jalisco: Un Estudio de Caso en Zapotlán el Grande. *Simposio Sobre Empresarios en México*. CIS-INAH (mimeo), México, D.F.
  1981 Los Estudios Regionales y la Antropología Social en México. *Relaciones* II(8):43–93.
  1986 Poder Local, Poder Regional: Perspectivas Socioantropológicas. In *Poder Local, Poder Regional*, edited by J. Padru and A. Vanneph, pp. 27–56. El Colegio de México/CEMCA, México, D.F.
  n.d. Cambio Social y Migración Internacional de Trabajadores: Aproximación al Estudio de Cuatro Regiones Agrarias de México (mimeo).
Díaz-Polanco, Héctor and Laurent Guye Montandon
  1978 *La Burguesía Agraria en México: Un Estudio de Caso en El Bajío*. Cuadernos del CES 22. El Colegio de México, México, D.F.
Djurfeldt, Göran
  1982 Classical Discussions of Capital and Peasantry: A Critique. In *Rural Development: Theories of Peasant Economy and Agrarian Change*, edited by John Harriss, pp. 139–159. Hutchinson, London.
Durán, Juan Manuel
  1982 Aspectos de la Migración en el Noroeste de Michoacán. Transformación Agrícola y Migración en la Ciénega de Chapala. Paper presented to the IV Coloquio de Antropología e Historia Regionales, El Colegio de Michoacán. (mimeo).
  1988 *¿Hacia una Agricultura Industrial?* University of Guadalajara, Guadalajara.
Eckstein, Salomón
  1966 *El Ejido Colectivo en México*. Fondo de Cultura Económica, México, D.F.

Escobar, Agustín
    1986 Patrones de Organización Social en el Mercado de Trabajo Manual de Guadalajara. In *Cambio Regional, Mercado de Trabajo y Vida Obrera en Jalisco*, Edited by Guillermo de la Peña y Agustín Escobar, pp. 147–189. El Colegio de Jalisco, Guadalajara.

Espín, Jaime L.
    1986 *Tierra Fría, Tierra de Conflictos en Michoacán*. El Colegio de Michoacán/Gobierno del Estado de Michoacán, Zamora.

Falcón, Romana Gloria
    1977 *El Agrarismo en Veracruz: La Etapa Radical, 1928-1935*. El Colegio de México, México, D.F.

Feder, Ernest
    1977 *El Imperialismo Fresa*. Ed. Campesina, México, D.F.

Fine, Ben and Laurence Harris
    1979 *Rereading Capital*. Macmillan, London and Basingstoke.

Forgacs, David (ed.)
    1988 *A Gramsci Reader: Selected Writings 1916–1935*. Lawrence and Wishart, London.

Foucault, Michel
    1979 *Discipline and Punish: The Birth of the Prison*. Peregrine Books, Harmondsworth.

Fowler Salamini, Heather
    1980 Revolutionary Caudillos in the 1920s: Francisco Múgica and Adalberto Tejeda. In *Caudillo and Peasant in the Mexican Revolution*, edited by David A. Brading, pp. 169–192. Cambridge University Press, Cambridge.

Friedrich, Paul
    1977 *Agrarian Revolt in a Mexican Village*, 2nd Edition. The University of Chicago Press, Chicago.

García Mora, Carlos
    1981 Tierra y Movimiento Agrarista en la Sierra Purépecha. In *Jornados de Historia de Occidente: Movimientos Populares en el Occidente de México, Siglos XIX y XX* , pp. 47–101. Centro de Estudios de la Revolución Mexicana "Lázaro Cárdenas," A.C., Jiquilpan.

Giddens, Antony
    1980 *The Class Structure of the Advanced Societies* (2nd edition). Unwin Hyman, London.

Gilly, Adolfo
    1983 *The Mexican Revolution*. Verso Editions, London.

Ginneken, Wouter van
    1980 *Socio-Economic Groups and Income Distribution in Mexico*. Croom Helm, London.

Gledhill, John
1981 Agrarian Change and the Articulation of Forms of Production: the Case of the Mexican Bajío. *Bulletin of Latin American Research* 1(1):63–80.
1985 The Peasantry in History: Some Notes on Latin American Research. *Critique of Anthropology* 5(1):35-56.
1987 State and Class Formation in Mexico, 16th to 19th Centuries: Frameworks for Comparative Analysis. In *Power Relations and State Formation*, edited by T.C. Patterson and C.W. Gailey, pp. 128–154. American Anthropological Association, Washington, D.C.
1988a Legacies of Empire: Political Centralization and Class Formation in the Hispanic-American World. In *State and Society: the Emergence and Development of Social Hierarchy and Political Centralization*, edited by John Gledhill, Barbara Bender, and Mogens Trolle Larsen, pp. 302-319. Unwin Hyman, London.
1988b Agrarian Social Movements and Forms of Consciousness. *Bulletin of Latin American Research* 7(2):257-276.

González, Luis
1968 *Pueblo en Vilo: Microhistoria de San José de Gracia*. Centro de Estudios Históricos, Nueva Serie 1. El Colegio de México, México, D.F.
1979 *Los Artífices del Cardenismo*. Historia de la Revolución Mexicana 14. El Colegio de México, México, D.F.
1984 *Zamora*. El Colegio de Michoacán/CONACYT, Zamora.

González de la Rocha, Mercedes
1986 Lo Público y lo Privado: El Grupo Doméstico Frente al Mercado de Trabajo Urbano. In *Cambio Regional, Mercado de Trabajo y Vida Obrera en Jalisco*, edited by Guillermo de la Peña and Agustín Escobar, pp. 191–233. El Colegio de Jalisco, Guadalajara.

Gordillo, Gustavo
1988 *Campesinos al Asalto del Cielo: Una Reforma Agraria con Autonomía*. Siglo XXI editores/Universidad Autónoma de Zacatecas, México, D.F.

Griffin, Keith
1974 *Land Concentration and Rural Poverty*. Macmillan, London.

Gutiérrez Pérez, Antonio and Yolanda Trapaga Delfin
1986 *Capital, Renta de la Tierra y Campesinos*. Ediciones Quinto Sol, México, D.F.

Hamilton, Nora
1982 *The Limits of State Autonomy: Post-Revolutionary Mexico*. Princeton University Press, Princeton.

Hamnett, Brian R.
1986 *Roots of Insurgency: Mexican Regions, 1750–1824*. Cambridge University Press, Cambridge.

Hernández Chávez, Alicia
1979 *La Mecánica Cardenista*. Historia de la Revolución Mexicana 16. El Colegio de México, Mexico, D.F.

Hernández, Manuel Diego
1982 *La Confederación Revolucionaria Michoacana del Trabajo*. Centro de Estudios de la Revolución Mexicana "Lázaro Cárdenas," A.C., Jiquilpan.

Hewitt de Alcantara, Cynthia
1980 Land Reform, Livelihood and Power in Rural Mexico. In *Environment, Society and Rural Change in Latin America*, edited by David Preston, pp. 21–36. John Wiley, Chichester.
1984 *Anthropological Perspectives on Rural Mexico*. Routledge and Kegan Paul, London.

Kahn, Joel S.
1985 Peasant Ideologies in the Third World. *Annual Review of Anthropology* 14:49–75.

Knight, Alan
1980 Peasant and Caudillo in Revolutionary Mexico. In *Caudillo and Peasant in the Mexican Revolution*, edited by David A. Brading, pp. 17–58. Cambridge University Press, Cambridge.
1986a *The Mexican Revolution. Volume I: Porfirians, Liberals and Peasants*. Cambridge University Press, Cambridge.
1986b *The Mexican Revolution. Volume II: Counter-revolution and Reconstruction*. Cambridge University Press, Cambridge.

Krauze, Enrique
1987 *Lázaro Cárdenas: General Misionero*. Biografía del Poder 8. Fondo de Cultura Económica, México, D.F.

Laclau, Ernesto
1985 New Social Movements and the Plurality of the Social. In *New Social Movements and the State in Latin America*, edited by D. Slater, pp. 27–42. FORIS Publications Holland, Dordrecht.

Linck, Thierry
1982 *Usura Rural en San Luis Potosí: Un Acercamiento a la Problemática de la Integración Campesina*. El Colegio de Michoacán, Zamora.

Long, Norman and Bryan Roberts
1984 *Miners, Peasants and Entrepreneurs: Regional Development in the Central Highlands of Peru*. Cambridge University Press, Cambridge.

Mandel, Ernest
1972 *Late Capitalism*. New Left Books, London.

Margulis, Mario
1979 *Contradicciones en la Estructura Agraria y Transferencias de Valor*. Jornadas 90. El Colegio de México, México, D.F.

REFERENCES CITED

Martínez-Alier, Juan
1977 *Haciendas, Plantations and Collective Farms*. Frank Cass, London.

Martínez Saldaña, Tomás
1980 *El Costo Social de un Éxito Político: La Política Expansionista del Estado Mexicano en el Agro Lagunero*. Colegio de Postgraduados, Chapingo.

Massey, Douglas S., Rafael Alarcón, Jorge Durand and Humberto González
1987 *Return to Aztlán: The Social Process of International Migration from Western Mexico*. University of California Press, Berkeley.

Mejía, Abram
1928 *Michoacán: Monografía del Estado*. Published privately, Morelia.

Meyer, Jean
1976 *The Cristero Rebellion: The Mexican People between Church and State, 1926–1929*. Cambridge University Press, Cambridge.
1981 La Segunda (Cristiada) en Michoacán. In *La Cultura Purhé*, edited by F. Miranda, pp. 245–75. El Colegio de Michoacán/FONAPAS Michoacán, Zamora.

Miller, Simon
1985 Revisionism in Recent Mexican Historiography. *Bulletin of Latin American Research* 4(1):77–88.

Moreno García, Heriberto
1980 *Guaracha: Tiempos Viejos, Tiempos Nuevos*. El Colegio de Michoacán/FONAPAS Michoacán, Zamora.
1989 *Haciendas de Tierra y Agua*. El Colegio de Michoacán, Zamora.

Nava Hernández, Enrique
1987 Cultura Política y Política Popular en Michoacán. Notas Para su Estudio. *Relaciones* VIII(31):25–60.

Ochoa, Alvaro
n.d. Política y un Poco de Agrarismo en la Bolsa de Guaracha, 1911–1940. (Mimeo).

Olivera de Bonfil, Alicia
1981 José Inés Chávez García, "El Indio." ¿Bandido, Revolucionario o Guerrillero?. In *Jornados de Historia de Occidente: Movimientos Populares en el Occidente de México, Siglos XIX y XX*, pp. 103–111. Centro de Estudios de la Revolución Mexicana "Lázaro Cárdenas," A.C., Jiquilpan.

Pahl, R.E.
1984 *Divisions of Labour*. Basil Blackwell, Oxford.

Paige, Jeffery M.
1975 *Agrarian Revolution: Social Movements and Export Agriculture in the Underdeveloped World*. The Free Press, New York.

Pardo Galvan, Sergio
1982 Hacienda, Escuela y Ejido: Guaracha-Emiliano Zapata, Michoacán.

418

La Escuela Práctica de Agricultura de Guaracha. In *Después de los Latifundios*, edited by Heriberto Moreno García, pp. 279–293. El Colegio de Michoacán/FONAPAS Michoacán, Zamora.

Paré, Luisa
1988　El Problema de la Tenencia de la Tierra en México: ¿Mito o Realidad? In *Las Sociedades Rurales Hoy*, edited by Jorge Zepeda Patterson, pp. 255–265. El Colegio de Michoacán/CONACYT, Zamora.

Pearse, Andrew
1975　*The Latin American Peasant*. Frank Cass, London.

Pearson, Ruth
1986　Latin American Women and the New International Division of Labour. *Bulletin of Latin American Research* 5(2):67–79.

Poulantzas, Nicos
1975　*Classes in Contemporary Capitalism*. New Left Books, London.

Preobrazhenski, Evgeni
1965　*The New Economics* (1925), edited by Alec Nove. Clarendon Press, Oxford.

Ramírez, Louis Alfonso
1986a　*Chilchota: Un Pueblo al Pie de la Sierra*. El Colegio de Michoacán/Gobierno del Estado de Michoacán, Zamora.
1986b　La Cañada de los Once Pueblos. In *Estudios Michoacanos II*, edited by C. Herrejón Peredo, pp. 119–144. El Colegio de Michoacán/Gobierno del Estado de Michoacán, Zamora.

Ramos Arizpe, Guillermo
1983　Testimonio de Trabajadores Michoacanos en Estados Unidos en los Años Veinte. *Boletín del CERM*. Centro de Estudios de la Revolución Mexicana "Lázaro Cárdenas," A.C., Jiquilpan.

Redclift, Michael
1986　Peasant Movements and Urbanisation in Contemporary Morelos: To What Do We Owe Our Ignorance? *Bulletin of Latin American Research* 5(1):95–100.
1987　*Sustainable Development: Exploring the Contradictions*. Methuen, London.

Rello, Fernando
1986　*El Campo en la Encrucijada Nacional*. SEP, Foro 2000, México, D.F.

Richards, Paul
1986　*Indigenous Agricultural Revolution*. Hutchinson, London.

Ronfeldt, David
1973　*Atencingo: The Politics of Agrarian Struggle in a Mexican Ejido*. Stanford University Press, Stanford.

Rosdolsky, Roman
1980　*The Making of Marx's "Capital."* Pluto Press, London.

REFERENCES CITED

Salmerón Castro, Fernando
1984 Haciendas Piloncilleras: Taretan y su Región en los Albores del Siglo XX. *Relaciones* V(19):61–94.
Sánchez Díaz, Gerardo
1981 Movimientos Campesinos en la Tierra Caliente de Michoacán, 1869–1900. In *Jornados de Historia de Occidente: Movimientos Populares en el Occidente de México, Siglos XIX y XX*, pp. 31–45. Centro de Estudios de la Revolución Mexicana "Lázaro Cárdenas," A.C., Jiquilpan.
Sanderson, Steven E.
1981 *Agrarian Populism and the Mexican State*. University of California Press, Berkeley.
1986 *The Transformation of Mexican Agriculture*. Princeton University Press, Princeton.
Scott, James C.
1976 *The Moral Economy of the Peasant: Rebellion and Subsistence in Southeast Asia*. Yale University Press, New Haven.
Semo, Enrique
1978 *Historia Mexicana: Economía y Lucha de Clases*. Ediciones Era, S.A., México, D.F.
Shanin, Teodor
1986 Chayanov's Message: Illuminations, Miscomprehensions and the Contemporary "Development Theory." In A.V. Chayanov, *The Theory of Peasant Economy*, Wisconsin reprint, pp. 1–24. The University of Wisconsin Press, Madison.
Sinkin, Richard N.
1979 *The Mexican Reform, 1855–1876: A Study in Liberal Nation-Building*. University of Texas Press, Austin.
Skocpol, Theda
1979 *States and Social Revolutions: A Comparative Analysis of France, Russia and China*. Cambridge University Press, Cambridge.
Solkoff, Joel
1985 *The Politics of Food: The Decline of Agriculture and the Rise of Agribusiness in America*. Sierra Club Books, San Francisco.
Tamayo, Jaime
n.d. Los Movimientos Populares y el Proyecto Neocardenista: La Influencia del Nuevo "Nacionalismo" en la Política Mexicana. Centro de Investigaciones Sobre los Movimientos Sociales. Unpublished, Guadalajara.
Tapia Santamaría, Jesús
1986 *Campo Religioso y Evolución Política en el Bajío Zamorano*. El Colegio de Michoacán/Gobierno del Estado de Michoacán, Zamora.
Therborn, Göran
1987 *El Poder de la Ideología y la Ideología del Poder*. Siglo XXI

Editores, Madrid. [English edition (1980) *The Ideology of Power and the Power of Ideology*. Verso, London.]

Tirado de Ruíz, Rosa
1971 Desarrollo Histórico de la Política Agraria Sobre Tenencia de la Tierra, 1910–1970. In *Bienestar Campesino y Desarrollo Económico*, edited by Ifigenia de Navarette. DAA, México, D.F.

Trigueros, Paz and Javier Rodríguez Piña
1988 Migración y Vida familiar en Michoacán (Un Estudio de Caso). In *Migración en el Occidente de México*, edited by Gustavo López Castro, pp. 201–21. El Colegio de Michoacán, Zamora.

Vergopoulos, Kostas
1978 Capitalism and Peasant Productivity. *The Journal of Peasant Studies* 5(4):446–65.

Walker, David
1985 An American Dilemma: Undocumented Mexican Immigration into the United States. In *Politics in Mexico*, edited by George Philip, pp. 171–193. Croom Helm, Beckenham.

Warman, Arturo
1976 *...Y Venimos a Contradecir: Los Campesinos de Morelos y el Estado Nacional*. CISINAH, Ediciones de la Casa Chata, México, D.F. [English edition (1980) *"We come to object."* Johns Hopkins University Press, Baltimore.]

Wolf, Eric R.
1955 *The Mexican Bajío in the 18th Century: An Analysis of Cultural Integration*. Middle American Research Institute Publication 17. Tulane University, New Orleans.
1969 *Peasant Wars of the Twentieth Century*. Harper & Row, New York.

Zaldivar Flores, José Antonio
1942 *Un Plan de Explotación para la Ciénega de Chapala*. Escuela Nacional de Agricultura, Chapingo (mimeo).

Zepeda Patterson, Jorge
1985 Los Pasos de Cárdenas: La Confederación Revolucionaria Michoacana del Trabajo. In *75 Años de Sindicalismo Mexicano*. Instituto Nacional de Estudios Históricos de la Revolución Mexicana, México, D.F.
1986 No Es el Mismo Agrario que Agrio, ni Comuneros que Comunistas, Pero se Parecen. In *Perspectivas de los Movimientos Sociales en la Región Centro-Occidente*, edited by Jaime Tamayo, pp. 323–77. Editorial Línea, México, D.F.
1987 Michoacán Antes y Durante la Crisis o Sobre los Michoacanos que no se Fueron de Braceros. *Relaciones* VIII(31):5–24.